MEMORY

Memory

Neuropsychological, Imaging, and Psychopharmacological Perspectives

Gérard Emilien, Cécile Durlach,
Elena Antoniadis, Martial Van der Linden
& Jean-Marie Maloteaux

Routledge
Taylor & Francis Group

LONDON AND NEW YORK

First published 2004 by Psychology Press

Published 2018 by Routledge
2 Park Square, Milton Park, Abingdon, Oxon OX14 4RN
52 Vanderbilt Avenue, New York, NY 10017

First issued in paperback 2018

Routledge is an imprint of the Taylor & Francis Group, an informa business

British Library Cataloguing in Publication Data
A catalogue record for this book is available from the British Library

Library of Congress Cataloging in Publication Data
Memory : neuropsychological, imaging, and psychopharmacological
perspectives / Gérard Emilien . . . [et al.].
    p. cm.
Includes bibliographical references and index.
  ISBN 1-84169-370-7 (hbk.)
  1. Memory. 2. Memory disorders. I. Emilien, Gérard, 1953–
QP406.M4565 2003
153.1′2–dc21

                        2003009714

Typeset in 10/12pt Times by Graphicraft Limited, Hong Kong

Cover design by Richard Massing

ISBN 13: 978-1-138-87750-4 (pbk)
ISBN 13: 978-1-84169-370-5 (hbk)

MIX
Paper from
responsible sources
FSC FSC™ C013985
www.fsc.org

Printed in the United Kingdom
by Henry Ling Limited

Contents

Introduction

The ability to store and recall information is one of the most amazing capacities of higher organisms. As human adults, we can remember events that happened in our earliest childhood. We can recall skills learned far in the past. Our memories encapsulate our sense of personal identity, our cultural identities, and the meaning of our lives. We can even be influenced by memories that we cannot explicitly remember. However, we all remember—of that there can be no doubt. Whether we remember accurately or inaccurately, in detail or in abstract, are questions that researchers have investigated for many years. The study of memory has a long history, with psychologists such as William James and Hermann Ebbinghaus using the tools of their day to try to understand some of its basic properties. Ebbinghaus made important innovations that enabled memory research to be conducted methodologically and he did what we recognise as the first experimental studies (Ebbinghaus, 1885/1909).

Research has clearly shown that memory and retention are dynamic processes that are relatively sophisticated even in very young children. Although neurophysiological immaturities constrain the young infant's perceptual abilities in the early postnatal months, babies are fully capable of storing and retrieving information in the visual world (Howe & Courage, 1993). Another more fundamental question is why do we forget? There are many animals that can survive without having memories of critical moments in their lives. Although they have no vivid memories of sexual encounters, loss of loved ones, and so on, yet they appear to survive with an adaptive fitness equal to our own. There should be reasons why humans have conscious recollection of the past. Perhaps a better understanding of the functions of memory would provide some explanations. New learning and memorisation are cognitive functions that, like attention, are multidimensional systems. Recent studies designed within the framework of cognitive psychology have yielded substantial insights regarding the cognitive and neurological substrates mediating normal and pathological human memory (Heindel et al., 1993). These studies have shown that memory should not be thought of as a single homogeneous entity but rather as being composed of many distinct interacting systems that are mediated by specific neuroanatomical substrates. Memory works by making links between information, fitting facts into mental structures and frameworks. The more one is actively remembering, the more facts and frameworks one holds, the more additional facts and ideas will slot easily into long-term memory. Remembering involves not only the ability to detect a recently seen item among a series of items but also the ability to discriminate information that is currently relevant from other information, both internally and externally generated, much of which is familiar to some degree. The theory based on cognitive neuroscience and neuropsychology categorises distinct memory systems.

THE TWO PRIMARY FORMATS OF MEMORY

Memory involves many complex subsystems by means of which an organism registers, stores, retains, and retrieves some previous exposure to an event or experience. These functions are highly specific but they do not work in isolation from other mental abilities and from mood states. Memories are stored in two primary formats: as "declarative" or language-accessible information and as non-language-based "procedural" or habit memories (Squire, 1987). Declarative memory encompasses the acquisition, retention, and retrieval of knowledge that can be consciously and intentionally recollected (Cohen & Squire, 1980). Such knowledge includes memory for events (episodic memory) or facts (semantic memory) (Tulving, 1983). Memory may be broadly divided into explicit (conscious) and implicit (unconscious) components (Squire, 1987). Explicit memory is revealed when performance on a task requires conscious recollection of previous experiences. It is measured by direct or explicit tests of memory, such as free recall, cued recall, or recognition, that refer to a prior episode (Graf & Schacter, 1985). Performance on explicit memory tests improves substantially from early childhood to adolescence and depends on factors such as the use of mnemonic strategies (Schneider & Bjorklund, 1998).

In contrast, non-declarative or procedural kinds of memory encompass the acquisition, retention, and retrieval of knowledge expressed through experience-induced changes in performance. Non-declarative memory concerns the process by which the brain encodes an experience and then later

influences behaviour without requiring conscious awareness. It is represented in tasks involving different forms of skill acquisition or simple conditioning procedures. Thus, implicit memory is an experience that you may not be able to consciously recall, yet it can be shown to be present. It has an automatic or reflexive quality and its formation and recall are not absolutely dependent on awareness or cognitive processes. Subjects should not have "retrieval intentionality", i.e., they do not intentionally search their memory for past experiences, but automatically reuse traces of past processing (Schacter et al., 1989). This type of memory accumulates slowly through repetition over many trials, is expressed primarily by improved performance, and cannot ordinarily be expressed in words. According to the "transfer-appropriate processing" (TAP) principle, this memory effect occurs because the same processing components are involved during both study and test (see Roediger & Srinivas, 1993). Implicit memory performance seems to exhibit few or no age-related changes from 3 to 14 years of age (see Graf, 1990).

One important form of non-declarative memory is priming, an improvement in identification, detection, or production of a stimulus resulting from its prior exposure (Tulving & Schacter, 1990). One principal account of how priming occurs is that it reflects the activation or strengthening of pre-existing representations in memory (Graf & Mandler, 1984). For example, exposure to a word might facilitate subsequent identification because the exposure activates its memory representation, which renders the representation more accessible (Morton, 1969). Priming effects are among the most well-studied implicit memory phenomena (Schacter, 1994). These effects are often classified as either perceptual or conceptual in nature. Perceptual priming tasks rely primarily on processing the features of the presented stimulus in order to evoke the facilitation. Conceptual priming tasks, in contrast, utilise semantic aspects of the stimulus, often evoking facilitation via "spreading activation" to semantically related concepts (Blaxton, 1989; Graf & Ryan, 1990; Graf & Schacter, 1985; Hasher & Zacks, 1979). Most priming tasks, in fact, involve both conceptual and perceptual processing components, but the relative contribution of each varies across tasks (Keane et al., 1991; Tulving & Schacter, 1990). The system of procedural memory is, more than likely, the type of learning that remains intact in amnesic patients. While declarative memory relates to the ability to store and recall or recognise specific images, events, or facts, procedural memory is based on information, which is accessible only by improvement in performance. These two types of memory can be clearly dissociated in patients with memory disorders.

THE PROCESSING OPERATIONS

The functional view of memory performance based on the information-processing approach in cognitive psychology describes human memory in terms of processing operations: encoding, consolidation, storage, and retrieval. Encoding is the initial laying down of the memory trace. It is the first stage of mnemonic processing when information is encountered. Consolidation refers to the process that can occur over several weeks or more, of establishing the permanence of a memory trace, during which time the memory trace is susceptible to modification (McGaugh & Herz, 1972; Squire et al., 1975). Storage involves the keeping of the memory trace over time. Retrieval is the process of bringing out a memory from storage into consciousness. A fundamental principle of memory holds that encoding and retrieval processes are strongly interdependent. A large number of behavioural studies show that memory performance is enhanced if the encoding conditions match the retrieval demands. For example, although semantic analysis of the study material benefits performance on most episodic tests, phonemic analysis can be more effective under certain retrieval conditions (Morris et al., 1977). Similarly, the kind of cues that will be effective at the retrieval stage depends on the extent to which the cue information overlaps the encoded information (Tulving & Thomson, 1973). One prevailing hypothesis suggests that rapid-eye-movement (REM) sleep is important in processing memory

traces (Maquet et al., 2000). REM sleep might be a privileged period for mammalian brain plasticity not only during development but also in adult subjects in learning situations (Marks et al., 1995).

TRADITIONAL MEMORY MODELS

Traditional memory models are based on duration and include short-term memory (STM) and long-term memory (LTM) (Squire & Zola-Morgan, 1991). STM is the temporary store of information that has limited capacity (or span). Information remains in STM for only half a minute or so, unless it is processed further. For this STM to become permanent, it requires attention, repetition, and associated ideas. Baddeley introduced the powerful concept that the appropriate way to characterise STM is as a "working memory" (Baddeley, 1986, 1990). The concept of working memory is an updated view of STM in that it stores and manipulates information in an "online" or constantly updating manner. Working memory is the cognitive mechanism that allows us to keep a limited amount of information active for a brief period of time. In Baddeley's model, working memory consists of three main components: the central executive, the articulatory loop, and the visuospatial scratchpad or sketchpad. The articulatory loop and the visuospatial sketchpad are "slave systems" in which verbal and visual information respectively is stored when the executive is overloaded. These components can be conceived as responsible for maintaining short-term information availability. The central executive may be considered as the mastermind of human cognition. It allocates attention to a task and performs information storage and computational functions within a given task. Thus, the central executive is assumed to be an attentional control system responsible for strategy selection, control, and coordination of various processing tasks.

On the other hand, in LTM, large numbers of facts and autobiographical events are maintained for years. LTM is considered to be of unlimited capacity and relatively permanent. The process of "long-term potentiation" is one way in which such alteration of connection strengths among neurons occurs (Milner et al., 1998). Duration of changes in the strengths of synaptic connections can vary, from quite brief levels of chemical alterations to extended intervals mediated by structural changes in neural connections. The cellular alterations resulting from learning and memory are called plasticity. They refer to an alteration in the efficiency of the synapses that can increase the transmission of nervous impulses, thus modulating behaviour. The term LTM is used to cover a very wide range of memory durations (i.e., from several minutes to many years) despite the evidence that memory processes vary across retention periods.

Additional concepts related to processing stages of memory are consolidation, a process that converts STM to LTM, and decay or forgetting, the gradual erosion of stored information. Thus, information storage in the nervous system is widely held to be based on enduring, activity-dependent changes in the number or downstream consequences of synaptic connections between neurons in the central nervous system. While memory is seemingly easily understood intuitively, it covers a whole world of complexity at the behavioural, neuroanatomical, and physiological levels. Many molecular sites in the brain are likely targets of metabolic change in LTM formation.

One focus in research into age differences in memory has been the question of whether older adults, compared to younger adults, have a similar capacity in STM. Some investigators have concluded that there are minimal age differences in the capacity of STM (Ogle, 1986; Poon, 1985). However, some investigators have also proposed that the key problem for the older adult is not one of decreased capacity in STM but the slowing down of central nervous system activity (Perlmutter & Hall, 1985; Salthouse, 1985). It seems that in STM, there is a decrease in both speed and flexibility of operations in older adults. In LTM, the main problems for the older adult seem to centre on the encoding of new information for long-term retention and its retrieval from LTM (Craik, 1977).

In recent years, investigators in memory research have become more cognisant of the multivariate nature of memory and are beginning to subscribe to the notion that no one hypothesis can adequately account for how our memory works. There has been evidence of interest in a much wider range of issues, such as the importance of individual differences, clinical memory testing and intervention, the development of neuropsychological models of memory, and the interaction of variables related to the individual subject, the learning/memory task, and the environment. The clinical assessment of memory requires developmentally appropriate tasks that can be offered in the form of a mental status examination, memory test batteries, neuropsychological test batteries, or other measures of memory. Often, such tasks examine the various dimensions of memory, such as timing (immediate, recent, or remote), aspects of processing (encoding, storage, or retrieval), strategies used (such as rehearsal and retrieval strategies), perceptual modalities required (visual, auditory) and ways in which memory performance affects the life of the individual involved.

THE BIOLOGICAL BASIS OF MEMORY

Extensive behavioural and neuroanatomical studies have revealed a number of different systems that process and store different types of information in the brain. Evidence from amnesic patients suggests that the medial temporal lobes/hippocampus and related limbic structures are necessary for conscious recollection, at least of information that was acquired recently. However, memory without conscious awareness can remain intact even if these structures are damaged. Thus, the declarative form of memory depends on medial temporal lobe structures, such as the hippocampus. In contrast, procedural forms of memory, classical conditioning, and non-associative memory do not involve awareness or conscious recall (recall refers to the ability to actively retrieve the information sought from memory stores). They are thought to be dependent on the function of cerebellum, amygdala, basal ganglia, and other systems (Graybiel, 1995; Knowlton & Squire, 1993; Salmon & Butters, 1995; Tulving & Schacter, 1990). It is now clear that there are a number of different forms or aspects of learning and memory that involve different brain systems. Under normal conditions, many of these brain-memory systems are engaged to some degree in memory formation but each of these brain systems is learning something different about the situation.

The cerebellar system is involved in the classical conditioning of skeletal responses. The amygdala is a memory structure that is pivotal in fear learning and mediates the behavioural and autonomic changes that occur in response to cues signalling danger. Emotional arousal activates the amygdala and such activation results in the modulation of memory storage occurring in other brain regions. The hippocampal system is concerned with learning about the situation and forming experiential or episodic memories about the events and their relationships in the context of the individual's ongoing experience. Current research indicates that hippocampal neural activity is necessary for both encoding (the process that transforms a stimulus into a format that can be retained by the brain), and retrieval of spatial memory and for either trace consolidation or long-term storage. Functional analysis of the hippocampus has shown that this medial temporal lobe structure is essential, for both humans and animals, in the acquisition and retention of complex spatial relationships (Cohen & Eichenbaum, 1993; Hirsh, 1974; Kim & Fanselow, 1992; Sutherland & Rudy, 1989). The cognitive mapping theory exemplifies this role by positing that the hippocampus is essential for the formation of cognitive maps of the environment (O'Keefe & Nadel, 1978). Consistently, damage to the hippocampus would result in impairment on any task that relies on the formation of a spatial map for successful performance.

Although lesion studies continue to provide new evidence on the functional neuroanatomy of memory, clinical studies using positron emission tomography (PET) or functional magnetic resonance imaging (fMRI) now permit the visualisation of memory processes in the human brain. Functional neuroimaging studies allow for the design of psychological experiments targeted at specific memory processes. To make inferences about the activation of particular brain regions during performance of behavioural tasks, investi-

gators generally measure changes in blood flow or blood oxygenation level in one experimental condition relative to another condition. Estimates of blood flow or oxygenation level can then be subtracted from one another, or assessed using various other analytical techniques. Acquisition of whole-brain images enables the characterisation of spatially distributed functional networks of activity. Moreover, analytical techniques have been developed that allow the characterisation of the effective connectivity between different brain regions during task performance (Büchel & Friston, 1997). Researchers are also devoting significant effort to further explaining the cellular and molecular mechanisms of memory, utilising behavioural, anatomical, physiological, cellular, and molecular studies. This greater understanding may undoubtedly provide better perspectives for the introduction of novel effective pharmacological interventions in the treatment of memory dysfunctions.

The clinical pharmacology of memory consists of a framework provided by a more basic pharmacology largely based on animal studies, and to a more limited extent, the application of derivative findings to studies in humans. Obviously, a pharmacology of facilitative drugs has more direct clinical relevance than a pharmacology of disruptive drugs, although the latter provide insight into such phenomena as amnesic processes and potential prevalence of specific drug interactions and adverse effects.

MEMORY DYSFUNCTIONS

The ability to learn new material is perhaps the single cognitive function most sensitive to any deviation from normality. The ability may be compromised in the context of brain disease, psychopathology, transiently acute stress, boredom, or fatigue, or in the context of non-neurological acute or chronic disease processes. Any cognitive problem that results in increased forgetfulness may elicit concern in patients about memory problems. It is the cognitive area of most frequent subjective complaint. Cognitive impairment in late life is a growing clinical problem, with Alzheimer's disease (AD) the most prevalent of the progressive dementias. Memory disorders are the commonest and most disabling feature of neurodegenerative disease. It is important to understand the signs of symptoms of mild cognitive impairment (MCI) and to differentiate the diagnosis from AD. In many people with MCI, the thinking and reasoning skills stay sharp but the memory, especially of recently acquired knowledge and information, declines. On the other hand, AD is a progressive neurological disease in which all areas of the brain shrink and decline in function. The disease may cause a decline in memory, thinking, and language skills, and in the ability to read and write. Thus, in people with MCI, only memory is impaired. It appears that the onset of cognitive decline correlates closely with the onset of neuronal loss in the hippocampus and entorhinal cortex, two areas that are particularly critical for memory processing (Price et al., 2001). Preclinical AD cases resemble very mild AD cases pathologically but do not have cognitive impairment or decline. In addition to MCI and AD, current information about memory disorders in semantic dementia, Huntington's disease (HD), and Parkinson's disease (PD) are discussed in Chapter 8. Semantic dementia is a recently described clinical syndrome characterised by an acquired progressive inability to name or comprehend common concepts with little or no distortion of the phonological and syntactic aspects of language. Relative sparing of other aspects of cognition such as episodic memory, non-verbal problem solving, and perceptual and visuospatial skills have also been observed. The cognitive locus of this syndrome appears to lie in the permanent store of LTM representing general world knowledge—semantic memory. Semantic dementia probably always represents a non-Alzheimer neurodegenerative process.

Researchers have taken a great interest in exploring the integrity of non-linguistic cognitive processes such as memory in patients with neurogenic communication disorders. Numerous types and severities of memory disorders may occur after brain damage. Patients with various neurogenic communication disorders are therefore at risk for memory impairments. Indeed, a growing literature has documented that memory abilities may be compromised in this population including those with aphasia, left or right hemisphere stroke, and traumatic brain injury (TBI). Concerning memory dysfunctions in neuropsychiatric diseases, it has been suggested that because flashbulb memories, drug-related flashbacks, palinopsia, vivid memories of a variety of psychiatric disorders, pain hallucinations, etc., have a number of phenomenological features, they may constitute a family of amnesic events sharing similar neurobiological mechanisms. Flashbulb memory is a recent name for the recollection, putatively unusually detailed both in terms of core content and background, of some specific social or personal events assumed to be of significance to the individual or the social group. Memory has been regarded as one of the major areas of cognitive deficit in schizophrenia (McKenna et al., 1995). Studies indicate memory impairment in schizophrenia to be common and disproportionate to the overall level of intellectual impairment (Gold et al., 1992; Rund, 1989). A study has even suggested the existence of a schizophrenic amnesia (McKenna et al., 1990).

Validated memory scales derived from clinical neuropsychology have contributed greatly to examination of each of these memory processes, and different patterns of impaired and preserved function have been found to be associated with specific disease processes (Delis et al., 1991a). For example, storage is particularly affected in AD, whereas retrieval is more severely impaired in subcortical diseases such as HD and PD. With such an approach, cognitive deficits can be detected several years before the clinical diagnosis of dementia. The neuropsychological profile may indicate the underlying neuropathology and allow for preventive treatment (psychological and pharmacological) interventions.

AIMS AND ORGANISATION OF THIS BOOK

This book reviews critically the impact of recent neuropsychological and biological discoveries on the understanding of various aspects of the normal human memory and its pathology. It attempts to provide the reader with a broad overview of our understanding of memory at various levels, from neuropsychological theories to molecules and functional neuroimaging. Too often these different approaches are treated separately. Often clinicians are not very familiar with the concepts and theoretical and research issues encountered by research neuroscientists. On the other hand, clinical psychopharmacologists who are developing potential cognitive enhancers for the treatment of various memory dysfunctions need to clearly understand current work performed in memory research and the terminology used by clinical neuropsychologists. The benefit would be the development of adequate technology in the assessment of memory in clinical trials of potential new pharmacological and rehabilitation treatments. Therefore, this book attempts to provide clinicians as well as neuroscientists with a broad view of the neuropsychology of memory and the psychobiological processes involved, as well as its treatment. The contribution of recent advances from imaging technology and psychopharmacology research is critically examined. The mechanisms involving intracellular signalling pathways that regulate synaptic strength are analysed and the specific roles of calcium, protein kinases, protein phosphatases, and retrograde messengers are emphasised. Differences in the memory dysfunctions of various neurodegenerative disorders are discussed.

There is now overwhelming evidence that individuals with neurodegenerative disorders, including Parkinson's disease (PD), Huntington's disease (HD), Alzheimer's disease (AD), and Korsakoff's syndrome exhibit diverse patterns of cognitive impairments that can include deficits of "executive function". Amnesic Korsakoff patients and patients with AD can display normal procedural learning (pursuit rotor learning, mirror reading) while being severely impaired on measures of declarative memory (story recall, category fluency,

word recognition). Conversely, individuals with neostriatal pathology (e.g., HD and PD) have less impairment on tasks of declarative memory (at least when tested with recognition tasks), and much greater difficulty on tasks involving procedural memory (mirror reading, pursuit rotor tasks, Tower of Toronto tasks) (Saint-Cyr et al., 1988). The focus of this book also includes research strategies that are useful for exploring how drugs such as the benzodiazepines and the cholinergics alter cognitive functions. The relevance of this research for understanding both normal and impaired memory functions is explored.

The book is divided into two parts. The first part discusses the neuropsychology and pharmacology of memory. The second part discusses the pathology of memory. In the section treating neurodegenerative diseases, discussion is focused particularly on AD, HD, and PD. The value of using a multidisciplinary perspective, one that makes use of methods and theory arising from cognitive science and cognitive neuroscience, psychopharmacology, clinical neuropsychiatry, and neuropsychology, is underlined. Bringing together cognitive, biological, and clinical information on memory, this book should be of benefit to all undergraduate and graduate students of memory. It should also be very useful to all those involved in the diagnosis and treatment of memory disorders including neurologists, psychiatrists, psychologists, research scientists, nurses, and students. Thus, it may be used as either a textbook for students or a reference guide for the clinician and neuroscientist involved in memory research.

ACKNOWLEDGEMENTS

The authors thank Dr Ing-Mari Tallberg, Huddinge University Hospital, Sweden, and Professor F. Craik, University of Toronto, for reviewing the manuscript and providing comments.

Part I

Neuropsychology and Pharmacology of Memory

1

What is Memory?

INTRODUCTION

In memory research, the initial impact of an experience on the brain has been called an *engram* (Schacter, 1996). Trace theory describes an encoding process in which the engram or memory trace has both a gist (a general notion) and specific details (Schacter, 1996). With time, the details of an experience may begin to fade away and become less tightly bound together. However, the gist may remain quite accurate and easily accessible for retrieval. When trying to retrieve an original memory, one may be calling up the gist at first and then later trying to reconstruct the details. This reconstruction process may be profoundly influenced by the present environment, the questioning context itself, and other factors such as current emotions (Christianson, 1991).

Remembering past events involves a large number of processes and their identification and interaction continues as a primary goal of today's memory research. One major set of these processes concerns "ecphory" (recovery of stored information); another has to do with what is called episodic "retrieval mode" or REMO (Nyberg et al., 1995; Tulving, 1983). REMO refers to a

neurocognitive set or state, and is a basic and pivotal necessary condition for remembering past events. Memory is an active process in which even the most concrete experiences are actually dynamic representational processes. Remembering is not merely the reactivation of an old engram. It is the reconstruction of a new neural-net profile with features of the old engram and elements of memory from other experiences, as well as influences from the present state of mind. This is particularly important for clinicians when interviewing patients about past events, including trauma. The gist of a situation may be recalled with great accuracy but the details may be more subject to bias from ongoing experiences.

Considering the importance of context in memory, we may define context as information associated with a specific memory that allows differentiation of that memory from other memories. Intrinsic context refers to features that are an integral part of the stimulus itself. In a face, for example, intrinsic contextual features would be eye colour, hair length, etc. In the case of words, intrinsic context would relate to the particular meaning extracted from the word at the time of learning. Extrinsic context corresponds to those features that include time of encounter and surroundings. Studies of memory dysfunctions and amnesia have concentrated on memory for extrinsic context.

Two fundamental ways of gaining access to past experiences may be distinguished: recollection of contextual details surrounding a previous encounter with a stimulus (source memory) and a general sense of familiarity that is sufficient to determine whether the stimulus was previously encountered even though contextual recollection is absent (item memory) (Atkinson & Juola, 1974; Tulving, 1985; Yonelinas, 1994). Item memory combined with source memory failure is a common experience in everyday life and plays an important role in such problems as faulty eyewitness identification, when a face perceived as familiar is assigned the wrong context. This distinction has implications for understanding the neural organisation of memory. Extensive neuropsychological research suggests that source memory can be dissociated from memory for particular items (Schacter et al., 1984; Shimamura et al., 1991).

Memory is not situated only in one structure in the brain; it is a biological and psychological phenomenon involving the association of several brain systems working together. Although it was initially believed that memory was a general property of the cerebral cortex as a whole, evidence from patients with temporal lobe damage was instrumental in establishing that there are different types of memory localised in the brain. Residual memory has been observed in these patients for both associative and non-associative forms of implicit memory. Despite the deficits in explicit memory tasks, these patients retain various forms of reflexive learning, including habituation, sensitisation, and classical conditioning, all forms that have an automatic quality. Recent studies have highlighted the differences in mechanisms and determinants between declarative and procedural memory (Tulving & Schacter, 1990) (see Figure 1.1 & Table 1.1).

In human memory, the mechanisms of forgetting are not so clear. Early in the cognitive revolution, one view was that STM is vulnerable to decay (Brown, 1958; Peterson & Peterson, 1959). Information "evaporates" with time unless it is actively maintained. Another view was that forgetting is caused by interference from distracting elements (Keppel & Underwood, 1962). Interference has dominated the memory literature but decay has not entirely been forgotten. Support for decay comes from evidence of forgetting in the absence of interference (Baddeley & Scott, 1971). Interference certainly remains a potent source of forgetting even at long delays. Decay and interference are probably functionally related (Altmann & Gray, 2002). If a target decays, it will interfere less with future targets.

The ways that we encode, store, retrieve, and forget information provide clues to what declarative memory is and how it functions. Declarative memory is memory for events, facts, words, faces, music, all the various pieces of knowledge that we have acquired during a lifetime of experience and learning. It is knowledge that can potentially be declared and brought to mind as a verbal proposition or as a mental image. Declarative memory encodes information about autobiographical events

TABLE 1.1		
Organisation of memory		
	Short term	Long term
Declarative Conscious, spoken (located in the hippocampus, neocortex, entorhinal cortex, basal forebrain, thalamus)	Working	Semantic, Reference, Episodic
Non-declarative or Procedural Habit, skill, classical conditioning, instrumental learning (located in the brainstem, cerebellum, cortex, basal ganglia)	+	+

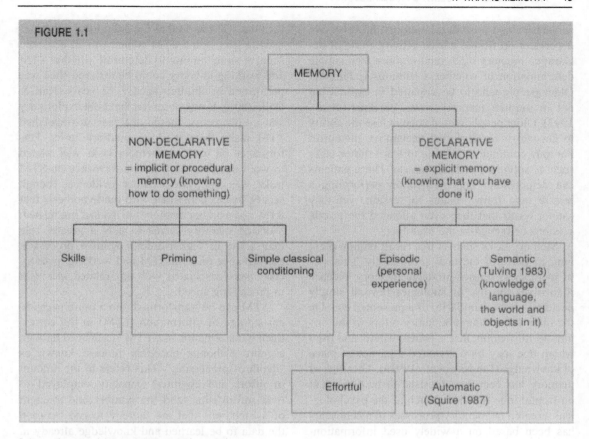

FIGURE 1.1

Schema for organising various types of memories.

as well as factual knowledge. Its formation depends on cognitive processes such as evaluation, comparison, and inference. Subjects are aware of the source and context of remembered information. Declarative memory can be recalled by a deliberate act of recollecting. It often can be concisely expressed in declarative statements such as "Last winter I visited my aunt in the countryside" (autobiographical event) or "All that glitters is not gold" (factual knowledge). It critically depends on structures in the medial temporal lobe. It is also called explicit or conscious memory. Research also suggests that episodic or explicit memory is characterised by the experience of specific features (e.g., colour, shape, semantic, time, location, and emotion) that comprise the event (Johnson & Raye, 1981). Thus, episodic memory depends on encoding multiple features and associations among

them. Furthermore, reflective activities (e.g., rehearsal, organisation, semantic judgements, and imagery) contribute to establishing such complex event representations. In contrast, procedural memory, which includes the ability to learn motor skills, does not. Procedural memory processes are, therefore, perhaps best characterised as "non-conscious memory" in order to distinguish them from repressed or dynamically unconscious memory processes (Clyman, 1991). They are specialised memory systems for processing patterns of perception, emotion, and action without the mediation of conscious attention or recollection. The distinctions between declarative and procedural memory are most apparent in amnesic patients. Amnesic individuals with bilateral medial temporal lobe lesions can learn procedural skills, whereas word list learning cannot be recalled. Both declarative and procedural memory, however, are dependent on frontal cortex activity. Tests of declarative memory often require more than simple determination of whether a stimulus is familiar. Older people tend to be impaired in explicit but not in implicit memory tests (Bäckman et al., 1997). Older people with dementia lose the ability to encode or recall verbal declarative memories but may continue to be able to learn motor tasks such as solving a difficult puzzle. These patients can demonstrate improvement in performing a puzzle task from session to session, yet they cannot recall that they even attended the puzzle sessions or recognise the examiner.

Memory tasks such as free recall require planning to perform the task successfully. This sort of memory is termed strategic memory because it involves the use of strategies beyond simply deciding on the familiarity of a presented cue. On the other hand, source memory refers to the origin of information, that is, when, where, and from whom one may have acquired a particular piece of knowledge (Lindsay et al., 1991a). This type of memory has been hypothesised to be dependent on frontal lobe function. Much of the psychological research on memory processes in recent years has been based on a widely used information-processing model, referred to as the "multimodal" memory store (Atkinson & Shiffrin, 1971). Incoming sensory information is initially held in preconscious, transient stores. Any information that is not lost is rapidly transferred (within milliseconds) to "short-term" or "primary" memory, where it is available for conscious processing, typically for periods of 10 to 20 seconds. Memory can be categorised as short-term (STM) and long-term (LTM). STM has limited capacity (only a few items), persists for a short time, and is believed to be related to a variety of short-term changes such as augmentation, synaptic facilitation, and post-tetanic potentiation (Zucker, 1989). STM and working memory are both central constructs in modern theories of memory and learning. STM refers to information in LTM that is activated above some threshold (Cowan, 1988, 1995). Activated information rapidly returns to an inactive state unless it becomes the focus of a limited-capacity attentional process. Working memory

includes STM as well as the attentional processes used to keep some STM contents in an activated state. A study aiming to determine whether STM and working memory could be distinguished was performed in children aged 7–13 years (Kail & Hall, 2001). It was observed that both exploratory and confirmatory factor analyses distinguished STM tasks from working memory tasks. Performance on working memory tasks was related to word-decoding skill but performance on STM tasks was not. The existing evidence, though scanty, seems consistent with the hypothesis that STM and working memory are distinct but related. Working memory seems to play a greater role than STM in higher-order cognitive processes. Performance on both STM and working memory tasks were associated with age-related increases in processing speed.

STM can be transformed into a more permanent storage of information (LTM) in the cortex. Such transformation into LTM is achieved through a more elaborate encoding process known as "depth of processing". This refers to the amount of effort and cognitive capacity employed to treat information, and the number and strength of associations that are thereby forged between the data to be learned and knowledge already in memory. This can be established with an elaborate encoding process that makes new information meaningful and therefore easy to consolidate. The greater the depth of processing, the greater the ability to recall learned information. LTM can be divided into an intermediate form, which is more easily disrupted, and a long-term form, which is resistant to disruption. In general, the formation of LTM takes several hours, during which time memories rely on short-term systems (Izquierdo & Medina, 1997). LTM is presumably mediated by persistent functional and structural changes in the brain. It is seemingly unlimited in its capacity and can retain many thousands of concepts and patterns, sometimes for a lifetime.

Another, slightly different model of LTM suggests two different facets of memory—episodic and semantic (Schacter & Tulving, 1994; Tulving, 1987). Episodic memory refers to information that is remembered within a particular temporal or spatial context (Tulving, 1983). It is autobiographical, that is, the recollection of information linked to an individual's personal experiences. It is called "episodic" because it is composed of a series of events (or an episode), which are sequentially ordered in time. Its time-linked nature is an important aspect and may comprise both reflections into the past or looking forward to the future (Tulving, 1989). Thus, episodic memory allows the mind to have a sense of space and time and to remember where things are and when they were there.

Semantic memory, on the contrary, is impersonal and not time-linked. It comprises an individual's repository of general information. The archetypal form of semantic memory is the process of using language, which calls on the individual's mental vocabulary and repertoire of knowledge of syntactical and semantic rules governing grammar, word order, meaning, and usage. On the other hand, episodic memory is more "plastic" than semantic memory. It may be affected by the process of recollection itself (e.g., by retrieval) or by a variety of factors that produce interference (e.g., distractors, anxiety) (Tulving & Schacter, 1990). Episodic and semantic memory share important features. They may for certain purposes be grouped together under the category of declarative memory (Tulving, 1983). Retrieval from procedural, perceptual representation system (PRS), and semantic memory is classified as implicit; that from STM and episodic memory is classified as explicit.

One useful concept of memory organisation is what some cognitive psychologists call a "schema". A schema is any pattern of relationships among data stored in memory. It is any set of nodes and links between them in the spider-web of memory that hang together so strongly that they can be retrieved and used more or less as a single unit. Theories of memory organisation suggest that activity knowledge organises autobiographical memory globally. According to these views, memories that share a participant, location, or time are only organised together if they also share an activity. If they do not, they are nested within their respective activity organisations locally rather than being organised together globally. However, this view is contradicted by a laboratory study that investigated the extent to which non-activity event characteristics organise event memories globally and provide direct access to these memories unmediated by activity (Lancaster & Barsalou, 1997). It was reported that people organise event memories globally in non-activity clusters, cross-classify events into multiple organisations, and pivot between activity and non-activity clusters. These results demonstrate the ability of individuals to organise events and also suggest that they may cross-classify event memories simultaneously into multiple global organisations. However, the representational and processing mechanisms that make such flexible performance possible need to be further understood.

Memories can also be divided into two additional categories: associative and non-associative. While both these categories cover many different subtypes, the essential difference is that in associative learning an animal learns the predictive nature of one environmental stimulus for another. The classic example of associative learning is Pavlovian associative conditioning, where Pavlov's dogs learned that a sound reliably predicted the delivery of food. The memorability of an event increases when that event is related to pre-existing knowledge, to existing beliefs or expectations, and/or other events at the time of encoding. Memory retrieval is enhanced by cues that are similar to the information supplied at the time of encoding. In addition, the memorability of an event increases when the event is relevant to expectations and beliefs about the event (Kihlstrom, 1994). Stressful events are often more memorable than ordinary daily life events. Cognitive theories have postulated that association and planning depends on the activation of representation units called "scripts" (Schank, 1982). Scripts are thought of as knowledge structures used for the representation of experienced events. They contain information about the temporal ordering, duration, and relative importance of events. Their structure is supposed to be similar to lexical or semantic knowledge representations in which individual items are linked by associative rules to form a network (Grafman, 1994).

Distinctions are also often made between verbal and spatial memory (i.e., memory for words versus spatial locations or pictures, respectively). More recently this distinction has been modified to reflect modality of input or an auditory versus visual distinction (The Psychological Corporation, 1997). As for the clinical relevance of these distinctions, there is a strong tendency to concentrate assessment on episodic and declarative memory rather than semantic and procedural memory, even though assessing these latter memory types can be very diagnostic in some memory disorders (Butters et al., 1988).

There are three ways in which information may be learned or committed to memory: by rote, assimilation, or use of mnemonic device. In the by rote approach, material to be learned is frequently repeated verbally so that it can later be repeated from memory without the use of any memory aids. When information is learned by rote, it forms a separate schema not closely interwoven with previously held information. That is, the mental processing adds little by way of elaboration to the new information, and that adds little to the elaboration of existing schemata. Learning by rote seems to be the least efficient way of remembering.

Through the assimilation method, the information is learned when its structure or substance fits into some memory schema already possessed by the learner. The new information is assimilated to the existing schema and can be retrieved readily by first accessing the existing schema, which may reconstruct it. Assimilation involves learning by comprehension. It is therefore a desirable method but it can only be used to learn information that is somehow related to one's previous experience.

Lastly, information may also be memorised by use of mnemonic techniques. A mnemonic device is any means of organisation or encoding information for the purpose of making it easier to remember. Mnemonic devices are useful for remembering information that does not fit any appropriate conceptual structure or schema already in memory. They work by providing a simple, artificial structure to which the information to be learned is then linked. The mnemonic device supplies the mental "file categories" that ensure retrievability of information. To remember, first recall the mnemonic device, then access the desired information.

SOME CONCEPTS OF MEMORY

Pairs of features that can be used to classify memory tasks and interventions are effortful versus automatic processing of information and the engagement of explicit versus implicit memory systems. The distinction between effortful versus effortless or automatic learning has been vigorously researched (Hasher & Zacks, 1979; Kausler, 1990; Parkin & Russo, 1990). Theoretical approaches to the study of memory make a distinction between automatic and controlled processes in remembering (Jacoby, 1991, 1998, 1999). Controlled processes are characterised by the intentional and conscious recollection of previously learned material. In contrast, automatic influences operate without intention, and lead to demonstrations of learning in the absence of any awareness of the learning episode. Initially, controlled and automatic memory processes were identified with remembering in direct and indirect memory tests (Ste-Marie et al., 1996). An example of a direct test is the traditional free recall procedure where participants are asked to recall studied material from an explicitly defined learning experience. Indirect tests make no such reference to any learning episode. Remembering is revealed by the facilitative effect of exposure to prior learning of which participants have no awareness (Richardson-Klavehn & Bjork, 1988). The findings generally indicate that normal ageing is associated with little loss of ability to learn new information through automatic processes. The concept of automaticity, in its original conception, has been criticised (Fisk, 1986). Parkin and Russo (1990) noted that most tasks used to demonstrate the lack of automatic processing have involved some form of conscious or explicit processing.

Studies on divided attention effects have found that performing a concurrent activity at the encoding stage of memory leads to a large decrement in later recall (Craik et al., 1996; Park et al., 1989). Performing a second activity at the retrieval stage of memory has provided some conflicting results. In some studies, divided attention at retrieval led to a decrement in memory performance, although not as severe as that associated with divided attention at encoding (Dywan & Jacoby, 1990; Moscovitch, 1994). However, in other studies, divided attention at retrieval had little effect on memory performance. This may suggest that retrieval is an automatic process (Baddeley et al., 1984; Craik et al., 1996). It is surprising that divided attention has such a large and consistent effect at encoding but a variable and sometimes much smaller effect at retrieval. Consequently, a large number of studies have been performed to better understand and clarify such an observation (Fernandes & Moscovitch, 2000; Moscovitch, 1992, 1994; Moscovitch & Umilta, 1990, 1991).

Schacter (1992) stated that explicit memory involves conscious recollection of previous experiences. It is typically assessed with recall and recognition tasks that require intentional retrieval of information from a specific episode. He defined implicit memory as an unconscious form of retention that may be measured with tasks that do not require conscious recollection of specific episodes. The dissociation of implicit and explicit memory has been described as resulting from two distinct anatomical memory systems (Tulving, 1985). This dissociation is derived from findings that an amnesic's implicit memory can be nearly normal while his or her explicit memory is severely impaired. A general consensus might be that in normal older adults, implicit memory appears to show either small or no decline compared with implicit memory performance in younger adults.

The transfer-appropriate procedures approach

Another hypothesis that has been proposed to explain implicit and explicit memory is the "transfer-appropriate procedures" (TAP) approach (Morris et al., 1977; Roediger et al., 1989). According to this hypothesis, explicit tests are seen as conceptually driven tasks that reflect meaning (Jacoby, 1983). Implicit tests are data-driven tasks that reflect perceptual processing. Therefore, performance on a test will increase if the test is similar in operation to the operation used in learning. Since different operations are used in implicit and explicit tests, different types of information are retrieved.

Tests designed to assess implicit memory can be classified according to the forms of information they access or the type of processing they require (perceptual vs conceptual). This distinction is emphasised by the TAP principle, which states that test of retention will benefit to the extent that the processing operations involved recapitulate or overlap those engaged during prior learning (see Roediger & McDermott, 1993a, b). According to the TAP account, for conceptual implicit tests that emphasise the semantic relationships between the studied and tested item (e.g., general knowledge questions, category production), the overlap in encoding and retrieval processes must occur at a semantic level in order to facilitate performance. In contrast, for perceptual implicit tests that emphasise a perceptual relationship between the studied and tested items (e.g., word or picture identification, word completion), the overlap in processes must occur at a perceptual level. The TAP framework can readily account for the finding that the perceptual similarity between study and test events (e.g., both being in the same mode of presentation) affects performance, whereas manipulations of meaning have no effect. The reverse is true for most conceptual tests (see Roediger & McDermott, 1993a, b). The perceptual/conceptual distinction is not meant as a dichotomy. Rather, it is more profitable to think of these as two separate dimensions that do not necessarily trade off against each other (see Craik et al., 1994). Performance in many implicit memory tasks relies on both conceptual and perceptual processes, for example, in recognition tasks, cued recall tasks, or priming of new associations.

The process dissociation framework

The process dissociation framework was designed to separate the effects of automatic and conscious influences on direct tests of memory. Jacoby and Kelley (1992) found that the likelihood of a word being used to complete a word stem (indirect test) is increased by prior presentation of the word. This effect is consistent even though a direct test shows no memory for the prior presentation. It was argued that these automatic influences may increase the likelihood of correct guessing on cued recall tests that are usually incorrectly viewed as reflecting only conscious processes.

Variables that will produce dissociations between recollection and automatic processes have been identified (Jacoby, 1991; Jacoby et al., 1993). One of these variables is attention allocated to stimuli at study. In these studies, the participants' ability to attend to the experimental stimuli was manipulated by dividing their attention. Manipulating attention allocation at presentation dramatically influenced recollection estimates. Participants in the divided-attention condition had recollection estimates that were virtually zero, but automatic influences were unaffected.

Using the process dissociation framework, it was demonstrated that amnesic recognition memory was largely based on estimates of familiarity, suggesting that the amnesic deficit lies primarily in failure to remember context (Verfaelli & Treadwell, 1993). However, this finding was criticised on the basis that the Jacoby procedure is difficult to interpret with amnesics with defective recognition memory (Roediger & McDermott, 1993a). There is good evidence to suppose that the amnesic syndrome can be associated with a failure to make use of context in memory, but the issue of whether this is an encoding or storage failure remains to be determined.

The component-process model

In an attempt to explain the puzzle of the interference effects of divided attention on memory at retrieval and encoding, the component-process model of memory has been proposed (Moscovitch, 1992, 1994; Moscovitch & Umilta, 1990, 1991). This model suggests that performance on explicit tests of memory is mediated by two main components. The associative cue-dependent component that is modular requires medial temporal lobe/hippocampal and diencephalic structures. The strategic component requires the prefrontal cortex, a central component that is under voluntary control. Being modular, the first component is domain-specific and operates mandatorily and automatically at encoding and retrieval. The strategic prefrontal cortex component is required to control this modular system and organise the

information it receives and emits. At encoding, it provides direct attention to the information that serves as the input to the medial temporal lobe/hippocampal system. Therefore, it is more resource-demanding than the modular process. Any concurrent task that diverts cognitive resources, by dividing attention during encoding, decreases the likelihood of that information being encoded adequately by the medial temporal lobe/hippocampal system, leading to poor memory (Bentin et al., 1998).

At retrieval, any cue that is consciously apprehended interacts with the memory trace via the medial temporal lobe/hippocampal structure if it is associated with it in a process known as ecphory. The product of that interaction is then delivered automatically to consciousness and experienced as a memory. However, a concurrent task can interfere with memory retrieval if, in addition to ecphory, prefrontal cortex strategic processes are required for successful retrieval (Moscovitch, 1994). The prefrontal cortex is required when the necessary retrieval cues are inadequate or not available. It is also needed to initiate a memory search, implement retrieval strategies, and monitor output from the medial temporal lobe/hippocampal system to determine its veridicality and consistency with the goals of the memory task. If the frontal lobe contribution to the memory test is minimal, then inference at retrieval is small or non-existent as the task can be performed by the modular medial temporal lobe/hippocampal system that operates automatically (Moscovitch, 1994).

Although the component-process model accounts for the asymmetry of the divided-attention effects at encoding and retrieval as well as for the variability of effects at retrieval, some investigators have questioned one of the model's assumptions (Anderson et al., 1998; Craik et al., 1996). It was reported that dividing attention during retrieval of a list of unrelated words led to only a slight decrease in number of words recalled but a marked increase in reaction time on the concurrent task (Craik et al., 1996). Therefore, it was concluded that retrieval on memory test was resource-demanding as indexed by the large reaction-time costs, yet was obligatory and immune to disruption because free recall was relatively unaffected by the concurrent task. Although consistent with the model's claim that ecphoric retrieval processes are obligatory, these findings indicate that they are also resource-demanding (non-automatic). It has also been suggested that free recall of words from LTM is not an automatic or obligatory process and that it is subject to interference effects under certain divided-attention conditions (Fernandes & Moscovitch, 2000). The magnitude of interference on free recall performance created under divided-attention conditions at retrieval depends on the similarity of material in the memory and concurrent tasks. However, under divided attention at encoding, any task that draws resources away from the memory task disrupts subsequent free recall performance to a similar degree. It was also pointed out that divided-attention effects do occur at retrieval but that they are material-specific. Memory tests that rely heavily on strategic prefrontal cortex resources are presumed to have a substantial strategic component whose operation is resource-demanding. On such tests of memory, divided-attention effects are observed at retrieval as long as the concurrent task itself is resource-demanding and thus draws resources away from the memory task. Examples of such tasks include recall of categorised lists, list discrimination, and release from proactive inhibition (Dywan & Jacoby, 1990; Jacoby, 1991; Moscovitch,1989, 1994; Park et al., 1989). Thus, divided attention at retrieval leads to relatively smaller interference effects than divided attention at encoding but the size of the effects depends on the material specificity of the concurrent task.

DECLARATIVE MEMORY

Working memory

The traditional concept of STM describes a more or less passive temporary memory store, the capacity of which is typically assessed via the immediate serial recall of lists of information. The concept of working memory, as well as being chronologically more recent, describes a more dynamic system concerned with the temporary

retention and transformation of information in support of cognitive activity (Baddeley & Hitch, 1974). Although STM and working memory clearly share a close relationship, both referring to transient memory, it has been argued on both empirical and conceptual grounds that there are nonetheless important distinctions to be made. STM tasks commonly require just the preservation of sequential order information. For example, the digit span task requires subjects to read or listen to lists of temporally separated digits and then repeat the sequence. In the span format, the number of list items increases until errors exceed threshold. Measuring working memory is less straightforward in that there are widely differing views as to what represents working memory. Nonetheless, the most common way of measuring working memory capacity involves working memory span tasks that essentially contain both a memory and a processing element. For example, the reading span task involves reading and comprehending sentences and remembering the sentence-final words for subsequent recall (Case et al., 1982; Daneman & Carpenter, 1980). Operation span involves solving arithmetic problems and remembering sums or accompanying words (Turner & Engle, 1989). Therefore, an important commonality of working memory span tasks is that they involve completing an additional processing task before each to-be remembered item becomes apparent. Working memory must keep track of which elements are activated at the same time, which ones were activated after which ones, and so on. In other words, the binding between activated features must be saved.

Working memory may be viewed as a gateway between sensory input and LTM (Baddeley, 1996). In particular, working memory is considered to be closely involved in the learning of novel information. However, a rather different interpretation of the LTM contribution to working memory performance has been proposed (Logie, 1996). It was suggested that working memory operates not as a gateway between sensory input and LTM but as a workspace (see Van der Linden, 1998). In this view, the storage components of working memory (the phonological loop and the visuospatial sketchpad) are not stores but rather they serve as temporary buffers for the information that has yet to be processed or is about to be rehearsed overtly. Thus, information that has been recently presented to the senses will activate the whole corresponding traces of LTM (visual, phonological, semantic, etc.), which then become available for temporary activation in the different components of working memory. This model provides an explanation of the intervention of LTM in span tasks by suggesting that the performance that depends on the phonological loop will be increased if semantic and visual information is simultaneously available for the other components of working memory. Logie's proposition constitutes an intermediate conception between Baddeley's multiple-component working memory model and the view which considers that working memory is nothing other than a temporary activation of representations and procedures in LTM (Kane & Engle, 2002).

Research on human working memory has been carried out at both behavioural and biological levels. Both avenues of research indicate that there are different kinds of working memories for different kinds of information. In particular, behavioural, neuropsychological, and neuroimaging evidence converges to indicate that there are separate systems for verbal and spatial information (Baddeley, 1996; Jonides et al., 1996). The verbal working memory is particularly important given the role that linguistic processes seem to play in higher cognitive processes. The study of a verbal system can be especially difficult, though, given that there can be no animal models to guide the effort. In this respect, imaging technology has been of great support.

Working memory is a limited-capacity system (able to hold only about seven recognisable items) capable of storing and manipulating information for only short periods of time (about 20 to 30 seconds without rehearsal) (Baddeley & Hitch, 1974). The core of the working memory model, the central executive, is assumed to be an attentional control system responsible for strategy selection and for control and coordination of the various processes involved in short-term storage and more general processing tasks. Baddeley (1986) has suggested that the supervisory attentional system (SAS) component of the attentional

control of action model proposed by Norman and Shallice (1986) might be an adequate approximation of the functions of the central executive system. Norman and Shallice (1986) assume the existence of two attentional control processes: the contention scheduling mechanism, which would be involved in making selections between conflicting routine actions, and the SAS, which would intervene when the selection of routine actions is not sufficient. By the early 1990s, cognitive-behavioural studies had provided evidence that verbal working memory contained a few distinct components, including a phonological rehearsal process (Baddeley, 1992; Jonides, 1995). Two other components of the working memory system (the articulatory loop or phonological loop and visuospatial sketchpad) also play significant roles in learning. The articulatory loop handles speech-based information whereas the visuospatial sketchpad handles visual (e.g., colour) and spatial (e.g., location) information. Thus, the articulatory loop may be described as a limited-capacity phonological store with an extremely brief memory trace (1–2 seconds), which very quickly decays unless it is refreshed by a rehearsal process involving subvocal speech.

Baddeley et al. (1998) have argued strongly that the phonological loop has evolved to support the acquisition by children of their native language and that it plays an important role in adult second-language learning. The visuospatial sketchpad is a mnemonic improvement system whereby the items to be remembered are recorded in visual terms and located as a specific visual scene. With rehearsal, information can be maintained in working memory indefinitely. According to Logie (1995), the visuospatial system comprises a visual temporary store that is subject to decay and to interference from incoming information, and also a spatial temporary store, which can be used to plan movement and also to rehearse the content of the visual store. In some respects, the structure of Logie's model is similar to that of the other documented slave system of working memory, the phonological loop. The visual cache, like the phonological store, provides a mechanism by which information can be rehearsed in working memory (akin to the role carried out by the phonological rehearsal process located in the phonological loop). One major difference between the two slave systems, however, is that whereas both subcomponents of the phonological loop are hypothesised to deal with information in a phonological code, the two subcomponents of the visuospatial sketchpad are believed to handle different types of information, giving rise to the visual and spatial distinction in working memory. In particular, the visual cache is thought to store information primarily about visual form and colour whereas the inner scribe is thought to store information about movement sequences. The visual cache is closely linked to the visual perceptual system while the inner scribe is involved in the planning and execution of movement. One other important feature of this model is the specification that information only enters visuospatial working memory through activated representations in LTM, rather than directly from the perceptual systems. Working memory has traditionally been evaluated by the digit-span test, in which a patient is asked to repeat back an increasingly longer series of digits. The patient's digit span is the length of the largest series of digits successfully repeated. In contrast, LTM can essentially be considered virtually unlimited in capacity, and is capable of storing strong experiences, factual knowledge, and skills over an entire lifetime.

This working memory concept differs from the previous notion of an STM store because it is more relevant to many everyday life situations than to specific memory tasks (e.g., as performed in the laboratory). One of the crucial contributions of the working memory model is the notion that numerous everyday activities (e.g., comprehension and resolution of a problem) require a combination of active processing and transformation as well as transient retention of relevant information. Another important component of working memory is the central executive, whose complex role is to integrate information from LTM and other involved systems and to plan, as well as to control, behaviour. Executive function comprises a broad class of mental processes involved in initiating and maintaining smooth information processing and coordinated actions in the central nervous system. They include strategic processes,

such as attention allocation, goal representation, and maintenance, and evaluative processes, such as performance monitoring. This latter can indicate the degree to which strategic processes need to be engaged to maintain stable performance.

There is considerable evidence for a division of the central executive of the working memory system into visual and verbal components (Shah & Miyake, 1996). Several studies have examined the performance of subjects with different verbal working memory capacities in syntactic processing in sentence comprehension tasks (Obler et al., 1991; Zurif et al., 1995). This literature provides evidence that the speed and accuracy of syntactic processing does not differ in a systematic way in normal subjects with different working memory capacities as measured by performance on sentence span tasks. In contrast, there is a suggestion in the data that low-capacity subjects may be more affected than high-capacity subjects by some sentential features, in particular the number of propositions in a sentence. The larger effect of the number of propositions in low-capacity than in high-capacity subjects suggests that low-capacity subjects have more difficulty with retaining information about the propositional content of a sentence in memory. Subjects whose verbal working memory capacity is reduced on standard tests of this function can retain the ability to use syntactic structure to determine sentence meaning. This is not only true in normal subjects (i.e., those without neurological problems), in whom the measurement of working memory may be unstable over time and lead to misclassification, but may also be observed in patients with AD and PD, whose verbal working memory and executive control functions are significantly impaired compared to normal subjects. A concurrent verbal memory load, either in normal subjects or in patients, does not disproportionately affect the processing of syntactically more complex sentences with reduced memory capacity. The working memory system involved in sentence interpretation is separate from that measured by standard tests of working memory. Thus, the central executive is like the manager who manipulates and coordinates information stored in the buffers for problem solving, planning, and organising activities.

Working memory plays an important role in consciousness, and impairments of working memory have been observed in several disorders, including schizophrenia, AD, and in alcoholics. A deficiency in the functioning of the central executive, reflected in a decreased ability to coordinate information from various different sources, may be an indication of memory impairments (Baddeley, 1988).

Reading comprehension deficits in learning-disabled (LD) readers have been attributed to impairments in working memory (Swanson & Alexander, 1997). Several studies suggest that LD readers have deficits in at least one component of working memory, the utilisation and operation of their articulatory loop. For example, LD readers are less able to generate pronunciations for unfamiliar or nonsense words than skilled readers, suggesting a deficient utilisation or operation of the phonological coding function of the articulatory control process (Gathercole & Baddeley, 1989; Rack et al., 1992). There is also evidence that a central feature of the dyslexic person's reading problems is a failure to develop adequate word-recognition skills (recognition involves determining whether a particular stimulus has previously been learned), a skill partially dependent on the articulatory system (Hansen & Bowey, 1994). A recent study that explores the contribution of working memory systems to the performance differences between LD and skilled readers reported poor performance of the LD readers (Swanson, 1999). They were observed to be inferior on virtually all composite measures of the articulatory, LTM, and central executive systems when compared to chronologically age-matched readers (Swanson, 1999). This study showed that the executive system accounts for significant variance in LD readers' comprehension performance. It further suggests that an executive system underlies some of the working memory and reading problems in children with learning disabilities.

The relationship between working and strategic memory has been suggested on the basis of findings in PD patients and aged normal subjects, both of whom have reduced working memory capacity and impaired strategic memory (Gabrieli et al., 1996b). Specifically, deficits in working memory have been proposed to impair the ability to perform the reasoning processes that are required when performing a strategic memory test. These deficits in working memory may arise from the impaired processing speed that occurs in PD and ageing, which may in turn be directly related to the depletion of frontal dopamine that occurs in both these conditions.

A plethora of studies has now demonstrated that the lateral frontal cortex is critically involved in certain aspects of working memory. This view emerged primarily from extensive lesion and electrophysiological recording on primates and from the study of patients with excisions of frontal cortex, although it has been largely confirmed by recent neuroimaging studies in normal human subjects (Petrides et al., 1993). Contemporary accounts, however, view working memory not as a unitary process but as a distributed system that depends critically on close and more posterior neural structures. Several multisynaptic connections between the prefrontal cortex (PFC) and the hippocampal formation have been described, with some speculations that these connections imply a reciprocal functional relationship in working memory (Goldman-Rakic, 1990; Goldman-Rakic et al., 1984). Damage to the hippocampus and related structures in rats produces severe and enduring deficits in spatial working memory tasks (Rawlins et al., 1983; Sahakian et al., 1990).

Neuroimaging technology has contributed much to our understanding of the neural bases of verbal working memory. These studies rest on a subtraction logic, in which two tasks are imaged, differing only in that one task presumably has an extra process, and the difference image is taken to reflect that process. These experiments indicate that verbal working memory consists of multiple components. One component involves the subvocal rehearsal of phonological information and is neurally implemented by left-hemisphere speech areas, including Broca's area, the premotor area, and the supplementary motor area. These experiments also provide some support for the hypothesis that, when a task requires the contents of working memory to be processed, the dorsolateral PFC is disproportionately activated (Smith et al., 1998). A PET study was designed to examine the cerebral areas subserving the updating function of the central executive with a running span task requiring subjects to watch strings of consonants of unknown length and then to recall serially a specific number of recent items (Van der Linden & Collette, 1999). It was observed that the most significant increase of rCBF (regional cerebral blood slow) occurred in the left frontopolar cortex (Brodmann's area 10) spreading to the left middle frontal (Brodmann's area 46). These results suggest that frontopolar activation underlies an updating process in working memory.

In principle, assessing working memory is simple: present a bit of information (a sample) to a subject, withdraw that information, wait for a period of time (a delay), then present that same bit of information along with a comparison bit, and ask the subject to identify which bit of information was presented previously (a choice). This process is then repeated across a number of trials. Only two bits of information are needed. Working memory will be required as long as the sample bit is selected randomly from trial to trial. This procedure forms the conceptual basis for memory paradigms known as delayed matching-to-sample. A common test of maintenance in working memory is the Sternberg task (Sternberg, 1969). Subjects are presented with a "memory set" of typically three to nine stimuli, which are then removed for several seconds before the appearance of a single probe stimulus. The goal for the subject is to decide whether or not the probe stimulus was one of the stimuli in the memory set. To isolate brain areas involved in maintenance from those involved in perceptual or motor components of the task, functional images obtained during the Sternberg task can be contrasted against those obtained in a control task in which the memory set and probe item are presented simultaneously, alleviating any memory requirements.

There is evidence that some working memory capacity emerges during infancy. Six-month-old infants can hold in working memory the spatial location of a cued target for as long as 4 seconds (Gilmore & Johnson, 1995). Mature functioning in working memory tasks emerges early during middle childhood, with considerable room for improvement through adolescence. Using a variety of prefrontal tasks that require working memory, a marked improvement from 4 years through early adolescence was shown (Luciana & Nelson, 1998). Indeed, it was observed that on a spatial working memory task and on more difficult Tower of London problems (i.e., those requiring four and five moves), the improvement from 8 years to adolescence/adulthood was at least as great as the improvement from 4 to 8 years. Similarly, 10- and 11-year-old children do not perform as well as adults on a test of visual working memory for pattern (Miles et al., 1996). In addition, in a study in which children between the ages of 7 and 15 were tested for spatial and verbal memory span, significant improvements in performance continued up through the oldest age group (Isaacs & Vargha-Khadem, 1989).

There are several differences between data from STM and working memory tests among children and adults. Working memory scores are often lower than their STM counterparts, sometimes half the value. More important, perhaps, working memory tasks are often better predictors of complex cognitive skills. In fact, a strong relationship between span measures and cognitive abilities has led some researchers to propose that working memory capacity may be an important component of the well-known psychometric concept of general intelligence, particularly its fluid aspects (Engle et al., 1999a, b). One's ability to temporarily maintain relevant information in mind has long been considered an indicator of one's intellectual capabilities (Jacobs, 1887). The fact that many widely used intelligence test batteries, such as the Wechsler Adult Intelligence Scale, include measures of temporary, short-term storage capacity such as forward and backward digit spans illustrates this point. Research has consistently demonstrated significant relationships between working memory and a range of abilities, including reading comprehension, language comprehension, reasoning, mental arithmetic, and general intelligence (Daneman & Carpenter, 1983; Logie et al., 1994; MacDonald et al., 1992). Among adults, STM is not consistently related to ability (Turner & Engle, 1989).

Developmental studies have also reported STM to be a weaker predictor of cognitive performance than working memory (Leather & Henry, 1994). A recent study performed in children between 8 and 11 years old compared STM and working memory across development in terms of absolute measures and intercorrelations between variables (Hutton & Towse, 2001). As indices of children's cognitive skills, STM and working memory were shown to be rather similar in terms of memory *per se*. However, this study highlights that what holds for working memory in adults may not be equally true for children and vice versa. Another line of evidence for the difference between STM and working memory in adults comes from another study that examined the relationship between verbal–numerical STM and working memory spans as well as their relations to general fluid intelligence (Engle et al., 1999). The main finding was that although STM and working memory span tasks correlate moderately with each other at the level of latent variables, they showed a clear separability and hence could not be considered the same. The nature of this difference is enhanced by the additional observation that the working memory span tasks were able to predict performance on general fluid intelligence tests. In addition, subsequent research has also demonstrated that performance on a working memory span task can reliably predict performance on various cognitive tasks that require deliberate, controlled processing in the face of distracting information (Kane et al., 2001; Tuholsky et al., 2001). Such findings suggest that, in the verbal domain, controlled attention ability may indeed be one important aspect of what makes the predictive power of working memory span tasks greater than that of STM span tasks.

The working memory model has been used to explain STM deficit both in normal ageing and in Alzheimer patients and to determine which component or components might be affected in either case (Anderson & Craik, 2000; Vallar & Papagno, 1995). In the first case, the elderly have a poorer performance when, for example, they are asked to carry out two tasks (dual task procedure) indicating that the central executive is performing less adequately in the elderly than in the younger group. In studies of Alzheimer's disease, it has been suggested that the low performance rates attained by AD patients in the Brown–Peterson task is due to a dysfunction of the central executive, which would otherwise allow the subject to review the items while doing the distracting tasks (Morris, 1986). Manipulating the complexity of the task, it was found that the more difficult it was, the lower the performance of AD patients in serial recall of the items. Studies have also examined the phonological loop and central executive functioning in this disease and have found a deficit in both components (Belleville et al., 1996; Collette et al., 1999b).

Episodic memory

The term episodic memory can be understood in two different ways. First, episodic memory may suggest a system that is different from the other major systems of human memory. The ability to travel mentally through time is an expression of the episodic memory system of the brain. The capacity to place events in time and to reference them may form the basis for self-awareness or consciousness. Thus, episodic memory is subserved by a distinct neurocognitive system that has evolved specially for mental time travel. Episodic memory enables individuals to remember their personal past, to consciously recollect experienced events and other happenings in subjectively apprehended space and time. It is a memory for personal events and its main characteristic is its dependence on autonoetic awareness, i.e., the kind of awareness that is known to normal subjects who consciously recollect these events by reliving them mentally (Tulving, 1985; Wheeler et al., 1997). In contrast, noetic awareness corresponds to the knowledge that an event occurred but without any conscious recollection; it is based on feelings of familiarity. The concept of autonoetic consciousness plays an important role in the discussion of episodic memory. Autonoetic consciousness is the capacity that allows adult humans to mentally represent and to become aware of their protracted existence across subjective time. When autonoetically aware, an individual can focus attention directly on his or her own subjective experiences. However, autonoetic consciousness is not limited to the past. It encompasses representation of the self's experiences in the past, present, and future. In summary, autonoetic consciousness affords individuals the possibility of apprehending their subjective experiences throughout time and perceiving the present moment as both a continuation of their past and as a prelude to their future.

The second case of episodic memory is that of a type of memory task and of performance on that task. The typical laboratory list-learning task in which participants are exposed to a collection of verbal items and then tested for what they have learned, by recall, recognition, or some kind of memory judgement, is often classified as an episodic memory test. Many of the verbal memory tests used by clinicians only involve retrieval (the process that activates and recovers stored information) from episodic memory. For instance, reading a list of words to a patient and then asking the patient to recall the words a minute later is an episodic memory test. This is because the patient must retrieve a specific list of words presented in a specific temporal (e.g., 1 minute) and spatial (in the same room) context.

A participant's performance on a so-called episodic memory task, such as recall or recognition of words encountered in a studied list, depends not only on episodic memory but also on other kinds such as semantic memory. Some studies showed that participants do not only consciously recollect words from a studied list, relying on episodic memory (Gardiner, 1988; Tulving, 1985). They can also simply "know" that some words occurred in the list, even if they are unable to have conscious recollection of the event of having studied the word.

Concerning episodic memory in children, it is likely that children cannot consciously recollect their past experiences before about the third year, despite the ability to recall the experiences (Wheeler et al., 1997). The development of episodic memory and autonoetic consciousness, similar to that of other brain functions, continues to mature throughout childhood. Although it may not be possible to say that newborn infants have no episodic memory, this system becomes fully functional by ages 2, 3, or 4. The development of episodic memory parallels the gradual growth of autonoetic consciousness and both mature slowly over time.

Given that children are not amnesic and much information is retained throughout childhood and into adulthood, infantile amnesia (defined as the inability of adults to remember experiences from their first few years of life) may be regarded as an issue of episodic remembering. Probably, an explanation for childhood amnesia is that the phenomenon results from a lack of autonoetic awareness in early childhood. Adults are only amnesic of their childhood in that they cannot mentally travel back in time to recollect events from the first few years of life as personally experienced happenings because in one sense the events were never personally experienced.

The exploration of age differences in episodic memory has recently included studies of both veridical memory (i.e., memory for information that was presented) and false memory (i.e., memory for information that was not presented). Several studies have demonstrated that compared with younger adults, healthy older adults have decreased veridical memory and relatively increased false memory (see Balota et al., 1999; Norman & Schacter, 1997; Tun et al., 1998). Using a repeated study–test procedure, it was reported that false recognition consistently increased across study–test trials in individuals with AD and consistently decreased across study–test trials in young adults (Budson et al., 2000). In addition, false recognition at first remained constant and then decreased across study–test trials in healthy older adults. Another study showed that when false memory was considered as a proportion of veridical memory, there was an increase in relative false memory as a function of age and dementia (Watson et al., 2001).

Semantic memory

Semantic memory includes a broad range of information about the world that is detached from personal experience as opposed to autobiographical reference. Semantic memory makes possible the acquisition, retention, and use of factual information about the world in the broadest sense. Spreading activation theories of the functional architecture of semantic memory assume that concepts are represented as nodes, and are interconnected by a network of links along which activation proceeds automatically (Collins & Loftus, 1975). In a properly working cognitive system, closely related semantic concepts are more strongly interconnected with each other than distantly related concepts and will be coactivated with a high probability.

A great deal of learning and memory may occur at the semantic (general knowledge) level alone without any intervention by episodic memory. Young children can acquire knowledge about the world efficiently and rapidly long before they develop the ability to recollect specific happenings from their past (Nelson, 1993; Perner & Ruffman, 1995). Piaget (1954) foreshadowed the concept of semantic memory with his discovery of object permanence in infants. Experiments suggest that the capacity for event memory in 1–2-year-olds not only exists but also is, in at least some meaningful ways, similar to that of older children and adults (Bauer & Wewerka, 1995).

Semantic memory and episodic memory have many features in common (see Table 1.2). Both represent large and complex systems, essentially unlimited in their capacity to hold and process information. They are unlike, for example, working memory, which has a limited capacity. Both are cognitive systems whose contents can be described in terms of objects and relations. Both model the world in the sense that a person can map their contents and make true–false judgements about individual propositions based on these contents. As a result, the two have been collectively referred to as declarative memory, or "remembering that", and dealt with as a unity distinguishable from procedural memory, or "remembering how". It may still be preferable to stick to the traditional view that there is only one kind of declarative memory and use the terms "episodic" and "semantic" for descriptive purposes only.

According to Tulving, episodic memory is an extension of semantic knowledge (Tulving & Markowitsch, 1998). Memory about the context of when and where the information was acquired is combined with the semantic knowledge that was gained on that occasion. Episodic memory cannot exist without semantic knowledge. Tulving's serial parallel independent model is based on the view that encoding of information is serial and that perceptual information about a viewed stimulus feeds only into the semantic system, which subsequently transmits information about the meaning of the item to episodic memory (Tulving, 1995; Tulving & Markowitsch, 1998). Therefore, the encoding of information into episodic memory is dependent on output from the semantic system. However, recent information from studies on semantic dementia showed that the manipulation of semantic knowledge had no significant impact on performance in episodic memory (Graham et al., 2000; Simons et al., 2001). These results are inconsistent with a hierarchical model of LTM and support a model in which episodic memory typically draws upon information from multiple systems, both semantic and perceptual. Some amnesic patients who have severely impaired or no functional episodic memory can nevertheless acquire new semantic information, especially when associative interference in learning is minimised or when "errorless" learning procedures are used (Baddeley & Wilson, 1994; Kitchener et al., 1998).

Prospective memory

Another concept, prospective memory, has received attention in neuropsychology. A distinction between retrospective and prospective remembering is drawn (Meacham & Leiman, 1982). Whereas retrospective memory refers to the recollection of information from the past (and most clearly resembles what has been referred to as declarative memory), prospective remembering concerns the recall of actions to be performed in the future. Prospective memory may be described as a kind of memory that is pervasive in daily activities in remembering to perform some intended action at a particular point in the future. Prospective memory can thus be conceptualised as involving the following stages: forming an intention, remembering the intention during an intervening period, and performing the intended action at the appropriate time (Hitch & Ferguson, 1991). Thus, prospective memory may be regarded as a separate form of LTM.

TABLE 1.2

Episodic vs semantic memory

Similarities	Differences
1. Both represent large and complex systems, essentially unlimited in their capacity to hold and process information.	1. Episodic memory is concerned with remembering, whereas semantic memory is concerned with knowing.
2. Cognitive operations involved in encoding of information are similar for both episodic and semantic memory.	2. Whereas man and animals possess well-developed knowledge-of-the-world or semantic memory, there is limited evidence that animals have the ability to consciously remember past events in the way people do.
3. Both can receive information for storage through different sensory modalities as well as from internally generated sources.	3. Young children acquire significant semantic memory before they become capable of adult-like episodic remembering.
4. Stored information in both systems represents aspects of the world.	4. Whereas semantic memory is present-oriented, episodic memory may be oriented toward the past, present, or future.
5. As cognitive systems, both differ from all forms of procedural memory.	5. Episodic remembering is often charged with much feeling of affection whereas such kinds of feeling may be absent in semantic knowing.
6. Information in both systems is accessible to introspection. An individual can consciously think about things and events in the world.	
7. The processes of both forms of memory depend critically on the integrity of the medial temporal lobe and diencephalic structures of the brain.	

Event-based prospective memory tasks are those for which some environmental event signals the appropriateness of the intended action (e.g., remembering to give a friend a message when you encounter the friend) (Einstein & McDaniel, 1990). By contrast, in time-based prospective memory tasks, a particular time or a particular amount of elapsed time signals the appropriateness of the intended action (e.g., a 10.00 a.m. doctor's appointment). The fundamental difference between prospective and retrospective memory tests lies in the relationship between the provision of instructions to retrieve information and the opportunity to demonstrate performance on the task. Explicit measures of retrospective remembering both require that to-be-remembered information must be encoded, and that the information is held and eventually retrieved. However, prospective remembering also requires that the instruction to activate retrieval must be retained and recalled across time (Einstein & McDaniel, 1990). Explicit retrospective remembering and instructions to retrieve are provided immediately prior to the opportunity to demonstrate retention. It is possible that variables interfering with the regular initiation of instruction retrieval would lead to dissociations between retrospective and prospec-

tive task performance. Time-based prospective memory tasks have been associated with significant age-related deficits and generally lower performance than observed in event-based tasks (Park et al., 1997). The elderly participants' poorer performance on a prospective memory task may be due to a failure to monitor time regularly because of attentional resource limitations (Einstein et al., 1995). Resources may be occupied by distracting, task-irrelevant intrusions.

A study designed to assess the degree of involvement of the neuropsychological systems in prospective remembering suggests that frontal functioning should play a key role in prospective memory performance (McDaniel et al., 1999). The involved executive functions might include encoding–planning the prospective memory task and inhibiting ongoing activity, and organising the execution of the intended activity This study also suggests that hippocampal functioning may influence prospective memory, perhaps in the service of retrieving the intended activity during presentation of the target event. Prospective memory may be viewed as a complex cognitive operation which draws on explicit or declarative memory and is controlled by frontal-based executive processes (Glisky, 1996).

Because prospective remembering is a core activity in everyday life, any deficit in this ability is likely to have severe consequences for an individual's ability to live independently in the community (Cockburn, 1995; Huppert & Beardsall, 1993; McDaniel et al., 1999). In practice, amnesic and demented patients have considerable problems executing any kind of prospective memory task. Accordingly, impairment in prospective memory is often an important target for assessment and rehabilitation in neuropsychological practice (Cockburn, 1995).

Graf and Uttl (2001) reported on one prospective function, called prospective memory proper, that they define in the spirit of James (1890). They regard vigilance and prospective memory proper as part of a continuum of possible prospective memory functions. At one end of this continuum, the prospective task dominates working memory and conscious awareness during the retention interval. At the other end (the prospective memory proper end), the plan is out of working memory during the retention interval and conscious awareness is focused on competing activities. It is postulated that what varies along the continuum is the proportion of available processing resources allocated to the prospective task during the retention interval. For vigilance, all or most of the available resources are allocated to the prospective tasks, whereas for prospective memory proper, all or most of the available resources are allocated to competing activities. It is further suggested that the development of instruments and methods that give separate indexes of the prospective and retrospective components of prospective memory tasks is urgently required.

Recognition memory

Recent research has provided a theoretical basis for the fractionation of memory function into recall and recognition components, although this dissociation is disputed (Aggleton & Brown, 1999; Squire and Knowlton, 1994). Recognition memory is a fundamental facet of our ability to remember. One model regards recognition memory as a unitary process directly linked to other forms of explicit memory and hence dependent on the same

systems (Donaldson, 1999; Hirshman & Master, 1997). It was argued that discrete hippocampal damage is sufficient to impair both recall and recognition (Squire & Knowlton, 1994). Following this model, recognition memory is an integral component of the class of memory lost in amnesia. An alternative approach is that there are different component processes within recognition memory (Gardiner & Parkin, 1990; Jacoby & Dallas, 1981). There is a widely held view that recognition depends on two independent processes: recollection and familiarity (Mandler, 1980).

Recollection involves retrieving associations between an item and features of the context defining the episode in which it was encountered, whereas familiarity involves the automatic attribution of previous experience based on more fluent processing of the remembered item. Recognition memory requires a capacity for both identification and judgement of the prior occurrence of what has been identified (Mandler, 1980). Only one of these processes maps onto the class of memory that is always lost in anterograde amnesia (Aggleton & Brown, 1999). If one encounters a person, one might recollect information about the person, such as when one previously met him or his name. It seems that subjectively it is possible to consider recognition memory as composed of at least two processes. The first is familiarity discrimination ("knowing"—I know you but I cannot remember when I first saw you). The second is recollective matching ("remembering"—I know I have seen you before because I can remember a specific episode). Aggleton and Brown suggest that damage limited to the hippocampal system (hippocampus, fornix, mammillary bodies, anterior thalamus) may leave recognition memory intact despite causing a severe recall deficits. Thus, it would be useful to employ the remember/know judgement paradigm to study the recollective processes captured in serial recall, paired associate recall, and other such measures of explicit memory to separate the likely "remember" and "know" components involved (Rajaram, 1993).

In a rather different theoretical context, Tulving (1983, 1985) proposed that these mental experiences reflect two kinds of consciousness, noetic and autonoetic consciousness, which are in turn properties of expressions of two distinct mind–brain systems, semantic and episodic memory. Hence, on this view, representations in two different mind–brain systems contribute to recognition memory. Tulving (1983, 1985) further suggested that people could use "know" and "remember" responses to report experiences of the two conscious states. Consequently, it has become established that reports of knowing and of remembering in recognition memory can be systematically dissociated and associated by many independent variables. A deeper level of processing increases remembering, without influencing knowing (Gardiner, 1988). Repetition test priming increases knowing without influencing remembering (Rajaram, 1993). Long versus short test-response deadlines increase both remembering and knowing (Gardiner et al., 1999). There are also systematic differences between knowing and remembering in different subject populations. Remembering but not knowing is reduced in older compared with younger adults and in certain clinical conditions such as schizophrenia (Huron et al., 1995). There is at least some evidence that these two subjective states of awareness involve quite distinct patterns of neuronal activation in the brain, as measured by event-related functional magnetic resonance imaging (Gardiner & Richardson-Klavehn, 2000; Henson et al., 1999).

Current research supports theories claiming that recognition memory involves the two components of remembering and knowing. These two components have been interpreted within a dual-process independence model developed by Jacoby (1991; Jacoby et al., 1997). According to this model, knowing reflects an automatic form of memory and remembering reflects a consciously controlled form of memory. The results have also been interpreted in terms of joint contributions to recognition memory made by semantic and episodic systems as conceived by Tulving (1983). Although there continue to be disagreements between these different views at both conceptual and theoretical levels, the results of current studies converge on the conclusion that knowing and remembering reflect qualitatively distinct memory traces.

The notion that there can be a specific deficit in recognition memory for faces is readily under-standable if one accepts that face recognition is modular (Moscovitch et al., 1997; Nachson, 1995). Neuroimaging studies have indicated that face recognition requires the use of multiple specific differential nodes on a complex memory circuit (Andreasen et al., 1996).

Autobiographical memory

The term autobiographical memory is used to focus attention on an individual's record of his or her own personal experiences as opposed to performance on standard laboratory tests such as free recall. It is a specific kind of episodic memory that refers to the recollection of experiences from an individual's life that are presumed to be of significance to the self-esteem (Baddeley, 1995). Autobiographical memories are the elements that ground the self. They are the elements that make us what we are, the mental representations that distinguish one individual from another. Of course there are other types of knowledge that do this as well: one's personal beliefs and experiences that separate one human being from another. Two twin brothers, for example, who live together will nonetheless have many different memories that reflect their personal projects and goals, whether conscious or not, during their life. The central point to emerge is that autobiographical memories are meaningful mental structures. As well as carrying personal meaning, they often carry a wider meaning for subgroups within society and even for society as a whole. How we are to model and understand this meaning is as yet unknown. Undoubtedly any model will eventually have to draw not only on experimentation from cognitive psychology, but also on systems of thought developed in psychoanalytic traditions of thinking and clinical psychiatry, which have for years addressed issues relating to autobiographical memory. Part of the answer lies in Pillemer's suggestion that autobiographical memories, and the ability to have them, provide a certain social intelligence that could not be delivered in any other way (Pillemer, 1998). In this social intelligence, the specifics of experience are preserved and can be re-examined, thought over, reconceptualised, and fed back into the group.

Autobiographical memories are specific, long-lasting, and usually of significance to one's self-concept. All autobiographical remembering involves a split between the present self that is remembering and the past self that is remembered (Reed, 1994). The way people see the past in autobiographical memory illuminates the relationship they currently perceive between the past and present, with implications for where they anticipate heading in the future.

Rubin et al. (1986) proposed a three-component model of autobiographical memory consisting of infantile amnesia, a retention component to account for the high frequency of memories from the most recent years, and a reminiscence component to explain over-representation of memories from adolescence. Individual differences in the way parents talk to their children about the past lead to individual differences in children's reporting skill. As children's self-understanding becomes more complex over time, more features are available to organise events in memory (Howe & Courage, 1993, 1997). Children's ability to use these self-features in conjunction with their increasing ability to maintain memories in storage results in the increases seen in children's autobiographical memory abilities from the age of 3 and beyond. The way in which adults talk to children about the past appears to play an important role in children's developing ability to report autobiographical memories (Harley & Reese, 1999).

In a typical autobiographical memory experiment, a participant is presented with a series of cue words and asked to respond with the first personal memory that each word elicits. By subsequently dating them, it is possible to see from what points in the participant's life the memories come. With the stronger bias that young people have for recent memories, their recall is typified by a propensity to recall from the very recent past. Most of the personally important events in life occur in the second and third decades: one goes to school, graduates, gets a job, gets married, has children, and so on. In addition, an incredible number of first experiences occur: first time driving a car, first romantic kiss, first job interview. The proliferation of these types of events causes the reminiscence peak (Jansari & Parkin,

1996). In effect, most of the crucial moments in one's personal history occur at this time. These memories are retrieved faster than other memories and first-time memories from childhood tend to be easier to retrieve than those from midlife.

The question of how these temporal landmarks may aid retrieval from autobiographical memory has been examined. Barsalou (1988) conducted a series of studies that showed that individuals recalled events on the basis of theme-related extended events (e.g., vacationing in Italy) more than activities (e.g., going to movies). Barsalou suggested that autobiographical memory consists of a collection of external events running concurrently and in parallel. The thematic knowledge structure proposed by Conway (1992) closely approximates Barsalou's (1988) concept of extended event time-lines. According to Conway, thematic knowledge is hierarchically organised in terms of lifetime periods. Autobiographical recollection may best be viewed as retrieval from within a hierarchy of nested events. Individuals move with varying degrees of fluency between different levels of the hierarchy. Thus, autobiographical memory appears to be hierarchically organised (Conway, 1992; Schooler & Hermann, 1992). The construction of autobiographical memories depends on access to an autobiographical knowledge base. Each layer of autobiographical knowledge, organised in hierarchical fashion, provides indices to the other levels and thus facilitates access. Retrieval of specific memories is mediated by a cyclical strategic series of events.

Because it is not possible to remember all of our experiences and because the same experience may be encoded and processed differently by different people, memory may be interpretive and driven at least in part by a person's goals and desires (DeSteno & Salovey, 1997). The content or subject matter of autobiographical memories may reveal themes that reflect an individual's most important concerns. In human motivation, the agency–communion contrast may describe the two central concerns of people. Agency refers to concerns about individual achievement and personal power as well as independence and distinction from others. Communion refers to concerns about relationships, interdependence, and connection to others. Ample evidence suggests that agentic and communal motives are linked to the content of autobiographical memories. For instance, researchers have noted that when subjects were asked to describe significant life experiences, agentic individuals recalled agentic experiences (e.g., self-mastery, losing face) whereas communal individuals recalled communal experiences (e.g., love or friendship, rejection) (McAdams et al., 1996; Woike, 1994). However, this pattern was reported for emotionally involving memories but not for everyday or neutral experiences (Woike, 1994).

Odours are particularly powerful autobiographical memory cues; they are specially evocative reminders of past experiences. Engen and Ross (1973) observed that whereas memory for odours, relative to stimuli from other perceptual modalities, was initially poor, subsequent testing revealed very little forgetting of the odours. When the distribution of autobiographical memories across the entire lifespan in a group of elderly participants was plotted, it was found that the peak number of memories retrieved appeared at an earlier age for odour cues (Chu & Downes, 2000). That is, odour-cued autobiographical memories are older. This led Chu and Downes to suggest that memory for odours differs in important ways from that for stimuli from other modalities. This hypothesis has since been corroborated by several other studies indicating that a separable memory system for olfaction exists and that odour memory may dissociate into different component subsystems (Lehrner et al., 1999; White, 1998). Because of the neuroanatomical projections between the olfactory processing regions and the limbic structures, odours may be especially privileged in their ability to directly influence the modulatory functions of the amygdala. Herz and Cupchik (1992) concluded that odour-evoked memories tended to be highly emotional, vivid, specific, rare, and relatively old.

Research in autobiographical memory suggests that gender-differentiated socialisation processes influence the content and complexity of representations of autobiographical emotional events in memory. Women recall more autobiographical memories of emotional events (Davis, 1999). The fact that they are generally faster in doing so strongly suggests that they engage in a greater degree of elaborative processing of personal, real-life emotional experiences than men do. From a very early age, girls are observed to be socialised to allocate more attentional and processing resources to emotional information than are boys (Brody & Hall, 1993). In addition, parents are more likely to use an elaborative narrative style when discussing past events with their young daughters than with their young sons (Fivush & Reese, 1992). Therefore, gender differences in autobiographical memory for emotional events may have their origins in early gender differences in the socialisation of emotion and in the nature of parent–child construction of past events. Autobiographical memories of emotional events appear as socially constructed memories that uniquely reflect the effects of gender-differentiated socialisation processes.

Autobiographical memory appears to be abnormal in depressed people, who tend to recall negative events more rapidly than positive events (Williams et al., 1997). Depressed people tend to be over-general in their recall even when cued to report specific events. Neuroimaging studies of the retrieval of autobiographical memories may reveal distinctive patterns of regional brain activation and may have particular relevance to clinical disorders characterised by cognitive deficits such as depression, anxiety, AD, and other conditions.

Mental imagery

Images may represent summary information in autobiographical memory that can be used to direct memory searches (Williams et al., 1999). They contain information that is richly informative about a represented event in the sense that information in the image facilitates access to other related events and themes. Thus, the information in the image may be employed by the retrieval process as a source of powerful cues with which to probe memory traces. A cue word high in imageability makes more probable the retrieval of specific autobiographical memories, because it establishes more links between general events and event-specific knowledge and in turn acts as a powerful index to direct the retrieval cycle. Cohen and Faulkner (1988) showed that for younger participants, age of memory was a significant predictor of memory vividness, with recent memories being much more vivid than remote memories. However, for their older participants (60 to 89 years old), this was not the case and other factors, such as frequency of recall, predicted vividness for them.

Tulving (1983) used the term "ecphory" to describe the process by which retrieval cues interact with stored information so that an image or a representation of the information in question appears. It is of interest to investigate whether in the intact human brain, the ecphory of presented autobiographical material will affect different brain regions compared with the retrieval of semantically closely similar material. A study designed to investigate the functional anatomy of autobiography material in normal volunteers showed that the right hemispheric network of temporal, together with posterior, cingulate, and prefrontal areas is engaged in the ecphory of affect-laden autobiographical information (Fink et al., 1996). This study provides strong evidence that right hemispheric temporal cortical areas are the key regions for autobiographical memory ecphory.

Visual STM may be considered as a limited-capacity system that maintains a record of recently presented visual information. LTM is a more durable store for well-learned information with no obvious limit on its storage capacity. Researchers have proposed that visual STM concerns the surface appearance of objects whereas LTM involves abstract, structural descriptions of objects (Humphreys & Bruce, 1989). Alternatively, it has been proposed that LTM stores surface as well as abstract descriptions (Kosslyn, 1980). According to Kosslyn (1994), visual mental imagery plays an important role in object recognition, activates the (primary) visual cortex, and shares spatial properties with representations of actual visual stimuli. Johnson and Raye (1981) developed a model that states how memories from internal and external stimulus sources (imagery and perception, respectively) can be distinguished. This can be achieved by comparing the amount of sensory, contextual, and semantic attributes of the item, because perception is in general more vivid than mental imagery. Memories for real experiences are richer in sensory details and contextual attributes than are memories for imagined experience (Johnson et al., 1993). The ability to discriminate between both types of event increases with the degree of sensory–perceptual information contained in memories for real events. Encoding conditions involving sensory–perceptual and semantic processing subsequently enhance recognition memory (McGinnis & Roberts, 1996).

PROCEDURAL MEMORY

The procedural system, an action system whose operations are expressed in the form of changes in overt behaviour, may function independently of cognition. Procedural knowledge expression is automatic. A number of studies have shown that certain tasks could be performed with minimal awareness following prolonged practice (Schneider & Shiffrin, 1977; Shiffrin & Schneider, 1977). The perceptual representation system (PRS) is critically involved in perceptual identification of objects, as well as in perceptual priming, that is, the enhancement of the efficacy of such identification through experience. Perceptual priming —non-conscious, early developing, presemantic perceptual learning—was discovered only recently. Thus, the PRS receives and makes available to other systems information about perceptual features of physical objects. It makes possible associative (e.g., stimulus–response) learning by furnishing one ingredient (the stimulus) for the basic unit of such learning.

Repetition priming

Repetition priming is a facilitation or bias in performance related to previous experience with a stimulus, measured in terms of response speed or accuracy at test. It is commonly subdivided into perceptual priming, which is based on the perceptual features of the stimulus (Roediger & McDermott, 1993a, b) and does not benefit from semantic encoding, and conceptual priming, which is based on semantic features of the stimulus and is not affected by changes in perceptual features.

Perceptual priming

Perceptual priming refers to the unconscious facilitation of performance following exposure to a target item or a related stimulus. Several different measures can be used to assess perceptual priming such as word identification, lexical decision, and word fragment completion. Perceptual priming may be tested using tasks such as perceptual identification, in which a word is presented for a brief time (< 100 ms) and the subject attempts to identify it. It may also be tested by word stem completion, in which a word stem is presented and the subject is asked to complete the stem with the first word that comes to mind. In the word stem completion task, subjects are required to complete a word stem (for example, Pre___) with the first word that comes to mind (Warrington & Weiskrantz, 1974). The stems are generally selected to have several possible completions. It is of interest to note whether prior presentation of an appropriate completion of a stem (for example, President) increases the probability of its generation. This is assessed by comparing the probability of completing stems with specific completions (targets), when these have (primed condition) or have not (unprimed/baseline condition) been presented in the experimental setting prior to the completion task (Schacter et al., 1993).

Memory retrieval as revealed by word stem completion priming (WSCP) has been referred to as "implicit". This is mainly because the test instructions do not ask the participants to actively think back to the previous study episode. Implicit retrieval is often contrasted with "explicit" retrieval as measured by standard episodic memory tasks in which subjects are told to recollect information from the study session. Perceptual priming is an unconscious form of human memory that deals with perceptual identification of words and objects, and may be considered as an expression of a PRS that interacts closely with other memory systems with which it has high affinity (e.g., semantic memory) (Tulving & Schacter, 1990). Some properties of the PRS suggest that this category of

memory develops early and is preserved late in life. It is relatively unaffected by the administration of drugs which may affect the other memory systems.

There is substantial evidence from both normative and neuropsychological studies that priming and declarative memory are functionally and neurally dissociable (Gabrieli et al., 1990; Schacter, 1990; Squire, 1987; Tulving & Schacter, 1990). In studies with young normal subjects, study-phase conditions such as semantic processing or stimulus generation enhance declarative memory, but have little or no effect on some kinds of priming (Rajaram & Roediger, 1993). On the other hand, some experimental manipulations can affect priming (e.g., study–test changes in modality or stimulus notation), but have little effect on declarative memory (Weldon & Roediger, 1987). Evidence for the neural dissociability of declarative memory and priming has come from studies of patients with amnesia due to bilateral damage to medial–temporal and diencephalic brain regions. Although these patients have a profound deficit on declarative memory tasks, they show normal priming on a variety of tasks, such as category exemplar generation, word association generation, word stem completion, word fragment completion, picture naming, and threshold identification (Graf et al., 1984; Keane et al., 1997; Schacter et al., 1994; Shimamura & Squire, 1984; Verfaellie et al., 1996). Densely amnesic patients who exhibit severe impairment on learning new information may exhibit near-normal learning and memory when tested by priming methods.

The notion that priming is intact in amnesic patients was challenged, based on a study of correlations among measures of priming, recognition memory, and resonance imaging of three different groups of patients (amnesic, AD, and HD patients) and controls (Jernigan & Ostergaard, 1993). It was concluded that it is questionable whether evidence from amnesic patients can provide support for the existence of separate memory systems, at least where such evidence is based on studies of priming. Such evidence may be complicated by the fact that amnesic patients process stimuli more slowly and less efficiently than control subjects, since amnesic patients perform more poorly than control subjects at baseline word identification. Moreover, priming can be mediated by a perceptual–structural representation system that may be spared in patients with AD, whereas priming mediated by a lexical–semantic memory system is impaired in these same patients (Keane et al., 1991; Schacter, 1990). Priming effects may depend exclusively on intact cortical representations, because they are reduced in patients with dementia resulting from early stage AD (Buckner et al., 1995). However, they are not reduced in amnesic patients with equivalently severe memory problems and in HD dementia patients. Neuroimaging data suggest that perceptual priming of visually presented stimuli depends on the extrastriate cortical visual pathways that are ordinarily involved in processing visual stimuli (Buckner et al., 1995). Visual priming appears to take place within perceptual processing systems, where neural changes occur well before information reaches the medial temporal lobe and diencephalic brain systems that transform visual perception into conscious visual memory. However, the question of what brain systems support baseline performance and priming still remains important for further work. Other studies that examined the perceptual identification thresholds of amnesic patients across a wide range of stimulus conditions and accuracy levels concluded that baseline thresholds and priming effects were fully intact for all amnesic patients except in a condition using small stimuli (1.1° × 0.25° of visual angle). In that condition, only the patients with Korsakoff's syndrome were impaired (Hamann et al., 1995; Squire et al., 1996). No systematic differences in perceptual identification performance between amnesic patients and control subjects were observed. Priming of perceptual identification is fully intact in amnesic patients. It was further hypothesised that priming is independent of the brain structures important for declarative memory that are damaged in amnesia.

A recent case study of patient EP, a profoundly amnesic patient who has no detectable declarative memory (he developed profound anterograde and retrograde amnesia after herpes simplex encephalitis), demonstrates that priming may operate nonconsciously and improve the ability to detect or identify recently presented stimuli (Hamann &

Squire, 1997). Priming and recognition tests that were matched with respect to test materials, test lists, and the kind of cues available at test were used. It was observed that on the priming tests, EP performed consistently at the same level as the controls and other amnesic patients for both studied and non-studied items. All three groups exhibited significant priming for both stem completion and perceptual identification. By contrast, EP performed at chance levels on the recognition tests. The percentage of correct scores (hits plus correct rejections) was 52%, 65%, and 81% for EP, amnesic patients, and control participants respectively. The amnesic group performed above chance but was impaired relative to the control group on both yes–no recognition and two-alternative forced-choice recognition. Thus, EP could not recognise as familiar the words he had read 5 minutes earlier, either to choose which of two words was familiar or, when asked, to say yes or no to indicate which words had been presented earlier. This study provides compelling evidence that priming depends on a separate and independent memory system from the system that supports declarative memory. Priming was fully intact in patient EP even though no declarative memory could be detected.

In a study that assessed repetition priming in two different tasks within a single experiment —one in which subjects named briefly (tachistoscopically) presented words, and one requiring naming of visually fragmented/degraded words— performance of amnesic patients, AD patients, and normal controls was assessed (Ostergaard, 1994). The two tasks produced very different patterns of priming effects, despite the fact that common study phases were used. The AD patients evidenced impaired priming in both tasks. However, in the degraded-word-naming task the deficit was only apparent under some experimental conditions. The amnesics produced priming effects that in absolute terms were similar to those produced by control subjects. Nevertheless, when group differences in overall performance level were considered in the tachistoscopic test, these patients also showed clear evidence of impaired priming. It was argued that the complex pattern of priming effects obtained is best explained by the characteristics of the retrieval cues provided by the tests. Generally, such characteristics may determine whether an experimental variable will affect measured priming. Therefore, this study highlights the fact that priming may not represent a form of retention that is selectively spared in amnesia. It also showed how several factors might converge to produce seemingly normal priming effects in memory-disordered patients. In general, priming measures vary in their sensitivity to experimental manipulations, such as delay between study and test, number of times the primed items are presented, and level of processing (Jacoby, 1983; Squire, 1987). It should perhaps not be surprising that such priming measures show different sensitivity to the experimental variable "amnesia". In other words, when no significant difference is found between amnesic patients and control subjects on a given measure, it is possible that the measure is not sensitive to a real underlying impairment.

Conceptual priming

Conceptual priming relies on the polymodal association cortices of the frontal, and temporoparietal regions. Conceptual priming has been tested using tasks such as category exemplar generation, in which a person is presented with a category name (e.g., animals) and asked to name members of that category. Priming in this task is noted when low-frequency studied items are generated on the test more often than are matched unstudied items. Patients with AD are impaired in tests of conceptual priming (Monti et al., 1996).

An important question concerns the capacity for showing priming for materials without pre-existing representations in memory in normal and pathological ageing. A study which assessed volunteers (20 patients with mild AD, 20 elderly controls, and 20 young control subjects) with a paradigm of priming for new verbal associations reported that neither the AD patients nor the normal elderly subjects demonstrated priming effects for new associations, while young subjects showed significant priming effects (Ergis et al., 1998). These results indicate that the absence of priming for new verbal associations is more attributable to an effect of ageing than to a specific effect of AD.

Skill learning

Skill learning involves the gradual acquisition of new abilities that generalise across a range of stimuli. Common everyday examples of skill learning include learning to ride a bicycle (motor skill learning), learning to read a novel alphabet (perceptual skill learning), and learning to play chess (cognitive skill learning). In skill learning tasks, subjects perform a challenging task on repeated trials in one or more sessions. The indirect or implicit assessment of learning is the improvement in speed or accuracy achieved by a subject across trials and sessions. As in priming, skill learning is thus independent of conscious recollection and is also spared in the amnesia that follows medial temporal lobe damage (Squire, 1987). Preservation of sensorimotor, perceptual, and cognitive skill learning in amnesia indicates that such learning for some skills is not dependent on declarative memory. Some of the neural systems underlying such skill learning have been identified in neuropsychological and neuroimaging studies.

Intact sensorimotor skill learning in amnesia has been well documented for mirror tracing, rotary pursuit, and serial reaction time (SRT). In mirror tracing, subjects trace a figure with a stylus while seeing only their hand, the stylus, and the figure reflected in a mirror. With practice, subjects trace the figure more quickly and make fewer errors (departures from the figure). Such skill learning is intact in patients with declarative memory problems due to amnesia or AD (Carrillo et al., 2001; Milner, 1962). In rotary pursuit, subjects attempt to maintain contact between a stylus and a target metal disk the size of a coin on a revolving turntable. With practice, subjects increase the time per trial that they are able to maintain contact with the disk. Rotary pursuit skill learning is intact in amnesia and in AD (Corkin, 1968; Heindel et al., 1989). In the SRT task, subjects see targets appear in one of four horizontal locations on a computer monitor and press one of four keys placed directly below those locations as soon as a target appears in the corresponding location. SRT learning is intact in amnesia but variable in AD patients (Ferraro et al., 1993).

This variability in AD performance may reflect dementia severity and perhaps specific impairment in spatial working memory.

Perceptual skill (e.g., learning to read mirror-reversed text) has also been studied in patients. Amnesic patients gain skill in reading such text at a normal rate, despite poor declarative memory for the particular words read or the episodes in which they gained their skill. On the other hand, patients suffering from HD have mildly impaired mirror-reading skill learning despite relatively good declarative memory for words read and the reading experiences (Martone et al., 1984). Cognitive skills may be acquired normally by amnesic patients but under relatively narrow circumstances. Amnesic patients have shown normal skill learning on Tower tasks that require planning and problem solving under some circumstances (Saint-Cyr et al., 1988).

The basal ganglia appear to be critical for a variety of motor, perceptual, and cognitive skills. The core structures of the basal ganglia include the dorsal striatum, ventral striatum, and globus pallidus. In addition, the substantia nigra, ventral tegmental area, and the subthalamic nucleus may be considered associated basal ganglia structures via their reciprocal connections with the core structures. Patients with basal ganglia disorders (e.g., Huntington's & Parkinson's diseases) exhibit impairments in a number of cognitive tasks (see Glosser, 2001). Evidence suggests that during learning, basal ganglia and medial temporal lobe memory systems are activated simultaneously and that in some learning situations competitive interference exists between the two systems (Packard & Knowlton, 2002).

Conditioning

The classical delay eyeblink conditioning has been greatly studied in animals and human volunteers. In the typical delay paradigm, a 250–500 ms tone (conditioned stimulus or CS) is repeatedly followed by an air-puff (unconditioned stimulus or US) delivered to the eye that reflexively elicits a blink, the unconditioned response (UR). The tone and air-puff coterminate. With repeated CS–US pairings, subjects learn to associate the tone with

the air-puff and initiate an eyeblink (conditioned response or CR) in response to the CS before the onset of the US. In the rabbit, electrophysiological activity in the cerebellum and in the hippocampus parallels the development of behavioural CRs (Disterhoft et al., 1986; McCormick & Thompson, 1987). Lesions of the cerebellar dentate interpositus nuclei prevent acquisition or abolish retention of the conditioned association. Results with human volunteers provide striking parallels with animal findings. Cerebellar lesions in human beings abolish delay eyeblink conditioning (Daum et al., 1993). Delay eyeblink conditioning is intact in amnesic patients with bilateral medial–temporal or bilateral thalamic lesions (Daum & Ackermann, 1994).

EMOTIONAL MEMORY

Research findings from neuropsychological, neuroimaging, drug, and neural stimulation studies indicate that emotional stimuli engage specific cognitive and neural mechanisms that enhance explicit memory. Emotional arousal influences memory via factors that act during memory encoding and factors that modulate memory consolidation. Environmental stimuli can be inherently dangerous or can be neutral but perceived as threatening because of past experiences. Emotional systems in the brain are pivotal in remembering stimuli and situations that signal danger and setting in motion defence responses that optimise the organism's survival. Across studies, the amygdala has been consistently implicated as playing a key role in enhancing explicit memory for both pleasant and unpleasant emotional stimuli through modulation of encoding and consolidation processes.

Fear is an important component of both normal and abnormal manifestations of behaviour. The emotional fear system detects the danger associated to cues and situations and coordinates behavioural and physiological adjustments designed to maximise chances of survival. This system can go awry and amplify the level of threat, or perceive threat in its absence, and confine the body in a state of fear (Öhman, 1992). It is possible that in cases of anxiety disorders, the generalisation of fear stems from a weakening of contextual constraints around the original fear experience (LeDoux, 1984). The hippocampus forms contextual representations, and hippocampal lesions lead to deficits in fear conditioning to context (Blanchard et al., 1970; Kim & Fanselow, 1992; Phillips & LeDoux, 1992; Selden et al., 1991; Sutherland & McDonald, 1990). Consistently, stress, a concomitant of fear, impairs the anatomy, physiology, and functioning of the hippocampus (Sapolsky, 1996). An understanding of the emotional memory circuitry involved in detecting danger is instrumental in producing treatments that can alleviate the suffering inherent in anxiety and fear disorders.

In the learning and memory literature it is well documented that the amygdala plays an important role in encoding and storing aversive memories (Davis, 1994; Fanselow & LeDoux, 1999; Maren, 2000, 2001). In contrast to this view, some findings suggest that the amygdala is not a memory storage site for aversive events (Cahill et al., 1999; Meunier et al., 1999; Vazdarjanova & McGaugh, 1998). However, it appears pivotal in the performance of fear responses in reaction to fearful stimuli both learned and unlearned. Other studies support the view that the amygdala does not play a central role in the performance of unconditioned fear responses (Antoniadis & McDonald, 2001; Maren, 1999; Sutherland & McDonald, 1990; Ursin, 1965; Ursin et al., 1981; Wallace & Rosen, 2001). Its role is of a mnemonic nature involved in the conditioning of fear to neutral cues. Through its connections to midbrain and brainstem areas involved in the unconditioned emergence of fear responses in rats, the central nucleus of the amygdala may control the conditioned emergence of these responses (Kapp et al., 1979; LeDoux et al., 1988). The former view stems from the hypothesis that the amygdala serves to modulate memory storage in other brain regions rather than acting as a permanent site of plasticity (McGaugh et al., 1996). There is some evidence supporting the hypothesis that the amygdala modulates plasticity in other brain areas (Packard et al., 1994). However, an underlying assumption to this hypothesis is that the plasticity that occurs during fear conditioning does not occur in the amygdala. It is hard to reconcile this with findings that fear conditioning induces changes in neuronal firing within the amygdala (Quirk et al., 1995, 1997).

Fear memory is a particularly rapid LTM formed during an aversive experience, for example, during Pavlovian fear conditioning. Fear conditioning studies in rats have been instrumental in identifying the neural underpinnings of fear and have laid the groundwork for the identification of the fear circuits in humans. Investigators have also studied anticipatory anxiety by using the acoustic fear-potentiated-startle paradigm that involves the anticipation of electric shocks without any shock delivery. Eyeblink responses were higher in amplitude and shorter in latency during shock anticipation than during safe periods (Grillon et al., 1991). Unpredictable shocks produced by unpaired CS–US conditions produce greater context conditioning. Converging evidence suggests that types of emotional memories may be stored in an implicit framework available for conscious recall only during the experiencing of particular affective states. A thorough understanding of the neural mechanisms involved in the indelible consolidation of traumatic events is fundamental. Pathological anxiety such as post-traumatic stress disorders (PTSD), phobias, and obsessive compulsive disorders can emerge in survivors of torture, childhood abuse, war veterans, victims of rape, and other forms of trauma. These disorders reflect a persistent disturbance of body and brain chemistry where traumatic experiences are re-experienced unaltered, confining people to a lifetime of misery. Dream stages of sleep are thought to play a central role in reorganising memory and reinforcing the connections between memory and emotion (Hobson, 1992).

In human fear-learning studies, autonomic changes in heart rate and sweat gland activity (skin conductance response) are triggered in response to unconditioned stimuli such as white noise and shock, as well as to conditioned stimuli (Grillon et al., 1991; Hodes et al., 1985; Öhman, 1992). Patients who have received unilateral lobectomy for epilepsy treatment show deficits in auditory fear conditioning (LaBar et al., 1995). This impairment cannot be accounted for by deficits in non-associative sensory or autonomic performance factors (LaBar et al., 1995). These findings suggest that in humans, temporal lobe structures, in particular the amygdala, are an important component in the emotional memory network. Patients with bilateral amygdalectomy were impaired at the acquisition of conditioned autonomic responses to visual or auditory stimuli, but did acquire the declarative facts about which stimuli were paired with the unconditioned stimulus. In contrast, a patient with selective bilateral damage to the amygdala and the hippocampus acquired neither the conditioned autonomic responses nor the facts about stimulus pairings. Damage to the amygdala also leads to impairments in the recognition of fear in facial expressions (Adolphs et al., 1995, 1999; Young et al., 1995).

Damage to the hippocampus in the absence of amygdala damage should impair explicit memory generally, but should not affect the emotional enhancement of explicit memory. That is, the amygdala should continue to modulate whatever residual memory function exists after hippocampal damage. This prediction has been confirmed. Amnesic patients with hippocampal damage show normal emotional enhancement of explicit memory despite their overall memory impairment (Hamann et al., 1997).

In a neuroimaging study of explicit emotional memory, Cahill et al. (1996) examined the relationship between brain activity at encoding and subsequent LTM for negative and neutral films in male subjects. Brain activity was assessed using PET while subjects viewed the films. Subjects who showed increased brain activity in the right amygdala remembered more of the emotional films on an explicit memory test administered 3 weeks later than did subjects with lower activity. This correlation was observed only for the emotional films. Interestingly, a follow-up study with women found the same correlation but in the contralateral hemisphere (left amygdala). This finding suggests that sex differences might exist in the lateralisation of emotional memory (Cahill et al., 2001). Another study examined the relationship between brain activity at encoding and later explicit memory for emotional and non-emotional picture stimuli

(Hamann et al., 1999). For both pleasant and unpleasant stimuli, bilateral amygdala activity during encoding was correlated with later enhancement of recognition memory for these stimuli assessed a month later but not with recall memory assessed immediately after scanning. This correlation was not observed for non-emotional stimuli. Hippocampal activity in this study was correlated with amygdala activity, supporting the view that the amygdala enhances explicit memory by modulating activity in the hippocampus. In summary, these neuroimaging studies have consistently reported the amygdala and related limbic areas to be involved in both the encoding and retrieval of emotional explicit memory for negative emotional stimuli and less frequently for positive stimuli. An issue for further research is to determine what differential roles, if any, the left versus right amygdala has in emotional memory encoding and retrieval.

Recent research has focused on how memories are shaped by a person's emotional state. "Mood-congruent memory" occurs when one's current mood aids the processing of material that has a similar emotional valence. Thus, a depressed mood heightens memory for unpleasant events, while elation heightens memory for pleasant events. Depression affects both the storage and retrieval of memories. Depressed people pay more attention to material that agrees with their current mood, causing it to be better learned. At retrieval, sad mood apparently provides internal cues that help call forth similar emotional memories. Mood congruency is especially powerful when remembering autobiographical events. Subjects recall personal memories more readily when the mood of those events matches their current mood state.

RETRIEVAL-INDUCED FORGETTING

Whenever an item cannot be rehearsed, for example during the overt recall of another item, the unrehearsed item tends to be forgotten over time. We broadly refer to that forgetting as "decay". The amount of decay may be related to the absolute amount of time that has passed without rehearsal. Faster retrieval of information may limit the amount of time during which decay can take place. In attempting to recall an event, the capacity of attention, the retrieval rate, and the decay rate could all come into play in determining performance. The act of remembering relies on a process of selection based on the mind's ability to separate the relevant from the irrelevant and to retrieve just the right memory to satisfy the current requirements of a task. Being able to forget information that turned out to be no longer relevant is as important to attaining performance goals as is being able to remember task-relevant information. As memory is involved with competing alternatives (e.g., one is trying to remember a friend's phone number), this task can be performed only if one has the capacity to impede the retrieval of unwanted information (telephone numbers). Otherwise, an irrelevant response is likely to result. Through the silent operation of inhibitory forces, people can prevent the unwanted retrieval of goal-irrelevant mental contents. Indeed, the actual act of remembering itself appears sufficient to inhibit the retrieval of related items in memory, a phenomenon that has been termed retrieval-induced forgetting. As memory is populated by a host of ostensibly similar items (e.g., phone numbers), recollection of a target item is clearly facilitated if one can inhibit the retrieval of potentially competing memories. Through the guided retrieval of specific items from memory, the accessibility of related material is diminished (Anderson & McCulloch, 1999). The act of remembering can prompt temporary forgetting or, more specifically, the inhibition of particular items in memory.

An important question in the study of directed forgetting is whether the differential memory performance for to-be-remembered and to-be-forgotten items is solely due to differential encoding or whether retrieval inhibition of to-be-forgotten items plays an additional role. Current data suggest that differential encoding alone cannot account for the effects of directed forgetting (Ullsperger et al., 2000). It is likely that items followed by an instruction to forget become inhibited and less accessible and therefore more difficult to retrieve.

Although retrieval inhibition has received the most attention in the directed-forgetting literature, it has been suggested that attentional inhibition also plays a role (Hasher & Zacks, 1988). Attentional inhibition is defined as the suppression of irrelevant information so that it will not enter working memory (Zacks et al., 1996). A similar process labelled "resistance to interference", which can be defined as efficiency in handling interference from multiple (including irrelevant) items trying to enter working memory, has been proposed (Wilson & Kipp, 1998).

MEMORY IN CHILDREN AND THE ELDERLY

Many reflective activities are thought to improve during childhood and decline in normal senescence, yielding an inverted U-shaped function for explicit memory (see Balota et al., 2000). The view that explicit memory is a U-shaped function of age is a reiteration of the Jacksonian principle of the development and dissolution of function (Jackson, 1880, reprinted in Taylor, 1958). This principle states that the last function to develop is the first to disappear after brain damage from injury, disease or ageing, whereas the first function to develop is the last to be affected when an organism undergoes demise. Because explicit memory is widely thought to be late maturing, it should also decline in old age if its developmental course is described by the Jacksonian principle (Tulving & Schacter, 1990). The notion that explicit memory improves during childhood, peaks in young adulthood, and declines in late adulthood as a mirror image of its order of appearance has been uncritically accepted for more than a decade (see Rovee-Collier et al., 2001). However, a recent study that examined age-related changes in explicit memory for three perceptual features (item identity, colour, and location) in individuals age between 4 and 80 years reported that the form of the explicit memory function across the lifespan varied with the perceptual feature tested and the type of task (Gulya et al., 2002). Item recognition was excellent at all ages but was significantly poorer for older adults than children, while colour recognition peaked in late childhood on the game-like task. It was reported that performance on explicit memory tests is not a consistent inverted U-shaped function of age across various features. Explicit memory performance depends on what is measured and how.

Children

Investigations conducted over the past few years have established that very young children have much better memory capabilities than was previously thought to be the case. Even infants and toddlers can encode, store, and retrieve a great deal of information about the events they experience (Howe, 2000). Recent work with toddlers, using elicited imitation tasks, in which action sequences that produce an event are demonstrated by an experimenter and subsequently reproduced by the children, has established that very young children form specific episodic memories and retain them for long periods of time (see Bauer, 1995). Such results contradict the assumption that children cannot remember their own lives before the age of 3 or 4 (Rovee-Collier & Shyi, 1992). However, although there is some emerging evidence that young children can report aspects of experiences that are encoded before the onset of productive language, it seems unlikely that such memories are retained among children who are much younger than 2 years of age at the time of the experience, at least over very long delays. Further, the information that is provided appears to be fragmentary and accompanied by inaccurate responses. For these reasons, it can be concluded that, at least in most instances, children cannot be expected to testify about events that transpired before they were at least 2 years of age.

Eisen and Goodman (1998) argue that what is memorable to any individual child, regardless of age, and hence most likely to be encoded, is anything that is personally significant to that child. Events or actions that affect a child's sense of well-being, safety, or social acceptance are considered to be personally significant and thus more likely to be remembered. Similarly, others indicate that aspects of an event are more likely to be encoded if they are interesting or distinctive either because they are unexpected or emotionally arousing to the child (Howe, 2000). What is central for a specific child depends on what is most relevant to that child, including the most threatening or most feared aspect of a traumatic experience.

In situations in which children lack knowledge about an event, interactions with adults may compensate for their developmental limitation. Conversations about an event between children and adults that occur as the event unfolds are a critical factor in determining the features that children encode and remember (Fivush, 1998). These ongoing jointly constructed conversations provide children with a better understanding of their experiences and help them to attend to important aspects of events. Indeed, several researchers have demonstrated this linkage between adult–child conversations and superior subsequent memory performance (Pipe et al., 1996; Tessler & Nelson, 1994).

With increasing age, there are corresponding changes in a variety of cognitive functions that affect the acquisition and storage of information in the memory system. Other influences being equal, older children will acquire more information from comparable exposure to an event and will maintain a stronger memory trace than will younger children. This effect can be attributed to age-related changes in processing speed as well as the availability of more efficient strategies and an increased knowledge base (Ornstein et al., 1997). The strength of the memory representation diminishes less over time for older as compared with younger children. As a result, stored representations of experiences become more difficult to access over time, especially among younger individuals (Howe & O'Sullivan, 1997).

The effects of event modality on children's memory and suggestibility have also been studied. The observation that young children more readily acquiesce to misleading questions, select misinformation as the correct response in multiple-choice or forced-choice tests, or incorporate misinformation into their open-ended accounts raises questions about the contributing factors (Goodman & Reed, 1986; Greenstock & Pipe, 1996). From a practical perspective, the possibility that children may misappropriate information from others into their own accounts has significant clinical and legal implications. A study was set up to examine how mode of events presentation impacts memory and the acceptance of misinformation as a function of the type of to-be-recalled items, age, and time (Gobbo et al., 2002). It was observed that 5-year-old children were more accurate than 3-year-olds, and those participating were more accurate than those either observing or listening to a narrative. The method of assessment, level of event learning, delay to assessment, and variables relating to the misled items also influenced the degree of misinformation effects. When children have been participants, and the effects of misinformation are assessed through open-ended recall, misinformation may have very little impact, particularly when children are questioned soon after the event.

Elderly

Four perspectives of how ageing affects various memory processes have been proposed (Light, 1991). These include theories attributing memory impairment to failures in metamemory (strategy used and memory monitoring), or to impoverished semantic encoding (due to problems in language comprehension), or to failures of deliberate retrieval (as opposing automatic, non-conscious recollection), or to diminished processing resources (due to reduced attentional capacity or cognitive slowing). The age at which changes in memory occur depends on the methods that are used to test the memory store. Difficult explicit memory tasks (e.g., delayed recall) demonstrate statistically significant differences in subjects in their 50s, in comparison to younger individuals (Albert et al., 1987). Age decrements are greater on recall than recognition tasks and this is true whether words or pictures are used. An age-dependent impairment in STM is somewhat more apparent during tasks that involve free recall rather than cued recall or recognition (Craik et al., 1987; Wahlin et al., 1995). Furthermore, episodic memory (e.g., recall of context-specific information such as a word list displayed 5 minutes earlier) falters substantially with age, whereas semantic memory shows only modest decline (Nilsson et al.,

1997; Perlmutter, 1978). In fact, when educational attainment is taken into account, decrements in the latter are almost non-existent (Bäckman & Nilsson, 1996). Explicit memory declines more dramatically with age than does implicit memory (Jelicic et al., 1996; Schugens et al., 1997). A study reported a 33% age-related decrement in cued recall, and an 11% age-related decrement in recognition, when comparing young and old subjects (mean age 19 vs 68) (Rabinowitz, 1986). Closer analysis of the data suggests that the older individuals are not forgetting what they learned more rapidly, but rather they are taking longer to learn the new information. Thus, if one allows older subjects to learn material well (i.e., to the point where few errors are made), they do not forget what they have learned more rapidly than the young (Albert, 1997; Petersen et al., 1992). However, if older subjects are not given the ability to learn material to the same level of proficiency as younger individuals, after a day the average older person will retain less information.

Executive functions such as working memory appear to be particularly vulnerable to the effects of normal ageing, a pattern that may reflect the disproportionate reduction in neuron density in the PFC and basal ganglia (Haug & Eggers, 1991; Van Gorp & Mahler, 1990). It has been suggested that central executive resources undergo a specific decrease whereas the storage capacities remain unaffected by ageing (Van der Linden et al., 1994). A study was designed to examine the effect of age on executive functions by using executive tasks inspired by the theoretical framework of Norman and Shallice (Andrés & Van der Linden, 2000; Norman & Shallice 1986). It was shown that elderly people present impaired performance on the executive tasks specifically designed to assess some of the supervisory attentional system functions, especially planning, inhibition, and abstraction of logical rules. The literature suggests a marked age-related decline in declarative, but only minimal decline in non-declarative memory tasks, although age differences in priming have been found that are, however, smaller than those found by direct measures of memory (recall, recognition) (Craik & Jennings, 1992; La Voie & Light, 1994). The age differences in episodic memory are obvious, whereas in semantic memory they appear only if tasks, in addition to memory, also involve conceptual or inferential processing (Craik & Jennings, 1992). Moreover, age differences have been shown to be particularly pronounced in source memory (Spencer & Raz, 1995). Source memory impairment in the elderly reflects difficulties in the recollection of the perceptual aspects of episodes (Schacter et al., 1994).

Various attempts have been made to establish a comprehensive neuropsychological framework to account for the general factors behind age-related changes in memory and other cognitive functions. A distinction of age-related cognitive changes has been made between "fluid intelligence" and "crystallised intelligence" (Horn, 1982). Fluid functions include those that challenge new learning, inductive reasoning, or speed of processing. The decline in these functions during ageing has been well documented (Salthouse, 1992). Crystallised functions that operate with previously acquired information, general knowledge, and comprehension tend to be preserved late in ageing (Baltes, 1991).

Normal age-related cognitive changes are defined as changes that occur in old age without any signs of overt disease affecting the central nervous system. Ageing is accompanied by slow and sometimes continuous changes in specific functions (e.g., the speed of learning and central processing) but little or no change in certain functions (e.g., crystallised intelligence). This mild alteration in cognitive abilities related to normal ageing does not have serious effects on the individual's social functioning. It does not lead to inability to maintain an independent lifestyle nor does it shorten life expectancy. The changes seen in normal ageing are clearly distinguishable from the changes in age-matched patients with mild dementia (Erkinjuntti et al., 1986).

Some longitudinal studies have demonstrated a rather high stability of intelligence during ageing (Schwartzman et al., 1987). Variability in neuropsychological test scores is greater in older subject groups (Morse, 1993). Thus, a large number of aged individuals also show cognitive performance comparable to the standards of younger adults, at least in some domains. The term "successful

ageing" has been introduced to take into account this heterogeneity among the elderly population. In usual ageing, extrinsic factors heighten the effects of ageing alone and in successful ageing, extrinsic factors play a neutral or positive role (Rowe & Kahn, 1987). Thus, cognitive changes might be better explained in terms of such factors as lifestyle, habits, diet, and psychosocial factors than by ageing *per se*.

Source memory

Ample evidence exists that source monitoring is greatly reduced with advancing age, as is monitoring other aspects of context. A finding quite likely attributable to differences in encoding abilities of young and older adults is the poorer ability of older adults to remember the source of information successfully retrieved (Hashtroudi et al., 1989). Source memory paradigms have proven to be particularly sensitive in detecting age-related change in memory function. Individuals are typically presented with words that have become familiar in different contexts. For example, some words may have been spoken in a male voice and others in a female voice or some actions may have been initially performed and others imagined. At test, participants are first asked whether they recognise an item as having been seen before (an old/new item) and then asked to designate the source of the items identified as "old". Almost invariably, older adults are more likely than younger adults to confuse the source of the recognised events (Craik et al., 1990; Schacter et al., 1994).

Source memory certainly falls into the domain of context encoding. Age differences have been reported in memory for whether the speaker was a man or a woman, the temporal order of events, or whether an action was performed or only imagined (Zacks et al., 2000). Whereas there is little disagreement that older adults are more vulnerable than younger adults to source memory error, the reasons for this are not clear. One view is that older adults have more difficulty discriminating between sources of familiarity due to deficits in the encoding of information or in the initial binding of that information to other neural traces associated with a specific event (Chalfonte & Johnson, 1996; Grady et al., 1995). Another view is that discriminating between sources of familiarity is only partially dependent on the quality of the memory trace (Dywan et al., 1994; Rubin et al., 1999). Such discrimination is heavily influenced by factors associated with the efficiency and organisation of retrieval strategies. Age-related changes in these processes are thought to reflect age-related changes to frontal lobe function and a decline in controlled relative to automatic response tendencies (Craik et al., 1990; Jacoby, 1999). Thus, a number of mechanisms have been proposed to explain the age-related decline in the contextual specificity of remembering events.

Older adults may be less likely or able to encode the context of a memory situation, and this failure may in turn impair retrieval. A study explored the effect of age on encoding, retention, and retrieval components of memory functioning in a sample of 156 healthy elderly subjects between the ages of 57 and 85 partitioned into four age groups (Mitrushina et al., 1991). Memory assessment on the subject's performance on the Rey Auditory Verbal Learning Test (RAVLT) was performed. This study reported significant group differences in recall on all five learning trials of the RAVLT, whereas rates of learning, forgetting, and recognition did not differ. Thus, the results of this study suggest faulty retrieval mechanisms, whereas encoding and retention processes did not prove to be affected by ageing. Dywan et al. (2002) recorded event-related potentials (ERPs) as individuals made source-monitoring decisions in a paradigm in which the influence of item familiarity and goal relevance could be separately assessed. Younger and older adults read a list of words and subsequently distinguished these words in a recognition test. It was observed that older adults generated far less differentiated ERP waveforms but with a markedly greater amplitude at frontal sites. Thus, ERPs do differentiate patterns of neural response in older adults from those in younger adults during source-monitoring tasks. These data may suggest that older adults have difficulty with source monitoring because they are less able to quickly or automatically suppress the cortical response to items that are not targets but are salient for the wrong reason. The problem is not simply one of faulty encoding but rather one of prolonged processing at test.

Close functional associations appear to exist between working memory, source memory, and episodic memory that may explain the more pronounced age-related decline in all of these systems in comparison to semantic memory. Regarding source memory impairment in older adults, a number of studies have shown that source memory is generally affected by ageing more than fact or item memory (McIntyre & Craik, 1987; Schacter et al., 1991b; Spencer & Raz, 1995; Trott et al., 1997, 1999). However, current research suggests that only a subset of the elderly show deficits in source memory, namely those with below average frontal function, and these deficits can be eliminated by requiring people at study to consider the relation between an item and its context (Glisky et al., 2001). These results provide convincing evidence of the importance of frontal function during the encoding of source and suggest that older adults with reduced frontal lobe function fail to initiate the processes required to integrate contextual information with focal context.

It has been proposed that the cognitive changes that occur during ageing resemble those seen in patients with reduced frontal lobe function (Veroff, 1980). A reduction in working memory processing, which is dependent on the frontal lobes, appears as the crucial factor for age-related changes not only in memory but in various other cognitive functions (Salthouse, 1990). Some investigators have also suggested that a reduction in the capacity to inhibit irrelevant influences might be an explanation for various age-associated cognitive changes (Dempster, 1992; Kramer et al., 1994). Frontal lobe function appears as the first to decline during normal ageing and this decline is attributed to defective attentional monitoring within high-level working memory (Daigneault & Braun, 1993).

Prospective memory

According to a widespread theoretical view, age-related changes in higher cognitive functions result from a decline in the availability of processing resources (Craik, 1983, 1986). Ageing may be associated with a decline in the capacity for processing information, and the requirements for processing capacity are greater for prospective than retrospective tests. However, in a recent study, 133 community-dwelling adults aged between 65 and 95 years old were examined with a large battery of tests of prospective and retrospective memory, as well as tests for indexing processing resources (Uttl et al., 2001). The results showed similar age-related declines in prospective and retrospective memory. There was only a weak correlation between prospective and retrospective memory. The age-related decline in processing resources was related more strongly to retrospective than prospective memory. The use and development of research methods that permit direct assessment of prospective memory would help to clarify the issue of the impact of ageing on prospective memory.

DISCUSSION

The episodic–semantic distinction attributes memory for facts to the semantic system and memory for personal experiences to the episodic system. Memory for personal experiences and memory for facts should therefore be dissociable. As numerous critics of the episodic–semantic distinction have pointed out, there is little evidence for such dissociation. To cite two counterexamples to this prediction, priming in general knowledge retrieval is influenced in the same way as free and semantically cued recall by experimental manipulations (Blaxton, 1985; Roediger & Blaxton, 1987). Memory for facts as well as for personal experiences is disrupted in both anterograde and retrograde amnesia.

Most tests of autobiographical recall are considered tests of episodic memory, as they focus on subjects' memories for personal events or episodes (Baddeley & Wilson, 1986). However, some doubts about the classification of autobiographical memory as "episodic" have been raised (Cermak, 1984). It was argued that episodic memories may devolve into semantic memories over time. Episodic memories may lose their orientation to time and place and eventually represent semantic forms of knowledge. If it true that episodic memories become semantic memories, then tests of remote memory would be biased towards episodic memory for recent periods and biased towards semantic memory for more distant time periods (Cermak, 1984). This renders the hypothesis of episodic and semantic memory rather ntriguing. Determining the time when episodic memories become semantic memories appears to be a rather difficult task.

There is now a large amount of evidence to suggest that working memory capacity contributes to proficiency in a wide range of cognitive tasks. For example, measures of working memory such as reading span and operation span correlate with performance in tasks such as language comprehension, solving maths problems, and writing (Adams & Hitch, 1997; Benton et al., 1984; Daneman & Merikle, 1996). It has also been proposed that it may be useful to conceptualise working memory capacity as the central information-processing component underlying fluid intelligence (Kyllonen & Christal, 1990). Perhaps one of the most influential ideas to emerge in cognitive psychology during the last few years is the viewpoint referred to as the knowledge-is-power hypothesis. The basic argument of the knowledge-is-power hypothesis is that domain knowledge is the primary determinant of success in cognitive endeavours. Some evidence suggests that both domain knowledge and working memory may contribute to performance differences in a wide range of cognitive tasks. Interestingly, recent research suggests that a high level of working memory capacity enhances the facilitative effect of domain knowledge on cognitive performance (Hambrick & Engle, 2002). This finding supports what can be termed the rich-get-richer hypothesis involving domain knowledge and working memory capacity. Thus, people with high levels of working memory capacity may be able to draw upon more pre-existing domain knowledge during cognitive performance than people with lower levels of working memory capacity. On the other hand, when the joint effects of domain knowledge and age on cognitive performance were assessed, there was no evidence to suggest that domain knowledge attenuated age-related differences in working memory performance (Hambrick & Engle, 2002). These data suggest that there may be conditions under which age has a negative effect on cognitive performance, even at high levels of domain knowledge.

Concerning the development of memory in children, it has been commonly assumed that memory storage of events of childhood is permanent and that early childhood memories, although gone from consciousness, are not forgotten (Loftus & Loftus, 1980). In fact, according to Freud, favourable therapeutic outcomes in adulthood hinge on the successful retrieval of these early childhood events (Freud, 1905/1953). Thus, autobiographical events from childhood remain intact but locked away safely in LTM. Current research suggests that neonates (and fetuses) can process and retain information in LTM for considerable periods of time. Studies of children's autobiographic recall of naturally occurring events have clearly established that children as young as 2 years can recall episodes for at least 6 months and that 3-year-olds can produce spontaneous or elicited well-structured narratives of previous events (Fivush et al., 1987; Mandler, 1983; Todd & Perlmutter, 1980). It has also been demonstrated that 2-year-olds provide coherent narrative accounts of past events regardless of whether those events occurred in the recent (e.g., 3 months ago) or distant past (e.g., 6 months ago) (Fivush et al., 1987). Although it cannot be claimed that memory development is complete early in life, there is ample evidence to support the hypothesis that childhood memory is sufficiently mature to support the types of encoding, storage, and retrieval necessary for long-term retention. Research is needed to identify how individual differences in specific cognitive and social/emotional domains influence children's performance at all phases of the memory process. For example, differences in how children cope with stressful experiences (e.g., active vs avoidant styles) may play a role in the amount and type of information that is encoded and thus what is recalled at a later time. Specifically, the use of dissociation as a coping strategy among children warrants further investigation.

The basic research on the development of visual self-recognition has involved measurement of infants' reactions to their mirror images (Bullock & Lutkenhaus, 1990). Coincident with mark-directed behaviour, infants begin to show self-consciousness (e.g., shy smiling and self-touching) when confronted with their images and by about 22 months of age will correctly label the image. Although the developmental trends for self-recognition in the second year of life are quite consistent, substantial differences may be noted. Mentally handicapped and autistic infants and children do not show self-recognition at least until they have achieved a developmental age of about 18 months, regardless of their chronological age (Loveland, 1987).

Another area of research into age differences has been the issue of whether older adults have a smaller capacity than younger adults in STM. Many investigators have concluded that older adults experience only a modest reduction, if any, in the capacity of STM (Ogle, 1986; Perlmutter & Hall, 1985; Poon, 1985). However, it appears that the key problem for the older adult is not one of decreased capacity in STM but the slowing down of central nervous system activity. Age differences are consistently found in studies when material has to be reorganised or manipulated and when attention has to be divided between two tasks. Obviously, there are adult age differences in both speed and flexibility of operations. In LTM, the main difficulty for the older adult seems to centre on the encoding of new information for long-term retention and its retrieval from LTM (Craik, 2002).

In the domain of implicit learning, it has been argued that amnesic patients who are severely impaired in explicit memory tasks such as recall and recognition may show normal performance in some implicit learning situations (Knowlton & Squire, 1996). In the same manner, a few studies have shown that performance of elderly people can be as good as those of young adult participants in implicit learning tasks. Cherry and Stadler (1995) studied young and elderly subjects in a serial reaction time task. It was shown that both groups performed at the same level for the learning of the sequence, although Cherry and Stadler also found individual differences in implicit learning. The higher-ability older adults (selected on the basis of their educational and occupational levels) obtained results similar to young adults, while lower-ability older adults showed less evidence of implicit learning. An earlier study reported no age-related differences in sequence learning (Howard & Howard, 1992). With the artificial grammar learning paradigm, young and elderly participants could discriminate as readily between grammatical and non-grammatical items in the classification task.

2

Neuropsychological Assessment of Memory

INTRODUCTION

Memory assessments are typically conducted within the context of a full neuropsychological evaluation that includes a general interview. Interviews are useful for determining subjective experiences of memory impairment, although memory complaints often occur in the absence of deficient performance on objective memory tests (Riedel-Heller et al., 1999; Schofield et al., 1997). Conversely, denial of memory problems due to lack of awareness is a frequent occurrence and does not obviate the need for memory testing (Lezak, 1995).

Forensic psychologists or psychiatrists may be asked to provide an opinion concerning the validity of an amnesia report. Evaluating reported memory impairment involves many sources of information, and psychological testing is necessary. Although the complaint of memory difficulty appears straightforward, "memory problems" expressed by patients often represent cognitive decline in any of several areas: speech, language, general intelligence, learning, recall, etc. Psycho-

logical testing can distinguish one cognitive deficit from another, but different tests are required to make these determinations. In a clinical setting, assessment of memory may serve various purposes including diagnosis and screening for impairment and determination of functional change. This, in turn provides information regarding ability to return to work, appropriateness of various rehabilitation interventions, establishment of feasible rehabilitation goals, and determination of funding and legal issues (Mayes & Warburg, 1992). Of critical importance in making these decisions is an understanding of exactly what the memory tests used actually measure, and when and for what purposes particular memory tests are appropriate.

A source of common confusion and theoretical challenge lies in the distinction between test instructions and memory processes. It is easy to classify a test as explicit when subjects are asked to intentionally retrieve memories from a specified episode, or as implicit when subjects are asked to perform a task and no reference is made to any prior episode. However, it is not easy to determine what kinds of memory processes are involved when performing the test. There are many examples where memory on an implicit task is correlated with memory on a related explicit test. A parsimonious interpretation is that these implicit tests invoke some of the same declarative memory processes typically invoked by explicit memory tests.

Performance on memory tests may vary as a function of intelligence. Virtually all memory tests place demands on directed and sustained attention that are necessary for proper registration of the information to be learned. Distinguishing between a primary memory disorder and an impairment of attention and concentration that secondarily disrupts memory may represent a challenge to the investigating clinician. Prior to concluding that a memory deficit exists, one must be certain that other cognitive impairments are not influencing the evaluation. For example, a patient with a significant attentional disorder, such as an acute confusional state, may not perform well on memory tests because of inattention rather than because of a fundamental memory disorder itself. Adequate attention is a prerequisite for most memory tasks, and disorders of attention can significantly influence performance. Erroneous conclusions regarding the presence or absence of memory disorders can be made in the setting of attentional disorders. Consequently, a total assessment of cognitive function is necessary as part of a memory evaluation. Depression and mood states may influence performance on certain memory measures. Finally, we must acknowledge that a detailed separation of memory assessment from other cognitive problems may often be impossible. The resulting memory measures may only represent an approximation of the severity of memory impairment *per se*. For the reason of comprehensiveness and to gain insight into possible cognitive comorbidity, neuropsychological investigations in a patient with presumed or confirmed memory dysfunction should include a thorough examination of language, visuospatial, and frontal functions as well as an assessment of mood state as a minimum supplement to memory testing.

It is beyond the scope of this chapter to provide a detailed description of every available memory test. We will rather focus on the reliability, validity, and normative data of the memory tests most commonly used.

TESTS AS DIAGNOSTIC TOOLS

There is a bewildering number of differences in the patterns of memory impairments that can be seen in patients with different neurological disorders, and properly interpreting these impairments can present a formidable challenge to the clinician. The memory systems framework that has been developed in clinical neuropsychology, and validated with neuropsychological investigations of memory deficit populations, provides a powerful clinical tool for the evaluation and classification of memory impairments in patient populations. Such tools may also be used for the assessment of the efficacy of drugs to treat memory disorders, as well as the adverse effects of drugs on memory in various clinical trials of new drugs. If memory impairment is noted in a test, more extensive testing is needed to describe what subprocesses are involved. In particular, the memory task should involve both verbal and non-verbal materials, an acquisition phase over several learning materials, free recall, cued recall, and recognition testing preferably with varying delay intervals. Tasks containing these components will enable one to determine the degree of memory impairment and also provide some information regarding the anatomical localisation of the disorder.

Cognitive deficits can be detected several years before the clinical diagnosis of dementia (Linn et al., 1995). Neuropsychological assessment at an early stage of dementia has the goal of determining a memory disorder that is not always associated with a memory complaint: It helps to characterise the memory disorder in light of the cognitive neuropsychology knowledge and to assess other cognitive functions with a view to integrating the memory disorder in a syndrome. Establishing the neuropsychological profile often indicates the underlying neuropathology. Assessing neuropsychological functions should include tests of each major cognitive domain. A qualitative analysis of the errors or types of failures in

TABLE 2.1

Some methods for testing learning and memory performances

Method	Type of task	Duration	Comments	References
Digit span	Repetition forwards or backwards of a series of single-digit numbers of increasing length: STM	About 5 minutes	Subtest of WAIS and of the Wechsler Memory Scale	Lezak, 1983
Rey's 15-word test	Repetition of a series of 15 words, 5 repetitions: STM	About 5 minutes	Parallel forms are available	Lezak, 1983
Selective reminding task	Repetition of a series of 10–12 words; only omitted words are repeated by the tester	About 10 minutes	More complex test for the tester and test subject	Buschke & Fuld, 1974
Benton visual retention test	Geometric shapes are shown for 10 seconds each and then have to be drawn from memory (drawing version) or picked out from several similar shapes (multiple-choice version)	5 minutes	Motor handicaps interfere with the drawing version but not with the multiple-choice version	Lezak, 1983
Paired associate learning	Words, numbers, etc., (each belonging to a stimulus word or number, shape, etc.) have to be learned	5–10 minutes	Recall of the associated words, etc. may be tested after minutes, hours, or days	Wechsler, 1945, 1987, 1997
Logical memory	Recall of a story with a specific number of elements	5 minutes	E.g., as part of the Wechsler Memory Scale	Wechsler, 1945, 1987, 1997

individual tasks is also required to differentiate between different diseases. In diagnosing the cause of dementia, it is important to distinguish between failures of storage (or retention) associated with damage to limbic and especially hippocampal structures, of retrieval associated with frontal–subcortical dysfunctions, and of STM associated with temporo-parietal lesions.

Storage disorders are characterised on testing by deficits on both recall and recognition and rapid loss of information at delayed recall. The patient shows limited benefit from cues of multiple-choice alternatives. Retrieval disorders are characterised by a difficulty in accessing information. STM disorders are characterised on testing by reduced memory span and rapid loss of information measured by the Brown–Petersen paradigm (Petersen & Petersen, 1959).

Memory may be assessed with a variety of individual tests each aimed at a subset of memory types or processes, or by a comprehensive single battery (see Table 2.1). It should be noted, however, that batteries may not evaluate all components of memory. Selection of individual tests or a standardised memory battery must be based on consideration of the referral question, the time available for the evaluation, the availability of suitable normative data, and the patient's ability level. In practice, most neuropsychological evaluations use individual tests, including components of memory batteries, rather than using an entire battery. Formal assessments for legal purposes or for social security may prefer a complete standardised battery. Due to the diagnostic utility of memory testing, clinicians are encouraged to evaluate assorted memory functions, such as storage, encoding, retrieval, or rate of forgetting, and to include assessment procedures for various types of memory such as episodic, semantic, and procedural memory.

MEMORY ASSESSMENT BATTERIES

Several available memory tests take the "battery" approach. The best-known, best-developed, and

most up-to-date is the Wechsler Memory Scale—
Revised (WMS–R) (Wechsler, 1987). Other common batteries are Memory Assessment Scales,
Remote Memory Battery, MMSE, and the
Rivermead Behavioural Memory Test (Denman,
1984; Wilson et al., 1985). These procedures are
termed "batteries" because they are collections
of several different short tests, each of which is
designed to examine different aspects of the learning and recall process.

Wechsler Memory Scales

The most widely applied memory test batteries
are the Wechsler Memory Scales (WMS). The
original version of the WMS has been revised
several times (WMS–R, WMS–III) (Wechsler,
1945, 1987, 1997). The WMS–R, published 42
years after the WMS, was viewed as an improvement because of the inclusion of a formal
delayed memory component to the test (Wechsler,
1987). The WMS–R is an individually administered clinical instrument for assessing major
dimensions of memory functions including immediate and delayed recall of verbal and non-
verbal stimuli. It consists of 13 subscales using
a weighted system involving multiplying the raw
score by a weight inversely proportional to the
standard error of measurement of the subtest. The
Visual Memory Score is composed of Figural
Memory, Visual Paired Associates I, and Visual
Reproduction I. The Attention/Concentration
Index comprises the Mental Control, Digit Span,
and Visual Memory Span. The Delayed Recall
Score consists of Logical Recall II, Visual Paired
Associates II, Verbal Paired Associates II, and
Visual Reproduction II. The General Memory
Score is derived from the Verbal Memory and
Visual Memory Scores. Reliability and validity
data are reported in the testing manual. Interrater
reliability was high (between 0.97 and 0.99) for
the two subtests (Logical Memory and Visual
Reproduction).

Russell's initial validation of the WMS–R consisted of the comparison of normal individuals to
a heterogeneous group of brain-damaged subjects
(Russell, 1975). Individuals with damage to the
left hemisphere tend to score substantially higher

on the Visual Reproduction Subtest (which Russell
renamed Figural Recall). Individuals with damage
to the right hemisphere tend to score considerably higher on the Logical Memory Subtest (which
Russell renamed Semantic Recall). Russell modified the WMS administration procedures so that
retention over time could be calculated separately
for semantic (logical memory) and figural (visual
reproduction) memory. Logue and Wyrick subsequently demonstrated the validity of the WMS–
R for the differentiation of normal elderly individuals and elderly demented patients (Logue &
Wyrick, 1979). The age range for these subjects
was 55 to 85 years.

Many studies support the validity of the WMS–
R subtests and indexes in the detection of memory
impairment. WMS–R subtests and indexes differentiate normal persons from individuals with
AD, PD, HD, and alcoholic Korsakoff's syndrome
(Butters et al., 1988; Tröster et al., 1995). In a
study that matched 31 elderly normal controls
and 25 patients with suspected AD who were
administered the WMS–R, it was observed that
the patient group performed significantly less well
than the control group on all WMS–R subtests
(Brinkman et al., 1983). A bimodal distribution
of percentage retained scores was noted in the
patient group but not the control group. This study
confirmed the findings of dementia-related deficits
in the later recall of information that had been
recalled initially, both with semantic and figural
information. The bimodal distribution of the data
in the patient group may reflect the necessity
of understanding the memory impairment of
Alzheimer-type dementia in terms of subcat-
egories of the disorder, rather than through mean
comparisons with highly variable groups. The
bimodal distribution suggests the necessity of
analysing subgroups of patients. The subtests have
also been found useful in distinguishing among
memory impairments associated with different
neurodegenerative disorders. The WMS–R is not
only useful in differentiating demented patients
from amnesics, but also in that saving scores
(i.e., percentage retained on delayed recall) for
the Logical Memory and Visual Reproduction
subtests distinguish AD from PD patients (Butters
et al., 1988).

The Information/Orientation subtest of the WMS–R contains orientation questions, as well as questions about autobiographical information (e.g., age, date of birth). The possibility that some benefit-seeking individuals may choose to feign impairments on these items is suggested by prior research showing that individuals simulating brain dysfunction may fail autobiographical questions (Rosenfeld et al., 1995; Wiggins & Brandt, 1988). Estimates of insufficient effort (assessment of effort and motivation to perform poorly or well) base rates in benefit-seeking populations demonstrate the utility of Information/Orientation as an indicator of suspicion of insufficient effort (Suchy & Sweet, 2000).

While the WMS–R is a great improvement over the original WMS, it has several psychometric weaknesses. The original normative sample is small. The reliability for most subtests is poor, yielding large errors of measurement. This suggests that the WMS–R provides only an approximate estimate of overall memory function (Elwood, 1991). The WMS–R's lengthy administration time has also been criticised for decreasing the instrument's utility when evaluating elderly, cognitively impaired patients and other populations whose attention spans and motivation may be limited (Loring, 1989). Thus, attempts have been made to produce and validate short forms of the WMS–R in an effort to decrease administration time while retaining the psychometric properties of the entire battery (Van den Broek et al., 1998; Woodard & Axelrod, 1995). It has been suggested that estimating General Memory and Delayed Recall scores using 3-subtest or 2-subtest equations decreases testing time without sacrificing reliability or clinical accuracy. A study was designed to cross-validate previous results in a mixed clinical sample as well as to examine the validity of the 2-subtest equations (Hilsabeck et al., 1999). Its results provide support for the use of the 3-subtest short form to estimate memory ability in normal and cognitively impaired patients; using only two subtests to estimate index scores resulted in a decline in predictive accuracy.

WMS–III (see Table 2.2) was developed, in part, to improve on the known difficulties with the WMS–R. It was improved with regard to stand-ardisation and content. The standardisation sample included a broader age range without interpolated norms. The newly developed scales demonstrated stronger internal consistency than did the WMS–R scales. Two new visual modality tests form 50% of the two principal memory indexes generated by the WMS–III. The test is co-normed with the Wechsler Adult Intelligence Scale—Third Edition (WAIS–III) allowing for direct comparisons across intellectual and memory domains. Several indexes (e.g., auditory immediate memory, visual immediate memory) can be calculated from subtest results. These indexes are intended to be the principal scores used to evaluate memory functioning (The Psychological Corporation, 1997). Because of ongoing controversy over the use and interpretation of these indexes, however, many clinicians choose to focus more on interpreting individual subtests rather than indexes.

Rivermead Behavioural Memory Test

The Rivermead Behavioural Memory Test (RBMT) was developed to detect impairment of everyday memory functions (Wilson et al., 1985, 1991). RBMT consists of 12 subtests and the tasks include remembering a name, an appointment, and a newspaper article, finding a hidden object, recognising faces, and remembering a route. The test is essentially atheoretical, focusing on practical applications of memory rather than a conceptualisation of the construct of memory. There are two ways for scoring the RBMT—a standardised score and a screening score. In the standardised score, each item is allocated 2 points for normal and complete responses, 1 point for borderline responses, and 0 points for responses deemed to be abnormal. A screening score is obtained by pass–fail scoring of the items. One-week test–retest reliability of the RBMT was 0.96 and reliability was 1.0. (Wilson, 1987). Performance on the RBMT correlates with therapist observations of memory failures and subjective ratings by patients and relatives, as well as with performance on other standardised tests of memory. Although originally designed for use with adults aged 16–69, norms are available for young people aged 11–14, older people aged over 70,

TABLE 2.2

Summary of Wechsler Memory Scales (WMS–III) subtests

Subtest	Description
1. Information and orientation	An optional subtest (i.e., does not contribute to the WMS–III indexes) requiring recall of well-learned personal information, as well as orientation to time, place, etc.
2. Logical memory	The clinician reads aloud two brief stories and the examinee must repeat the stories immediately, and after a 25–35-minute delay. Responses are scored for literal or near-literal recall. Supplementary scoring for thematic material examines learning and recall of more general conceptual material vs specific story elements. A recognition test for story material is presented after delayed recall.
3. Verbal and paired associates	A list of unrelated word pairs is read to the examinee in a series of four learning trials. Learning is tested by telling the examinee the first word of each pair and asking for recall of the second word (cued recall) in immediate and delayed conditions.
4. Word lists	An optional word list learning task.
5. Faces	The subject views a series of photographs of faces, some of which are repeated, and must indicate whether each face is "old" (i.e., seen earlier in the series) or "new" (i.e., seen for the first time). Delayed recognition is assessed 25–35 minutes later.
6. Family pictures	The subject views scenes of families engaged in basic activities (e.g., picnic). The picture is then removed and the subject must recall immediately, and after a 25–35-minute delay, the scenes (i.e., characters, location, and activity information).
7. Visual reproductions	An optimal subtest in which the subject views line drawing for 10 seconds each, then reproduces the drawings both immediately and after a 25–35-minute delay. Included are recognition, discrimination, and copy components that may identify confounds of constructional apraxia or visuoperceptual deficits.
8. Letter–number sequences	A list of 2–8 intermixed letters and single-digit numbers is read to the subject who must reorganise and recite (1) the numbers in ascending order and then (2) the letters in alphabetical order. This working memory task requires two simultaneous cognitive processes: holding and reordering the stimuli.
9. Spatial span	A visual STM (forward span) and working memory (backward span) in which the subject views 9 identical cubes placed randomly on a surface. The clinician taps out a prescribed sequence on the cubes which the subject must then mimic. The clinician begins with a sequence of 2 cubes and progresses as high as 9 cubes, if the subject can mimic the pattern correctly. In backward span, the subject mimics each sequence in reverse order.
10. Digit span	An optional subtest often used to index basic attention as well as short-term auditory memory span.
11. Mental control	An optional subtest that examines the speed and accuracy of recall of overlearned information (e.g., alphabet, days of the week). It also includes dual task demands (e.g., counting by sixes).

and patients with impairments of language or perception (Cockburn et al., 1989, 1990). A modified version has been prepared for children aged 5–10 years (Wilson et al., 1991). The children's version of the behavioural memory test (RBMTC) has good interrater and parallel form reliability (Wilson et al., 1993). It can be used to answer such questions as whether there is evidence that a child has memory impairment compared to his or her peers or whether there is improvement or deterioration of memory functioning over time. As the measurement of rate of change is often the principal objective in neuropsychological rehabilitation, preferably in comparison to the group or the functional situation aimed at, the availability

of stratified norms to enhance the adequate interpretation of test performance of the RBMT has been proposed (Van Balen et al., 1996).

The Rivermead Behavioural Memory Test—Extended version (RBMT–E) is also built on the ecologically valid format of the RBMT (Wilson et al., 1999). It is also designed to assess subtle impairments of everyday memory performance.

The RBMT has adequate validity in distinguishing normal persons from those with cerebral dysfunction and in detecting mild and moderate dementia (Huppert & Beardsall, 1993; Wilson et al., 1989). Lezak considers the RBMT to be very good at discriminating moderate from severe impairment but useless for identifying subtle or small memory deficits because it is not unusual for patients with head injuries or recently retired patients with multiple sclerosis to perform at perfect or near-perfect levels (Lezak, 1995). However, a study that appraised the everyday memory of 119 adults with diagnosed brain injuries showed that the RBMT is very accurate in classifying severity of memory impairment as rated by clinicians (Makatura et al., 1999). A study also showed that the RBMT was as robust as the WMS–R in differential discrimination of patients with memory problems (Pérez & Godoy, 1998). Despite the proliferating interest in prospective memory and its relevance to everyday clinical deficits, the RBMT is the only memory test widely used in clinical practice that explicitly tests prospective remembering. This test incorporates three tasks that assess prospective memory: remembering where a belonging is hidden and asking for it to be returned, asking for the next appointment time when an alarm sounds, and delivering a message. Although these tests from the RBMT have been used in several neuropsychological studies of prospective memory, they provide only a limited range of scores and are unlikely to be sensitive to deficits in less impaired patients (Huppert & Beardsall, 1993; Kinsella et al., 1996).

Despite these apparent advantages, the RBMT is also noted to have several shortcomings. As the RBMT has only a two- or three-point scoring range, it has been criticised for lacking sensitivity at both the high and low ends of memory functioning and being most relevant for patients with moderate memory disorders (Lezak, 1995). This test has less sensitivity in mild head injuries and is not well suited to differential diagnosis of memory dysfunctions (e.g., AD) because these disorders are typically described according to theoretical memory models rather than their pragmatic outcomes. A more taxing version of the test, sufficiently sensitive to pick up small decrements in memory within the normal range of memory functioning, would therefore have considerable usefulness.

The RBMT–E, like the RBMT, includes subtests evaluating the ability to remember a route around a room, both immediately and after a delay, and associated subtests involving remembering to

pick up messages and deliver them along the way. These subtests present a difficulty for some patients with restricted mobility. A study was designed to facilitate the use of the RBMT–E with people who have impaired mobility by devising substitute tasks for the route and message subtests that do not require the individual to move around, and by presenting normative data for these substitute tasks (Clare et al., 2000a, b). This study showed that where mobility problems preclude the use of the route and message subtests of the RBMT–E, the "model" tasks can be substituted and profile scores calculated. This approach will allow clinicians to obtain a full spectrum of subtest scores for the RBMT–E with mobility-impaired patients, thus permitting an estimation of a total profile score. The RBMT–E may be a useful clinical tool to aid therapists in the assessment of subtle impairments of everyday memory performance following brain injury (Wills et al., 2000).

Memory Assessment Scales

The Memory Assessment Scales (MAS) is an individually administered battery of tasks developed to assess several areas of cognition (Williams, 1991). Functions of memory that are assessed include attention, concentration and STM, learning and immediate memory, and delayed recall.

Preliminary data reported in the manual suggest that the MAS subtests and summary scores are sensitive to closed head injury, stroke, and PD. Patients with PD scored at least one standard deviation below the average of normal individuals on every summary score and they tended to score lower than those with closed head injury or stroke.

Remote Memory Battery

Remote Memory Battery (RMB) is a frequently used measure of remote memory (Albert et al., 1979). This battery consists of three subtests that require the identification of famous individuals and recollection of public events from the past. On the first test (Famous Faces), individuals are shown photographs of people who became famous at various times and they are asked to name these individuals. The second test consists of a questionnaire that requires recollection of public events from the same time periods tested on the Famous Faces test. The third test is a multiple-choice questionnaire pertaining to similar information tested in the first two subtests. Phonemic and semantic cues are provided to patients if they are unable to provide correct answers on the first two tests.

The Mini-Mental State Examination Scale

One of the simplest and most universal tests is the Mini-Mental State Examination (MMSE) (Folstein et al., 1975). MMSE includes a selection of short items testing different aspects of cognitive function: orientation, repetition and recall of words, attention, language (several items), and constructional ability (Folstein et al., 1975). The test consists of two sections that, together, contain 11 tasks of cognition. The first section involves verbal responses and addresses orientation, memory, and attention. The second section involves the ability to respond to verbal and written commands, such as write a sentence and copy a polygon (Folstein et al., 1975). Although the MMSE was designed for use with hospitalised patients, the scale has attained widespread use among clinicians and researchers concerned with primary care and community settings (George et al., 1991; Murden et al., 1991; Tangalos et al., 1996). Time to administer the screening ranges from 5 to 10 minutes and the instrument can be administered by a clinician or a nurse. Scores range from 0 to 30. The score used is the sum of the scores of all items. The MMSE has also been adapted for use in paediatric settings (Ouvrier et al., 1993). Since its introduction, the MMSE has been used in three ways, each related to one another. First, it is used to provide rapid assessments of cognitive status in clinical settings. Second, it is used as a dementia screening device in which low scores on the MMSE identify respondents with a high probability of fulfilling clinical criteria for a mental disorder or other condition (Gallo et al., 2000; Tombaugh & McIntyre, 1992). Third, the MMSE operationally defines cognitive impairment through the assignment of cut-points (George et al., 1991). Through this third use, the

MMSE has been instrumental in the development of an epidemiology of cognitive impairment (Bassett & Folstein, 1991; Whitfield, 1996). A study designed to report the percentile distribution of the MMSE scores in older people by age, sex, and educational level estimated from longitudinal data showed that performance on the MMSE was related to age in men and women (Dufouil et al., 2000). In women, at age 75, MMSE score ranged from 21 (10th percentile) to 29 (90th percentile). At age 95, the range was 10 (10th percentile) to 27 (90th percentile). The upper end of MMSE distribution was slightly modified with age whereas the lower end of the distribution was very sensitive to age effects. A similar pattern was observed in both sexes. Such norms can be used as reference values to determine where an individual's score lies in relation to his or her age and educational level.

An MMSE score of 27 or higher is usually taken as excluding mental impairment, while one of 23 or lower generally indicates sufficient cognitive decline for the diagnosis of dementia to be made in epidemiological studies (Folstein et al., 1985). A study showed that among residents of nursing homes, the average MMSE score for the cognitively impaired was 9.97 and the average score for the cognitively intact was 21.34 (Phillips et al., 1993). In a study that investigated the association between MMSE scores and diagnosis, computed tomographic scans, or EEG findings in geropsychiatric patients (age $\geq$ 65), it was reported that patients who had abnormal findings on CT scans or EEG had lower MMSE than patients with normal findings (Yang et al., 2000). MMSE is a useful screening instrument for organicity in geropsychiatric inpatients. A study suggested a mathematical representation of AD decline and showed that AD progression over time can be modelled using a cubic or a logarithmic function of the MMSE score (Mendiondo et al., 2000). Additional analyses suggest that patient factors affect rates of AD progression over time, and younger patients and more educated patients progress more rapidly, while sex has little impact on the disease progression. Such estimations of disease course are useful when comparing different populations for both clinical and research purposes.

MMSE has disadvantages for the screening of vascular dementia (Roman et al., 1993). It emphasises language and verbal memory, it lacks the recognition part of memory, it has no timed elements, and it is not sensitive to impairments in executive functions or mental slowing. It has limited sensitivity for detecting subtle or mild cognitive impairment and even mild dementia (Tombaugh & McIntyre, 1992). For example, among mildly demented patients with probable AD, 27% obtained scores at or above the median age- and education-adjusted MMSE score of the population (McKhann et al., 1984; Welsh et al., 1991). The MMSE may have particularly limited utility in differentiating between those patients with subtle cognitive impairments versus those with normal cognitive function (Brodaty et al., 1998; Kukull et al., 1994).

To complete the test successfully, the older adult must have adequate hearing and vision and they must demonstrate sufficient musculoskeletal function to be able to hold a pencil and to write (Dellasega & Morris, 1993). Ten percent of the elderly population had somatic or mental symptoms that contributed to poor performance on the MMSE and difficulties increased sharply with age (Räihä et al., 2001). When screening elderly subjects for cognitive impairment, Molloy et al. (1991) found that the Standardised MMSE (StMMSE), a modified version of MMSE, provided better reliability (intraclass correlation 0.90) than did the MMSE. Physical disabilities that may affect performance on the MMSE and StMMSE are arthritis, multiple sclerosis, or paralysis from a stroke (Dellasega & Morris, 1993). These findings are of particular interest to clinicians who evaluate the individual for dementia but also to those who use the MMSE in research or who develop assessment instruments.

MMSE may be used to assess the longitudinal stability of cognitive impairment in schizophrenia because the test–retest reliability of this scale is extremely good at different retest intervals (Folstein et al., 1975; Harvey et al., 1995). MMSE has become a frequently used test in longitudinal studies of schizophrenia and therefore it may be useful in the long-term assessment of treatment effects in patients with schizophrenia. MMSE is the most widely used scale in population-based dementia. However, as AD progresses, it has limited applicability because patients perform at floor levels. Therefore, based on the MMSE, a new version, the Severe Mini-Mental State Examination (SMMSE) has been devised to briefly assess cognitive domains relatively preserved in moderate to severe AD (Harrell et al., 2000). The SMMSE has advantages over other batteries used to assess this population, in that it is brief (i.e., less than 5 minutes to administer) and easily administered.

Few researchers have estimated correlates of the MMSE (DePaulo et al., 1980; Dick et al., 1984; Folstein et al., 1975). Folstein et al. (1975) reported moderately high correlations for the MMSE with WAIS Verbal and Performance IQs. DePaulo et al. (1980) reported moderate values for the MMSE with Memory Quotient of the WMS and with WAIS Performance IQs. A less robust correlation was found between the MMSE and WAIS Verbal IQs. Dick et al. (1984) reported moderate correlations between WAIS Performance IQs and the MMSE scores and again a less robust relationship with WAIS Verbal IQs.

Mattis Dementia Rating Scale

The Mattis Dementia Rating Scale (MDRS) is a standardised, clinical mental status examination that provides a global measure of dementia derived from subscores for five cognitive capacities: attention, initiation and perseveration, construction, conceptualisation, and memory (Mattis, 1976). The MDRS was designed as a screening instrument to detect the presence of brain pathology in impaired geriatric patients. It was developed to determine the degree of cortical deficit in those individuals with extremely low scores on the WAIS and the WMS. It is sensitive to frontal and fronto-subcortical impairments. In the first report of this scale, 20 patients with organic mental syndromes and 11 normal subjects were examined with the WAIS and the MDRS (Coblentz et al., 1973). In the patient group, the correlation between the full-scale WAIS and the MDRS was 0.75, indicating that at least half the variability in this scale was predictable from a knowledge of intellectual level. In the same study, test–retest reliability for the MDRS was determined on a different group of 30 patients with findings consistent with AD. The MDRS was administered twice with a 1-week interval and the test–retest correlation was 0.97, indicating a high degree of reliability. A particular benefit to the clinician in using this test is the availability of cut-off scores for each of the five indices and the total score of the MDRS, thus facilitating interpretation of performance compared to normative data.

The MDRS has been widely used in the United States for detecting and staging dementia (Shay et al., 1991; Smith et al., 1994; Woodard et al., 1996). High test–retest reliability has been confirmed and normative data have been published (Mattis, 1976; Schmidt et al., 1994). Given the advantages of MDRS over the brief standardised mental status examination, it has been translated and culturally adapted for use with elderly Chinese in Hong Kong (Chan et al., 2003). A number of studies have demonstrated that the MDRS reliably discriminates between patients with moderate to severe cognitive dysfunction and healthy control subjects, and even between types of dementia (Connor et al., 1998; Kertesz & Clydesdale, 1994; Smith et al., 1994; Van Gorp et al., 1999). A study that sought to expand on previous research that examined the clinical utility of the MDRS with older, urban medical patients has provided normative data for this scale, stratified by age (61–94 years) and education (Bank et al., 2000). In this study, which included a large percentage of African Americans as well as a broad range of education levels, it was shown that demographic variables accounted for 19% of the MDRS total score variance. Age and years of education accounted for significant unique variance in MDRS total score variance, consistent with previous research (Lucas et al., 1998). This study provides additional evidence of the significant influence of age and education on MDRS total score performance and highlights the importance of matching a patient's demographic background to the normative sample with which his or her test score is being compared. Consideration of this factor will certainly lead to more accurate diagnostic conclusions and improvement in patient care.

Free and Cued Selective Reminding Test

The best instrument for assessing memory disorders in early dementia is probably the Free and Cued Selective Reminding Test (FCSRT) (Grober et al., 1997). Unlike most clinical memory tests that do not control cognitive processing, this test includes a study procedure in which patients search for items (e.g., grapes) in response to cues (e.g., fruit) that are later used to elicit recall of items not retrieved by free recall. The unique feature of the FCSRT is its emphasis on encoding specificity during learning and recall. Encoding specificity requires that information be processed in a precise manner (i.e., semantically) during learning. The FCSRT then uses semantic categories as cues for items failed during free recall.

Encoding specificity is a powerful technique that, in normal controls, produces efficient learning and memory. However, in diseased states such as senile dementia, Alzheimer's-type brain regions that are essential for these cognitive processes (i.e., medial temporal structures) are characteristically impaired. Theoretical reasons exist to expect that tasks that maximise encoding specificity such as the FCSRT might be particularly sensitive to early AD. Bushke (1984) and Petersen et al. (1992) have shown the effectiveness of encoding specificity using the FCSRT paradigm among normal older adults. Performance on the FCSRT distinguishes dementia from normal ageing with accuracy (Petersen et al., 1994). The FCSRT detects subtle memory changes prior to a person becoming sufficiently impaired to merit a possible or probable AD diagnosis (Petersen et al., 1995; Tuokko et al., 1991). A study designed to estimate the relative rates of dementia in initially non-demented subjects with and without memory impairment defined by baseline free recall from the FCSRT showed that poor performance on free recall from this test predicts dementia (Grober et al., 2000). A longitudinal evaluation of 264 initially non-demented elderly volunteers was performed with clinical and psychometric examinations every 12 to 18 months for up to 10 years. Survival analyses indicated that subjects with impaired free recall at baseline had developed dementia (relative risk = 75.2, 95% CI = 9.9 to 567) over 5 years of follow-up at dramatically higher rates than subjects with intact free recall after adjusting for age, gender, and education. Moreover, the test (immediate recall, free and cued recall, learning slope, recognition, delayed free and cued recall) provides a characterisation of the memory impairment that distinguishes AD from subcortical dementia and from fronto-temporal dementia (Pasquier, 1996; Pillon et al., 1993). Age-adjusted norms for persons aged 56–98 years on the FCSRT have been presented (Ivnik et al., 1997). These data were obtained via several research projects that are known collectively as Mayo's Older Americans Normative Studies (MOANS). These norms will certainly increase the usefulness of the FCSRT test in clinical and research assessment of various memory dysfunctions.

FCSRT has promise as a culture-fair memory test. Education was unrelated to any FCSRT variable in the Mayo Clinic older adults normative study and explained < 2% of the variance in free recall among non-demented elderly (Ivnik et al., 1997; Grober et al., 1998). Free recall was also unrelated to black or white race in the Einstein Ageing Study (Grober et al., 1998).

The Gottfries–Brane–Steen Scale

The Gottfries–Brane–Steen (GBS) Scale is a comprehensive global assessment tool for evaluating dementia symptoms and is based on a semi-structured interview and observation of patients (Gottfries et al., 1982). The scale consists of subscales measuring intellectual (12 items), emotional (3 items), and activities of daily living (ADL) functions, primarily items of self-care (6 items) as well as 6 items of behavioural and psychological dementia. Scoring of the GBS scale may be performed during or after an approximate 20-minute interview with the patient by the rater with caregiver input. The observer's estimation of the patient's present or recent clinical status (the time should be defined) on each item is scored on a 7-point scale where 0 represents the absence of any impairment of symptoms and 6 represents maximal impairment or maximal symptoms. This

is similar to the Likert-type scale of the Clinician's Interview-Based Impression of Change with caregiver input (CIBIC–plus) (Schneider et al., 1997). To aid scoring, anchor points (short descriptions) are defined for each item for 0-, 2-, 4-, and 6-point scores. The items are defined explicitly but in a non-technical language so that the scale may be used by various healthcare personnel. The scores from the assessment are transferred to a "GBS-profile" which may be used to obtain a general overview of the degree of dementia in individual patients or specific patient groups.

The GBS–Total score has been employed in clinical trials of anti-dementia drugs to assess patients' global functioning and also to assess psychological therapy programmes (Dehlin et al., 1985; European Pentoxifylline Multi-infarct Dementia Study, 1996; Karlsson et al., 1988; Koponen et al., 1989; Ohkura et al., 1995; Ragneskog et al., 1996; Saletu et al., 1990; Urakami et al., 1993). A particular advantage of the GBS scale over global assessments is that individuals' domains of cognition, emotion, function, and behavioural symptoms can be assessed in isolation.

The scale is shown to be highly reliable across a variety of healthcare professionals and languages, and is sensitive to changes over time. It gives comprehensive information on global, cognitive, functional, and psychobehavioural characteristics of demented patients. It is an appropriate assessment tool to follow the course of dementia over the long term and can be used to evaluate the long-term efficacy of anti-dementia drugs in clinical trials.

INDIVIDUAL MEMORY TESTS

Buschke Selective Reminding Test

The Buschke Selective Reminding Test (BSRT) was developed to assess verbal memory, specifically list learning (Buschke, 1973; Buschke & Fuld, 1974). The BSRT has traditionally consisted of 12 learning trials. In the most commonly used version, participants are instructed to listen to a list of 12 words and then repeat as many words as can be remembered (Hannay & Levin, 1985). On each trial, the participant is reminded only of the words that were not recalled on the previous trial. The test is discontinued after 12 trials or after the participant recalls all 12 words on two consecutive trials. However, no theoretical or rational basis has been presented for a selection of 12 as the requisite number of trials to administer. A study designed to gather data on independent healthy elderly people, aged 65–75 showed that on selective reminding, women did significantly better than men on most dependent measures (Banks et al., 1987). Men and women showed a significant decrease from last trial recall to recall following a 15-minute delay.

The validity of the BSRT has been demonstrated in several clinical populations, including brain injury, Alzheimer-type dementia, multiple sclerosis, and epilepsy (Beatty et al., 1996a, b; Dikmen et al., 1995; Drane et al., 1998; Masur et al., 1990). It has considerable clinical utility in differentiating normal ageing from dementia and has promise as a useful tool in the preclinical detection of Alzheimer-type dementia (Masur et al., 1989). The sum of recall and delayed recall were the BSRT measures best able to predict dementia with sensitivities of 47% and 44% respectively (Masur et al., 1990). Additionally, Sass et al. (1995) reported a significant correlation of 0.62 between BSRT long-term retrieval and volumetric cell density of CA1 in the left hippocampus of patients undergoing left temporal lobectomy for medically refractory epilepsy. The BSRT has a sensitivity of 80% and specificity of 95% in patients with PD relative to healthy elderly controls (Masur et al., 1989). The BSRT was not useful for differentiating AD from HD. It is particularly valued for its sensitivity to pharmacological agents in drug trials of aged or demented individuals (Stern et al., 1987; Thal et al., 1983).

In addition to its clinical utility in the evaluation of memory disorders, the test has been employed in pharmacological studies that assessed possible memory-enhancing effects of experimental drugs as well as in studies that assessed the adverse effects of commonly prescribed psychotropic drugs (Block & Berchou, 1984; Peters & Levin, 1977, 1979; Pomara et al., 1989; Thal & Fuld, 1983). Typically, these treatment studies required several equivalent test forms to administer predrug and multiple postdrug assessments. A study that evaluated the equivalence of five forms of the BSRT in 45 normal young and 45 normal elderly subjects reported that the forms generally correlated well with one another and were of comparable difficulty, suggesting adequate test equivalence (Deptula et al., 1990). Four of the five forms were particularly well matched.

However, this test may be too lengthy to use as a bedside procedure. The development of BSRT short forms may minimise this disadvantage (Larrabee et al., 2000; Smith et al., 1995). A study utilising a 10-item, 6-trial version of the BSRT reported good discrimination between normal subjects and patients with AD or HD (Paulsen et al., 1995). Current research suggests that fewer trials of the BSRT would provide information highly consistent with that provided by 12 trials while reducing administration time (Smith et al., 1995). Shortening the BSRT to six or eight trials would not deprive the clinician of important behavioural observations, yet it would decrease the length of frustration experienced by the patient.

Delayed Word Recall Test

A procedure that is brief and efficient for bedside use is the Delayed Word Recall Test (DWRT) (Knopman & Ryberg, 1989). This involves the presentation of a set of 10 common nouns, one word at a time. In response to reading each word on a 3″ × 5″ index card, the patient is then required to generate a sentence using the word. A second exposure of the list using this same format follows immediately. The patients are again asked to generate a sentence using the word, even if it is the same sentence as the one they generated on the previous list. This aspect of the task is meant to induce the patient to process the words semantically. After a 5-minute interval filled with other mental status examination activities, free recall of the 10-word list is tested. No cues or prompts are given to the patient. Thus, the DWRT was designed to maximise the likelihood of poor delayed free recall performance in AD patients while minimising the likelihood of poor performance in normal elderly subjects (Knopman & Ryberg, 1989).

A study reported 98% overall predictive accuracy in 42 AD patients and 42 elderly control subjects (Coen et al., 1996). In an extension of the original test, Coen et al. (1996) added a delayed four-choice recognition component which offers clinical and practical advantages over the free recall measure alone. The recognition measure performed almost as well as the free recall measure in discriminating control subjects and patients (overall predictive accuracy = 96%). It was also shown that both DWRT recall and recognition measures were highly sensitive and specific in distinguishing very mild AD patients from depressed/dysthymic patients (Coen et al., 1997). However, a study designed to assess the ability of the DWRT to separate a group of 50 patients with early AD from 50 elderly patients with major depression in a between-subjects experimental design failed to differentiate clearly between the two disorders (O'Carroll et al., 1997). The DWRT is not specific enough to clearly distinguish those patients with early AD from elderly patients with major depression.

Rey–Osterrieth Complex Figure and Rey Auditory Verbal Learning Test

The Rey–Osterrieth Complex Figure (RCF) was designed to assess visuospatial constructional ability and visual memory (Lezak, 1983; Rey, 1941). This test requires copying and reproduction from memory of the complex figure with 18 scorable units. Administration involves having the subject copy the complex figure, then without prior warning, reproduce it from memory. Some investigators give both immediate and delayed recall trials, others only delayed recall trials. The delayed recall interval ranges from 3 to 45 minutes. Scoring is recorded for order and number of completed units. Interscorer reliability was 0.80 for copy, 0.93 for immediate recall, and 0.96 for delayed recall trials (Berry et al., 1991). One-year test–retest reliability ranged from $r = 0.47$ to 0.59 for immediate and delayed recall; split-half and internal consistency reliability estimates range from 0.80 to 0.84

for immediate and delayed recall (Berry et al., 1991). Extensive normative data are available for children and adults (Lezak, 1995). The RCF has proven useful in the study of normal child development (Waber & Holmes, 1986). Atypical child development has also been investigated using the RCF (Prior & Hoffmann, 1990). The RCF is useful with adults as well. It has proven to be sensitive to a wide range of nervous system insults, including hippocampal sclerosis, Wernicke's encephalopathy, Alzheimer's-type dementia, mild head injury, lateralised strokes, and lateralised seizure foci (Fastenau & Fisk, 1997; Leininger et al., 1990; Miller et al., 1993; Parkin et al., 1993). A study designed to compare specific aspects of visuoconstructional deficits in patients with AD, patients with vascular dementia, and normal age-matched subjects using the RCF showed that the AD patients and patients with vascular dementia had significant deficits in all six RCF scoring categories compared with normal controls (Cherrier et al., 1999). Patients with AD exhibited a pattern of deficits similar to that of patients with vascular dementia, with the exception that the AD patients had increased left-sided errors or inattention. It was suggested that left hemispatial inattention contributes to impaired performance on visuoconstructional tasks in AD.

The RCF has been useful in detecting visuoconstructional and visual memory impairment in persons with brain injury, psychiatric disturbance, and PD (Grossman et al., 1993; Meyers & Meyers, 1995). Squire and Slater (1978) found psychiatric inpatients performed significantly worse with a 16–19 hour delay condition on this test following bilateral and right unilateral electroconvulsive therapy. A study designed to assess visual memory disturbance in different forms of schizophrenia compared the RCF performance in acutely psychotic, chronically psychotic, outpatient schizophrenia, and controls with disorders other than schizophrenia (Silverstein et al., 1998). There were no group differences on the copy condition of the RCF. However, the chronic schizophrenia group utilised more abnormal copying strategies than the outpatient or non-schizophrenia groups. The chronic schizophrenia group demonstrated significantly poorer recall than the outpatient or non-schizophrenia groups, and a trend towards poorer performance than the acute schizophrenia group. These data suggest that chronic schizophrenia patients are characterised by more severe memory impairment than are non-chronic schizophrenic patients. Visual memory disturbance in chronic schizophrenia is not solely a function of encoding difficulties.

A study reported that patients with right unilateral temporal lobectomies were impaired relative to normal controls and to patients with left temporal lobectomies on a 40-minute recall (Jones-Gotman, 1986). In a factor analysis, the RCF immediate and delay loaded onto a visuospatial perceptual/memory factor with immediate and delay WMS Visual Reproduction and Benton Line Orientation (Berry et al., 1991). In another study that examined the role of perceptual and organisational factors in three amnesic groups of patients (Korsakoff, medial temporal, and anterior communicating artery aneurysm) on the RCF test, it was observed that while both the anterior communicating artery aneurysm and Korsakoff groups had poorer copy accuracy and organisation than controls, only the Korsakoff patients' copy accuracy was worse than the other two amnesic groups (Kixmiller et al., 2000). While the Korsakoff patients' visuoperceptual deficits could partially clarify this group's poor performance at immediate recall, the Korsakoff group's comparatively worse performance at delayed recall could not be explained by poor copy accuracy, reduced visual organisation or even the combined influence of both variables. This is an important finding considering that there is a tendency to attribute any unique memory performance by Korsakoff patients to their executive dysfunction, especially when this group is compared to other etiologically distinct amnesic patients.

Although the RCF has proven to be a very useful tool, it lacks recognition and matching trials which can help clarify contributions of perception and memory retrieval to defective memory recall performances. Fastenau (1996) expanded the administration of the RCF by adding recognition and matching trials to the existing copy, immediate recall, and delayed recall trials of the Rey. This elaborated administration is collectively called the Extended Complex Figure Test (ECFT). In addition to showing strong reliability and validity, the RCF and ECFT have been shown to be robust with respect to several variations in administration and with respect to different scoring systems for the Rey figure drawings (Fastenau et al., 1996). In a study in which both the RCF and ECFT were administered to 211 healthy adults (aged range 30–85 years), it was shown that age and education effects were evident on all trials (Fastenau et al., 1999). In this study, age-appropriate norms are presented using Osterrieth's 36-point scoring, and overlapping cells and convenient tables for converting raw scores to scaled scores.

The Rey Auditory Verbal Learning Test (RAVLT) is a brief, easily administered measure of verbal learning and memory (Rey, 1964). The test consists of 15 common nouns which are read aloud to the examinee at the rate of one per second for five consecutive trials, each followed by a free recall period. Upon completion of trial V, an interference list of 15 words is presented in the same manner as the first, followed by a free recall of that list. On the sixth trial the examinee is asked to recall as many of the words as possible from the first list. Finally, a story incorporating all the words from the initial list is presented and the examinee is instructed to identify any words he or she recognises from the first list. In addition to scores on Trials I through to V, which may be used to plot a learning curve, the RAVLT provides the opportunity to score for the total number of words recalled following interference (Trial VI), the total number of words recognised in the story, and the total number of words recalled after a half-hour delay (Lezak, 1976). The RAVLT provides measures of registration, verbal learning, overall verbal memory functioning, immediate and delayed recall, and recognition. It requires only 10 to 15 minutes of administration time and children as young as 5 years can usually complete the test. Rey's data are based on a sample of Swiss children (Rey, 1964). Current normative data for the adult population have recently become available. Query and Megran (1983) provided norms for male hospital inpatients. They reported a gradual decline in RAVLT scores as the subject's age increased. A study compared the performance of adult men and women on the test (Bleecker et al., 1988). Age and sex accounted for a significant proportion of variance on each trial.

Initial studies of the RAVLT suggest its validity and clinical utility. Mungas (1983) found the test identified different patterns of deficits in groups of amnesics, brain trauma victims, Attention Deficit Disorder patients, schizophrenics, and non-psychotic psychiatric patients. The RAVLT effectively differentiated non-neurological from mixed neurologically impaired subjects (Powell et al., 1991). As an independent measure, it established its clinical efficacy by correctly identifying 74% of the sample population (using the Trial V score). Specifically, in this sample RAVLT Trial V discriminated between control subjects and brain-impaired patients better than any individual measure in either the Halstead–Reitan or Dodrill batteries. The validity of the RAVLT in detecting memory impairment has also been demonstrated in patients with AD, PD, and traumatic brain injury (Bigler et al., 1989). In a study that investigated the use of the RAVLT in distinguishing between demented patients with PD and those with AD, it was noted that elderly controls performed better than did patients with moderate AD, severe AD, or PD on all measures of the RAVLT (Tierney et al., 1994). The moderate-AD group performed better than did the severe-AD group on the five learning trials of list A. Unlike the controls and PD patients, both AD groups showed a greater recency than primacy effect, and both performed equally poorly on recall of List A after List B had been presented. The pattern of performance among AD and PD patients reveals that individuals with AD evidence problems with all aspects of memory (i.e., encoding, storage, and retrieval) while patients with PD demonstrate a retrieval deficit. Relatively poor free recall, but adequate scores on recognition, suggest the latter. Another study confirmed the predictive utility of the RAVLT with AD patients (Haddad & Nussbaum, 1990). The scores obtained on the RAVLT made it possible to identify cognitively impaired elderly people who would benefit from a rehabilitative group therapy experience.

Clinical experience over the past few years with the RAVLT has led to the conclusion that Rey's norms are too high for the population of children on current versions of Rey's word lists (Rey, 1964). A study designed to assess performance of English and French subjects aged 5 to 16 on the RAVLT showed that Rey's (1964) norms were too high for current use (Bishop et al., 1990). There was a high positive correlation between age and RAVLT performance. IQ correlated moderately with RAVLT scores. French subjects did less well compared to English subjects but IQ was a confounding factor. However, the RAVLT is a valuable addition to neuropsychological test batteries as well as psychoeducational assessments. The delayed recall trial is the most sensitive to memory or learning impairment.

The California Verbal Learning Test

The California Verbal Learning Test (CVLT), a relatively new neuropsychological memory assessment based on methods and constructs of cognitive science, is a multiple-trial recall and recognition word-list learning test. The CVLT involves learning, recalling, and recognising a 16-item list of words representing four semantic categories (e.g., tools, fruits) (Delis et al., 1987; Elwood, 1995). To assess auditory verbal learning, the word list is read aloud by the clinician and the patient immediately recalls as many items as possible. Five such trials are administered. Performance is quantified in terms of the slope of the increase in words recalled across trials. Subsequent to learning trials, the patient is presented with, and must immediately recall, a new list of 16 words. This second list permits examination of proactive (i.e., words from the list being recalled in the second list) and retroactive interference (i.e., words from the second list being recalled during recollection of the first list in subsequent trials). Next, the patient is asked to recall all items from the first list, and then in a second phase (cued recall), is requested to recall items when given category cues. These trials assess retrieval abilities under less structured (i.e., free) and more structured (i.e., cued) conditions. In this way, the CVLT may quantify and provide data for memory performance indices such as primacy–recency effects, rate of acquisition across trials, consistency of item recall across trials, recognition and recall performance, and semantic and serial clustering.

The commonly used norms presented in the CVLT manual consisted of a combination of several independently collected subject samples (Delis et al., 1987). It included 273 (104 men, 169 women) neurologically intact subjects. These norms have been described as limited because they are based on a relatively small sample size with less than desirable representativeness, and thus caution is advised in their clinical use (Delis et al., 1987; Elwood, 1995). Information regarding ethnicity was not analysed in the CVLT norming process but ethnic minorities are believed to be poorly represented in this sample. The lack of information regarding the contribution of ethnicity may lead to misclassification of memory impairment, especially within ethnic minority populations. Recently, demographically corrected norms for the CVLT have been presented (Norman et al., 2000). There were 906 subjects, of whom 549 were Caucasians (61%) and 357 were African Americans (39%). Tables and regression equations were offered to convert raw scores into T-scores corrected for age, gender, education, and ethnicity (Norman et al., 2000). A study that examined the test–retest stability of the CVLT in a normal elderly sample (mean age was 72 years) performed a retest after one year (Cellucci et al., 2001). Mean total recall did not change and the stability coefficient was 0.64. Thus, the CVLT total recall measure was moderately stable.

A meta-analysis of the memory literature reported the CVLT to be among the most sensitive of all tests to cognitive deficits associated with abnormal ageing (Christensen et al., 1991). The CVLT not only assesses, through recall and recognition trials, the amount of verbal information learned, but also provides various indices of how information is learned by characterising the strategies used and the types of errors made.

The CVLT has been used to explore the verbal learning and memory capabilities of patients with AD, Korsakoff's syndrome, PD, schizophrenia, bipolar disorder, epilepsy, and alcoholism (Delis et al., 1991a; Dupont et al., 1990; Hermann et al., 1988; Karaken et al., 1996; Kramer et al., 1989a, b; Masserman et al., 1990). Clinical investigations have demonstrated the validity of the CVLT in identifying verbal learning and memory deficits in patients with AD, HD, and PD (Bondi et al., 1994a, b; Kramer et al., 1989b). CVLT is also useful in revealing a clear pattern of memory deficits in PD patients with typical profiles characterised by severely impaired learning, high intrusion error rates, and poor retention over delay intervals (Delis et al., 1991a). Furthermore, these three characteristics have proven to be quite effective for differentiating AD patients from individuals with progressive basal ganglia disease and depression. Some studies have focused on CVLT performance in the traumatically brain injured (Crosson et al., 1988; Vanderploeg & Eichler, 1990). In a study that compared memory disorders of three patient groups suffering from brain lesions (left prefrontal cortex lesion, left arteria cerebri posterior lesion, and right hemispheric lesion) with a word list corresponding to the CVLT, it was shown that a discriminant analysis correctly classified 86.11% of the patients (Hildebrandt et al., 1998). Consistent with previous studies, it was shown that patients with left prefrontal cortex lesions were significantly impaired in encoding and recall (Shimamura, 1994; Wheeler et al., 1997). It was also suggested that left prefrontal cortex lesions also result in verbal memory disorders as far as free recall is concerned and that the CVLT helps to detect this disorder (Hildebrandt et al., 1998). The CVLT can be used to detect proactive interference in TBI individuals (Numan et al., 2000). Confirmatory factor analysis of eight competing latent variable models suggested that a four-factor model (composed of Attention Span, Learning Efficiency, Delayed Recall, and Inaccurate Recall) fits the data relatively well (Wiegner & Donders, 1999). The CVLT is also a sensitive and multifactorial measure of learning and memory after TBI.

The quantification of numerous verbal learning and memory processes and the provision of good validity information are major strengths of the CVLT. In addition, an alternative form of CVLT that would be useful in retest situations has been developed (Delis et al., 1991b).

A children's version of the CVLT, the California Verbal Learning Test—Children's Version (CVLT–

C) has been found to be useful for detecting verbal learning and memory deficits in neurologically impaired children (Delis et al., 1994). The reliability of the CVLT–C appears to be acceptable with average values of coefficient alpha ranging from 0.72 to 0.85 (Delis et al., 1994). Norms are currently available for children 5 years and older. The potential clinical utility of this test for 4-year-old children has also been demonstrated (Goodman et al., 1999). Among the groups studied are children with fetal alcohol syndrome, TBI, autism, attention deficit hyperactivity disorder, and language impairment (Loge et al., 1990; Mattson et al., 1996; Minshew & Goldstein, 1993; Yeates et al., 1995).

Fuld Object Memory Evaluation

The Fuld Object Memory Evaluation (FOME) was developed especially for persons 70 years and older, and to be useful with nursing home and community residents (Fuld, 1981). It is an instrument that assesses an older individual's ability to recall information across repeated trials via a selective reminding format. Thus, the FOME is a selective reminding test in which patients are asked to remember 10 common objects (ball, bottle, button, scissors, key, ring, playing card, nail, cup, and matches) that they identify tactually and visually prior to the first recall trial. An object that is misnamed after visual confrontation is corrected by the examiner. After the objects are placed back into the bag, the subject is then presented with a distractor task, during which he/she is required to generate words belonging to one of several categories: names of people, names of foods, things that make one happy, names of vegetables, and things that make one sad. During each recall trial, the subject is given 60 seconds to recall all of the contents of the bag. The subject is then selectively reminded of those items that are not recalled and administered another distractor test. This sequence of recall trials followed by selective reminders and distractor tasks continues for five trials and the total number of target items recalled across the five trials is tabulated. The entire five trials of the FOME take approximately 20 minutes to administer whereas administration

of the first trial alone takes approximately 5 minutes.

The FOME has been found useful for differentiating both dementia and depression from healthy ageing (La Rue, 1989; La Rue et al., 1986). A study that investigated the usefulness of the FOME as culture-free showed that this test has a high degree of sensitivity—95.9% for mildly impaired Spanish-speaking patients and 95.5% for English-speaking patients diagnosed with mild AD (Loewenstein et al., 1995). Fuld and colleagues (1988) found the test useful in diagnosing dementia in a sample of Japanese elders. The Japanese subjects were similar in age, education, mental status, and FOME performance to a sample collected in the United States. Sensitivity of the FOME also greatly exceeded that of the Folstein MMSE in this mildly impaired dementia group. Thus, the FOME is free of cultural bias and AD patients from different language groups obtain virtually identical scores on it (Lowenstein et al., 1995). A study designed to compare performances on the FOME with other memory measures to assess convergent validity and to determine discriminant validity of the FOME on factors such as education, race, and gender was performed in 146 consecutively admitted elderly people (Wall et al., 1998). Convergence was found with other standardised measures of memory, as significant correlations were found between FOME scores and Logical Memory from the WMS–R and the Memory Scale of the MDRS. The results were consistent with previous research suggesting that the FOME is useful with persons with lower levels of formal education and those from culturally diverse backgrounds. The FOME remains a useful measure in the geriatric battery for persons of ethnic diversity who have limited formal education as an assessment of a person's capacity to acquire information.

A study examined performance on the FOME using a less educated and more ethnically diverse sample than was utilised in the normative study (Summers et al., 1995). Discriminant function analysis results revealed that the cognitively intact group scored significantly higher on the FOME than did the cognitively impaired patients. Cut-off scores at levels of adequate specificity, however, revealed low sensitivity. These data suggest that the FOME is an easy memory test but has a low ceiling. Those patients who do not have significant cognitive impairment may still perform well. If a person performs poorly on this examination, they are likely to be experiencing significant impairments in memory functioning. But a person may perform within normal limits and still be experiencing a degenerative cortical dementia. Consequently, this assessment should not be used as the only measurement of memory functioning in neuropsychological evaluations of the elderly.

A modification of the FOME test was developed for use with middle-aged adults (35–55 years) (Davenport et al., 1988). To avoid the ceiling effect that occurs when the 10-item FOME is used with adults in age groups, the test was made more difficult by increasing the number of items to 15. This version of the test was difficult enough for even high-functioning adults to need multiple trials to memorise all items. Thus, with such a normative data base, this version—the FOME-15—may prove to be a valuable tool to be used in individuals during middle adulthood, when memory processes can be impaired as a consequence of disease or as a side-effect of pharmacological agents.

Benton Visual Retention Test

The Benton Visual Retention Test (BVRT) evaluates visual memory, visual perception, and visuo-constructive abilities (Sivan, 1992). There are three, roughly equivalent, alternative forms. Each comprises 10 unique designs and four different administration methods as follows: (A) reproduction after a 10-second exposure, (B) reproduction after a 5-second exposure, (C) copying during exposure, and (D) reproduction after a 10-second exposure and 15-second delay. The most popular administration approach is administration A where each design is displayed for 10 seconds, with the subject drawing the design from memory immediately afterwards. In spite of the face-valid memory component to the task, factor analyses have demonstrated that administration A of the BVRT loads primarily on a visual–perceptual–

motor factor and secondarily on a memory–concentration–attention factor (Larrabee et al., 1985).

The BVRT has a number of advantages that account for its continuing popularity. It is a sensitive indicator of the presence of brain dysfunction (Heaton et al., 1978; Tamkin & Kunce, 1985). Furthermore, error types can be of localising significance, that is, patients with unilateral neglect may consistently omit peripheral figures appearing only on one side (Benton, 1974; Spreen & Strauss, 1991). Scoring criteria are more explicit than other similar tests of visual memory (Spreen & Strauss, 1991). The total number of designs drawn correctly out of 10 possible is scored in an all-or-none fashion, with subjects receiving a credit of either 1 or 0 for each individual design. The scoring allows for both quantitative, that is, total number of errors committed, as well as qualitative analyses. Six major types of error are explicitly described in the manual including: (1) omissions and additions, (2) distortions, (3) perseverations, (4) rotations, (5) misplacements, and (6) size errors (Benton, 1974). There is also provision made for noting whether an error occurred on the right or left side. These well-defined scoring criteria have allowed for excellent interrater reliabilities for both number correct (0.96) and total number of errors (0.97) (Swan et al., 1990). An important advantage of the BVRT that sets it apart from most other currently available tests of visual memory is the presence of multiple parallel forms. Multiple forms of equivalent difficulty are needed to minimise practice effects when performing serial cognitive assessments for measuring treatment effects and/or disease progression/recovery (Crook et al., 1992; Youngjohn et al., 1992). Although interform correlations are respectable, ranging from 0.79 to 0.84, the different forms do not appear to be equally difficult, with Form D being slightly more difficult than Form C (Benton, 1974).

The BVRT is frequently included in neuropsychological test batteries for differentiating dementia from the effects of normal ageing because it has been demonstrated to have good discriminant validity for this purpose (Youngjohn et al., 1992a, b). It has also been used to differentiate persons with one apolipoprotein E ε4 allele from those with none (Soininen et al., 1995). Patients with right hemisphere lesions performed worse on this measure than patients with left hemisphere lesions (see Benton, 1974; Lezak, 1995). In addition to its sensitivity to memory dysfunction, one notes other advantages such as explicit scoring criteria, parallel forms, and high interrater reliability (0.96 for number correct) (Youngjohn et al., 1993).

Total errors on the BVRT are known to increase in normal ageing. The rate of decline was gradual at younger ages but was especially pronounced after age 70 (Arenberg, 1978). These findings were extended to women in later stages (Giambra et al., 1995; Robertson-Tchabo & Arenberg, 1989). In a study designed to examine the differential increase in seven specific error categories for 2000 participants in the Baltimore Longitudinal Study of ageing, significant age differences for all types of BVRT errors in men and women ranging from 20 to 102 years of age were shown (Resnick et al., 1995). Cross-sectional analyses indicated that all types of errors increased significantly across age groups. The overall increase in errors with age was similar for men and women. Another study that examined relationships between demographic and diagnostic variables and BVRT in older adults aged 55 to 97 years derived extended geriatric norms for BVRT total correct scores adjusted for parameters that contributed significantly to the variance (Coman et al., 1999). It was shown that age and education but not gender were significantly associated with BVRT performance in both normals and normals with memory concerns. The BVRT is one of several procedures that have been recommended by a NIMH workgroup for the identification of individuals suffering from Age-Associated Memory Impairment (Crook et al., 1986).

Concerning children, norms have been provided for administration A (immediate reproduction of designs following a 10-second exposure) and administration C (copy of exposed designs). These norms are for children and adolescents 8–14 years old, and are based on expectations given IQ level. The BVRT has been investigated using several paediatric clinical groups. The measure has demonstrated utility in differentiating children with brain damage as compared to those with emotional disturbance (Rowley & Baer, 1961). A study that examined the clinical use of the BVRT for 130 children and adolescents with learning difficulties who were between the ages of 8 and 13 years of age showed that this test was also sensitive to developmental patterns (Snow, 1998). The results support the use of the BVRT with children and adolescents with learning difficulties.

Wisconsin Card Sorting Task

The Wisconsin Card Sorting Task (WCST) was developed by Berg (1948) as an objective measure of the ability to deduce abstract categories and to shift cognitive set. It is the prototypical executive functions task in neuropsychology. It has been suggested that this test is sensitive, if not specific, to prefrontal lobe dysfunction (Anderson et al., 1991; Heinrichs, 1990; Milner, 1963). In this test, subjects are asked to match cards according to three categories (colour, shape, and number). The examiner tells subjects if cards have been placed correctly or incorrectly but does not reveal the sorting strategy, which must be inferred from the feedback provided. Once 10 consecutive cards have been categorised correctly, the sorting principle changes, without warning or comment from the examiner. All sorts according to the previous strategy now receive negative feedback and subjects are expected to shift eventually to a new categorisation principle. The most widely used and sensitive variable derived from the WCST is a measure of perseveration obtained by counting the number of times a subject sorts according to a previously correct principle despite negative feedback from the examiner (Heaton et al., 1993).

The WCST has been used to characterise neuropsychological deficits in a wide range of disorders, including those with clear focus neuropathology (e.g., focal brain lesions) and those in which the neurological substrates are more hypothetical (e.g., schizophrenia). The WCST is used to examine these kinds of abilities for both clinical and research purposes. It has been used as a measure of abstract reasoning among normal adult populations. Norms for non-pathological adult populations have been published (Heaton, 1981; Spreen & Strauss, 1991). In addition, it is reported to be sensitive to hypoactivation of the frontal cortex in schizophrenia (Weinberger et al., 1986). Studies of the WCST in schizophrenic patients have generally found significant impairments, particularly in chronic patients, but this finding also holds true for acute schizophrenic patients (Goldberg et al., 1987; Morice, 1990; Saykin et al., 1994; Weinberger et al., 1986). Schizophrenics show perseverative impairments on the WCST, failing due to a tendency to continue to sort along the previously correct stimulus dimension. Some studies suggest that performance failure on the WCST is probably a reflection of physiological frontal lobe deficits in schizophrenic patients rather than a reflection of poor motivation (Goldberg et al., 1987; Llonen et al., 2000). A simple instruction such as verbalisation of a sorting strategy or verbal reinforcement may enhance executive function and impact WCST performance in patients with schizophrenia (Everett et al., 2001; Perry et al., 2001). Thus, these results on the WCST may suggest that the cognitive deficits in schizophrenia are not fixed but reversible. These data have implications for the cognitive remediation of patients with schizophrenia.

Spreen and Strauss (1991) presented norms for 60 elderly subjects aged 60 to 94, although no information about the variables of educational level or gender was given. It was suggested that performance appears not to decline significantly until late in life. A study reported that the eldest group (75–85 years) performed the most poorly of subjects aged between 17–87 years (Haaland et al., 1987). The WCST scores should be interpreted within the context of patient gender, education, and age (Boone et al., 1993). Interest in the cognitive and developmental effects of early frontal lobe injury among children has also increased interest in the use of the WCST as a potential measure of executive function among school-age children. Chelune and Baer (1986) published information on developmental norms for the WCST for children between the ages of 6 and 12 years. They emphasised that by the time the children were 10 years old, their performance

on the WCST was no different from that of normal adults. Rosselli and Ardilla (1993) applied the WCST to 233 children aged between 5 and 12 in Colombia. They reported that the children's performance on the WCST varied with age. By about 11–12 years of age, performance was also similar to that of young adults. A recent study presented norms for the WCST in 6–11-year-old children in Taiwan and made comparisons of WCST performance between children in Taiwan and the USA (Shu et al., 2000). The scores of the WCST were mostly age-dependent and associated with underlying CNS maturity level. In Chinese culture the father has a more powerful role than the mother in a family, and the father's education level had a significant effect on some variables (correct number, categories completed, percent conceptual level response, perseverative response, and perseverative error) of the WCST. Thus, the results of this study may facilitate the WCST as a clinical or research instrument in combination with other procedures to examine aspects of cognitive and neuropsychological functioning of school children.

The WCST has a potential problem with specificity. It may not always distinguish intact from impaired subjects. For example, it is not uncommon to have a bright, intact subject achieve few categories on the WCST because they are testing very complicated sorting rules (Nelson, 1976). Although such a subject would not necessarily make an excessive number of perseverative responses, their performance would not look entirely normal. The WCST has also a specificity problem with patients with different kinds of brain damage. In several studies, it does not discriminate patients with focal frontal damage from those with diffuse damage (Heaton et al., 1993). It has even failed to discriminate patients with focal frontal damage from patients with focal non-frontal damage (Anderson et al., 1991). The WCST has also a sensitivity problem. Some patients with documented frontal lesions and dramatic "frontal" problems in everyday life may perform completely normally on the WCST (Damasio et al., 1991). Finally, the WCST suffers from a ceiling problem and poor reliability in school-age populations, although its reliability was considerably higher in a population with more impaired scores (Pennington et al., 1996). To avoid misdiagnoses, we need norms that allow us to take into account the relative contribution of age, education, and gender in terms of the patient's score and adjust the raw score accordingly.

Due to practical and financial constraints, a number of abbreviated versions of the WCST have been introduced and cogent arguments can be made for one over another in certain situations. However, the single deck, 64-card WCST (WCST–64) appears to be the most logical and practical short form (Greve, 2001). It is the test to which the existing WCST literature is most likely to generalise. Psychological Assessment Resource has recently published a new manual with comprehensive norms for the WCST–64.

The Alzheimer's Disease Assessment Scale

The Alzheimer's Disease Assessment Scale (ADAS), another important neuropsychological test, was constructed as a severity scale applicable to patients diagnosed as suffering from AD (Mohs & Cohen, 1988; Rosen et al., 1984). It is a good representative of the sort of scale containing both cognitive and non-cognitive items. The scale consists of 21 items—11 pertaining to the cognitive section (ADAS–cog) and 10 to the interview-based ratings of behavioural symptoms (ADAS–ncog). The ADAS and its subscales are not designed for use as a diagnostic tool. However, scores on the scale discriminate patients with clinically diagnosed AD from non-demented subjects (Zec et al., 1992). Its sensitivity to detect change has been documented by longitudinal data. On average, AD patients show an increase in ADAS–cog scores of approximately 7 to 8 points per 12-month interval (Pena-Casanova, 1997). Due to its sensitivity to change and facility to use, ADAS has become one of the most widely used research tools for the assessment of treatment efficacy in large clinical trials of pharmacological treatment of AD. In a large-scale multicentre clinical trial, ADAS was noted to clearly demonstrate reliability and validity in the assessment of symptom severity in AD patients (Weyer et al., 1997). Its reliability and validity have been established

in the original English version. The test–retest and interrater reliability of the English ADAS scale, ADAS–cog, and non-cognitive subscales are good. The interrater reliability of the ADAS–cog is 0.989 (Mohs & Cohen, 1988; Rosen et al., 1984). Its test–retest reliability is 0.915, which is much better than that of the non-cognitive subscale, which is 0.588. Versions in Japanese, Greek, German, French, Spanish, Dutch, Swedish, Chinese, Icelandic, Finnish, Danish, and Hebrew have also been developed (Chu et al., 2000; Homma, 1992; Manzano et al., 1994; Tsolaki et al., 1997).

The ADAS–cog is more elaborate than the MMSE, but many of the criticisms aimed at the MMSE are also appropriate for the ADAS, in particular those concerning the use of posterior measures and the probability of ceiling effects in minimal and mild AD. Unlike the MMSE, the ADAS assesses to a limited extent the capacity of episodic memory. However, the cueing paradigm, of interest for minimal and mild AD, is not employed and there is no evaluation of consolidation capacity (with the delayed recall paradigm). Furthermore, the ADAS has no quantitative and thorough evaluation of semantic memory, and no evaluation of working memory, autobiographical memory, or personal semantic memory. This lack of measures sensitive to the first stages of the disease, and specifically, the lack of memory system measures in the ADAS has already been reported (Mohr et al., 1995a, b).

METAMEMORY

There has been a growing interest in metamemory or the knowledge that one has about one's own memory skills and ability (Cavanaugh & Murphy, 1986). It is assumed that such knowledge may determine how an individual performs in memory tasks. Hence, metamemory may involve general memory judgements and task-specific appraisal of one's memory capabilities (Nelson, 1996). Most studies have investigated metamemory by means of self-report questionnaires.

In terms of defining and measuring metamemory, it has yet to be clearly established that self-perceptions about one's memory can be isolated from self-perceptions such as self-esteem, from affected states such as depression, and from traits such as social desirability that may influence questionnaire responses. Although metamemory is thought to consist of a number of dimensions, the number and interrelationships of the dimensions have not been determined, nor whether the same dimensions are being measured in the various studies. Finally, there is the question of the link between measures of metamemory and actual performance in memory tests. Generally, when such a relationship has been reported, the link between the two has been rather weak, with correlations in the range 0.20 to 0.30 (Hultsch et al., 1987). Despite this low relationship, which shows that metamemory cannot be used as a substitute for traditional tests, the metamemory construct is still worth investigating. Self-report questionnaires have shown that individuals see their memories not as completely good or poor but as a set of abilities, some of which are good, some of which are poor. Therefore, a memory profile can be obtained from such questionnaires and this may be more useful than a single total score. Given the potential significance of memory, there is a need for well-developed self-report measures of metamemory that are reliable, valid, and applicable to clinical and research settings.

An important area of research on metamemory and ageing is the degree to which individuals of different ages accurately predict their ability to remember recently studied materials (see Hertzog & Dixon, 1994; Lovelace, 1990). Individuals with high levels of metacognitive accuracy ought to be able to use accurate monitoring to control and regulate their strategies for learning and retrieving information from memory (Schneider & Presley, 1989). Optimal self-regulation should lead to higher levels of memory performance. Two different kinds of prediction have been frequently elicited in developmental research. With the global predictions approach, people judge how many items of an entire study list they will subsequently recall. With the item-by-item predictions method, people predict the likelihood of subsequent recall separately for each item. A study designed to assess the effects of age on different kinds of

metacognitive prediction accuracy showed that older adults monitored learning effectively (Connor et al., 1997). Relative to younger adults, they showed equally accurate immediate judgements of learning, produced an equivalent delayed judgement of learning effect, and showed equivalent upgrading in the accuracy of their global prediction from before to after study of test materials.

The metamemory questionnaires

The Metamemory in Adulthood Questionnaire (MIA) contains 108 items that describe memory issues and changes relevant to healthy ageing (Dixon et al., 1988). The seven subscales provide information about an individual's knowledge of general memory processes and tasks, frequency of memory strategy use, and self-rated memory ability. The MIA also assesses the perceptions of memory stability over time, anxiety regarding memory, memory and achievement motivation, and locus of control in memory abilities. Good psychometric data have been presented for the factor structure, reliability, and validity for this test (Dixon et al., 1988).

The Memory Functioning Questionnaire (MFQ) is another metamemory scale that contains 64 items distributed across four subscales (Gilewski et al., 1990). It assesses subjective appraisals of frequency of forgetting in different situations, the seriousness of the consequences of forgetting in these situations, comparison of present and past memory functioning, and frequency of memory strategy use. Psychometric evidence supports the factor structure, reliability, and validity of this test (Gilewski et al., 1990; Zelinski et al., 1990).

Additional self-report questionnaires provide information primarily about the frequency with which various memory mistakes occur. These include the Memory Assessment Clinics Self-rating Scale (MACSS), the Everyday Memory Questionnaire (EMQ), and the Cognitive Failures Questionnaire (CFQ) (Broadbent et al., 1982; Crook & Larrabee, 1990, 1992; Martin, 1986).

There are several drawbacks with the use of these self-report memory questionnaires, especially in clinical settings. Since some of these questionnaires were developed primarily for research purposes, the items included do not necessarily reflect aspects of memory that are amenable to clinical memory intervention. Several of the questionnaires include items that are not applicable to some individuals, such as public speaking, reading novels, driving, or working. It can be difficult to interpret the results of a questionnaire when not all items are answered. The considerable amount of time required to complete a long questionnaire such as the MIA could adversely affect compliance especially in older or cognitively impaired individuals. Finally, many of the metamemory questionnaires do not assess common emotional reactions to memory such as frustration, irritation, unhappiness, or pleasure.

A new scale, the Multifactorial Memory Questionnaire (MMQ) has been devised to assess three dimensions of self-reported memory including overall contentment or satisfaction with one's own memory ability (MMQ–Contentment), perception of everyday memory ability (MMQ–Ability), and use of everyday memory strategies and aids (MMQ–Strategy) (Troyer & Rich, 2002). This questionnaire requires about 10 minutes to be completed. It represents an improvement over other memory self-report instruments because it encompasses a number of features in combination (i.e., multidimensionality, clinical relevance, brevity, and ease of administration) that are rarely found in other questionnaires. Evidence for the reliability and validity of the MMQ in healthy older adults has been shown (Troyer & Rich, 2002). The psychometric strengths of the MMQ make this questionnaire useful in both clinical and research settings.

DISCUSSION

One of the central problems for research in the assessment of memory regards the methodology employed to measure memory deficits and in particular the sensitivity, validity, and reliability of test procedures. The demands on psychometric test materials are well known. They have to be reliable, i.e., these instruments are supposed to

measure a given variable in an accurate, consistent, reproducible manner. Forms of reliability include internal consistency (the extent to which items comprising a scale measure the same construct), test–retest, interrater, and parallel forms reliability. Furthermore, neuropsychological test materials have to be valid. They should be able to measure what they were intended to measure. Finally, as memory impairment progresses in neurodegenerative disorders, memory tests must have the ability to detect clinically important changes in a reliable way.

Cross-cultural or multinational studies of dementia have been confronted by the problem that memory tests designed in one language and normed in one culture may not be applicable to the group under investigation. Although AD affects individuals of all races and cultures, the instruments used to assess its clinical features have been mainly developed with members of the English-speaking White middle class. It appears that no standard tests for memory fulfil all the desired psychometric properties. Bohnstedt et al. (1994) compared the MMSE scores and clinical diagnosis of White, Black, and Hispanic dementia patients and found that MMSE scores for Black and Hispanic patients underestimated their cognitive capabilities relative to the White patients. A study showed that Hispanic AD patients perform significantly worse than non-Hispanics in terms of total MDRS score, scores on the MDRS subscales for Conceptualisation and Memory, and on serial subtraction (or backward spelling item) of the MMSE (Hohl et al., 1999). While mildly to moderately demented Hispanic and non-Hispanic patients obtained comparable scores on the MDRS, severely impaired Spanish-speaking patients obtained significantly lower MDRS scores than their English-speaking counterparts. The discrepancy in the MDRS scores of the severely impaired Hispanic and non-Hispanic patients might reflect a cultural bias in the test or educational differences between the groups. Research interested in ethnic differences in MMSE suggests that neighbourhood type may be a predictor of cognitive impairment (Espino et al., 2001). The geographic context in which people live, including neighbourhood context, may be related to their level of cognitive functioning. Thus, it was shown that Mexican Americans were 2.2 times more likely than European Americans to have MMSE scores < 24 (Espino et al., 2001). However, once neighbourhood was added to the statistical model, the ethnic difference noted in MMSE scores was no longer statistically significant. Observed ethnic differences in the prevalence of MMSE-classified cognitive impairment appeared to be primarily a function of ethnic differences in the prevalence of lower educational levels and types of neighbourhood residence.

A source of common confusion and theoretical challenge lies in the distinction between test instructions and memory processes. It is easy to classify a test as explicit when subjects are asked to intentionally retrieve memories from a specified episode, or as implicit when subjects are requested to perform a task and no reference is made to any prior episode. However, it is not easy to determine what kind of memory processes are involved when performing the test. There are many examples when memory on an implicit test is correlated with memory on a related explicit test. Obviously, these implicit tests invoke some of the same declarative memory processes typically invoked by explicit memory tests. There are several theories and methods that address the distinction between implicit tests that measure processes associated with or dissociated from declarative memory (Bowers & Schacter, 1990; Cohen & Eichenbaum, 1993). Nevertheless, these approaches cannot at present satisfactorily predict whether a specific implicit test will or will not invoke declarative memory processes.

The issue of how to measure the expression of memory other than by verbal recall has been hotly debated for some time. Currently, many researchers are of the opinion that the requirements that expressions of memory be "verbal and conscious" are unnecessary. Investigators examining children's memory, human amnesic syndromes, and the ageing of implicit and explicit memory and activity memory have also rejected "verbal and conscious" as necessary components in the expression of memory (Howard, 1988; Howe & O'Sullivan, 1990; Kausler & Lichty, 1988; Shimamura et al., 1990).

Using metamemory questionnaires, both age and sex differences in adults' self-perceptions of their memory functioning were reported (Hultsch et al., 1987). In comparison with younger adults, older adults considered they had less memory capacity and also reported that their memory had declined over the years. Also, there was some evidence that older adults believed they had little control over their memory (i.e., that they could not improve it or prevent it from getting worse). Regarding sex differences, women reported better remembering of past events and greater use of strategies. They also emphasised that it was important to have a good memory and to do well on memory tasks. Women also showed a higher level of anxiety in situations that place demands on memory.

Most of the memory tests have adequate validity in detecting memory impairments in elderly persons. At this time, the RCF and CVMT should be used with caution in elderly individuals pending further investigation of their reliability and validity in the elderly population. The test–retest stability of most of the memory tests falls below the recommended minimum cut-off for tests used in clinical decision making, which suggests that relatively large test–retest differences are needed in order to conclude that a significant change in memory functions has occurred over time. As repeated assessments are commonly used to evaluate memory deterioration due to disease, good test–retest normative data are urgently required.

In recent years, a concern has developed about the "ecological validity" of research studies in memory and the extent to which traditional laboratory tests of memory reflect performance in everyday situations (Schooler & Schaie, 1987). Researchers have tended to move away from the traditional laboratory measures of memory performance, such as digit span and word lists, and to utilise material that appears to have more direct relevance to everyday living. Diversity of areas investigated in current attempts to increase the ecological validity of research into memory includes memory for motor activities and memory for events. The relationship between prose recall and everyday activities has also been investigated. Other areas of investigations include memory for television programmes, differences between experts and novices, and efficiency of retrieval. Concerning memory for television programmes, the most important discovery was that older adults did retain information from watching television (Stokes & Pankowski, 1988). They remembered 56% of the main ideas and 43% of the subordinate ideas in the immediate recall test, and 48% of the main ideas and 30% of the subordinate ideas after 1 week. The results showed no significant correlations between age and any recall measures. Only previous education was significantly positively related with the number of ideas recalled immediately and after 1 week's delay. Regarding the differences in memory between experts and novices, the results of studies in problem solving appear consistent in a variety of situations, such as playing chess and bridge, music, physics, electronics, architecture, and radiological interpretation and diagnosis (Glaser, 1987; Hoyer, 1987; Salthouse, 1985). It seems that the amount and organisation of knowledge specific to the area of expertise in LTM, rather than a superior capacity in working memory, provides the basis for the differences between experts and novices.

There remains a need for the development of ecologically based memory tests. The WMS–R is considered to be a reasonably good test of memory impairment but it does not correlate with memory performance in real life. In other words, the WMS–R measure does not disability and therefore does not address rehabilitation issues. The RBMT, on the other hand, measures disability in that it includes analogues of real-life tasks. The RBMT is one of the few tests that have been developed primarily with ecological validity in mind (Wilson et al., 1985). It seeks to provide measures of the practical effects of impaired memory and can thus be used for monitoring memory changes with treatment (Lezak, 1995). The RBMT includes mostly practical memory tasks such as name-free associations; remembering a hidden belonging, an appointment, a newspaper article, faces and routes, and to deliver a message; as well as an orientation section. Thus it reflects real-life problems and is a good predictor of both independence and employment (Schwartz & McMillan, 1989; Wilson, 1991). The test has

four parallel forms and supplemental norms have been developed for the 70–94 age range (Cockburn & Smith, 1989).

Two CANTAB (Cambridge Neuropsychological Test Automated Battery) tests, the Paired Associate Learning (PAL) and Delayed Matching to Sample (DMTS) have been used in a longitudinal study to assess memory in AD (Fowler et al., 1995, 1997; Sahakian et al., 1988). It was shown that both tasks were more sensitive to decline among questionable dementia patients than were traditional measures such as the WAIS–R and WMS–R. The performance of approximately half of the questionable dementia patients on the PAL task worsened whilst that of the remaining subjects remained stable. It was therefore hypothesised that worsening performance on PAL may be an early indicator of AD (Fowler et al., 1995, 1997). A recent study confirmed that scores on a test of visuospatial PAL very accurately classified individuals as belonging to either the AD or the combined depression/control group (Swainson et al., 2001). The PAL test appears as sensitive and specific for AD and preliminary data also suggest that it may be sensitive to the specific memory deficits of prodromal AD. Another recent study that analysed eight widely used memory measures showed each to have moderate predictive power in differentiating between patients with mild dementia and healthy normal controls (Derrer et al., 2001). However, when these instruments were combined in a logistic regression analysis, three of them had substantial predictive power. Together, the Word List Acquisition, WMS–T Logical Memory II and WMS–R Visual Reproduction II were 97.26% accurate (100% sensitive and 94.59% specific) in distinguishing these two groups. The Word List Acquisition is a brief test that alone had high accuracy (92%). These memory tests are highly useful in the diagnosis of mild dementia.

The development of neuropsychological tests of visual memory has lagged behind the development of tests of verbal memory, with doubts being raised about the construct validity of all commonly used visual memory tests (Lezak, 1995). For example, the Visual Reproduction subtests of the WMS–R and the BVRT have been found to load on a general memory factor or a visuoperceptual/visuoconstructional factor rather than on an independent visual memory factor (Wechsler, 1987). As another example, the criterion-related validity of the visual subtests from the WMS–R and the RCF test has been questioned because of the insensitivity of these tests to impaired performance in patients with right temporal-lobe lesions (Lee et al., 1989; Wechsler, 1987). Visual memory can be validly assessed using a recognition test of previously presented

Chinese characters, at least for those with no knowledge of this language (Eadie & Shum, 1995). This approach would overcome the confounding of memory functions with visuoconstructive abilities criticised in a number of visual memory tests using reproduction of stimulus materials (Loring & Papanicolaou, 1987). It would also overcome the problems of interjudge agreement in scoring responses often encountered in tests using reproduction (Loring & Papanicolaou, 1987).

Neurological Assessment
of Memory

INTRODUCTION

Studies of patients with brain lesions have provided the foundations of our knowledge about the biological organisation of human memory. Lesions have produced dramatic and often unexpected mnemonic deficits that provide clues about which brain regions are necessary for which memory processes. The behaviour of memory-impaired patients with brain lesions, however, does not delineate what process the injured tissue subserves. The behaviour reflects what uninjured brain regions can accomplish after the lesion. In addition, naturally occurring brain lesions often impair multiple brain systems, either by direct insult or by disconnection of interactive brain regions. It is therefore difficult to determine which defect is the consequence of which part of a lesion. Despite that, lesion studies continue to provide new evidence—functional neuroimaging studies using positron emission tomography (PET) or functional magnetic resonance imaging (fMRI) now permit the visualisation of memory processes in the healthy brain. The goal of some of this work has been to "map" the brain in the sense of assigning specific function to structures by selectively activating or deactivating them while people perform various tasks. It is important to acknowledge that what is measured is not neuronal activity but local haemodynamic changes such as blood flow, in the case of PET, and blood oxygenation in the case of fMRI.

The study of the functional neural basis of declarative memory has disclosed several brain regions that provide critical contributions to declarative memory abilities. The regions to which damage results in amnesia can be divided into three groups: medial temporal lobe structures, diencephalic structures, and basal forebrain structures (see Figures 3.1–3.3, and some possible association between memory systems and neuroanatomical substrates in Table 3.1). Visual information is stored in the occipital cortex, tactile information in the sensory cortex, auditory information in the middle temporal gyrus, and olfactory information in the orbitofrontal cortex. Often eclipsed by some of its more famous neighbours such as the medial temporal lobe and hippocampus, the retrosplenial cortex has nevertheless maintained its standing as one of the key brain regions classically comprising the limbic system.

FIGURE 3.1

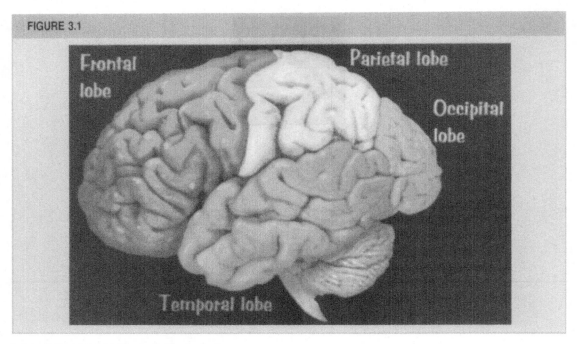

Lobes of the cerebral cortex in the human brain.

FIGURE 3.2

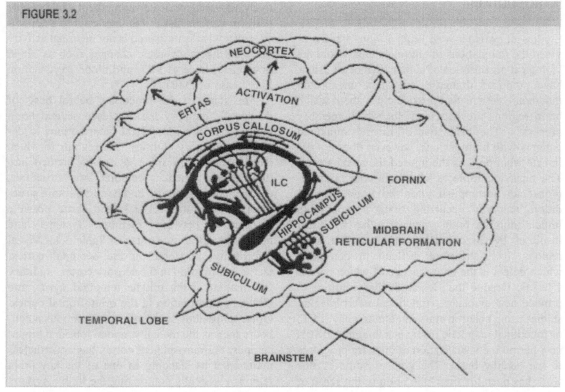

Human brain: Output from the hippocampus travels via the fornix to the intralaminar complex (ILC) of the thalamus, the midbrain reticular formation, and the limbic nuclei. This activation effected via the fornix conveys "flagging" messages to the extended reticular-thalamic activation system (ERTAS).

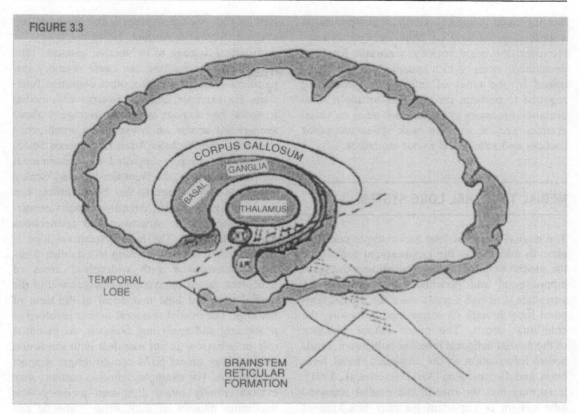

FIGURE 3.3

Human brain: The thalamus sits atop the brainstem at the centre of the brain, surrounded by the basal ganglia and limbic structures. Most of the neocortex and white matter of the left hemisphere have been removed to reveal these subcortical structures. The thalamus lies closest to the midline of the hemisphere; the basal ganglia are situated more laterally (towards the outside).

It forms part of the cingulate cortex, an anatomically and functionally heterogeneous structure (Vogt et al., 1992). It is clear that patients with lesions primarily involving the retrosplenial region are notable for significant memory problems (Masuo et al., 1999; Vogt et al., 2000). That lesions of the retrosplenial cortex can give rise to memory problems and in some cases amnesia highlights its close anatomical links with the medial temporal region and points to a crucial role in memory processing.

Interest in identifying neuroanatomical locations for emotional memories suggests that they are closely linked to the amygdala, which enables associations between complex/multimodal sensory information and affective states related to fear or reward (Gaffan et al., 1988; Kesner et al., 1989; LeDoux et al., 1988). Stimulation of the amygdala

in humans frequently elicits the recall of emotionally charged memories (Gloor et al., 1982).

The demonstration that amnesic patients can acquire and retain several memory skills despite their severe episodic memory deficits provides strong evidence that procedural memory appears to be mediated, at least in part, by a corticostriatal system involving reciprocal connections between the neocortex and the basal ganglia. Damage to this corticostriatal system has been found to produce impairments in perceptuomotor skill learning and other tasks that involve the generation and refinement (i.e., learning) of motor programmes to guide behaviour (Heindel et al., 1993; Squire & Zola, 1996a). Damage to this system also produces impairment on probability-classification learning tasks that do not require overt motor learning. Taken together, these studies indicate that the basal ganglia is a critical component of a general procedural or habit-learning system. However, the brain regions important for non-declarative memory in a specific task are determined by the types of information processing required to perform the task. For example, non-declarative memory in a visual task relies on visual cortices and in a motor task relies on motor cortices and subcortical motor structures.

MEDIAL TEMPORAL LOBE SYSTEM

The medial temporal lobe has multiple components. In addition to the hippocampal formation, the medial temporal lobe also includes the parahippocampal and perirhinal cortices, and the amygdala. Cortical signals enter the medial temporal lobe through its major input structure, the entorhinal cortex. The major output structure of the medial temporal lobe, the subiculum, sends neural information to the amygdala, basal forebrain, and diencephalon (Van Hoesen et al., 1991). It appears that the role of the medial temporal lobe system is important for only one kind of memory. It is essential for conscious recollections of recently occurring facts and events (declarative memory) but not for a large collection of non-declarative memory abilities (e.g., skills and habits, simple classical conditioning, and priming). Medial temporal lobe lesions may result from resection, anoxia, herpes simplex encephalitis, infarction, or sclerosis.

The mechanisms underlying priming and skill learning do not rely on the conscious recollection of the original experience and do not seem to involve medial temporal lobe structures. In contrast, declarative memory, which consists of the ability to store new memories of specific events (episodic memory) as well as new facts and knowledge (semantic memory) depends on medial temporal lobe structures in the hippocampal region (Squire & Zola-Morgan, 1991). This region, including the hippocampus, parahippocampal cortex, perirhinal cortex, and entorhinal cortex, has reciprocal connections (directly or indirectly) with the dorsal and ventral stream visual areas as

well as with equivalent areas in the other sensory systems (Suzuki & Amaral, 1994).

Bilateral damage to the medial temporal lobe or diencephalic midline can cause memory impairment without affecting other cognitive functions. For example, amnesic patients with medial temporal lobe damage can obtain average or above average IQ scores on conventional intelligence tests (e.g., the Wechsler Adult Intelligence Scale) and yet be severely impaired on conventional memory tests (e.g., the Wechsler Memory Scale). Empirical work suggests that brain lesions can produce highly specific cognitive deficits exquisitely related to the structures and connections that are damaged. The medial temporal lobe is needed at the time of learning to establish functional connections with widespread areas of neocortex, based on synaptic changes within the medial temporal lobe that occur at the time of learning. The medial temporal lobe is involved in processing and analysing; however, its essential role in behaviour is not manifest with the lesion methodology unless STM can no longer support recollection. For example, amnesic patients may exhibit entirely intact digit-span memory—the maximum number of digit items someone can recall in order immediately after their presentation (Cave & Squire, 1992). Similarly, amnesic patients with medial temporal lobe lesions were fully intact at identifying words flashed briefly on a computer screen (Hamann et al., 1995). They exhibited normal performance across a wide range of accuracy. However, patients with damage to the temporal lobes often have difficulty naming objects and retrieving information about object-specific characteristics (Hart & Gordon, 1990; Hodges et al., 1992). This suggests that object-specific information may be stored, at least in part, in the temporal lobes.

Lesion studies identify three key features of medial temporal lobe function. Medial temporal lobe lesions spare STM while impairing LTM. The deficit can be described as profound forgetfulness. It emerges most clearly after some time has elapsed beyond the moment of learning. Medial temporal lobe function is involved in memory for a limited period of time after learning. When a medial temporal lobe lesion is sufficiently de-

TABLE 3.1

Possible neuroanatomical and neurochemical substrates of memory systems

Memory system	Possible neuroanatomical substrate	Possible neurotransmitter involvements	References
Working memory Central executive system	Frontal lobes (prefrontal areas)	Dopamine Noradrenaline Others?	Malapani et al., 1994 Coull et al., 1995 Goldman-Rakic, 1995a, b Riekkinen et al., 1998a
Articulatory loop: Verbal rehearsal	Left middle and inferior frontal gyri Left supramarginal gyrus	Acetylcholine Others?	Cohen et al., 1994a, b Stern et al., 1992 Ruchkin et al., 1997 Jonides et al., 1993
Phonological buffer	Temporal-occipital lobes and prefrontal areas	Unknown	
Visuospatial sketchpad "What" system "Where" system	Parietal-occipital lobes and prefrontal areas		Christensen et al., 1992; Crosson, 1992
Episodic memory General	Medial temporal lobes and diencephalic midline or limbic system	Acetylcholine	
Encoding and consolidation	Hippocampus, parahippocampal gyrus, entorhinal area, amygdala, mammillary bodies, septum, anterior and dorsal-medial thalamic nuclei, cingulate gyri and orbito-frontal regions	Catecholamines and vasopressin (encoding)	Forette et al., 1992
Retrieval	Frontal regions	Catecholamines	
Semantic memory General	Neocortex	Unknown	Squire & Zola-Morgan, 1991; Crosson, 1992
Autobiographical memory General (retrograde memory for personal events)	Anterior and posterior temporal lobes (except medial structures); parietal and occipital lobes, brain stem mesencephalic structure	Unknown	De Renzi & Lucchelli, 1993; Hunkin et al., 1995; Goldberg et al., 1981
Implicit memory Skill learning	Left primary motor cortex Left supplementary motor area Left pulvinar thalamus	Unknown	Grafton et al., 1992
Verbal priming Data-driven processes	Occipital lobes	Non-acetylcholine	Russo & Spinnler, 1994; Christensen et al., 1992
Conceptually driven processes	Medial temporal lobes	Unknown	Keane et al., 1995

layed after learning, memory is not affected. This finding of temporally graded retrograde amnesia has been obtained using different species. Tasks such as object discrimination learning in monkeys, context-specific fear conditioning in rats, acquired food preference in rats, maze learning in mice, and trace conditioning of the eyeblink reflex in rabbits have been used (Cho et al., 1993; Kim et al., 1993, 1995; Winocur, 1990; Zola-Morgan & Squire, 1990). In contrast, there is no evidence for temporally graded retrograde amnesia following a neocortical lesion.

Another defining feature of medial temporal lobe function is that damage to this region produces a memory impairment that is global and multimodal. Memory is impaired regardless of the kind of material that is presented (e.g., objects, words, or designs) and the sensory modality in which information is presented (Suzuki et al., 1993). Bilateral lesions produce a global amnesia that extends to verbal and non-verbal information. Global amnesia impairs the ability to acquire both episodic and semantic memories, such as the meaning of words and concepts

(Gabrieli et al., 1988). Work with monkeys and humans has led to the observation that the severity of memory impairment increases as more components of the medial temporal lobe memory system are damaged. The severity of impairment was greater following damage within the medial temporal lobe that also included all the adjacent cortical regions (e.g., the perirhinal, entorhinal, and parahippocampal cortices) (Zola-Morgan et al., 1993).

Studies on the role of the medial temporal lobe in the memory system suggest that this part of the brain performs a critical function beginning at the time of learning to establish a long-term declarative memory (Mishkin, 1982; Squire, 1987). Its role continues after learning for a lengthy period of reorganisation and consolidation whereby memories stored in neocortex eventually become independent of the medial temporal lobe memory system. This process, by which the burden of long-term permanent memory storage is gradually assumed by the neocortex, ensures that the medial temporal lobe system is always available for the acquisition of new information. Such a hypothesis suggests that lesions of the medial temporal lobe interfere only with the long-term storage of new memories. Patients like HM, who due to the severity of his epilepsy had the medial temporal lobes of his brain removed to prevent almost constant seizures, retain a reasonably good memory of earlier events (Milner, 1985; Scoville & Milner, 1957; Squire, 1987). He showed deficiency in declarative memory—he cannot recollect new events in his life or new facts about the world but is able to learn new visuomotor skills (e.g., reading in a mirror after several practice sessions) without awareness of having been previously tested. Patient HM's case triggered several important hypotheses that have significantly impacted the study of the neuroanatomical basis of memory. HM's deficits were initially attributed to his hippocampal damage (resulting from his bilateral medial temporal lobectomy). This was the first case implicating the hippocampus in memory. The view that mnemonic functions are diffusely represented throughout the forebrain was challenged. The findings from HM triggered many studies to investigate the role of the hippocampus in learning

and memory in both animals and men. They provided the first evidence that implicit memory could survive in the absence of explicit memory. The implication of the medial temporal lobes in memory consolidation was suggested.

The first lesions in most cases of AD may occur in the medial temporal lobe and this may account for amnesia being the most common initial problem in AD (Hyman et al., 1984). Unlike patients with pure amnesia, AD patients have a dementia defined by the compromise of at least one additional, non-mnemonic function. Further, AD patients also have early damage to cholinergic neurons in the basal forebrain and lesions in that area cause declarative memory impairments (Arendt et al., 1983). Therefore, it is not appropriate to ascribe the amnesia in AD exclusively to medial temporal injuries.

Postmortem analysis of medial temporal damage in patients with well-characterised amnesias shows that damage restricted to a small part of the hippocampal region, the CA1 field, is sufficient to produce clinically significant anterograde amnesia. More extensive damage to additional medial temporal structures aggravates the severity of the anterograde amnesia and the temporal extent of the retrograde amnesia. When lesions extend beyond the hippocampal region into the entorrhinal and perirhinal cortices, retrograde amnesia extends back one or two decades (Corkin et al., 1997; Rempel-Clower et al., 1996).

Neuroimaging studies provide convergent evidence about the participation of medial temporal regions in declarative memory. Medial temporal activations are observed during intentional memory retrieval (Schacter et al., 1996a, d; Squire et al., 1992). These activations are associated with successful memory retrieval. Activations are greater when people make memory judgements for studied than for novel materials and for well remembered than for poorly remembered words. Medial temporal activations also occur during the encoding of memories. The encoding activations appear to index stimulus novelty. They are greater for stimuli seen initially rather than repeatedly (Stern et al., 1996; Tulving et al., 1994b). Neuroimaging studies suggest that proper name retrieval deficits are typically associated with the most anterior regions of the left temporal lobe (temporal pole)

(Semenza et al., 1995). Activation of the left temporal pole during proper name production was also observed during a PET study (Damasio et al., 1996). A more posterior temporal region showed increased activation during animal naming, and an even more posterior region showed increased activation during naming of tools. These observations raise the intriguing possibility that retrieval blocks associated with attempts to name different kinds of items (e.g., individual persons, animals, tools) may reflect inhibition of slightly different temporal regions. Imaging studies are beginning to provide information about the specific contributions of different components of the medial temporal memory system to declarative memory. The finding that different medial temporal structures make different contributions to declarative memory may help to explain why extensive lesions, which may compromise multiple declarative memory processes, yield more severe anterograde and retrograde amnesias.

Neuroimaging data also indicate that the medial temporal area is involved in encoding novel events into episodic memory (Stern et al., 1996). The medial temporal region is also thought to play a role in pattern completion at retrieval. However, the neuroimaging data on medial temporal contributions to episodic retrieval are not entirely clearcut. Many studies have failed to observe medial temporal activity during retrieval and have implicated the medial temporal area in the successful recollection of recently acquired information (Schacter et al., 1996a, d; Ungerleider, 1995). Unfortunately, these clinical studies seldom include detailed neuropsychological and behavioural information from established personality questionnaires. Increased activity in the medial parietal lobe, the precuneus, is commonly reported in functional imaging memory studies (Buckner et al., 1996; Fletcher et al., 1995a, b). This has been interpreted as being associated with the retrieval of visual imagery in episodic memory. This was confirmed in a study in which the recall of imageable word pairs, but not of non-imageable word pairs, was associated with significant activation of the precuneus (Fletcher et al., 1995). All functional imaging studies of topographical memory encoding report the precuneus as active. Activity in this region may relate to the construction of an internal representation of large-scale environments, and seems compatible with the role of the precuneus in imagery.

The hippocampus

The hippocampus has long been considered to be critically involved in memory storage. Hippocampal long-term potentiation (LTP) has been proposed to be a potential neural mechanism for memory storage (Lynch & Baudry, 1984; McNaughton, 1983; Teyler & Discenna, 1986). It is part of the limbic system and is connected to other brain areas through two main pathways, the fornix and perforant path (Gilman & Newman, 1992). The entorhinal cortex itself is the major source of afferents to the hippocampus. As a consequence these connections along with a number of direct perirhinal–hippocampal projections ensure that the perirhinal and parahippocampal cortical areas are a major source of hippocampal inputs. Additionally, the hippocampus has extensive reciprocal connections with the entorhinal, perirhinal, and parahippocampal cortices (Suzuki & Amaral, 1994). These interconnections help to reinforce the view that the hippocampus along with the perirhinal, parahippocampal, and entorhinal cortices function as a closely integrated unit subserving aspects of memory, including recognition (Squire & Zola-Morgan, 1991). In one of the most often cited models, the parahippocampal, perirhinal, and entorhinal cortices form a reciprocal network with the hippocampus to create a "medial temporal memory system" (Squire & Zola-Morgan, 1991). Although the hippocampus and the perirhinal cortex will often function as interacting components of an integrated recognition memory system, there are increasing indications that their contributions are different and can be dissociated (Brown & Aggleton, 2001). Importantly, evidence from animal studies suggests that a system centring on the perirhinal cortex is concerned with discriminating the familiarity and recency of occurrence of individual stimulus items, whereas a system centring on the hippocampus is concerned with judging the prior occurrence of constellations of stimuli. The evidence relating to the hippocampus for spatial arrangements of stimuli includes spatial information (the place

TABLE 3.2

Some tasks sensitive in infraprimate mammals to hippocampal damage

Tasks	References
Water maze	Morris et al., 1986
Odour discrimination	Eichenbaum et al., 1986; Lynch, 1986
Event timing	Olton et al., 1987
Cue relationships	Sutherland et al., 1989
Spatial memory	O'Keefe & Nadel, 1978
Spatial alternation	Aggleton et al., 1989
Radial arm maze	Becker et al., 1980
Conditional learning	Ross et al., 1984
Discrimination reversal	Berger & Orr, 1983
Trace classical conditioning	Moyer et al., 1990; Solomon et al., 1986
Contextual conditioning	Kim & Fanselow, 1992; Phillips & LeDoux, 1992

where they occur), so that recognition memory for episodes would correspondingly be expected to be affected by hippocampal lesions. This system is crucial for the rapid acquisition of new information about facts and events. The role of the hippocampus is to bind together different components of the memory. Later expansions of this model have acknowledged some linkage with medial thalamic regions but no apparent role has been provided for hippocampal outputs to the mammillary bodies and anterior thalamus via the fornix (Zola-Morgan & Squire, 1993). It is therefore presumed that these connections are not necessary for the recall of episodic memory.

The hippocampus is composed of two major regions, the hippocampus proper (Ammon's horn) and the dentate gyrus. Ammon's horn contains mainly the stratum pyramidal (a narrow cell layer consisting of pyramidal neurons and interneurons) and the stratum radiatum (apical dendrites of neurons). It is further divided into four subfields called cornu ammonis (CA) 1–4 (CA1, CA2, CA3, CA4) (Isaacson, 1987). The dentate gyrus is located at the end of the band of hippocampal pyramidal neurons and is composed mainly of granule cells (Brown & Zador, 1990). Further research led to findings that the hippocampus has three major afferent pathways (perforant fibre pathway, mossy fibre pathway, and Schaffer collateral fibre pathway) running from the subiculum to the CA1 region. A brief high-frequency train of stimuli to any one of these pathways increases the excitatory postsynaptic potentials in the hippocampal neurons, an increase that can last for hours and,

in the intact animal, for days and even weeks. This facilitation, which is called LTP, is the best model available for a cellular basis for learning and memory. Hippocampal cells readily demonstrate plastic events associated with learning. For example, pyramidal neurons of the CA1 sector display LTP, change firing during classic conditioning, and show induction of protein kinase C (PKC) synthesis in response to learning (Berger et al., 1983; Buzsaki, 1989; Olds et al. 1989). Depth electrode recordings from patients show that some hippocampal units increase their activity in the recall phase of memory tasks (Halgren et al., 1978). Studies on monkeys suggest that the hippocampus may also be important for providing a snapshot memory of relative spatial relationships in complex scenes (Gaffan & Harrison, 1989; Parkinson et al., 1988). In the human brain, the right hippocampus appears more closely related to spatial memory, whereas the left hippocampus is more closely associated with memory for verbal material (Smith & Milner, 1989).

A number of tasks in mammals are sensitive to hippocampal damage (see Table 3.2). Damage to the hippocampus results in learning deficits in a variety of tasks involving goal-directed navigation, such as the Morris water maze tasks, the eight-arm radial maze, and place discrimination tasks (Harley & Martin, 1999; de Hoz et al., 2003). It is also involved in discrimination learning, which also requires the processing of relationships between stimuli, such as contextual conditioning tasks, various non-spatial mnemonic tasks, and the negative patterning discrimination task

(Antoniadis & McDonald, 2001). Although it is difficult to generalise, common threads in many of these tasks include relational memories, i.e., memories for relations among stimuli and events, and memories that utilise spatial/contextual information, both of which would seem reasonable analogies of human declarative memory in lower animals. Converging evidence supports the idea that the hippocampus is a pivotal structure in memory formation (Mishkin, 1982; Scoville & Milner, 1957; Squire, 1992). The spatial hypothesis of hippocampal functions as best exemplified by the cognitive mapping theory suggests that this medial temporal lobe area is essential in human and animals for the acquisition of complex spatial relationships (O'Keefe & Nadel, 1978). Active movement leads to the development of place-coding and direction-coding hippocampal cells (O'Keefe & Dostrovsky, 1971). Allocentric maps stored in the hippocampus enable flexible navigation by encoding several and alternative routes to the same destination. Indeed, place-coding cells within the rat and primate hippocampus have been found to exhibit spatially localised firing (O'Keefe & Dostrovsky, 1971).

Classical conditioning

Regarding the role of the hippocampus in classical conditioning studies, research suggests that neuronal unit cluster recordings in hippocampal fields in CA1 and CA3 increase in discharge frequency very rapidly during training trials (Berger & Thompson, 1978; Berger et al., 1976). This growth of hippocampal unit response forms a predictive "temporal model" of the learned behaviour response. The growth of the hippocampal unit response is, under normal conditions, an invariable and strongly predictive concomitant of subsequent behavioural learning. This increase in neuronal activity in the hippocampus becomes significant by the second or third trial of training, long before behavioural signs of learning develop, as would be expected of a declarative memory system. Studies in humans with brain damage show that hippocampal–medial temporal lobe lesion subjects are massively impaired on conditional discriminations in eyeblink conditioning (compared with frontal lesion or normal controls)

but not on acquisition or simple discriminations (ruling out deficits in response inhibition) (Daum et al., 1991, 1992). The deficits seen in eyeblink conditional discriminations in humans and discrimination reversal in rabbits reflect deficits in declarative memory (Daum et al., 1991, 1992).

Large bilateral lesions of the hippocampus in animals made before training markedly impair learning of the trace conditioned response (CR) but lesions made 1 month after training have no effect on memory of the trace CR (Kim et al., 1995). These results are strikingly consistent with the literature concerned with the declarative memory deficit following damage to the hippocampal system in humans. These deficits have two key temporal characteristics. They are profound and permanent anterograde amnesia and profound but clearly time-limited retrograde amnesia. Subjects have great difficulty learning new declarative tasks/information. They have substantial memory loss for events for some period just preceding brain damage (1 or more years in humans, 2–3 months for monkeys) but relatively intact memory for earlier events (Zola-Morgan & Squire, 1990).

Spatial navigation

Removal of the hippocampus in rats produces devastating impairments on spatial navigation tasks and on tests of spatial working memory that rely on the animal being able to make a recency discriminations about locations it has visited (Liu & Bilkey, 1998, 1999). In contrast to its effects on recognition memory, removal of the perirhinal cortex in rats often has no apparent effect on spatial tasks (Bussey et al., 1999; Glenn & Mumby, 1998). Even when deficits are observed, they are less severe than those after hippocampectomy (Liu & Bilkey, 1998, 1999). So when recognition memory judgements involve spatial information, the hippocampus and not the perirhinal cortex is the critical structure.

Human patients with damage to the hippocampus show spatial learning impairments (Maguire, 1997). Activation of the left hippocampus has been noted in neuroimaging studies of navigation but this activity was not found to correlate with any navigation measures (Ghaem et al., 1997; Grön et al., 2000). In contrast to the left, the right hippocampus has been shown to correlate with the accuracy of the path taken to goal destinations in a virtual reality town, while the right parahippocampal gyrus is most active during the memory for landmarks (Maguire et al., 1998; Mellet et al., 2000). While accepting that the right human hippocampus is not exclusively concerned with navigation, way-finding does seem to be one of its major concerns. In accordance with this idea, a neuroimaging study reports hippocampal activation during spatial navigation in a computerised virtual environment (Maguire et al., 1996). Goal finding was either direct or indirect. To assess the flexibility of the cognitive map, in the indirect condition, direct goal routes were precluded by the blockade of certain streets. Successful performance was associated with right hippocampal and inferior parietal activation for both direct and detour way-finding conditions. These findings suggest that the right hippocampus provides an allocentric representation of the environment that allows the computation of accurate direction from any start point and the right inferior parietal cortex uses this information to compute the correct body turns to enable movement towards the goal. Previous findings show that lesions to the right inferior parietal cortex result in deficits of the ability to represent or act on an object located with regards to the left–right body axis (Burgess et al., 2000).

Evidence from recent PET scanning studies suggest that the hippocampal formation is associated with some aspect of the actual recollection of an event (Schacter, 1997). The hippocampus has been proposed to maintain a cognitive map of the spatial layout of learned environments. Complex spike cells within the rat hippocampus have been found to exhibit spatially localised firing (O'Keefe & Dostrovsky, 1971; O'Keefe & Nadel, 1978).

Role in declarative memory

The most common current view of the memorial functions of the hippocampal–medial temporal lobe system is that declarative memories are stored there for some period of time, perhaps due to processes of synaptic plasticity like LTP. For an element of LTM to become a part of permanent explicit memory, a process called cortical consolidation must occur (Abel et al., 1998). According to this consolidation process hypothesis, these memories may then eventually be transferred or consolidated to other brain regions for permanent storage, the cerebral cortex being the most commonly suggested site. It appears that the hippocampus plays a time-limited role in memory formation. It serves to bind together the various elements of complex episodic memories. This binding process is necessary in the short term for traces to be consolidated, but eventually the traces become independent of the hippocampus. Although the specific mechanism by which this "cortical consolidation" process occurs has not been clearly elucidated, cortical consolidation may require a non-conscious activation or rehearsal process that allows representations to be stored in the "association cortex" (Kandel, 1989). This region of the cerebral cortex appears to integrate representations from a variety of parts of the brain. In cortical consolidation, information is finally free of the need for the hippocampus for retrieval. This consolidation process appears to depend on the stage of rapid-eye-movement sleep stage that is thought to be attempting to make sense of the day's activities (Karni et al., 1992; Winson, 1993).

Adult patients with lesions in this structure cannot recall facts and events that occurred months to years before the lesion (e.g., surgery). However, their remote declarative memories (for example, their childhood events) are usually unaffected by the lesions. These lesions have another devastating impact in patients: Without a functional hippocampus, patients are unable to create new declarative memories. Severe anterograde amnesia can be caused by damage to the CA1 field alone, whereas retrograde amnesia seems to require more extensive areas of damage (Rempel-Clower et al., 1996). With respect to anterograde memory, there are numerous studies, involving a wide range of paradigms, in which hippocampal damage severely impaired LTM while sparing STM (Milner, 1972; Winocur, 1995). The predicted pattern for premorbid memory has also been reported frequently but there have been conflicting results (Kim & Fanselow, 1992; Reed & Squire, 1998; Rempel-Clower et al., 1996). Several investigators failed to observe time-dependent, retrograde amnesia following hippocampal damage, reporting instead a flat gradient in which memory loss was comparable over all the intervals studied (Gaffan, 1993; Kartsounis et al., 1995).

It has also been postulated that the hippocampus is the site that mediates the storage of memories for episodes and factual knowledge of the world (Tulving, 1987). Thus the domain of the hippocampus appears to be limited to episodic and semantic memory formation. According to this episodic hypothesis of hippocampal memory formation, semantic knowledge can be acquired by way of the surrounding cortex even in the face of impaired episodic capabilities. This hypothesis also states that damage to the hippocampus would result in a selective impairment of episodic memory, whereas damage to the semantic (i.e., cortical) system would impair both semantic and episodic memory. In contrast to the episodic hypothesis of hippocampal memory function, a relational hypothesis suggests that the hippocampus supports the formation of relational representation between all kinds of stimuli (Eichenbaum et al., 1999). A key feature of hippocampal-dependent relational representations is that they are quickly learned and allow for inferential relationships between representations that can be used in novel situations. Like the episodic hypothesis, this hippocampal-dependent relational representations proposal suggests that the hippocampus plays an essential role in signalling the unique sets of relationships that make up an episode. Unlike the episodic hypothesis, it postulates that the hippocampus is also important for extracting common features across episodes and therefore plays a critical role in semantic memory as well as in simpler forms of recognition and associative memory. In contrast to the relational functions of the hippocampus, the role of the surrounding cortices is described as being important in maintaining the persistence of individual stimuli in memory (Eichenbaum, 2000). This relational view of hippocampal function is reminiscent of the hypothesis of Squire and Zola, who argue that the individual structures of the medial temporal lobe contribute to many aspects of declarative memory including both semantic and episodic memory (Squire & Zola, 1998).

Repetition comparisons have been derived from the assumption that at time of encoding, there is much more information to be encoded from a novel stimulus than from stimuli that have been repeatedly viewed by the participant. Imaging studies have shown significant novelty-driven activations for scenes, words, and object–noun pairs (Dolan & Fletcher, 1997; Gabrieli et al., 1997; Kopelman et al., 1998; Tulving et al., 1994c). In accordance with the usual hemispheric differences found in the literature, lateralisation occurs for verbal tasks (i.e., they are left lateralised) whereas scene activations appear bilaterally. Concerning episodic retrieval, research has shown that there is greater hippocampal activation for episodic retrieval versus matched non-episodic lexical or semantic verbal tasks (Blaxton et al., 1996; Squire et al., 1992). In addition, significantly increased hippocampal activation has been found for episodic retrieval relative to viewing stimuli where no operations or tasks were to be performed for figural and spatial materials (Maguire et al., 1996; Schacter et al., 1995).

Recognition memory underlies our ability to detect that a stimulus has been experienced previously. Although it is widely accepted that the perirhinal and entorhinal cortices surrounding the hippocampus are important for recognition memory, the role of the hippocampus itself in this form of memory has been controversial (Leonard et al., 1995; Murray & Mishkin, 1998; Suzuki et al., 1993). Current findings suggest that the hippocampus plays a key role in many forms of recognition memory. The involvement of the hippocampus in recognition may depend on a complex set of factors including the type of lesion, the training history, and the particular strategy the animal is using to solve the task. Further, the findings point to the trend showing that the recognition tasks that are naturally acquired by the animal more clearly reveal the dependence of these tasks on the hippocampus.

Because neuropsychological studies indicate that the hippocampal region is more important for the initial storage, or encoding, of information than for its retrieval, one might expect to find this distinction reflected in the results of activation studies. In fact, there is some support for this idea from a recent study of face memory, which showed right hippocampal activation during encoding but not during subsequent recognition of faces (Haxby et al., 1996). It has been proposed that tasks that require people to process novel stimuli will also lead to hippocampal activation, because novel information is usually encoded for storage in memory (Tulving et al., 1994). It has been hypothesised that the role of the hippocampus is to bring together memory elements from diverse neocortical areas at the time of retrieval of explicit memory (Zola-Morgan & Squire, 1990). Thus, the hippocampal complex plays a critical role in solving this binding problem by providing a mechanism to link the physically separated neocortical fragments. Over time, this need dissipates and the hippocampal component is rendered unnecessary (McClelland et al., 1995; Squire et al., 1984; Teyler & DiScenna, 1986).

Some investigators have concluded that the variable findings associated with retrograde amnesia are related to the extent of damage to the hippocampal complex, which includes the hippocampus itself as well as the rhinal cortex and parahippocampal gyrus (Nadel & Moscovitch, 1997). It was indicated that, for animals and humans, temporally graded retrograde amnesia is found most often in cases where damage to the hippocampal complex is limited, whereas large lesions to the structure reliably produce more extensive memory loss. On the basis of this evidence, Nadel and Moscovitch (1997) proposed a modification to the traditional consolidation process model of hippocampal function. In the multiple trace hypothesis they suggested that, in addition to its involvement in the consolidation of new information, the system participates in the long-term storage of that information. According to this view, such memory traces are represented as spatially distributed interactions between the hippocampal complex and neocortex that persist for as long as those memories exist. On the other hand, semantic or context-free memories can become independent of the hippocampal complex as the consolidation hypothesis predicts. An important element of this model is that old memories, because they are activated often and in various ways, acquire redundant elements within the circuitry. As a result, such memories can

withstand partial damage to the hippocampus and are vulnerable only when damage is large enough to disrupt a substantial number of traces. This approach accounts more readily for the very long retrograde amnesia gradients often observed in amnesia. In contrast, recently formed memories are represented in fewer traces, have a less developed circuitry, and are susceptible to smaller lesions. Thus, within the traditional model, episodic and semantic memory are treated as more or less equivalent with respect to their neural underpinnings (McClelland et al., 1995; Squire, 1992). The multiple memory trace proposed, in contrast to the standard consolidation hypothesis, that the hippocampal complex is always involved in the storage and retrieval of episodic memories, independent of their age. On the other hand, and consistent with standard consolidation hypothesis, it is believed that long-term interactions between the hippocampal complex and neocortex can influence the stabilisation of semantic memories within neocortex. This position emphasises a critical distinction between episodic and semantic memory, both of which are influenced by the hippocampal complex. However, only one of them becomes independent of this brain region in the course of consolidation.

Neuroimaging studies revealed a nuanced assessment of hippocampal function. Based on studies in patients with medial temporal lobe damage who failed in their efforts to recollect information, it was initially assumed that effort to recollect should result in hippocampal activity. However, it appears that effort was not the key factor in producing hippocampal activation. Rather, success in recollection appears to be related to activation of the hippocampus. The use of imaging that makes it possible to obtain anatomical information from living patients suggests that the hippocampal region of amnesic patients may be damaged. Certain studies have shown that this brain region is shrunken and atrophic in some patients (57% of normal size) (Press et al., 1989; Squire et al., 1990). Although the resolution of most fMRI and PET studies does not allow for the identification of most specific structures within the hippocampus involved in episodic memory, there has been some attempt to identify particular regions of activation related to different mnemonic processes. A meta-analysis reported a fairly consistent pattern with encoding activations being predominantly (91%) in the anterior portion of the hippocampus, with retrieval activations being predominantly (91%) in the posterior portion of the structure (Lepage et al., 1998). However, another study reported less convincing data (Schacter & Wagner, 1999). Here 58% of encoding activations in the anterior hippocampus and 80% of retrieval activations in the posterior portion were observed. Such variability may be due to the inherently different paradigms used in employing the fMRI and PET techniques. Clearly more work needs to be done to identify the specific mnemonic functions related to different regions of the hippocampal complex.

Functional imaging techniques provide a new window on brain function and the potential possibility to image memory systems *in vivo* in the neurologically normal and pathological human brain. Attainment of this goal has important pragmatic applications as well as offering insight into the underlying mechanisms of memory. Functional brain imaging in humans is beginning to reveal a network of brain regions that subserves topographical learning: the medial parietal lobe, the posterior cingulate gyrus, occipitotemporal areas, the parahippocampal gyrus, and the right hippocampus (Maguire, 1997). The right hippocampus is clearly involved in processing spatial layouts over long as well as short time-courses. It participates in both the encoding and the retrieval of topographical memory.

The amygdala

Experimental work in animals and humans suggests that the amygdaloid complex may play a crucial role in emotional memory, particularly memory of events arousing strong emotions (Bechara et al., 1995; Mori et al., 1999). This research implicates stress hormones and the amygdaloid complex as key interacting modulators of memory consolidation for emotional events. Generally inactive in unemotional situations, this system is activated during and after an emotionally arousing event and appears to regulate declarative-memory storage processes in other brain regions. According to McGaugh and collaborators, the amygdala regulates the storage or consolidation of information in other brain regions (McGaugh et al., 1995). This hypothesis posits that emotional arousal activates the amygdala. Such activation results in modulation of memory storage processes occurring in brain regions influenced by the amygdala. The amygdala is part of a system that serves to regulate the strength of memories in relation to their emotional significance. It is not generally involved in memory but rather plays a selective role. It is involved when it is activated by emotional arousal. This view emphasises that the amygdala is not involved in the retrieval or expression of emotionally influenced memory. The critical role is that of modulating memory consolidation (Cahill & McGaugh, 1996). Furthermore, several studies of patients with Urbach–Wiethe disease (a rare hereditary disorder that produces bilateral brain damage confined to the amygdaloid complex region) in which the amygdala is selectively damaged also suggest a central involvement of the amygdala in emotional memory in humans (Adolphs et al., 1997; Cahill & McGaugh, 1998; Markowitsch et al., 1994). Therefore, it may be hypothesised that the amygdala is not a site of long-term explicit or declarative-memory storage, but serves to influence memory storage processes in other brain regions, such as the hippocampus, striatum, and neocortex.

Considerable evidence from animal studies suggests that the amygdala has a crucial role in enhancing the strength of LTM for emotional stimuli through the interaction of peripheral adrenergic systems with cholinergic, opioid–peptidergic, and GABAergic systems in the amygdala (Cahill & McGaugh, 1998; Packard & Teather, 1998). In spite of a general consensus on the amygdala's importance in emotional memory, there are only a few studies exploring the role of the amygdala in episodic memory performance in humans.

The advent of different brain-imaging techniques such as positron emission topography (PET) and single or event-related functional magnetic resonance imaging (fMRI), marked an advance in understanding the neurobiological substrates of emotional learning in humans. Functional neuroimaging studies have shown activation of the amygdala in reaction to the presentation of fearful facial expressions and during classical conditioning. Amygdala activation in response to emotional stimuli occurs in the absence of explicit awareness (for review see Büchel & Dolan, 2000).

The use of event-related fMRIs allows scientists to measure responses evoked by single stimuli or differential responding, and in parallel scientists have assessed the activation of autonomic fear responding such as fluctuations in skin conductance response (SCR). Amygdala activation during this form of associative fear conditioning provides evidence that the neural substrates involved in aversive learning show continuity across species (Büchel & Dolan, 2000; LaBar et al., 1995). A study that used PET to examine the relationship between amygdala activity during memory encoding of pleasant and aversive stimuli, and enhanced long-term episodic memory (recall and recognition) for these stimuli, confirmed and extended previous findings (Hamann et al., 1999). It demonstrated that activity in the left as well as right amygdala is related to enhanced episodic memory for aversive stimuli, and that this relationship is specific to emotional stimuli. The amygdala is involved in encoding memory for emotionally arousing, pleasant stimuli in humans and its role in this encoding process is significantly greater than has been appreciated previously. The data indicate that the amygdala in humans is important in modulating memory for events according to their emotional importance regardless of whether the nature of the emotion is pleasant or aversive. Its relationship with the hippocampus is consistent with the notion that the amygdala may exert its influence on episodic memory for emotionally arousing stimuli in part through modulation of the hippocampal–medial temporal lobe memory systems (Cahill & McGaugh, 1998; Packard & Teather, 1998).

Fear conditioning

Fear conditioning is a powerful model of emotional memory. In Pavlovian fear conditioning, an animal learns to fear a conditioned stimulus (i.e., a tone) after its association with an unconditioned stimulus, such as a foot shock. After several such pairings, the tone comes to elicit stereotyped fear behaviours such as freezing, response suppression, and autonomic changes (LeDoux, 2000). Some studies have shown that fear conditioning leads to increases in the strength of synapses between neurons of the auditory thalamus and the lateral amygdala (McKernan & Shinnick-Gallagher, 1997; Rogan et al., 1997). The lateral amygdala is thought to be one of the sites where information about the conditioned and unconditioned stimuli converges. Experiments with brain slices also uncovered evidence for training-dependent increases in the strength of auditory thalamus–lateral amygdala synapses in conditioned rats (McKernan & Shinnick-Gallagher, 1997).

A number of studies have suggested that an intact amygdala is important for the acquisition and expression of conditioned aversive responses (see Fendt & Fanselow, 1999; LeDoux, 1998). Lesions of the amygdala complex disrupt conditioned freezing (LeDoux, 1995). The critical role of the amygdala in fear conditioning to aversive stimuli such as electric shocks has been established in rats (Davis et al., 1987). In humans, Urbach–Weithe patients and patients with amygdala resections showed little or no fear conditioning (Bechara et al., 1995). The fear-conditioning deficit was dissociated from declarative memory because the patient had excellent declarative memory for the experimental experience (e.g., for the stimuli). In contrast, amnesic patients without amygdala damage demonstrated intact fear conditioning but impaired declarative memory for their experimental experience (Bechara et al., 1995). Thus, the role of the amygdala in fear conditioning appears to be critical.

The amygdala participates not only in explicit memory for aversive stimuli but also in implicit memory for aversive stimuli tested via fear conditioning. Patients with amygdala lesions show selective deficits in the identification of fearful or angry facial expressions or prosody (Adolphs et al., 1994; Scott et al., 1997). Amygdala activations occur in PET and fMRI studies during the perception of fearful facial expressions or scenes

(Morris et al., 1996b). The amygdala appears to have a widespread role in processing negatively salient stimuli.

BASAL FOREBRAIN

The basal forebrain is located superior to the optic chiasm and includes the medial septal nuclei, anterior hypothalamus, part of PFC, nucleus accumbens, nucleus basalis of Meynert, and the diagonal band of Broca (Delis & Lucas, 1996). Neurons in this system provide the major cholinergic innervation to cortical and limbic structures. These structures send projections to all association cortices, hippocampus, and amygdala. Because these cholinergic neurons have a strong modulatory effect on the hippocampus and other structures, it has been proposed that lesions to the basal forebrain may effectively reduce neural activity in the hippocampus.

Lesions in the basal forebrain, as sometimes follow aneurysms of the anterior communicating artery, can cause significant amnesia (Volpe & Hirst, 1983; Zaborszky et al., 1999). Studies of basal forebrain lesions in animals are also equivocal with regard to the role of this region in declarative memory function (Aigner et al., 1991; Baxter et al., 1995). Therefore, it is likely that the basal forebrain plays some role in declarative memory function, but the precise nature and extent of this participation remains to be specified. A study showed that selective removal of cholinergic neurons in the basal forebrain in rats may not be sufficient to produce a deficit in spatial working memory (Chappell et al., 1998). In that study, despite multiple small injections of an immunotoxin (192 IgG-saporin) at the locations of cholinergic neurons in the medial septal area producing a cholinergic depletion, the rats had no impairment in the spatial working memory task, even when delays ranging from 60 seconds to 8 hours were imposed within a trial. These results are pertinent to the long-standing view that links degeneration of cholinergic neurons to memory impairment (see Baxter & Gallagher, 1997).

Case studies have shown that dense amnesia can occur from rupture, stroke, or repair of this vessel, and that anterograde without retrograde memory loss can occur when the basal forebrain is lesioned (Alexander & Freedman, 1984; Damasio et al., 1985). In addition, the basal forebrain has been implicated in AD, in which inexorably progressive memory loss is the major feature (Delis & Lucas, 1996). Yet investigations of monkeys with basal forebrain cholinergic system lesions do not completely support the hypothesis that this system is responsible, to some degree, for learning and memory. However, extensive damage in the nucleus basalis of Meynert does disrupt mnemonic abilities (Voytko et al., 1994). Cognitive and electrophysiological studies of the basal forebrain cholinergic system of monkeys indicate that the most convincing cognitive role for the nucleus basalis of Meynert is in attention, as has been proposed for the rodent nucleus basalis of Meynert (Olton et al., 1988; Pang et al., 1993). Impairments in attention are now recognised as an early and significant feature of patients with AD (Jorm, 1986; Nebes & Brady, 1989; Parasuraman & Haxby, 1993).

DIENCEPHALON

The limbic thalamus including the anterior, medial dorsal, and other thalamic nuclei contains neurons that project directly to the cingulate cortex. This thalamocortical system is involved in different learning and memory processes such as active avoidance tasks, instrumental learning, and spatial tasks. Diencephalic amnesia may appear to be very complex since neuropathological evidence has implicated several structures, namely the mammillary bodies, the anterior thalamic nuclei, the medial dorsal thalamic nucleus, and the parataenial thalamic nucleus (Aggleton & Sahgal, 1993). A number of adjacent tracts (the mammillothalamic tract and the internal medullary lamina) have also been implicated (Savage et al., 1997). Unfortunately, there are still no amnesic cases with confirmed, circumscribed damage in just one of these structures. The extended diencephalic–hippocampal system is critical for the efficient encoding and hence normal recall of new episodic information (Aggleton & Brown, 1999). Damage to different parts of this system produces similar memory impairments. Amnesia associated with diencephalic damage typically results in a severe loss of recognition.

The diencephalon has been implicated in the type of amnesia that results from neuropathological impairments related to Korsakoff's syndrome (see Squire, 1981). Findings from Korsakoff patients highlight that structures in areas other than the medial temporal lobe are involved in the formation of declarative memories. Damage to the dorsomedial thalamus can impair memory formation. Patient NA was the first studied case of medial thalamic damage caused by a miniature fencing foil that entered his brain through his nostril. Damage appeared in his left medial thalamus, bilaterally to the mammillary bodies and the mammillothalamic tract. Although his STM was intact, the difficulty resided in forming long-term declarative memories. Converging evidence from human cases as well as animal models suggests that damage to the medial dorsal nucleus of the thalamus produces severe anterograde amnesia (Winocur, 1990; Zola-Morgan & Squire, 1990). Evidence suggests that the thalamus plays a fundamental role in the encoding operation that occurs early during the learning process. In a food preference memory task, rats with dorsomedial thalamic lesions showed a mnemonic deficit when the surgery was performed immediately after the training phase. However, if the interval between acquisition and surgery is extended to 2 days, the animals are unlikely to display memory loss if there is sufficient time to acquire the information. Findings from human studies also suggest that medial thalamic damage interferes with new learning by disrupting the process of encoding new information (Huppert & Piercy, 1978; Wetzel & Squire, 1980).

A study showed that Korsakoff patients and control subjects did not differ in their picture recognition performance provided that the Korsakoff group was given supplementary time to inspect the pictures during the acquisition phase (Huppert & Piercy, 1979). This finding suggests that Korsakoff's syndrome is associated with a deficit in the acquisition or encoding phase and not the retention phase. A direct comparison between Korsakoff patients and HM, a patient with extensive medial temporal lobe damage, showed that when the Korsakoff group was brought to learning criterion by additional training trials, thereafter the group retained the information normally while HM showed a retention deficit (Huppert & Piercy, 1979).

FRONTAL LOBES AND PREFRONTAL CORTEX

The frontal lobes are anatomically represented by those areas of the cortex anterior to the central sulcus, including the main cortical areas for the control of motor behaviour. The anterior cingulate gyrus can be considered part of the medial frontal lobe. The term "prefrontal cortex" is most appropriately used to designate the main cortical target projections for the mediodorsal nucleus of the thalamus. This area is also sometimes referred to as frontal granular cortex. Brodmann areas 9–15, 46, and 47 (BA9–15, BA46, and BA47) denote it (see Figure 3.4). Whereas the frontal lobes are greatly involved in encoding, the PFC is more involved in working and strategic memory. Several independent lines of research point to the prefrontal regions—especially the orbitofrontal cortex in the right hemisphere—as a crucial area for integrating memory, attachment, emotion, bodily representation and regulation, and social cognition (Baron-Cohen, 1995; Damasio, 1994; Schore, 1994; Tucker et al., 1995; Wheeler et al., 1997). Patients with PFC lesions are impaired in processing some aspects of script knowledge, particularly the temporal ordering of actions or the ability to discard irrelevant actions that do not fit within the script's internal structure (Allain et al., 1999).

Based on clinical and neuroanatomical evidence, the functions of the frontal lobe can be broadly subdivided into three levels (Stuss & Benson, 1986). Functions at each level serve a supervisory role over other functions and domains

FIGURE 3.4

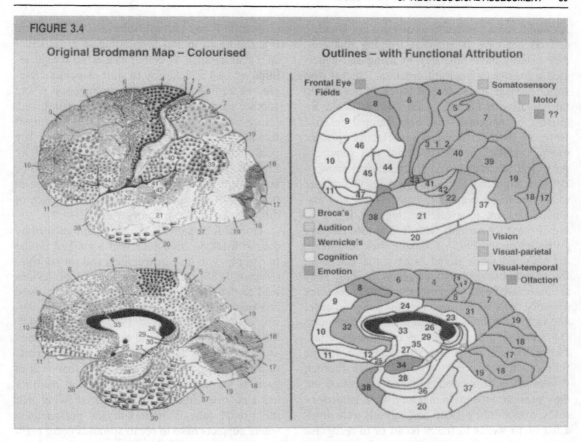

Outlines with functional attributions of Brodmann areas in the human brain. Brodmann classified brain regions based on their cytoarchitecture (basically, the appearance of the cortex under the light microscope). It is important to note that Brodmann's areas were identified purely based on visual appearance, which is not necessarily related to function.

that are localised more posteriorly. At the first level, functions include the ability to organise and maintain information in a fixed sequence and to integrate diverse types of information into a meaningful representation. Within this same level, medial frontal structures affect motivation and drive, including the ability to initiate cognitive and motor activities. A second independent level equivalent to a class of operations is often labelled as executive functions. These functions represent a higher order than those at the first level because they provide conscious control and direction for the integrated behaviour of total brain operations. They are especially important during non-routine situations that require novel solutions (Norman & Shallice, 1986). The most widely used test of psychologically frontal functioning, the WCST, is

assumed to measure abilities manifested largely at this level because the test uses a novel and complex task that requires goal selection and hypothesis testing along with cognitive flexibility and inhibition of salient responses. A third proposed level of prefrontal function consists of what is commonly called self-awareness, the ability to introspect on one's own thoughts and to realise the relation of self to one's social environment (Stuss & Benson, 1986). The abilities are intimately related to autonoetic consciousness, which is the awareness of self. It is not known which regions of the frontal lobes are especially critical for self-awareness but probably the most anterior regions are importantly involved.

Clinically important patterns of memory deficits occur in patients with frontal lobe lesions.

Although these patients typically are not amnesic and do not have anterograde learning problems, they usually have difficulty in using self-generated strategies to recall information. Patients who suffer damage to the frontal lobes do not exhibit the pervasive and disabling amnesia that is characteristic of patients with hippocampal lesions. However, their performance on selective episodic memory tasks, specifically those that require a great deal of strategic and organisational manipulation, is impaired. Episodic processes that require memories to be evaluated, transformed, and manipulated seem to evoke the highest degree of impairment for patients with frontal lobe damage (Wheeler et al., 1995). Frontal cortex lesions do not cause the same global amnesia that can result from medial temporal/diencephalic lesions. They are associated with impairments in more complex memory tasks such as memory for temporal order and tasks with high levels of interference (Incisa Della Rochetta & Milner, 1993; Janowsky et al., 1989a, b). One of the specific behaviour deficits following frontal lobe damage is attention disorder. Patients show distractibility and poor attention and they present with poor memory. In a laboratory study, frontal-lobe patients and controls were given a list of 15 words to freely recall or to recognise (Shimamura et al., 1990). Free recall was somewhat worse in the frontal-lobe patients than in controls while recognition performance was equal. However, a different test required participants to reconstruct the order in which the words were presented and in this test, frontal-lobe patients were grossly impaired.

Strategic memory tasks may require subjects to reason about their memories. There is evidence that the frontal lobes are important in reasoning. Frontal-lobe patients perform poorly on problem-solving or reasoning tasks that require the generation, flexible maintenance, and shifting of plans such as the WCST and the Tower of London Test (Milner, 1963; Shallice, 1982). Patients with frontal lobe damage are impaired at developing novel cognitive plans or strategies for solving tasks. They also have difficulty using feedback to modify their behaviour or adjust their strategy to solve a problem. Indeed, they persevere in their response strategy even if it has not been reinforced. This propensity is best exemplified in the WCST. There is a failure to inhibit responding to a particular card feature such as colour that is no longer reinforced, and an inability to shift response strategies according to the new contingency where another card feature such as form is reinforced. Neuro-imaging studies have shown prominent frontal-lobe activations when people reason as they perform problem-solving tasks (Baker et al., 1996; Prabhakaran et al., 1997). Thus, the frontal lobe contribution to strategic memory may be one of problem solving and reasoning in the service of difficult declarative memory demands.

Frontal-lobe patients are also distinguished by their risk-taking behaviour, and a marked failure to comply with task instructions and follow rules (Milner, 1985). In primates, frontal-lobe lesions lead to deficits in delayed response test; delayed non-matching to sample and a more complex version of this task (Mishkin, 1982, Petrides, 1994). Indeed, electrophysiological studies reveal that area 46 of the PFC is active during the delay intervals in delayed-response tests, an activity that ends as soon as the animal responds. Temporal memory has also been studied in humans, showing that the frontal lobe is important for performance where subjects have to recall stimulus order presentation, a mnemonic function referred to as temporal memory. Hemispheric asymmetry exists for this function whereby the left frontal lobe seems pivotal for verbal recency and the right frontal lobe for non-verbal/pictorial recency. Lastly, a striking feature of frontal-lobe damage is the ensuing personality, social, and behavioural changes as most strikingly exemplified in the case of Phineas Gage (Sanfey et al., 2003). Frontal-lobe damage results in two types of personality change. Left frontal-lobe damage most often results in pseudo-depression, and involves symptoms such as apathy, indifference, lack of initiative, and low verbal output. Right frontal-lobe damage most often results in pseudo-psychopathy and involves symptoms such as coarse language, lack of restraint, promiscuous sexual behaviour, and poor social conduct.

Patients with frontal-lobe lesions may recall or recognise the information at a normal level yet show a disrupted memory regarding the source

(Janowsky et al., 1989a, b; Shimamura et al., 1990). Populations in which frontal damage exists such as Korsakoff patients and normal elderly also demonstrate problems in remembering sources (Meudell et al., 1985; Rabinowitz, 1989).

PET and fMRI studies consistently demonstrate that specific areas within left frontal cortex are active when subjects intentionally memorise words (Dolan & Fletcher, 1997; Kelley et al., 1998). An open question that has often been asked is how, and to what degree, cortical areas outside the medial temporal lobes contribute to conscious remembering. Left frontal activations, especially in the anterior portion of the inferior prefrontal gyrus, have been found when subjects perform tasks that enhance memory for the encoded information (Demb et al., 1995; Gabrieli et al., 1996a; Kapur et al., 1994a, b, c). There is greater left prefrontal activation when subjects make semantic (deep) versus non-semantic (shallow) decisions about words. A greater left prefrontal activation is also noted when subjects study words with a mild versus severe division of attention or generate versus read words (Petersen et al., 1989; Shallice et al., 1994). Left frontal cortex has been consistently associated with encoding of verbal materials (Tulving et al., 1994). PET studies show that the left ventrolateral frontal cortex is selectively activated during the acquisition of word series, but these same areas are not activated during the retrieval of this information. In one of the first lesion studies inspired by imaging findings, it was found that patients with left frontal lesions were impaired at making the same semantic judgements that had yielded left frontal activations in healthy subjects (Swick & Knight, 1996). Although the left frontal activation is also evident for non-verbal stimuli such as faces, it seems likely that this activation is most closely linked to semantic processes associated with language (Haxby et al., 1996). This kind of activation, which may also be considered one of semantic memory retrieval, occurs in the right PFC of patients who are right-hemisphere dominant for language (Desmond et al., 1995).

A consistent but poorly understood activation occurs in right frontal cortex during intentional declarative or episodic retrieval of memory for words, faces, scenes, or meaningless objects (Haxby et al., 1996; Schacter et al., 1995; Shallice et al., 1994; Tulving et al., 1996). These robust activations were unexpected because they applied to verbal and non-verbal memories and because right frontal lesions have modest effects on declarative memory. It has been difficult to specify the nature of the retrieval conditions that yield right frontal activations. In some studies, the activations occur during memory judgements for old studied stimuli relative to new unstudied stimuli (Rugg et al., 1996; Tulving et al., 1994b, c). Such activations are considered to reflect retrieval success that was greater for old than new stimuli. In other studies, they occur equally for well-remembered old stimuli, poorly remembered old stimuli, and new stimuli (Kapur et al., 1995; Nyberg et al., 1995). This pattern of results is interpreted as reflecting retrieval attempt or mode that occurs irrespective of the memorial status of the stimulus. One speculative interpretation is that right frontal retrieval activations reflect working memory processes that guide or evaluate the products of episodic memory. Such an interpretation would posit a special role for right frontal cortex in the working memory aspects of intentional retrieval.

Memory disturbances following frontal damage have been noted to varying degrees, depending on the exact kind of memory test. In particular, memory difficulties are observed in frontal patients when the test requires recollection of a particular context (e.g., remembering who made a particular statement) or judgement of the timing of an event (Shimamura et al., 1991). However, patients with frontal damage often perform well on many other tests of memory, such as simple recognition of past items. Because remembering intention relies, to a large extent, on self-regulated executive and supervisory attentional processes, often assumed to be prefrontal lobe functions, damage to the frontal regions may also cause impairments in prospective memory. It is therefore possible that patients with near normal memory but frontal damage will have problems with prospective remembering (Tröster & Fields, 1995). Perseveration of certain memory abilities following frontal damage has often been contrasted to the profound amnesia that can follow damage to the medial temporal lobes. One speculation as to how the frontal cortex is implicated is that the critical cascade driving human memory formation occurs only when frontal activity provides information to medial temporal lobe structures. The medial temporal lobe may then function to bind together processed information from frontal and other cortical regions to form lasting, recollectable memory traces. Thus, both regions would be critical to the conception of a memory. Lack of participation of either brain region would disrupt memory formation. The interaction of frontal and medial temporal regions, rather than the isolated contribution of either region, seems to be crucial for the effective formation of memories that contribute to consciousness of life events.

Working memory

Brain-imaging studies, using PET and fMRI, have implicated the human PFC in working memory (Courtney et al., 1997, 1998). Imaging studies investigating the roles that prefrontal regions might play in working memories suggest that the posterior midfrontal region has been activated during a wide range of working memory tasks, including verbal, spatial, and object (Cohen et al., 1997; McCarthy et al., 1996; Smith et al., 1996a). This region seems to contribute to working memory processes independent of the type of information. On the other hand, the inferior prefrontal region, which is close to a ventrolateral prefrontal area, appears to be involved in the encoding and retrieval of information held in posterior cortical areas (Owen et al., 1996; Petrides et al., 1993). Verbal semantic functions have also been associated with this inferior frontal area (Demb et al., 1995). The left PFC is commonly activated during encoding of information, and the right PFC is activated during retrieval, regardless of whether the material is verbal or visual (Buckner et al., 1995; Fletcher et al., 1995a, b; Haxby et al., 1996; Moscovitch et al., 1995). It has been proposed that prefrontal activation during retrieval is correlated specifically with the effort of attempting to retrieve information from memory rather than the conscious recollection of the retrieved information (Kapur et al., 1995).

In the working memory, it has been suggested that the PFC performs the executive functions—an observation suggested by studies of patients who have suffered frontal lobe damage (D'Esposito, 2000). These individuals often show severe difficulties in executive functions that require working memory such as planning and organising. They are also easily distracted or find it difficult to switch their attention away from a task. This hypothesis has also received support from studies of cognition in primates (Friedman et al., 1990; Goldman-Rakic, 1984; Goldman-Rakic & Porrino, 1985). A PET study was designed to distinguish precisely the functions of the central executive from the storage function of the slave systems (Collette et al., 1999a). It was shown that the manipulation of information induced an activation in the right (BA 10/46) and left (BA 9/6) middle frontal gyrus and in the left parietal area (BA7). The interaction between the storage and ma-nipulation conditions did not show any significant modification inactivation. These results are in agreement with the observation that central executive functions are distributed between anterior and posterior brain areas but could also reflect a simultaneous involvement of controlled (frontal) and automatic (parietal) attentional systems.

Interest in better understanding of the role of the two different working memory systems (the articulatory loop/phonological store and visuo-spatial sketchpad) has led to some debates (Paulesu et al., 1993). It was hypothesised that engagement of the phonological store or "verbal buffer" is associated with activation of the left inferior parietal cortex. Rehearsal of the contents of this phonological store through inner speech activates predominantly the left inferior posterior frontal region (Broca's area). On the other hand, visuospatial memory activates right-sided structures, including right inferolateral prefrontal and lateral premotor cortices as well as right inferior parietal and dorsolateral occipital cortices. The identification of subcomponents of the working memory indicates that "internal speech" is associated with activity of Broca's area (Paulesu et al., 1993). The "phonological store" localises to the inferior parietal cortex. Verbal tasks often activate the left PFC Brodmann area (BA44,

Broca's area), which may be involved in phonological rehearsal (Awh et al., 1996; Fiez et al., 1996; Paulesu et al., 1993). They also activate left parietal BA40, which may be involved in phonological storage. Object tasks tend to activate the temporal–occipital regions (BA37) whereas spatial tasks tend to activate the parietal–occipital regions (BA7 and 19). This pattern is consistent with the distinction between a ventral pathway for object processing ("what") and a dorsal pathway for spatial processing ("where") (Ungerleider & Mishkin, 1982).

Several recent studies have focused on the distinction between two fundamental working memory processes: the passive maintenance of information in STM and the active manipulation of this information (D'Esposito, 2000). Available evidence suggests that ventrolateral PFC is associated with maintenance (as well with response selection and interference), whereas dorsolateral PFC is associated with manipulation (as well as with maintenance) (D'Esposito et al., 1999; Postle et al., 1999). Activity in dorsolateral PFC has been shown to vary as a function of load (i.e., number of items held in working memory) showing an increase or inverted U response (Callicott et al., 1999; Rypma et al., 1999). Additionally, certain forms of psychopathology associated with prominent affective symptoms such as schizophrenia and depression are also associated with dorsolateral PFC-mediated working memory dysfunction (Perlstein et al., 2001).

Performing two tasks simultaneously makes demands on working memory, most probably reflecting the switching between information appropriate for one or other task (Baddeley, 1986). Patients with frontal lesions may be disproportionately impaired in dual task performance, supporting a frontal role in these aspects of working memory (McDowell et al., 1997).

Imaging studies of working memory using non-verbal material have focused on differences between the maintenance of spatial and object information. In a study using a spatial Sternberg task, activations were seen in several right hemisphere regions, broadly homologous to those seen in verbal maintenance tasks (Jonides et al., 1993). These included the right parietal cortex, right dorsal premotor cortex, and right ventrolateral

frontal cortex. The frontal cortex activations resulting from comparison of the Sternberg task with its control are sometimes bilateral for both verbal and spatial material. However, the left–right verbal–spatial lateralisation is normally clearer when direct comparisons of verbal and spatial material are made. Similar findings were reported in a direct comparison of visuospatial and verbal Sternberg tasks (Smith et al., 1996). The networks of parietal, dorsal premotor, and ventrolateral frontal cortex regions were left and right lateralised for verbal and spatial tasks, respectively.

Using an object version of the Sternberg task to test memory for abstract shapes (for which spatial location was irrelevant), activations that were predominantly left lateralised, including the inferior parietal cortex, inferior temporal cortex, and left ventrolateral frontal cortex, were observed (Smith & Jonides, 1995a). In a direct comparison of object and spatial maintenance, participants were presented with two abstract shapes and, after a 3-second delay, a single probe shape prompting a yes–no response (Smith & Jonides, 1995b). In the test of object working memory, the task was to decide whether the probe matched one of the memory set in shape (regardless of its location on the screen). In the test of spatial working memory, the task was to decide whether the probe matched one of the memory set in its location (regardless of its shape). The regions more active in the object task than in the spatial task were the left posterior parietal cortex and left inferior temporal cortex, a subset of the areas implicated in the study (Smith & Jonides, 1995a, b). The areas more active in the spatial task were the right ventrolateral frontal cortex and the right posterior parietal, right anterior occipital, and right premotor cortices.

A recent study was designed to examine spatial working memory with fMRI in 8- to 11-year-old children (Nelson et al., 2000). It was demonstrated that prepubescent children show a pattern of brain activation that is remarkably similar to that of adults (i.e., dorsal aspects of the frontal cortex, posterior parietal area, and anterior cingulate cortex). In contrast, in the non-spatial working memory task with children, more ventral aspects of the PFC were activated (Casey et al., 1995). Taken together, these studies suggest that the division of labour of the dorsal and ventral streams is already evident in the PFC before puberty.

In summary, functional imaging of human working memory has provided considerable evidence that broad anatomical divisions within the lateral frontal cortex subserve different processes. Ventrolateral frontal cortex, for example, is more often activated during tasks requiring maintenance and dorsolateral frontal cortex is more often activated during tasks requiring manipulation. This is more consistent with the view of Petrides than with that of Goldman-Rakic (Goldman-Rakic, 1987; Petrides, 1994). Nonetheless, there also appears to be a lateralisation of frontal cortex processes according to the type of material. Although the frontal cortex activations are often bilateral (relative to baseline tasks), direct comparisons of verbal and spatial tasks suggest that left ventrolateral frontal cortex is primarily concerned with the maintenance of verbal information and right ventrolateral frontal cortex with the maintenance of spatial information. The maintenance of object information is sometimes left lateralised, though the overall pattern is less clear. Indeed, one problem with human experiments is the potential for subjects to recode visuospatial stimuli verbally, effectively converting an object task, for example, into a verbal one. One solution may be to combine imaging of visuospatial tasks with concurrent articulatory suppression to prevent verbal recoding of the stimuli. Another possibility is that process-specific and domain-specific specialisation exist within the human dorsolateral frontal cortex but the current resolution of imaging techniques is unable to distinguish them.

Imaging studies have also supported the dissociations between storage and rehearsal of verbal and spatial information proposed by neuropsychological models. The demands of storage engage posterior brain regions, including the parietal, temporal, and occipital lobes, whereas rehearsal engages a network of regions that include ventrolateral frontal cortex.

Respective roles of dorsal and ventral prefrontal cortex

It has been proposed that ventral PFC is functionally divided in a dorsal/ventral fashion according to the type of cognitive operation that must be performed on information held in working memory (Petrides, 1994). Two competing ideas concerning functional specialisation of frontal cortex in working memory are the "domain-specific" and "process-specific" hypotheses. These hypotheses concentrate in particular on dissociations between ventral and dorsal regions of lateral frontal cortex.

According to the domain-specific hypothesis, frontal cortex is the primary site of working memory processes and different regions within frontal cortex process different types of information (Goldman-Rakic, 1987, 1998). Specifically, ventrolateral frontal cortex is believed to be responsible for the maintenance of stimulus form (object information) whereas dorsolateral frontal cortex (also known as principal sulcus or middle frontal gyrus) is believed to be responsible for the maintenance of stimulus location (spatial information). The dorsolateral PFC is involved in explicit recall, as shown by working memory tasks (Goldman-Rakic, 1988). This hypothesis is based largely on electrophysiological data. It is an extension of the object–spatial ("what" versus "where") visual processing streams found in posterior regions (Mishkin et al., 1983). The object–spatial ventrolateral frontal cortex/dorsolateral frontal cortex distinction reflects all components of working memory: the "attentional, memorial, and response control mechanisms" (Goldman-Rakic, 1998).

The alternative, process-specific hypothesis proposes that the difference between ventrolateral frontal cortex and dorsolateral frontal cortex lies not in the type of material being maintained but in the type of processes operating on that material (Petrides, 1994, 1995a, b). According to this hypothesis, ventrolateral frontal cortex supports processes that transfer, maintain, and match information in working memory. This information may have been perceived recently or retrieved from LTM. However, dorsolateral frontal cortex supports more complex processes operating on information that is currently maintained in working memory such as monitoring and higher-level processing.

Empirical studies have supported the notion that ventral PFC mediates maintenance processes whereas dorsal PFC is recruited when additional processing of information, such as manipulation or monitoring, is necessary (D'Esposito et al., 1999; Owen, 1997). A study that used an event-related fMRI in volunteers to explore the relative roles of dorsal and ventral PFC regions during specific components of a working memory task showed that brain activity that correlated with each of the components of the task (encoding, delay, response) was identified (Rypma & D'Esposito, 1999). In a group analysis, effects of increased memory load were noted only in dorsal PFC in the encoding period. Activity was lateralised to the right hemisphere in the high but not the low memory-load condition. One source of variability was the subject's memory retrieval rate. Dorsal PFC plays a differentially greater role in information retrieval for slower subjects, probably because of inefficient retrieval processes or a decreased quality of mnemonic representations. It was therefore hypothesised that dorsal and ventral PFC play different roles in component processes of working memory.

Using a combination of lesion studies, tract tracing, studies of cerebral metabolism, and single cell recordings in awake behaving monkeys, it was demonstrated that the dorsolateral PFC (the principal sulcus or Walker's area 46) plays a key role in working memory. It was proposed that the segregation of spatial and object information processing between parietal and temporal cortices, respectively, is maintained within the PFC for working memory (Goldman-Rakic, 1995a). Thus, dorsal PFC, specifically cortex within the principal sulcus (BA46), is proposed to be specialised for spatial working memory, whereas ventral PFC, specifically the inferior convexity (BA12), is specialised for object working memory.

A study that used fMRI in normal volunteers was designed to investigate whether the same, or different, areas of the lateral PFC are involved in visual spatial and visual non-spatial working memory when the executive processing is the same (Owen et al., 1998). The view that spatial and non-spatial working memory may be mediated, respectively, by mid-dorsolateral and mid-ventrolateral regions of the frontal lobe. In this study, which examined the activation patterns within the frontal cortex in two working memory tasks that required monitoring of information within working memory,

the monitoring requirements of the two tasks were carefully matched. However, in the spatial working memory task, performance depended on remembering the locations of the stimuli. In the non-spatial working memory task, location was irrelevant for performance requiring memory for visual patterns. The results indicate that two working memory tasks that have the same monitoring demands yield increased activity in the mid-dorsolateral frontal cortical region, regardless of whether the stimulus material is visual spatial or not. These data are consistent with findings from behavioural-lesion studies in primates that demonstrated the critical nature of the mid-dorsolateral frontal cortex for the monitoring of information within working memory (Petrides, 1995a). Functional working memory tasks in humans have consistently been associated with activation of the dorsolateral frontal cortex (BA46) and, more variably, with activation of other prefrontal areas (e.g., BA9, 10, 44, 45, and 47). These observations and the density of memory cells in the PFC may lead to the mistaken conclusion that the PFC is the centre or location of working memory. However, these prefrontal cells are components of widespread memory networks, including posterior cerebral elements that support perceptual representations and anterior elements that support the neural representations of motor acts and behavioural sequences (Fuster, 1995). In fact, imaging studies suggest that both prefrontal and parietal cortices play a role in active maintenance of STM (Cohen et al., 1997; Courtney et al., 1997). There is a continuum of functional specialisation for perceptual and mnemonic processing from the occipital to the prefrontal regions.

Strategic memory relies crucially on the dorsolateral PFC. Evidence for the involvement of PFC in strategic memory derives from lesion and neuroimaging studies. Patients with lesions to dorsolateral PFC are impaired on tests of strategic memory such as free recall, temporal order memory, and frequency and source judgements (Janowsky et al., 1989a, b; Shimamura et al., 1990; Smith & Milner, 1988). These patients often perform normally on recognition tests that are believed to be less strategically demanding than recall or temporal order tests (Shimamura et al., 1990). Dorsolateral PFC is also active in normal healthy individuals during cued recall and recognition tasks as evidenced by use of PET (Rugg et al., 1996).

In summary, imaging data are consistent with the hypothesis that the ventrolateral PFC is primarily involved in simple STM operations whereas dorsolateral PFC is primarily involved in executive functions and monitoring (Owen, 1997; Petrides, 1994, 1995a, b). By contrast, the hypothesis that ventrolateral PFC is associated with object working memory and dorsolateral PFC with spatial working memory has been challenged. A recent study reported evidence for the object/spatial distinction in posterior regions (i.e., temporal vs parieto-occipital) but not in PFC (Postle & D'Esposito, 1999). Imaging studies have produced good evidence for material-specific stores in posterior brain regions and some evidence for a left–right lateralisation of frontal cortex regions for the rehearsal of verbal and spatial information, respectively. Contrary to suggestions from primate studies, there is little evidence for ventral–dorsal object–spatial distinction in non-verbal maintenance tasks in humans. Rather, frontal cortex activation associated with the maintenance of object information appears to be more left lateralised relative to that for the maintenance of spatial information. The frontal cortex region most consistently associated with the simple maintenance of verbal material is the left ventrolateral frontal cortex. The ventrolateral frontal cortex is often associated with the maintenance of spatial and object information (on the right for spatial information), though dorsolateral frontal cortex is also sometimes activated in these cases (Belger et al., 1998).

Episodic memory

Findings from both lesion and imaging studies support the general idea that the frontal lobes play some critical role in the episodic system. Current research suggests that damage to the frontal lobes does not lead to deficits in storage and retention given adequate encoding at input and proper cues at retrieval. These functions are mediated by the medial temporal lobes/hippocampus. Instead, memory disorders following frontal lesions are

associated with those aspects that are dependent on intact organisational and strategic processes at encoding and retrieval. Thus, recognition and cued recall are typically intact. What is impaired is memory for temporal order, for free recall of organised lists or stories, and for information that is specified by minimal distant cues or that requires monitoring to differentiate between relevant items (Moscovitch & Winocur, 1992; Shimamura et al., 1991). An increasing amount of evidence indicates the existence of links between the operations of episodic memory and the frontal lobes of the brain (Tulving, 1985). PFC has also been implicated in episodic memory retrieval. Neuroimaging studies have consistently revealed evidence of prefrontal activity during episodic retrieval, especially in the right hemisphere. Electrophysiological studies using ERPs have provided converging evidence (Johnson et al., 1996; Nyberg et al., 1996; Wilding & Rugg, 1996). Research has resulted in a preliminary hypothesis of episodic memory, which suggests that the frontal lobes underlie a special kind of consciousness called autonoetic consciousness, which allows healthy human adults to both mentally represent and become aware of their subjective experiences in the past, present, and future. Autonoetic consciousness is crucial for the complex abilities, including the possibility of performing mental time travel in the personal, subjective way that is the hallmark of retrieval from episodic memory. It is the autonoetic awareness, supported by the frontal lobes, that makes recollective experience what it is.

Imaging studies suggest that encoding and retrieval engage PFC, medial temporal lobe, and parieto-occipital regions (Cabeza, 2000). Prefrontal activations tend to be left lateralised during encoding and right lateralised during retrieval, a pattern known as hemispheric encoding/retrieval asymmetry (HERA) (Nyberg et al., 1996, 1998; Tulving et al., 1994a). It has been suggested that the right lateralisation of retrieval activity described in the HERA model is primarily driven by retrieval mode or REMO activations (Lepage et al., 2000). The HERA pattern holds not only for verbal materials but also for non-verbal ones (Nyberg et al., 1996). This is despite the fact that, orthogonally to the HERA pattern, there are other data showing hemispheric asymmetry for cognitive processing of different kinds of information. Words are processed predominantly in the left hemisphere whereas unfamiliar faces are processed in the right hemisphere (Wagner et al., 1998). The HERA model implies that frontal lobes are heavily involved in episodic memory processes, thus confirming earlier suggestions that this might be the case (Schacter, 1987; Squire, 1987). However, left prefrontal cortex is also activated during episodic retrieval depending on the reflective demands of the task (Cabeza et al., 1997, 2000; Nolde et al., 1998). Thus, left PFC activations are likely when the reflective demands are relatively complex (e.g., processes that are engaged when episodic memory tests require more detailed, deliberate analysis of activated information, maintenance of information while being evaluated, or the initiation of systematic self-cueing to retrieve information). This pattern suggests a "cortical asymmetry of reflective activity" (CARA) hypothesis (Nolde et al., 1998). The specific processes with which the left and right PFC are associated might be best considered in the context of more general component-process architectures rather than as processes dedicated to any one particular function such as episodic retrieval.

During episodic memory retrieval, age-related decreases in activation were typically found in right PFC and right parietal regions, whereas age-related increases in activation were typically found in left PFC, as well as in bilateral anterior cingulate and cuneus/precuneus regions. Given that PFC activity was usually right lateralised in younger adults, age-related decreases in right PFC activity coupled with age-related increases in left PFC activity often led to a more symmetric pattern of PFC activity in older adults (Bäckman et al., 1997; Cabeza et al., 1997, 2000). In contrast with PFC, medial temporal lobe activity was preserved in older adults, consistent with evidence that medial temporal lobe regions show less age-related structural decline than PFC (Bäckman et al., 1997; Cabeza et al., 2000; Raz et al., 1997).

With regard to the standard episodic memory tests of recall and recognition, patients with frontal lobe damage are solely impaired on tests of recall. Recognition tests, where success depends on stimulus familiarity and not on any overt type of memory strategy, are performed equally well in patients with frontal-lobe damage and controls. On the other hand, recall tasks or any other task requiring self-organisation or strategies to aid in remembrance are impaired. This principle is most clearly understood by examining one useful strategy for improving recall for a list of words. When presented with a list of words, a patient may group the list into categories of semantic meaning such as sports versus furniture. However, patients with frontal-lobe lesions, despite normal recognition memory for these words, are severely impaired on free recall and exhibit deficits in the subjective organisation that aids recall (Gershberg & Shimamura, 1995).

Semantic memory

There is considerable evidence for the involvement of the left frontal cortex in the semantic processing of verbal material. Patients with damage to the left PFC often have difficulty retrieving words in response to specific cues (e.g., words beginning with a specific letter, the names of objects belonging to a specific semantic category), even in the absence of a frank aphasia (Baldo & Shimamura, 1998). This suggests that the left PFC plays a general, albeit crucial, role in retrieving lexical and semantic information. The earliest functional neuroimaging evidence came from PET studies of language processing in which subjects were presented with nouns and required to generate semantically appropriate verbs (Petersen et al., 1988; Raichle et al., 1994). A study comparing semantically based decisions on words with pitch-based decisions on tones showed activations across widespread regions of left frontal cortex (Binder et al., 1997). Activations in left PFC BA45 may reflect semantic processing and those in left PFC BA44 (i.e., Broca's area) articulatory processes during word generation (Cabeza & Nyberg, 2000; Martin, 2000). Temporal activations in BA21 are common for both verbal and pictorial stimuli, suggesting amodal semantic processing (Cabeza & Nyberg, 2000). Thus, performing semantic tasks commonly activates a wide expanse of left lateral PFC. More recently, evidence has accumulated suggesting that an anterior and inferior prefrontal region (roughly equivalent to Brodmann's area BA47 and the inferior aspect of BA45) may be involved selectively in semantic processing. This region may serve as a "semantic working memory system" responsible for retrieving, maintaining, monitoring, and manipulating semantic representations stored elsewhere (Gabrieli et al., 1998; Poldrack et al., 1999; Wagner, 1999). Evidence supporting this view comes from studies showing that the left inferior prefrontal cortex (LIPC) is more active when the subjects make semantic judgements to words than when they make nonsemantic judgements to the same words. The phenomenon is observed even when the tasks are equated for difficulty (Demb et al., 1995; Gabrieli et al., 1996; Poldrack et al., 1999). Additional evidence comes from studies that find repetition-related decreases (and more efficient processing) in LIPC activity with repeated performance on semantic, but not nonsemantic tasks (Demb et al., 1995; Wagner et al., 2000).

Although these findings are broadly consistent with the hypothesis that this region may subserve a number of working-memory-like processes, the precise role of LIPC is difficult to determine from these reports. Moreover, patients with LIPC lesions are impaired when required to generate verbs to nouns with high, but not low, selection demand (Thompson-Schill et al., 1998). Because high-selection-demand tasks also place greater demands on retrieval, these findings may reflect retrieval demands, rather than selection demands *per se*. Some studies suggest that using semantic classification and word generation tasks, repeated performance of the same task (i.e., repeated generation of an action word to the same concrete noun) resulted in decreased activity in the LIPC (Demb et al., 1995; Wagner et al., 2000). However, crossing the tasks (i.e., generating an action word to a concrete noun when the subjects had previously generated a colour word to that noun) produced increased LIPC activity, even though the same concept and set of attributes were retrieved under both conditions. Thus, when recently selected information was irrelevant, selection demands and LIPC activity increased, whereas when recently selected information was relevant,

selection demands and LIPC activity decreased. In contrast, temporal lobe activity decreases when the same concept is retrieved, regardless of the type of feature that has to be selected. Taken together, these findings are consistent with the idea that LIPC is involved in the selection among competing semantic features (colour and action object associates) stored in temporal cortex. Interestingly, the location of the selection-related LIPC activity is actually in the dorsal aspect of BA44, placing it posterior and superior to the semantic working memory region identified by Gabrieli and collaborators (Gabrieli et al., 1998; Wagner, 1999). This suggests that the process of selecting among competing alternatives may occur in a different cortical region than other working memory processes.

Several studies dissociated the neural correlates of different kinds of knowledge. Knowledge about animals was associated with occipital activations and knowledge about tools with PFC activations (Damasio et al., 1996; Martin et al., 1996). Knowledge about colour was associated with colour perception regions in the fusiform gyrus and knowledge about actions with motion perception regions in the temporo-occipital cortex (Martin et al., 1995).

A study explored functional divisions within the left frontal cortex using simple semantic (abstract/concrete decisions), phonological (syllable counting), and low-level perceptual control (uppercase/lowercase) judgements that required minimal strategic processing (Poldrack et al., 1999). Direct comparison of the semantic and phonological conditions revealed a more anterior ventrolateral frontal cortex activation associated with semantic judgements. A broad division of ventrolateral frontal cortex was therefore proposed, into a posterior region concerned with phonological production (common to both semantic and phonological tasks) and a more anterior region concerned specifically with semantic processing. The semantic contribution to successful encoding may derive specifically from the anterior regions of ventrolateral frontal cortex. These findings suggest that we are beginning to make progress in identifying the distributed cortical networks associated with semantic object representations, and the networks underlying our ability to retrieve, select, and operate upon them.

Skill learning

Motor skill learning is associated with the activation of motor areas of the frontal lobes, notably the premotor and supplementary motor cortex (lateral and medial BA6) (Cabeza & Nyberg, 2000). Regions of the parietal lobes have also consistently been involved in motor skill learning and fronto-parietal interactions have been emphasised.

Frontal role in the "remember–know" procedure

The "remember–know" procedure was introduced to investigate the conscious experience accompanying memory retrieval (Tulving, 1985). Participants in this procedure indicate with a remember (R) judgement those stimuli that evoke recollection of a specific episode in which the stimuli were experienced previously. For stimuli thought to have been experienced previously, but which do not evoke recollection of a specific episode, volunteers make a know (K) judgement. R judgements typically entail memory for the spatiotemporal context in which stimuli occurred or the mental associations triggered by their occurrence (source) memory (Johnson et al., 1993). Little is known about the neural substrates that mediate R and K judgements. Whereas one study reported that amnesics with damage to the hippocampal formation or diencephalon showed reduced levels of both R and K judgements, another indicated that amnesics showed reduced levels of R but not K judgements (Knowlton & Squire, 1995; Schacter et al., 1997a, b). These results can be reconciled by scoring R and K judgements under the independence assumption, for which amnesics show reduced levels of both recollection and familiarity (Yonelinas et al., 1998). A frontal role in recollection is suggested by studies showing that frontal patients are disproportionately impaired at retrieval of source information (Shimamura et al., 1990). A recent fMRI study in normal human volunteers was designed to identify brain regions that exhibit differential haemodynamic responses according to whether participants recognise stimuli from a previous study episode (Henson et al., 1999). It was reported that both R and K judgements for studied words were associated with enhanced responses in left prefrontal and left parietal cortices relative to N judgements for unstudied words. R judgements for studied words were associated with enhanced responses in anterior left prefrontal, left parietal, and pos-terior cingulate regions relative to K judgements. K judgements for studied words were associated with enhanced responses in right lateral and medial PFC relative to both R judgements for studied words and N judgements for unstudied words, a difference that can be attributed to greater monitoring demands when memory judgements were less certain. It was argued that the responses of different brain regions could dissociate according to the phenomenology associated with memory retrieval. Thus, the subjective classification of stimuli afforded by event-related techniques allows neuroscientists to begin to address the conscious experience accompanying memory retrieval with a scientific approach.

Left versus right prefrontal cortex

The major impact of the studies using neuroimaging technological advancement is that they have provided evidence for the important implication of the PFC in both memory encoding and memory retrieval (Tulving et al., 1994b, c). These two memory functions are performed in different hemispheres (different lateralisation of functions). Further studies on the neuroanatomical location of episodic and semantic memory using PET indicate that free-ranging mental activity (e.g., random episodic memory or uncensored thinking about experience) produces large activation in association cortex (right and left frontal, parietal, angular/supramarginal, and posterior inferior temporal regions) (Andreasen et al., 1995a, b). The major difference between semantic and episodic memory is activation of Broca's area and the left frontal operculum by semantic memory (Andreasen et al., 1995b). The more specific activation of these centres by the semantic memory may be due to greater involvement in the search for recall of words.

Left frontal cortex has been consistently associated with encoding of verbal materials (Tulving et al., 1994b, c). However, considering frontal involvement in non-verbal memory, memorisation of materials associated with different codes can activate distinct regions of left and right frontal cortex. Early studies examining memory encoding showed evidence for the engagement of left frontal cortex. This functional lateralisation formed part of the influential HERA generalisation, which associates greater left than right frontal cortex activation with episodic encoding, and greater right than left activation with episodic retrieval (Tulving et al., 1994). Furthermore, the left lateralisation during encoding is found whether or not subjects are aware that their recall will be tested later. Left frontal activation is found in both incidental and intentional memory encoding (Kapur et al., 1994; Shallice et al., 1994). It is easy to forget that the original formulation of HERA was specific to "verbal and verbalisable" material. Speculation as to whether this model would be apposite for other types of material was not discussed. Some studies have suggested that encoding-related left frontal cortex activation may generalise to other types of stimuli. Studies involving semantic processing of pictorial stimuli, for example, have also produced left-sided activations (Grady et al., 1998; Vandenberghe et al., 1996). These pictures may have been verbalised. If this is correct, the Tulving hypothesis was correct. Encoding nameable objects produced bilateral frontal cortex activation and encoding unknown (unnameable) faces produced right rather than left frontal cortex activation (Kelley et al., 1998; Wagner et al., 1998). This lateralisation by material is similar to that seen in working memory.

Memorisation of unfamiliar faces and texture patterns, neither of which can be easily associated with a verbal label, activates right frontal regions (Kelley et al., 1998; Wagner et al., 1998). Of particular interest is the finding that memorisation of nameable objects (items that can be associated with both verbal and non-verbal imagery-based codes) often elicits bilateral activation of frontal cortex (Kelley et al., 1998). An intriguing interpretation of this finding is that distinct brain regions of frontal cortex will, for a single event, code the multiple kinds of information available. These studies also permit the observation of lateral differences. Left frontal activity predicted which words would be remembered, whereas right frontal activity predicted which picture scenes would be remembered (Brewer et al., 1998; Wagner et al., 1998). Taken together, these studies suggest that, depending on the kind of information being memorised, multiple lateralised regions within frontal cortex may participate in encoding.

CEREBELLUM AND CEREBELLAR CORTEX

Current research suggests that the cerebellum is necessary for learning, retention, and the expression of classical conditioning of the eyeblink and other direct responses (Ito, 1984, 1989, 1994; Ito et al., 1982). A recent study made use of the mutant Purkinje cell degeneration (pcd) mouse strain (Chen et al., 1996). In this mutant, Purkinje neurons are normal throughout pre- and perinatal development. At about 2–4 weeks postnatal, the Purkinje neurons in the cerebellar cortex degenerate and disappear (Landis & Mullen, 1978). For a period of about 2 months after this time, other neuronal structures appear relatively normal. Thus, during this period of young adulthood, the animals have a complete functional decortication of the cerebellum. The pcd mice learned very slowly, and to a much lower level, than wild-type controls, but showed extinction with subsequent training to the conditioned stimulus (CS) alone. Thus, the cerebellar cortex plays a critically important role in normal learning but some degree of learning is possible without the cerebellar cortex.

Several lines of evidence support the hypothesis that a process of long-term depression (LTD) in cerebellar cortex is a mechanism involved in memory storage in classical conditioning of discrete behavioural response. Similarly, several lines of evidence support such a role for cerebellar cortical LTD in adaptation of the vestibulo-ocular reflex (Ito, 1984, 1989). The cerebellum learns and stores complex, multijoint movements (Thach et al., 1992). The cerebellum may be critically involved in many other forms of learning including cardiovascular conditioning and discrete response instrumental avoidance learning (Steinmetz et al., 1993; Supple & Leaton, 1990). This may be extended to maze learning, spatial learning and memory, and adaptive timing (Goodlett et al., 1992; Keele & Ivry, 1990; Lalonde & Botez, 1990; Pellegrino & Altman, 1979). There is also a growing literature implicating the cerebellum in complex processes (Schmahmann, 1997).

Learning how to perform complex behavioural acts clearly requires the cerebral cortex and basal ganglia. It is envisioned that these structures learn to detect and register events and contexts that are potentially useful in planning and programming motor actions (Houk & Wise, 1995). The cerebellum, once provided with this information through the cortico-ponto-cerebellar pathway, must learn how to use it in an optimal fashion to orchestrate its own participation in complex motor acts.

THE IMPACT OF IMAGING TECHNOLOGY

PET and fMRI have distinct advantages and disadvantages. fMRI has superior spatial and temporal resolution, and recent advances now allow characterisation of the time course of brain activation in individual subjects. PET requires separate MRI scans for anatomical localisation, whereas anatomical and functional images are collected in the same session in fMRI studies, giving fMRI more precise localisation abilities. fMRI is also non-invasive whereas PET requires administration of radioactive material to the subject. PET and fMRI take advantage of the fact that neural activity leads to a relative increase in local blood flow. In PET, a radionuclide (such as ^{15}O) is injected into the bloodstream, and regional cerebral blood flow is measured with detectors that respond to the coincident emission of photon pairs emitted when positrons (created when the radionuclide breaks down) are annihilated (Raichle, 1994). fMRI relies on the different magnetic characteristics of oxyhaemoglobin and deoxyhaemoglobin in the bloodstream. The increase in local blood flow related to neural activity causes an increase in the ratio of oxy- to deoxyhaemoglobin (Moseley & Glover, 1995). Because the paramagnetic property of deoxyhaemoglobin results in greater magnetic susceptibility, the increase in the oxy- to deoxyhaemoglobin ratio results in an increase in magnetic resonance signal using a T_2-weighted pulse sequence. Therefore, PET is sensitive to changes in blood flow and fMRI is sensitive to blood oxygenation-level-dependent (BOLD) changes in the magnetic properties of blood. Both techniques allow relatively precise localisation of the observed changes in haemodynamic response.

PET studies have reported both cerebellar and medial-temporal activations associated with delay conditioning that parallels the development of behavioural CRs (Blaxton et al., 1996; Logan & Grafton, 1995). Delay eyeblink conditioning is not diminished by the basal ganglia lesions in HD patients (Woodruff-Pak & Papka, 1996). It does diminish across the normal adult lifespan and is virtually abolished in AD (Woodruff-Pak et al., 1990).

MRI has shown that the left planum temporale region of the brain is larger in musicians than in non-musicians (Schlaug et al., 1995). If this results from a change in cortical organisation, the left temporal area in musicians might have a better-developed cognitive function than the right temporal lobe (Elbert et al., 1995). A recent study showed that adults who received music training before the age of 12 have a better memory for spoken words than those who did not, thus providing preliminary evidence that music training may have a long-term effect on the improvement of verbal memory (Chan et al., 1998). Investigation of the effects of the age at which music training begins, and of the duration of training, may provide a better explanation for this result.

Neuroimaging investigations that examined true and false recognition with PET and fMRI also noted that patterns of brain activity were highly similar during the two forms of recognition, including some evidence of medial temporal lobe activation during both true and false recognition (Schacter et al., 1996b, 1997a). Frontal lobe activation was quite prominent in each of the PET and fMRI studies of false recognition.

A recent study used fMRI to examine the individual patterns of brain activation associated with successful autobiographical memory retrieval in normal volunteers (Maddock et al., 2001). It was shown that the caudal part of the left posterior cingulate cortex was the most strongly activated region in all volunteers. These findings are consistent with prior studies showing posterior cingulate cortex activation during autobiographical memory retrieval (Andreasen et al., 1995b; Conway et al., 1999; Maguire & Mummery, 1999). These data support the hypothesis that the posterior cingulate cortex plays an important role in successful memory retrieval.

Differences in brain activation of young and elderly subjects

PET studies differentiate in brain activation between young and older individuals and there were differences emphasising the low recall condition (Chan-Paley & Asan, 1989; Rosene, 1993). Most striking was the difference between the groups in the low recall minus baseline comparison, which produced blood flow increases bilaterally in the anterior frontal lobe (centring on area 10), for the young subjects but not the older ones. By contrast, the older subjects demonstrated unilateral blood flow increases in the right posterior frontal lobe (centring on area 46) and the right motor area (centring on area 4/6). These differences in frontal activation between the young and older adults may reflect differences in retrieval strategies when subjects are attempting to recall information that is not well learned. Age-related alterations in subcortical nuclei that project to the cortex seem to be the more likely explanation for these findings (Chan-Palay & Asan, 1989; Rosene, 1993). There is substantial neuronal loss in selected subcortical regions involved in neurotransmitter systems important for memory function such as the basal forebrain and the locus ceruleus. Investigators comparing young and old subjects using PET scanning have demonstrated that several frontal lobe regions exhibit compensatory hypermetabolism during working memory tasks in older subjects (Furey et al., 1997; Graf &

Uttl, 1995). They also showed that the clinical effects of cholinergic drug effects on working memory (improvement with physostigmine and impairment with scopolamine) produce corresponding modifications in these compensatory metabolic patterns. These results may suggest that age-related working memory disturbances involve disruption of executive as much as encoding and retrieval systems in the brain.

Sentence comprehension declines with age and there is much evidence to support the hypothesis that elderly subjects are significantly more impaired than younger subjects at understanding grammatically complex sentences (Obler et al., 1991). An fMRI study designed to assess the neural basis for sentence comprehension in healthy elderly subjects monitored regional brain activity in young (22.6 ± 4.9 years) and elderly (63.5 ± 10.8 years) subjects matched for sentence comprehension accuracy while they answered a simple probe about written sentences (Grossman et al., 2002). The sentences varied in their grammatical features and their verbal working memory demands. Differences in activation patterns for elderly compared to younger subjects were due largely to changes in brain regions associated with a verbal working memory network. While the elderly had less left parietal recruitment than younger subjects, left premotor cortex and dorsal portions of left inferior frontal cortex showed greater activation in elderly compared to younger subjects. Younger subjects recruited right posterolateral temporal cortex for sentences with a long noun-gap linkage. The elderly subjects additionally recruited right parietal cortex for this sentence-specific form of working memory. These findings are consistent with the hypothesis that the neural basis for sentence comprehension includes dissociable but interactive neural networks supporting core written sentence processes and related cognitive resources in working memory. The elderly with good comprehension appear to up-regulate portions of the neural substrate for working memory during sentence processing to achieve comprehension accuracy that equals that of young subjects. Thus, in healthy ageing, the human communication system demonstrates critical adaptive changes in its neural substrate to maintain comprehension accuracy.

Comparing the performance of young normal subjects and elderly volunteers with AD patients on episodic memory assessment with fMRI technology, it was suggested that hippocampal activation during encoding and frontal lobe activation during recognition were related to successful performance on the recognition task and not to group membership (Corkin, 1998). However, advanced age in the elderly normal subjects and AD groups was associated with diminished extent of activation and diminished significance of signal intensity in the hippocampus and parahippocampal gyrus. Recognition in AD patients, but not in elderly normal subjects, was associated with diminished extent of activation and diminished significance of signal intensity in the PFC. In both elderly subjects and AD patients, no recruitment of new cortical areas that were not activated in young subjects were observed. Therefore, it was suggested that prefrontal activation might index voluntary, intentional, and effortful retrieval processes.

An observation in several studies is that lateralised patterns of brain activity tend to be less pronounced for old than for young adults. This phenomenon has been described as hemispheric asymmetry reduction in old adults (HAROLD). In the case of episodic memory retrieval, HAROLD summarises evidence that PFC activity is right lateralised in young adults but bilateral in old adults. This has been observed for word-pair cued-recall, word-stem cued-recall, word recognition, and face recognition (Cabeza et al., 1997; Kapur et al., 1995; Madden et al., 1999). Current research also suggests that HAROLD onsets in middle age, probably prior to age 50 (Dixit et al., 2000). During working memory, HAROLD was found for both verbal and spatial tasks (Reuter-Lorenz et al., 2000). A pessimistic view of HAROLD is that the elderly have difficulty engaging specialised neural mechanisms, whereas an optimistic opinion is that bilateral PFC activation signals functional compensation. Old adults may compensate for neurocognitive deficits by recruiting both PFCs

for tasks in which young adults recruit only one PFC (Cabeza et al., 1997).

Brain systems mediating perceptual and conceptual priming

Several recent functional neuroimaging studies have explored priming on a variety of implicit retrieval tasks. Converging evidence suggests that priming is associated with changes in posterior cortical regions that are involved in perceptual processing; some of the same regions may contribute to explicit memory. However, whereas priming was accompanied by blood flow decreases in the word-stem completion study, it was accompanied by blood flow increases in an object decision study. The reason for this discrepancy is not entirely clear. One possibility is that blood flow increases in old object decision minus new object decision comparison are related to some process other than priming. The finding that stem completion priming was accompanied by blood flow decreases may suggest that the processing of primed stimuli requires less metabolic activity and possibly fewer neurons than priming of nonprimed stimuli. The idea also receives support from experiments with non-human primates, showing that when they passively view stimuli that become increasingly familiar, the responses of some neurons in the inferior temporal cortex gradually decrease (Desimone et al., 1995). Not all priming phenomena are necessarily accompanied by blood flow reductions, but the appearance of reductions across different task and stimulus conditions is striking. It has also been suggested that priming and object decisions about structurally possible objects may involve inferior temporal regions (Schacter et al., 1991a).

Patients with AD are often impaired on certain forms of implicit memory, such as word-stem completion priming (WSCP). Lesion data suggest that deficient WSCP may be associated with abnormal functioning in posterior neocortex (Schacter et al., 1996a, d). Using PET, a study was designed to provide direct evidence that AD-related deficits in WSCP are associated with changes in brain activity during task performance

(Bäckman et al., 2000). The results demonstrated that both normal old and AD patients showed significant priming, although the size of the priming effect was reduced in AD. This study indicated that compared with normal adults, AD patients showed reduced priming on a word-stem completion task. The normal old showed decreased activity in right occipital cortex (area 19) whereas the AD patients showed increased activity in this region during priming. To the extent that decreased activity priming reflects an experience-dependent reduction of the neuronal population involved, these results suggest that shaping of the relevant neurons is slower in AD, possibly as a result of inadequate initial-stimulus processing.

Neuroimaging studies also indicate that separate cortical areas mediate perceptual and conceptual priming. Priming on visual word-stem completion tasks is associated with reduced activity, relative to baseline word-stem completion, in bilateral occipito-temporal regions (Schacter et al., 1996a, d; Squire et al., 1992). Priming on conceptual tasks is associated with reduced activity in left frontal neocortex on tasks involving abstract/concrete decisions about words and living/non-living decisions about words and pictures (Gabrieli et al., 1996a; Wagner et al., 1997). Reduced activity in left frontal neocortex is also observed after generation of verbs to nouns and generation of semantically related words (Blaxton et al., 1996; Raichle et al., 1994). Amnesic patients who show normal priming when making abstract/concrete decisions about words also show a priming-related reduction in left frontal cortex (Gabrieli et al., 1996a).

DISCUSSION

Memory appears to be stored in the same distributed assembly of brain structures that is engaged in initially perceiving and processing what is to be remembered. There is still no technique that allows one to pinpoint a memory directly in the mammalian brain. We cannot as yet locate the sites where memory of some particular object is stored. Nevertheless, studies of humans and animals with brain lesions, and newer imaging techniques, have consistently made an important point. The brain regions in cortex that are involved in the perceiving and processing of colour, size, shape, and other object attributes are close to, if not identical to, the brain regions important for remembering objects. Broadly, memory phenomena have been categorised as explicit or implicit. Thus, explicit memories for experience involve the hippocampus–medial temporal lobe system and implicit basic associative learning and memory involves the cerebellum, amygdala, and other systems. Overall, both the lesion data and functional neuroimaging of healthy volunteers point to a neural model in which semantic knowledge is stored in distributed neural networks with regions in the temporal lobes, particularly the left temporal lobe, at the core. Other cortical areas seem to be recruited into the representational network as a function of the intrinsic properties of the object or concept that is being instantiated. Under normal conditions, however, many of these brain–memory systems are engaged to some degree in learning situations. But each of these brain systems is learning something different about the situation. The cerebellum is necessary for classical conditioning of discrete behavioural responses (eyeblink, limb flexion) under all conditions. However, in the "trace" procedure, where a period of no stimuli intervenes between the conditioned stimulus and the unconditioned stimulus, the hippocampus plays a critical role. Analysis of the role of the cerebellum in basic delay conditioning (stimuli overlap) indicates that the memories are formed and stored in the cerebellum.

In the domain of remote memory, amnesic patients have equal difficulty in retrieving recent episodic and semantic memories but older events and knowledge can sometimes be retrieved (Reed & Squire, 1998). Episodic memories can be affected by time with better preservation of distant events compared with more recent memories. However, a model in which amnesia is caused by a selective impairment to episodic memory does not predict this. These neuropsychological findings strongly suggest that Tulving's original hypothesis regarding the organisation of human LTM, in which episodic and semantic memory are neurologically and psychologically distinct, is incorrect (Tulving, 1972, 1983). In order to accommodate these conflicting findings from amnesia, some investigators have suggested a neuroanatomically based hypothesis in which medial temporal lobe structures (i.e., the hippocampus, subiculum, and entorhinal cortex) play a temporary, time-limited role in the acquisition of human LTM (Graham & Hodges, 1997; Reed & Squire, 1998). Thus, the hippocampal complex is necessary for the retrieval of recently experienced events but is not involved in the retrieval of older episodic and semantic memories. On the other hand, regions of the neocortex are thought to be the permanent repository of memory (Squire & Alvarez, 1995). This hypothesis provides a reasonable clarification for why patients with damage to the hippocampal complex show a temporally graded loss of memory, with recent memories affected more severely than older memories. However, the time-course of this transfer needs to be specified. Although this type of process may well help to explain the differential loss of information over weeks and months, it seems highly unlikely that it can explain temporal gradients of retrograde amnesia that extend over several decades.

Although amnesics show preservation of motoric forms of classical conditioning and several kinds of skill learning and memory, it seems likely that these kinds of memory are primarily mediated by the basal ganglia and cerebellum. Motoric classical conditioning and skill memory are likely to depend on very different kinds of memory representation, as the cerebellum and basal ganglia are organised very differently from the neocortex, where most aspects of explicit memories are likely to be stored.

Support for the hypothesis that episodic memory required interhemispheric integration whereas semantic memories are more unilaterally localised comes from imaging studies. Tulving et al. (1994a) have proposed a HERA model of verbal episodic memory wherein the left and right hemispheres, particularly the prefrontal lobes, are differentially involved in semantic and episodic memory encoding and retrieval. Tulving et al. (1994) suggested that the left PFC is responsible for both the encoding and retrieval of semantic memories. Conversely, they also suggested that episodic encoding versus retrieval is associated with the left versus right hemispheres, respectively. Thus, semantic versus episodic memories appear to be associated with intrahemispheric versus interhemispheric processing, respectively, lending further support to the hypothesis that episodic memory requires integration of the cerebral hemispheres whereas semantic memory does not.

Recent studies have also clarified the involvement of the medial temporal lobe in encoding and retrieval (Cohen et al., 1999). A meta-analysis of PET data concluded that encoding activations tend to engage more anterior hippocampal regions and retrieval activations more posterior hippocampal regions, a pattern called the hippocampal encoding/retrieval (HIPER) model (Lepage et al., 1998). Although earlier fMRI results appeared inconsistent with this model, two recent fMRI studies provide support for HIPER (Dolan & Fletcher, 1999; Saykin et al., 1999; Schacter et al., 1999; Strange et al., 1999).

Advances in the study of the cognitive neuroscience of memory reveal the functional neural architecture of normal human memory and clarify why focal or degenerative injuries to specific memory systems lead to characteristic patterns of mnemonic failure. Although lesion studies continue to provide new evidence, functional neuroimaging studies using PET or fMRI now permit the visualisation of memory processes in the healthy brain. Functional neuroimaging studies allow for the design of neuropsychological investigations targeted at specific memory processes.

Imaging technology may be useful in the future in the diagnosis and perhaps prediction of dementia (de Leon et al., 1993; Jobst et al., 1992). fMRI can be useful in differentiating AD from other dementias. In fact, parieto-temporal hypometabolism and right/left (or left/right) asymmetry in AD are the most consistent findings in the functional neuroimaging literature (Mazziotta et al., 1992). Current research using the above techniques and similar ones offer the potential for improved diagnostic as well as predictive uses. Serial PET scans of patients with AD show progression of the metabolic decline that correlates with clinical deterioration. Moreover, the abnormal metabolic pattern is observed several years before clinical confirmation of the disease (Haxby et al., 1990; Kuhl et al., 1987). Because PET scanning produces a consistent pattern of parietal and temporal deficits, it is currently being used in some clinical settings to increase the likelihood of a diagnosis of AD in the presence of mild to moderate cognitive impairment.

Although imaging technologies have contributed greatly to our understanding of memory, the interpretation of imaging data is not straightforward. It is not possible simply to measure brain activity from PET during performance of a single task and then draw meaningful conclusions about the neural underpinnings of that task based on the resulting brain image. Such a procedure does not specify those components of the image that were produced from the task instructions and those that were already present. Therefore, experiments are typically performed using a "subtraction method". There is a great deal of psychological interpretation involved in understanding the meaning of an activation, i.e., in specifying what mental process is signified by an activation. Most imaging studies report activations arising from the difference between two tasks. At least two cognitive tasks are required of each participant in a PET comparison. Ideally, the tasks are identical except for a single component. The challenge for PET researchers is to design two tasks that differ by only one meaningful component. After subtraction, the resulting image shows the pattern of activation that is assumed to represent the localised blood flow associated with the different component between the two tasks. PET implies that if a brain region is shown to have a higher blood flow on Task A than on Task B, then that region is more active in Task A. The resulting brain map is only as meaningful as the analysis of the cognitive ingredients of the compared tasks. The manipulation of mental operations of participants within the PET scanner represents another means to investigate the relation between cognition and neurophysiology.

A recent study that used sensitive priming measures obtained with the fade-in task to better define the neural bases of deficits in priming and recognition memory was performed by Jernigan et al. (2001). The results suggested that damage in both hippocampal and amygdala/entorhinal areas as well as damage in the diencephalon and the nucleus accumbens all contributed independently to the severity of recognition-memory deficits. Both caudate nucleus damage and hippocampal damage contributed independently to increased naming latency. Finally, only damage in the hippocampus appeared to result in decreased word priming. These data may represent some evidence against the hypothesis that word priming represents a form of memory unaffected by damage to the medial temporal lobes.

Physiological and Pharmacological Assessment of Memory

INTRODUCTION

Hebb's rule (1949) states that learning and memory are based on modifications of synaptic strength among neurons that are simultaneously active. This implies that enhanced synaptic coincidence detection would lead to better learning and memory. There are about 10^{11} neurons in the brain and each neuron establishes about 10^3 to 10^4 connections to other neurons. Neuroscience research has demonstrated that neurons are arranged in distributed networks of brain regions to govern human behaviour (Mesulam, 1998). Modulation of neuronal activity via neurotransmitters is a fundamental mechanism of brain function. Although there are many more neurotransmitter systems in the brain, clinical neuroscience in the study of memory is particularly concerned with the monoaminergic (dopaminergic, noradrenergic, and serotonergic), cholinergic, glutamatergic, and GABAergic systems. These various systems can be divided into two groups based on their anatomical characteristics. The first group of neurotransmitter

systems comprises the dopaminergic, noradrenergic, serotonergic, and cholinergic neurons. These four systems originate from small groups of neurons, densely packed in circumscribed areas of the forebrain or brainstem, which project to their target areas typically by long-ranging projection fibres. Because neurotransmitter-specific projection systems reach selected neural systems, their mechanism leads to more circumscribed effects. The second group includes the glutamatergic and GABAergic systems. Their neurons are by far the most prevalent and most widely distributed types in the human brain. Their modulation affects many neural systems and they are very implicated in learning and memory.

The activity of receptors and ion channels influences gene and protein expression in neurons. Second messengers (calcium, cyclic AMP) regulate the activity of protein kinases (proteins that transfer phosphate groups to a substrate protein) and phosphatases (proteins that remove phosphate groups from a substrate protein). In all cases studied to date, the activation of neurotransmitter receptors changes the state of phosphorylation of neuronal proteins. One group of proteins regulated by phosphorylation are the transcription factors that operate by recruiting the transcription initiation complex and RNA polymerase to particular genes. Among the best-studied transcription factors in the brain is the Ca^{2+} and cyclic AMP-responsive element binding protein (CREB) (Montminy et al., 1990). The study of CREB has provided us with an insight into the complex consequences of transcription factor activation and gene expression on higher brain function. Activated by phosphorylation, CREB regulates the expression of several target genes (e.g., genes for peptide neurotransmitters, enzymes involved in neurotransmitter synthesis, and growth factors). The discovery that CREB plays a pivotal role in processes such as learning and memory provided a link between gene regulation and cognitive function (Frank & Greenberg, 1994; Stevens, 1994).

Working memory does not require the transcription and translation processes that enable genes to promote protein production (Milner et al., 1998). Working memory is thought to be mediated by transient chemical alterations in synaptic "connectivity" or the functional strengths of connections among associated neurons. In contrast, encoding into LTM appears to be dependent on gene activation with the resultant production of proteins and alteration in synaptic structure and hence structural neuronal connectivity. Formation of consolidated memory involves a complex set of cellular events, including second messenger pathways, post-translational modification of protein in the cytoplasm, and regulation of gene expression in the nucleus. In most animal systems, protein synthesis is required within a narrow time window if LTM is to form (Davis & Squire, 1984). Combined with neurochemical evidence, these observations suggest that LTM is stored in a distinct region of the brain as physical changes in synapses. It is likely that most neurotransmitters can influence memory negatively or positively to some degree, but only a select few play prominent roles. In addition to classic neurotransmitters, other neuropeptides and trophic proteins probably influence memory by activating neuronal membrane receptors and second messenger systems.

MONOAMINERGIC RECEPTORS

Dopaminergic, noradrenergic, and serotonergic pathways to the hippocampus and neocortex have long been known to regulate mood and emotion through dopamine D_1, adrenergic β, and serotoninergic 5-HT_{1A} receptors respectively. As is known, memory depends a lot on mood and emotion, and a number of animal studies suggest that the central noradrenergic systems have a major role in memory and learning. For example, depletion of cortical norepinephrine (noradrenaline) is associated with an impairment of learning in the rat (Anlezark et al., 1973). Although the precise interpretation of these results remains unclear, many other studies have also shown changes in the pattern of learning and extinction to be associated with cortical norepinephrine depletion (Leconte & Hennevin, 1981; Robbins et al., 1982). The biogenic amine projections to the cortex from the brainstem, containing norepinephrine, dopamine, or serotonin, also play important supporting roles to enhance memory formation.

Dopamine

Dopamine is the immediate metabolic precursor of epinephrine (adrenaline) and norepinephrine. It is a neurotransmitter and possesses important intrinsic pharmacological properties. There are three main neuronal systems in the brain that use dopamine as the neurotransmitter. The nigrostriatal pathway arises from dopamine-containing cell bodies in the substantia nigra and sends axons to the caudate-nucleus–putamen complex (the neostriatum) (see Figure 4.1). This pathway forms part of the extra-pyramidal system of the brain. The cell bodies of the neurons that form the mesolimbic forebrain system are concentrated in the ventral tegmentum of the midbrain close to the substantia nigra. The cell bodies of the neurons that form the tubero-infundibular system lie within the region of the arcuate nucleus of the hypothalamus. To date, five dopamine receptors (D_1–D_5) have been discovered.

Dopamine is the most studied neurochemical system for working memory. In CA1, enhance-

FIGURE 4.1

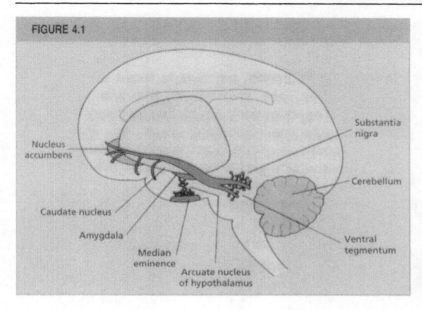

Sagittal section of the human brain showing the dopaminergic pathways.

ment of dopamine D_1 receptor binding has been shown 3–6 hours post-training (Bernabeu et al., 1997). The mesolimbic dopamine projection from the midbrain to the frontal lobes plays a prominent role in working memory (Goldman-Rakic, 1995a, b). It has been widely reported that increasing dopamine levels in human subjects facilitates working memory performance (Luciana et al., 1992, 1998). However, the relative role of D_1 and D_2 dopamine receptors in modulating working memory is yet to be clarified in humans. In a study, normal volunteers received either an acute oral dose of 0.1 mg pergolide (a combined D_1/D_2 receptor agonist) or 2.5 mg of bromocriptine (a D_2 receptor agonist) (Muller et al., 1998). An improvement in spatial working memory in subjects treated with pergolide but not bromocriptine was observed. It was concluded that pergolide administration could be attributed to a modulatory effect of D_1 receptors. This may highlight the more prominent role for D_1 receptors in working memory.

On the basis of evidence suggesting that dopamine receptor agonists may facilitate working memory, it would follow that dopamine receptor antagonists may impair working memory performance. Using a sample of 34 young male volunteers, the effect of the D_2 dopamine antagonist

sulpiride on spatial working memory was assessed (Mehta et al., 1999). It was reported that spatial working memory, as assessed by a sequence generation task, was impaired following both 200 and 400 mg doses of sulpiride compared to placebo. Another study showed that following a 3 mg oral dose of a D_2 antagonist, haloperidol, a decrease in performance on the spatial working memory task compared to placebo as measured by a decrease in accuracy of identifying the location of cue was noted (Luciana et al., 1998). This decrement was observed at delays of 8 and 16 seconds, but not at a delay of 5 seconds.

Regarding the impact of ageing on memory, although neuronal loss appears to be minimal in the hippocampus with age, recent reports suggest alterations in specific receptor types that may play a role in memory function (Gazzaley et al., 1996). There is an age-related decrease in dopaminergic binding sites in the caudate nucleus and the substantia nigra and a loss of neurons in the substantia nigra of about 6% per year (McGeer et al., 1977; Severson et al., 1982). Systematic age-related reductions of D_2 binding in the caudate and putamen were noted (Bäckman et al., 2000a, b). Changes in dopamine levels or neurotransmission may cause age-related changes in cognitive flexibility. Age-related decrease in D_2 receptors

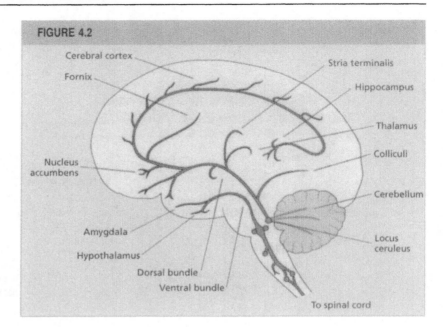

FIGURE 4.2

Cerebral cortex
Fornix
Stria terminalis
Hippocampus
Thalamus
Colliculi
Nucleus accumbens
Cerebellum
Amygdala
Locus ceruleus
Hypothalamus
Dorsal bundle
Ventral bundle
To spinal cord

Sagittal section of the human brain showing the noradrenergic pathways.

may also contribute to age-related cognitive decline by affecting frontal-lobe function (Volkow et al., 1998, 2000). A study reported that patients with MCI had improvement in global cognitive function when treated with the dopamine agonist piribedil (Nagaraja & Jayashree, 2001). These results support the role of age-related dopamine decline in cognitive impairment of the elderly.

Recently, the cortical effects of working memory have also been examined for the dopaminergic system. Using fMRI, it was observed that following bromocriptine administration, there were reductions in task-related brain activity in the parietal and occipital cortexes during the maintenance component of a working memory task (Kimberg et al., 2001). These data may suggest that the manipulation of dopamine may modify brain activity during the maintenance component of working memory. There is no doubt that brain imaging may aid better understanding of the pharmacology of memory.

Epinephrine and norepinephrine

Epinephrine (adrenaline) is a potent stimulant of both α- and β-adrenergic receptors and its effects on target organs are thus complex. Norepinephrine (noradrenaline, *l*-adrenaline, levarterenol) is the chemical mediator liberated by mammalian postganglionic adrenergic nerves. It differs from epinephrine only by lacking the methyl substitution in the amino group. Major noradrenergic pathways in the brain arise from the cell bodies in the locus ceruleus (see Figure 4.2). From there, fibres project rostrally to form a dorsal bundle with branches leaving to the cerebellum, thalamus, hypothalamus, and hippocampus. Neurons in the locus ceruleus have been associated with the maintenance of attention and vigilance, and noradrenergic mechanisms in the brain have been shown to be involved in the process of reinforcement that facilitates learning.

Extensive evidence from studies of memory of inhibitory avoidance training in rats indicates that several neuromodulatory systems interact with the noradrenergic system in the amygdala in modulating memory storage (Introini-Collison et al., 1996). A large number of studies using a variety of training tasks have demonstrated that post-training systemic injections of epinephrine enhance memory (McGaugh, 1983; McGaugh & Gold, 1989). Epinephrine effects on memory are also blocked by peripherally administered propranolol, as would be expected because propranolol readily enters the brain (Introini-Collison et al., 1992). However, the finding that epinephrine effects on memory are blocked by sotalol, a β-adrenergic antagonist that does not readily enter the brain, suggests that epinephrine effects are initiated by activation of peripheral β-adrenergic receptors. It has been hypothesised that epinephrine activates β-adrenergic receptors located on vagal efferents that project to the nucleus of the solitary tract (NST) (Ricardo & Koh, 1978). Thus, projections from the NST would release norepinephrine within the amygdala. Consistent with this hypothesis, inactivation of the NST with lidocaine blocks the effects of epinephrine on memory (Williams & McGaugh, 1993). Other β-adrenergic agonists that enter the brain, including dipivefrin and clenbuterol, enhance memory when administered post-training (Introini-Collison et al., 1992). Dipivefrin effects are blocked by propranolol but not by sotalol. Post-training intra-amygdala infusions of clenbuterol enhance memory storage (Introini-Collison et al., 1991, 1996). These findings support the hypothesis that epinephrine effects on memory storage are mediated by the amygdala. The effects involve activation of the release of norepinephrine within the amygdala. Metyrapone (a drug that inhibits 11β-hydroxylase, a rate-limiting enzyme in corticosterone synthesis) pretreatment blocked the memory-enhancing effects of amphetamine, 4-OH-amphetamine (a peripherally acting amphetamine derivative), and epinephrine but did not affect retention performance of otherwise untreated animals. Post-training injections of different doses of epinephrine (0.0001–1 mg/kg) produced a dose-dependent memory enhancement for inhibitory avoidance training and metyrapone blocked the memory-enhancing effects of all these doses. These data provide evidence that the sympathoadrenal and adrenocortical systems are intimately coupled during the processes of memory storage.

Norepinephrine and other β-adrenergic agonists administered to the amygdala, after training dose-dependently, enhance retention (Liang et al., 1995). These effects are also time dependent; they affect retention when given shortly after training but have no effect if given several hours later. Intra-amygdala infusions of the β-adrenergic antagonist propranolol or depletion of norepinephrine in the amygdala by N-2-chloroethyl-N-ethyl-bromobenzylamine (DSP-4) block the memory-enhancing effect of the adrenergic stress hormone epinephrine (Liang et al., 1995). Moreover, intra-amygdala infusions of propranolol as well as specific β_1- or β_2-adrenergic antagonists also block the effects on memory of drugs affecting opioid peptidergic and GABAergic systems (McGaugh et al., 1995).

Epinephrine has a modulatory effect on memory function and its administration after a learning task influences retention with an inverted U-shaped curve. Retention is enhanced at moderate doses and impaired at high doses (Gold & Van Buskirk, 1975; Liang et al., 1986). Low-dose injection (0.2 μg) of norepinephrine into the amygdala facilitates memory function in an inhibitory avoidance task, while higher doses (0.5 μg) impair memory function (Liang et al., 1990). In summary, epinephrine and norepinephrine released during stress enhance the formation of memory traces. A focal lesion of catecholamine fibres by infusing 6-hydroxydopamine into the principal sulcus disrupts spatial working memory in young monkeys, and working memory performance of the lesioned monkeys can be normalised by treatment with α_2 agonists, such as clonidine or guanfacine (Arnsten et al. 1988; Brozoski et al., 1979). Accordingly, agonists at α_{2A} receptors (e.g., clonidine and guanfacine) have been shown to improve PFC function in non-human primates whereas antagonists at α_2 receptors (e.g., yohimbine) have been shown to impair PFC function or antagonise the beneficial actions of agonists (see Mao et al., 1999). A recent study was designed to investigate whether acute oral administration of clonidine (0.5 or 2 μg/kg) can improve performance of PD patients in two tests of "frontal" function, spatial working memory and attentional set shifting (Riekkinen et al., 1999). The results showed that clonidine (2 μg/kg) stimulated spatial working memory accuracy. However, it had no effect on attentional set shifting or visual recognition memory. In contrast, clonidine was more effective in stimulating spatial working memory in severe PD patients while these patients were off dopaminergic medication. These results may suggest that disrupted activation of α_2 adrenoceptors contributes to the impairment of spatial working memory in PD.

Persisting emotional memories (especially fear) depend to a large extent on a specific structure in the limbic system (the amygdala) and are promoted by a particular type of modulatory influence such as stress hormone (Cahill & McGaugh, 1996, 1998). Drug studies also suggest that release of stress hormones that influence activity within the amygdala may contribute importantly to persisting emotional memories (Cahill et al., 1996; Cahill & McGaugh, 1998). For example, in one study, it was shown that propranolol interfered with retention of emotional but not non-emotional aspects of a story (Cahill et al., 1996). The neurophysiological basis of emotional memory (memory storage for events that arouse emotions) appears to be associated with the activation of β-adrenergic receptors and the amygdaloid complex (McGaugh et al., 1993). An experimental study in normal human volunteers indicated that β-adrenergic blockade selectively impaired LTM (1 week) for an emotionally arousing story (Cahill et al., 1994). Patients suffering from Urbach–Wiethe disease show selective impairment of memory for emotional material (Babinsky et al., 1993; Markowitsch et al., 1994). Current findings on the neurophysiological basis of human emotional memory con-

firm the opinion that the influence of emotional arousal involves β-adrenergic receptor activation and influences associated with the amygdaloid complex (Cahill et al., 1995). It also appears that these processes are not necessary for normal memory retention in non-emotionally arousing situations.

Serotonin

Serotonin (5-HT, 5-hydroxytryptamine), a monoamine neurotransmitter that mediates a wide range of physiological functions, seems to be implicated in mood, and in normal and dysfunctional cognitive processes (Flood et al., 1998). In the past few years, seven distinct families of serotonin have been identified ($5-HT_1$–$5-HT_7$) and subpopulations have been described for several of these. At least 15 subpopulations have now been cloned. Cell bodies that contain serotonin are clustered in the raphe nuclei and groups of axons that follow the same pathway to innervate the different cerebral regions (see Figure 4.3).

Serotonin appears to play a role in memory and cognition as made evident after administration of serotonin $5-HT_{2A}$/$5-HT_{2C}$ or $5-HT_4$ receptor

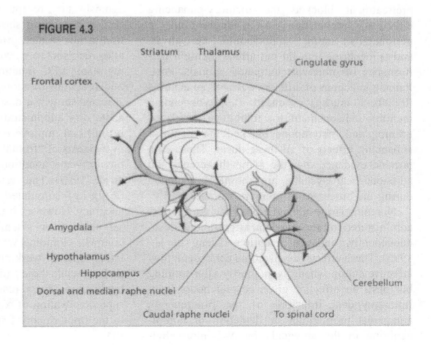

FIGURE 4.3

Frontal cortex

Striatum   Thalamus

Cingulate gyrus

Amygdala

Hypothalamus

Hippocampus

Dorsal and median raphe nuclei

Caudal raphe nuclei

To spinal cord

Cerebellum

Sagittal section of the human brain showing the serotonergic pathways.

agonists or 5-HT$_{1A}$ or 5-HT$_3$ receptor antagonists (Meneses, 1999). 5-HT also appears to participate in modulating the activity of septal efferents to the hippocampal formation, a pathway that is of considerable importance to mnemonic processes and that is known to degenerate in AD. Such 5-HT-cholinergic interactions may offer a pharmacological substrate for memory-enhancing drugs (Cassel & Jeltsch, 1995).

5-HT$_{1A}$ receptors

The highest densities of the regional distribution of 5-HT$_{1A}$ receptors in the brain of various species are in the hippocampus, septum, amygdala, and cortical limbic areas. Some neurobiological demonstrations have also shown that 5-HT$_{1A}$ receptors are expressed in a subpopulation of cholinergic neurons belonging to the medial septum/diagonal band of Broca (Kia et al., 1996).

Considerable progress is being made towards an understanding of the role played by 5-HT$_{1A}$ receptors in cognition, especially hippocampal 5-HT$_{1A}$ receptors. Stimulation of 5-HT$_{1A}$ receptors has detrimental effects on working memory (Herremans et al., 1995). Both systemic and intrahippocampal injections of 8-OH-DPAT [8-hydro-2(di-N-propylamino)tetralin], a specific 5-HT$_{1A}$ agonist have previously been found to impair rats' acquisition in spatial memory tasks, a deficit attributable to the activation of postsynaptic 5-HT$_{1A}$ receptors. Activation of these receptors has a detrimental effect on learning and working memory whereas their inactivation selectively antagonises these effects and those associated with cholinergic dysfunction.

5-HT$_{1B/1D}$ receptors

The 5-HT$_{1B}$ (formerly named 5-HT$_{1D\beta}$) and 5-HT$_{1D}$ (formerly named 5-HT$_{1D\alpha}$) receptors occur in brain areas associated with cognitive processes (Martin et al., 1998). The 5-HT$_{1B}$ receptor is predominantly located on axon terminals. In the hippocampus, 5-HT$_{1B}$ mRNA is found in CA1 pyramidal cells (Boschert et al., 1994). In particular, 5-HT$_{1B}$ heteroceptors located on hippocampal terminals of septal cholinergic neurons decrease the release

of acetylcholine, whereas those located on axon terminals of glutamatergic CA1 pyramidal cells have been found to control transmission between CA1 and the subiculum (Aït Amara et al., 1995; Boeijiga & Boddeke, 1996; Cassel et al., 1995). The recent availability of specific antagonists for this receptor is a valuable tool for pharmacological investigations (Skingle et al., 1996).

Some findings suggest that presynaptic 5-HT$_{1B}$ (or 5-HT$_{1D}$?) receptor stimulation decreases learning consolidation, while postsynaptic 5-HT$_{1B}$ receptor stimulation seems to facilitate this process (Meneses, 1999a, b; Meneses & Hong, 1997; Meneses et al., 1997). The exact roles of pre- and postsynaptic 5-HT$_{1B/D}$ receptors and the maximal effect on 5-HT neurotransmission achievable with a 5-HT$_{1B/D}$ receptor antagonist deserve further attention.

5-HT$_2$ receptors

The 5-HT$_2$ receptors family includes three subtypes: 5-HT$_{2A}$ (formerly named 5-HT$_2$), 5-HT$_{2B}$ (formerly named 5-HT$_{2F}$), and 5-HT$_{2C}$ (previously included in the 5-HT$_1$ family and named 5-HT$_{1C}$). This classification has made clear that most of the existing drugs for these receptors are nonselective and behave as mixed agonist/antagonist, neutral antagonist, and/or inverse agonist (Meneses, 1998, 1999).

The 5-HT$_{2A}$ and 5-HT$_{2C}$ (5-HT$_{2A/2C}$) receptors are of close homology. They are present in high concentrations in cortical areas. A study reported a positive enhancing effect on memory in animal studies when the task is difficult and generates a low level of acquisition (Harvey, 1996). This may suggest the use of 5-HT$_{2A/2C}$ agonists as therapeutic tools for the treatment of severe memory deficits in humans. At the systems level, the activation of 5-HT$_{2A/2C}$ receptors induces a facilitatory effect on cholinergic release in the rat frontal cortex (Hirano et al., 1995).

5-HT$_3$ receptors

5-HT$_3$ receptors occupy a somatodendritic subcellular position and are widely distributed in the cortex and all subfields of the hippocampus

(Morales et al., 1996). A study demonstrated that in the entorhinal cortex, 5-HT$_3$ receptors (probably located on GABAergic interneurons) tonically inhibit acetylcholine release (Ramirez et al., 1996). As a consequence, 5-HT$_3$ antagonists exert an indirect disinhibitory effect on acetylcholine release. Among the 5-HT ligands, only 5-HT$_3$ antagonists had previously been found to clearly improve learning and memory or to antagonise the effects of anticholinergics or age-induced memory loss in rodents and primates (Barnes et al., 1990). The cognitive-enhancing property of the 5-HT$_3$ receptor antagonist ondansetron in aged rats is significant and selective in cognitively impaired animals when compared to a cholinergic agonist (Fontana et al., 1995). However, ondansetron failed to attenuate the scopolamine-induced impairment in a Stone maze and has been abandoned due to lack of efficacy in AD patients (Teccott et al., 1998). It has been suggested that the effective action of 5-HT$_3$ receptor antagonists may be task-dependent and require chronic treatment (Costall & Naylor, 1997).

5-HT$_4$ receptors

The 5-HT$_4$ receptor is present in the limbic system, particularly in the septohippocampal formation. The number of hippocampal 5-HT$_4$ receptors is reduced in patients with AD (Wong et al., 1996). 5-HT$_4$ agonists increase the release of acetylcholine in the rat frontal cortex, but not in the striatum, and increase the extracellular level of 5-HT in the hippocampus (Eglen et al., 1995; Van Ge & Barnes, 1996). RS67333, a selective 5-HT$_4$ agonist, antagonises the performance deficit induced by atropine in rats on the Morris water maze (Eglen et al., 1995). This effect is reversed by RS67532, a selective 5-HT$_4$ antagonist. The 5-HT$_4$ agonist RS17017 has been found to enhance working memory in both young and aged monkeys performing a delayed matching-to-sample task (Terry et al., 1998).

5-HT$_6$ receptors

5-HT$_6$ receptors are the latest serotonin receptors to be identified by molecular cloning. Their high affinity for a wide range of drugs used in psychiatry, coupled with their distribution in the brain, has stimulated significant interest. The first behavioural studies of possible 5-HT$_6$-mediated function have been attempted using antisense oligonucleotides targeted to the 5-HT$_6$ receptor subtype (Bourson et al., 1995). In these studies, the rats exhibited a behavioural phenotype consisting of an increased number of yawns and stretches. This behaviour was blocked by atropine, suggesting a role of the 5-HT$_6$ receptor in the control of cholinergic neurotransmission. If so, then the 5-HT$_6$ antagonist might be useful in the treatment of depression, anxiety, and memory disorders. As the new pharmacological tools become widely available, a better understanding of the role of 5-HT$_6$ receptors in cognition will be sketched.

CHOLINERGIC RECEPTORS

Acetylcholine is the endogenous neurotransmitter at cholinergic synapses and neuroeffector junctions in the central and peripheral nervous systems. Cholinergic neurotransmission is mediated by two classes of receptors, the G-protein coupled muscarinic family and the ligand-gated ion channel nicotinic family. Most studies have focused on muscarinic acetylcholine receptor (mAChR) subtypes because this family has more established roles in central cholinergic transmission and functions such as learning and memory (Bartus et al., 1982). The molecular diversity of mAChRs became evident with cloning of a family of five genes, m1–m5, encoding highly related but distinct receptor subtypes (Bonner et al., 1987). The mAChR subtypes mediate a diversity of pre- and postsynaptic actions in hippocampus.

Most of the cholinergic fibres in the human cerebral cortex originate in the nucleus of Meynert (see Figure 4.4). A second major pathway leads from the septum to the hippocampus. Studies using lesions consistently showed that a destruction of "cholinergic areas" produced learning impairments parallel to those observed after administration of anticholinergic drugs. Aged rats, either impaired or non-impaired in a spatial memory task, showed

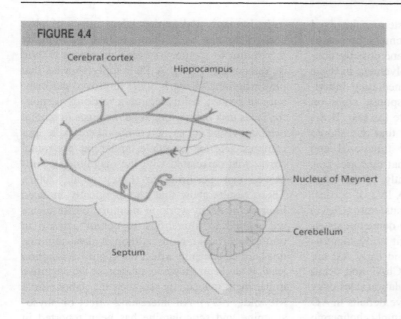

FIGURE 4.4

Cerebral cortex

Hippocampus

Nucleus of Meynert

Cerebellum

Septum

Sagittal section of the human brain showing the cholinergic pathways.

a pronounced sensitivity to pharmacological blockade of central cholinergic neurotransmission, which resulted in severe deficits in spatial navigation in the water maze (Nilsson & Gage, 1993). Since the same behavioural deficit was produced by cholinergic blockade in young rats with septal lesions, it was concluded that the impaired water maze performance seen in the aged rats during cholinergic blockade resulted from impaired function in the septohippocampal system. This pathway consists of cholinergic fibres originating in the medial septal nucleus and the nucleus of the diagonal band. These fibres synapse on cholinoceptive cells in the hippocampal formation (Lewis & Shute, 1967; Shute, 1975).

The discovery that cholinergic neurons in the basal forebrain degenerate in AD led to expanded research on the cholinergic pharmacology of learning and memory (Blokland, 1996; Fibiger, 1991). The cholinergic hypothesis states that basal forebrain neurons are severely affected in AD and this results in a cerebral cholinergic deficit that underlies the memory loss and other cognitive symptoms that are hallmarks of the illness (Bartus et al., 1982). Although there is no question that muscarinic receptor antagonists such as scopolamine can transiently impair performance on a variety of declarative memory tasks, there are

many apparent inconsistencies in the literature concerning the psychological mechanisms that underlie the observed deficits (Blokland, 1996; Fibiger, 1991). The very few psychopharmacological studies on the effects of scopolamine on non-declarative memory performance suggest that scopolamine primarily affects declarative and not procedural memory function (Nissen et al., 1987). This assumption is corroborated by the finding that procedural memory assessment did not differ in Alzheimer patients and healthy controls (Christensen et al., 1992).

Cholinergic neurotransmission has important roles in the brain (see Table 4.1). Animal studies

TABLE 4.1

Some roles and function of cholinergic neurotransmission in the brain

- Acetylcholine modulates attention, novelty seeking, and memory via basal forebrain projections to the cortex and limbic structures.
- Alzheimer's disease and anticholinergic delirium are examples of a deficit state. Blocking the metabolism of ACh by AChE strengthens cognitive functioning in Alzheimer's disease patients.
- Brainstem cholinergic neurons are essential for the regulation of sleep–wake cycles via projections to the thalamus.

suggest that the cholinergic system is involved in a variety of learning and memory processes such as acquisition, STM, LTM, and possibly consolidation. Furthermore, its involvement in these processes seems to be that of mediating inhibition, more likely sensory than response inhibition although it is difficult to separate the two. However, it is important to consider that one should not assume there is a unitary functional and anatomical cholinergic system that mediates performance behaviour independently of the other neurotransmitter systems. In AD, loss of cortical and hippocampal choline acetyltransferase (ChAT) activity has been correlated with dementia severity and disease. However, a recent study suggests that cognitive deficits in MCI and early AD are not associated with the loss of ChAT and occur despite regionally specific upregulation (DeKosky et al., 2002). The earliest cognitive deficits in AD involve brain changes other than simply cholinergic system loss. The cholinergic system is capable of compensatory responses during the early stage of dementia. Thus, the up-regulation in frontal cortex and hippocampal ChAT activity could be an important factor in preventing the transition of MCI subjects to AD (DeKosky et al., 2002). However, although many muscarinic effects have been identified in memory circuits, including a diversity of pre- and postsynaptic actions in hippocampus, the identities of the molecular muscarinic acetylcholine receptor subtypes responsible for any given memory function remains elusive. All five muscarinic acetylcholine receptor genes (m1–m5) are expressed in the hippocampus, and subtype-specific antibodies have enabled identification, quantification, and localisation of the encoded proteins. The m1, m2, and m4 muscarinic acetylcholine receptor proteins are most abundant in forebrain regions and they have distinct cellular and subcellular localisations suggestive of various pre- and postsynaptic functions in cholinergic circuits. The subtypes are also differentially altered in postmortem brain samples from Alzheimer's disease cases. Further understanding of the physiology of the failing synapses in Alzheimer's disease together with the development of new subtype-selective drugs may provide more specific and effective treatment of the disease.

In humans, a dose-dependent effect of physostigmine has been demonstrated, particularly in relation to memory storage processes (David & Yamamura, 1978). A PET study showed that physostigmine (1 mg/h dose) improved performance in healthy volunteers on a working memory for faces task and in functional changes in medial occipital visual cortex, left temporal cortex, hippocampus, anterior cingulate, and right prefrontal cortex that correlated with the magnitude of improved task performance (Furey et al., 2000). These results show that cholinergically induced improvements in working memory performance are related to alterations in neural activity in multiple cortical regions. Although physostigmine does not consistently affect the cognitive function level, it has been shown to antagonise the cognitive impairment induced by scopolamine (Ghoneim & Mewaldt, 1977). An interesting effect of physostigmine and scopolamine has been reported in trained chess players (Liljequist & Mattila, 1979). Physostigmine (20 mg/kg, IV) impaired the performance of good players but there was improved solution to chess problems in players with low performance levels. On the other hand, scopolamine (6 μg/kg, IV) impaired the performance of all players. When combined, the two drugs appeared to cancel out each other's effects. In studies of LTM, it has been demonstrated that cholinergic blockade impairs acquisition and active retrieval, but not recognition of information from durable storage (Rusted & Warburton, 1988). This is consistent with the hypothesis that the cholinergic system is controlling the functional state of the cortex for processing.

The use of the acetylcholine precursor choline, and the choline precursor lecithin has represented a rather controversial subject. There is little substantive evidence to support either dietary agent as a successful treatment modality in the senile dementias. However, stimulation of the cholinergic system, by administration of nicotine, improves performance on tasks of sustained and selective attention and facilitates durable storage of information under conditions of both pre- and post-trial administration (Rusted et al., 1995; Warburton, 1992). Nicotine is the prototypic nicotine acetylcholine receptor (nAChR) agonist, which may enhance cognition by direct effects on attention and by interacting with the presynaptic nAChR to facilitate the release of acetylcholine, glutamate, dopamine, norepinephrine, serotonin, and GABA, the transmitters that have been implicated in learning and memory (Samuels & Davis, 1998; Wonnacott, 1997; Wonnacott et al., 1989). Nicotine has been found to improve memory function in rats, monkeys, and humans (Levin, 1992; Wonnacott et al., 1989). Acute nicotine administration increases the activity of dopamine release in the striatum, whereas nicotinic antagonist administration has been found to inhibit dopamine release from both striatal and mesolimbic structures (Ahtee & Kaakkola, 1978; Haikala & Ahtee, 1988). D_2 receptors seem to be particularly important in this regard. Nicotine and nicotinic agents have been shown to possess neuroprotective effects, which are probably mediated by stimulation of the α7 nicotinic receptors. A study suggested that nicotine may act to inhibit the deposition of β-amyloid in vitro (Salomon et al., 1996). Nicotine can be administered to patients with cognitive dysfunction via skin patch or injection to assess efficacy, as a proof of principle, for possible treatments to improve cognitive performance.

GLUTAMATE RECEPTORS

Glutamate, the excitatory amino acid neurotransmitter, is one of the most important memory molecules because of its profound effect on the excitability of almost all neurons and the special role it plays in the hippocampus and medial temporal lobe structures (McDonald & Johnston, 1990). Current research has implicated glutamate and two of the major classes of glutamate receptors, NMDA and AMPA (α-amino-3-hydroxy-5-methylisoxazole-4-propionic acid), in long-term potentiation (LTP) induction and maintenance (Malenka & Nicoll, 1993). The efficiency of transmission at these glutamatergic synapses can either be weakened (long-term depression or LTD) by prolonged, low-frequency stimulation or strengthened (LTP) by brief, high-frequency stimulation of the afferent pathway (Malenka, 1994).

Two distinctive properties of the NMDA receptor is that it is both ligand and voltage gated and that its associated ionophore is more permeable to Ca^{2+} than to Na^+ and K^+ (Mayer & Westbrook, 1987). The NMDA receptors are heteromeric complexes consisting of subunit 1 (NR1) and various NR2 subunits (Nakanishi, 1992; Hollmann & Heinemann, 1994). The NR1 subunit is essential for channel function, whereas the NR2 subunit regulates channel gating and Mg^{2+} dependency (Monyer et al., 1992). Overexpression of the NMDA receptor 2B (NR2B) in the forebrains of transgenic mice leads to enhanced activation of NMDA receptors (Tang et al., 1999). Enhanced NMDA receptor function in the forebrain improves learning and memory (Tang et al., 1999). Although NMDA receptors are essential for the initiation of LTP, expression of LTP is mediated primarily by AMPA receptors. It was consistently reported that learning induced selective and region-specific increases in AMPA binding within hippocampus (Cammarota et al., 1995; Tocco et al. 1991). Evaluation of the full time course revealed enhanced AMPA binding in CA1 shortly after training (0.5–2 hours) followed by a longer lasting increase in CA2 and CA3 (0.5–24 hours and 0.5–48 hours, respectively) and in dentate gyrus (2–48 hours). The early CA1-specific increase in AMPA binding coincided with an increase in glutamate receptor 1 (GluR1) subunit expression (Bernabeu et al., 1997; Cammarota et al., 1998). Blockade of NMDA receptors in the amygdala prevents fear conditioning, suggesting that an NMDA-dependent form of synaptic plasticity in the amygdala might contribute to fear conditioning (Fanselow & Kim, 1994). Glutamate-mediated neurotransmission is significantly compromised in the neocortex and hippocampus of AD patients, a factor that may contribute to the cognitive deficits associated with the disease (Palmer & Gershon, 1990).

A study in rats implanted with minipumps containing a range of concentrations of an NMDA receptor antagonist D-AP5 (D-2-amino-5-phosphonopentanoate) and subjected to both behavioural and electrophysiological testing showed a significant impairment of spatial memory (Davis et al., 1992). The results clearly established that

D-AP5 impairs spatial learning in a linear dose-dependent manner, highly correlated with its corresponding impairment of hippocampal LTP *in vivo*. In healthy volunteers, ketamine, another NMDA receptor antagonist, uniquely induces positive and negative symptoms similar to those associated with schizophrenia (Newcomer et al., 1999). Ketamine decreases episodic memory performance by impairing encoding, but not retrieval processes (Hetem et al., 2000). Ketamine might mimic the memory impairment associated with acute, but not chronic forms of schizophrenia.

Several studies in a variety of non-human species (mice, rats, monkeys) have reported that the NMDA receptor transmitter system becomes hypofunctional with advancing age (Magnusson & Cotman, 1993; Saransaari & Oja, 1995). Age-related decreases in binding parameters have been reported, including decreases in binding to the NMDA site, using agonists and antagonists, in the neocortex and hippocampus of rodents and primates. Depending on species, this generally appears to reflect a decrease in the number of binding sites, rather than changes in affinity, and generally reflects greater decreases in the cortex than in the hippocampus. In humans, a 36% decrease in Bmax for [3H]MK801, reflecting a decreased number of PCP binding sites, was observed in a study that compared 10–20-year-olds and individuals in their 90s (Piggott et al., 1992). These results generally support the hypothesis that age-related decreases in NMDA receptor function could contribute to age-related decreases in memory and learning and suggest the need for further research in this area in clinical populations.

Long-term potentiation

Most of the electrophysiological studies in the hippocampus have focused on two phenomena, long-term potentiation (LTP) and long-term depression (LTD). LTP is broadly defined as a persistent increase in synaptic strength. It is usually seen experimentally as an increase in the excitatory postsynaptic potential (EPSP) response to a test stimulus following a brief, high-intensity stimulation of a presynaptic cell. Slow, weak stimulation of CA1 neurons also brings about long-term

changes in the synapses, in this case, a reduction in the sensitivity. This is called LTD. On the other hand, LTP refers to the increase in the amplitude of a glutamatergic excitatory postsynaptic response that is induced by repeated stimulation of that synapse or by coactivation of two sets of synapses in an associative manner (Bliss & Lomo, 1973). LTP is specific to the activated synapses and persists for many hours to days. LTP, as commonly studied in hippocampal slices, is only a model system for the far more complex and highly regulated long-term synaptic changes that may accompany learning in vivo in structures such as the hippocampus. Although LTP measured in vitro does not always faithfully reflect its in vivo counterpart, measurements of LTP in hippocampal slices remain a highly useful model. Many researchers consider LTP to be an excellent model of how memory might work at the cellular level (see Table 4.2).

Current research on the molecular basis of memory suggests that memories can be stored in nerve networks through changes in the strength of synapses (Bliss & Collingridge, 1993). Under normal conditions, synaptic excitation is exclusively mediated by glutamate receptors of the so-called AMPA class. Patterns of stimulation that elicit LTP, however, result in an activation of not only AMPA receptors but also the class of glutamate receptors sensitive to NMDA. These receptors are unique in that they permit a large influx of calcium ions into the postsynaptic cell. The mechanism by which memory storage takes place involves Ca^{2+}/calmodulin-dependent protein kinase II since it is localised at synapses, and the known autophosphorylation properties enable it to undergo long-term modification. Ca^{2+}/calmodulin-dependent protein kinase II is the principal protein of the postsynaptic density, a transmembrane structure that is physically linked to postsynaptic membrane in the specialised synaptic region. It is this region that probably contains the NMDA and non-NMDA channels that mediate synaptic transmission, which increases the likelihood of its importance in the role of controlling synaptic strength by phosphorylating synaptic channels and thus its implication in memory storage (Craig et al., 1993; Kennedy, 1993).

TABLE 4.2

A summary of some of the properties of long-term potentiation (LTP)

LTP	• Bliss and Lomo discovered LTP in the hippocampus in 1973 • A candidate cellular mechanism of memory • An enduring (>1 hour) increase in synaptic efficacy that results from high-frequency stimulation of an afferent (input) pathway
Experimental design	• Stimulate a bundle of presynaptic axons, e.g., hippocampal perforant path • Use extracellular recording electrode to measure monosynaptic EPSP, e.g., dentate gyrus
Events in LTP	• Calcium entry into the postsynaptic cell • Activation of the NMDA receptor • A variety of second messenger cascades • Enhanced presynaptic neurotransmitter release and/or increased receptor responses on the postsynaptic side
Calcium entry into the postsynaptic cell is necessary for LTP	• NMDA receptor activation opens a calcium channel • Calcium chelators block the induction of LTP • Increasing calcium concentrations induce LTP-like phenomenon
LTP requires a variety of second messengers	*Protein kinase C (PKC)* • PKC inhibitors block LTP • Increase in PKC after LTP *Ca2+/Calmodulin-dependent protein kinase II (CaM II)* • Inhibitors of CaM II block LTP
Ways to test LTP as a mechanism for learning and memory	• Correlate the ability to induce LTP with the ability to learn • Test the effect of LTP in induction on learning • Test the effect of learning on LTP • Test the effects of blocking LTP on learning and memory • Test memory of knockout mice that are defective in LTP
The ability to induce or sustain LTP is correlated with memory	• Spatial memory in developing rats emerges at the same time that the hippocampus is functional and capable of LTP • Old rats have poor LTP and poor spatial memory
Blockade of LTP can block memory	• NMDA antagonists block spatial memory • Many drugs impair both LTP and memory

The activation of NMDA receptors appears to stimulate an elevation in cyclic guanosine monophosphate (cGMP) in the hippocampus which can be blocked by inhibitors of nitric oxide synthase (East & Garthwaite, 1991). Given that stimulation of NMDA receptors results in elevated cGMP levels in the hippocampus and these elevations require calcium/calmodulin-dependent enzyme, it is likely that nitric oxide (NO) is involved in LTP (Snyder & Bredt, 1991). In support of this position inhibitors of nitric oxide have been shown to influence LTP (Haley et al., 1992). However, there have been several failures to confirm these results (Haley et al., 1993; Musleh et al., 1993). Although differences in temperature and stimulation protocols may have contributed to these negative results, they could also be explained by variations in NO synthase production within regions of the hippocampus (Holscher, 1997). A study that used a knockout strain of mice lacking both endothelial and neuronal NO synthase showed a marked

reduction in LTP, thus supporting the hypothesis that NO synthase is an important retrograde messenger in synaptic plasticity (Son et al., 1996).

The breeding of mice lacking the α-Ca^{2+}/calmodulin-dependent protein kinase II (gene knockout model) has made it possible to study the role of α-Ca^{2+}/calmodulin-dependent protein kinase II in behavioural learning and memory (Silva et al., 1992). The gene knockout model in mice has made it possible to examine the relationship of the two second-messenger kinases (the calcium/calmodulin kinase and the tyrosine kinase) to LTP in the hippocampus and learning in the intact animal. Ablation of the gene for the alpha subunit of the Ca^{2+}/calmodulin kinase leads to loss of LTP. Animals deficient in this gene also show a deficiency in spatial learning. On the other hand, no deficit in learning simple visual discrimination tasks, which does not involve the hippocampus, was observed. Similarly, ablation of *fyn*, the gene coding for a cytoplasmic tyrosine kinase, results in blunting of LTP and learning. Recently, a preclinical study also confirmed that mice lacking NMDA receptors in hippocampal area CA1 are deficient in spatial memory and that they also have non-spatial memory deficits which are overcome by environmental enrichment (Eichenbaum & Harris, 2000). By electron microscopy, environmental enrichment was shown to increase the number of synaptic connections within hippocampal area CA1 in normal mice, and also in the mutant mice, even without NMDA receptors. Enrichment improved learning performance in control mice and almost eliminated the memory deficits observed in the CA1 NMDA receptor-knockout mice. These data represent a beginning in the attempt to bridge molecular mechanisms to memory and cognitive experience.

The discovery of relatively selective NMDA antagonists therefore provides a means, at least in principle, by which to assess the role of hippocampal LTP in normal memory formation. Synaptic potentiation can be divided into several temporal stages that use different mechanisms: short-term potentiation (STP), which lasts only 15–30 minutes, early phase LTP (E-LTP) which is stable for up to 2–3 hours, and late-phase LTP (L-LTP) which can last for 6–8 hours in hippocampal slices. The induction of E-LTP involves the activation of NMDA receptors and a subsequent postsynaptic increase in Ca^{2+} (Bliss & Collingridge, 1993; Huang et al., 1996). This increase in Ca^{2+} activates a number of protein kinases and other enzymes (e.g., adenylate cyclase) thought to trigger the biochemical cascade of events that result in the long-lasting enhancement of synaptic transmission. Both presynaptic and postsynaptic mechanisms can play a role, depending on the location of the pathway in the brain (Nicoll & Malenka, 1995). Postsynaptic mechanisms involve the combined action of NMDA and non-NMDA-type glutamate receptors that are activated by glutamate. The NMDA-type glutamate receptor is special because it requires the combined actions of glutamate and glycine accompanied by depolarisation of the electrical potential of the neuronal membranes it resides. Depolarisation occurs if non-NMDA receptors called AMPA receptors are stimulated vigorously. Infusion of drugs that block NMDA receptors into the hippocampus of rats blocks both NMDA LTP and spatial memory (Steele & Morris, 1999). STP and E-LTP do not require gene expression or new protein synthesis, whereas L-LTP does (Bailey et al., 1996).

NMDA receptor blockers were shown in many cases to also disrupt memory formation (Davis et al., 1992). Using the competitive NMDA antagonist AP5 (D, L-2-amino-5-phosphonopentanoic acid), it was shown that a dose of the D-isomer was sufficient to block LTP and induced a selective impairment in spatial but not non-spatial learning or memory (Morris et al., 1986). Subsequent experiments indicated that the drug impairs acquisition rather than recall of spatial memory and that the drug dose required to induce a clear behavioural impairment closely matches the dose required to block LTP in hippocampus (Morris, 1989). There are now several demonstrations that intraventricular administration of the NMDA-antagonist D-AP5 can resemble the effects of hippocampectomy (Steele & Morris, 1999). Both manipulations impair spatial learning or memory in reference memory designs, while sparing visual cue-guided task performance on the elevated T-maze, although AP5 administration, unlike hippocampectomy or fornix section, leaves task performance normal unless an additional retention delay is incorporated (Aggleton et al., 1986; Rawlins & Olton, 1982). In reference memory designs, NMDA antagonists can selectively impair acquisition while sparing task performance (Shapiro & Caramanos, 1990). In working memory designs, drug administration can impair performance of differential reinforcement of low rates and T-maze alternation tasks that have already been acquired (Rawlins, 1985; Tonkiss & Rawlins, 1991; Tonkiss et al., 1988). Such impairment would be expected if the drugs impaired a temporarily memory store in hippocampus that is necessary for successful performance of these tasks.

There are strikingly parallel and persisting increases in glutamate AMPA receptor binding on hippocampal membranes in the hippocampal subfields in both eyeblink conditioning (well-trained animals) and in vivo expression of LTP by stimulation of the perforant path projection to hippocampal dentate gyrus. The pattern of increased binding is similar in both paradigms (Baudry & Davis, 1991; Maren et al., 1993; Tocco et al., 1992). Glutamate NMDA receptors play the critical role in induction of LTP (at least in dentate and CA1) and also appear to be involved in acquisition of the trace eyeblink CR (Baudry & Davis, 1991; Thompson et al., 1990).

At least three protein-synthesis-dependent waves of memory consolidation, which take place within the hippocampus, have been proposed (Riedel & Micheau, 2001). These waves lead to the production of many novel proteins. Considering the consolidation of the memory trace, increases in AMPA receptor expression may be the products of immediate and intermediate waves of memory consolidation over minutes or days. Longer-lasting memories with extended consolidation periods, in addition, draw on a third wave. It is believed that metabotropic glutamate receptors are a product of this late wave and enable long-term consolidation of memory (Riedel & Micheau, 2001).

Several studies reported that infusions of the AMPA receptor antagonist 6-cyano-7-nitroquinoxaline-2, 3-dione (CNQX) into the amygdala prior to retention tests impair inhibitory avoidance performance and fear-potentiated startle (Izquierdo et al., 1993; Kim et al., 1993).

Synaptic re-entry reinforcement hypothesis

At the molecular level, LTM is widely believed to be expressed in the form of synaptic structural changes resulting from a single molecular cascade. It is postulated that learning triggers a molecular cascade consisting of receptor activation, transient changes in levels of protein phosphorylation, new protein synthesis, and gene expression. This single cascade hypothesis has guided research in the past decades. However, a single molecular cascade triggered within the hippocampus during learning might not be sufficient to explain the consolidation of LTM in the brain. For example, hippocampus-mediated consolidation of long-term memories occurs over a time-scale of weeks in animals and years in humans (Haist et al., 2001; Squire et al., 1989). Synaptic structures in the adult brain are not stationary; synaptic receptors and proteins are turned over regularly. Thus, it is not clear whether structural changes resulting from a single molecular cascade can be sustained in the presence of such dynamic turnover processes

for a long period to complete cortical memory consolidation.

Recently, animal studies have shown that the formation of long-lasting memories was severely disrupted if the CA1-hippocampal NMDA receptor was knocked out selectively during the initial post-training weeks (Shimizu et al., 2000). On the other hand, inducible knockout of the CA1-hippocampal NMDA receptor during the fourth week post-training had no effect on the retention or retrieval of 1-month-old hippocampal memories. In consistency with lesion studies, these data may suggest that the hippocampus becomes dispensable once memories have been sufficiently consolidated in the cortex (Anagnostaras et al., 1999). Considering that the activation of the NMDA receptors in CA1 is not crucial for basal synaptic transmission, these observations have led to the synaptic re-entry reinforcement (SRR) hypothesis (Shimizu et al., 2000; Wittenberg & Tsien, 2002). This hypothesis suggests that memory consolidation requires multiple rounds of NMDA-receptor-dependent synaptic modification to reinforce the synaptic changes initiated during memory acquisition. The hippocampus, by forming its reinforced memory traces, could act as a coincidence-regenerator to provide coherent input inducing reinforcement of synaptic connections between cortical neurons via cortical SRR. It can be conceived that one triggering mechanism for the SRR could be conscious recall. If a particular event is recalled more frequently, it will be remembered more efficiently and for longer. Another triggering mechanism could be the subconscious reactivation of the hippocampus/cortex during sleep. Although the SRR process was initially described for the consolidation of hippocampus-dependent memory traces, the same process might occur in other brain regions involved in hippocampus-independent LTM formation.

GABAergic RECEPTORS

Gamma-aminobutyric acid (GABA) is the primary mediator of inhibitory neurotransmission in the central nervous system. GABA-A receptors are found especially in brain and neural tissue.

They represent hetero-oligomeric protein complexes consisting of GABA and benzodiazepine receptors coupled to an integral chloride channel. There are some indications that the central GABAergic system may play a key role in cognitive processes, including memory formation and consolidation (Johnston, 1992). The GABA-A agonist muscimol administered to entorhinal cortex was reported to induce amnesia or block memory of habituation and inhibitory avoidance in animals (Izquierdo & Medina, 1991). On the other hand, GABA antagonists like bicuculline were found to be strong memory-activating agents (Cruz-Morales et al., 1993).

Indirect GABA modulators such as benzodiazepine agonists have also been studied. Experimental and clinical data showed that benzodiazepines are generally strong amnesic agents (Lister, 1990; Venault et al., 1986). Benzodiazepines are known to act on the $GABA_A$ receptor complex. It is well established that benzodiazepines impair memory (Izquierdo et al., 1990; Lister, 1985). Moreover, benzodiazepine antagonists or inverse agonists exert memory-enhancing properties (Venault et al., 1986).

Ethanol is known to stimulate GABAergic transmission through enhancing the effects of GABA, thus producing anxiolytic-like effects and deleterious effects on memory and learning (Nevo & Hamon, 1995).

NEUROSTEROID AND PEPTIDE RECEPTORS

Improved awareness of the distribution and function of steroid receptors in the brain has led to increasing recognition of direct effects of corticosteroids on the CNS, including effects on mood, behaviour, brain excitability, and cognition. Recent studies suggest that steroids produced locally in the brain (termed neurosteroids) may regulate neuronal excitability (Mellon, 1994). As for the peptides, the discovery during the 1980s of numerous novel peptides in the brain, each capable of regulating one or another aspect of neural function, produced considerable excitement among neuroscientists (see Guillemin, 1978; Hökfelt

et al., 1994). It has been difficult to develop synthetic agonists or antagonists that will interact with specific receptors for peptides. However, the recent development of non-peptide antagonists of cholecystokinin, neurotensin, and members of the tachykinin family offer promise of future success (Hökfelt et al., 1994; Steinberg et al., 1994).

Dehydroepiandrosterone (DHEA) and dehydroepiandrosterone sulfate (DHESS), largely adrenally derived substances, serve as precursors for both androgenic and estrogenic steroids. Their effects, depending on their absolute levels in blood in man and stimulated release by ACTH, are reduced in ageing and during prolonged acute stress (Parker et al., 1985; Roberts, 1986). A preclinical study showed that post-training intracerebroventricular (ICV) administration of DHEA in dimethylsulfoxide (2 µl) prevented the amnesia for footshock active avoidance training (FAAT) caused by the same volume of dimethylsulfoxide alone (Flood et al., 1988). DHEA significantly enhanced retention of FAAT in weakly trained mice whether injected ICV or subcutaneously (SC) immediately post-training or given in the drinking water for a 2-week period. In the latter instance, DHEA was shown to facilitate retention of FAAT without enhancing acquisition. DHEA administered ICV occluded the amnestic effects of anisomycin (inhibitor of protein synthesis) and scopolamine (muscarinic cholinergic antagonist). There was a time-dependence of the facilitatory effects of post-training ICV administration of DHEA on retention of FAAT, significant enhancement of retention being observed when it was given either immediately (within 2 min) or at 30 and 60 min after training, but not at 90 or 120 min. DHEA given ICV also improved retention for step-down passive avoidance. However, anecdotal reports from patients do not support the hypothesis that DHEA improves memory. It can be stated that the effect of DHEA on cognition remains controversial. It seems fair to say that, at this point, there may be a relationship between DHEA but there is no evidence to suggest that DHEA is an alternative to the pharmacological treatment of memory impairment.

The anti-µ-receptor-mediated action of κ-opioid receptors has also been reported in learning and memory processes in the brain. In behavioural studies, selective activation of the μ-receptor by morphine impairs working-memory associated spontaneous alternation performance in mice, but dynorphin, at otherwise ineffective doses on the control performance, significantly improves the drug-induced memory impairment (Itoh et al., 1994). Dynorphin also improves memory dysfunction in the animal model of amnesia (Ilyutchenok & Dubrovina, 1995; Ukai et al., 1997). These dynorphin effects are reversed completely by pretreatment with nor-binaltorphimine.

Studies in vitro on neurons in the hippocampus have shown that μ- and κ-receptor agonists have opposite actions on LTP: opioids acting on the μ-receptor facilitate the induction of LTP, while U69593 or dynorphin inhibits LTP in a norbinaltorphimine-reversible manner (Simmons & Chavkin, 1996; Weisskopf et al., 1993). It is not known how these cellular actions of μ- and κ-receptor agonists are related to the modulation of memory processes by these agonists at the behavioural level.

Opiate receptor agonists, when administered after training in a learning task, impair retention, while opiate receptor antagonists, such as naloxone, enhance retention (Castellano, 1975). Opiate antagonists (naloxone) enhance retention of recently acquired information when injected into the amygdala (Introini-Collison et al., 1989). The evidence that opioid peptides and opiates inhibit the release of norepinephrine suggests that opiate agonists and antagonists may influence memory storage by modulating the release of norepinephrine within the amygdala. β-adrenergic antagonists infused into the amygdala block the memory-enhancing effects of naloxone administered either systemically or intra-amygdally (Introini-Collison et al., 1989; McGaugh et al., 1988).

Nerve growth factor (NGF)-related systems in brain, particularly with respect to NGF-responsive cholinergic neurons located in the basal forebrain, appear to play an important role in learning and memory processes (Nilsson et al., 1992). NGF is the original member of a growing family of polypeptide growth factors—including brain-derived neurotrophic factor (BDNF) and neurotrophins 3 (NT-3) and 4, 5 (NT-4/5) referred to collectively as the neurotrophins (Lindsay et al., 1991b; Terry

et al., 1993). A study reported that the selective destruction of over 95% of NGF receptor-containing neurons in the basal forebrain (using a cytotoxin coupled to an antibody raised against the low affinity NGF receptor) was sufficient to produce a significant spatial memory deficit in rats (Nilsson et al., 1992). While these findings more correctly implicate NGF-responsive systems as opposed to cholinergic systems in learning and memory, it is true that over 90% of the NGF receptor-containing neurons present in the basal forebrain are cholinergic, suggesting that the loss of sufficient numbers of forebrain cholinergic neurons may by itself lead to important deficits on at least some learning and memory tasks. Intracerebroventricular infusions of NGF improve performance on certain learning and memory tasks in aged animals perhaps via increases in cholinergic activity mediated by direct effects on basal forebrain cholinergic neurons (Fischer et al., 1991; Williams et al., 1991). These data support the concept that factors which affect NGF or NGF receptor expression are likely to have an effect on learning and memory processes. A decrease in NGF activity may well contribute to age- and disease-related cognitive decline. Recent studies indicate that NGF receptor and its high-affinity signal transducing receptor (transmembrane protein tyrosine kinase or trkA) are reduced in end-stage AD (Chu et al., 2001; Mufson et al., 2000). Individuals with MCI and AD displayed significant decreases in trkA mRNA relative to aged-matched controls, indicating that alterations in trkA gene expression occur early in the disease process (Chu et al., 2001). The magnitude of change was similar in MCI and AD cases, suggesting that further loss of trkA mRNA may not necessarily be associated with the transition of individuals from non-demented MCI to AD. Nevertheless, the lass of trkA mRNA in MCI and AD was significantly correlated with function on a variety of episodic memory tests (Chu et al., 2001).

Glucocorticoids

Central actions of corticosteroids, which are secreted from the adrenal glands in high amounts after stress, are exerted via two receptors: the high-affinity mineralocorticoid (MR) and the lower-affinity glucocorticoid receptors (GR) (de Kloet, 1991; McEwen et al., 1986). The two receptors are involved in specific aspects of information processing. MRs play a role in behavioural reactivity during novel situations (Oitzl et al., 1994). Importantly, activation of GRs caused by the stress associated with a learning tasks facilitates consolidation of information (Sandi & Rose, 1994; Sandi et al., 1997; Shors, 2001). Consequently, if one interferes with GR activation that occurs in association with a learning task by treatment with exogenous GR antagonists or by knocking out the GR, consolidation is impaired (Oitzl et al., 1997; Roozendaal & McGaugh, 1997; Tronche et al., 1999). Although the role of MR and GR activation in cognition is well established, the molecular mechanism underlying corticosteroid actions on learning and memory is presently not entirely clear. Task-related facilitating effects of corticosterone on spatial memory indeed depend on DNA binding of the glucocorticoid receptor rather than on protein–protein interactions of the receptor with other transcription factors (Oitzl et al., 2001). Although it cannot be excluded that both processes may be involved in a coordinated fashion, obviously interrupting the DNA-binding capacity of the receptor is sufficient to induce cognitive impairment.

A likely mechanism for hormones (e.g., the excessive and prolonged release of glucocorticoids in patients without a clear organic base for amnesia) to affect memory is during prolonged stress. These hormones have numerous receptors especially in memory and affect related regions such as the hippocampus and amygdala (Haas & Schauenstein, 1997). Indeed, prolonged, severe stress, as in combat veterans, may even lead to brain damage exactly in these medial temporal regions implicated in memory processing (Markowitsch, 1995). Cumulative exposure to high glucocorticoid levels throughout life disrupts electrophysiological function, leading to atrophy and ultimately death of hippocampal neurons, all of which can cause severe cognitive deficits in hippocampus-dependent learning and memory (Squire, 1992). Training in aversively motivated learning tasks is also known to stimulate the

adrenocortical system, resulting in increased plasma levels of corticosterone (Roozendaal et al., 1991). There is extensive evidence that glucocorticoids modulate memory consolidation (Roozendaal & McGaugh, 1996; Sandi & Rose, 1994).

The amygdala is involved in mediating the memory-modulating effects of glucocorticoids (Roozendaal et al., 1996). A study was designed to examine whether the glucocorticoid-induced effects on memory storage depend on β-adrenergic activation within the amygdala in rats (Quirarte et al., 1997). Microinfusion (0.5 μg in 0.2 μl) of either propranolol (a non-specific β-adrenergic antagonist) or atenolol (a $β_1$-adrenergic antagonist), administered bilaterally into the basolateral nucleus of the amygdala (BLA) before training blocked the enhancing effect of posttraining systemic injections of dexamethasone (0.3 mg/kg) on 48-hour memory. Such effects were also observed after microinfusion of zinterol (a $β_2$-adrenergic antagonist) in similar conditions. These findings provide evidence that glucocorticoids and the noradrenergic system are involved in modulating memory storage. Further, they indicate that the BLA is a locus of interaction between these two systems in regulating memory. Systemic injections of dexamethasone enhanced avoidance retention when administered immediately after training. As dexamethasone has a high affinity for glucocorticoid receptors (GRs), these findings are consistent with the hypothesis that long-term storage of information is strengthened by posttraining activation of GR-sensitive pathways (Lupien & McEwen, 1997).

Both acute and chronic cortisol elevations induce cognitive deficits in human populations (Lupien & McEwen, 1997; Wolkowitz et al., 1997). A study was designed to investigate whether prolonged cortisol elevation and memory impairment in normal elderly humans correlate with a decrease in hippocampal volume (Lupien et al., 1998). It was demonstrated that elderly human subjects showing increasing cortisol levels over years with currently high cortisol levels are impaired on hippocampal volume. They have a 14% reduction in hippocampal volume, compared to elderly subjects who show decreasing cortisol levels over years with currently moderate cortisol levels. The magnitude of the decrease in hippocampal volume in the increasing/high cortisol group was comparable to that previously reported for elderly subjects with age-related MCI (Wolkowitz et al., 1997). Therefore, increases in cortisol secretion in later life may initiate MCI or mild cognitive-related hippocampal atrophy.

The hippocampus is not only a target for gluco-corticoids but is also involved in their regulation (Jacobson & Sapolsky, 1991; Sapolsky, 1992). Lesions to the hippocampus are associated with increased basal corticoid levels and the hippo-campus has been implicated in regulating gluco-corticoid release during stress (De Kloet, 1991). Thus, hippocampal atrophy is both a result of and a contributory cause of increased basal gluco-corticoid levels.

AD patients show an inverse relationship be-tween mean 24-hour cortisol levels and severity of cognitive decline, which is associated with pro-gressive hippocampal degeneration (Davis et al., 1986).

Vasopressin and oxytocin

Vasopressin and related peptides are ancient hormones in evolutionary terms and they are found in species that do not concentrate urine. Vasopressin and oxytocin are synthesised in the perikarya of magnocellular neurons in the supra-optic nucleus and paraventricular nucleus; the two hormones are synthesised predominantly in separate neurons. It is likely that vasopressin plays a role as a neurotransmitter and/or neuromodulator (Gash et al., 1987). Vasopressin may participate in the acquisition of certain learned behaviours (Dantzer & Bluthé, 1993). Data suggest vaso-pressin has a role in memory processes through secretion into the third ventricle with receptors in the periventricular grey matter (the same highly thiamine-dependent tissue that is damaged in Korsakoff's syndrome) (De Wied et al., 1975). Exogenous vasopressin and its analogues, when injected intraventricularly, facilitate the consolida-tion of learned responses. Vasopressin injected 3 hours before or after a task involving new learning increases resistance to extinction. The time course

of vasopressin's effects suggests that it affects the consolidation phase of new learning. Vasopressin also facilitates passive avoidance behaviour, while oxytocin has the opposite effect (De Wied & Croiset, 1991; Pitman et al., 1993).

In animal studies, vasopressin has been shown to facilitate memory consolidation, presumably through its selective action on the hippocampus, and the suggestion of its application as a thera-peutic medium in memory dysfunction has been made (Legros et al., 1978; Oliveros et al., 1978). The application of vasopressin to studies of memory function in man, without clinical or measured biochemical changes, has suggested that intranasal installation of 16 IU of lysine-8-vasopressin significantly improved the perform-ance of 12 patients on attention tasks, motor performance, and visual retention, recognition, and recall (Legros et al., 1978). Vasopressin has also been used with some success in the treatment of alcoholic as well as post-traumatic amnesias (Oliveros et al., 1978). Vasopressin has been used with reported success in the treatment of Korsakoff's syndrome (LeBoeuf et al., 1978). The treatment involves nasal spray administration of the vasopressin three times per day. Replication of these data is necessary. Recently, a study de-signed to examine the influence of post-learning administration of vasopressin (40 IU, intranasally) on the consolidation of declarative memories in healthy young human volunteers (aged 19–27 years) during different intervals of sleep and waking was performed (Gais et al., 2002). Although no effect of vasopressin on memory consolidation was observed, the EEG activity indicated a significant arousing influence of vasopressin. These data may suggest that if vasopressin affects memory function, it might do so primarily at the stage of encoding of the materials to be learned but it leaves unaffected processes of consolidation.

This research approach has provided for a "vasopressin" hypothesis of Korsakoff's syndrome where the amnesia results from low levels of vasopressin due to periventricular tissue damage. Both effector as well as some receptor grey matter is destroyed, to varying degrees, by the characteristic lesions of Korsakoff's syndrome, thereby influencing the potential responsiveness of such sites to therapeutic vasopressin. Amnesic syndromes so common in older adults seem correlated with lowered blood levels of vasopressin in men and women over 50 years old.

Selective cholecystokinin agonists

Several behavioural studies have reported an involvement of cholecystokinin (CCK)-related peptides in the modulation of learning and memory processes. Most used memory tests based on aversive or appetitive stimuli. CCK8 and caerulein have been shown to protect against amnesia induced by electroconvulsive shock, scopolamine, NMDA antagonists, or protein kinase inhibitors in the passive avoidance test (Itoh & Katsuura, 1987, 1989; Katsuura & Itoh, 1986; Takashima et al., 1991). Peripheral injection of CCK8 was also shown to improve consolidation memory processes in a rat memory model on habituation of exploratory activity (Voits et al., 1995). In contrast to these peptides devoid of receptor selectivity, CCK4, which interacts with the CCKB receptor type, was reported to produce memory impairment in the passive avoidance response after central or systemic injection and to potentiate scopolamine-induced amnesia in the radial maze (Hadjiivanova et al., 1995; Harro & Oreland, 1993). In addition, the selective CCKA antagonist, devazepide, injected intraperitoneally, was found to induce a deficit in memory in the Morris water maze and in the passive and active avoidance tests (Itoh et al., 1992). Similar results were obtained using CCK4, CCK8, and devazepide in a memory model based on olfactory recognition in the rat (Lemaire et al., 1992, 1994). It was therefore suggested that an endogenous balance could exist between CCKA-mediated facilitative and CCKB-mediated disruptive effects in memory processes.

Indeed, the modulation of memory processes by CCK through CCKB2 receptors could offer a new perspective in the treatment of attention/memory disorders associated with ageing or with neurodegenerative diseases. The brain CCK8 contents are reduced in aged subjects (Greenstein et al., 1991). Furthermore, it was shown that a CCK analogue, ceruletide, increased electrophysiological markers of attention (Schreiber

et al., 1995). In Alzheimer patients, CCK8 concentrations are decreased in some cerebral cortex regions (Mazurek & Beal, 1991).

Relationships between the cholecystokininergic system and other neurotransmitters in memory processes have also been described. The increase in spontaneous alternation behaviour induced by BC264 was abolished by selective dopamine D_1 (SCH23390) and D_2 (sulpiride) antagonists (Ladurelle et al., 1997). In the two-trial memory test, the opposing effects induced by BC264 and BC197 were suppressed by dopamine D_2 antagonists or agonists, respectively, but not by dopamine D_1 antagonists or agonists suggesting that the effects of both CCKB agonists are mediated by dopamine D_2 receptors in this test.

PROTEIN KINASES, GENE TRANSCRIPTION, AND PROTEIN SYNTHESIS

Distinct cellular and molecular mechanisms underlie different temporal phases of hippocampal LTP. Induction requires elevated postsynaptic calcium, early maintenance is mediated by the elevation of protein kinases and later phases depend on gene transcription and protein synthesis (Bliss & Collingridge, 1993; Frey et al., 1996; Lynch et al., 1983; Soderling & Derkach, 2000). Consistent with the assumption that synaptic plasticity provides the neural basis for long-term information storage in the brain, several forms of LTM involving hippocampal and cortical structures also depend on protein synthesis (Meiri & Rosenblum, 1998).

One of the signalling cascades implicated in the early stages of hippocampal LTP and certain forms of learning and memory is the protein kinase C (PKC) pathway (Van der Zee et al., 1997). PKC is a phospholipid-dependent enzyme that plays a central role in activity-dependent neuronal plasticity. In view of the many similarities between the hippocampal biochemistry of memory and that of LTP, the suggestion arose that PKC may be involved in memory formation. In a study that evaluated the levels of conventional PKC isozymes (α, βI, βII, γ) in synaptic plasma membrane (SPM) fractions isolated from hippocampus, rats were subjected to a one-trial inhibitory avoidance paradigm (Paratcha et al., 2000). It was observed that at 0, 30, and 120 minutes after training, there was a significant increase in the total amount of PKCβ1 (Soderling & Derkach, 2000). Densitometric analysis of the immunoblots showed an increase of 142 ± 11% at 0 min, 193 ± 16% at 30 min, and 156 ± 6% at 120 min after training relative to shocked control values. No changes were found in PKCβI level in SPM fractions of the shocked animals relative to naive control values. In addition, bilateral micro-injections of a fairly selective inhibitor of PKCβ1 isozyme into the CA1 of the dorsal hippocampus produced amnesia when given 10 min before training, or 50, 110, but not 170 min after training. These data demonstrate the participation of PKCβI in the early synaptic events responsible for the acquisition and consolidation of an inhibitory avoidance learning, and suggests a putative role of this presynaptic isozyme in associative learning and memory.

The evidence also suggests that protein kinase A (PKA) and phosphatases PP1 and PP2A "gate" the long-term stability of synaptic changes (Bailey et al., 1996; Silva et al., 1998). For example, inhibitors of PKA impair early stages of LTP. This inhibition can be overcome by inhibitors of phosphatases PP1 and PP2A (calcineurin) (Blitzer et al., 1995). The data suggest that at low levels of cAMP, the calcium/calmodulin-dependent phosphatase calcineurin dephosphorylates target proteins, including PP1 phosphatase inhibitor 1 (I-1). Dephosphorylation by calcineurin inactivates PP1 phosphatase inhibitor 1 and allows PP1 in turn to dephosphorylate a wide range of target proteins such as the calcium/calmodulin-dependent kinase II that are required for LTP induction. Therefore, phosphatase activity seems to block long-term synaptic changes. In contrast, when the concentration of cAMP (as produced by calcium-stimulated adenylyl cyclase) is high, PKA promotes long-term synaptic changes by phosphorylating and therefore activating PP1 phosphatase inhibitor 1, which then blocks PP1 (Blitzer et al., 1998).

Recent work suggests that the mitogen-activated protein kinase/extracellular-regulated kinase (MAPK/ERK) cascade, a complex kinase cascade implicated in cell differentiation and proliferation, is essential for long-term synaptic plasticity and for certain types of learning (Atkins et al., 1998; Blum et al., 1999). Although MAPKs were initially identified as mediators of cell differentiation and proliferation in mitotic cells, ERK1 and ERK2 are most highly expressed in the postmitotic neurons of the adult mammalian CNS (Boulton et al., 1991; Fiore et al., 1993). Immunohistochemistry studies have demonstrated that in neurons, ERK2 is localised to the soma and dendritic trees of neurons in the cortex, hippocampus, striatum, and cerebellum (Fiore et al., 1993). Several additional members of the MAPK family have been cloned including p38/HOG, JNK/SAPK (c-jun- N-terminal kinase/stress-activated protein kinase and ERK5) (Han et al., 1994; Kyriakis et al., 1994; Zhou et al., 1995). Although many scientists use the terms ERK and MAPK interchangeably, it is important to differentiate among the various members of the MAPK family that are regulated by distinct mechanisms and have different effectors, giving each pathway a distinctive function in the cell. The term MAPK now refers to the superfamily, with ERKs, JNK/SAPKs, and p38s as the main subfamilies.

Atkins et al. (1998) reported that ERK2 phosphorylation was increased in rat hippocampus 1 hour after training using either a cued or cued-plus-contextual conditioning paradigm. It is important to note that this increase was not due to the handling of the rats or to the footshock itself. Thus, the MAPK cascade is required for fear conditioning—an inhibitor of ERK activation, SL327, led to a blockade of memory formation upon testing with either the cued or the contextual conditioning paradigms. These results showed that the MAPK cascade is required for long-term fear memory. In subsequent studies, these initial findings have been confirmed and greatly extended using intraventricular injection of an inhibitor of ERK activation in the rat, intra-amygdalar infusion of an inhibitor of ERK activation in the rat, and using systemic administration of SL327 in the mouse (Schafe et al., 1999, 2000; Selcher et al., 1999). Moreover, there is abundant crosstalk between kinase pathways, suggesting that MAPK/ERK may be a point of convergence integrating PKC, PKA, and calcium/calmodulin-dependent kinase signals in addition to the activity of individual signalling systems (Roberson et al., 1999). In cell lines, MAPK/ERK translocates to the nucleus once it has been activated, in which it can regulate transcriptional activity of many immediate early genes (Treisman, 1996). A recent study confirmed that MAPK/ERK activation is required for LTP-dependent transcription regulation (Davis et al., 2000). Induction of LTP in the dentate gyrus in vivo leads to rapid phosphorylation and nuclear translocation of MAPK/ERK. Following a similar course, the two downstream transcriptional targets of MAPK/ERK, cAMP responsive element binding (CREB) and the ternary complex factor Elk-1, a key transcriptional regulator of serum response element (SRE)-driven gene expression, were hyperphosphorylated. It is suggested that LTP is regulated by two parallel signalling pathways, the MAPK/ERK-Elk-1 pathway targeting SRE and the MAPK/ERK-CREB pathway targeting cAMP response element (CRE).

Transcriptional activation and protein synthesis in the amygdala have proven essential for the formation of fear memory (Bourtchuladze et al., 1994; Schafe et al., 1999, 2000). In addition, fear memory can be enhanced through localised overexpression in the basolateral complex of the mouse amygdala (BLA) of the transcription factor CREB at the time of conditioning (Josselyn et al., 2001). A study that described changes of gene expression that occur in the BLA during the formation of fear memory showed that the formation of Pavlovian fear memory is associated with changes of gene expression in the BLA, which may contribute to neural plasticity and the processing of information about both conditioned and unconditioned fear stimuli (Stork et al., 2001). In particular, a key enzyme of monoamine metabolism, aldehyde reductase, and the protein sorting and ubiquination factor praja1 showed pronounced and learning-specific induction 6 hours after conditioning training.

Long-term memory

The molecular pharmacological approach has also led to a dissection of the mechanisms involved in STM and LTM processes in CA1 and the entorhinal cortex (Izquierdo et al., 1998). Several treatments given into CA1 or the entorhinal cortex were found to block STM without altering LTM, which points to a separation of the two systems. Other studies point to molecular linkages between STM and LTM (Izquierdo et al., 1998). Clearly, all this is beyond the reach of lesion or imaging studies, and is of great potential clinical interest.

Previous pharmacological studies showed that the synthesis of new proteins is a pivotal requirement of LTM (Davis & Squire, 1984). Evidence from a variety of species suggests that LTM formation reflects a synaptic growth process mediated by a cascade of gene expression. The MAPK/ERK cascade is also involved in the formation in the insular cortex of long-term memories for taste (Hettinger & Frank, 1992; Rosenblum et al., 1993). The insular cortex is thought to be the location of the consolidation of long-term taste memory; this memory is usually tested using the conditioned taste aversion paradigm. Berman et al. (1998) have shown that presentation of an unfamiliar taste leads to activation of ERK in the insular cortex within 30 minutes. Furthermore, they showed that inhibition of ERK activation in the insular cortex impairs conditioned taste aversion when tested up to 120 hours after training. These data suggest that ERK is involved in insular cortex-dependent LTM.

Cyclic AMP responsive element binding protein

Cyclic adenosine 3', 5'-monophosphate (cAMP) signalling has a key role in determining which synaptic changes become stable and long lasting (Bailey et al., 1996; Silva et al., 1998). Studies with *Aplysia*-cultured neurons suggested that cAMP responsive element binding protein (CREB) is one of the transcription factors activated during the induction of LTM (Dash et al., 1990). CREB is a family of transcription factors that regulate the synthesis of a number of proteins, including inducible transcription factors, when phosphorylated (CREB-P). According to this hypothesis, learning-induced activity in the appropriate neural circuits activates second-messenger pathways including cAMP. One target of this biochemical activation is CREB. Depending on the mix of activator and repressor isoforms of CREB, particular training protocols can release CREB activator from its inhibitory constraints, thereby initiating the remaining cascade of gene-regulatory events. Hence, CREB acts as a molecular switch for LTM formation. Studies in mice have also demonstrated the requirements for CREB in several different forms of memory (Bourtchuladze et al., 1994; Kogan et al., 1997). Genetic and pharmacological studies in mice and rats suggest that CREB is required for a variety of complex forms of memory, including spatial and social learning, thus indicating that CREB may be a universal modulator of processes required for memory formation (Silva et al., 1998). CREB's involvement in memory formation is not restricted to certain forms of memory, such as aversive conditioning, but appears to have a much broader impact on memory formation. Studies of CREB function are starting to identify not only the mechanisms responsible for its activation in neurons, but also the molecular processes that its transcriptional products trigger.

The role of CREB during memory formation has received further support from experiments in rats. In a study in which antisense oligonucleotides specific for CREB transcripts were injected directly into the hippocampus, it was shown that LTM of another hippocampus-dependent task (Morris water maze) was disrupted (Guzowski & McGaugh, 1997). Similarly, LTM of conditioned taste aversion was disrupted by injecting these oligonucleotides into the amygdala (Lamprecht et al., 1997). A recent study measured the phosphorylated CREB (CREB-P) in the hippocampus following inhibitory avoidance training in normal and fornix-lesioned rats (Taubenfeld et al., 1999). It was observed that in unoperated rats immediately after training, hippocampal CREB-P increased to 152.3 ± 12.4% of levels in control animals that entered the dark chamber but received no shock. Thus persistent elevation in CREB-P was specifically associated with consolidation of inhibitory avoidance memory. Further analysis also showed that unlike levels in controls, the levels of CREB-P in hippocampal of rats with fornix

lesions did not increase either 0 or 6 hours after training (108.7 ± 11.2%, 80.1 ± 6.7). Immunohistochemistry confirmed that fornix lesions prevented CREB-P induction by training in CA1 and dentate gyrus, as no induction was noted in any hippocampal subregions in lesioned rats. Thus, fornix lesions prevent hippocampal CREB phosphorylation induced by inhibitory avoidance training.

Early genes

Following induction of LTP in the dentate gyrus, a cascade of genes is activated at different time points (Davis & Laroche, 1998). The transient activation of immediate early genes is believed to be a critical step in these successive waves of gene expression. Zif268 (also known as krox-24, EGR-1, or NGFI-A) is one such immediate early gene, encoding a zinc finger transcription factor (O'Donovan et al., 1999). Recent studies have provided evidence that Zif268 mRNA is upregulated in the hippocampus and in the behaving rat following exposure to a novel stimulus and in the inferior temporal gyrus of the monkey during associative learning (Hall et al., 2000; Miyashita et al., 1998). It appears that activation of Zif268 is required for the expression of long-term but not short-term synaptic and behavioural plasticity (Jones et al., 2001).

DISCUSSION

LTP is operationally defined as a long-lasting increase in synaptic efficacy which follows high-frequency stimulation of afferent fibres. Other characteristics of LTP, including its rapid induction, persistence, and correlation with natural brain rhythms, provide circumstantial support for this connection to memory storage. One extensive review states that LTP is an increase in synaptic efficacy at monosynaptic junctions, occurring as a result of afferent fibre tetanization (Teyler & DiScenna, 1987). Although these definitions are generally accepted and often used, they do not capture the range of conditions that are considered to reflect the induction of LTP. Much of the research aimed at elucidating the role of LTP in memory has focused on the hippocampal formation, presumably because LTP was discovered there and for some time was considered unique to that region. Since then, it has been determined that LTP at two of the major synaptic regions in the hippocampus (the dentate gyrus and area CA1) is, in part, dependent on calcium influx through the NMDA type of glutamate receptor and channel. Thus, some researchers have focused on the role of NMDA-dependent forms of LTP in memory, often stating that LTP is a NMDA-dependent phenomenon (Johnston et al., 1992). To add to the confusion, even in the dendate gyrus and CA1, LTP can be induced in the absence of activation of the NMDA receptor provided there is an alternate means of intracellular calcium accumulation, such as strong depolarisation and subsequent influx of calcium through voltage-dependent channels or the release of Ca^{2+} from intracellular storage pools (Bortolotto et al., 1995; Wierazko & Ball, 1993). Thus, defining LTP based on its NMDA-dependence seems unnecessarily limiting and may be misleading with regard to a role for LTP in memory.

The notion that LTP was a substrate of learning and memory arose, in part, from the proposition that enhancing synaptic transmission would be an effective way to "construct" and retrieve specific memories in a neuronal network (Hebb, 1949; James, 1892). If this suggestion was correct, one would expect that enhancing synaptic transmission would improve memory formation. Recently, this hypothesis was tested with a class of drugs known as ampakines. These drugs enhance synaptic transmission by increasing the mean open time of the AMPA type of glutamate receptor. It was observed that the drugs facilitated learning in a number of tasks, from olfactory discrimination to maze learning (Staubli et al., 1994; 1995). In a classical conditioning task, it was found that rats treated with the drug displayed an enhanced responsiveness to discrete sensory cues. When the sensitisation to cues was removed (by lowering the intensity of the conditioned stimulus), facilitated acquisition of conditioned eyeblink response occurred (Shors et al.,

1995). It is noted that the drug was injected peripherally and thus the increase in synaptic transmission occurred throughout the brain (Staubli et al., 1995). Thus, the drug could not by itself form the "memory" because it would not affect specific synapses. It could nonetheless prime the network such that subsequent memories are more easily induced. These results are consistent with the idea that enhancing synaptic neurotransmission (inducing LTP-like phenomena) increases the neural representation of cues in the brain, which incidentally improves learning when the cues are relevant. Consistent with the more general assumption that the efficacy of synaptic transmission should directly influence the rate of learning, a strong correlation between the strength of the synaptic integration between the two sensory systems and the capacity to form an association between stimuli presented in those sensory modalities was also reported (Matzel et al., 1996).

Traumatic stress can result in long-term changes in brain regions involved in memory (Bremner et al., 1995a, b). Monkeys and other animal species exposed to extreme stress have been found to have damage to the CA2 and CA3 subfields of the hippocampus (Uno et al., 1989). Such damage is due to a relationship between high levels of glucocorticoid and stress. These structural changes are associated with deficits in memory. It is well established that memory storage is also modulated by post-training systemic injections of drugs affecting opiate, GABAergic, and cholinergic systems (McGaugh & Cahill, 1997).

Concerning the effects of GABAergic drugs on memory, hypotheses that a degree of anxiety or stress may be necessary for learning may be drawn (Izquierdo & Medina, 1991). It would appear that memories being labile immediately after acquisition are susceptible to both deleterious and facilitatory influences. This will finally determine which memory is eventually stored and therefore memory consolidation is likely to be a mechanism of brain integration between memory and anxiety. Like the action of exogenous GABA-inhibiting drugs, this endogenous process has an impact on balance between central inhibitory and facilitatory systems and therefore may serve as a principal mechanism of memory activation and regulation.

Norepinephrine probably has an important function in the memory functions of the hippocampus due to its concentration and wide distribution. The neuropharmacology and neurophysiology of norepinephrine-dependent limbic systems may be the key to a unified theory of memory consolidation. Extensive evidence suggest that adrenergic, glucocorticoid, opioid, and GABAergic influences on memory storage are mediated by norepinephrine release within the amygdala. Several neuromodulatory systems regulate memory storage by influencing the release of norepinephrine and the subsequent activation of muscarinic receptors within the amygdala. The amygdala appears as a critical site for integrating the interactions of several neuromodulatory systems influencing memory storage. The evidence that LTP can be induced in the amygdala, as well as that drugs that block LTP also attenuate fear-based learning when administered into the amygdala prior to training, suggests that neural changes mediating fear conditioning may be located within the amygdala

(Fanselow & Kim, 1994; LeDoux, 1995; Maren & Fanselow, 1995).

Studies of molecular mechanisms of learning and memory have illustrated the existence of both positive and negative regulators of synaptic plasticity and memory storage. Kinases such as the calcium/calmodulin-dependent protein kinase II, the PKA, and the MAPK are positive regulators, critical for the initiation of many forms of synaptic plasticity and for learning and memory (Abel et al., 1998; Lee et al., 2000). On the other hand, phosphatases such as the calcium/calmodulin-dependent calcineurin and PP1 are thought to be negative regulators, inhibiting both synaptic plasticity and memory storage (Ikegami & Inokuchi, 2000). Initial clues as to the antagonistic role of kinases and phosphatases came from pharmacological and genetic studies indicating that PKA is required for the expression of persistent LTP because of its role in suppressing an endogenous phosphatases cascade (Blitzer et al., 1995; Abel et al., 1997).

5

Drug-induced Memory Alteration

INTRODUCTION

Over the past three or four decades, there has been increasing interest in the neuropharmacological regulation of memory. This field received a considerable impetus in the 1980s, with the identification of possible cognitive enhancing agents or "smart drugs". The group of preparations already observed to display memory-enhancing effects in experimental learning situations is very large with diverse mechanisms of actions. Among others, the list includes cholinergic agonists at the muscarinic and nicotinic receptors, cholinesterase inhibitors such as physostigmine, calcium channel blockers such as nimodipine, neurotransmitters such as norepinephrine, $GABA_B$ receptor blockers such as CGP 36742, peptides such as vasopressin and corticotropin, glucose, and not least, the large group of so-called nootropics including oxiracetam and piracetam (Beversdorf et al., 1998; Delis et al., 1987; Frith & Happé, 1994; Hermelin & O'Connor, 1970; Lord et al., 1994; O'Connor & Hermelin, 1967; Roediger & McDermott, 1995).

Empirical findings have established that increases in blood glucose levels subsequent to peripheral endocrine events may contribute towards the enhancement of memory storage processes (White, 1991). Glucose is the major source of energy for the brain and is essential to the normal functioning of the central nervous system (Sieber & Traystman, 1992). Glucose crosses the blood–brain barrier by facilitated transport and it is utilised in a wide range of biochemical processes. For example, it is a substrate for the synthesis of the neurotransmitter acetylcholine, which has been widely associated with learning and memory (see Drachman & Leavitt, 1974; Hasselmo & Bower, 1993). More generally, it has been suggested that blood glucose regulation may be a useful indicator of an individual's level of cognitive functioning (Hall et al., 1989; Scholey et al., 2001). There is evidence from studies of ageing, age-related illnesses, and diabetes that impaired glucose regulation may be associated with deficits in cognitive functioning, with particular emphasis placed on deficits in memory functioning (Ryan & Williams, 1993). Glucose administration can enhance memory in elderly rats and humans and glucose can attenuate the amnesia induced in rats given scopolamine, a cholinergic antagonist (Hall et al., 1989; Wenk, 1989; Winocur, 1995). In addition, glucose administration significantly enhanced the performance of participants with

AD on several memory functions: for example, orientation, recall, narrative prose, and word recognition (Manning et al., 1993). A study showed that elevated insulin without hyperglycaemia enhances memory in adults with AD and indicates that insulin is essential for hyperglycaemic memory facilitation (Craft et al., 1999).

A large variety of various other drugs and nutrients may have a negative impact on memory. Benzodiazepines, the most prescribed anxiolytics, cause anterograde amnesia (Cahill et al., 1995; Izquierdo & Medina, 1991, 1997). Other $GABA_A$-receptor complex-binding drugs like barbiturates, muscimol, and ethanol also present anxiolytic and some amnesic properties (Devinsky, 1995; Commissaris, 1993; Izquierdo & Medina, 1997; Media et al., 1996). This double effect is also common to competitive and non-competitive NMDA-receptor antagonists, anxiolytic glycine-site antagonists at the NMDA-receptor, and β-adrenergic blockers (Anthony & Nevins, 1993; Cahill & McGaugh, 1996; Ohno et al., 1996).

The progression to cocaine addiction and its chronically relapsing nature is often attributed to frequent and intense bouts of drug craving that are triggered by environmental and internal stimuli (Pickens & Johanson, 1992). Places, people, actions, and sensations associated with past drug use and their collection as episodic memories represent conditioned cues that trigger drug craving as a conditioned response.

BENZODIAZEPINES

The administration of benzodiazepine antagonist flumazenil or inverse agonists methyl- and butyl-beta-carboline 3-carboxylate resulted in significant improvement of memory and learning in various learning tests. Benzodiazepines' influence on memory for inhibitory avoidance training appears to be mediated by the amygdala (Izquierdo et al., 1990). Infusions of the benzodiazepine midazolam into the amygdala induce memory impairment, and intra-amygdala infusion of the GABAergic antagonist bicuculline methiodide blocks the benzodiazepine effect (Dickinson-

Anson et al., 1993). In a study, differential effects of pharmacologically induced changes in dopaminergic, GABAergic, and cholinergic activity in the brain on declarative (object and face recognition, immediate and delayed word recall) and procedural memory processes (compensatory tracking) were investigated (Rammsayer et al., 2000). In a double-blind design, one of 3 mg of haloperidol, 11 mg of midazolam, 1 mg of scopolamine, or placebo were administered to 80 healthy volunteers randomly assigned to one of the four drug conditions. Although all three drugs produced a detrimental effect on immediate and delayed word recall, recall performance was substantially more impaired by the benzodiazepine midazolam than by either haloperidol or scopolamine. While recognition of faces was affected by none of the drugs, performance on object recognition was significantly decreased by midazolam as compared to placebo. All drugs markedly impaired procedural learning but again the observed effect was most pronounced with midazolam. Additional analyses of measures of subjective activation, cortical arousal, and psychomotor performance argued against the assumption that the observed memory-impairing effects were secondary to drug-induced sedation. The overall patterns of results revealed those memory processes that are much more susceptible to changes in GABAergic than in dopaminergic or cholinergic neurotransmitter activity.

The benzodiazepines might simulate, or model, the form of memory dysfunction (e.g., impaired acquisition of information in explicit memory tasks, normal priming and skill learning, and normal semantic memory) that is expressed in the typical amnesic patient. There is some evidence that benzodiazepines may impair some frontal functions such as recency judgements (File et al., 1992). However, whereas benzodiazepines have been repeatedly shown to spare various forms of motor, perceptual, and cognitive skill learning, studies of the effects of these drugs on perceptual priming and on retrieval processes are controversial. While diazepam seems to be devoid of action on perceptual priming, lorazepam does have a deleterious effect, suggesting that the two benzodiazepines might have differential memory effects (Sellal et al., 1992). In addition, there is evidence that some benzodiazepines may have some disruptive effect of information from episodic memory, even though this retrieval effect is much smaller than the impact of benzodiazepines on acquisition functions. These effects that are expressed at the time of retrieval depend on the task and level of training, and the time at which memory is tested. There was also some evidence that benzodiazepines may even disrupt retrieval of information from semantic memory (File et al., 1992). However, this possibility needs further investigation and the effect is likely to be only minor. It is suggested that the apparent sparing of semantic memory after administration of benzodiazepines could relate to the fact that benzodiazepines mainly impair acquisition. Unfortunately, there have been no systematic experiments on their effects on acquisition of semantic memory.

Many benzodiazepines can provoke dose-dependent anterograde amnesia. They impair episodic memory but spare STM, semantic memory (as assessed by word-fluency tasks), and procedural memory (Curran, 1991; Ghoneim & Mewaldt, 1990; Lister, 1985). Episodic memory impairment is due to a disturbance of the acquisition, but not the retrieval, of new information (see Table 5.1 for some examples of drugs affecting/improving memory). The benzodiazepines also produce impairments in other aspects of cognition, particularly psychomotor performance (Hindmarch, 1980; Johnson & Chernik, 1982).

Benzodiazepine receptor ligands produce a consistent "birectional" effect on memory. In human and animal studies, inverse agonists such as the β-carbolines improve memory performance in selected paradigms while certain compounds with agonist activity (similar to benzodiazepines) impair memory (Duka, 1991; Holmes & Drugan, 1991; McNamara & Skelton, 1992). Benzodiazepine receptor antagonists (with little or no intrinsic activity) such as flumazenil block the amnestic effects of the benzodiazepines (Curran & Birch, 1991). In fact, it has been reported that flumazenil when given alone may enhance memory performance in rats perhaps because of the antagonism of naturally occurring benzodiazepines-like substances by flumazenil (Prather et al., 1992). The amnestic effects of the benzodiazepines may be

localised neuroanatomically in the amygdala, a structure densely populated with GABA receptors and believed to be involved in the mediation of anxiety as well (Tomaz et al., 1992).

The temporary anterograde amnesia induced by single doses of these drugs has long been viewed positively by anaesthetists, who administer benzodiazepines as premedications and appreciate the fact that patients remember little of their surgical experience. Much research interest has been shown in understanding the amnesic properties of the benzodiazepines, and the question of how single doses of these drugs impair certain aspects of memory whilst sparing others has been greatly studied. These drugs impede the acquisition of new information (anterograde amnesia). The degree and duration of these effects following an acute dose depends on several factors (e.g., dosage and route of administration, the memory assessment used, the times postdrug at which information is presented and retrieval is required, characteristics of the subject/patient involved). In general, tasks requiring remembering a few items for a period of seconds such as digit span and block span are unaffected by benzodiazepines. However, in other complex tasks where information needs to be manipulated whilst it is retained, a reduction in the speed with which information is processed, rather than qualitative effects on components of working memory, is observed (Curran, 1991).

Short-term storage and working memory

The benzodiazepines do not appear to affect the storage capacity of STM as measured by relatively simple tests such as digit recall (Curran et al., 1987).

Most studies of working memory have not found benzodiazepine-induced deficits in storage capacity (Curran et al., 1991; Rusted et al., 1991). However, drug-induced decrements in speed have been consistently reported (Taylor et al., 1967). Benzodiazepines definitely produce impairments in attention and vigilance that have been strongly correlated with the amnesic effects of the drugs in some studies (Preston et al., 1989; Rich & Brown, 1992).

TABLE 5.1

Some drugs that may impair or improve memory

Drugs	Type of memory impaired/improved	Comments	References
IMPAIRED MEMORY			
Lorazepam and diazepam	Explicit and implicit memory	Volunteers were randomly allocated to oral dose of lorazepam (2.5 mg), diazepam (0.3 mg/kg, 18–27 mg) and placebo. Testing commenced 90 minutes following drug administration. Diazepam and lorazepam significantly impaired performance on explicit memory measures, compared to placebo.	Le Roi et al., 1999
Intrahippocampal DPAT, intra-entorhinal CNQX, MUS, & NAN	Block STM without altering LTM	Rats were tested twice to see whether they had retained the memory of electric footshock: once at 15 hours after training, to measure STM, and once at 24 hours after training to measure LTM. The results show for the first time that STM and LTM mechanisms are separated.	Izquierdo et al., 1998
Methylenedioxymethamphetamine (MDMA or "Ecstasy")	Verbal and visual memory	24 abstinent MDMA users and 24 control subjects were compared on several standardised tests of memory (WMS–R, Rey auditory verbal learning test, & the RCF). Abstinent MDMA users have impairment in verbal and visual memory and the extent of impairment correlates with the degree of MDMA exposure.	Bolla et al., 1998
Ethanol and temazepam	LTM	In this double blind five-period design, volunteers took part in five sessions. At least 2 days apart, they received by mouth either ethanol calculated to produce peak blood ethanol concentrations of 80 mg/100 ml, ethanol at 0.75 the dose used in the previous condition, temazepam, 20 mg, temazepam 15 mg and placebo. Dissociations occur between ethanol and temazepam, ethanol producing more errors at a similar degree of slowing performance.	Tiplady et al. 1998
IMPROVED MEMORY			
Citicoline	Facilitates recovery of function and cognition after traumatic brain injury	Description of individual cases in whom the administration of citicoline (cytidine-diphosphocholine) appeared to enhance recovery after TBI. Patients significantly recovered after taking citicoline so that memory and new learning greatly improved and their cognitive status may be considered entirely functional and above average.	Spiers & Hochanadel, 1999 Alvarez et al., 1997

CNQX: AMPA (α-amino-3-hydroxy-5-methyl-4-isoxazole propionic acid) receptor antagonist 6-cyano-7-nitro-quinoxaline-2, 3-dione, 0.5 μg; MUS: GABA$_A$ (γ-aminobutyric acid type A) receptor agonist muscimol, 0.5 μg; DPAT: the serotonin 1A receptor agonist 8-hydroxy-2-(di-n-propylamino) tetralin, 2.5 μg; NAN: the serotonin 1A receptor antagonist 1-(2-methoxyphenyl)-4-(4-(2-phthalimido) butylpiperazine, 2.5 μg.

Long-term storage

Concerning the long-term effects of benzodiazepines on memory of anxious patients, a study of long-term users (> 6 months) of benzodiazepines indicates that a measure of cumulative intake on benzodiazepines correlated negatively with level of learning over trials in a word recall task (Golombok et al., 1988). Benzodiazepines block the improvement in performance that normally accompanies practice on cognitive tasks (Curran et al., 1994; Tata et al., 1994).

The most consistently demonstrated effect of the drugs across multiple studies is a dose-dependent anterograde impairment in the acquisition of newly learned information into episodic stores of explicit memory (Cole, 1986). Thus, benzodiazepines impair performance on tasks assessing episodic memory. The more demands a task places on episodic memory, the more apparent are the deteriorating effects of benzodiazepines (Curran et al., 1998). This can be demonstrated on both visual (e.g., picture recognition) and verbal (e.g., word list, paired-associate learning) tests. If individuals are required to process information at different depths, from the relatively superficial to the relatively deep, benzodiazepines will result in fewer words being subsequently recalled, but the pattern of recall will be the same as normal (Curran et al., 1998). However, following acquisition, forgetting rate is not affected by benzodiazepines (Brown et al., 1983). Deficits in the encoding of contextual information (e.g., a person can remember another person's face or a new fact but cannot recall where they met that person or learnt that fact, a phenomenon also known as source amnesia) have been suggested as a possible mechanism for benzodiazepine-induced impairment of episodic memory (Brown & Brown, 1990). The various approaches to differentiate sedation amnesia support the notion that benzodiazepines have specific effects over and above their sedative effects. In a study that compared three dose levels of flunitrazepam (1, 2, and 4 mg), it was found that memory impairments occurred even at the lowest dose, whereas accompanying attentional impairments were produced only at the higher doses (Smirne et al., 1989).

Despite their impairing effect on the learning of new information (anterograde amnesia), benzodiazepines do not produce retrograde impairments of memory (information acquired before the drug is taken) (Ghoneim & Mewaldt, 1990; Polster, 1993). Retrieval of well-established knowledge (semantic memory) is generally intact following drug administration. Benzodiazepines also do not affect procedural learning in perceptual-learning tasks (e.g., mirror learning) or in anagram-solving tasks; learning curves on drugs tend to parallel those on placebo (Weingartner & Wolkowitz, 1998). However, although there is some evidence that conceptual priming is intact following benzodiazepines, fitting with the hypothesis of preservation of semantic memory, lorazepam produced impairment in perceptual priming tasks, which depend on a different memory system, the perceptual representation system (Brown et al.,

1989). This is in contrast to other benzodiazepines (alprazolam, triazolam, diazepam, oxazepam, midazolam) which have been found to leave perceptual priming intact (Stewart et al., 1996; Vidailhet et al., 1994).

Intravenous diazepam has been studied in patients prepared for oral surgery (Driscoll et al., 1972). There was evidence for an anterograde amnesia on the day of the surgery, for oral injections (53.9%) and use of an oral elevator (40.3%). When tested on a 1-week postsurgical follow-up visit, there was 70.6% amnesia for the oral injection. Psychomotor performance using a modified Bender Gestalt test was also carried out on this study. A peak psychomotor deficit was observed after diazepam injection, with complete recovery by 1.5 hours after injection. This finding partially separates the psychomotor components of the cognitive task from the consolidation process involved in the operative situation. A study designed to investigate the degree of amnesia seen in patients undergoing minor oral surgery with intravenous midazolam sedation showed that overall, the sedated patients exhibited significantly greater amnesia for the surgical procedure (Nadin & Coulthard, 1997). However, this study also confirmed that midazolam can produce profound anterograde amnesia in many patients and that the degree of memory loss can be high for both artificial and meaningful stimuli. This amnesia may be unpredictable and reliable amnesia should not therefore be guaranteed for all patients. Memory loss appears to be related to the dose of midazolam administered rather than the level of sedation achieved. Higher doses (> 5 mg) were associated with more consistent amnesia.

In a study designed to investigate the effects of diazepam and lorazepam in 48 volunteers, it was reported that both diazepam and lorazepam significantly impaired performance on explicit memory measures, compared to the placebo group (Le Roi et al., 1999). Only lorazepam significantly impaired performance on implicit memory task. Impairments in both implicit and explicit measures were reported to be due to drug effects rather than drug-induced sedation. It was also suggested that, possibly, a differential cortical distribution of lorazepam and diazepam receptors could account for their differential amnesic effects.

In a study that used tasks involving free and cued recall and mental imagery, there was a significant deficit in the learning of new material with a dose of 0.3 mg/kg of diazepam (Petersen & Ghoneim, 1980). However, there was no appreciable impairment of recall for previously acquired tasks. The effects of intravenous diazepam appear to show a consistently rapid-onset (2–3 minutes), brief (20–30 minutes), anterograde amnesia with the duration of the amnesia being increased as a function of increases in dose (Gregg et al., 1974). This effect may be compared with that of lorazepam which when given orally as well as intravenously has a delayed onset of effect (30–40 minutes) and produces a prolonged amnesia lasting up to 270 minutes. As compared with other preoperative benzodiazepines, lorazepam produced the greatest frequency of failure to recall the journey to the operating room (10% with 2 mg, 65% with 4 mg), and to recall the intravenous injection (10 and 70% respectively for 2 and 4 mg). Whereas diazepam (10 or 20 mg, IV) exerts its greatest amnesic effect (85%) by 60 minutes after administration, as does flunitrazepam (0.5 or 1 mg), lorazepam (1, 2, or 4 mg) has its greatest effect (35–90%) by 90 minutes postinjection (McKay & Dundee, 1980).

Flunitrazepam, principally used as a hypnotic, impaired morning recall of several tasks presented when the subjects were awakened during the night (Bixler et al., 1979). It is apparent that the benzodiazepines used as either preanaesthetic agents or hypnotics can exert potent anterograde memory effects.

Benzodiazepines do not alter retrieval function from episodic memory for information learned prior to or during drug exposure (Lister & File, 1984; Preston et al., 1988). In those studies that have reported such deficits, it appears that these findings were likely the result of interpretation and scoring procedures (Block & Berchou, 1984). Similarly, the drugs do not impair recall from context-independent semantic memory (knowledge memory) (Weingartner et al., 1992).

Procedural memory

Procedural memory does not seem to be affected by some benzodiazepines (Lister & File, 1984).

Most studies have reported that the benzodiazepines do not affect implicit memory performance whereas a few others have observed some effects (Brown et al., 1989; Fang et al., 1987; Knopman, 1991; Weingartner et al., 1992). The reasons for these conflicting results are not understood but may be due to differences in the methodologies employed to assess implicit memory function.

Perceptual priming studies show that some benzodiazepines such as lorazepam and midazolam impair perceptual priming while others such as diazepam and oxazepam have little or no deleterious effect (Curran & Birch, 1991; Curran & Gorenstein, 1993; Danion et al., 1989; Knopman, 1991). The deleterious effect of lorazepam is not due to a contamination of the implicit task by explicit memory and it seems to be independent of sedation. Lorazepam has been shown to impair priming by disturbing the acquisition but not the retrieval of information (Vidailhet et al., 1994). These results suggest that some but not all benzodiazepines do impair the functioning of the specialised processing structures that underlie the "perceptual representation system" (Sellal et al., 1992).

BARBITURATES

Pentobarbital has been rather generally applied to behavioural studies in animals and man with a variety of effects. Rats given pentobarbital (13 mg/kg) acquired conditioned avoidance responses without any drug effect but avoidance behaviour after acquisition was reduced if the drug administration was continued (Holmgren & Condi, 1964). The memory span in man was reduced by pentobarbital (100 mg, IV) (Quarton & Talland, 1962; Talland & Quarton, 1965).

Secobarbital, particularly when administered at bedtime, has been shown to exert anterograde amnesic effects as assessed the following morning (Bixler et al., 1979). After being given 100 mg of secobarbital, subjects were later awakened, asked to complete four tasks (e.g., sharpen a pencil, describe a familiar topic, write a cheque, describe an important event) and were then allowed to return to sleep. The next morning the subjects were awakened and asked to recall the tasks. A significant recall decrement occurred among those subjects that were given secobarbital at bedtime.

In general, except for some studies in which a state of barbiturate dependency constitutes a basis for the effect of an agent on learning or memory, barbiturates tend to impair acquisition and interfere with the retention of learned behaviour. With barbiturates the performance of learned responses, which depend on a motor component, appears to be facilitated whereas a verbal or associative component of acquired behaviours appears impaired. The extent of impairment in the latter case seems to relate to blood levels of the barbiturate at those times that performance is measured.

ANTICHOLINERGICS

Anticholinergic drugs have been shown to impair STM processes in both animals and man (Sitaram et al., 1978). Considerable psychopharmacological evidence shows that antagonists of the muscarinic acetylcholine receptor interfere with memory function in humans, primates, and rodents (Aigner et al., 1991; Kopelman, 1986). Drugs such as scopolamine, which attenuate CNS cholinergic function through non-selective blockade of muscarinic receptors, impair performance on a variety of memory tasks and are useful tools for studying the role of acetylcholine in memory function. The dose–response relationship for memory impairment by anticholinergic drugs is an increasing function across the clinically used dose range (McEvoy & Freter, 1989). In a study in healthy young human volunteers, it was demonstrated that intravenous scopolamine impaired LTM while leaving immediate memory intact (Drachman, 1977). This deficit was reversed by physostigmine, a short-acting acetylcholinesterase inhibitor that enhances synaptic cholinergic function. In another study in normal volunteers, scopolamine caused significant dose- and delay-dependent impairments resembling those associated with normal ageing and AD (Robbins et al., 1997).

Studies in normal controls suggest that the major effects of anticholinergic drugs are on STM, especially on the encoding and storage of

information (Caine et al., 1981; Drachman, 1977; Drachman & Sahakian, 1979). In a review, it was concluded that there is clear evidence for an anticholinergic information storage impairment (Warburton, 1987). However, evidence of a retrieval rather than an encoding problem caused by anticholinergic-induced disruption of the organisation of material at input has also been provided (Rusted & Warburton, 1989). Whatever phase of processing may be defective, there is significant impairment in episodic memory for visuospatial material and for verbal material, whether written or spoken (Kopelman, 1986). A serial position effect on list learning has been reliably reported. Recall performance is disrupted for items in the early and middle portions of the list, with no significant impairments at the end (Frith et al., 1984; Jones et al., 1979; Mewaldt & Ghoneim, 1979). Recall performance has shown some selective disruption for lists of unrelated words, though not for lists of related words (e.g., with similar meanings or sounds) (Frith et al., 1984). A substantial literature now exists in humans and animals demonstrating that cholinergic agonists can reverse the effects of scopolamine on LTM tasks and that cholinergic lesions or anticholinergic drugs impair performance on such tasks. However, long-term anticholinergic therapy probably does not result in irreversible damage to STM (van Herwaarden et al., 1993). Memory improves significantly after withdrawal of long-term anticholinergic therapy.

In a study designed to differentiate between sedative and anticholinergic effects of antidepressants (amitriptyline 37.5, 70 mg; trazodone 100, 200 mg; viloxazine 100, 200 mg and protriptyline 10, 20 mg) in acute dosage, it was reported that although both amitriptyline and trazodone impaired performance on episodic memory tasks, the effect of amitriptyline was significantly greater and this may reflect specific anticholinergic action over and above global sedative effects (Curran et al., 1988). The two more sedating compounds viloxazine and protriptyline produced global impairments on test of attention, manual motor speed, recording skills, and primary memory. It has been suggested that anticholinergics should be stopped when an old patient with such treatment develops chronic memory disturbance and/or intelligence impairment (Nishiyama et al., 1998). Anticholinergic therapy should not be resumed on patients who have suffered from chronic memory disturbance induced by previous anticholinergic therapy.

BETA-BLOCKERS AND ALPHA-2 AGONISTS

Propranolol, a beta-adrenergic blocker, impaired normal subjects' recall of emotionally arousing (but not neutral) elements of a story (Cahill et al., 1994). It was suggested that adrenergic function in the amygdala mediates memory for emotional material and that beta-blockers may produce poor memory particularly for emotionally valent information.

Studies in man suggest that unlike benzodiazepines and anticholinergics, clonidine, an alpha-2 agonist, did not impair free recall of word lists, nor did it impair STM or retrieval from remote semantic memory (Frith et al., 1984). However, it did induce a marked impairment of paired associate learning particularly when novel associations had to be learned. After treatment with clonidine, subjects typically gave inappropriate associations. The pattern of performance is similar to that observed in amnesic patients. The patients are unable to learn verbal paired associates if they are unrelated but learn as well as controls when words are combined according to their semantic or phonetic properties.

CORTICOSTEROIDS

Cognitive deficits following acute administration of corticosteroids have been described in preclinical studies and in humans (Lupien & McEwen, 1997; Lupien et al., 1995). Prolonged exposure to high concentrations of glucocorticoids can site-specifically accelerate pathological changes in the hippocampus and may impair spatial memory in rats (Luine et al., 1994; Sapolsky & McEwen, 1986). Even brief exposure to glucocorticoids can diminish feedback sensitivity to the hypothalamic–pituitary–adrenal axis leading to higher circulating

glucocorticoid concentrations and potential hippocampal damage (Sapolsky et al., 1990). These effects are probably not a direct consequence of glucocorticoid exposure but rather the result of a number of possible cellular insults, including inhibition of glucose transport into hippocampal neurons and glia, the potentiation of excitatory amino acid killing of hippocampal neurons, and most pertinent to the effect on memory, the modulation of both hippocampal LTP and primed burst potentiation by adrenal steroids (Diamond et al., 1992; Pavlides et al., 1993; Watanabe et al., 1992). There is sufficient evidence from clinical studies to suggest that memory impairment may result from both endogenous and exogenous hypercortisolaemia. Memory impairment is evident in patients receiving high-dose steroid therapy for various medical problems and in patients with Cushing's syndrome, presumably a result of spontaneous overproduction of corticosteroids (Starkman & Schteingart, 1981; Varney et al., 1981). Additionally, there is an association between elevated cortisol levels, memory dysfunction, and reduced hippocampal volume as assessed by MRI in patients with Cushing's syndrome (Starkman et al., 1992).

Concerning the elderly population, it has also been suggested that ageing can lead to a significant increase of endogenous cortisol levels and that this increase is significantly related to a decrease in declarative memory performance (Lupien et al., 1995). In a study, corticosteroid Type I and Type II receptors were decreased during senescence and this effect may be due to the rise in circulating plasma corticosteroid concentrations (De Kloet & Veldhuis, 1984). Specifying the nature of the memory deficits observed with changes in cortisol levels in ageing could possibly lead to sensitive markers of normal and pathological brain ageing and memory dysfunctions.

While several studies of the effects of acute stress and corticosteroids on human cognition have documented a deleterious effect on declarative memory performance, this finding is not unequivocal (Beckwith et al., 1986; de Kloet et al., 1999; Lupien et al., 1999). On the contrary, a great deal of animal research documents a facilitating effect of corticosteroid on memory performance (Micco

& McEwen, 1980; see Roozendaal, 2000). Most of these studies used aversive conditioning paradigms in which emotional arousal was a key component of the learning experience and memory enhancement. It is postulated that this enhanced memory for emotional events is due to an interaction between amygdala activity and the stress hormones (both epinephrine and corticosteroids) (see McGaugh, 2000). In a recent study, following administration of cortisol (20 mg) or placebo, human participants were exposed to pictures varying in emotional arousal (Buchanan & Lovallo, 2001). Elevated cortisol levels during memory encoding enhanced the long-term recall performance of emotionally arousing pictures relative to neutral pictures. These data extend previously reported work in animals suggesting that corticosteroids may enhance the formation of memory for emotionally related events.

METHYLENEDIOXYMETHAMPHETAMINE

Methylenedioxymethamphetamine (MDMA or ecstasy) is a popular recreational drug of abuse that is known in animals (and possibly in humans) to severely damage serotonin axons in the hippocampus and other brain regions implicated in learning and memory (e.g., thalamus) (McCann et al., 1994; Steele et al., 1994). In a study designed to investigate whether individuals with a history of extensive MDMA use showed evidence of memory impairment, 24 abstinent MDMA users and 24 control subjects were studied on several standardised tests of memory (Bolla et al., 1998). The results of this study showed that abstinent MDMA users have impairment in verbal and visual memory, and the extent of memory impairment correlates with the degree of MDMA exposure and the decrease in brain serotonin, as evidenced by cerebrospinal 5-hydroxyindoleacetic acid measurements.

There is a growing evidence that chronic recreational use of ecstasy is associated with sleep disorders, depressed mood, persistent elevation of anxiety, impulsiveness and hostility, and selective dysfunction of episodic memory, working memory,

and attention (Morgan, 2000). Some of these problems may remit after abstinence, but residual neurotoxicity and decline of serotonergic function may result in premature cognitive decline and recurrent psychopathology. Another study designed to investigate the effects of moderate and heavy MDMA use, sex differences, and long-term effects of MDMA use on serotonin neurons in different brain regions confirmed that heavy use of MDMA is associated with neurotoxic effects on serotonin neurons (Reneman et al., 2001). MDMA use could lead to decreases in the density of brain serotonin transporters and that men and women differ in their susceptibility to the neurotoxic effects of MDMA. In women, use of MDMA is associated with dose-related decreases in densities of brain serotonin transporters. Such a reduction was also seen in men, but this finding was not significant. The use of MDMA in quantities regarded as moderate does not lead to significant reductions in densities of serotonin transporters in men. Thus, women might be more susceptible than men to the neurotoxic effects of MDMA. However, MDMA-induced neurotoxic changes in several brain regions of women ex-MDMA users might be reversible, but the possibility that they might be long-lasting or only partly reversible in the parieto-occipital cortex and occipital cortex cannot be excluded.

ETHANOL

In considering the relationship between ethanol and the process of learning and memory, a distinction between the acute and chronic effects of this agent becomes useful. There are probably several forms of ethanol amnesia. Two forms have been described: a state-dependent and a "blackout" form (Ryback, 1970). The former indicates that stimuli learned during a state following ethanol ingestion are best recalled in a similar later ethanol state. There is some controversy as to the genuine nature or universality of the state-dependent concept, particularly in view of the obvious fallacy that the ethanol state, where performance is maximally compromised, should confer a unique synaptic circumstance where memory is better recalled.

The blackout amnesia induced by ethanol refers to a profound STM deficit associated with an acute elevation in the blood ethanol level. Under these circumstances, prompted recognition fails to provide for recall. Hypoglycaemia, hypomagnesia, dehydration, pH change, and so on all represent possible factors that may result from the elevated blood ethanol. Such factors may account either individually or collectively for the observed amnesia.

The combination of ethanol abuse and nutritional deficiency serves as a basis for Wernicke's disease and Korsakoff's syndrome characterised, among several neurological findings, by a disorder of memory. It is apparent, therefore, that memory disturbances resulting from the chronic effects of ethanol involve structural changes. In general, the most debilitating effects have been shown in the offspring of mothers reporting the heaviest and chronic use of alcohol (Little & Streissguth, 1981). Approximately 30–45% of the children of alcoholic mothers have been observed as having fetal alcohol syndrome (FAS). The FAS children exhibited mental-age-inconsistent abilities in the comprehension and use of grammatical markers both in repetition and in spontaneous verbal STM tasks. Further, the FAS subjects also demonstrated reduced capacity to process and store critical elements when compared with non-FAS children (Becker et al., 1990).

Impaired performance by alcoholics has been reported on a wide range of tasks that engage some aspect of visuospatial function. These include tests that require visuospatial construction such as object assembly and block design tests from the Wechsler Adult Intelligence Scale (Stringer & Goldman, 1988; Wechsler, 1981). Impairments are also noted on copying complex designs such as Rey–Osterrieth figure, and other tasks that require visuospatial learning of symbols or designs (Sullivan et al., 1992). A study designed to understand the processes that might be responsible for the deficits in visuospatial cognition exhibited by chronic alcoholics reported that their deficits in spatial cognition do not seem to arise from dysfunction in any localised brain region (Beatty et al., 1996a). Small but potentially important dysfunctions in fundamental aspects of spatial information processing such as scanning and use of visual imagery were noted. It has also been suggested that cognitive function in alcoholics may be compromised not just by the effects of chronic alcohol consumption but also by other factors such as negative affect and attentional problems (Parsons & Nixon, 1993). Additional study of the deficits in scanning and using information from visual images are necessary to clarify the clinical importance of these subtle cognitive impairments.

The similarity in findings for alcoholic and normal ageing individuals led to the hypothesis that alcoholism may result in premature ageing of the brain (Ellis & Oscar-Berman, 1989). According to one version of the premature ageing model (the accelerated ageing hypothesis), alcoholism may accelerate age-related cognitive decline regardless of the age at which problematic drinking begins (Noonberg et al., 1985). According to another version (the increased vulnerability hypothesis), vulnerability to alcoholism-related brain damage is magnified in problematic drinkers over age 50, which is after the normal manifestations of ageing generally begin (Klisz & Parsons, 1977). Thus, older people who abuse alcohol may suffer proportionately greater age-related cognitive decline than their non-alcoholic peers, whereas younger alcoholic individuals are not expected to show cognitive impairments relative to younger control participants. The accelerated ageing and the increased vulnerability hypotheses of the premature ageing model may differ in the prediction of the age of onset for alcoholism-related cognitive and memory decline.

CAFFEINE

The most widely used stimulant in the general population is caffeine, which is available in many food sources, including coffee, tea, and chocolate. Participants report that a moderate dose of caffeine makes them more awake, alert, and attentive. Caffeine is highly lipid soluble, and thus crosses the blood–brain barrier quickly. Brain levels remain stable for at least an hour, with a slow, steady clearance over 3 to 4 hours and longer (see Nehlig et al., 1992). Caffeine is a non-specific antagonist for adenosine receptors, which are distributed widely throughout the cortex. Regions mediating sleep, mood, and concentration, including the dorsal and medial raphe nuclei and the locus ceruleus, show substantial increases in activity at low doses of caffeine and these increases probably collectively account for the general increase in alertness and well-being reported by individuals after ingesting caffeine (Nehlig, 2000).

In humans, caffeine (1.5 g) given 2.5–3 hours prior to presenting a list of nonsense syllables to be learned, provided for better learning of those stimuli for which there were pleasant associations and also an increase in the number of consonants learned (Tolman, 1917). There appear to be considerable interindividual differences in the effects of the caffeine in coffee on simple learning functions in humans. Coffee given 20, 100, or 140 minutes prior to adding or memory span tasks increased the accuracy with which performance occurred but there was considerable variability in the magnitude of the effect. It would be difficult to generalise from such studies and speculate about the potentially facilitative effect of coffee consumption on tasks requiring learning or depending on the efficiency with which memory consolidation takes place. Just as there are wide variations in the caffeine content in different coffees, so there are individual differences in the absorption, duration of effect, and magnitude of central action. The central effects of caffeine and coffee appear to depend on the activation and behavioural baselines on which the drug is superimposed.

DISCUSSION

All of the benzodiazepines cause memory deficits. The pattern of deficits is that of an anterograde amnesia. Most patients taking benzodiazepines do not complain of memory problems, although it has been noted that the problems are often quite subtle and thus patients may not be aware of them. The magnitude of these effects is dependent on multiple variables, but from a clinical standpoint, the most salient issues are likely dosage, time of drug ingestion, length of therapy, the age of the individual, and concomitant drug use. The benzodiazepines do not affect the memory of events that have occurred prior to taking the drug. They do not have any effect on one's store of knowledge or prior experience. They do not affect the retrieval of such information. In general, clinicians must be vigilant for the amnesic effects of benzodiazepines as patients are often unaware of them. Patients should be warned about the possibility of their occurrence, particularly when they occupy roles that require large amounts of learning.

Unfortunately, relatively few studies have been devoted to the possible memory effects of non-benzodiazepine anxiolytics. Animal data suggest that the serotonin 5-HT$_{1A}$ receptor partial agonist buspirone also disrupts acquisition avoidance learning and retention, leading to the question of an unavoidable link between anxiety, memory, and learning (Venault et al., 1986). Indeed, in contrast with anxiolytics, anxiogenic drugs notably β-carbolines, promote learning capacity in rats (Bass et al., 1992). As the same limbic structures (amygdala, hippocampus, and septum) are implicated in both anxiety and memory, it is probably illusory to expect anxiolytics with no adverse effects on human cognition.

Unlike the benzodiazepines, anticholinergic drugs such as scopolamine impair the retrieval of previously stored information as well as the acquisition of new memory (Weingartner, 1985).

There is extensive evidence that many central nervous system stimulants enhance LTM when administered to animals shortly after training in inhibitory avoidance tasks as well as other types of learning tasks (McGaugh, 1973, 1989). Such findings support the hypothesis that the drugs influence memory by modulating neurobiological processes underlying memory consolidation.

Part II

Pathology of Memory

6

Memory Dysfunctions

INTRODUCTION

Memory dysfunctions may affect the ability to recall both past events (retrospective memory) and future events and intentions (prospective memory). Forgetting to complete a wide variety of tasks may result in a loss of independence, limited employment prospects, and anxiety.

The two major brain regions that have generally been implicated in human memory dysfunction include the diencephalon and the hippocampi. The dysmnesic syndromes that involve these structures include impairment of long-term data storage, disruption of the encoding of short-term into long-term storage, or a loss of decoding or access to the long-term data storage. Dysmnesia is the preferred term describing a partial memory loss, in contrast to the term amnesia, which implies a total memory loss. Amnesia may be viewed as an extreme on a broad continuum of dysmnesic syndromes where mild dysmnesic illnesses occur more commonly than total amnesia. Memory disorders belong to the most common symptoms after brain damage (see Table 6.1) but can be found in a number of dissociative states as well (Markowitsch, 1995). While interest among

clinicians and researchers has tended to focus on retrospective memory, it has been suggested that memory dysfunctions affecting prospective memory are also very disabling and may significantly undermine a patient's independence (Mateer et al., 1987; Raskin & Sohlberg, 1996).

FORGETTING

Types of forgetting include transience, absent-mindedness, and blocking. Transience involves decreasing accessibility of information over time, absent-mindedness entails inattentive or shallow processing that contributes to weak memories of ongoing events or forgetting to do things in the future. Blocking refers to the temporary inaccessibility of information that is stored in memory.

There is no doubt that retrieval failure plays an important role in forgetting. Some experiences may be rendered temporarily inaccessible because of interference from related experiences. It is well established that cues and hints can elicit recall of seemingly forgotten memories (Koutstaal & Schacter, 1997; Postman & Underwood, 1973). However, it seems likely that information is also

TABLE 6.1

Conditions that can result in amnesia

Condition	Putative lesion	References
	Medial temporal lobe	
Surgical resection	Hippocampal formation, surrounding cortices	Helmstaedter et al., 1997
Herpes simplex encephalitis	Hippocampal formation, surrounding cortices	Mimura et al., 1997
Hippocampal sclerosis	Hippocampal formation	Davies et al., 1999
Anoxia	Hippocampal formation	Squire & Zola, 1996
Posterior cerebral artery infarct	Hippocampus	Bogousslavsky & Regli, 1988
Electroconvulsive therapy	Hippocampal formation	Squire, 1981
Transient global amnesia	Hippocampus (temporary ischaemia)	Kapur et al., 1998
Closed head injury	Hippocampal formation, surrounding cortices, fibre tracts	
	Diencephalon	
Korsakoff's syndrome	Mammillothalamic tract, mediodorsal thalamus, internal medullary lamina	Fadda & Rossetti, 1998
Thalamic infarct	Thalamus, mammillothalamic tract	Markowitsch et al., 1993a, b
	Basal forebrain	
Alzheimer's disease	Basal forebrain, hippocampal formation	Zaborszky et al., 1999
Anterior communicating artery aneurysm	Basal forebrain	Abe et al., 1998

lost from storage over time; loss of information may be particularly likely to occur when individuals do not "use" a memory (Schacter, 1996). Memories that are not retrieved and rehearsed may slowly dissipate over time. Although there is no direct evidence for such dissipation in studies of humans, neurobiological evidence from preclinical studies has revealed loss of synaptic connectivity over time (Bailey & Chen, 1989).

The exact cause of rapid forgetting within working memory has long been debated and some evidence suggests that it involves different mechanisms from long-term forgetting (Crowder, 1989). In many cases of STM loss, the observed deficit can be attributed to a specific component of working memory known as the phonological loop which is necessary for holding small amounts of speech-based information (Baddeley et al., 1998). Patients with damage to the phonological loop usually have a lesion in the lower part of the left parietal lobe, and they exhibit rapid forgetting of speech-based information. Patients with damage to the phonological loop also have difficulty with long-term vocabulary acquisition and related aspects of language learning (Gathercole & Baddeley, 1994).

Because absent-mindedness lapses involve forgetting to execute a planned action at some point in the future, they are typically referred to as failures of prospective memory (Brandimonte et al., 1996). Absent-minded errors of prospective memory can have important everyday consequences, as when elderly patients forget to take prescribed medications (Park & Kidder, 1996).

Blocking constitutes one of the most subjectively compelling of memory's problems in the sense that individuals are acutely aware of the block at the time it occurs. The most thoroughly investigated example of blocking is the tip-of-the-tongue (TOT) state. In a TOT state, individuals are unable to produce a word or a name, but they have a powerful subjective conviction that the item is available in memory. Blocking appears to be especially pronounced in old age and the incidence of TOT states increases with ageing (Brown & Nix, 1996). Recently, the term mnestic block syndrome was suggested and a case of a patient with no detectable brain damage but who manifested continued and severe anterograde and retrograde memory disorders together with an inhibition in his thinking processes was described (Markowitsch et al., 1999). Mnestic block syndrome condition may be considered related to an altered brain metabolism which may include alterations in various neurotransmitters and hormonal systems (e.g., GABA-agonists, glucocorticoids, acetylcholine) which have numerous receptors especially in memory and affect-related regions such as the hippocampus and amygdala (Haas & Schauenstein, 1997; Herman & Cullinan, 1997).

Tip-of-the tongue state

The tip-of-the tongue (TOT) state is a relatively common type of speech error in which a word retrieval failure is coupled with a strong feeling of knowing and often with a considerable sense of frustration at the inaccessibility of the desired word. Typically, an individual can access semantic and syntactic properties of the TOT word and partial phonological properties such as initial sound or number of syllables, although the complete phonology remains inaccessible (Vigliocco et al., 1997). Resolution of a TOT is as compelling as the TOT onset when it occurs spontaneously with the target word popping into mind at a time when retrieval attempts have been abandoned (Burke et al., 1991). TOTs are a hallmark of old age, increasing in frequency with normal ageing and ranking as older adults' most annoying cognitive failure (Burke et al., 1991; Heine et al., 1999; Lovelace & Twohig, 1990). This age-related increase in TOT states may be particularly pronounced when individuals attempt to retrieve names (Maylor, 1990).

The vulnerability of phonological retrieval to failure has been explained in the transmission deficit (TD) model of TOTs in terms of the strength of the connections that transmit priming to phonological representations (Burke et al., 1991). According to the TD model, TOTs occur when the strength of the connections among phonological nodes is too weak to transmit sufficient priming for activation of the complete phonology of the TOT target word. The strength of the connections to nodes determines the rate and amount of priming transmitted to them and is an important determinant of what information in memory becomes available (Mackay, 1987). Recent and frequent activation of nodes (e.g., in production of a word) strengthens connections, therefore increasing priming transmission whereas ageing weakens connections, reducing priming transmission (Burke & Mackay, 1997).

PARAMNESIA

During the 19th century, the generic term paramnesia was used to refer to a group of clinical phenomena amongst which déjà vu, confabulations, delusions, and hallucinations of memory remain the more salient. Paramnesia denotes false memory. This term was coined by Emil Kraepelin (1887) in analogy of terms such as paranoia, paraphasia, and paraphrenia, as a general term to explain pseudoreminiscences or illusions and hallucinations of memory (Burnham, 1889). The most common paramnesias are déjà vu and jamais vu, with the latter being the less frequent of the two.

However, current research has neglected this area of investigation. These states are considered in DSM–IV as being related to dissociation. Déjà vu remains a curiosity seen in some forms of epilepsy and occasionally in normal people affected by fatigue. Delusions of memory and hallucinations of memory are sometimes mentioned in the literature. However, because these phenomena do not figure as "symptoms" in most current nosologies, they are no longer searched for, and hence their incidence and prevalence in clinical populations are unknown. The conceptual, historical, and clinical information published suggests that it might be clinically worthwhile to return to these phenomena not only in relation to patients explicitly complaining of memory disorders but also in subjects with functional psychosis, as they might provide the clinician with new phenomenological markers.

Distortion and false recognition

Many factors may hinder the accurate recollection of a memory. The same knowledge that enables us to encode and retrieve information may impede the accurate recall of information. Knowledge or expertise on a topic can influence recollection. The retrieval process incorporates current information that serves to make sense of the past. A new interpretation of past events can be formed that conforms to current knowledge and as a consequence influences the recollection of past events. The retrieval and rehearsal of information leads to the consolidation of long-term memories. However, if false information is infiltrated within such recollections, false information can be rehearsed and can lead to the formation of false memories.

Distortion or inaccuracy includes misattribution, suggestibility, and bias. Misattribution involves attributing a recollection or idea to the wrong source. One example of misattribution may be that individuals can remember correctly an item or fact from a past experience but misattribute the fact to an incorrect source. For instance, people may assert that they saw a face in one context when they encountered it in another, or that they perceived an event that they only imagined. Source confusions of this kind can be particularly pronounced in older adults (Schacter et al., 1997a, b). Source confusions can have important implications in everyday life, as exemplified by cases of erroneous eyewitness identifications in which a person seen in one context is mistakenly "transferred" to another (Ross et al., 1994). A second type of misattribution is characterised by an absence of any subjective experience of remembering. People sometimes misattribute a spontaneous thought or idea to their own imagination, when in fact they are retrieving it, without awareness of doing so, from a specific prior experience. This phenomenon of cryptomnesia is exemplified in everyday life by instances of unintentional plagiarism (Marsh & Landau, 1995). A third type of misattribution occurs when individuals falsely recall or recognise items that never happened. A number of research studies have produced laboratory demonstrations of false recall and recognition in which individuals claimed to have seen or heard sentences that had not been previously presented (Bransford & Franks, 1971; Norman & Schacter, 1997; Posner & Keele, 1968; Seamon et al., 1998). Striking false recognition effects have been replicated and explored in a number of laboratories. Studies of brain-injured patients have revealed that damage to the frontal lobes is often associated with a selective increase in source memory errors (Janowsky et al., 1989a, b; Schacter et al., 1984, 1996b, c).

Suggestibility refers to memories that are implanted as a result of leading questions or comments during attempts to recall past experiences.

Suggestibility in memory refers to the tendency to incorporate information provided by others, such as misleading questions, into one's own recollections. Suggestibility is closely related to misattribution in the sense that the conversion of suggestions into false recollections must involve misattribution. However, misattribution can occur in the absence of overt suggestion.

Bias refers to the distorting influences of present knowledge, beliefs, and feelings on recollection of previous experiences. Bias involves retrospective distortions and unconscious influences that are related to current knowledge and beliefs (Schacter, 1999). False recognition occurs when individuals claim that a novel word, object, or event is familiar, and intrusions and confabulations occur when people produce non-studied information in memory experiments (intrusions) or narrative descriptions of events that never happened (confabulations).

Although neuropsychological studies of memory disorders have long been concerned with the status of recognition memory after brain damage, it is only recently that systematic investigations of false recognition in patients with brain lesions have appeared (Curran et al., 1997; Schacter et al., 1996). Excessive levels of false recognition have also been reported in studies of patients whose cerebral hemispheres have been surgically separated (Phelps & Gazzaniga, 1992).

Early studies of ageing memory reported that elderly adults show increased false recognition of semantically related distractors in paradigms, whereas young adults show relatively small false recognition effects. Recent studies have replicated these findings and extended them to paradigms that produce high levels of false recognition even in younger adults (Isingrini et al., 1995; Schacter et al., 1997a, b). The inability of explicit warnings to impact illusory recollections shows that the false memories cannot be attributed simply to a criterion shift (Neuschatz et al., 2001). The implications of these results in terms of memory theory are that memory researchers must consider how accurately memory reports correspond with what was encountered during encoding. Although this qualitative approach needs to be developed more specifically, it still represents a giant step towards constructing precise models and theories that can account for the phenomenological experience associated with true and false memories.

Confabulations

Two phenomena are conventionally included under the name of confabulation. The first type concerns untrue utterances of subjects with memory impairments. Often provoked or elicited by the interviewer, these confabulations are accompanied by little conviction. They are believed by most clinicians to be caused by the conscious or unconscious needs to cover up for some memory deficit. The second type concerns confabulations with fantastic content and great conviction, as seen in subjects with functional psychoses and little or no memory deficit. Little is known about the epidemiology of either type of confabulation.

Occasional amnesic patients fail to adapt behaviour to current reality. They invent untrue stories about their recent doings and describe impossible plans for the day. These patients insist on the veracity of their stories and often act according to them. These false ideas have been called spontaneous confabulations (Schnider et al., 1996). The patients typically consider themselves in different places, assume earlier dates, and indicate other reasons for hospitalisation than their memory impairment. Whether the stories seem simple or fantastic, they can always be traced back to fragments of actual experiences. A 58-year-old woman hospitalised following rupture of an anterior communicating artery aneurysm was convinced that she was at home and had to feed her baby (Schnider et al., 1996). But her "baby" was over 30 years old at the time. A tax accountant with extensive traumatic destruction of the orbitofrontal cortex inadvertently left the hospital in the conviction that he had a meeting with the county's financial director (Schnider et al., 1996).

Confabulations usually draw upon bits and pieces of the patient's actual past experiences, with episodes confused in time and place, but confabulated autobiographical memories may sometimes incorporate knowledge acquired from other sources. Confabulations are typically not intentionally produced and do not appear to be measured attempts to attract attention or compensate for memory loss. Patients typically present confabulations without awareness that their memories are false, and are more generally unaware of their own memory deficits (McGlynn & Schacter, 1989). Confabulation usually occurs together with anterograde amnesia (i.e., poor memory of recent events). Confabulations may sometimes contain bizarre content that patients tend to accept as veridical (Kopelman, 1987a, b). Although the mechanism of confabulatory false recall effects remains poorly understood, source confusions may play a role. As individuals repeatedly think about or imagine an event, they may retrieve fragments of other actual events, without recognising them as such.

Several studies described provoked confabulations and illusory memories after dorsolateral prefrontal, medial temporal (hippocampal area), and other brain lesions but also in healthy subjects (Moscovitch & Melo, 1997; Roediger & McDermott, 1995; Schacter et al., 1996b, c). That is, provoked confabulations have no anatomic specificity. By contrast, all patients described in the literature with sufficient detail to conclude that they had the syndrome of spontaneous confabulation, had lesions involving anterior limbic structures, in particular the orbitofrontal cortex or its connections. Spontaneous confabulations are most closely associated with the effects of aneurysms of the anterior communicating artery. If the aneurysm ruptures, it can cause lesions of the ventromedial frontal lobes and the basal forebrain. How such lesions could lead to confabulations has been unclear. One explanation is that the current memory traces—which are often recently acquired ones—are weak, so that older representations intrude during the retrieval process. Confabulators not only fail to check their retrieved memories properly, but are also defective in their ability to specify the required memory with the necessary precision before retrieval (Burgess & Shallice, 1996; Norman & Schacter, 1996). However, the results of a recent study suggest that mental associations that were previously acquired but are currently irrelevant, are normally suppressed, so as not to interfere with whatever pertains to "now" (Meunier et al., 1997). It has been hypothesised that this suppression mechanism is lost in confabulators. These findings are related to phenomena described in monkeys with orbital lesions, who fail to suppress habits that no longer bring any rewards. Such a mechanism would presumably be part of an error-correction process. A recent study that used repeated runs of a continuous recognition task to measure the ability to distinguish currently relevant from previously encountered information showed that spontaneous confabulators steeply increased false-positive responses from run to run and failed to suppress this interference even after 30 minutes (Schnider & Ptak, 1999). This indicates that spontaneous confabulators experience information encountered 30 minutes ago as if it had just been presented in the current test run, the "present". These results are compatible with the idea that spontaneous confabulations reflect a defective monitoring process on memory retrieval, that is, a failure to monitor the veridicality of thoughts. Spontaneous confabulators may specifically fail to suppress mental associations that do not pertain to the present; memories thus seem to be as real and pertinent for present behaviour as representations of current reality.

The view that confabulations are verbal statements conveying erroneous information about world or self remains a popular one. At least two alternative views can be proposed, that confabulations are just involuntary, mechanical, tic-like verbal utterances like those seen in Tourette's syndrome, and that they are utterances issued by a speaker within a dialogical context, usually that of patient and clinician. However, since the intentional component is central to the semantics of confabulation, the tic model seems inadequate. The old view that confabulations are generated by embarrassed amnesic patients covering up for their deficit, could be interpreted as meaning that confabulations are speeches through which patients try to persuade their clinical interlocutors that they have normal memories.

Most patients with spontaneous confabulation eventually stop confabulating and regain correct orientation in time and space and the ability to refer thinking and acting to ongoing reality (Schnider et al., 2000). The cessation of spontane-

ous confabulation depends on the lesion site; it may last only a few weeks after isolated damage of the anterior orbitofrontal cortex but months after combined basal forebrain and posterior orbitofrontal cortex damage. Nonetheless, continued spontaneous confabulation is rare.

Hallucinations

Hallucinations are a principal feature of psychosis. Hallucinations, at least those encountered in psychiatric practice, cannot be regarded as random discharges from a diseased brain, but rather as the distorted output of a complex cognitive system. One of the most important symptoms associated with schizophrenia is auditory hallucinations, which are reported by approximately 50–80% of patients (Alpert, 1986). For some, this symptom only emerges during an acute psychotic state, while for others it can persist for years. In either case, significant distress and functional disability frequently result.

Other hallucinatory phenomena include palinopsia and palinacusis. Palinopsia is defined as the recurrence, after varied intervals, of the image of a previously seen object (Michel & Troost, 1980). For example, a patient who had peeled a banana saw multiple vivid bananas projected on the walls shortly after. Complex scenes such as a man walking in front of a window have also been reported. These hallucinated images are actually a replica of the original stimulus even when, in the case of moving objects, their speed may be augmented (Cleland et al., 1981). Palinopsia has been conceptualised as a release phenomenon probably associated with retrochiasmatic lesions of the visual pathways (Vaphiades et al., 1996). The fact that palinopsic images may frequently display movement suggests that this disorder reflects a dysfunction of the visual memory rather than of the visual system (Maillot et al., 1993).

In palinacusis, patients report voices, music, or random noises indistinguishable from the original stimulus (Malone & Leiman, 1983). However, no attempt has been made to verify the accuracy of these forms of hallucinations.

Hallucinations also occur during sleep. Hypnagogic (from the Greek *hypo*, sleep, and *gogic*, enter into) hallucinations are of the visual, auditory, or tactile modality and occur during sleep paralysis at the initial sleep stage. Hypnopompic (*pompic*, leading away) hallucinations also occur during sleep paralysis but towards the end of sleep when the individual is awakening. Hallucinations of this sort are reported to involve a frightening or horrifying experience. These types of hallucinations are an integral part of narcolepsy, a sleep disorder. An odd aspect of these sleep hallucinations is that the individual is conscious of the events that occur during the experience.

Disorders of face memory and delusions

Disorders of face memory and face perception have been the subject of much neuropsychological investigation. The most extensively studied of these is prosopagnosia—a condition characterised by the inability to identify all familiar faces, including famous persons, friends, family, and even the prosopagnosic's own face (Bodamer, 1947). The critical lesion sites in prosopagnosia involve right ventromedial occipitotemporal regions which include the inferior temporal cortex and medial temporal lobe limbic areas (De Renzi et al., 1994). Neuropsychological studies have also documented an association between false recognition and right frontal lobe dysfunction (Rapcsak et al., 1999). These frontal patients, in striking contrast to the lack of conscious facial recognition described in prosopagnosics, mistakenly believe that unfamiliar faces are familiar (Young et al., 1993).

In a small subset of psychotic patients, false recognition can lead to frank misidentification which can reach delusional proportions as in the case of Frégoli delusion (Courbon & Fail, 1927). The hallmark of Frégoli delusion is the recognition of a familiar other in a stranger. The patient believes that the familiar other is able to take on different physical forms and adopt another's appearance. It has been suggested that Frégoli delusion develops when spurious feelings of familiarity evoked by novel faces are combined with the retrieval of incorrect biographic details (Rapcsak et al., 1999). A related phenomenon called the delusion of intermetamorphosis is marked by the false belief that a person has been transformed

physically and psychologically into another (Courbon & Tusques, 1932). Patients report the presence of physical similarities between the original and misidentified individuals, and a dynamic transformation occurring between the two. Finally, the Capgras delusion, a subtly different form of misidentification from the Frégoli delusion and intermetamorphosis delusion, is characterised by the delusional belief that a significant other has been replaced by an impostor who bears a close physical resemblance to the original (Todd et al., 1981). Again, small misperceived differences, for instance in physical appearance and behaviour, are frequently used to distinguish the impostor from the loved one. Neuroanatomical evidence from studies of recognition memory in psychotic patients suggests that delusional misidentification syndromes like Capgras, Frégoli, and intermetamorphosis delusions emerge when right hemisphere dysfunction is substantial relative to left hemisphere preservation (Edelstyn et al., 1996).

AMNESIA

Amnesia can arise from several aetiologies (see Table 6.1). It may result from head injury, ischaemic attacks, embolisms, tranquillisers, alcohol, and electroconvulsive shock. Although memory difficulties may accompany damage to many parts of the brain, circumscribed amnesia without other neuropsychological impairment typically follows injury to the medial temporal lobe, basal forebrain, and the diencephalon. Another significant cause of amnesia is herpes encephalitis that preferentially damages the limbic system, particularly the medial temporal lobes. When encephalitis causes mainly unilateral temporal lobe damage, circumscribed retrograde amnesia results. Qualitatively similar findings have been described for mainly right or left sided lesions (O'Connor et al., 1992; Yoneda et al., 1992).

In diagnosing the cause of memory deficits or dementia, it is important to distinguish between failures of storage (or retention), associated with damage to the limbic and especially hippocampal structures, retrieval associated with frontal–subcortical dysfunctions, and STM associated with temporo-parietal lesions. Storage disorders are characterised on testing by deficits in both recall and recognition and rapid loss of information. Retrieval disorders are characterised by a difficulty in accessing information, and STM disorders are characterised on testing by reduced memory span and rapid loss of information as measured, for example, by the Brown–Petersen paradigm (Petersen & Petersen, 1959). Neuropsychological studies have demonstrated normal working memory abilities in patients with dense amnesia despite virtually non-existent LTM for new events (Baddeley & Warrington, 1970). The reverse pattern of impaired working memory and intact LTM has been observed in other clinical cases. For example, patients with damage to the left supramarginal gyrus of the inferior parietal lobule exhibit poor retention, produce phonemic paraphasias, and have reduced auditory verbal span, deficits indicative of an impaired phonological store (Murray et al., 2001; Vallar & Papagno, 1995). Deficits in the storage of visuospatial information (e.g., poor spatial localisation) have been observed in patients with posterior lesions, primarily of the right hemisphere (De Renzi et al., 1977).

Many amnesic patients have anterograde amnesia. Anterograde amnesia can be defined as a profound defect in new learning with impairment in the conscious, deliberate recall of information (Bauer et al., 1993). Damage in more than one brain region can result in anterograde amnesia, and neuropathological studies have repeatedly highlighted the medial temporal lobes and the medial diencephalon (Aggleton & Brown, 1999). However, patients usually retain some skill-learning abilities that may facilitate rehabilitation. Various behavioural patterns indicate that this type of amnesic syndrome is not a single entity. Amnesic patients vary in the severity and extent of their retrograde amnesia—a loss of information gained before the onset of the amnesia or the inability to retrieve previously acquired information. Retrograde losses of memory in amnesia are usually temporally graded in that they are most severe for time periods closest to amnesia onset. This varies markedly across patients and it has to

be admitted that its anatomical and functional determinants are still not well understood. In addition to cases with definite and neuroanatomically visible brain damage, there is a wide variety of amnesic cases without demonstrable brain lesions (e.g., patients with concussions), transient global amnesia, or with so-called psychogenic forms of amnesia (Markowitsch, 1990; Russell, 1971; Schacter & Kihlstrom, 1989). Cases with anterograde amnesia usually occur after bilateral, profound damage of so-called bottleneck structures within the limbic system—the medial diencephalon, the medial temporal lobes, and possibly also the forebrain (Markowitsch, 1995). Cases with retrograde amnesia occur after bilateral damage of fronto-temporal cortical regions, usually predominant on the right side (Kroll et al., 1997). Most of the available data on retrograde amnesia in subjects with bilateral temporal lobe injury indicate that the extent of retrograde amnesia is proportional to the size of the lesions. Furthermore, a number of aetiologies (Korsakoff's syndrome, anoxia after severe heart attack) may result in combined anterograde and retrograde memory impairments (Mayes et al., 1997).

Recently, an increasing number of patients has been reported with functional amnesia, that is amnesia of unknown or unsure aetiology and without evidence of brain damage (Markowitsch et al., 1998). A number of patients have also been reported with retrograde amnesia that is not accompanied by a typical anterograde amnesia (Kapur, 1992). Such disorder was termed "focal retrograde amnesia" and this refers to a memory impairment in which the primary deficit is a loss of remote memory with performance on anterograde tests only mildly impaired (Kapur, 1992). A problem with this type of disorder, however, is that some of the patients may be suffering from psychogenic disorders resulting from psychological trauma or they may be malingering, in some way faking or dissimulating memory impairment. However, once these possibilities have been discounted, there remains a range of cases where focal retrograde amnesia occurs in the context of known brain injury (Kapur, 1992; Kapur et al., 1994a, b, c). There are essentially two types of patient showing this unusual deficit: those with identifiable brain lesions and those who appear to have developed the disorder from extremely minor injuries (Parkin, 1996). Examining the former group, there is some evidence that structures in the anterior and inferior temporal neocortex are damaged in patients with this kind of disorder, although more posterior temporal neocortex lesions have been reported to cause a similar deficit (De Renzi & Lucchelli, 1993). The performance of these patients on tests of anterograde memory is not normal although it is far better than that found in amnesics. De Renzi and Lucchelli's patient not only showed retrograde amnesia, but also showed an impaired ability to retain new memories over a period of weeks despite normal performance on standard tests sensitive to anterograde amnesia, which are given at relatively short delays. The existence of this atypical kind of anterograde amnesia needs to be confirmed as does its relationship with retrograde amnesia. The implications that this form of memory deficit have for our understanding of the amnesic syndrome need to be worked out.

A study designed to examine sentence memory as a function of linguistic processing complexity in amnesic patients used sentence length as well as lexical and syntactic complexity in two sentence-repetition experiments (Shapiro et al., 1992). The results showed that amnesic subjects performed more poorly than alcoholic control subjects. Both subject groups were affected by increases in length (particularly the nonargument kind), by the cleft sentence type, and by verb complexity. Amnesic performance was particularly affected when complex sentences were involved and performance significantly decreased when these sentences contained nonargument length increases. Further, amnesic subjects showed considerable sensitivity to the argument/adjunct distinction, with adjuncts posing more difficulty. These data demonstrate a sentence memory deficit in severe anterograde amnesics. The deficit involved the memory system that mediates, at the very least, sentence repetition and perhaps extended to more common postures of sentence comprehension and production.

The findings from functional neuroimaging (especially PET) in the study of amnesia not only support the data from the classic clinico-anatomical approach but have also revealed hypometabolism in unlesioned brain regions (Paller et al., 1997). For instance, hypometabolism of the left supramarginal gyrus in patients with permanent amnesic syndrome may reflect a disconnection mechanism and may explain, at least in part, the intriguing phenomenon of retrograde amnesia, particularly prominent in the Wernicke–Korsakoff syndrome (Paller et al., 1997; Baron et al., 1986).

An important feature of the amnesic syndrome is impaired acquisition of new declarative knowledge, including information about specific events and episodes as well as information about factual material. In this sense, it is sometimes stated that the impairment in amnesia involves both episodic and semantic memory (Baddeley, 1982; Squire, 1992). Nevertheless, amnesic patients can usually acquire some semantic information, albeit at an abnormally slow rate. For example, new learning has been demonstrated for factual statements and for computer vocabulary (Glisky et al., 1986; Hayman et al., 1993). Global amnesia impairs the ability to acquire both episodic and semantic memories, such as the meaning of words and concepts (Gabrieli et al., 1988). Some patients are much more impaired in free recall than in recognising previously presented information. They deny any failure of their memory, and sometimes confabulate spontaneously and in memory tests. This type of amnesia (contextual amnesia) has been reported in patients with orbitofrontal and basal forebrain damage (Damasio et al., 1985; DeLuca & Diamond, 1995; Shoqeirat & Mayes, 1991). It has also been reported in some patients with paramedian thalamic infarction (Hodges & McCarthy, 1993; Parkin et al., 1994) and in the early course of Wernicke–Korsakoff syndrome (Shimamura & Squire, 1987; Victor et al., 1989). These patients fail to store the temporal order and the context of information acquired, a disorder that, in an attenuated form, was also observed in patients with dorsal prefrontal lesions sparing the orbitofrontal area (Milner et al., 1985; Shimamura et al., 1991). Thus, the patient's amnesia is based on an inability to store the context of information acquired rather than the information itself. On the other hand, some patients also fail to recognise and feel entirely unfamiliar with previously presented information (indicating deficient information storage). They are very concerned about the failure of their memory and do not spontaneously confabulate. Examples of such a memory dysfunction were seen in patients with severe amnesia after medial temporal lobe damage (Schnider et al., 1994; Scoville & Milner, 1957).

The ability to recall the source of learned information has been shown to be dissociable from memory for the learned information itself. It has been demonstrated that some amnesic patients are unable to recall when or where they had learned certain "facts" several minutes after they were presented, although they are able to learn the facts themselves (Schacter et al., 1984). This phenomenon was called "source amnesia". It was noted that the deficit was often associated with signs of frontal lobe dysfunction. Source amnesia has been shown to be related to executive dysfunction in amnesic patients, independent of aetiology (Schacter et al., 1984).

The question of whether perception of emotional stimuli is normal in amnesia and whether emotional arousal has the same enhancing effects on memory in amnesic patients as it has in healthy volunteers has been investigated (Hamann et al., 1997). Perception and memory were assessed using the standardised International Affective Picture System (IAPS) stimuli in a group of nine amnesic patients (including four Korsakoff's patients), two postencephalitic patients (both had sustained bilateral damage to the amygdaloid complex), and two groups of controls (Hamann et al., 1997; Lang et al., 1988). Thus 40 standardised colour pictures were presented while volunteers rated each picture according to emotional intensity (arousal) and pleasantness (valence). An immediate free-recall test was given for the pictures, followed by a yes–no recognition test. The results of that study suggest that emotional judgements are intact in amnesia, even in patients with bilateral damage to the amygdala. Amnesic patients experienced the same memory enhancement from emotional arousal as healthy controls. It may be hypothesised that the emotional arousal effect is modulated by brain structures that are intact in amnesia.

It is generally believed that patients with organic amnesia who are severely impaired on explicit memory tests are less impaired, and frequently normal on various implicit tests (Brooks & Baddeley, 1976; Weiskrantz & Warrington, 1979). A widespread interpretation of this finding is that implicit memory is based on the automatic activation of pre-existing memory representations (Graf et al., 1982). However, in a recent study, the priming performance of amnesics was examined using the fade-in task (Ostergaard, 1999). The results showed that baseline naming was slower and priming effects were larger in the slow than in the fast fade-in conditions. The most important findings were that in the slow fade-in condition, the amnesic patients evidenced significantly reduced priming compared to control participants. In an experiment in which the number of study repetitions was manipulated, the amnesic patients evidenced impaired simple priming. Unlike the controls, their priming effects were not enhanced by further repetitions of the items. These findings suggest that the memory that is measured as priming is not intact in patients with clinical memory impairment. The apparent dissociation between priming and explicit memory performance is due to strong effects on priming measures of such factors as the amount of task-relevant perceptual or lexical information that is available to participants. Memory-impaired patients often appear to have normal priming because the priming effects in the control participants are constrained by their superior perceptual and lexical skills. Previously published reports of normal priming in amnesic patients may be an artefact of priming scores being inflated by baseline information-processing impairments (Ostergaard, 1994; Ostergaard & Jernigan, 1993). Therefore, it may be argued that implicit and explicit memory are mediated by the same brain mechanisms, especially the medial temporal lobe. By this view, the distinction between implicit and explicit memory need not reflect the contribution of distinct brain systems.

Dissociative amnesia

Psychogenic amnesia, classified as dissociative amnesia in DSM–IV has been the subject of few published studies (American Psychiatric Association, 1994; Mai, 1995). Dissociative amnesia refers to amnesia for a traumatic experience that has a psychological origin. Whereas dissociative amnesia refers to a process of forgetting following a traumatic experience, a dissociative state refers to an altered state of consciousness occurring during a traumatic experience. Dissociation is the more general term referring to the separation of any normally integrated psychological processes, encompassing both dissociative amnesia and dissociative state.

Large gaps in memory, known as amnesia episodes, which occur in dissociative identity disorder (DID, formerly multiple personality disorder) also indicate that dissociation is related to abnormal memory. The dissociative amnesia is typically retrograde rather than anterograde—one or more discrete periods of past information become unavailable. The memories lost are generally associated with traumatic or stressful events. The criteria in the DSM–IV for dissociative amnesia are one or more episodes of inability to recall important personal information, usually of a traumatic or stressful nature, that is too extensive to be explained by ordinary forgetfulness or age. The disturbance is not due to multiple personality disorder or to an organic mental disorder (blackouts during alcohol intoxication). There is rather a close functional resemblance between dissociative amnesia and dissociative fugue. The memory loss in fugue states is more robust and often involves the autobiographical memory in such a way that people do not remember who they are or how they got into a certain situation.

Reports of dissociative amnesia are common in the legal system. Amnesia is reported in a significant proportion of cases involving murder or attempted murder (e.g., Bradford & Smith, 1979). Estimates of memory impairment in homicide cases range from 10% to 70%; Bradford & Smith, 1979; Parkin, 1987). Patients with a history of childhood sexual abuse have very high levels of amnesia prior to memory retrieval. In a study by Williams, it was shown that as many as 38% of abuse survivors did not remember significant episodes of abuse many years after the event (Williams, 1995). There tends to be an age re-

lation to significant amnesia. The younger the age at the time of trauma, the greater the likelihood of amnesia. It is commonly reported that dissociative amnesia usually involves personal events and information, rather than general knowledge or skill (Spiegel et al., 1993). The gaps in memory are organised according to affective rather than temporal dimensions. Three key issues in dissociative amnesia have been recognised. The memory loss is for a discrete period of time; there is a dense unavailability of memories that were clearly at one time available; explicit memory for what is wrong might be lacking.

One common explanation for amnesia in perpetrators of homicide and childhood sexual abuse is that they have "repressed" the memories. According to Freud (1922), repression involves a traumatic event being actively buried in the unconscious, a process independent of ordinary forgetting. Although this explanation for amnesia is interesting, scientific scepticism over the validity of repressed memories is steadily increasing (Loftus et al., 1998). Despite opposing arguments, there have been no studies that convincingly demonstrate the validity of repression. Further, its theoretical bases are not consistent with the current scientific understanding of memory (Loftus et al., 1998). It is becoming clear that memory is fundamentally constructive rather than operating like a storehouse (Porter et al., 2000).

Posthypnotic amnesia

Hypnotised subjects respond to suggestions from the hypnotist for imaginative experiences involving alterations in perception and memory. The field of experimental and clinical hypnosis adds a different type of amnesia called hypnotic amnesia. Hypnosis is well known for its sometimes striking or impressive phenomena such as catalepsy, rigidity, hallucinations, time distortion, hypermnesia, age regression, and post-hypnotic amnesia (Kihlstrom, 1997).

Posthypnotic amnesia refers to subjects' difficulty in remembering, after hypnosis, the events and experiences that transpired while they were hypnotised. Posthypnotic amnesia is not an instance of state-dependent memory, but it does seem to involve a disruption of retrieval processes similar to the functional amnesias observed in clinical dissociative disorders. However, implicit memory is largely spared and may underlie subjects' ability to recognise events that they cannot recall (Kihlstrom, 1997). Hypnotic hypermnesia refers to improved memory for past events. However, hypermnesia suggestions increase false recognition, as well as subjects' confidence in both true and false memories. The clinical and forensic use of hypermnesia to enhance memory in patients should be discouraged (Kihlstrom, 1997).

Transient global amnesia

In most cases of amnesia, the severity of the memory deficit remains stable over a period of years, but there are conditions such as transient global amnesia where recovery occurs. Global amnesia, associated with bilateral lesions to limbic–diencephalic brain structures, is characterised by a relatively circumscribed deficit in LTM for new information. Rare cases of unrecognised head trauma or transient ischaemic attack without other neurological deficit may mimic transient global amnesia (the sudden onset of an isolated amnesic episode). Its course is benign (Nausieda & Sherman, 1979). It appears that transient global amnesia may be caused by temporary bilateral dysfunction of medial temporal lobe structures, including the hippocampus, entorrhinal cortex, and parahippocampal gyrus (Fisher, 1982). This dysfunction is most likely due to ischaemia, perhaps caused by vertebrobasilar hypoperfusion or migrainous vasospasm of vertebrobasilar vessels (Caplan et al., 1981; Crowell et al., 1984). Several cases of transient global amnesia that involves a sudden onset of disorientation and bewilderment have been reported (Fisher & Adams, 1964; Logan & Sherman, 1983). This type of amnesia is characterised by a patient's inability to learn new material, by their repeated asking of questions that have been answered and being able to recall events that antedate the onset of the episode. Repeated questions such as "What is happening to me?" combined with an inability to learn new information herald this entity. General fund of knowledge is preserved and except for a short retrograde amnesia preceding this event, the patient is otherwise neurologically intact. Transient global amnesia occurs in middle aged and elderly men more commonly than women (Fisher & Adams, 1964). The condition, which is still not clearly understood, can emerge in times of severe stress, pain, or emotion, and has been attributed to migraine, epilepsy, drug use, hypoglycaemia, stroke, and neoplasms but is still not clearly understood. Fortunately, these patients normally improve spontaneously, within a few hours, and are neurologically normal the following day.

In the clinic, transient global amnesia is typically assessed by means of recall and recognition tests that require retrieval of recently learned information. Globally amnesic patients demonstrate impairments in both recall and recognition tasks, suggesting that recall and recognition, and familiarity, rely on the integrity of the medial temporal–diencephalic brain regions. Patients with global amnesia also manifest retrograde amnesia. Frequently, remote memories are better preserved than memories for events that occurred shortly before brain injury.

In transient global amnesia, interpretation of the PET data is presently difficult because so few studies have assessed both metabolism and cognitive impairment during the acute phase of the episode and the PET findings differ from one case to another. Nevertheless, these data suggest a dysfunction of a large network implicated in episodic memory. The hypometabolism affects a distributed network including the hippocampal region, the thalamus, and the prefrontal cortex but with a different pattern in each case (Eustache et al., 1997, 1999) Although the clinical pattern seems comparatively stereotyped during the acute phase, the impairment may not be similar in all cases. Moreover, the nature of the impairment seems to evolve during the episode, notably with respect to the recovery phase, in which retrograde amnesia seems to recover before anterograde amnesia (Kapur et al., 1998). The timing of the PET study will no doubt be an important methodology to clarify the relationships between cognitive and PET data when enough cases are collected.

Visual memory-deficit amnesia

Vision and visual imagery play a central role in a variety of memory tasks (Rubin, 1995). Although visual images do not guarantee accuracy, the successful retrieval of a visual image may lead a subject to classify a memory as being from a real event that actually occurred, rather than from an event that did not occur but was just thought about. The experience of recollecting an autobiographical memory coincides with the successful retrieval of a visual image (Brewer, 1996). People tend to report recollecting an event only if they have a visual image of that event. Biographical memory appears to rely on visual imagery to a much greater extent than other sensory modalities.

A form of amnesia called visual memory-deficit amnesia, caused by damage to areas of the visual system that store visual information, has been described (Rubin & Greenberg, 1998). Because it is caused by a deficit in access to stored visual material and not by an impaired ability to encode or retrieve new material, it has the otherwise infrequent properties of a more severe retrograde than anterograde amnesia with no temporal gradient in the retrograde amnesia. Although rare, this disorder is frequent enough to establish that its properties distinguish it from the other types of amnesias.

Korsakoff's syndrome

Korsakoff's syndrome results from prolonged and excessive alcohol intake. The thiamine (B_1) deficiency has a direct toll on the brain, specifically on the medial thalamus and possibly on the mammillary bodies of the hypothalamus (Victor et al., 1989). The most common symptoms associated with this syndrome include anterograde as well as retrograde amnesia, confabulations, and a general sense of apathy. In such patients the neurological disorder is not so perceptible, as individuals seem normal, with average IQ and attentiveness. Korsakoff's syndrome has long been recognised the prototype of diencephalic amnesia, although it is now recognised that Korsakoff's syndrome commonly involves cortical atrophy, especially the frontal lobes and damage to other brain regions

(Parkin, 1991). In addition to their anterograde memory deficit, Korsakoff's syndrome patients have severely impaired retrograde memory. This retrograde amnesia is typically temporally graded with memory for events in the more distant past preserved relative to memory for more recent events (Butters & Granholm, 1987; Parkin, 1991). Patients with Korsakoff's syndrome have a striking anterograde and retrograde amnesia, often with marked confabulation but preserved attention, personality, social functioning, STM, and non-declarative memory. Gliosis of the mammillary bodies, with cell loss in dorsomedial, median pulvinar, and lateral dorsal nuclei of the thalamus is the underlying neuropathology (Okazaki, 1989).

Both source memory impairments and compromised "frontal lobe" functioning have been demonstrated in alcoholic Korsakoff's syndrome, a disorder in which frontal lobe atrophy and deafferentation of PFC from thalamic nuclei are well established (Shimamura & Squire, 1987; Shimamura et al., 1988). Korsakoff patients, like other amnesics, exhibit severe impairments in the ability to learn new information.

Korsakoff's syndrome is mostly seen in chronic severe alcoholics who become severely deficient in thiamine or vitamin B_1. Massive doses of thiamine supplements may abort the damage but cannot reverse the effects even after a lengthy period of treatment ranging from 10–20 years. Korsakoff's syndrome may also occur following a sudden carbohydrate loading (glucose, in particular) and often, though not always, presents with some or all of the features of Wernicke's encephalopathy (i.e., confusion, ophthalmoplegia, and ataxia). Consequently, administration of intravenous thiamine is the standard treatment of acute confusional states because thiamine rapidly reverses this condition and prevents the profound amnesia seen in Korsakoff's syndrome.

REPRESSION AND DISSOCIATION

Repression and dissociation are processes central to some theories and approaches to therapy. According to these theories and approaches, memories of traumatic events may be blocked out unconsciously and this leads to a person having no memory of the events. However, memories of these traumatic events may become accessible at some later time. Although some clinical observations support the notion of repressed memories, empirical research on memories generally does not. Moreover, the scientific evidence does not allow general statements to be made about any relationship between trauma and memory. Nevertheless, a recent case study demonstrates that some form of repression or dissociation of the memory of childhood sexual abuse beyond mere forgetting does exist (Bull, 1999). This case showed that a 40-year-old woman with no history of mental illness recovered memories of childhood sexual abuse by her father through a call from her youth pastor in whom she had confided as an adolescent. This reminder triggered a severe depression, suicidal action, and the need for hospitalisation.

False memory syndrome

The false memory syndrome refers to the recovery of memories of childhood sexual abuse, usually during adulthood, with the help of a therapist. These memories are often used as the basis of allegations against the perpetrators of the abuse, often many years after the alleged events. The term false memory suggests that these memories are implanted by therapist in the minds of patients who seek help (Winbolt, 1996).

Various memory recovery techniques have been employed by therapists to retrieve these memories. These methods have included hypnosis, dream interpretation, and guided imagery. A significant correlation has been found between the number of memory recovery techniques used and the percentage of women who recalled sexual abuse during therapy (Poole et al., 1995). Once a patient believed that they had been abused, the usual approach was to close off all other means of confirming what had happened with external sources. Patients were encouraged to confront the alleged abuser and then to cut off all contact. Therapists would refuse to see parents to hear their side of the story, on the grounds that it would interfere with their relationship with the client.

However, remembering is not a simple process of retrieving something as if from a filing cabinet. Memory is reconstructive, not reproductive. This entails that each time one remembers something, calls up a memory, one actually reconstruct those images, those thoughts, those feelings, and that process may be influenced and modified in the light of our experiences since the original event. Therefore, many factors such as emotional arousal, expectation, suggestion, motivation, the methods used, and the circumstances in which a memory is retrieved may influence retrieval.

Some authors have claimed that psychotherapists practising "recovered memory therapy" created false memories of abuse through leading questions or excessive insisting (Loftus et al., 1994). These therapists reportedly believe that psychopathology is related to childhood trauma and that the goal of therapy is to help patients remember incidents of previously forgotten abuse from childhood. They explained the loss of memory of abuse as secondary to "repression" or dissociative amnesia. This process, variously termed repression, dissociative amnesia, or psychogenic amnesia, is sometimes discussed without question, as if everyone knew it to be true.

Several studies suggest that traumatic experiences may be forgotten and later recalled (Madakasira & O'Brian, 1987; Van der Kolk & Kadish, 1987; Wilkinson, 1983). The amnesia may last for hours, weeks, or years. Since the memories are held in a dissociated form, they may be triggered by stimuli that match sensory or affective elements associated with the trauma. Therefore, the evidence on memory processes that is available suggests that false memories may indeed occur. True memories could be forgotten and then brought to active memory by events or understandings occurring many years after the event. Memories that are reported either spontaneously or following the use of special procedures in therapy may be accurate, inaccurate, fabricated, or a mixture of these. The level of belief in memory or the emotion associated with the memory does not necessarily relate directly to the accuracy of the memory. The available scientific and clinical evidence does not allow accurate, inaccurate, and fabricated memories to be distinguished in the absence of independent corroboration. The Ramona case where a father successfully sued two therapists and a hospital for allegedly implanting false memories of childhood sexual abuse in his bulimic daughter showed the potential risk of the recovered memory therapy (Pope & Hudson, 1996). Thus, because there is no reliable method for distinguishing "true" from "false" memories in the absence of external corroborative evidence, clinicians who work with clients (both adults and children) whose symptoms or allegations suggest the possibility of childhood trauma are urged to exercise great caution in pursuing this possible interpretation. Explanations for the symptoms or allegations other than abuse should always be examined. Moreover, clinicians should inform their patients of the possibility of false memories.

Changes in brain regions involved in memory may underlie many of the symptoms of stress-related psychiatric disorders, including symptoms of amnesia (Bremner et al., 1993). There are a variety of reasons to believe that memories of abuse in traumatised patients might be different from normal memories. Several studies have shown that events after the laying down of the memory trace, such as provision of misleading information, are associated with alterations in recall. This has led to the conclusion that misleading information "overwrites" or "replaces" the original memory trace (Loftus et al., 1987). Thus, it is possible to construct convincing pseudo-memories for events that never occurred. However, some researchers in the field agree that although it is a rare occurrence, a memory of early childhood abuse that has been forgotten can be remembered later. The mechanisms by which both of these phenomena happen are not well understood and at this point, it is not possible without other corroborative evidence to distinguish a true memory from a false one.

PERSISTENCE AND INTRUSIVE RECOLLECTIONS

Whereas memory problems such as transience, absent-mindedness, and blocking refer to forgetting a fact or event that one wants to forget, persistence involves remembering a fact or event that one would prefer to forget. Persistence is revealed by intrusive recollections of traumatic events, rumination over negative symptoms and events, and even by chronic fears and phobias. Studies of traumatic memories reveal that failures to forget can sometimes be even more disabling than forgetting itself (Krystal et al., 1995).

Persistence also occurs in less extreme situations than post-traumatic disorder. Disturbing emotional events that are not necessarily traumatic, such as pictures that elicit negative affect, are sometimes remembered in greater detail than are positive pictures. In a study in which participants were instructed not to think about a particular item or object (e.g., don't think about white bears), a rebound effect was noted. The initially suppressed item is subsequently produced at higher levels than are items for which no suppression instructions are provided (Wegner & Erber, 1992).

Current mood and emotion can influence persistence. Just as current feelings can distort recollections of past emotions, they can also increase the accessibility of memories whose affective tone is congruent with a current mood state (Mineka & Nugent, 1995). Some evidence also indicates that the persistence of negative memories can be enhanced by ruminative tendencies in individuals with dysphoric moods (Lyubomirsky et al., 1998; Williams, 1997).

Flashbulb memory

Flashbulb memory refers to the vivid recollections that humans may have of events considered to be of particular significance to the individual or group. For an event to create a flashbulb memory, it must be "surprising", "consequential" with a high level of "arousal" as perceived relevance to the individual (Brown & Kulik, 1977). These memories are described as having a photographic quality and as being accompanied by a perfect-detail apparel of contextual information (weather, background music, colour, clothes worn, etc.) pertaining to the time and place where the event was first known. In summary, a stimulus or event that caused a high degree of surprise and reinforced by consequentiality may generate a flashbulb memory that is strengthened by rehearsal. Whether a special visual memory system is involved in the formation of flashbulb memories is unclear. A study reported that 58% of subjects rated visual images as being "as vivid as normal vision" (Rubin & Kozin, 1984). On the whole, flashbulb memories seem more accurate and stable than ordinary memories (Bohanon & Simons, 1992). The great number of details constituting flashbulb memories, their clarity and durability suggest that a particularly efficient encoding took place (see Finkenauer et al., 1998). However, they are not immune to change; for example, the regular finding of a change in "visual perspective" or shift towards an "observer's perspective" (for example, the subject reports the memory as if he or she was actually watching it from the outside) suggests that flashbulb memories undergo reconstruction.

It has been suggested that emotional arousal plays a role in the vividness and accuracy of flashbulb memories (Rubin & Kozin, 1984). However, it is unclear whether emotions are directly involved in memory encoding or simply increase rehearsal frequency. Some evidence from clinical practice supports the "encoding hypothesis". Recollections of panic attack by anxious patients are sometimes as detailed as flashbulb memories. The way in which emotions modulate memory encoding also remains unclear. In the short term, emotional arousal seems to have a detrimental effect on memory, but in the long term, the effect is reversed as emotions seem to attenuate the rate of forgetting (Heuer & Reisberg, 1992). The vividness of memory components, regardless of "relevance", also seems to be enhanced by emotional arousal. The memory enhancement caused by emotional arousal probably involves activation of the β-adrenergic system as it was shown that propranolol significantly impaired memory for an emotionally arousing story but did not affect memory for an emotionally neutral story (Cahill et al., 1994). The locus for such activation is the amygdala (Quirarte et al., 1997).

Flashbulb memory is often discussed as a particular instance of autobiographical memory, that is, memory for the events and experiences of one's personal past (Neisser & Libby, 2000). In most studies of flashbulb memory, however, the emotionality arousing event itself is not personally experienced, and what is of interest is memory for the reception of information about the event—when, where, and from whom the news was heard. Flashbulb memory may thus represent a special case of source memory (Brewer, 1992). Studies of source memory and emotion, perhaps, incorporating functional neuroimaging, may be able to cast further light on the processes and brain regions involved in flashbulb memory.

Flashback

The term flashback was initially introduced to describe returns of visual imagery for prolonged periods after the immediate effect of hallucinogens has worn off (Frankel, 1994; Horowitz, 1969). Flashbacks could also occur in the taste, smell, touch, kinaesthetic, and auditory modalities. During the 1980s, flashbacks were used to refer to the revisualisation of the trauma scene that occurred with realistic intensity in PTSD (Burstein, 1985). However, the indeterminateness of the concept allowed for the inclusion of a variety of other PTSD symptoms such as nightmares, illusions, and vivid imagery. The high frequency with which visual experiences are reported obscures the fact that these patients also experience auditory and olfactory phenomena. Flashbacks may be triggered by fatigue, certain mood states, and by environmental cues assumedly related to the original situation, suggesting the operation of a context-dependent retrieval mechanism such as, for example, the sound of a helicopter for a Vietnam veteran. Victims of trauma often report anxious dreams, in which the traumatic event is relived in vivid multisensory images accompanied by the same emotions as those of the original event. Although reported as an accurate playback, these experiences are also subject to a switching of perspective.

Obsessions and compulsions

Obsessions are defined as recurrent and persistent distressing thoughts, impulses, or images, not due to real-life worries alone, that cannot be suppressed or ignored by these patients. They are perceived as originating from within their own minds. Compulsions are defined as repetitive behaviours or mental acts that the person feels driven to perform in response to an obsession or to comply with rigid rules. Typical compulsions are hand washing, counting or ordering of items, checking of door locks or stove knobs, repetitive rubbing, touching, or blinking. Patients suffering from obsessive compulsive disorder can become so incapacitated by their obsessions and compulsions that, by the time they finally seek treatment, they are close to despair.

DISCUSSION

Much research on memory dysfunctions concerns deficits that occur after the time of brain injury or the presumed onset of the disease, that is anterograde amnesia. However, much less is known about the ability of patients to recollect information acquired prior to the onset of disease. The practical consequences of marked impairment in remote memory (i.e., retrograde amnesia) are likely to be more serious for an elderly person with dementia than are equally severe anterograde memory deficits. For example, a patient's failure to remember any of the items on a grocery list does not increase the caregiver's burden. This patient would not be expected to do the shopping anyway. On the other hand, if the dementia patient repeatedly wanders away from home and cannot find the way back (a failure of remote visuospatial memory), the burden on the caregiver is great. Institutionalisation of the patient may be necessary.

Psychogenic amnesia (dissociative amnesia) has received little attention in the literature. In contrast to organic amnesia in which acquisition of new information (anterograde memory) is usually impaired, the memory disturbance in psychogenic amnesia is often characterised by a defect of autobiographical memory, either globally or with respect to a specific situation (Kopelman, 1995). Involvement of new episodic learning, semantic

memory, and procedural memory may vary among patients with psychogenic amnesia. Accordingly, there may be some difficulties in differentiating psychogenic from organic amnesia (Kopelman, 1987a, 1994). It has been proposed that it is important to consider behavioural responses to memory rehabilitation as well as neuropsychological findings in differentiating psychogenic amnesia from an organic one (Izumi et al., 1998).

Individuals may have recollections in which they lack an understanding of how the contextual cues have led to specific events being recalled. The exploration of these memories may be carried out by searching for a match between the features present at the time of retrieval and at the time of the original event. In this manner, the prefrontal regions may attempt to create accurate assemblies of representations. Whether accurate or not, they may carry a sense of the self recalling the past. Such subjective sensations may be part of imagination, dreaming, and accurate or inaccurate recollection. Importantly, representations resembling those of the past are reassembled during the process of recollection. Retrieval is thus a "memory modifier". The act of reactivating a representation can allow it to be stored again in a modified form (Bjork, 1989). The frontal lobes carrying out the integrating, executive, and socially constructive memories of the self can directly shape the nature of autobiographical recollections and past memories. These processes explain one way in which our memories, things we may regard as facts, can actually change over time. This may also explain how repeated questioning regarding a possible experience of abuse can lead a child or an adult to confuse recollections of the stories told from the retrieval of elements of the initial experience. To better understand the issue of the validity of memories of childhood abuse, research should be performed to provide clarification of the mechanism by which accurate or inaccurate recollections of events may be created. Research is required to ascertain how trauma and traumatic response impact the memory process. Whether some people are more susceptible than others to memory suggestion and alteration, and if so, why, should also be clarified.

7

Ageing and Memory Impairment

INTRODUCTION

As individuals age into their 60s and beyond, they often complain of forgetfulness (see Table 7.1). Such age-related cognitive decline is common and generally does not progress to dementia (Larrabee & Crook, 1994). Older persons may take longer to remember things, but most of them continue to recall and recognise information well. Investigators have rather consistently noted several "normal" intellectual changes in late life and these may include slowing of reaction or cognitive processing, deterioration in so-called fluid intelligence, and impairment in certain aspects of STM (i.e., secondary or delayed recall) (Baltes, 1993; Birren & Fisher, 1991; Poon, 1985; Salthouse, 1996; Schaie, 1983). A study found that 31% of cognitively intact community-residing elders reported memory complaints, and 47% of those with cognitive impairment acknowledged memory difficulties (Schofield et al., 1997). In general, these self-perceptions of memory loss are valid, both with respect to current memory function and as predictors of impending cognitive decline. Although the effects of senescence on memory can be mitigated somewhat by education and training,

the differences between young and old individuals persist; they are to some degree related to slowing in the speed of central processing (Bryan & Luszcz, 1996; Graf & Uttl, 1995). In normal ageing, while in general the registration of new information and retrieval of older material remains relatively unaffected, the forgetting of new information occurs more rapidly.

The effects of age on behavioural performance and event-related potentials (ERP) recorded during a working memory task using digits presented either acoustically or visually, were studied in 37 healthy subjects with an age range from 19 to 71 years (Pelosi & Blumhardt, 1999). With increasing age, psychological tests showed a progressive decline in visuospatial performance and both auditory and visual reaction times increased. There were multiple and varying effects of age on both early and late ERP components. For both auditory and visual responses, increasing age was associated with an increased amplitude of early positive waves (auditory P100 and visual P145) and, in the oldest subjects, significant delays of the major late positive waves. Although performance in working memory was apparently unaffected by age, as judged by behavioural parameters (apart from slowing of the reaction times), ERPs

TABLE 7.1

Memory functions and their sensitivity to ageing processes

Type of memory function	Description	Declines with age	References
Free recall	A differential memory organisation deficit may underlie the age differences in free recall among individuals varying in locus of control when they are performing an intentional learning task; Age differences in recall under visual and haptic conditions.	Yes	Amrhein et al., 1999
Cued recall or recognition	Item-associated stimuli or other cues provided or items presented mixed with nontarget distractor items.	Min.	
Episodic	Recollection of context-specific information (e.g., word lists recall after a 5-minute delay).	Yes	Stadtlander et al., 1998
Semantic	Retrieval of vocabulary or general knowledge.	No/Min.	Foos & Sarno, 1998
Explicit	Conscious recall of specified information.	Yes	
Implicit	Unconscious recollection of facts/skills acquired during earlier exposures.	No	
Working	Although performance in working memory was apparently unaffected by age, as judged by behavioural parameters, ERPs revealed significant changes in both early and late electrical brain processes associated with working memory as age increases. These changes, which were not symptomatically manifest and only revealed by sensitive tests, may represent subtle dysfunction of working memory.	Yes	Pelosi & Blumhardt, 1999

revealed significant changes in both early and late electrical brain processes associated with working memory as age increases. These changes, which were not symptomatically manifest and only revealed by sensitive tests, may represent subtle dysfunction of working memory.

A number of clinical labels have been proposed to describe subclinical cognitive deficits. Earlier concepts such as "benign senescent forgetfulness", "age-associated cognitive memory impairment" (AAMI), "age-associated cognitive decline" (AACD) consider such mild cognitive deficits to fall within the limits of normal ageing (Crook et al., 1986; Kral, 1958, 1962; Levy, 1994). However, the "normality" of these subclinical states has been called into question because subjects with objectively demonstrated deficits have been shown to be at increased risk for neurodegenerative disease. They showed quantitative and qualitative differences in cerebral imaging, and share common biological and environmental risk factors (Ritchie & Touchon, 2000). The concept of mild cognitive impairment (MCI) has been proposed to link subclinical cognitive impairment to pathological states (Petersen et al., 1999).

The concept of MCI has predominated in the United States where large-scale research programmes have been initiated. The aim was to provide treatment and therefore to reduce the risk of progression to senile dementia. In Europe, reference is more often made to AAMI and AACD, states linked rather to the normal biological ageing process. MCI may represent an interesting concept to both clinicians and scientists as it is assumed to be pathologically based and therefore amenable to treatment intervention.

There is some evidence that vascular factors may be important in the development of cognitive impairment. Some longitudinal studies have pointed to a relationship between elevated blood pressure and development of AD later in life (Kivipelto et al., 2000; Launer et al., 2000; Skoog et al., 1996). Some longitudinal studies investigated the relationship between midlife blood pressure and late-life cognitive function in nondemented subjects. These studies have described an association between elevated systolic blood pressure, elevated diastolic blood pressure, both elevated systolic blood pressure and diastolic blood pressure or hypertension in general at midlife, and impaired cognitive performance in late life (Elias et al., 1993; Kilander et al., 1998; Launer et al., 1995). In these studies, cognitive performance was defined by a variety of neuropsychological tests instead of being based on clinical or diagnostic concepts.

NORMAL AGEING

Research in which the effects of age on working memory were assessed has shown consistent age differences in working memory performance. Children, adolescents, and older adults all have smaller memory spans than do young adults (Craik & Jennings, 1992; Hale et al., 1997; Salthouse, 1994). Relative to young adults, both children and older adults show more pronounced age deficits in spatial memory than in verbal memory. Although the mechanisms underlying the relationship between processing speed and working memory are not fully understood, it has been suggested that faster processors may activate and covertly rehearse information more quickly than slower processors (Salthouse, 1994). Studies also suggest that at all ages, individuals with larger spans show larger interference effects than do their peers with smaller spans (see Jenkins et al., 1999). Perhaps studies that examine how both age and individual differences in memory span are related to differences in processing speed may help to better understand the nature of ageing and working memory.

Among the multiple mechanisms proposed to account for some of the cognitive deficits in normal ageing is age-related decline in ability to use mental imagery (Craik & Dirkx, 1992). Investigations of mental rotation in young and elderly individuals provide ample evidence of age-related decline in performance. Older adults are slower in mental rotation and experience progressively greater slowing as a function of the angle of rotation than their young counterparts (Hertzog & Rypma, 1991; Puglisi & Morrell, 1986). Working memory plays an important role in mental rotation tasks and mental imagery in general. Ageing is associated with a reliable drop in this resource (Salthouse, 1994). Age-related deficits in working memory, in conjunction with a reduction in processing speed, have been proposed to play a critical role in age-related cognitive declines (Salthouse, 1994, 1996). In addition, age-related declines in performance on spatial visualisation tasks are predicted by reduction in both capacity and executive aspects of working memory. Thus, it is possible that age-related deterioration of working memory underlies the observed deficits in mental imagery. The magnitude of these declines appears to be uniform across a broad range of task difficulty and is mediated by individual differences in working memory (Briggs et al., 1999).

A study on normal ageing suggests that staying in close contact with people and remaining involved in meaningful activities predicted successful ageing (Kahn & Rowe, 1998). Because a large component of the study's definition for successful ageing was cognitive success, such activities will likely promote brain health as well. Neuropathological studies show that during normal ageing, the hippocampus loses some of its neurons (20–30% by the age of 80 years) and the remaining neurons develop signs of pathology (senile plaques and neurofibrillary tangles) (Squire, 1987). These findings suggest that forgetfulness in elderly individuals might at least in part be due to hippocampal dysfunction. It has been observed that age-related decline in memory performance correlated with regional electroencephalographic (EEG) changes in the frontal and temporal areas (Albert et al., 1987). Imaging studies of the medial temporal lobe and the hippocampus have further confirmed that atrophy in these regions is common in elderly persons and might contribute specifically to memory dysfunction (Launer et al., 1995a, b). The greatest loss of neurons and reduction in brain volume during ageing is seen in the frontal lobes (but also in subcortical structures, the thalamus, and the basal ganglia) (Coffey et al., 1992; Haug et al., 1983). Another view is that the number of cells is not dramatically reduced but they shrink in size (Sofroniew et al., 1987). Similar patterns of inefficiency in frontal lobe function occur in young children, older adults, and patients with frontal lobe lesions (Dempster, 1992).

Correlation of latency of the P300 component of cognitive event-related potentials with cognitive dysfunction appears to be well established. The P300 latency is correlated negatively with mental function in normal subjects. Latency increments are observed as cognitive capability decreases because of ageing (Goodin, 1990; Pfefferbaum et al., 1990). Meta-analysis studies confirmed the finding that P300 latency constantly increases with ageing, with an average increment of 2 ms/y of life (Polich, 1996). Severe P300 delays are observed in demented patients in comparison to age-matched control subjects (Neshige et al., 1988; Polich et al., 1990).

AGE-ASSOCIATED MEMORY IMPAIRMENT

Impairment in recent memory due to a reduction in storing ability and deficits in retrieval processes has been known as benign senile forgetfulness (BSF). Thus, the term BSF was introduced to distinguish subjects with mild memory decline from those with more severe "malignant" changes and also from those with normal functions (see Koukolik, 1992; Gottfries, 1988). However, the concept of BSF was not operationalised until the National Institute of Mental Health (NIMH) work group was set up to describe this phenomenon more precisely and proposed the concept of "age-associated memory impairment" (AAMI) as a diagnostic entity (Crook et al., 1986). The criteria of AAMI include the presence of subjective memory decline, objective evidence of memory loss (in a well-standardised memory test, a score at least one standard deviation below the mean of younger adults), and adequate intellectual function. Other criteria should also include the absence of dementia or other memory-affecting disease in a person aged 50 years or older. Thus, the AAMI diagnosis identified persons with subjectively and objectively evidenced memory loss without cognitive decline impairing enough to warrant the diagnosis of dementia. The criteria leave open the question of progression in the condition. The detailed AAMI criteria are presented in Table 7.2.

Some researchers have regarded both neurobiological and neuropsychological observations in ageing studies as evidence of a continuum between normal ageing, MCI, and dementia (Von Dras & Blumenthal, 1992). Since the proposition of the criteria, a substantial body of research has been conducted involving subjects with AAMI. The construct of AAMI has been used in studies aiming to characterise age differences in memory, brain structure, neuroimmunology, and cerebral metabolism (Larrabee & Crook, 1994; Parnetti et al., 1996; Reisberg et al., 1988b). It is estimated that AAMI might affect most of the over-50 population to some degree (McEntee & Crook, 1990). A prevalence rate of 35% for AAMI in subjects aged 65 years or over was reported. However, another study reported much lower prevalence rates for AAMI (Barker et al., 1995). A prevalence rate of 15.8% for AAMI in 50- to 64-year-old and 24.1% in 65- to 79-year-old subjects was reported. The low figures were mainly explained by the high proportion of subjects meeting some of the exclusion criteria since memory test performance identified as many as 79% of the participants in the AAMI category.

Although AAMI was originally defined to refer to a subpopulation of normal older people, there is some evidence that AAMI may be considered as a discrete entity, distinguishable from normal ageing. Soininen et al. (1994), in an MRI study, found that AAMI subjects presented minor structural volumetric abnormalities of the hippocampus when compared with age-matched controls. Parnetti et al. (1996), using magnetic resonance spectroscopy found lower values of N-acetyl-aspartate in the temporo-parietal areas in AAMI and AD compared with controls and intermediate hippocampal volumes for AAMI compared with those for normal ageing and AD. Finally, a study reported increases in the frequency of the apolipoprotein E (apo E) ε4 allele in the AAMI group when compared with controls and the distribution was similar to AD patients (Förstl et al., 1995). Apo E also influences cognitive profiles in AAMI subjects, with those carrying the ε4 allele performing worse in declarative and procedural memory tests (Bartrés-Faz et al., 1999). Apolipo-

TABLE 7.2

Proposed criteria for the diagnosis of age-associated memory impairment

Inclusion criteria

a. Males and females at least 50 years of age.

b. Complaints of memory loss reflected in such everyday problems as difficulty remembering names of individuals following introduction, misplacing objects, difficulty remembering multiple items to be purchased or multiple tasks to be performed, problems remembering telephone numbers or post codes, and difficulty recalling information quickly or following distraction. Onset of memory loss must be described as gradual, without sudden worsening in recent months.

c. Memory test performance that is at least 1 SD below the mean established for young adults on a standardised test of secondary memory (recent memory) with adequate normative data. Examples of specific tests and appropriate cut off scores are listed below, although other measures with adequate normative data are equally appropriate.
Test Cut-off score:
Benton Visual Retention Test (A) 6 or less
Logical Memory Subtest of the Wechsler Memory Scale (WMS) of 6 or less
Associate Learning Subtest of the WMS 13 or less

d. Evidence of adequate intellectual function as determined by a scaled score of at least 9 (raw score of at least 32) on the Vocabulary subtest of the Wechsler Adult Intelligence Scale.

e. Absence of dementia as determined by a score of 24 or higher on the Mini-Mental Scale Examination.

Exclusion criteria

a. Evidence of delirium, confusion, or other disturbances of consciousness.

b. Any neurological disorder that could produce cognitive deterioration as determined by history, clinical neurological examination, and if indicated, neuroradiological examinations. Such disorders include AD, PD, stroke, intracranial haemorrhage, local brain lesions including tumours, and normal pressure hydrocephalus.

c. History of any infective or inflammatory brain disease, including those of viral, fungal, or syphilitic aetiologies.

d. Evidence of significant cerebral vascular pathology as determined by a Hachinski Ischaemic score of 4 or more, or by neuroradiological examination.

e. History of repeated minor head injury (e.g., in boxing) or a single injury resulting in a period of unconsciousness for 1 hour or more.

f. Current psychiatric diagnosis according to DSM–III criteria of depression, mania, or any major psychiatric disorder.

g. Current diagnosis or history of alcoholism or drug dependence.

h. Evidence of depression as determined by a Hamilton Depression Rating Scale score of 13 or more.

i. Any medical disorder that could produce cognitive deterioration, including renal, respiratory, cardiac, or hepatic disease; diabetes mellitus unless well controlled by diet or oral hypoglycaemics; endocrine, metabolic or haematological disturbances or malignancy not in remission for more than 2 years. Determination should be read on complete medical history, clinical examination (including electrocardiogram), and appropriate tests.

j. Use of any psychotropic drug or any other drug that may significantly affect cognitive function during the month prior to psychotropic testing.

National Institute of Mental Health Work Group (Crook et al., 1986).

protein E ε4 dose was significantly correlated with the rate of hippocampal atrophy, suggesting a gene dose effect in accelerated brain atrophy in dementia (Mori et al., 2002). This observation has implications for therapeutic approaches in AAMI and AD and should be taken into consideration in longitudinal studies including clinical drug trials.

Although many studies have supported the theoretical construct of AAMI, other investigators have doubted the usefulness of the AAMI diagnosis. Revisions in the defining criteria to reduce the variability in the AAMI population to enhance the reliability of the diagnosis have been suggested (Caine, 1993; O'Brien & Levy, 1992). AAMI may be too sensitive in detecting less-well-educated individuals and older people with high levels of psychopathology (Franceschi & Canal, 1996; Koivisto et al., 1995). It may also be too broad, and identify a highly heterogeneous group of normal older people (O'Brien & Levy, 1992). There is evidence that the AAMI rates are modified depending on which test was used during the diagnosis and that the probability of diagnosing the entity increases as the number of tests used (Blackford & La Rue, 1989; Smith et al., 1991). Thus, further research is warranted. In particular, follow-up studies of AAMI subjects have been recommended (Nichol, 1995; O'Brien, 1994).

TABLE 7.3

Diagnostic criteria for ageing-associated cognitive decline (AACD)

1. A report by the individual or a reliable informant that cognitive function has declined.
2. Onset of decline must be described as gradual and must have been present for at least 6 months.
3. Difficulties in any one of the following areas: memory and learning; attention and concentration; thinking (e.g., problem solving, abstraction); language (e.g., comprehension, word finding); visuospatial functioning.
4. Abnormality of performance on quantitative cognitive assessments (for example, neuropsychological tests or mental state evaluation) for which age and education norms are available for relatively healthy individuals. Performance must be at least 1 SD below the mean value for the appropriate population.
5. Exclusion criteria: None of the abnormalities listed above of a degree sufficient for the diagnosis of mild cognitive disorder or dementia to be made. (There must be no objective evidence from physical and neurological examination or laboratory tests, and no history of cerebral disease or damage, or of systemic physical disorder known to cause cerebral dysfunction). Other exclusion criteria would be as follows: (a) depression, anxiety or other significant psychiatric disorder that may contribute to the observed difficulties; (b) organic amnestic syndrome; (c) delirium; (d) postencephalitic syndrome; (e) postconcussional syndrome; (f) persisting cognitive impairment due to psychoactive substance use or the effects of any centrally-acting drug.

Working Party of the IPA in collaboration with WHO (Levy, 1994).

AGEING-ASSOCIATED COGNITIVE DECLINE

A task force of the International Psychogeriatric Association (IPA) in collaboration with the World Health Organisation (WHO) has proposed diagnostic criteria for "age-associated cognitive decline" (AACD) (Levy, 1994). The diagnosis of AACD is based on a more comprehensive assessment of cognition than that of AAMI. Impairment in any major cognitive domain is sufficient for identifying AACD. The cognitive functions that are assessed in the AACD criteria are memory and learning, attention and concentration, thinking, language, and visuospatial function (see Table 7.3).

AACD and AAMI must also be differentiated from the various other diagnostic classifications that have been proposed (Ebly et al., 1995). The best established of these classifications are "mild cognitive impairment" (MCI) and "age-related cognitive decline" (ARCD). ARCD is included in the DSM–IV (American Psychiatric Association, 1994) and is defined as "an objectively identified decline in cognitive functioning consequent to the ageing process that is within normal limits given the person's age". However, no more detailed criteria are included in the DSM–IV and no studies employing this construct have been conducted. Some evidence suggests that patients with AAMI have an increased risk of developing dementia, a

finding that has generated considerable concern and provided the impetus for rigorous investigation (Green, 1995).

MILD COGNITIVE IMPAIRMENT

Interest has been generated in understanding the boundary or transitional state between normal ageing and AD (Petersen, 1995). A large group of elderly cognitively impaired subjects do not meet the criteria for dementia or other specific neurological and psychiatric disorders. Reported prevalence rates for mild dementia or "mild cases of cognitive impairment" are much higher than for dementia and could also be wrongly assessed by inadequate specification (Mowry & Burvill, 1988). Several descriptors including MCI, incipient dementia, and isolated memory impairment have been used (Flicker et al., 1991; Minoshima et al., 1997; Tierney et al., 1996a, b). The terminology "mild cognitive impairment" refers to subjective memory disturbances verified by objective deficits of memory at testing (Flicker et al., 1991). Some authors seem to label any slight cognitive impairment as a mild case of dementia but few such cases progress to dementia. In defining dementia, one has to exclude this very important group of subjects not yet demented but with "mild cognitive impairment". Estimates for "mild dementia" or "mild cognitive impairment" are derived using different methods and vary widely, from a low 10% for the population over 70 years old to a high of 50%. A recent study reported that the prevalence of MCI was estimated to be 3.2% and AACD 19.3% (Ritchie et al., 2001). MCI was a poor predictor of dementia within a 3-year period, with an 11.1% conversion rate. Individuals with MCI constituted an unstable group, with almost all subjects changing category each year. Discriminant function analysis failed to identify a homogeneous clinical group. On the other hand, patients classified as AACD represented a more stable group, with a 28.6% conversion rate to dementia over 3 years (relative risk = 21.2). It was argued that the MCI criteria perform poorly when applied to a representative population sample. Modifications to current diagnostic criteria to increase their capacity to detect incipient dementia were suggested.

Current data point to a role for midlife vascular risk factors in the development of MCI in late life. A recent study designed to investigate the impact of midlife elevated serum cholesterol levels and blood pressure on the subsequent development of MCI by applying the MCI criteria devised by the Mayo Clinic Alzheimer's Disease Research Centre performed an average follow-up of 21 years of 1449 subjects aged 65 to 79 years old (Kivipelto et al., 2001). It was reported that 6.1% of the population (average age, 72 years) met the criteria for MCI. Midlife elevated serum cholesterol level (≥ 6.5 mmol/L) was a significant risk factor for MCI. The effect of blood pressure approached significance.

A neuropathological study showed that subjects with MCI have a range of histological findings, from those seen in normal brain ageing to those that characterise AD (Petersen et al., 1997). Computed tomography has demonstrated a smaller medial temporal lobe volume in MCI subjects than in the normal elderly. A SPECT study has shown that temporo-parietal perfusion in MCI subjects is intermediate between that seen in normal elderly subjects and AD patients (Celsis et al., 1997). Quantitative electroencephalography has shown similar pattern in AD and MCI patients, clearly

different from that observed in normal elderly subjects (Jelicic et al., 1996). A study using proton-magnetic resonance spectroscopy (^{1}H-MRS) have shown an increase in the grey matter myo-inositol/creatine ratio in MCI subjects compared with normal controls (Kantarci et al., 2003). Recently, such findings have been confirmed in a study that showed that MCI is different from normal brain ageing, having a white matter biochemical pattern similar to AD (Cantani et al., 2001). MCI seems to be associated with medial temporal lobe changes that represent reliable predictors of dementia in these individuals (Jack et al., 1999). The results of a recent study also showed that MCI individuals present higher prevalences of apo E $\varepsilon4$ alleles and are more cognitively impaired beyond the memory domain when compared with AAMI (Bartrés-Faz et al., 2001). The examination of the presynaptic cholinergic marker choline acetyltransferase in the brains of individuals with no cognitive impairment, with MCI, and with mild-to-moderate AD was also performed (DeKosky et al., 2002). The results showed elevated choline acetyltransferase activity (suggesting up-regulation of cholinergic systems) in the frontal cortex and hippocampus of individuals with MCI. It was observed for the first time that cholinergic systems may be upregulated in MCI individuals and that the loss of this apparent compensatory response may mark the conversion of MCI to diagnosable AD. In addition to this involvement of cholinergic system, MCI individuals share other features of AD (memory impairment, increased frequency of the apolipoprotein E $\varepsilon4$ allele, medial temporal atrophy, and cerebral metabolic abnormalities) (Morris & Price, 2001; Petersen et al., 1996). MCI represents a more homogeneous condition than does AAMI, a finding that is further supported by follow-up studies (Hänninen et al., 1995; Nielsen et al., 1998; Petersen et al., 1995, 1999). Thus, MCI subjects represent a clear high-risk population for developing dementia and can be considered to represent an intermediate state between AD and normal ageing (Petersen et al., 1996; Smith et al., 1996b).

Early diagnosis of dementia relies on the documentation of mild impairments of memory and other cognitive processes. Memory and executive dysfunction showed the greatest decline over time in individuals who would clinically manifest AD 1.5 years later (Chen et al., 2001). These findings highlight the importance of executive dysfunction in the disease process and might facilitate early detection of AD. These data may also help to understand the underlying evolution of the early neurodegenerative process. The results of several studies indicate that these individuals with MCI are at an increased risk for developing AD ranging from 1% to 25% per year (Dawe et al., 1992). This variability in rates probably reflects differing diagnostic criteria, measurement instruments, and small sample sizes. Unfortunately, these "preclinical" memory impairments or early stage of dementia are often confounded by the decline occurring in normal ageing or by difficulties of interpretation associated with a low intelligence quotient or level of education, or with depression. The use of efficient neuropsychological screening test to predict such early stage dementia is crucial to start effective preventive treatment. Until recently, clinicians and researchers had difficulty in diagnosing MCI as there was no agreed upon definition for the condition. However, from established characteristics, five diagnostic criteria for MCI have been suggested (Petersen et al., 1999). They include memory complaints, abnormal memory for age, ability to carry out normal activities of daily living, normal general cognitive function, and lack of dementia.

Diagnostic criteria for MCI include cut-off scores on memory tests, scores aimed at identifying individuals with pathological memory and which identify individuals with a higher risk of progression to dementia. In a study comparing the cognitive test results of people with MCI to those of healthy normal controls and mild AD patients, MCI participants performed worse on memory measures than healthy normal people, scoring roughly equivalent to patients with mild AD (Callahan et al., 1995). However, measurements of activities of daily living revealed MCI scores equivalent to healthy normal people and superior to those with AD. A measure commonly utilised to diagnose MCI is the Clinical Dementia Rating Scale (CDR). The CDR was initially designed as a staging instrument for the dementia of AD and rates the severity of dementia as absent (CDR = 0), questionable (CDR = 0.5), mild (CDR = 1), moderate (CDR = 2), or severe (CDR = 3) (Morris, 1993). While MCI patients typically score a CDR of 0.5, there is some heterogeneity in this classification, as some with this score would warrant a diagnosis of probable AD. This heterogeneity springs from the fact that some portions of the CDR test for memory impairments and thus register MCI patients, while other sections test for more global cognitive functions in which those with probable AD score poorly. Thus patients diagnosed with AD who have a CDR of only 0.5 are more likely to be impaired ($\leq$ 1 standard deviation below normal) on other measures of cognition as well as verbal IQ, performance IQ, Mini-Mental State Exam (MMSE), and Dementia Rating Scale. A recent study that investigated the retrieval and encoding of episodic memory in normal ageing and patients with MCI suggests that encoding of episodic memory is vulnerable to being impaired in MCI patients (Wang & Zhou, 2002). There was significant decline in the function of orientation, language, and praxis besides memory impairment in the MCI group. Impairment of encoding and retrieval of episodic memory was also observed in the MCI group. It was suggested that MCI might be a transitional state from normal ageing and AD.

A study that used the SIDAM (also called SISCO) score (Structured Interview for the Diagnosis of Dementia of the Alzheimer type, multi-infarct dementia, and dementias of other aetiology, according to the DSM–III–R and ICD–10) reported that for "mild cognitive impairment", a SISCO between 34 and 47 (ICD–10: 34–51) was found (Zaudig, 1992). The SISCO covers more cognitive functions than the MMSE and is more useful in detecting even "mild cognitive decline". It was therefore suggested that the SIDAM could be used as a short diagnostic instrument for measurement and diagnostic of dementia and MCI. A study designed to characterise clinically subjects with MCI cross-sectionally and longitudinally studied 76 consecutively evaluated subjects with MCI compared to 234 healthy control subjects and 106 patients with mild AD (Petersen et al., 1999). This study reported that the primary distinction between control subjects and subjects with MCI was in the area of memory, while other cognitive functions were comparable. When the subjects with MCI were compared with the patients with very mild AD, memory performance was similar, but patients with AD were more impaired in other cognitive domains as well. Longitudinal evaluations showed that the subjects with MCI declined at a rate greater than that of the controls but less rapidly than the patients with mild AD. Therefore, it may be suggested that subjects with MCI may constitute a clinical entity that can be categorised for pharmacological treatment interventions. Another interesting longitudinal study directly compared change in different cognitive abilities and other key clinical milestones in individuals with MCI to those without cognitive impairment (Bennett et al., 2002). The results showed that on average, subjects with MCI had significantly lower scores at baseline in all cognitive domains. Over an average of 4.5 years of follow-up, 30% of subjects with MCI had died, a rate 1.7 times higher than those without cognitive impairment. The results also indicated that 34% of subjects with MCI developed AD, a rate 3.1 times higher than those without cognitive impairment. Furthermore, subjects with MCI declined significantly faster on measures of episodic memory, semantic memory, and perceptual speed but not on measures of working memory or visuospatial ability as compared with normal control elderly subjects. These data suggest that MCI is associated with an increased risk of death and incident AD and a greater rate of decline in selected cognitive functions.

MAINTAINING COGNITIVE VITALITY WITH AGEING

Memory loss is not inevitable with ageing. Staying mentally and physically active are the main preventives. Most people can keep their mental capacities from declining just by doing simple things like walking, reading the newspapers, and getting help for problems like depression and stress. Simple recommendations to prevent age-related memory loss include lifelong learning (the intellectual stimulation that comes from doing memory exercises and playing intellectually stimulating games), exercise (this increases blood supply and oxygen to the brain), and daily activities (remaining active with travelling, volunteering, gardening, and joining social events). Other important prevention measures are stress reduction (meditation and muscle relaxation training can be helpful), sleep (sleep disorders may interfere with cognitive function), and emotional stability (depression is particularly common in elderly people and should be treated adequately if protracted). Finally, a balanced diet is very important.

DISCUSSION

The definition of "normal ageing" is problematic since the typical "normal" control group of elderly individuals is also likely to include a few subjects with some brain disorder (Lezak, 1995). Beside the purely memory defects, elders' underperformance in memory tests may be under the influence of a significant number of extra-memory factors such as of motivation, absence of familiarity with the testing procedures, sensory defects, and depression. Research into the relationship of "normal" changes with those resulting from degenerative diseases, especially AD, relates to the debate about the continuum from normal ageing to dementia. Several authors have suggested that a short battery of neuropsychological tests should be used for dementia screening instead of a cognitive scale or only one individual test (Morris et al., 1989; Stern et al., 1992a, b). However, despite satisfying results in case-control studies, it has been difficult to establish a method for dementia screening that would be at the same time sensitive and specific enough at the population level.

Elderly subjects evidence a clear decline in explicit memory (Light, 1991). On the other hand, several investigators have detected no age effects on priming measures (Light & Singh, 1987). It has been suggested that this pattern of memory change bears a qualitative resemblance to the pattern of deficits seen in amnesic patients (Light & Singh, 1987). However, other investigators have found a significant decline in priming in older compared to young individuals (Davis et al., 1990; Hultsch et al., 1991). Such findings have led to comparisons between memory impairments in normal ageing and in AD and it has been suggested that AD may represent a more severe or accelerated form of normal age-related memory decline associated with degeneration in the medial temporal lobe system.

The validity of the AAMI construct is still dubious. Several aspects of the diagnostic criteria are disputable. The AAMI diagnosis appears to identify a very heterogeneous group of subjects of only vague clinical or theoretical significance. The relevance of the AACD diagnosis remains to be evaluated in further studies. More reliable diagnostic approaches are needed in studies trying to identify risk factors for dementia or to find treatment for very early dementia. The diseases that progress to dementia may in their course from normality to dementia resemble AAMI, the amnesic syndrome, or diminished cognitive capacity. Because there is a need to treat such patients before they meet the criteria for mild dementia, concepts and definitions of possible milder categories are needed. There does not seem to be any rationale for waiting until a patient meets criteria for dementia before treatment is started. On the contrary, treatment should begin as soon as the diagnosis is suspected.

Considering the assessment of elderly patients, cohort differences may also occur in test-taking characteristics. Older subjects may be unfamiliar with standardised testing, making them more anxious or less motivated in test sessions. They might be more vulnerable to fatigue. However, some problems are also evident in longitudinal studies. The repeated administration of neuropsychological tests appears to result in significant practice effects. Longitudinal studies have suggested that MCI determined by clinical and neuropsychological tests is useful in predicting dementia from 2 to 3 years before the condition is manifest clinically (Bickel & Cooper, 1994; Flicker et al., 1991). Observed mild cognitive decline also appears to be associated with a greater risk of mortality in very old age groups (Johansson et al., 1992). However, assessment methods that rely on neuropsy-

chological batteries may not detect subtle impairments because test performance may not reflect the patient's impaired ability to carry out customary activities of daily living. It is also important to assess how these patients appraise their memory function and to enhance their sense of control over their memory abilities because one's sense of control can influence motivation and memory performance (Lachman, 2000; West et al., 2000). A history of declining cognitive and functional performance in relation to that individual's previous abilities, however, can be sensitive to early-stage dementia even when cognitive test performance is within a normal range (Crum et al., 1993; Morris et al., 1996a; Tierney et al., 1987). This history usually is obtained from someone who knows the individual well, such as a family member.

Evaluation procedures that are based exclusively on neuropsychological tests rather than collateral source information may not detect subtle cognitive and functional decline in MCI or in putatively nondemented individuals. Further, numerous studies have shown that a large proportion of patients diagnosed with mild to moderate AD lack full awareness of their progressive cognitive decline (DeBettignies et al., 1990; Kotler-Cope & Camp, 1995; Kiyak et al., 1994). A study designed to evaluate the predictive utility of self-reported and informant-reported functional deficits in patients with MCI for the follow-up diagnosis of probable AD showed that in patients with MCI, the patient's lack of awareness of functional deficits identified by informants strongly predicts a future diagnosis of AD (Tabert et al., 2002). These data may suggest that clinicians who evaluate MCI patients should obtain both self-reports and informant reports of functional deficits to help in prediction of long-term outcome.

A role for genetic factors as modificators of cognition during ageing has been suggested (Helkala et al., 1996). The value of studies combining behavioural and neurobiological assessments in the same subject to define the neural basis of age-related cognitive changes and to identify the factors that promote successful ageing has been emphasised (Rapp & Amaral, 1992). Although sensitive clinical and neuropsychological assessment approaches can be very helpful in this regard, hopefully the development of a biological marker that relates directly to the clinical and pathological changes in AD may ultimately further help to identify prodromal and preclinical states. These states may be the optimal targets of eventual disease-modifying interventions. Until more of that work is completed it will be difficult to develop treatment strategies specific to the MCI condition. Furthermore, conducting clinical trials on MCI presents a unique ethical dilemma as such studies require treatment of subjects without disease with potentially potent drugs for long periods of time.

Several studies of neuronal number in the hippocampus and entorhinal cortex have shown that there is essentially no neuronal loss with ageing but substantial cell and volume loss in AD (Kordower et al., 2001; West et al., 1994). In the entorhinal cortex, in particular, marked cell loss was found in mild AD cases—Clinical Dementia Rating (CDR) 0.5 (Gomez-Isla et al., 1996; Kordower et al., 2001). Since a high proportion of MCI patients might represent the preclinical stage of AD, it is extremely important to find early markers such as neuropathological or neurocognitive changes which may help to characterise the early phases of AD. For this reason, a study that investigated levels of a biomarker in subjects with MCI reported that individuals with MCI have increased brain oxidative damage before the onset of symptomatic dementia (Pratico et al., 2002). The isoprostanes, sensitive and specific markers of in vivo lipid peroxidation, have been found to be increased in cerebrospinal fluid, blood, and urine of patients with a clinical diagnosis of AD (Pratico, 1999). These levels were highly correlated with other biomarkers of AD pathology and with the severity of the disease (Pratico et al., 2000). Assessing subjects with MCI who attended the Memory Disorders Clinic, Pratico et al. (2002) found significantly higher 8, 12-iso-iPF$_{2\alpha}$-VI levels in cerebrospinal fluid, plasma, and urine of subjects with MCI compared with cognitively normal elderly subjects. Thus, it appears that measurement of this isoprostane may identify a subgroup of patients with MCI with increased lipid peroxidation who are at increased risk to progress to AD.

The results of an MRI study that assessed the hippocampal volume as an index of Alzheimer neuropathology suggest that volumetric measures of the hippocampus may be useful in identifying nondemented individuals who satisfy neuropathologic criteria for AD as well as pathological stages of AD that may be present decades before initial clinical expression (Gosche et al., 2002). Another interesting study that aimed to assess whether reduced glucose metabolism (rCMRGlu) and cognitive functioning could predict development of AD in patients with MCI followed 20 MCI patients for an average interval of 36.5 months (Arnaiz et al., 2001). Logistic regression indicated the two variables that most effectively predicted future development of AD were rCMRGlu from the left temporo-parietal area and performance on the block design. These combined measures provided an optimal 90% correct classification rate whereas rCMRGlu or neuropsychology alone showed 75% and 65% correct classification, respectively. This finding offers a practical relevance for an easy identification of subjects at risk of developing dementia.

Memory Dysfunctions in Neurodegenerative Diseases

INTRODUCTION

Dementia was initially thought of as a unitary behavioural syndrome, characterised by a homogeneous decline in intellectual functions, regardless of aetiology. Subsequently, clinical studies of cognition in dementias suggested that the pattern of dysfunction in dementia was heterogeneous, depending largely on whether the pathological process affected predominantly cortical or subcortical structures. Dementia is defined as decline of memory and other cognitive functions in comparison with the patient's previous level of function, implying a change between two or more assessment points (McKhann et al., 1984). Evaluation of dynamic change over time, by accounting for potential confounders, is clinically more meaningful than a single assessment. There are many kinds of dementia documented, with the traditional breakdown being 70% AD, 20% vascular disease, and 10% other (made of uncommon conditions and the so-called reversible dementias). Fronto-temporal dementia (FTD) is the second cause of primary degenerative dementia, after AD

with or without Lewy bodies (Neary et al., 1998). FTD was often confused with AD and rarely diagnosed during life, although differentiating FTD from AD is feasible even on the basis of retrospective historical information obtained from relatives of patients (Barber et al., 2002). Dementia of the Alzheimer's type and multi-infarct dementia (MID) are usually considered to be the two most frequent forms of dementia, even if recent anatomoclinical an neuropathological studies have shown that vascular lesions alone are probably unable to provoke a clear clinical syndrome of dementia (Nolan et al., 1998; Ott et al., 1998; Snowdon et al., 1997). As a consequence of the different locations of neurofibrillary tangles and senile plaques, and of lacunar infarcts, AD and MID patients have different neuropsychological profiles. Poorer performance is usually found in AD patients on episodic memory tasks and to a lesser extent, on tasks of language, on tasks of constructional apraxia, and on tasks requiring visuospatial abilities (Gainotti et al., 1989, 1992; Kertesz & Clydesdale, 1994; Looi & Sachdev, 1999). Inferior performance is observed in MID patients on tasks involving executive functions, attention, and psychomotor speed (Almkvist et al., 1993; Gainotti et al., 1992; Villardita, 1993). A recent study confirmed that while psychomotor speed and the lower (sensorimotor) levels of attention are preferentially impaired in subcortical forms of dementia such as MID, the higher levels of selective and divided attention are more markedly disrupted in the Alzheimer type of dementia (Gainotti et al., 2001).

A recent study that was designed to assess STM and LTM in FTD and AD patients showed that FTD patients demonstrated a genuine memory deficit, with impaired digit span, encoding deficit, and retrieval strategy difficulties but preserved implicit verbal and visual priming (Pasquier et al., 2001). STM and free recall were similarly decreased in FTD and AD but cues provided more benefit to FTD than to AD. Encoding was more impaired and the forgetting rate was faster in AD than in FTD. Priming was also lower in AD than in FTD. Thus, this study outlined a differential pattern of memory deficit in FTD and AD.

A variety of conditions have been labelled as subcortical dementias, including progressive supranuclear palsy (PSP), HD, PD, Wilson's disease, idiopathic basal ganglia calcification, and multiple sclerosis (Albert, 1978; McHugh & Folstein, 1975). The subcortical dementias are characterised as involving predominantly the basal ganglia, white matter, and/or brainstem structures, and as causing disturbances in arousal, attention, retrieval, motivation, mood, and motor programming (Cummings & Benson, 1984). These fundamental deficits result in psychomotor slowing, memory impairment, difficulty in actively manipulating novel information, lack of efficiency in accessing old knowledge, and emotional changes (e.g., depression, apathy). This pattern of impairment is said to be different from that of patients with cortical dementias, of which AD is the hallmark. Therefore, a distinction was drawn between "cortical vs subcortical" dementias and the term "subcortical dementia" came to refer to a variety of dementias associated primarily with subcortical pathology early in the course of these diseases (e.g., PD, HD, and multiple sclerosis), which were thought to lead to similar patterns of cognitive impairment (Cummings & Benson, 1984).

The validity of the subcortical–cortical dementia distinction is still a matter of controversy. Criticism of this dichotomy has been made primarily on neuroanatomical grounds (Whitehouse, 1986). Some patients with PD, for example, have been found to have cortical neuropathological changes similar to those found in AD patients (Boller et al., 1980). In addition, pathological changes in subcortical structures, most notably the cholinergic nucleus basalis of Meynert, have been discovered in AD patients (Coyle et al., 1983). Thus, it has been shown that subcortical and cortical dementias do not involve exclusively subcortical or cortical pathophysiology, especially considering the complex interconnections between subcortical and cortical structures. However, metabolic studies have shown that subcortical dementias involve greater subcortical than cortical hypometabolism whereas cortical dementia (e.g., AD) is characterised by the opposite pattern (Benson et al., 1983). A number of studies, in fact, have found clear distinctions in explicit memory performance between AD and HD patients, AD and PD patients, and AD and PSP patients (Butters et al., 1988a, b; Filley et al., 1989; Pillon et al., 1986). Overall, AD patients typically displayed severely impaired immediate free recall, rapid forgetting of information over time, and recognition memory impairment as severe as their free recall deficits. Subcortical dementia patients often exhibited immediate free recall deficits as severe as those seen in AD, but showed superior retention over time and marked improvement on recognition testing compared with free recall. AD patients also give higher rates of intrusion errors, particularly on delayed-recall trials (Kramer et al., 1988).

Although AD is the most common cortical neurodegenerative condition that affects semantic memory, there are also reports of focal neurodegenerative processes that degrade semantic networks (Hodges et al; 1992; Snowden et al., 1989). The term semantic dementia was used to describe several cases of progressive focal atrophy that presented with prominent and circumscribed impairment of semantic memory. The core features include impairment of semantic memory manifest in anomia, impaired single-word comprehension, reduced category fluency, and degraded fund of general knowledge. Other features include a relative sparing of syntax and phonology, intact perceptual and non-verbal problem-solving abilities, and "relatively preserved" episodic memory. The focal and progressive changes in semantic memory that are manifest early on in the disease course, as well as the sites and nature of the neuropathology, set this condition apart from the progressive amnesic dementia characteristics of typical AD. The disease process seems to initially strike at the temporal lobe core of the neural networks that subserve semantic memory storage.

The particular clinical presentation of a dementing syndrome often suggests the specific condition. For example, AD is typically characterised by memory loss, language impairment, and visuospatial disturbances. Patients may also appear indifferent and suffer from delusions and agitation, particularly during the later stages of the disease. By contrast, in fronto-temporal dementia, there are marked personality changes with relative preservation of visuospatial skills but loss of function. In dementia with Lewy bodies, the patient often experiences prominent visual hallucinations, delusions, fluctuating mental status, and neuroleptic sensitivity.

ALZHEIMER'S DISEASE

AD is a disease of the elderly. Age is the single most important risk factor for AD, with the prevalence of AD increasing almost exponentially between the ages of 65 and 85 (Katzman & Kawas, 1994). It is estimated that AD affects about 2% of people between the ages of 65 and 70, increasing to 3% between 70 and 75, and to about 10–15% by age 85 and over (Kolb & Wishaw, 1991). The prevalence of AD is greater in women: in fact, the woman:man ratio has been reported to be almost 3:1 for patients over 75 years old (Filley, 1997). Although the onset and course of the disease is similar for the sexes, women often score lower in cognitive/neuropsychological testing than men of comparable age, education, family history, and duration of symptoms (Filley, 1997). In addition to age, several other risk factors for AD

have been identified. The ε4 allele of the apolipoprotein gene located on chromosome 19 is over-represented in AD patients. Patients with the epsilin 4/4 genotype have a more than 10-fold higher risk of dementia and patients with the epsilon 3/4 genotype have a 1.7-fold increased risk of dementia as compared with individuals with the epsilon 3/3 genotype (Slooter et al., 1998). A recent study reported that apolipoprotein E ε4 dose was significantly correlated with the rate of hippocampal atrophy, suggesting a gene dose effect (Mori et al., 2002). A positive family history of AD represents another risk factor. Individuals with a first-degree relative with AD are almost four times more likely to develop AD than those without such a family history (Van Duijm et al., 1991).

The hallmark neuropathological lesions of AD are neurofibrillary tangles (NFTs) and neuropil threads (NTs), both of which are composed of hyperphosphorylated tau arranged in paired helical filaments as senile plaques composed of β-amyloid peptides. A recent study reported that phosphorylated tau pathology in the ventromedial temporal lobe develops prior to the onset of clinical dementia, and their presence is associated with cognitive impairment, particularly impairment of episodic memory (Mitchell et al., 2002). This finding is important as it demonstrates the clinical relevance of neurofibrillary pathology in ageing and early dementia. Thus, it appears that neuropathology and cognitive changes in AD are continuous correlated variables.

It has been suggested that in familial AD, cognitive decline predates symptoms by several years and that verbal memory deficits precede more widespread deterioration (Fox et al., 1998). In this 6-year period study, 63 subjects underwent serial assessments. During the study, 10 subjects developed symptoms of episodic memory loss and subsequently progressed to fulfil criteria for possible and probable AD. Subjects who later became clinically affected already had significantly lower verbal memory and performance IQ scores at their first assessment when they were ostensibly unaffected. Subsequent assessments showed progressive decline in multiple cognitive domains. Blinded evaluations of serial imaging showed the appearance of diffuse cerebral and medial temporal lobe atrophy in individuals once they were clinically affected. This study therefore suggests that verbal memory loss is detectable some years before symptoms appear and that verbal memory test could be used as a predictor of which subjects would develop AD. The finding of early verbal memory deficits accords with imaging and autopsy reports of early hippocampal involvement in AD. Most clinicians agree that the line between incipient dementia and cognitive changes associated with normal ageing is a fuzzy one. This can only be drawn by a comprehensive neuropsychological evaluation. In addition to memory evaluation, tests should include a standardised assessment of functions like intelligence, language, visuospatial abilities, and executive and sensorimotor functions.

The dementia of AD typically includes anterograde and retrograde amnesia early in its course. The aetiology of symptomatic changes, prognosis, symptomatology, and assessment all vary depending on the disease stage. Additionally, the range of utility of assessment measures and treatment side effects vary with stage. The Global Deterioration Scale (GDS) is a clinical staging instrument frequently employed (see Table 8.1) (Reisberg et al., 1982, 1988a, b). Deficits in recent memory are typically the first symptoms of AD and may be clinically reported as misplacing objects, repeating questions and statements, and forgetting names. When clinical neuropsychological tests are used to evaluate memory in AD patients, it is clear that recall and recognition performances are impaired in both the verbal and non-verbal domains (Storandt & Hill, 1989; Wilson et al. 1983). Impairments in visuospatial memory are often experienced as getting lost. This anterograde amnesia reflects impaired encoding and consolidation of the material. Patient groups with minimal and mild AD were found to be impaired on autobiographical memory (Greene et al., 1995; Sagar et al., 1988). Patients in the minimal and mild stages show a temporal gradient, with stronger deficits for recent events (late adult) than for events of childhood and early adult life.

The first stage of memory capacity that can be distinguished is that in which elderly individuals

TABLE 8.1

Global Deterioration Scale (GDS) for age-associated cognitive decline and Alzheimer's disease

GDS	Clinical characteristics	Diagnosis
1 No cognitive decline	No subjective complaints of memory deficit. No memory deficit evident on clinical interview.	Normal
2 Very mild cognitive decline	Subjective complaints of memory deficit, most frequently in the following areas: (a) forgetting where one has placed familiar objects. (b) forgetting names one formerly knew well. No objective evidence of memory deficit on clinical interview. No objective deficit in employment or social situations. Appropriate concern with respect to symptomatology.	Normal ageing
3 Mild cognitive decline	Earliest clear-cut deficits. Manifestations in more than one of the following areas: (a) patient may have become lost when travelling to an unfamiliar location. (b) co-workers become aware of patient's relatively poor performance. (c) word and name finding deficit becomes evident to intimates. (d) patient may read a passage or book and retain relatively little material. (e) patient may demonstrate decreased facility remembering names upon introduction to new people. (f) patient may have lost or misplaced an object of value. (g) concentration deficit may be evident on clinical testing. Objective evidence of memory deficit obtained only with an intensive interview. Decreased performance in demanding employment and social settings. Denial begins to become manifest in patient. Mild-to-moderate anxiety frequently accompanies symptoms.	Compatible with incipient AD

TABLE 8.1 (CONT'D)

GDS	Clinical characteristics	Diagnosis
4 Moderate cognitive decline	Clear-cut deficit on careful clinical interview. Deficit manifest in the following areas: (a) decreased knowledge of current and recent events. (b) may exhibit some deficit in memory of one's personal history. (c) concentration deficit elicited on serial subtractions. (d) decreased ability to travel, handle finances, etc. Frequently no deficit in the following areas: (a) orientation to time and place. (b) recognition of familiar persons and faces. (c) ability to travel to familiar locations. Inability to perform complex tasks. Denial is dominant defence mechanism. Flattening of affect and withdrawal from challenging situations occur.	Mild AD
5 Moderately severe decline	Patient can no longer survive without some assistance. Patient is unable during interview to recall a major relevant aspect of their current life; e.g.: (a) their address or telephone number of many years. (b) the names of close members of their family (such as grandchildren). (c) the name of the high school or college from which they graduated. Frequently some disorientation to time (date, day of the week, season, etc.) or to place. An educated person may have difficulty counting back from 40 in 4s or from 20 in 2s. Persons at this stage retain knowledge of many major facts regarding themselves and others. They invariably know their own names and generally know their spouse's and children's names. They require no assistance with toileting or eating, but may have difficulty choosing the proper clothing to wear.	Moderate AD
6 Severe cognitive decline	May occasionally forget the name of the spouse upon whom they are entirely dependent for survival. Will be largely unaware of all recent events and experiences in their lives. Retain some knowledge of their surroundings: the year, the season, etc. May have difficulty counting by 1s from 10 both backward and sometimes forward. Will require some assistance with activities of daily living: (a) may become incontinent. (b) will require travel assistance but occasionally will be able to travel to familiar locations. Diurnal rhythm frequently disturbed. Almost always recall their own name. Frequently continue to be able to distinguish familiar from unfamiliar persons in their environment. Personality and emotional changes occur. These are quite variable and include: (a) delusional behaviour, e.g., patients may accuse their spouses of being an imposter or may talk to imaginary figures in the environment or to their own reflection in the mirror. (b) obsessive symptoms, e.g., person may continually repeat simple cleaning activities. (c) anxiety symptoms, agitation, and even previously non-existent violent behaviour. (d) cognitive abulia, e.g., loss of willpower because an individual cannot carry a thought long enough to determine a purposeful course of action.	Moderately severe AD
7 Very severe cognitive decline	All verbal abilities are lost over the course of this stage. Early in the stage, words and phrases are spoken but speech is very circumscribed. Later there is no speech at all—only grunting. Incontinent of urine; requires assistance toileting and feeding. Basic psychomotor skills (e.g., ability to walk) are lost with the progression of this stage. The brain appears no longer to be able to tell the body what to do. Generalised and cortical neurological signs and symptoms are frequently present.	Severe AD

Reisberg et al., 1982; 1988.

have neither subjective complaints of cognitive impairment nor objective clinically manifest symptoms. These persons are considered at stage 1 of the GDS. The progressive deterioration characteristic of AD might affect different cognitive functions at different periods during its course, as would be expected from the pathological evolution of the disease (Braak & Braak, 1996; Locascio et al., 1995; Perry & Hodges, 1996). There is little or no neuronal loss in ageing or preclinical AD but substantial loss in very mild AD (Price et al., 2001). A recent study that examined neuron numbers in the entorhinal cortex and CA1 in preclinical AD showed that AD results in clinical deficits only when it produces significant neuronal loss (Price et al., 2001). Longitudinal studies measuring cognitive decline in AD patients as measured by annual rate of change (ARC) scores on mental status examination or global cognitive tests have shown that such information is fundamental to understanding the natural history of the disorder, planning patient care, and evaluating the effectiveness of clinical interventions (Galasko et al., 1991; Yesavage & Brooks, 1991). A meta-analysis showed that a pooled estimate of ARC in AD patients was 3.3 points (95% confidence interval: 2.9–3.7) on the MMSE (Han et al., 2000). The effect size of ARC was related to the initial MMSE score of the study population and the number of assessments.

In the second stage of identifiable cognitive capacity, elderly individuals have subjective complaints of cognitive impairment without any clinically overt or manifest deficit (GDS stage 2). At stage 3, cognitive deficits are subtle but manifest in the course of a detailed clinical interview. Stage 4 on the GDS is characterised by deficits that become clearly manifest in the course of a detailed clinical interview. Deficits occur in the ability to manage the complex activities of daily life. Stage 5 also termed the early dementia phase encompasses patients whose cognitive deficits are of sufficient magnitude that they no longer can survive on their own without assistance. All of the cognitive and emotional features observed at the previous stage occur with increased magnitude and frequency at this stage. At stage 6, deficits are of sufficient magnitude to interfere with the basic

activities of daily life. Traditional adult cognitive test measures yield uniformly "bottom scores" and mental status assessments also show floor effects. In the final stage (GDS stage 7), individuals require continuous assistance with all basic activities of daily life. Traditional psychometric assessments invariably result in bottom scores at this stage as well as mental status assessments.

Among the host of degenerative processes occurring in AD, reproducible cholinergic deficits are consistently reported, appear early in the disease process, and correlate well with the degree of dementia (Francis et al., 1999). These findings have contributed to the "cholinergic hypothesis" of AD. In addition, cholinergic neurons appear to be involved in β-amyloid precursor protein processing and consequently, abnormalities in these neurons may lead to β-amyloid deposition and formation of toxic neuritic plaques. The underlying neuropathology of AD begins in medial temporal and limbic structures and spreads in a fairly systematic way. Early stages primarily involve entorhinal cortex and hippocampus and can be asymptomatic (Braak et al., 1996). The memory impairment in AD may be a direct result of disconnection of the hippocampus from its input; the entorhinal cortex (the major input pathway into the hippocampus) exhibits extensive pathology in AD. However, other regions important for memory are also damaged in AD; therefore, it is difficult to attribute the memory deficit exclusively to medial temporal damage. Abnormally low metabolic activity in the posterior cingulate cortex has been consistently observed in AD, and may be the earliest metabolic abnormality detectable by functional imaging in that disorder. Future studies should assess the possible clinical value of autobiographical memory retrieval tasks as fMRI probes of the functional status of this region in individual patients being evaluated for early AD.

Neuropathological alterations have been found in the amygdala of patients with dementia of the Alzheimer type, including the presence of neurofibrillary tangles and neuritic plaques (Unger et al., 1991). Amygdala atrophy was detected in autopsied patients with advanced AD and also in vivo in patients with early phase of the disease (Cuenod et al., 1993). Given the pathological alterations seen in the amygdala of AD patients, some kind of emotion processing impairment is to be expected in these patients. Indeed, some investigators have demonstrated a defective processing of emotional cues in AD patients, including an impairment in the processing of facial expressions (Cohen et al., 1997; Tillfors et al., 2001). On the other hand, it was shown that AD patients living in Kobe when the earthquake happened were able to remember this experience with a strong emotional content (Ikeda et al., 1998). Recently, a study was designed to examine whether AD patients can benefit from the emotional content of visual stimuli in a picture recognition test (Abrisqueta-Gomez et al., 2002). In normal subjects it was expected that affectively loaded pictures would be recognised better than neutral stimuli, but in AD patients, on the contrary, the affective content of stimuli should not facilitate their performance because the amygdala is presumably affected. The results showed that the total pictures correctly recognised by the AD patients (75.4% of the target pictures) was smaller than that of the controls (96.4%). Controls recognised more emotional pictures than indifferent pictures. These results suggest that emotional content enhanced recognition of pictures in normal subjects, whereas for the Alzheimer's subjects the emotional significance attached to the pictures was of no benefit to enhancing recognition. On the other hand, several studies have suggested that the influence on memory is preserved at least in part in AD (Kazui et al., 2000; Moayeri et al., 2000). Boller et al. (2002) designed a study to investigate whether the emotional content of a text can influence memory in patients affected by AD and whether this effect is related to attentional processes as assessed by ERP. The results suggest relatively preserved emotional processing in patients with AD. They also indicate that the emotional content of a context can influence memory performance. There was no evidence that this effect is mediated by attention as measured by ERP.

Experimental studies have demonstrated that on any memory tasks that requires conscious or controlled retrieval, patients with AD will be severely impaired (Simon et al., 1994). Thus, on any memory task that involves explicit and retro-

spective free or cued recall, patients with AD are impaired. Apart from the memory deficits that are comparable to those of amnesic patients in AD, the results of some studies suggest that memory impairment in AD may include priming deficits as well (Keane et al., 1991; Ostergaard, 1994). Since AD patients exhibit significant post-rolandic neocortical degeneration, as well as medial temporal lobe atrophy, it has been suggested that their priming deficits may reflect damage to a memory system located within temporal–parietal and/or occipital cortical regions (Keane et al., 1991). However, several findings are in conflict with these conclusions. Reports of normal or near-normal priming in AD patients on some tasks indicate that their priming performance may not invariably be compromised (Keane et al., 1991; Ober & Shenaut, 1988). The results of a 6-year longitudinal study that examined memory for a single routine activity of daily living in people with AD showed that there are large differences in the rate of action-based memory decline with substantial preservation of performed recall of the everyday task, even in the more severe phases of the disease (Rusted & Sheppard, 2002). The pattern of memory impairment suggests a benign degradation of the memory trace with omissions including the most common category of errors and this result is contrasted with the more dramatic action disorganisation syndrome associated with frontal injury. Clearly, as memory for the event degrades over time, it is the less important details that are lost, while the key elements of the event are retained. Thus, memory for action-based events or "scripts" is generally considered to be hierarchically structured. As dementia progresses, an individual becomes increasingly dependent on local cues which reduce the cognitive demands of the situation to a manageable level.

Several lines of evidence suggest that aspects of life experience such as educational or occupational attainment provide a "cognitive reserve" against the clinical manifestation of the neuropathological changes of AD. Higher educational and occupational attainment has been associated with a reduced risk of incident dementia (Evans et al., 1993 Letenneur et al., 1994; Stern et al., 1994). Furthermore, imaging studies suggest that given comparable clinical severity of dementia, AD pathology is more advanced in patients with higher educational and occupational attainment (Alexander et al., 1997; Stern et al., 1992a, b, 1995). These findings suggest that the degree of reserve might influence the level of pathological severity at which clinical manifestations of AD emerge. A recent study designed to determine whether the rate of decline in performance on a memory test is more rapid in AD patients with higher versus lower educational and occupational attainment was performed in a total of 177 patients, who were tested yearly for up to four study visits with the selective reminding test (Stern et al., 1999). It was observed that memory declined more rapidly in AD patients with higher educational and occupational attainment. This observation adds support to the view that the discontinuity between the degree of AD pathology and the observed clinical severity of AD is mediated through some form of reserve.

Working memory deficits in AD can be demonstrated using a variety of procedures. AD patients show poor performance on verbal memory span tasks. STM deficits probably arise from central executive impairment (Baddeley et al., 1986, 1991a, b). AD patients also show a decrease of visuospatial span capacity but the nature of the deficit has not been precisely identified (Ergis et al., 1995).

Many studies have shown that patients with AD, HD, and PD display different patterns of preserved and impaired memory performance (Kramer et al., 1989a, b; Pillon et al., 1993). In STM, as assessed by digit and block span, AD and HD patients are usually impaired, while PD patients may be normal. The performance on the Brown–Peterson task is impaired in HD, AD, and demented PD patients but not in non-demented patients (Beatty, 1992). In LTM, although AD and HD patients display similar level of short-delay recall, HD patients show superior verbal recognition, slower forgetting rate, and a lower number of intrusions and false recognitions than AD patients (Moss et al., 1986; Pillon et al., 1993). Recognition is also more preserved in PD than in AD (Caine et al., 1977; Pillon et al., 1993, 1996, 1997). AD patients are more impaired in tests that depend on the integrity of semantic

knowledge compared to HD patients, whose poor performance in episodic and semantic memory tasks has been associated with a general retrieval deficit (Hodges et al., 1990). Both PD and HD patients have mildly deficient encoding, intact storage, and marked difficulty in initiating systematic retrieval strategies (Masserman et al., 1990). However, HD patients have greater free recall impairment, a deficient rate of improvement across learning trials, increased perseveration rate, reduced primacy effect, and disproportionate improvement on recognition testing.

Episodic memory

Episodic memory is often globally weakened in AD, although some patients may present selective deficits of verbal or visual memory in the first stages of the disease (Baddeley et al., 1991; Becker & Lopez, 1992; Greene et al., 1996). Episodic memory deficits in persons who will develop AD have been observed for both verbal and nonverbal materials as well as in different retrieval conditions including free recall and recognition (Bäckman & Small, 1998; Fuld et al., 1990; Grober et al., 2000; Small et al., 1997; Tierney et al., 1996a, b). In a study that sought to determine the course of the preclinical episodic memory deficit in AD, the results indicate that AD is characterised by a long preclinical period during which episodic memory deficits are detectable (Bäckman et al., 2001). The magnitude of these deficits appears to be quite stable, at least up to 3 years before diagnosis. This may reflect the fact that those anatomophysiological events that eventually result in clinically diagnosed AD accumulate at a relatively slow rate.

Several hypotheses have been proposed to account for this impairment of episodic memory in AD, which might affect both encoding and retrieval of information, and would result from attentional deficiencies, working memory dysfunction, semantic difficulties, or neglect of contextual information (Van der Linden, 1994). Although episodic memory deficits occur in both cortical and subcortical dementia syndromes, these deficits result from damage to different memory systems. The deficit in AD is a true impairment in the episodic memory system due to direct damage within the medial temporal lobes. Early perturbations of episodic memory in AD appears likely to be due to a disruption of the medial temporal structures and particularly of the paralimbic rhinal cortex which is the earliest affected by neurofibrillary tangles (Braak & Braak, 1991; Delacourte et al., 1999). Consequently, AD is both quantitatively and qualitatively similar to the consolidation deficit that occurs in patients with circumscribed amnesia. Thus, like amnesic patients, AD patients show a little improvement in acquiring information over repeated learning trials and a tendency to recall only the most recently presented information in free recall tasks. A failure to demonstrate normal improvement in performance when memory is tested with a recognition rather than a free recall format and a rapid forgetting of information over time are also observed. AD patients also display a severe retrograde amnesia that is temporally graded, with memories from the distant past being better remembered than more recent memories. A study designed to assess various aspects of episodic memory and particularly sensitivity to semantic cueing, in patients with various degrees of cognitive deterioration compared with normal elderly subjects confirmed that a severe amnesic syndrome occurs very early in AD, even in a subgroup of patients who did not meet the criteria for dementia (Tounsi et al., 1999). It was shown that free recall performance (commonly measured by most studies in AD), characterised in all subgroups by a floor effect, is not likely to be an appropriate index in pharmacological trials. The strong relationship between sensitivity to cueing and the severity of the disease makes this index more appropriate than free recall to the qualitative assessment of episodic memory function in pre-demented AD patients and at different stages of AD. Sensitivity to cueing would therefore be the most sensitive index of episodic memory in AD.

Some studies suggest that an encoding deficit, rather than increased forgetting, underlies the poor performance on episodic memory tasks in AD (Christensen et al., 1998; Granholm & Butters, 1988; Greene et al., 1996). It may therefore be important in AD to assess factors such as meta-memory that operate during encoding. One cause of the deficit might be that people with AD fail to control and monitor memory during encoding. Several studies have examined metamemory functioning in AD (Bäckman & Lipinska, 1993; Lipinska & Bäckman, 1996; Pappas et al., 1992). Previous research claiming that there is a metamemory deficit in AD has been based on paradigms in which metamemory judgements are compared with performance. These methods confound predictive accuracy with very poor memory performance. However, in a recent study in which this confound is removed by focusing on the sensitivity of metamemory judgements to item differences at encoding, rather than on predictive accuracy, no evidence of a metamemory deficit at encoding in AD was observed (Moulin et al., 2000). Thus, this study emphasises that episodic memory impairment in AD, particularly the encoding deficit, is not exacerbated by a metacognitive deficit.

In most amnesic patients, anterograde memory deficits are accompanied by marked retrograde memory deficits (Kapur et al., 1989). However, a number of patients may present with minimal retrograde deficits or with isolated retrograde memory deficits. It has also been suggested that recent memories are more vulnerable than remote memory especially in dementia. In a paper that describes retrograde memory performances of AD patients and FTD patients, it was found that encoding (immediate cued recall) and free recall were as deficient in AD as in FTD (Thomas-Antérion et al., 2000). However, total recall was better in FTD than in AD because cueing was more efficient in FTD than in AD. AD patients forgot more words 20 minutes after learning than FTD patients. AD patients recognised fewer words than FTD patients did. Logical memory test and Benton visual memory test results were as deficient in FTD as in AD patients. Concerning frontal tests, FTD patients did not differ from AD patients in verbal fluency task and in the trail making test. However, AD patients were quicker and made fewer errors than FTD patients.

A recent study has analysed the pattern of errors committed in the Brown–Peterson task by an AD patient group in order to determine whether it differed from the control group and whether such a difference has any functional significance (Sebastian et al., 2001). The quantitative results showed that AD patients had a lower performance level in the three retention intervals than controls but a significant interaction between group and interval was not found, indicating that the rate of forgetfulness was similar in the two groups. In the qualitative analysis, errors were categorised as confusions, perseverations, omissions, and order alterations. Contrary to other studies, where an AD forgetfulness tendency of omissions was observed, an excess of perseveration indicating problems in the central executive was observed (Dannenbaum et al., 1988; Kopelman, 1985; Sebastian et al., 2001). The high rates of perseverations in a single series (even more than five times) would seem to suggest a clear inability by the patient to renew or update the contents of working memory. The greater prevalence of omissions in AD patients may be a reflection of an encoding or storage deficit, as the distractor task employed (counting forwards one by one) alters the patient performance in series as short as two letters. Taken as a whole, the results suggest that the performance deficit shown by AD patients in the Brown–Peterson task is primarily due to a difficulty in renewing or updating the contents of working memory.

Recently, a study designed to investigate neural correlates of subjective memory complaints with fMRI in patients seeking attention for the first time showed that fMRI of episodic memory can demonstrate hippocampal malfunction in AD patients not only in contrast to healthy elderly but also in contrast to patients with subjective memory complaints resulting from major depression (Grön et al., 2002). The investigators used repetitive learning and free recall of abstract geometric patterns during fMRI to assess episodic memory in the participants. Comparison of healthy elderly or depressive patients with AD patients revealed superiority of hippocampal activation. Contrasting AD patients with normal elderly people showed bilateral prefrontal activity as a correlate of futile compensation of episodic memory failure. It was suggested that failure of hippocampal recruitment for episodic memory performance may be a practical and valid marker in groups of patients with very early AD. Subjective memory complaints may

be classified objectively and very early with fMRI of episodic memory in groups of patients with AD and depressive syndrome. However, such findings will require confirmation in further studies in order to be considered a useful procedure to establish the differential diagnosis of the individual patient.

Remote memory

In general, remote memory remains relatively intact early in the course of AD. With disease progression, a slight temporal gradient becomes evident. The remote memory impairment in AD is a temporal gradient, with recall of recent events being more severely impaired than recall of more remote events (Beatty & Salmon, 1991). In moderate to severe AD, the temporal gradient disappears and patients show marked retrograde amnesia for all decades of life (Butters et al., 1995). This general pattern of impairment has been demonstrated for memory for famous faces and public events, visuospatial information, and auto-biographical information. By contrast to AD, the remote memory impairment in PD has generally been characterised as temporally limited, with a gradual decline in performance across only the most recent decades (Sagar et al., 1988).

Studies investigating component processes of remote memory have reported that AD participants were impaired in memory for photographs depicting historical events (content memory) and for the dates on which these events occurred (contextual memory) whereas PD patients were selectively impaired in contextual memory (see Sagar et al., 1988). A study designed to examine the severity of deficits in remote memory in patients with probable AD using newly designed scales for autobiographical memory and memory for famous people and well-known events reported several important findings (Dorrego et al., 1999). Surprisingly, even patients with very mild AD had significantly more severe deficits in memory for public events than age-comparable normal control subjects. Deficits were similar across decades and no significant gradient was found. In addition, AD patients had significantly more severe deficits in autobiographic memory than age-comparable normal control subjects. A significant gradient was found, with AD patients having significantly better recall of early memories than more recent ones. AD patients showed a significantly better performance on the recognition section of the Remote Memory Scale compared with the free recall, suggesting that retrieval deficits and damage to memory traces may both play an important role in the impairment of remote memory in AD. Further, the deficits in both types of remote memory were significantly correlated with deficits in verbal naming. It was concluded that memory deficits in AD may be related to both retrieval deficits and damage to memory traces.

A study designed to investigate content and contextual memory for remote public figures and events as assessed with a modified version of the Presidents Test in patients with AD or PD has examined the contribution of executive functioning, semantic memory, and explicit anterograde memory to remote memory (Fama et al., 2000). It was confirmed that the AD group had temporally extensive deficits in content and contextual remote memory not accountable by dementia severity. It was argued that different component processes characterise remote memory. Various mnemonic and non-mnemonic cognitive processes contribute to remote memory performance. Anterograde and remote memory processes are probably dissociable and differentially disrupted by neurodegenerative disease.

Semantic memory

A consensus has emerged from several convergent lines of research that semantic memory is impaired without exception at some point during the AD course. Numerous methods have been employed to assess the integrity of semantic memory in AD (Nebes, 1989). Perhaps the most fruitful and noteworthy paradigms have been studies of naming ability, category fluency, priming, and more recently, multidimensional scaling models of semantic networks (Martin & Fedio, 1983).

Naming

A naming disturbance has been recognised as one of the core clinical features of AD (Wilkins &

Brody, 1969). The anomia tends to be a relatively early manifestation of the disease. It progressively worsens over the disease course and is strongly correlated with overall dementia severity (Chertkow & Bub, 1990; Nebes, 1989). In clinical practice, anomia is commonly measured with tests of confrontation naming ability such as the Boston Naming Test (BNT) on which AD patients are impaired (Hodges et al., 1990, 1991; Kaplan et al., 1983). The nature of the anomia in AD may derive from three different sources: perceptual misidentification, impaired lexical access and loss of semantic stores. Current evidence strongly points to the degradation of semantic stores as the principal cause of anomia. A study compared the naming error patterns of AD patients, HD patients, and controls (Hodges et al., 1991). It was observed that whereas the few errors normal controls made were predominantly semantic-category (e.g., dice for dominoes) and circumlocutory errors, the AD patients made a significantly greater proportion of semantic-superordinate errors (e.g., blow for harmonica). The HD group, by contrast differed from normal controls only in their increased rate of visually based errors (e.g., fountain pen for asparagus), implying that for these patients the deficit is primarily perceptual. On the other hand, it was argued that the AD error pattern implies a defect at the level of semantic knowledge such that specific item knowledge is lost and only more general superordinate category knowledge remains. This is consistent with the semantic storage disorder (Warrington & Shallice, 1984). In addition to studies of the types of naming errors, stronger evidence for a fundamental semantic memory breakdown in AD comes from studies of the consistency of errors. The demonstration that AD patients lose knowledge pertaining to specific words across multiple probes has been taken as evidence of actual degradation of semantic stores (Huff et al., 1986).

Category fluency

Word-list generation or verbal fluency tasks have been widely used to assess lexical retrieval capacities (Benton, 1968; Newcombe, 1969). The procedure typically requires the subject to generate as many words as possible in 1 minute, constrained by a cue provided by the clinician. For letter (or phonemic) fluency, the subject is asked to produce words that begin with a given letter (e.g., A) whereas for category (or semantic) fluency the subject is requested to generate exemplars of a given category such as fruits and vegetables (Benton & Hamsher, 1976; Goodglass & Kaplan, 1972). Fluency tasks are considered very demanding, as they require some combination of attention, retrieval strategies, working memory, and intact semantic stores (Hodges et al., 1992; Randolph et al., 1993). Current data suggest that AD patients are disproportionately impaired on category fluency as compared to letter fluency. This pattern reflects degradation in the semantic stores that are primarily tapped by the category fluency task. A recent study that examined the categorisation processes that AD patients use during assessments of semantic memory requested patients to decide the category membership of test stimuli for categories with poorly defined or fuzzy boundaries (e.g., vegetable) and for categories with well-defined boundaries (e.g., female) and then to judge the representativeness of the test stimulus for its chosen category (Grossman et al., 2001). A subgroup of AD patients showed a typical pattern of impaired semantic memory compared to healthy controls and experienced difficulty deciding the category membership of test items from fuzzy categories. Among these patients, no deficit in category membership decisions about items taken from well-defined categories was observed. These data are most consistent with the hypothesis that rule-based categorisation difficulty limits semantic memory in AD.

Semantic priming

Priming is observed when response speed is affected by semantically related primes that precede the target stimuli. For example, the time taken to read the word "doctor" is shorter when the preceding word was "nurse" as opposed to an unrelated word. Thus, semantic priming paradigms used in recent investigations of AD and other memory-impaired patients generally fall into two classes—those that assess the influence of priming on subsequent response speed and those that assess the influence of priming on the subsequent retrieval of words.

It has been hypothesised that if semantic systems were disrupted in AD, then these patients should demonstrate diminished priming (Nebes, 1989). The majority of studies that have looked at the influence of semantic priming on subsequent processing speed have concluded that AD patients and controls benefit in a similar fashion from priming manipulations (Nebes et al., 1986, 1989). On the other hand, studies investigating the influence of semantic priming on subsequent measures involving the retrieval of words have concluded that AD patients exhibit a deficit relative to controls, patients with HD, and patients with Korsakoff's syndrome (Heindel et al., 1989; Salmon et al., 1988).

A priming task involving a word-stem completion paradigm was administered to patients with AD, patients with HD, and normal control subjects (Randolph, 1991). The task was done under conditions of both implicit and explicit recall. Explicit and implicit recalls were positively correlated in all three groups. After controlling for explicit recall ability through statistical procedures, AD patients were found to be normally susceptible to the effects of priming on implicit recall. HD patients, however, exhibited significantly increased susceptibility to priming, suggesting that they may have carried out the implicit task in a manner different from that of normal controls and AD patients. AD patients were also found to supply words of significantly lower association strength than the other two groups in a "free association" task using words from a published list of word association norms. This degradation of semantic memory was strongly correlated with explicit performance, suggesting that explicit, implicit, and semantic memory functions decline in parallel in AD.

Differences in implicit memory between AD, PD, and HD patients are also reported (Heindel et al., 1989; Soliveri et al., 1992). A double dissociation was observed in AD and HD: most often lexical, semantic, and pictorial priming were impaired in AD but not in HD patients, whereas HD patients were impaired on motor skill learning (i.e., pursuit motor) which is preserved in AD patients (Heindel et al., 1988, 1989).

Multidimensional scaling

In one of the newest forms of inquiry into semantic memory in AD, multidimensional scaling techniques have been used to render spatial models of semantic network structure. Multidimensional scaling refers to a set of multivariate techniques that transform some index of psychological similarity between pairs of stimuli into distances between points in a spatial representation that models subjects' schematic organisation of the stimuli (Shepard et al., 1972). Thus, multidimensional scaling can be thought of as providing a map that reflects the hidden structure in the data (Kruskal & Wish, 1978).

Multidimensional scaling techniques have shown promise for clarifying the breakdown in the structure of semantic knowledge in AD patients. Multidimensional scaling offers graphic modelling of semantic organisation. Preliminary results suggest that it may capture an aspect of semantic structures that has important prognostic value.

Prospective memory

Deficits in retaining material held in primary or STM for periods of up to about 30 seconds have been demonstrated in AD using a variety of well-known tests (Morris, 1994). Patients with AD display pervasive impairments on measures of memory span, tests using the Peterson–Brown distractor techniques and indices of recency effects in free recall tasks, which have an impact on their ability to perform many activities in their everyday lives (Knight, 1992). Failure of the executive functions in working memory in AD appears to be part of a more generalised disruption in processing on any tasks that requires executive function. Thus, many patients with AD show features of the dysexecutive syndrome that are seen in patients with predominantly frontal lobe damage. These observations suggest that AD patients will have specific difficulties with prospective memory tests.

Procedural memory

In order to explore the neurological correlates of motor skill learning, a study compared the ability of AD, HD, and amnesic patients to learn the motor skills underlying performance of a pursuit rotor task (Heindel et al., 1988). The results of the study showed that AD and amnesic patients demonstrated rapid and extensive motor learning across trials and that this learning was equivalent to that of normal control subjects. The preserved motor skill learning exhibited by the AD and amnesic patients was consistent with previous reports (Corkin, 1968; Eslinger & Damasio, 1986). This indicates that this form of procedural memory is not dependent on the medial temporal lobe structures damaged in both of these disorders, nor on temporal, parietal, or frontal association cortices affected by AD. In contrast to the AD and amnesic patients, HD patients were impaired in learning the motor skills underlying pursuit rotor task performance. This motor learning deficit suggests that this form of procedural memory may be mediated by the corticostriatal system that is severely compromised in HD (Bruyn et al., 1979).

Comorbidity with depression

Current surveys suggest that the occurrence of clinical depression in patients who eventually are diagnosed with probable AD may be as high as 15–20% (Allen et al., 1997; Migliorelli et al., 1995). Depressive symptoms can be either reactive or biological in origin. The biological changes involve neuronal loss in adrenergic, serotonergic, and dopaminergic systems. Reactive depression can be a response to the experienced cognitive and environmental changes associated with AD and is often observed early in the course of the illness. As the dementia advances, delusions become more common, occurring in up to 40% of AD patients (Folstein & Blysma, 1994). Suspiciousness and fixed paranoid ideation are perhaps the most prevalent type of delusion and often consist of the patient accusing others of stealing from him or her. More severely demented AD patients also have visual and auditory hallucinations.

A sizeable number of patients with clinical depression experience memory failure, and current surveys suggest the second most important cause of "treatable" dementia in the elderly is depressive illness (Friedland, 1993). Patients with depression-induced dementia perhaps fall into a subgroup with increased risk of age-associated difficulties, and perhaps with lifelong structural irregularities that only become manifest in the context of depression. There are no commonly accepted neuropsychological markers that set AAMI apart from cognitive impairments in early or preclinical organic dementia. Conversely, not enough is known about AAMI patients who subsequently are diagnosed with depression, and what role this has as a predictor of organic disease. During a depressive episode, disturbances in visuospatial functions initially occur in the context of relatively undiminished verbal semantic skills, while disruptions of executive functions become more prominent as the illness deepens. As depression relents, so memory impairment remits in most patients with pseudodementia, although a number of cases will deteriorate further. These patients may coincide with AAMI patients who similarly go on to develop dementia in the context of depression. It is still unclear how profiles on cognitive diagnostics (e.g., MMSE, WAIS, CAMCOG) can be shown to reliably distinguish between reversible and irreversible patients, and whether such profiles can be used to avoid misclassifying other depressed patients in preclinical stages of AD (des Rosiers et al., 1995).

Imaging

Advances in neuroimaging have contributed to the clinical diagnosis of AD. MRI has provided a way of discrimination between normal ageing and AD (Sandor et al., 1992). AD patients have significantly more parietal lobe and insular atrophy than do control subjects (Foundas et al., 1996). The most effective MRI indices have focused on medial temporal structures which include entorhinal cortex, parahippocampal cortex, hippocampal formation, and amygdala. All of these structures are typically smaller in AD patients than in age-matched controls. For example, a study

reported that AD was associated with 33% reduction in the size of the amygdala and a 20% decrease in the size of the hippocampus (Smith et al., 1999). Changes in the amygdala also appear to correlate with impairments in emotional memory in AD patients, even after correcting for overall brain atrophy and cognitive deterioration (Mori et al., 1999).

The diagnostic utility of MRI measures remains to be established. Many studies have reported age-related reductions of the hippocampus in healthy subjects and AD patients (Golebiowski et al., 1999; Mu et al., 1999; Smith et al., 1999). Therefore, reduction of hippocampus volume with age may decrease our ability to use this volume to distinguish AD patients from healthy elderly controls. However, by combining hippocampus and entorhinal cortex, a study showed that it was possible to classify AD patients and normal controls with 90% accuracy (Juottonen et al., 1999). Recently, Hampel et al. (2002) have suggested that age transformation of hippocampus and amygdala volume may improve diagnostic accuracy in AD. Using an orthogonal rotational transformation of the coordinate system, values of the MRI-determined volumes of hippocampus–amygdala formation (HAF) were transformed according to the age of the subjects. The results showed that the age-transformed HAF volume predicted AD in a subject with MCI with later biopsy-confirmed AD. It was argued that this easily applicable technique may increase the diagnostic accuracy for a subject by taking into account the independent effect of age on hippocampus and amygdala volume. However, differentiating between AD patients and normal elderly individuals can often be done quite effectively with clinical data, and performance on memory tests may be more sensitive to early AD than neuroimaging (Visser et al., 1999; Zakzanis, 1998).

Recently, the technique of magnetisation transfer ratio (MTR) was proposed as an additional predictor for abnormal cognitive decline in the elderly (Kabani et al. 2002). Magnetisation transfer is a technique that generates contrast dependent on the phenomenon of magnetisation exchange between semisolid macromolecular protons and water protons (Wolff & Balaban, 1989). In clinical scans, the relaxation properties of this pool of hydrogen atoms and the rate at which it exchanges magnetisation are typically assessed by a combined measure called a magnetisation transfer ratio (MTR). MTR has been used extensively in assessing subjects with multiple sclerosis since it is believed to provide greater pathological specificity than conventional MRI. Using this procedure, it was shown that the MTR of white matter was significantly lower in the AD group (Kabani et al., 2002). The grey matter volume was significantly lower in the AD group compared to controls (387.29 ± 26.04 cm^3 vs 532.93 ± 20.53 cm^3) and MCI (464.64 ± 16.93 cm^3). No significant differences were found in the white matter volume between the three groups. It was therefore suggested that the MTR methodology may be used as a novel approach to improve early diagnosis of AD.

SEMANTIC DEMENTIA

Semantic dementia is a recently documented syndrome associated with non-Alzheimer degenerative pathology of the polar and inferolateral temporal neocortex with relative sparing (at least in the early stages) of the hippocampal complex (Hodges et al., 1992). Patients typically show a progressive deterioration in their semantic knowledge about people, objects, facts, and the meanings of words. Yet, at least clinically, they seem to possess relatively preserved day-to-day (episodic) memory (see Table 8.2). Patients are well oriented and demonstrate good recall of recent life events,

though their language difficulties often result in poor performance on bedside and formal tests of verbal memory. Recall of autobiographical details has recently been shown to be temporally modulated, with sparing of recent events and impairment of more distant memories (Greene et al., 1995; Snowden et al., 1996). In particular, recent investigations of recognition memory in patients with semantic dementia have demonstrated that new episodic learning for pictures of nameable objects can be normal despite the severe breakdown of semantic knowledge that is the hallmark of the disease (Graham et al., 2000; Simons & Graham, 2000). This is in marked contrast to the preservation of early memories that is often seen in patients with dementia of the Alzheimer's type (Greene & Hodges, 1996; Snowden et al., 1996). These results are problematic for current theories of LTM organisation which hold that normal episodic memory should not be possible in the context of degraded semantic knowledge about the to-be-remembered material (Tulving, 1995). Patients with semantic dementia invariably perform poorly on tests of naming and this is true whatever the modality of presentation of the item to be named (Lambon Ralph et al., 1998). Production is always more affected than comprehension. Both are highly dependent on word fluency and familiarity.

Hodges et al. (1994) investigated whether the immediate recall of words was influenced by semantic knowledge by asking a patient (PP) with semantic dementia to repeat lists of words that were either all "known" or all "unknown". Known words were defined as those that PP had used correctly in spontaneous speech. Unknown words

---

TABLE 8.2

Core features of semantic dementia

1. Selective impairment of semantic memory causing severe anomia, impaired spoken and written single-word comprehension, reduced generation of exemplars on category fluency tests, and an impoverished fund of general knowledge about objects, persons, and the meaning of words.
2. Relative sparing of other components of language output and comprehension, notably syntax and phonology.
3. Normal visuo-perceptual and spatial skills, working memory, and non-verbal problem-solving abilities.
4. Relatively preserved autobiographical and day-to-day (episodic) memory.

Hodges et al., 1992.

were defined as those that she had never used spontaneously during the testing sessions and which she failed to comprehend in word–picture matching tasks. The results showed that PP was significantly better at repeating the lists of known words compared with the unknown words. Interestingly, PP tended to make phonological errors and incorporate phonemes from one word in the list into another when recalling unknown words and a number of errors were perfect spoonerisms. For example, she repeated "mint, rug" as "rint, mug". Hodges et al. (1994) suggested that semantic degradation might affect stored representations within the phonological output lexicon. According to their account, words are not represented as whole units in the phonological output lexicon but as sets of phonological elements. These phonological elements usually emerge together correctly. Every time a word is spoken the constituent phonological elements are activated together and every time a word is spoken the pattern of phonological elements is associated with a particular semantic representation which could also provide a binding function within the network (the semantic glue hypothesis). A deterioration in meaning will eliminate an important source of coherence that holds the phonological elements together to form words.

Evidence concerning the pathological basis of semantic dementia is still scant, although earlier speculation that this was unlikely to reflect a variant of AD is upheld. Two cases that have been subject to postmortem in Cambridge have shown changes consistent with Pick's disease and a meta-analysis of 13 cases from the literature revealed that all had Pick bodies or nonspecific histological changes without either Alzheimer's or Pick's pathology (Hodges et al., 1998). In terms of the integrity of neuroanatomical structures at postmortem, while on the one hand there is consensus about the involvement of the anterior temporal regions, temporal pole, and inferomedial temporal cortices, there is variability in the degree of reported hippocampal pathology (Hodges et al., 1998; Snowden et al., 1996). Although some investigators have reported severe involvement of the hippocampus, others have reported absolute and relative sparing of this structure, respectively (Graff-Radford et al., 1990; Harasty et al., 1996; Scheltens et al., 1990).

In marked contrast to their performance on tests that require semantic memory, normal or near-normal scores can be obtained on tests of auditory–verbal STM (digit span). Normal or near-normal scores may also be observed on other tests such as non-verbal problem solving (Raven's Progressive Matrices), visuospatial abilities (Rey-Osterrieth Complex Figure), and non-verbal memory (e.g., memory for designs or the faces component of the Recognition Memory Test) (Lezak, 1983; Raven, 1962; Warrington, 1984). Despite clear evidence that recognition memory for objects can be preserved in semantic dementia, other studies have indicated that recognition memory for faces may be impaired (Evans et al., 1995; Warrington, 1975). A recent study has confirmed preserved face recognition memory in semantic dementia so long as atrophy was confined predominantly to the left temporal lobe (Simons et al., 2001). Patients with structural damage to the right temporal lobe were typically impaired, with the status of the hippocampus and parahippocampal gyrus (including the perirhinal cortex) on the right being critical. However, early stages of semantic dementia are often compatible with complete preservation of normal day-to-day existence while in many cases the symptoms have necessitated early retirement from employment. As the disease process advances, changes in behaviour and social conduct become evident and patients typically degenerate to a state of severe global dementia. At the later stages of the disease, many patients may develop a fixation with food and time, displaying bizarre ritualistic eating habits, and often gaining substantially in weight (Hodges et al., 1992). There are obvious similarities between such behaviour and that exhibited by patients with the Klüver-Bucy syndrome (hyperorality and sexual disinhibition), a syndrome that may follow severe bilateral temporal lobe damage from any cause (Cummings & Duchen, 1981). An alternative explanation is that with disease progression, damage to the orbito-frontal regions becomes increasingly pronounced.

PARKINSON'S DISEASE

Parkinson's disease (PD) has received attention primarily as a neurological movement disorder but it is becoming more well known that it also affects cognitive processes to a point where normal age-related changes in cognitive functioning seem to be accentuated (Passafiume et al., 1986; Taylor et al., 1987). It is rarely diagnosed before the age of 40 but shows an increasing prevalence from age 50 to 79. The prevalence in this age group has been estimated to be somewhere between 0.3 and 1.8 percent. Four general types of symptoms characteristic of PD include tremor, akinesia or bradykinesia, rigidity of movement, and loss of normal postural reflexes. It is generally acknowledged that memory impairment is seen in PD, although the occurrence is not invariable and severity tends to be less than seen in AD. Performance on the BVRT was compared between those with PD and age-equivalent controls (Netherton et al., 1989). The results support the notion that PD is associated with change in visuospatial memory, beyond that predicted by age *per se*. A study designed to provide accurate descriptions of the abnormalities that can be observed in the various types of memories in PD by using batteries of validated and standardised neuropsychological tests showed that various components of memory are altered in therapeutically controlled and undemented or undepressed Parkinsonians (Allain et al., 1995a, b). Statistically significant results revealed an impairment in explicit memory (verbal recall of words and drawings) with preserved recall of faces. Implicit memory was also deficient in association tests (sound–form, arithmetical alphabet) and maze tests. Other studies showed that deficits are primarily seen on tests that require conscious control of processing and retrieval, such as traditional free recall tests of word lists and on tests of procedural learning (Beatty et al., 1989; Harrington et al., 1990). It is also apparent that the most pervasive deficits that PD groups show on neuropsychological testing are revealed on tests of executive functioning.

Parkinsonians are impaired at tasks involving internal clues (i.e., when they have to establish a strategy based on self-oriented internal control). Current hypotheses about the cognitive mechanisms underlying PD memory dysfunction fall into two broad categories, one postulating a failure in retrieval operations associated with basal ganglia pathology, and the other postulating a deterioration in executive functions (e.g., self-initiated strategic information processing) associated with frontal and/or fronto-striatal pathology. However, there is a subtle distinction between the "frontal executive" and "subcortical retrieval" interpretations of PD memory deterioration. Whereas the traditional retrieval deficit hypothesis suggests that PD compromises access to stored memories, the frontal hypothesis proposes that the strategies required to initiate and/or maintain efficient retrieval and other cognitive operations are deficient.

A study investigated the neuropsychological correlates of hippocampal atrophy in PD patients (Riekkinen et al., 1998b). Verbal memory was measured with a list learning test. The list learning test consisted of a nine-word list that was read aloud to patients three times. Immediately after the tester had finished reading the words, the patient repeated three times and a maximum correct score was 27. The patient was asked to again repeat the words 6 minutes later (delayed recall, maximum correct score nine words). The subjects were scanned with a 1.5 T Magnetom. The results were calculated using normalised volumes of the amygdala and hippocampus (volume of the hippocampus/the area of both hemispheres in MRI taken at the level of the anterior commissure). The results show that hippocampal atrophy correlated with impaired memory scoring in PD patients. The memory-impaired patients have smaller hippocampi than other PD patients do. The performance of PD patients in spatial working memory and attentional set-shifting correlated with the severity of motor defect, and not with hippocampal atrophy. The results suggest that failure of verbal/visual memory may be related to hippocampal atrophy in PD. On the other hand, the defect in spatial working memory and attentional set-shifting may be sensitive to dysfunction of "fronto-striatal" systems in PD patients.

Some authors describe positive correlations between the extent of memory loss and the severity of hypokinesia, rigidity, tremor, and postural abnormalities, while others hold that no such correlations exist (Keiburtz et al., 1994; Korsakova & Moskvichyute, 1985; Reid et al., 1989; Riklan et al., 1989). Thus, there are no generally accepted concepts relating to the association of memory impairment with motor disturbances. No relationship has yet been established between the severity of memory loss and the duration of disease (Glozman et al., 1994; Cummings, 1988; Keiburtz et al., 1994; Korsakova & Moskvichyute, 1985).

Dementia is found in 20–40% of patients with PD (Louis et al., 1997). The aetiology remains unknown but both cortical and subcortical pathologies may contribute. In PD with dementia, the nature of memory impairment is qualitatively different. Verbal memory is affected both in terms of active reproduction and recognition of words. The inefficacy of organising methods is regarded as an important sign of defects in memory trace consolidation (Knopman, 1991; Kopelman, 1987a, b). This latter is typical for the Alzheimer's type of dementia and is probably associated with a deficit of acetylcholinergic "innervation" of structures in the hippocampal circuit (Kopelman, 1986; Kopelman & Corn, 1988). In addition, PD with dementia is more frequently associated with signs of loss of recall selectivity (element substitution, irrelevant insertions, series contamination) suggesting a more diffuse dysfunction of the frontal lobes of the brain with marked impulsivity. Comparative clinical studies of patients with different neurodegenerative diseases may help to clarify the underlying aetiology of the dementia syndrome in PD with dementia. A study that compared the profile of neuropsychiatric symptoms in patients with PD with dementia and patients with AD reported that AD and PD with dementia have different neuropsychiatric profiles (Aarsland et al., 2001). Hallucinations were more severe in PD patients while aberrant motor behaviour, agitation, disinhibition, irritability, euphoria, and apathy were more severe in AD. Delusions increased with more severe motor and cognitive disturbances in PD

with dementia. Dementia often occurs in patients with PD and estimates of its prevalence averaged about 40% when structured tests such as the Folstein Mini-Mental State Exam (FMMSE) were used to assess dementia (Cummings, 1988). It was also noted that dementia associated with PD presents as a variable group of disorders superimposed on an underlying subcortical dementia. Another report suggested that in some patients with PD, there are corresponding symptoms that resemble those of AD (Mahler & Cummings, 1990). But whatever its prevalence or manifestations, little research has been conducted on cognitive intervention for dementia associated with PD.

The retrieval deficit hypothesis

PD patients typically demonstrate impaired recall for verbal material such as word lists, prose passages, and paired associates, but their recognition of the same material is only slightly impaired, if at all (Buytenhuijs et al., 1994; Cohen et al., 1994a, b; Tsai et al., 1994). This performance pattern stands in contrast to the impaired recall and recognition observed in AD (Bondi et al., 1994a, b). On the other hand, PD patients without significant cognitive impairment have relatively normal rates of forgetting, and tend not to commit a large number of intrusion errors, which is an index of heightened sensitivity to proactive interference. Although PD patients with dementia show more rapid rates of forgetting and commit more intrusion errors than do PD patients without dementia, these abnormalities are still not as pronounced as in AD when the groups' overall severity of dementia is comparable (Pillon et al., 1993). In addition, whereas the remote memory loss in AD is characterised by a temporal gradient, with relative preservation of more distant memories, retrograde amnesia in PD, like HD, is equally severe for all past decades (Beatty et al., 1988). These findings tend to support the hypothesis that memory impairment in PD is primarily a function of retrieval deficits, a mechanism thought common to several "subcortical" dementias. That retrieval deficits underlie recall impairments in PD has also been supported by the finding that non-PD patients with focal basal ganglia lesions show impaired recall but intact recognition memory (Dubois et al., 1995). In contrast, memory impairment in "cortical" dementias such as AD is thought to reflect disturbed encoding, consolidation, and storage of memories.

The deficiencies observed in PD are associated with the use of procedures involving declarative and motor material in learning and automation (Thomas et al., 1996). A recent study designed to investigate if the impaired memory for spatial location in PD is domain-specific or dependent on "strategic processes" suggested that the memory deficit for spatial location observed in PD results mainly from a disturbance of strategic processes and from decreased attentional resources (Pillon et al., 1998). The fact that these processes are also impaired in recently diagnosed pharmacologically untreated patients suggests the implication of the nigrostriatal dopaminergic system and associated striatofrontal neuronal circuits in these deficits.

Working memory has also been reported to be impaired in PD patients (Owen et al., 1997). A recent study was designed to assess recall memory, immediate recognition memory, and delayed recognition memory for words derived from semantically related categories in a sample of non-demented patients with PD and age- and education-matched control participants (Stebbins et al., 1999). It was shown that PD patients had intact immediate but impaired delayed recognition memory performance. PD patients were also impaired on tests of free and cued recall, working memory (listening span test & digit ordering test), and measures of psychomotor speed (symbol digit modalities test oral version). It was hypothesised that the dissociation in declarative memory performance between immediate recall and recognition in PD is not based on the type of test but rather on the greater processing requirements the recall process places on executive working memory. When the task demands of a recognition test are modified so as to augment dependence on executive working memory, such as by including a delay between study and recognition test, PD patients evidence impaired recognition.

Although the PD sample's memory was "generally intact", deficits were observed on immediate recall of two prose passages, on a spatial delayed recognition task (DRT), and on the Rey Auditory Verbal Learning Test (RAVLT) (Rey, 1964; Taylor et al., 1986). Deficits were also noted on a word list learning and memory test.

The frontal hypothesis

PD even at an early stage impairs performance in tests measuring functions mediated by the "fronto-striatal" systems, such as spatial working memory and attentional set shifting (Agid et al., 1987; Alvarez et al., 1995). This impairment may reflect the severity of striatal dopaminergic loss and impaired functions of "fronto-striatal" loops. However, in PD the frontal dopamine projections are also adversely affected, suggesting that the progressive dysfunction of striatal and frontal dopamine transmission may both contribute for the impaired performance in "frontal" tests (Alexander et al., 1986; Double et al., 1996). It appears that frontal dysfunction in PD compromises the ability to generate efficient strategies on tasks requiring self-initiated planning (Taylor et al., 1986). The notion that a frontally mediated impairment in the ability to generate efficient strategies is at the root of PD memory impairments has been supported (Buytenhuijs et al., 1994; Karamat et al., 1991). Experimental studies of PD patients' performance on "frontal" memory tests provide the most convincing evidence to date that fronto-striatal dysfunction underlies select memory impairments in PD.

Some studies have attempted to directly establish a link between brain physiology and memory test performance in PD (Cummings, 1993; Zola-Morgan & Squire, 1993). The proposal that PD memory deficits are related to cognitive changes associated with frontal dysfunction is attractive from anatomical and pathological standpoints. The striatum and frontal cortex are intimately connected via a series of parallel circuits and some of these subcortical circuits are in turn connected to regions important for memory, such as entorhinal cortex (Cummings, 1993; Zola-Morgan & Squire, 1993).

Evidence from a range of cognitive tasks has led to the hypothesis that PD patients are impaired in shifting set on tasks such as the WCST, which is known to be sensitive to frontal lobe dysfunction (Gotham et al., 1988; Taylor et al., 1986). Impairment has also been reported in PD patients on a wide range of other executive tasks that involve set shifting (Cronin-Golomb et al., 1994). In a study designed to investigate the nature and extent of executive impairments in PD patients and matched control subjects, two tasks involving strategic processing, deductive reasoning, and memory updating were utilised (Channon, 1997). This study showed that PD patients differed significantly from controls in solving two- and four-dimensional deductive reasoning problems, and they showed impairment in memory updating. PD patients gave fewer correct solutions to the reasoning problems for both serial and parallel presentation. The serial presentation permitted examination of omission and false positive error rates in deducing possible rules at each stage of the problems. This suggests that PD patients made more errors than controls, both by omitting possible rules and by including rules that feedback had already shown to be incorrect. Therefore, the concept of impaired set shifting does not appear to provide an adequate characterisation of the nature of the observed PD deficits. An increased focus of attention on the availability and efficiency of working memory resources may be more fruitful.

The frontal executive deficit hypothesis cannot adequately account for all memory impairments in PD, and that a more parsimonious theoretical account might invoke a distinction between prospective and declarative memory impairments. There may be three subgroups of PD patients, one demonstrating prospective memory dysfunction only, one with declarative memory dysfunction only, and one with prospective and declarative memory dysfunction. Consequently, PD might provide a useful model within which to investigate the relationship between prospective and declarative memory. Indeed, in an attempt to better understand cognitive dysfunctions in PD, several authors have suggested subgrouping PD on the basis of cognitive impairment patterns. Three subgroups of PD patients appear to exist: those with dementia, those with circumscribed cognitive deficits, and those who are cognitively intact (Dubois

et al., 1991). Only a subset of PD patients develops dementia, with prevalence estimates ranging from 20% to 30% (Mohr et al., 1995b).

Whether memory deterioration in PD is a "true" memory impairment has been questioned. Some authors have suggested that this impairment is a feature secondary to executive deficits (e.g., an inability to generate efficient strategies demanded by tasks involving self-initiated planning) associated with frontal dysfunction (Pillon et al., 1993; Taylor et al., 1990). The debate about the relative merits of the retrieval and executive deficit hypotheses, and about the neural basis of PD memory impairment, is unlikely to be resolved soon. To some extent, this discussion parallels the continuing controversy about whether the frontal lobes serve a primary function in memory (Shimamura, 1994).

Comorbidity with depression

In patients with PD, the relationship between depression and neuropsychological deficits has been investigated. PD or HD have a seemingly higher prevalence of depression than AD. The initial degree of depression in PD may even predict subsequent declines in cognitive performance and abilities of daily living (Tröster et al., 1995). A recent study investigates the possible influence of depression on tests of episodic memory, in patients with PD (Boller et al., 1998). Three groups of patients (controls, non-depressed PD, mildly to moderately depressed PD) were studied. Neuropsychological tests included tests of STM and LTM in verbal and non-verbal modalities. The two groups of PD patients performed significantly worse than controls on the memory tests, but there were no differences between the depressed and non-depressed PD patients. Severity of depression may be the critical variable in predicting cognitive impairment and rate of decline. Cognitive impairment in depressed PD patients is only found beyond a certain threshold (Starkstein & Mayberg, 1993).

Semantic memory

Like HD patients, PD patients are impaired on mechanical aspects of speech and overall output but lexical–semantic aspects of language such as vocabulary, grammar, and syntax aspects of language tend to be essentially intact (Bondi & Tröster, 1997).

When PD patients are compared with AD patients carefully matched for age and dementia severity, most studies show that PD patients are less impaired on confrontation naming measures (Wilson et al., 2003). Generally, when naming deficits are present in PD they tend to be mild and have been associated with depressive symptoms.

Procedural memory

PD is accompanied by cognitive disorders that may affect procedural memory. A study designed to show that in PD declarative as well as procedural memory is severely impaired used three tests (inverted reading, Braille reading, and sound–form association) to explore memory (Allain et al., 1995a, b). The results obtained, compared with those of the young and aged controls, show that PD is associated with marked deficits in both declarative and procedural memory. Declarative memory impairment was similar to that observed in the control population (healthy elderly subjects, age-matched with the PD patients) but more marked in PD patients. The procedural memory deficit was linked with age and pathology. Face recognition, consistently with a previous study was highly impaired (−50%) (Raoul et al., 1992). The deficits observed were more like a loss of automatism than procedural impairment *stricto sensu*. Theoretically, this procedural memory impairment in Parkinsonians could account for the loss of certain motor automatisms and above all participate in the breakdown and interrelations of a number of neuropsychological abnormalities that have been shown in Parkinsonians (Cooper et al., 1991). It would be interesting to study akinesia and the loss of motor automation from the angle of a major impairment of procedural memory.

HUNTINGTON'S DISEASE

George Huntington described the salient features of the disease bearing his name in 1872.

Huntington's disease (HD) is an inherited, autosomal dominant, neurodegenerative disorder characterised primarily by a progressive deterioration of the neostriatum (caudate nucleus and putamen) and by progressive neurological impairment. Onset is typically in adulthood and the symptoms consist of the appearance of abnormal movements (chorea, from the Greek "to dance"), psychiatric manifestations (a tendency to insanity and suicide), and dementia. HD is a progressive neurodegenerative disorder characterised by neuronal loss in neostriatum, particularly the head of the caudate nucleus (Vonsattel et al., 1985). This forebrain nucleus has strong reciprocal connections to the dorsolateral PFC (Alexander et al., 1997). Whether the cognitive impairments of HD patients are due to intrinsic neostriatal cell loss or to secondary atrophy and/or deafferentation of PFC remains an area of intense research. Children of patients with HD have a 50% risk of themselves developing the disease. The HD gene defect places it in a novel category of disease: trinucleotide triplets repeat diseases, in which there is an abnormal expansion of a series of nucleotide triplets within the DNA. The disease is caused by an abnormal number of repeats of the trinucleotide sequence CAG in the gene IT15 on chromosome four. Individuals with more than 39 CAG repeats will develop HD. Cognitive losses include intellectual speed, attention, and STM. In addition to marked memory deficits, HD patients usually display anomia, agnosia, apraxia, and severe visuoconstructive deficits, especially as the disease progresses (Cummings & Benson, 1984).

There is a growing body of research suggesting that cognitive decline may precede the onset of motor symptoms in HD (Campodonico et al., 1996; Kirkwood et al., 1999). For example, presymptomatic gene carriers showed deficits in delayed and immediate recall in verbal memory tasks of the WMS (Hahn-Barma et al., 1998). Individuals showing impaired performance on subtests of the WMS had significantly longer CAG repeats than those who did not show impairments. On the basis of these findings, it was suggested that individuals who are closer to onset (i.e., have a greater number of repeats) were more cognitively impaired than individuals further from onset. Individuals who are presymptomatic but known to have the gene mutation also showed deficits in general intelligence tests, and memory and language tasks (Jason et al., 1997). Again, CAG repeat length was correlated with cognitive test performance and individuals with more repeats scored lower than those with fewer repeats.

Experimental studies provide major support for the relative sparing of recognition performance in HD (Butters et al., 1978, 1985, 1986). Moss et al. (1986) found verbal recognition memory span to be normal in HD, but not in AD. It has been suggested that this relative preservation of verbal recognition in HD may be characteristic of the "subcortical dementias" and may differentiate HD from AD and other "cortical dementias" (Cummings, 1990; Cummings & Benson, 1984). In a study designed to examine the ability of HD patients to learn new "facts" about famous people as well as the source of these facts, it was reported that fact recall did not differ significantly between HD patients and healthy control subjects (Brandt et al., 1995). However, erroneous source attribution was more common among the HD patients. Like frontal lobe damage patients, HD patients have impaired memory for the source of learned information. Volumes of the left caudate nucleus on MRI scans correlated with fact recall and source memory measures. Cognitive dysfunctions characteristic of patients with frontal lobe lesions are noted in the dementia of HD and are thought to result from disruption of frontal–striatal pathways secondary to caudate degeneration (Alexander et al., 1986; Berent et al., 1988; Brandt & Bylsma, 1993; Starkstein et al., 1992).

A study was designed to compare patients with HD and AD matched for level of dementia on tests of executive function (Lange et al., 1995). It was observed that patients with HD are significantly inferior to patients with AD in three tests of cognitive function (spatial working memory, visual discrimination/attentional set shifting, and the Tower of London). Whereas recall of patients with AD tended to be worse on the Kendrick object learning test, the two groups were equivalent on tests of sensorimotor ability and delayed matching to sample performance. By contrast, the patients with HD were significantly worse on tests of pattern and spatial recognition, simultaneous matching to sample, visuospatial paired associates, and on three tests sensitive to frontal dysfunction —namely the Tower of London test of planning, spatial working memory, and a visual discrimination learning and reversal paradigm. The impairments in these tests, however, did not always qualitatively resemble those seen in patients with frontal lobe damage and may be more characteristic of primary neostriatal deficit. In the visual discrimination paradigm, the patients with HD were significantly worse than the patients with AD at the simple reversal stage, where they displayed significant perseveration to the previously rewarded alternative. The results are consistent with the observation that patients with HD exhibit deficits in tests sensitive to frontostriatal dysfunction and that this form of intellectual dysfunction is qualitatively distinct from that seen in AD.

To determine whether asymptomatic individuals at very high genetic risk for HD have demonstrable cognitive abnormalities, the Hopkins Verbal Learning Test was used to assess verbal learning and memory in 76 asymptomatic adults at risk for HD (Rothlind et al., 1993). The results of this study suggest that healthy individuals who will almost certainly develop HD generally do not show evidence of impairment in verbal memory prior to clinical onset of the disease.

Episodic memory

In contrast to AD, the apparent episodic memory disorder associated with HD actually results from damage to the central executive component of the working memory. This damage produces a general difficulty in initiating a systematic retrieval strategy when recalling information from episodic memory. Although these patients, like AD patients, have difficulty in learning and recalling information in a free recall task, they exhibit a marked improvement in performance when memory is tested with a recognition format (minimising retrieval demands). They are able to retain information over a delay in near normal fashion. In addition, HD patients suffer only a mild degree of retrograde amnesia, with difficulty retrieving information from any decade of their lives. HD patients do not display a true episodic memory impairment because the medial temporal lobe structures are intact. Rather, HD patients possess working memory system deficits associated with frontal lobe dysfunction due to frontostriatal damage inherent in the disease.

Semantic memory

HD patients may display impaired performance on some standard measures of semantic memory but on careful assessment, these apparent dysfunctions tend to be attributable to initiation and retrieval problems rather than to an actual degradation of the semantic knowledge.

Naming and category fluency

A review of existing studies failed to demonstrate a significant anomia in HD, at least among patients with overall mild to moderate dementia (Brown & Marsden, 1988). However, more recent studies indicate that HD patients do demonstrate some apparent naming impairment (Hodges et al., 1990). In a study, groups of AD and HD patients were matched on overall dementia and followed longitudinally for one year (Hodges et al., 1990). It was found that the HD patients were mildly impaired on the BNT but their anomia did not progress as rapidly over the year as did the AD patients' anomia. Error analysis revealed that the HD patients' anomia was fully attributable to an increased proportion of visually based errors (Podoll et al., 1988). Hence, at least among mildly demented HD patients, poor performance on confrontation naming measures appears to stem from the primary visuoperceptual problem HD patients are known to have (Brouwers et al., 1984).

A significant component of the fluency deficits in HD patients is attributable to retrieval problems rather than semantic degradation *per se* (Randolph et al., 1993).

Semantic priming and multidimensional scaling

A mutidimensional scaling study showed that the HD patients' semantic map for animal terms was highly similar to that of normal controls (Chan et al., 1993). In contrast to the AD group, the HD group used the identical dimensions, and cluster analysis revealed the same clusters as the normal controls, suggestive of intact semantic organisation for mildly demented HD patients.

Procedural memory

In a study designed to examine various aspects of procedural memory in HD patients using a maze-learning paradigm, it was found that although the HD group showed normal learning curves for a specific maze route, they were deficient in generalising the cognitive skills across mazes (Bylsma et al., 1990). They failed to improve performance on a maze with a predictable route relative to mazes with unpredictable routes. It was hypothesised that the basal ganglia is an important structure in mediating the ability to generalise skills and appreciate patterned organisation in to-be-acted-upon stimuli.

DISCUSSION

Although AD is often thought of as a unitary or homogeneous syndrome, nothing could be further from the truth. In fact, some researchers have posited that AD may have multiple aetiologies and subtypes. Different patterns of cognitive dysfunction have also been reported (Fisher et al., 1997; Martin et al., 1986). Cluster analyses have identified three neuropsychological subgroups, such as patients with predominantly language impairment, patients with predominantly spatial impairment, and a diffuse subtype. Longitudinal studies have indicated that these patterns show stability over time (Fisher et al., 1997). However, despite the advances in understanding the various forms of dementia, reliable algorithms for differential diagnosis do not exist. It remains the responsibility of the clinician to recognise the various typical and atypical forms of AD. Differential diagnosis is often a dynamic ongoing multidisciplinary process.

Word-reading threshold determination discriminates mild AD subjects from normal elderly controls and correlates with severity of cognitive impairment (Massoud et al., 2002). Word-reading threshold was significantly longer in the AD group (122.6 ± 70.8 ms) in comparison with elderly normal controls (53.8 ± 15.9 ms). A word-reading threshold limit of 85 ms correctly classified 11/12 elderly normal controls and 10/13 AD subjects. Four of the 13 mild cognitive impairment subjects also exceeded this threshold and all four progressed to AD within a 2-year follow-up (Massoud et al., 2002). The word-reading threshold test may have diagnostic and prognostic utility in early AD and MCI subjects.

AD and HD impair performance on semantic memory tasks and, according to one view, AD disrupts the storage of semantic memories, whereas HD disrupts the retrieval of semantic memories (Rohrer et al., 1999). In this study in which participants generated category exemplars (e.g., kinds of fruit) for 1 minute, and response latencies were evaluated, it was shown that AD patients produced a larger proportion of responses earlier in the recall period, consistent with the view that AD patients quickly exhaust their limited supply of items in storage. On the other hand, HD patients produced a larger proportion of their responses late in the recall period, consistent with the hypothesis that HD slows retrieval. Another study that aimed to compare the pattern of spared and impaired memory functions in AD, HD, and PD, assessed explicit memory in various situations of acquisition (free encoding or controlled encoding) and retrieval (immediate and delayed free and cued recall recognition) conditions (Pillon et al., 1993). It was observed that in a free encoding situation, higher numbers of intrusions and false recognitions occurred in AD patients but in the retrieval condition, cued recall and recognition scores were significantly higher in PD and HD than in AD patients. Memory performance correlated significantly with executive function test scores in HD and PD but not in AD. The results suggest that the amnesia syndrome in AD was compatible with lesions of hippocampus and temporal cortex but the inefficient planning of memory processes of HD and PD might result from a striato-frontal impairment.

Prior-item intrusion errors represent the perseveration of previously presented materials into an individual's ongoing current performance on cognitive tasks. Although increments in these and other types of intrusion errors have been reported in several neurological populations, some studies have reported that such errors may be diagnostic of the early stages of dementia of the Alzheimer type (Butters, 1985; Shindler et al., 1984). It has been demonstrated that dementia-of-the-Alzheimer-type patients produce numerous intrusion errors on list learning and object memory tests, mental status examinations, and on several verbal subtests of the Wechsler Adult Intelligence Scale (Fuld, 1983). Indications of the possible diagnostic importance of intrusion errors have also been provided by the finding of significant correlations between these error tendencies and low choline acetyltransferase (ChAT) levels and the number of senile plaques in the brains of elderly nursing home patients (Fuld et al., 1982). In a study designed to assess the diagnostic value of intrusion errors of AD patients, the tendency of the AD and HD patients on a memory task was evaluated (Jacobs et al., 1990). Results indicate that both patient groups produced more prior-figure intrusion errors than did normal elderly controls and that AD patients made significantly more intrusion errors in their reproductions than did HD patients matched for overall severity of dementia. Using a cut-off proportion score of 35%, 100% of the normal elderly control subjects, 84% of HD, and 60% of DAT patients were classified correctly. When only the patient groups were included in the analysis, the cut-off proportion score of 35% successfully classified 70% of HD and AD patients. Thus, it appears that prior-figure intrusion errors are of maximum usefulness when they occur in combination with other deficits associated with AD such as rapid forgetting rate and anomia. The presence of prior-figure intrusion errors may be of great diagnostic support in distinguishing AD from HD and perhaps other forms of "subcortical dementia".

Both PD and HD are examples of extrinsic "frontal" disorders. Both involve basal ganglia rather than PFC pathology, yet both produce executive function deficits, presumably because of close connections between the PFC and the basal ganglia. So, neuropathology outside the PFC appears to be able to produce dysfunction in the PFC because the PFC is part of a complex system. Nonetheless, each is a distinct disorder in terms of aetiology, the exact nature of the neuropathology within the basal ganglia, behavioural symptoms, and course. Future studies should seek to investigate these potentially important functional differences further by relating them to what is known about the differential neuropathology in each condition. Such investigations, when combined with information derived from clinical neuropsychology, and neurobiology, should certainly provide a significant focus for future research and may lead ultimately to a better understanding of the distinctive roles played by the frontal cortex and the striatum in the operation of the "fronto-striatal" functional loops. For example, it has been shown that the striatum is involved in more than simple pairwise associations and that it has the capacity to process higher-order knowledge (Peigneux et al., 2000). It has also been suggested that the striatum is not only involved in the implicit automatisation of serial information through PFC–caudate nucleus networks but also that it plays a significant role for the selection of the most appropriate responses in the context created by both the current and previous stimuli, thus contributing to better efficiency and faster response preparation in the serial reaction time task (Peigneux et al., 2000).

Finally, patients with cortical and subcortical dementia syndromes can also be differentiated by the functional status of their procedural memory system. HD patients are impaired on a number of procedural memory tasks, such as motor skill learning, prism adaptation, and weight biasing, which involve the generation and refinement (learning) of motor programs to guide behaviour. In contrast, all of these tasks are performed normally by AD patients. Furthermore, patients with subcortical dementia are also deficient in acquiring the cognitive (non-motor) skills necessary to perform a probabilistic categorical classification learning task, although patients with circumscribed amnesia retain this ability. The impaired procedural learning associated with subcortical dementing diseases such as HD is due to damage within basal ganglia structures, whereas the procedural memory system is normal in cortical dementias such as AD since the corticostriatal systems remain intact.

One possible agenda faced by PD research guided by a declarative/prospective memory distinction is the delineation of how executive functions, prospective memory, and declarative memory are related. More specifically, research might address which executive functions relate to prospective memory impairment, and whether the same executive functions significantly impact declarative memory. The identification and comparison of processes underlying prospective and declarative memory might be of mutual benefit both to clinical neuropsychology and behavioural neurology.

9

Memory Dysfunctions in Neurogenic Communication Disorders

INTRODUCTION

Communication disorders in children are both diverse and complex. The majority of children with specific language impairments (SLI) are considered to have broadly intact non-verbal skills while showing primary deficits in one or more areas of language. Difficulties in acquiring phonological and grammatical skills are widely noted. Deficits in semantic and pragmatic development are also widespread. A study in a population of children with SLI reported that the cognitive deficit most common in that group was a deficit in verbal STM as indicated by digit span (Haynes & Naidoo, 1991). STM skills in normally developing children have been linked with vocabulary acquisition, language comprehension and reading development (Gathercole & Baddeley, 1989). Gathercole and Baddeley (1994) argued that children with SLI have poor vocabulary knowledge resulting from difficulties in acquiring and retaining new words in their phonological forms. If adequate phonological STM skills are a prerequisite for normal vocabulary development, a deficit in STM skills will make it harder for the child with SLI to learn new words and patterns of word sequences. Furthermore, it was also stated that this sort of STM limitation may present a substantial obstacle to comprehension by restricting the ability to keep in mind the necessary background information established by prior words in the sentence and by preceding sentences (Cowan, 1996).

Linguistic performance, characteristically compromised in aphasia, has been defined as the product of language capacities, processing capacities, and memory storage (Zurif et al., 1979). A model that takes into account the relationship between such complex cognitive activities, at least to some extent, is the working memory model of Baddeley and Hitch (1974). In this model, working memory refers to a system of limited capacity which is utilised for the temporary storage and manipulation of information (Baddeley, 1992). The phonological loop formed the basis of much of the initial research related to working memory and aphasia.

Evidence accumulated suggesting that a reduced or deficient memory frequently accompanies aphasia, possibly resulting from impairment of the phonological loop (Gordon, 1983; Rothi & Hutchinson, 1981). It was suggested that short-term verbal memory impairment in conduction and Broca's aphasia might reflect a failure to rehearse information verbally in STM (Heilman et al., 1976). It was reasoned that, in a memory task in which there was a delay prior to recall, those patients who could verbally rehearse would fare better than those patients who could not. In a study that includes fluent and nonfluent aphasic individuals, better performance by the fluent aphasic individuals because of their use of verbal rehearsal was observed (Rothi & Hutchinson, 1981). In another experiment designed to investigate the presence of a disrupted phonological loop in aphasia, it was found that, in contrast to individuals with fluent aphasia, non-fluent aphasic individuals failed to demonstrate several of the effects found in normal subjects which, according to Baddeley (1990), support the existence of the phonological loop (Martin, 1987). For example, the non-fluent aphasic individuals failed to demonstrate a phonological similarity effect (the phonological similarity effect refers to the finding that memory span is longer for a phonologically dissimilar word series "day, pen, cow, foot" than for a phonologically similar word series such as "man, pan, can, fan"). The non-fluent individuals also showed a reduced word length effect relative to fluent aphasic individuals (the word length effect refers to the finding that memory span varies inversely with word length).

Patients with aphasia often complain of memory impairment and their families often confirm that the patients have trouble recalling previously known names and events and learning new information. Many instances of memory problems in these patients are a reflection of their aphasia, word-finding difficulties, and poor comprehension of a request rather than actual amnesia for events. Even though most brain lesions that produce aphasia are located outside limbic circuits believed to be critical for memory, there are reasons to view the complaints of poor memory in aphasic patients as more important than simply a reflec-

tion of underlying aphasia. Memory complaints often persist despite good language recovery (Beeson et al., 1993; Risse et al., 1984). Verbal memory processes may rely on some of the same neural systems that serve language processes even though these processes are located outside limbic circuits. Colombo et al. (1990), for example, reported that monkeys with lesions in auditory association cortex had impaired complex auditory memory despite unaffected auditory perception. Verbal learning deficits in humans after damage to language-specific association cortex may reflect similar processes. Many aphasic speakers exhibit poor performance on auditory–verbal STM tasks. On the other hand, memory impairments may also negatively influence the functional communication abilities and response to treatment of adults with neurogenic communication disorders (Goldenberg et al., 1994). Thus, speech–language clinicians as well as other care professionals must be cognisant of the types of memory problems that may occur in their patients.

APHASIA

The complex interactions of memory and language have been demonstrated in several ways. First, children with acquired aphasia often have very poor academic performance (impaired acquisition of facts and skills) even when language recovery is good (Cranberg et al., 1987; Woods & Carey, 1979). Second, using recognition tasks that avoid the necessity for verbal responses, severe aphasics show impairments in both verbal and non-verbal memory (Cermak et al., 1984; Meier et al., 1990). Third, even mildly aphasic patients may have impaired short- or long-term verbal memory when recall tasks such as selective reminding procedure are used (Beeson et al., 1993; Risse et al., 1984).

Many studies in aphasia have documented impaired STM for both auditory and visual–verbal material and have identified factors that may influence the severity of these deficits. A study reported that patients with fluent aphasia, like non-brain-damaged adults, were better at recalling easy versus hard-to-articulate word lists (Martin & Feher, 1990). In contrast, ease of articulation had no effect on the STM performance of patients with non-fluent aphasia. These results suggest that STM problems in aphasia may reflect difficulties with covert articulatory rehearsal. The type of aphasic linguistic deficit may also influence STM abilities. Another study reported that on word list recall tasks, aphasic patients with phonologic deficits showed a robust primacy effect (i.e., recall of words from the beginning of a list thought to be based on storage at semantic levels) whereas aphasic patients with semantic deficits had an enhanced recency effect (i.e. recall of words from the end of a list thought to be based on storage at phonological levels) (Martin & Saffran, 1997). It was proposed that different recall profiles reflected different memory strategies. Patients with phonological deficits relied more strongly on the integrity of their lexical–semantic system, whereas patients with semantic deficits relied on their phonological systems.

The selective preservation or impairment of word or digit repetition is a defining feature of the two classical aphasic syndromes, transcortical aphasia and conduction aphasia. In transcortical sensory aphasia, repetition of single words and word lists is preserved despite there being a marked comprehension impairment. Furthermore, in the class of transcortical sensory aphasics whose deficit is at the level of single word comprehension, there may be no difference in the ability to repeat lists of words that are known or lists of words whose meaning has been forgotten as a consequence of the disease (Warrington, 1975).

In conduction aphasia, an inability to repeat either polysyllabic words and/or lists of digits may be the only significant deficit with other aspects of language functioning being relatively well preserved. Conduction aphasia is an aphasic disturbance that is seldom present in isolation (Kohn, 1992; Shallice & Butterworth, 1977). Impairment in the ability to repeat word lists and polysyllabic words does not invariably co-occur. Repetition difficulty in conduction aphasia has been attributed to a deficit of STM by some investigators whereas others have viewed the difficulty as primarily a linguistic deficit (Cappa & Pasquali, 1998;

Goodglass, 1993). It has been argued that there are at least two identifiable subclasses of conduction aphasic (Shallice & Warrington, 1977). In those patients with difficulty in repeating polysyllabic words the deficit appears to be one at the level of speech production. In the other class of patients single word repetition is normal although "span" for auditorily presented lists of verbal material is selectively impaired. This pattern of performance has been identified with an impairment in auditorily verbal STM (Vallar & Baddeley, 1984). There have been a number of studies addressing the neuroanatomical basis of conduction aphasia. The consensus seems to be that conduction aphasia occurs from damage to the supramarginal gyrus, the posterior superior temporal gyrus, or both (Albert et al., 1981; Palumbo et al., 1992). A study reviewed 25 cases that had common involvement of the posterior end of the Sylvian fissure (Green & Howes, 1978). Damasio and Damasio (1980) stressed in their six cases of conduction aphasia the damage to the insula and the absence of involvement of more posterior structures such as the angular gyrus (area 39) and the posterior portions of the second and third gyri (area 37).

Unlike long-term retention of verbal information, STM is vulnerable to fast decay. Presumably, introducing a delay would negatively impact repetition difficulty if the problem with repetition in conduction aphasia is one that is memory-based. A case study showed that the patient's repetition errors did not differ following immediate, 5-second, and 10-second delay conditions, which suggests that delay did not interfere with his ability to retain the phonological form of the word (Barresi & Lindfield, 2000). Thus, these data tend to support a linguistic rather than a memory basis for the repetition difficulty in this patient with conduction aphasia.

An interesting study reported an analysis of verbal learning and memory in 16 patients with mild aphasia (Ween et al., 1996). It was hypothesised that phonologic deficits are associated with impaired STM and that lexicosemantic deficits are associated with encoding and possibly retrieval of information from LTM. Thus, subjects were classified according to phonological and lexicosemantic abilities, tested on a variety of STM and LTM tasks, and their behavioural deficits correlated with lesion location. It was found that aphasia deficits impaired both STM and LTM. Phonological impairment affected only digit span performance. Lexicosemantic deficiencies impaired self-organised encoding of word lists. Memory dysfunction was not associated with specific lesion locations. It was suggested that persistent verbal-memory impairments accompanying even mild residual aphasia may be responsible for much of the difficulty mildly aphasic patients experience returning to vocational, academic, and social life. The co-occurrence of these deficits may probably reflect their underlying dependence on similar processing systems.

The relationship between the site of lesion and type of verbal memory disorders in aphasic patients has also been studied. Both Risse et al. (1984) and Beeson et al. (1993) compared patients with anterior and posterior lesions. Short-term verbal memory was tested using digit span and verbal learning was assessed by free recall of a nine-word list with selective reminding of unrecalled items (Buschke, 1973). The results of these studies suggest that anterior lesions are associated with impaired long-term retention and posterior lesions with STM deficits. However, another study that compared aphasic patients with either anterior or posterior lesions in a series of verbal STM and LTM task was also performed (Ween et al., 1996). Aphasic patients were impaired compared to normal controls but no association was found between memory impairment and lesion site.

Working memory

Language comprehension abilities in aphasia could be predicted by working memory capacity (Caspari et al., 1998). It has also been suggested that aphasic patients who do poorly on working memory span tests often do well at comprehending sentences with complex syntactic structures (Caplan & Waters, 1994). Therefore, there must be a memory system specific to syntactic processing and separate from a general working memory.

It was argued that working memory does play a role in aphasia but that this role needs to be more finely analysed taking into account separate working memory systems for different linguistic processes.

Daneman and Carpenter (1980) examined the integrative function of the central executive by measuring working memory capacity. They defined the capacity of working memory as the total amount of resources that could be allocated to support concurrent processing and storage of information. They suggested that an individual draws on a common but limited pool of resources, first to process incoming information and then to store its product temporarily until task completion. Thus, the more efficient the processing, the more resources there would be available for storage. If these resources were measurable, their assessment would be an index of working memory capacity. In accordance with this hypothesis, the more efficient processors would demonstrate larger working memory capacities whereas less efficient processors would demonstrate smaller working memory capacities. A task was devised to measure working memory capacity, which incorporated both storage and processing (Daneman & Carpenter, 1980). Their results demonstrated that working memory capacity measurements that considered both processing and storage were better able to predict reading performance than were the older traditional list span measurements. A recent study was designed to determine if differences in working memory capacity could be demonstrated in the aphasic population using a task similar in deign to Daneman and Carpenter's (1980) reading span task and whether or not reading or listening span in the aphasic population has the same correlational relationship to silent reading comprehension and general oral language ability as found by Daneman and Carpenter (1980) in the normal population (Caspari et al., 1998). Strong positive correlations were observed between working memory capacity, reading comprehension, and language function. The data support the hypothesis that the ability of aphasic individuals to comprehend language is predictable from their working memory capacities.

Semantic and episodic memory

Within the framework of the classical distinction between episodic memory and semantic memory, it has been argued that these two memory systems are organised in a hierarchical way (Tulving, 1983, 1984). The hierarchical hypothesis assumes that episodic memory is a specific subsystem of semantic memory and therefore implies that episodic memory cannot exist without semantic memory. Although this hypothesis has been challenged, the experimental evidence against it is still scant (Squire, 1987).

In addition to pure language impairment, aphasic patients are known to show semantic memory deficits and also episodic memory deficits in the verbal domain and in the nonverbal domain (Riege et al., 1980; Risse et al., 1984; Warrington & Shallice, 1984). However, the nature of episodic memory deficit in aphasia is still unclear.

In a study designed to investigate the influence of semantic encoding on recognition memory performance in a population of aphasic patients, the investigators aimed to see whether, holding constant the material variable, subjects' performance on a semantic association task would be correlated with the performance on a recognition (episodic) memory task (Dalla Barba et al., 1996). The results showed that aphasics, regardless of their type of language disturbance, show some episodic memory deficit. A further analysis also showed that patients who were impaired on the semantic association task did significantly worse on the episodic memory task than controls and than patients who were unimpaired on the semantic association task. It was suggested that the aphasic patients' episodic memory deficit reported in this study and other studies may represent a sequel of semantic memory impairment (Riege et al., 1980; Risse et al., 1984). Thus, as far as meaningful to-be-remembered stimuli are concerned, a semantic memory deficit affects performance on episodic memory. Episodic memory may depend on the integrity of semantic memory. It is in this sense that Tulving's hierarchical hypothesis must be interpreted (Tulving, 1983).

RIGHT HEMISPHERE DISORDERS

Right hemisphere brain damage can produce a variety of communication problems including difficulties comprehending and producing discourse, processing figurative language, and using prosodic information (Myers, 1999; Tompkins, 1995). These communication problems may not be purely language-based in all cases but rather represent the direct or indirect effects of a variety of cognitive impairments such as deficits of perception, attention, and memory abilities (Joanette et al., 1990). Considerable research has shown that patients with damage to the right hemisphere have difficulty in following the implications of conversation and deriving implicit meaning from the relevant context. This work has shown that the right hemisphere plays a crucial role in influencing the interpretation of utterances used in conversation and in distinguishing internal emotional states (Molloy et al., 1991). For example, stroke patients with right hemisphere damage display considerable difficulty in interpreting indirect requests and commands. They also often do not recognise the relevance of the theme of a story in understanding narratives (Winner et al., 1998).

It is generally accepted that, after right brain damage, STM and LTM for nonverbal or "not easily verbalised" material is more affected than memory for verbal material (Lewis-Jack et al., 1997; Rausch, 1985). Right-hemisphere-brain-damage patients, particularly those with temporal lobe damage, may have difficulty with immediate or delayed recall of visual information such as complex visual figures, spatial expressions, as well as auditory information such as the melody or rhythm of songs, and prosodic voice qualities. Problems remembering nonverbal material in other sensory modalities such as olfaction have also been reported (Rausch et al., 1977).

A case study reported on a patient who demonstrated a pattern consistent with pure conduction aphasia (Stefanis et al., 1997). Visuospatial memory was very poor but improved in follow-up testing. Head CT and MRI showed infarction of the right lateral temporal lobe, suggesting that the patient had a "mirror" crossed aphasia. A classically non-dominant hemispheric function, visuospatial memory, was also affected, suggesting that the right hemisphere mediated both language and visuospatial memory. It was suggested that language and modality-specific memory functions may lateralise independently of each other.

Name recognition

Names are thought to be represented in the brain differently from common nouns. Although this hypothesis is supported by both theoretical and empirical arguments, the brain areas that are relevant for the recognition of personal names and in particular the extent of the right hemisphere involvement, remain controversial.

Several cases of anomia (the inability to name target items) that was selective for personal names have been reported as a result of brain lesion (Fery et al., 1995; Micelli et al., 2000). Although one has to consider that these were deficits of name production that need to be distinguished from name comprehension or recognition, there is also some evidence that has been taken to argue for a neurological dissociation of names and words in recognition (Brédart et al., 1997). A study reported that in four globally aphasic patients, preserved recognition of personal names but not other words was observed in a picture to word matching task (VanLancker et al., 1991). In part, because of the extensive left hemispheric lesions that were seen in these patients, it was subsequently hypothesised that personal name recognition was mediated predominantly by the right hemisphere (VanLancker, 1991). In a further study, right brain damaged patients were found to be inferior to left brain damaged patients when they had to point to a facial picture (of an array of 10) that corresponded to an auditorily presented personal name. From these results, a right hemisphere advantage for personal name recognition was inferred (VanLancker et al., 1991). However, a recent study that investigated asymmetries both for names and common nouns concluded that although familiar names may be represented by brain systems that differ from those representing common nouns, there is no evidence for a distinct role of the right hemisphere in the recognition of names (Schweinberger, 2002).

Face recognition

Bodamer (1947) named the condition prosopagnosia (literally, loss of person knowledge; from Greek *prosopon* meaning person and *agnosia* meaning ignorance). Subsequent work has shown that the right cerebral hemisphere plays a predominant role in analysing and learning complex visual material such as familiar faces. The most complete hypothesis of face recognition posits an initial structural encoding followed by several analytical processes (carried out by face recognition units), which probably act in parallel, followed by recognition and naming (Bruce & Young, 1986). This model focuses on functional requirements in facial recognition and does not attempt to designate which cerebral hemisphere is responsible for a particular analytical component, although many of the units are likely to be organised by the right hemisphere (Anderson et al., 2000).

Evidence that the right cerebral hemisphere has a major responsibility for learning and remembering familiar faces comes from studying patients with lateralised brain damage and from tachistoscopic studies in which normal participants view lateralised visual stimuli that are sent initially to one or the other cerebral hemisphere (Benton & Van Allen, 1968; Rizzolatti et al., 1971). Recent studies showing activation of the right fusiform gyrus in face tasks support these conclusions (Kim et al., 1999; O'Craven & Kanwisher, 2000). However, although there is a convergence of findings that the right hemisphere is superior to the left hemisphere in face analysis and face memory, both the left and right cerebral hemispheres appear to possess mechanisms that allow them, in isolation, to recognise certain classes of faces. In the case of unilateral right hemisphere lesions in adulthood, patients may be extremely impaired in learning of new, previously unknown faces but they are usually still able to recognise, for example, family members, perhaps by using mechanisms located in the intact left hemisphere (Benton & Van Allen, 1968). It should be noted that clinical observations and CT scan findings in living patients have suggested that right hemisphere damage alone may be capable of producing a complete loss of memory for faces, including family members (De Renzi, 1986; Landis et al., 1986).

Specification of the neuroanatomical components responsible for the right hemisphere mechanisms that are involved when confronted with a face stimulus will require further study. Imaging studies in intact and brain-damaged patients may provide the answer by showing which areas are activated when a face is presented in the right visual field.

TRAUMATIC BRAIN INJURY

Traumatic brain injury (TBI) refers to any brain damage caused by an external force that may produce a variety of temporary or permanent physical, cognitive, and behavioural impairments (National Head Injury Foundation Task Force on Special Education, 1989). The neurological consequences of TBI include sensory, motor, and/or autonomic deficits depending on the severity of the initial trauma. The cognitive sequelae are also diverse, but some of the most common problems involve memory impairment, difficulties in attention and concentration, language and visual perceptional deficits, and frontal lobe functions including problem solving, insight, judgement, and information processing. It has been well established that memory deficits are a reliable consequence of TBI (Richardson, 2000). Difficulties in remembering people's names are among the memory problems reported most frequently. These include difficulties in retrieving the names of familiar persons as well as in learning the names of newly met persons (Brooks, 1984; Wilson, 1987a, b).

LTM impairments are very common after TBI (Richardson, 2000). In particular, most patients with TBI, regardless of injury severity will have episodic or "events" memory deficits. Anterograde amnesia or difficulties remembering or learning new information whether it is episodic versus semantic or verbal versus nonverbal in nature, is another frequent TBI symptom (Richardson, 2000;

Shum et al., 2000). For most patients with mild TBI, these mnemonic deficits do not persist beyond the period of post-traumatic amnesia (i.e., acute recovery period during which the patient is disoriented and cannot remember day-to-day events). In more severe cases of TBI, these deficits endure, affect performance on a variety of daily tasks, and are the most frequent subjective complaint of both patients and caregivers. Recent reports indicate that 54–84% of individuals with severe TBI suffer from memory difficulties and 53% of patients and 79% of their families report persistent memory deficits even after 7 years post-injury (McKinlay & Watkiss, 1999; Oddy et al., 1985). Memory deficit is also a major factor in failure to return to work and is a predictor of successful completion of rehabilitation and vocational training (McKinlay & Watkiss, 1999; Ryan et al., 1992). Age of injury plays an important role. Thus children who suffer a TBI at a younger age are more impaired in learning and memory than children who suffer a TBI at an older age (Lehnung et al., 2001).

In a retrospective study that compared the results of two groups of left hemisphere damaged patients (acute and chronic) with the results of a normal control population in a series of memory tasks, the question of whether the locus of lesion —anterior, posterior, or deep—correlated with different memory impairments was investigated (Burgio & Basso, 1997). The issue of whether LTM for prose and for word lists be differentially impaired was also studied. The results showed that both brain-damaged groups were significantly impaired in all memory tasks (except for chronic patients in the story-learning task) compared to controls. The presence of aphasia and locus of lesion (anterior, posterior, and deep) had no effect on the memory impairment, with only one exception of paired-associate learning that was better performed by non-aphasic than aphasic patients. Finally, chronic patients performed significantly better than acute patients only in the Corsi's learning task. Chronic patients with a mean length of illness of 2 years and 9 months were still significantly impaired compared to normal controls in digit span, paired-associate, and spatial learning. However, chronic patients were not more severely impaired in language tasks than acute patients when examined with memory tasks, although they may have had more severe language disorders that partly recovered with time. It was concluded that memory disorders are long-lasting although for some of the patients some partial recovery has taken place.

Several investigators have postulated that memory impairment in individuals with TBI is a result of deficiency in acquisition of information (i.e., impaired acquisition hypothesis). Generally, these studies have focused on measures of learning ability (i.e., encoding strategies). For example, it has been suggested that individuals with TBI exhibit a decreased learning curve, reduced semantic clustering ability, and deficiencies in the ability to apply encoding strategies spontaneously (Blachstein et al., 1993; Crosson et al., 1988; Goldstein et al., 1989). In contrast to studies that assess acquisition, other investigations have supported the retrieval failure hypothesis of memory impairment (Kear-Caldwell & Heller, 1980; Levin et al., 1979). These studies, which report that compromised memory in persons with TBI may be a function of impairments in the retrieval in the retrieval of information, are often based on findings of intact recognition performance in the presence of impaired recall performance (Baum et al., 1996; Gass, 1995). However, these conclusions were challenged by findings indicating that a discrepancy between recognition and recall performance does not accurately identify the presence of retrieval deficits in the patients with TBI (Wilde et al., 1995). An examination of data supporting the retrieval hypothesis shows that investigators typically fail to control for differences in learning ability between individuals with TBI and control groups. A study designed to examine whether impaired memory in individuals with TBI is caused by impaired initial acquisition or compromised retrieval from long-term storage showed that memory impairment after TBI is caused primarily by deficiencies in initial acquisition of verbal information rather than in compromised retrieval (DeLuca et al., 2000). Thus, these data support the impaired acquisition hypothesis of memory dysfunction in patients with TBI whereby memory dysfunction is primarily attributed to deficiencies in the initial acquisition of verbal information rather than in retrieval failure.

Awareness of deficits

Impairment in awareness of deficit generally refers to the explicit verbal denial of an illness or impairment (i.e., anosognosia) or a lack of concern about a deficit (i.e., anosodiaphoria). In general, individuals with TBI rate themselves as more behaviourally and cognitively competent than do their relatives or therapists (Gasquoine & Gibbons, 1994). Although unawareness of deficit is inversely related to emotional dysphoria among individuals with TBI, it also is inversely related to rehabilitation success and return to work postinjury (Prigatano, 1996). Individuals with TBI who show positive gains from rehabilitation are described as developing a realistic awareness and acceptance of their cognitive difficulties, and a willingness and ability to learn compensatory strategies (Prigatano et al., 1984).

DISCUSSION

There is evidence that different forms of memory (i.e., STM, LTM, and working memory) for both verbal and non-verbal material may be impaired in aphasia. However, there is a critical need for further delineation of the nature of memory problems in aphasia and how these mnemonic deficits may affect the language abilities and treatment responses of aphasic patients. The results showing a relationship between working memory capacity and reading and language impairment in aphasia suggest the fruitfulness of further exploration of cognitive resource allocation theory in aphasia. Future research in the area of working memory and aphasia should consider the individual contributions of processing and storage to comprehension (Waters & Caplan, 1996). Such information might shed further light on whether or not working memory can be viewed as a single processing resource that supports all cognitive activities or whether it is divided into several separate resource pools that support specific cognitive activities, such as, for example, online psycholinguistic processing.

Research indicates that patients with right hemisphere brain damage are at risk for a variety of both non-verbal and verbal memory deficits. Because attention deficits are well documented after right hemisphere brain damage, and there is a close relationship between attention and other cognitive abilities such as memory, it is suspected that memory impairments after right hemisphere brain damage may be quite prevalent (Caplan & Waters, 1994; Lyon & Krasnegor, 1996; Myers, 1999). Right hemisphere lesions are more commonly associated with disturbances of directed or spatial attention. Additionally, the right hemisphere has long been identified as playing a key role in mediating aspects of executive function (Lezak, 1982).

One of the most difficult issues on TBI for family and sometimes for medical staff involved in treatment is to understand how cognitive impairment can be significant even in the presence of relatively minor orthopaedic injuries. It is for that reason that patients with minor brain injuries are sometimes referred to as the walking wounded. For all intents and purposes, the brain-injury patient may look normal to the family. It is very important that the clinical staff educate the family about cognitive impairments and offer reassurance regarding the "normal" aspects of the clinical presentation as well as the expected course of recovery. Common memory profile for TBI patients includes impaired LTM (i.e., retrograde

and anterograde amnesias) and working memory, but relatively preserved STM and non-declarative memory abilities. At the same time, diverse patterns of memory deficits are possible, given the great variation in location and extent of brain damage associated with TBI. Brain-injured patients also suffer from a non-specific slowing of information processing that has been documented extensively in a range of studies (Van Zomeren & Brouwer, 1994). Whether impaired performance in complex tasks is due to a deficient activation of low-level routine skills, related for example to slowing of information processing, or to a specific disorder in higher-level cognitive abilities is still controversial (Schwartz et al., 1998). Several studies have reported beneficial effects of treatments for attentional deficits following TBI. Mateer et al. (1990) described five TBI cases who received treatment 1–5 years after their injury. The postacute rehabilitation programme included individual and group cognitive remediation for attention and memory deficits over a period of 8 months. Following treatment, these five subjects made clinically significant gains on 60% of the neuropsychological measures of attention, memory, and general intellectual functioning administered. It appears that intervention based on a cognitive neuropsychological model of working memory may be effective in the remediation of attention deficits after TBI (Cicerone, 2002). Future research must continue to focus on determining the impact of memory deficits and their treatment on the communication skills of patients with TBI.

10

Memory Dysfunctions in Psychiatric Diseases

INTRODUCTION

The most common psychiatric disorders in which memory impairment may be seen are schizophrenia, depression, and anxiety. The objective cognitive impairment is often mild with alterations in such functions as attention, STM, and speed of processing. Examination of memory biases for disorder-congruent information suggests that characteristic cognitive styles can distinguish among various psychopathologies. For example, an implicit memory bias has been typically associated with anxiety and an explicit memory bias has been found to be more characteristic of depression (Williams et al., 1997). Implicit memory processes activate stored information, thereby improving its accessibility though not necessarily affecting its direct retrievability. Conversely, explicit memories involve conscious, deliberate recall of information that was elaborated at the time of encoding and are therefore more available due to embellishment from contextual cues. Anxiety is marked by a non-conscious, automatic, preattentive bias towards threat cues that may

prime such information in implicit memory tests (Mathews et al., 1989). However, this defensive attentional mechanism thwarts further processing of anxiety-provoking stimuli and so no explicit memory bias appears for such material. In contrast, depression is characterised by conscious elaboration of sad material that increases its availability for explicit directed recall. However, these specific memory effects in anxiety may not generalise across diagnostic categories. Although the hypothesis of an implicit but not explicit memory bias for disorder-congruent material has been replicated in generalised anxiety disorder (GAD), others have found both implicit and explicit memory biases for relevant stimuli in panic disorder (Cloitre & Leibowitz, 1991; MacLeod & McLaughlin, 1995). Methodological inconsistencies across studies might account for these discrepant memory effects (Becker et al., 1999).

Over the past few years, knowledge about autobiographical memory functioning in the emotional disorders has steadily accumulated (see Williams, 1996). There have been indications that impairment in ability to recall specific autobiographical memory is a clinically significant phenomenon.

Research has focused on the relative inability of some patients to retrieve specific autobiographical memories even when they are explicitly instructed to do so. Instead these patients respond to cue-words (e.g., happy) with so-called overgeneral memories, that is memories reflecting several occurrences or a category of situations rather than one specific event. Overgeneral memory was originally described in suicidal patients (Williams & Broadbent, 1986). This phenomenon was first described in a study that investigated the issue of why overdose patients display relatively long latencies to retrieve personal memories, especially in response to positive cue words (Williams & Broadbent, 1986). That initial study has been replicated with suicide attempters, and tendencies to retrieve inappropriately general memories, compared with control groups, have since been discovered among patients suffering from a variety of psychological disorders (Williams, 1996). These tendencies have been found among patients suffering from depression and among adult survivors of childhood sexual abuse (Goddard et al., 1996; Henderson, 1996; Kuyken & Brewin, 1995; Kuyken & Dalgliesh, 1995). Subsequent research found overgeneral memory to be a characteristic of depression and post-traumatic stress disorder (PTSD) (Goddard et al., 1996; McNally et al., 1995).

SCHIZOPHRENIA

Schizophrenia, the most severe of the mental illnesses, is a psychotic disorder characterised by late-adolescent or early adult onset and has, in most cases, a chronic course. The deficient processes involved in this disorder are clinically silent until the onset of prodromal or psychotic symptoms, at which time neuropsychological testing demonstrates the presence of cognitive deficits that are often chronic and apparently irreversible (Goldberg et al., 1993). The clinical picture of schizophrenia has led many authors to speculate that particularly the negative features of schizophrenia reflect deficits in executive functioning (e.g., Andreasen, 1989). An increasing number

of studies document impairments on tests such as the Wisconsin Card Sorting Test (WCST) in schizophrenia (Goldberg et al., 1987; Morice, 1990). Weinberger et al. (1986) found that patients were impaired on the task and there was no increase in regional blood flow in dorsolateral prefrontal cortex relative to controls during card sort performance. This result has often been quoted to support the view of "hypofrontality" in schizophrenia.

Memory deficits observed in schizophrenia are not restricted to a single element of memory but strike different systems, such as declarative memory, procedural memory, and working memory (Goldberg et al., 1993; McKenna et al., 1990; Tamlyn et al., 1992). McKenna et al. (1990) and Tamlyn et al. (1992) reported significant correlations between declarative memory deficits and both formal thought disorders and negative symptoms, while Goldberg et al. (1993) found that negative symptoms also correlate with procedural memory impairment. An interesting study was designed to investigate learning and memory using a wide number of neuropsychological measures in monozygotic pairs of individuals discordant for schizophrenia compared to normal pairs of monozygotic twins (Goldberg et al., 1993). A significant correlation between many measures of memory and global level of social and vocational functioning within the discordant group were observed. Thus, cognitive impairment is a central manifestation of the schizophrenic illness that impacts on the quality of life of the patient. Apart from the potential utility of indicating the degree or severity of neuropsychological deficiency, the measurement of cognitive processes and its impairment may also serve as an indicator or marker of vulnerability to schizophrenia in normal individuals at high risk of schizophrenia.

Information processing

Negative thought disorder appears to reflect a disturbance in generating a discourse plan that requires selecting ideas to be expressed, retrieving concepts or ideas from LTM, and connecting such ideas to a logical format (Levelt, 1989). Generating a discourse plan is thought to involve the retrieval of conceptual information from working memory and/or LTM (Levelt, 1989). Thus, one factor that could influence the generation of a discourse plan is the ease of retrieving conceptual information to be expressed in speech. Discourse coherence disturbances may reflect deficits in the ability to maintain a discourse plan and to monitor the ongoing content of speech. Both negative thought disorder and disturbances in discourse coherence among schizophrenic patients reflect deficits in specific components of language production (Barch & Berenbaum, 1997). The presence of structure improves the maintenance of a discourse plan, such as by fewer discourse coherence disturbances, but does not improve the initiation of a discourse plan (e.g., no decrease in negative thought disorder).

In a recent study designed to investigate what type of cognition might be most strongly associated with thought disorder in schizophrenia, the authors questioned whether thought disorder resided in the semantic system or elsewhere (Goldberg et al., 1998). All patients and normal controls received tests of executive function and working memory, including the WCST and the Letter–Number Span test, a test of deployment of attentional resources. They also received tests of semantic processing and language comprehension, including the Peabody Vocabulary Test, the speed and capacity of language processing test, the Boston Naming Test, and tests of semantic verbal fluency and phonologic verbal fluency. The normal subjects were compared with the schizophrenic patients who were rated as having mild thought disorder or moderate to severe thought disorder. While differences between the schizophrenic subgroups and the comparison subjects were observed on nearly all tests, a large difference in effect size between the two schizophrenic subgroups was apparent only in the verbal fluency difference score. Since the fluency measure discriminated between the groups with high and low levels of thought disorder, it was hypothesised that clinically rated thought disorder in schizophrenia may result from semantic processing abnormalities. Language disorder present in schizophrenia may occupy an important place in the treatment of cognitive processes of schizo-phrenic patients. A recent study concluded that verbal memory deficits can be ameliorated by memory exercises in some patients with schizophrenia (Wexler et al., 2000).

In tests of learning processes, patients with schizophrenia had an inferior ability to repeat material presented just once, in comparison with the standardisation sample (Hawkins, 1999). However, they did relatively better with repeated presentations than patients with AD or Korsakoff's syndrome. The learning slope for patients with schizophrenia demonstrated an ability to learn and memorise increasing amounts of material with repeated exposure that is inconsistent with new pronounced memory impairment. Patients with schizophrenia exhibit new learning deficiencies. However, the Wechsler Memory test performances of the schizophrenics are not substantially weaker than their performances on measures of general intellectual functioning which also typically fall below the population average (Hawkins, 1999). The memory difficulties observed appear to be reasonably consistent with the levels of deficit reported in other domains such as in speeded information processing, rapid responding, novel problem solving, and executive functioning (Goldberg et al., 1991). They do not approach the memory impairment exhibited by patients with AD or Korsakoff's syndrome.

Sensory memory

Relatively few studies have addressed sensory memory function in schizophrenia. The most compelling finding involves a masking paradigm in which the presentation of a target stimulus is followed immediately by a second stimulus, the mask. The length of exposure to the target is gradually reduced until it is no longer acknowledged by the subject. In healthy controls, the threshold of perception occurs at about 100 ms. In patients with schizophrenia, the threshold is 2.5 times greater (Widlocher & Hardy-Bayle, 1989). Work in this area would suggest that while individuals with schizophrenia exhibit some impairment of sensory memory, this deficit involves not the actual formation of sensory impressions, but rather their immediate processing.

Short-term memory

Deficits have generally been reported for delayed response tasks that measure the maintenance of visuospatial representations over time. Park and Holzman (1992), for example, found that in a task involving visual stimuli, subjects with schizophrenia performed less well than either manic-depressive or control subjects. In tests of serial recall, however, results have been mixed, as they have also been for tasks involving the Brown–Peterson interference task (Flemming et al., 1995; Park & Holzman, 1992; Stip et al., 1995). Verbal STM function has been noted to be relatively preserved in schizophrenia, whereas the deficit in LTM is significant (Tamlyn et al., 1992; Goldberg et al., 1993).

Long-term memory

Subjects with schizophrenia consistently show a performance deficit on LTM tasks whether the material in question is verbal or non-verbal (Goldberg et al., 1989; Saykin et al., 1992). Moreover, recall is impaired not only for recently learned items but also for older material (McKenna et al., 1990). Schwartz et al. (1991) have shown that, among chronic schizophrenics, there is a disturbance of the temporal ordering of information, suggesting a possible disturbance of episodic memory.

Schizophrenia impairs episodic memory in its critical feature, autonoetic awareness (Huron et al., 1995). A recent study was designed to provide direct evidence that the impairment of autonoetic awareness associated with recognition memory in schizophrenia is related to a defective binding between separate aspects of events (Danion et al., 1999). An experiential approach was used in a memory task assessing content and source recognition in 25 schizophrenic patients and 25 normal subjects. The results showed that schizophrenic patients exhibited an impaired recognition memory. There was a reduction in frequency of autonoetic awareness, its consistency throughout recognition of objects and source, and its relationship to source discrimination accuracy. Recognition was based largely on noetic aware-

ness. Therefore, patients with schizophrenia were unable to link the separate aspects of events into a cohesive, memorable, and distinctive whole. This deficiency of relational binding leads to a quantitative and qualitative impairment of autonoetic awareness. Patients' impaired relational binding and hence impaired conscious awareness may be the result of deficient elaborate processes at encoding, a deficiency consistently reported in schizophrenia (Russel & Beekhuis, 1976; Traupmann et al., 1976). The impact of the alteration of recognition memory in schizophrenia may explain why memory impairments of schizophrenic patients are so consistently related to inadequate functional outcomes in their daily lives (Eichenbaum, 1997). Because recognition and conscious awareness might be severely disrupted in schizophrenia, a past event cannot be used with great flexibility for guiding and controlling behaviour, affects, and beliefs, which may in turn be inappropriate inasmuch as they can be driven only by false memories and noetic awareness.

Semantic memory is also known to be impaired in schizophrenia. Although the disturbance is relatively minor, it has been shown repeatedly from tests of semantic fluency to tasks involving naming, word-to-picture matching, and definition (Chapin et al., 1992; Clare et al., 1993; Kenny & Meltzer, 1991). Most investigators, however, have attributed the functional deficit not to the semantic store itself, but rather to some disturbance of semantic processing. These studies suggest that there is no clear corruption of semantic information in schizophrenia but that the access to semantic memory may be impaired (Allen et al., 1993). This impairment is attributable to a disorganisation of the semantic systems and to defective processes acting on semantic memory such as those involved in the initiation and/or the organisation of search strategies. However, in their studies of face naming, Laws et al. (1998) observed a heterogeneous performance pattern. The results obtained for some of the patients suggested a store deficit whereas for others there was evidence of an access disorder. It was suggested that this may reflect a quantitative difference in deficit severity with the more impaired patients displaying the more storelike profile and the less impaired patients showing the more accesslike profile.

A recent meta-analysis, which included 70 studies measuring LTM (free recall, cued recall, and recognition of verbal and non-verbal material) and STM (digit span), showed that schizophrenia and memory dysfunction are significantly associated as evidenced by moderate to large effect sizes (Aleman et al., 1999). The performance of patients with schizophrenia was more than 1 standard deviation lower than that of normal comparison subjects on tasks of recall memory. The results indicate memory impairment in schizophrenia to be wide-ranging and consistent across task variables, such as level of retrieval support (free recall, cued recall, or recognition), stimulus type (verbal versus non-verbal), and retention interval (immediate versus delayed). The extent of the memory impairment may appear to be in accordance with a pattern of generalised dysfunction rather than a differential deficit (Blanchard & Neale, 1994). Clinical variables such as medication, duration of illness, patient status, severity of psychopathology, and positive symptoms did not appear to influence the magnitude of memory impairment. Thus, the memory impairment in schizophrenia is of a considerable robustness and is not readily moderated by variables that may seem relevant. The substantial memory deficit in schizophrenia is likely to have repercussions on therapy and rehabilitation. A thorough understanding of the cognitive deficits in schizophrenia may prevent the failure of future treatments. For example, insight-related or other therapies that require advanced learning and memory functions are almost certain to be ineffective.

Executive function and memory

Frontal/executive impairments have been observed in schizophrenia (Morice & Delahunty, 1996). Executive function includes the capacity to both devise and carry out solutions to problems whose solutions are not immediately obvious (e.g., problems that may require abstract reasoning). Three functions are gaining greater recognition as executive functions—cognitive shift (or flexibility), forward planning, and working memory—and

much work is being performed to better understand their implications in schizophrenia. The increased perseverative error scores by schizophrenia patients performing the WCST has been of particular interest. Poor WCST performance has been linked both to cognitive inflexibility and to left dorsolateral PFC dysfunction (Weinberger et al., 1986). A study of frontal executive impairment in schizophrenic patients indicated that 64.7% of schizophrenia patients and no controls were impaired on WCST with respect to perseverative errors (cognitive flexibility) (Morice & Delahunty, 1996). However, 76.5% of schizophrenia patients and no controls were impaired on the Tower of London test with respect to targets achieved in minimum moves (forward planning). Further cognitive assessment indicated that the schizophrenic patients were significantly impaired compared to controls on two tests of working memory, Alphabet Span and Sentence Span. Using a cutoff derived from the mean score for the controls, 65% of schizophrenia patients proved to be impaired on Sentence Span. A significant percentage (94%) was impaired on one or more of the three tests of executive functioning used. It was hypothesised that schizophrenia represents a loss of, or a failure to acquire, the ability to process complex information.

The assessment of the effect of a graded memory task on brain activation of schizophrenic patients is an important subject to study. In an experiment in which schizophrenic patients and volunteers underwent scanning while learning and recalling word lists of variable length, it was observed that all patients showed perfect recall with word lists of up to four words (Fletcher et al., 1998). Beyond this, performance declined, with the steepest fall in the impaired schizophrenic patients. As task demands increased and performance deteriorated, schizophrenic patients failed to show an increasing frontal response. The more demanding tasks may have engaged frontally mediated strategies that the schizophrenic patients did not or could not adopt. Therefore, the abnormal PFC activation under more demanding conditions may reflect a motivation deficit occurring as the task becomes too difficult for a patient. A striking observation in the study performed by

Fletcher et al. was that a region showing impaired activation, the posterior parietal region (Brodmann area 40), was specific to the impaired schizophrenic group (Fletcher et al., 1998). Posterior parietal activations are a common finding in functional imaging studies of memory retrieval and the significant decrease of activation in the impaired schizophrenic group may reflect an impairment in LTM retrieval processes in schizophrenia (Shallice et al., 1994).

Several studies have considered recall and recognition memory impairment in schizophrenic patients. Some studies have reported impaired recall along with normal recognition in patients relative to controls (Beatty et al., 1993; Koh, 1978). A similar pattern of impairment has also been observed in patients with frontal-lobe lesions (Jetter et al., 1986). However, recognition deficits in schizophrenic patients, especially when more severely disturbed patients were assessed, have been reported (Gold et al., 1992). A greater memory deficit in schizophrenic patients than in controls has been reported when a delay intervened between learning and recall stages. This appeared in both verbal and visuospatial performance (Brébion et al., 1997). Regarding verbal memory, all these storage deficits were also found in tasks with delays of at least 30 minutes. The deficits in recall in schizophrenic patients may result from an inability to encode information in an organised way (Koh, 1978). Investigation of the mechanisms involved in verbal memory impairments in schizophrenia suggests that a major deficit in encoding appeared in the patient group, with a lesser use of deep encoding and a lesser efficiency of superficial encoding (Brébion et al., 1997). The early phase of storage and the retrieval function appear not to be affected. The overall memory performance in schizophrenics appears to be related to the depth of encoding (Brébion et al., 1997).

The assessment of verbal and nonverbal memory in schizophrenic patients has shown word and tone working memory deficits in schizophrenia (Wexler et al., 1998). Using word list immediate recall, tone delayed discrimination, and word and tone serial position tasks, it was observed that patients who performed normally on the screening test of perception and attention performed normally on both non-verbal tests but had significant deficits on both verbal tests. On the other hand, patients who performed poorly on the screening test had highly significant performance deficits on all the memory tests. This observation is interesting as it shows two subgroups of memory deficit patients; one subgroup of patients has a selective deficit in auditory verbal memory despite performing normally on an auditory non-verbal memory test. Most importantly, these patients did not suffer from global auditory processing problems, as might result from perceptual or attentional dysfunction, and their verbal memory deficits cannot be explained by nonspecific performance factors. Furthermore, the memory deficit itself is not global in those patients because their performance on the tone memory tests was intact. The second group of patients in this study showed deficits in multiple aspects of cognitive function suggestive of failure in early stages of information processing.

Clinical findings suggest that spatial working memory deficits in schizophrenia have been well replicated (Chey et al., 2002; McDowell & Clementz, 1996). A recent study was performed to examine verbal working memory, as measured by performance on the backward digit span task, in schizophrenia patients and their biological relatives (Conklin et al., 2000). It was found that schizophrenics had a shorter forward digit span length than both the first-degree relatives and the nonpsychiatric comparison participants. Schizophrenia patients also had a shorter backward digit span length than their first-degree relatives who, in turn, had a shorter backward digit span length than the non-psychiatric comparison participants. Most important, the non-psychotic first-degree relatives of the schizophrenia patients exhibited impaired verbal working memory. Impaired performance on the backward digit span task, a simple measure of verbal working memory, appears to be associated with the diathesis for schizophrenia and may be a valuable indicator of susceptibility for this disorder. Additionally, performance on the backward digit span task may be used as an endophenotypic marker for the schizophrenia genetic diathesis.

Cognitive deficits and negative symptoms

The cognitive deficits that are characteristic of schizophrenia suggest a frontal–medial–temporal dysfunction (Goldberg & Gold, 1995). It was suggested that "hypofrontality" characterises schizophrenia because it was observed that patients with prominent negative symptoms did not mount a significant increase in perfusion to their left mesio-frontal cortex during performance in neuropsychological tests such as the Tower of London task (Andreasen et al., 1992). This was in contrast to both normal control and schizophrenic patients with less prominent negative symptoms who demonstrated a regional increase in perfusion. These findings seem to indicate that hypofrontality is related to negative symptoms, and highlight the utility of neuropsychological assessment in the study of schizophrenia.

A certain degree of statistical correlation exists between cognitive deficits and negative symptoms which may reflect a common biological abnormality, such as dysfunction of the frontal cortex or a common association of the two with a third factor such as poor cooperation (Perlick et al., 1992). Severity of negative symptoms was found to be strongly correlated with poor performance on the WCST as reflected by a high proportion of perseverative errors, perseverative responses, and a low number of completed categories (Berman et al., 1997). On the other hand, positive symptoms are more closely associated with poor performance on the digit span, particularly the digit span forward (Berman et al., 1997). In recent studies, the value of the WCST as a predictor of rehospitalisation and stability of negative symptoms in schizophrenia has been demonstrated (Lysaker et al., 2003a, b).

Research has addressed the question of whether schizophrenic patients can improve their performance on neuropsychological tests after receiving coaching instructions (Summerfelt et al., 1991). Comparisons of pre- and postinstruction cognitive test scores indicated that the schizophrenic patient group were able to improve their performance significantly on the tests after coaching (Shean et al., 2002). Symptom dimensions were predictive of improved postinstruction test per-

formance beyond the impact of the level of preinstruction scores. Symptoms of disorganisation and negative symptoms were related to lack of ability to improve performance on one or more of the tests. Positive symptoms and premorbid adjustment were associated with improved postinstruction performance

Cognitive deficits as markers of vulnerability

First-degree relatives of schizophrenic patients are of special interest in the search for indicators of vulnerability to schizophrenia, as they have a risk of developing schizophrenia that is about 10 times that of the general population (Kendler & Diehl, 1993). Various observations suggest that the neuropsychological variables may be important endophenotypes for schizophrenia. Studies of schizophrenic patients and their non-affected relatives have yielded several phenotypes (e.g., eye tracking dysfunction and neuropsychological impairments including attentional and working memory deficits) that might aid the identification of genes (Cornblatt & Keilp, 1994; Holzman et al., 1984; Levy et al., 1994; Park et al., 1995). A recent study comparing neuropsychological performance of stable schizophrenics and their biological full siblings with normal controls also suggest that in the sibling group, the observed impaired neuropsychological deficits may represent indicators of the genetic vulnerability to schizophrenia (d'Amato et al., 1998). These findings further indicate that the deficiency of the neuropsychological performance of the siblings is related to the genetic factors.

Working memory in fact seems to possess the crucial elements to be a trait marker of schizophrenia. Spatial "working memory" deficit has been observed in relatives of schizophrenic patients and has been found to be related to smooth pursuit eye tracking (SPEM), probably the most powerful vulnerability indicator for schizophrenia (Levy et al., 1993; Park & Holzman, 1993; Park et al., 1995). On the other hand, no deficit in WCST has been consistently observed in schizophrenic patients' first-degree relatives and no consistent associations between SPEM alterations and WCST impairment have been found (Franke et al., 1992; Stratta et al., 1997).

Although it is acknowledged that schizophrenic patients as a group demonstrate a variety of cognitive deficits that can be observed at the onset of the illness, it is still unclear how these cognitive deficits progress with older age (Heaton & Drexler, 1987). The assessment of cognitive functions by neuropsychological tests such as MMSE has suggested that intellectual functions in cohorts of schizophrenic patients did not markedly decline (Hyde et al., 1994). Other studies suggest that there is a stability or an amelioration of symptoms in chronic schizophrenic patients with advancing age (Harding et al., 1987; Lindenmayer et al., 1997). These findings support the notion of schizophrenia as a disorder with a relatively stable psychopathological course, once established, and one that is only minimally affected by age and length of illness. Apart from the confirmation that there is no progression of impairments in cognitive functioning in older schizophrenic patients, these observations also suggest that the hypothesis of a dementia-like course of the cognitive functions in schizophrenia should be excluded.

Imaging

Research performed by Weinberger's group indicates that schizophrenia patients display abnormal dorsal prefrontal cortical fMRI response while performing spatial working memory tasks (Callicott et al., 2000). They observed that with increasing task difficulty (i.e., increasing working memory load), the schizophrenia patients display greater dorsal prefrontal cortex fMRI activation and poorer accuracy. A study using fMRI was designed to test the hypothesis that PFC dysfunction contributes to both working memory and LTM deficits in individuals with schizophrenia (Barch et al., 2002). This study also examined whether deficits in working memory and LTM in schizophrenia are equally severe for verbal and nonverbal materials. Performance of both working memory and LTM tasks revealed disturbed dorsolateral PFC activation in schizophrenia although medial temporal deficits were also present. Some evidence was found for more severe cognitive and functional deficits with verbal than non-verbal stimuli, although these results were mixed.

A study that measured rCBF with ^{99m}Tc-HMPAO SPECT in 18 schizophrenic patients and 16 healthy controls during paired-associate verbal memory tasks showed that patients with a recent history of hallucinations showed increases in rCBF to the left basal ganglia during the memory challenge (Busatto et al., 1995). However, non-hallucinating patients and healthy volunteers tended to show reduced rCBF to that area. Thus, rCBF activation studies provide evidence that increased basal ganglia activity may be a brain dysfunctional correlate of monitoring deficits underlying hallucinatory phenomena in schizophrenia. PET and SPECT techniques can also be used to map the distribution of receptors for several transmitters in the living brain, after the administration of radiolabelled ligands that selectively bind to specific receptor populations. In a study that used a ^{123}I-Iomazenil SPECT study on 15 schizophrenic patients and 12 healthy controls, weak evidence of reduced GABA$_A$ binding in several cortical regions in the schizophrenic group was noted (Busatto et al., 1996). The intensity of hallucinations and delusions was more strongly associated with diminished GABA$_A$ binding specifically in the left medial temporal region. These results suggest the implication of medial temporal abnormalities in the genesis of hallucinations. They further indicate that diminished GABAergic inhibition may be a possible neurochemical correlate of the excessive medial temporal activity observed with hallucinations in schizophrenia.

Future research will need to determine how abnormalities in dorsolateral PFC and medial temporal cortex as well as other brain regions are related in schizophrenia. It will be important to determine whether impaired activation in one or more of these regions reflects the downstream effects of primary deficits in other regions as opposed to a fundamental disturbance in the functional or structural integrity of a region.

ANXIETY

The presence of distracting, task-irrelevant thoughts is a common feature of anxiety. Individuals with elevated anxiety perform less efficiently than low-anxious controls on a range of cognitive tasks where speed is measured (e.g., standard Stroop colour-naming tasks and reading speed) (Calvo et al., 1994; Martin et al., 1991). It has been proposed that state anxiety influences task performance (Eysenck & Calvo, 1992). As worry occupies some of the limited capacity available to the working memory system, this negatively impacts tasks that rely heavily on the working memory system. The adverse effects of anxiety will be evident on tasks carried out in conjunction with a task treated as more "primary", as this reduces the capacity available for further tasks.

Obsessive compulsive disorder

Obsessive compulsive disorder (OCD) is characterised by recurrent unwanted thoughts and repetitive, ritualistic behaviours that lead to severe impairments in daily functioning. Various lines of evidence suggest that fronto-striatal systems of the brain are involved in this disorder (Savage, 1998; Tallis, 1997). A number of studies have provided evidence for deficits in learning and memory, especially for non-verbal information in OCD patients (Dirson et al., 1996; Savage et al., 1996). A study suggests that OCD patients' impairments in free recall are also associated with deficits in the ability to organise information during encoding, especially when complex non-verbal information is involved (Savage et al., 1999). That is, despite their ability to copy a complex geometric figure (Rey–Osterrieth) accurately, individuals with OCD tended to assemble the figure by copying small unrelated details rather than core elements such as a basic rectangle. Poor organisational strategies strongly predicted subsequent deficits in immediate free recall (Savage et al., 1999). A recent study that aimed to determine the pattern of memory deficits in OCD showed that these patients were impaired in immediate and delayed free recall, exhibited slowed rates of verbal learning and deficits in organisation over long delays, and had preserved verbal recognition memory (Deckersbach et al., 2000). The results show that OCD patients were significantly impaired in both verbal and non-verbal memory performances. They suggest that deficits

in organisation in OCD are not restricted to the nonverbal domain but extend to verbal information and memory as well. Deficits in organisational strategies are consistent with fronto-striatal dysfunction models in OCD.

OCD patients are often uncertain whether they have performed an action or whether they have merely imagined performing it. Doubt as to whether a memory has arisen from perception or from imagination may motivate compulsive checking of locks, doors, and so forth. Researchers have tested if OCD is characterised by a deficit in reality monitoring, the process whereby a person determines whether a memory originates from perception or from imagination (Johnson & Raye, 1981). Although these individuals may encounter no difficulties in encoding or retrieving a memory trace, they may have difficulty ascertaining the source of the trace. Compulsive checking may therefore result from the defect in the ability to distinguish between memories of doing from memories of imagined doing. However, recent studies suggest that OCD patients seem characterised by confidence deficits or by an intolerance of uncertainty, but not by a deficit in distinguishing memories of doing from memories of imagined doing (Brown et al., 1994; Constans et al., 1995).

A study designed to determine whether patients with OCD have difficulty retrieving specific autobiographical memories requested patients with OCD and healthy controls to retrieve specific personal memories in response to cue words having positive (e.g., happy) or negative (e.g., anxiety) valence (Wilhelm et al., 1997). It was observed that OCD patients exhibited greater difficulty retrieving specific personal memories than did healthy control participants regardless of cue word valence. Moreover OCD patients took longer than controls to retrieve specific autobiographical memories. However, additional analyses revealed that these overgenerality effects were not a function of OCD *per se*. They were related to a comorbid diagnosis of major depression. The difficulty in retrieving specific autobiographical memories exhibited by OCD patients might reflect excessive cognitive capacity consumption due to preoccupation with intrusive thoughts typical of major depression.

Panic disorder

Anxiety-disordered individuals suffer from recurrent, unwarranted thoughts about personal harm. People with panic disorder think they are about to die or "go crazy" in the midst of their attack. Researchers have tested whether patients remember standardised threat words better than standardised non-threat words relative to normal control subjects. In a study, panic disorder patients and normal controls were requested to rate the self-descriptiveness of adjectives either related (e.g., nervous) or unrelated to anxiety before performing either a high-arousal (i.e., exercise step-test) or a low-arousal (i.e., relaxation task) (McNally et al., 1989). After the arousal manipulation, subjects received a surprise free recall test for the previously rated material. The results revealed that panic patients exhibited better memory for anxiety than for non-anxiety adjectives whereas control subjects exhibited the opposite pattern. This bias tended to be greatest in patients who had undergone the arousal induction. These data imply that panic disorder is characterised by a memory bias for threatening information. Such findings were supported by another study reporting that panic disorder patients showed an explicit memory bias for threatening words as compared to controls (Becker et al., 1999). Physical anxiety symptoms were the disorder-relevant words that revealed the strongest memory bias in the panic disorder patient group. The panic disorder patients remembered more words referring to bodily symptoms than did the control participants, whereas both groups remembered about the same number of neutral and positive words. The memory bias shown by the anxiety patients was therefore highly selective and cannot be explained by a general bias towards emotional words.

Since the attack in panic disorder is not triggered by any external event, it could be proposed that most panic attacks have an endogenous mechanism that could be conceived as either biochemical or cognitive. In a recent study designed to explore the relationship between panic disorder and memory, anxiety and fear were induced in the participants (30 patients with panic disorder, 12 healthy volunteers, 12 with GAD, and 12 with major depression) with verbal description of one or more fearful situations (Berksun, 1999). They were asked in a neutral manner what they felt if they thought of themselves in such situations. The results of this study showed that none of the patients in the panic disorder group could recall any acceptable fearful event or episode in their past. All but one person among healthy volunteers and all the patients with conditions other than panic disorder could recall one or more fearful event or episode in a period as brief as 30 seconds. A possible hypothesis embracing this observation is that the fear-relevant emotional–autonomic cluster in these panic patients is not cognitively linked to the fearful events or the scenarios of the past life memory traces. Panic patients are unable to recall or produce any themes or scenarios other than the simple apprehension of a heart attack or a similar fear. Thus patients with panic disorder have a defect in fear-relevant episodic memory, and their panic attacks arise from automaticity in recollecting fear-relevant emotional–automatic clusters. The cluster as a component of fear appears to have been dissociated from cognitive structure, episodic or informative memory trace, or from information structure.

Post-traumatic stress disorder

Post-traumatic stress disorder (PTSD) is a specific anxiety disorder of significant prevalence and morbidity that develops following exposure to extreme emotional trauma (American Psychiatric Association, 1994). Three symptoms clusters characterise the disorder, all of which represent direct or indirect effects of memory processes: (1) persistent re-experience of the traumatic event, (2) persistent symptoms of increased arousal, and (3) persistent avoidance of stimuli associated with the trauma that may include amnesia for an important aspect of the traumatic event.

Adult PTSD patients often report a wide range of cognitive problems in memory, concentration, attention, planning, and judgement (Bremner, 1999; Bremner et al., 1993a, b). New research directions indicate that some people with PTSD are characterised by deficits in autobiographical memory functioning (McNally et al., 1994). An inability to retrieve specific memories about one's past hampers current daily problem-solving issues. It is likely that it underlies the phenomenon of future foreshortening. Clearly, PTSD may be conceived as a clinical condition that involves both memory intensification for the core traumatic event and memory impairment for the context surrounding the trauma. The latter comprises dissociation of the experience from ordinary autobiographical memory. Because disturbances of episodic memory for peritraumatic events are not explained by the fear-conditioning model, it has been presumed that these conscious memory disturbances are secondary symptoms that develop as psychological defences to suppress and avoid the primary symptoms of intensified memory or intrusive re-experience of the trauma.

A study that employed the RBMT to examine cognitive factors in children and adolescents aged 11 to 17 years who met DSM–III–R and ICD–10 criteria for PTSD showed that the patients had poorer overall memory performance compared to controls (Moradi et al., 1999). Patients with PTSD scored lower on the total score of the RBMT compared to controls and to the norms of the RBMT. The cumulative percentage scores of the RBMT showed that about 78% of PTSD patients were under-performing and fell into the categories labelled "poor memory" compared to 13% of controls. Regarding performance on the specific subtests, PTSD patients were worse on orientation and prospective memory. Obviously, the presence of the intrusion, avoidance, and hyperarousal symptoms of the PTSD interferes with everyday memory performance and possibly development of reading skills.

The right hippocampal volume of the patients with combat-related PTSD was 8% smaller than that of the comparison subjects, but there was no significant difference in the volume of comparison structures, including temporal lobe and caudate (Bremner et al., 1995b). Deficits in free verbal recall (explicit memory), as measured by per cent retention on the WMS logical component, were associated with smaller right hippocampal volume in the PTSD patients but not in the comparison subjects.

The coupling of memory intensification and amnesia might appear to be a paradox that is unique to psychopathology. Indeed, PTSD is a special case of the normal operation of memory systems. A neurobiological model explaining the memory phenomena characteristic of PTSD may emanate from a classic observation termed the von Restorff effect, the augmentation of memory for one novel item in an otherwise neutral or homogeneous stimulus field (Wallace, 1965). One important finding of studies using the von Restorff paradigm is the co-occurrence of intensification of memory for a sufficiently arousing critical stimulus with memory impairment for a temporally proximate neutral stimulus. Basing on the von Restorff paradigm, a model to account for the memory mechanisms in PTSD has been proposed (Layton & Krikorian, 2002). With respect to the relationship between emotional stimulation and neurophysiology, this model suggests that the amygdala is increasingly recruited as a function of emotional intensity. At modest levels of arousal, the amygdala potentiates hippocampal function and increases memory. This phenomenon corresponds to the flashbulb effect, the enhancement of episodic memory for events that are moderately emotionally arousing (Brown & Kulik, 1977). At greater levels of stimulus intensity, the amygdala begins to inhibit hippocampal consolidation of memory both for the emotional stimulus and for proximate neutral stimuli. Beyond this level as the amygdala is increasingly activated and the hippocampus increasingly suppressed, information will be less well consolidated in episodic memory. Thus, this model emphasises that the amygdala is the locus of consolidation of the core of the traumatic experience. The amygdalar inhibition of hippocampal function at high levels of emotional arousal mediates diminution of conscious memory of peritraumatic events.

It has been suggested that pharmacological manipulation of neurotransmission could be clinically useful in post-traumatic syndromes by disrupting the consolidation of traumatic experiences into LTM (O'Brien & Nutt, 1998). In animal models, NMDA channel or specific peptide receptor blockers inhibit the physiological and behavioural corollaries of PTSD (Adamec, 1997). However, the timing of the drug therapy may be important. Drug treatment started beyond the critical periods may be too late in preventing the laying down of the brain traces that constitute PTSD. The observation that upon reactivation long-term fear memories are vulnerable to disruption offers the possibility of pharmacological treatment well beyond the initial trauma. Such new findings are exciting as they may likely open new effective methods of treatment of neuropsychiatric disturbances of memory.

Generalised anxiety disorder

Although findings of an implicit memory bias for threat words in generalised anxiety disorder (GAD) are fairly robust, the data regarding an explicit bias in this disorder are less consistent. An explicit memory bias for threat words was replicated across separate GAD samples under conditions recommended as ideal for detection of memory biases in studies of anxiety: namely, incidental learning and free recall (Becker et al., 1999). However, contrary to previous trends in the literature, a recent study reported a marked bias in the GAD group towards recall of the threat words (Friedman et al., 2000). Many studies of memory bias in GAD have used very brief stimulus exposure times to which an active response is required (Borkovec et al., 1998). In contrast, the protracted passive viewing of the task in this present study may have overridden the avoidant aspects of worry and so resulted in enhanced retention of threat words.

Physiological arousal has been studied in the alterations of memory in GAD (Becker et al., 1999). In that report, the GAD group developed a conditioned heart rate deceleration in anticipation of threat words, a physiological change that suggests facilitation of stimulus intake. Furthermore, these individuals also exhibited a heart rate acceleration in response to the threat words which in accord with models that linked increased adrenergic activity with enhanced memory might have improved stimulus retention. The adaptive value of this mechanism presumably entails the selective recall of salient emotional events such as threatening encounters. In GAD, defensive cognitive operations occur at multiple stages of information processing. There is a preattentive bias towards detection of threatening stimuli and excessive rumination of stored threat information. This combination may account for the convergent findings of an implicit memory bias in GAD as well as positive findings of an explicit memory bias in GAD under certain conditions.

DEPRESSION

The impact of depression on memory and other aspects of cognition has been demonstrated in many studies (Burt et al., 1995; Starkstein et al., 1989). For example, research participants diagnosed with major depressive disorder scored significantly lower than a nonpatient control group on a visual memory task (Shah et al., 1999). Individuals with major depressive disorder also scored significantly lower than an age- and IQ-matched group of control subjects in the areas of verbal fluency, visual memory tasks, spatial span tasks, working memory tasks, and tasks involving executive function (Elliot et al., 1996). Severe depression in the elderly is often accompanied by complaints of memory loss and mild cognitive deficits on neuropsychological testing. Depression and dementia can coexist, however. The assessment of various memory functions such as recall, recognition, strategy use, remote memory, or meta-memory appear especially important in differential diagnosis.

STM or the retention of small amounts of information over very short durations has been found to be unaffected among depressive patients (Austin et al., 1992; Channon et al., 1982). LTM or performance on supraspan memory tasks seems to be more prone to impairment (Austin et al., 1992). It is now commonly accepted that depression is associated with a number of deficits in episodic memory and learning (see Goodwin, 1997). This finding is consistent across most studies and appears to involve both explicit verbal and visual memory in patients with both melancholic (endogenous) and non-melancholic (non-endogenous) depression (Austin et al., 1999). Impaired delayed memory as opposed to preserved immediate recall has also been found among depressive patients (Cohen et al., 1982). However, some studies have also reported no dissociation between immediate and delayed recall (Gass & Russell, 1986). A study aiming to examine the degree and patterns of memory impairment among adult patients with major depression compared with healthy controls reported that the depressed patients' generalised view of their memory capability was strongly underestimated, whereas online metamemory accuracy by which one perceives and makes inferences about one's performance was adequate (Kalska et al., 1999). It was also reported that besides showing signs of cognitive slowing, the patients were especially vulnerable to visual memory impairment, whereas verbal memory, STM, and recall by recognition were often unaffected. Implicit memory tasks also appears to be spared (Danion et al., 1995; Hertel & Hardin, 1990; Ilsley et al., 1995).

Clinical observations suggest that depressed patients are troubled by the frequent, spontaneous recall of a limited repertoire of negative memories that are emotionally highly charged rather than by their ability to recall negative memories easily when they try to do so. Depressed and control subjects also differ in their recall of positive material, with the control subjects recalling relatively more positive memories than the depressives (Williams et al., 2000). These differences between depressives and controls in the recall profiles for negative and positive materials are seen by many researchers as being indicative of depressive realism in that the depressed subjects have an accurate and realistic picture of the world (Mischel, 1979). On the other hand, normal subjects process the world in a positively self-serving manner (Alloy & Abramson, 1988).

A concept that has been commonly applied in clinical theorising is that of the schema. The major proponent of the schema concept is Beck (Beck, 1976; Beck et al., 1979). It has been suggested that depression is associated with a negative self-schema that biases memory in mood memory experiments. This has been investigated experimentally by examining memory bias for trait words on which subjects have rated themselves (including a control condition in which they have rated other people or made no ratings at all) (Derry & Kuiper, 1981). It was shown that clinically depressed patients have a self-referent recall bias towards negative words, whereas for controls the bias is towards positive words encoded with respect to others. Beck's theory, in which depressive schemata play an important part, is powerful in explaining many of the empirical findings. Results of clinical studies accord with the observation that depressive people tend to have a negative view about themselves and this includes their capacities and other performance outcomes (Grut et al., 1993; Niederehe & Yoder, 1989; O'Connor et al., 1990). There is some evidence that depressed patients are less skilful in accurately predicting and rating their cognitive performance than nondepressed people, and less able to change their memory performance according to received feedback (Roth & Rehm, 1980; Slife & Weaver, 1992).

People with major depressive disorder, including those who have recently attempted suicide, have difficulty retrieving specific autobiographical memories in response to cue words (Williams, 1996). A recent study designed to investigate to what extent depression and childhood trauma are implicated in overgeneral autobiographical memory showed that a clinical diagnosis of current major depression rather than self-reported childhood trauma predicts decreased autobiographical memory specificity (Wessel et al., 2001). These data support previous reports of relatively poor autobiographical memory performance in clinically depressed patients (Brittlebank et al., 1993; Goddard et al., 1996; Kuyken & Dalgliesh, 1995). Difficulty accessing specific personal memories is related to emotional disturbance (Williams, 1996). It strongly predicts failure to recover from depression. The more overgeneral a patient's memory tends to be, the more unlikely it is that he or she will improve (Brittlebank et al., 1993). Overgenerality is also related to poor interpersonal problem-solving skills, a deficit associated with depression (Schotte et al., 1990). From this, the possibility that overgeneral autobiographical memory in adults may arise or persist in part from early childhood adversities has been suggested (Williams, 1996). A recent study demonstrated that overgeneral memory is a feature of first episode major depression in adolescents which may persist following remission (Park et al., 2002). The implications of these findings for the course and outcome of major depression into young adult life require further investigation with long-term experimental designs.

Relapse is common in depression and incomplete recovery is a risk factor for relapse. Remission may be defined as a short-term improvement in symptoms within an overall episode of illness during which patients remain vulnerable to relapse, while recovery is defined as a period of sustained improvement associated with the end of the episode of illness. Remission from depression is accompanied by a reduction of memory intrusion but not of memory avoidance (Spenceley & Jerrom, 1997). One reason remitted depressed patients remain vulnerable to relapse may be because they are still having to expend effort avoiding the reactivation of distressing autobiographical memories. Full recovery from depression may not be possible until there is a reduction in the accessibility of the memories indicated by a reduction both in intrusion and in deliberate attempts at avoidance.

Suicidal subjects have difficulty picturing the future in a specific way compared to matched controls, a difficulty that affects their responses to positive, negative, and neutral cues (Williams et al., 1996). The degree of difficulty in generating specific images of the future is found to be correlated with the extent to which subjects fail to retrieve specific autobiographical memories from the past. Hopelessness about the future plays a central role in suicidal behaviour. Hopelessness mediates the relationship between depression and suicidal intent within suicidal populations (Salter & Platt, 1990). Hopelessness has been found to predict repetition of parasuicide 6 months later and completed suicides up to 10 years later (Beck et al., 1989; Petrie et al., 1988). Suicidal individuals may have a cognitive deficit that compounds their problem by making it more difficult for them to imagine their future sufficiently concretely to generate specific plans and goals.

The impact of depressive subtype on task performance has been explored in a small number of studies. Some studies using the Newcastle scale to define subjects with endogenous and non-endogenous depression found impairment of complex reaction time in subjects with endogenous depression alone (Byrne, 1977; Cornell et al., 1984). Fromm and Schopflocher (1984) also using the Newcastle criteria, and Rush et al. (1983) using the Research Diagnostic Criteria, reported that patients with endogenous depression were more impaired on all cognitive tasks (Trails, Stroop test, visual recall, and complex attention) than patients with non-endogenous depression. The relationship between severity and depression subtype is a further confounder. Thus, while some studies reported only frontal deficits in their patients with narrowly defined endogenous or melancholic depression, these disappeared after covarying for Hamilton scores indicating that this pattern of frontal deficits was more likely to be present as a result of depression severity rather depressive subtype (Austin et al., 1992, 1999). A useful probe of the effects of severity *per se* is provided by the significant diurnal variation in mood seen in many patients with melancholia where depressed mood is typically worse in the day. It has been demonstrated that these patients perform less well on most cognitive tasks in the morning compared to the evening, with the opposite finding in controls (Moffoot et al., 1994).

Findings from activation studies in normal control subjects and patients with depression are strongly suggestive of a close integration between the dorsolateral prefrontal cortex and the subgenual cingulate in depression (Teasdale et al., 1999). Thus, it was reported in normal subjects that certain components of the medial prefrontal cortex (including the anterior cingulate) appear to be involved in the cognitive induction of a negative affect, thereby implying close integration between the dorsolateral and limbic circuits. Mayberg et al. (1999) examined the impact of negative mood induction both in normal control subjects and those patients who had recovered from depression, on cerebral perfusion. Induced sadness was associated with an increase in subgenual cingulate cerebral blood flow and a decrease in dorsolateral prefrontal cortex, while recovery from depression was associated with the reverse pattern. A focus on the interactions between motivation, affect, and cognitive function may allow greater understanding of the interplay between key aspects of the dorsal and ventral aspects of the prefrontal cortex in depression.

ATTENTION DEFICIT HYPERACTIVITY DISORDER

Attention deficit hyperactivity disorder (ADHD) is the most common childhood psychiatric disorder (DSM–IV) and persists into adulthood for 30–50% of those affected. According to epidemiological studies, it has a prevalence of 1–7% (Hinshaw, 1994). Sex ratios in referred samples have been reported to be as high as 9:1 (males:females) but an epidemiological study found a sex ratio of 3:1 (Szatmari et al., 1989). The cardinal symptoms of ADHD are hyperactivity, impulsivity, and distractibility as reported by parents, teachers, and health care professionals. In terms of natural history, the age of onset is usually in toddlerhood with a peak "age of onset" between ages 3 and 4 (Palfrey et al., 1985). Symptoms of ADHD may appear earlier, even *in utero*. It is becoming clearer that ADHD is a chronic disorder across the lifespan and that the clinical pattern observed in adults is similar to that observed in school-aged children. A substantial body of evidence suggests that certain core symptoms of ADHD are related to dysfunction of prefrontal regions of the brain and connections to the striatum, possibly extending to limbic structures. Functional neuroimaging studies have identified anomalies of frontal metabolic activity indexed by diminished cerebral blood flow or glucose metabolism (Ernst et al., 1994). The clinical relevance of these findings is supported by neuropsychological reports indicating that ADHD is commonly associated with selectively impaired performance on measures of executive function and working memory (Shue & Douglas, 1992). Neuropsychological studies of ADHD suggest that it involves a dysfunction in working memory (Barkley et al., 1996). Recent reports also point to differential involvement of right hemisphere processes in ADHD. Several neuroimaging studies have noted asymmetries that particularly implicate

pathophysiology of right frontostriatal circuitry (Castellanos et al., 1994, 1996).

One possible hypothesis of brain mechanisms in ADHD is that the executive function deficit of ADHD children is caused by functional hypofrontality, which in turn is caused by either structural and or/biochemical changes in the prefrontal lobes and is detectable as reduced frontal blood flow (Zametkin & Rapoport, 1986). A recent study that used a functional neuroimaging approach with a working memory probe to investigate the pathophysiology of ADHD reported that regional cerebral blood flow (rCBF) in men with ADHD were more widespread and primarily located in the occipital regions (Schweitzer et al., 2000). This study suggests that individuals with ADHD recruit novel neural pathways while organising less efficient strategies to solve working memory tasks. Extrastriate activations also suggest the primary use of visual imagery in ADHD individuals to perform the addition task. Further experimental studies are needed to dissect the executive function deficit in ADHD and test its specificity.

The continuance of many core ADHD symptoms into adulthood is well established and suggests continuing impact of underlying neural dysfunction, presumably involving the same brain regions as implicated in children. While neuroimaging data from longitudinal studies is currently lacking, cross-sectional comparisons of ADHD children and adults indicate significant concordance in terms of behavioural symptomatology, neuropsychological patterns of impairment, associated pathophysiology indexed by functional neuroimaging studies, and response to pharmacological treatment (Bellack & Black, 1992; Epstein et al., 1997). Thus, the current child-based models appear to provide a reasonable framework for understanding neurobiological manifestations of ADHD in adults.

DISCUSSION

Although recall biases for threat are common in panic disorder and PTSD, they rarely occur in other anxiety-disordered groups. Researchers have failed to find emotion-congruent recall biases in GAD, social phobia, or specific (e.g., spider) phobia (Mogg & Mathews, 1990; Rapee et al., 1994; Watts & Coyle, 1993). Moreover, even panic patients have sometimes not shown an emotion-congruent free recall or cued recall bias (Rapee, 1994). Widely varying emotion-congruent memory effects across diagnostic categories demand explanation. Relative to GAD and phobic patients, those with panic disorder and PTSD may simply be unable to avoid recalling disturbing information. They may exhibit involuntary explicit memory for threat. That is, threat-related material may come to mind with little or no effort.

Cognitive impairment has been shown to exert a considerable effect on a patient's psychosocial status (Goldberg & Gold, 1995). Confronted with such cases, the challenge for the neuropsychologist is to provide data from observations and a battery of sensitive validated cognitive tests which give clues to the nature of the brain dysfunctions that underlie the signs and symptoms associated with neuropsychiatric disorders. The use of these neuropsychological techniques may greatly further enhance our assessment of cognitive impairment in psychiatric diseases and more accurately monitor pharmacological treatment outcome in these diseases. The extent and stability of the association between schizophrenia and memory impairment suggest that the memory dysfunction may be a trait rather than a state characteristic. Hypothetically, some degree of memory dysfunction may already be present in subjects at risk for schizophrenia. Future research must concentrate on this issue to explore the possible implications with regard to prescreening for schizophrenia. There is evidence that verbal memory is a rather strong predictor for functional outcome in schizophrenia. Improving memory may be beneficial for everyday functioning.

Research into subtype-specific cognitive dysfunction in schizophrenic patients suggest that whereas all schizophrenic patients showed significant deficits in verbal learning (Rey auditory verbal learning test), which may indicate a temporal–hippocampal system dysfunction as a common denominator in both schizophrenic subtypes, patients with paranoid schizophrenia demonstrate more intact intellectual abilities. Although it is widely accepted that schizophrenic patients as a group demonstrate a variety of cognitive deficits that can be observed at the onset of the illness, it is still unclear how these cognitive deficits progress with age (Goldberg et al., 1988; Heaton & Drexler, 1987). There are some indications that the cognitive deterioration found in older schizophrenic patients reaches a state with little or no evidence of progression over time, despite age effects (Chaikelson & Schwartzman, 1983). Longitudinal studies in schizophrenia show a stability or an amelioration of symptoms of chronic schizophrenic patients with advancing age (Ciompi & Muller, 1976; Harding et al., 1987; Winocur et al., 1987). Future research might use neuropsychological profiles to assess the organisation of thought and behaviour to subtype the schizophrenia spectrum. This approach may help with treatment planning, as well as understanding the aetiology of the illness. Cognitive impairment in schizophrenia greatly impedes psychosocial performance and eventual reintegration into society. Thus, the cognitive features of schizophrenia are especially relevant based on their resulting social and vocational disability and should, in turn, become key targets in the development of new therapeutic modalities.

The suggestion is that anxiety operates mainly on automatic processes while depression operates mainly on strategic processes. Because attention is largely automatic and memory largely strategic, this explains why the effects of anxiety are stronger on attention while those of depression are stronger on memory. However, two important differences need to be discussed. First, automatic thoughts take up processing resources (e.g., the effects of test anxiety on cognitive performance) while central to the definition of automatic processing is that it takes up minimal resources (Mayer, 1977). Second, automatic thoughts tend to intrude into consciousness whereas automatic processes occur outside of the subject's awareness. So far this hypothesis has been encouraging. Although memory is largely strategic, there are forms of memory that are relatively automatic. As predicted from this hypothesis, anxiety only affected the implicit memory task (Matthews et al., 1989). It would be predicted that depression in contrast would affect only the strategic recall task, although this remains to be tested. This hypothesis may seem oversimplified, but it illustrates the kind of theoretical breadth that the data now call for.

Overgeneral memory does not seem to be confined to individuals with major depressive disorder. People with a primary diagnosis of combat-related PTSD also show deficits in retrieving specific personal memories (McNally et al., 1994, 1995). Overgenerality may be present in any psychiatric disorder characterised by intrusive cognition, regardless of whether cognitive disturbances arose as a consequence of trauma.

11

Treatments

INTRODUCION

Psychological and physiological events can either strengthen or weaken the formation of memories. Some of these events, such as arousal, may occur immediately before or during the perception of a salient stimulus, enabling an organism to better attend to the stimulus and thus learn about it more efficiently (Eysenck, 1982). From the psychological perspective, a sense of control over memory functioning is at the heart of an adaptive view of memory (Cavanaugh & Green, 1990). From this perspective, memory is seen as a body of skills that can be developed and maintained with effort. A view of memory as a body of acquirable skills may predispose people to persist in developing strategies to cope with memory problems and to make adaptive attributions in the face of difficulties. These tendencies may protect people against decreases in efficacy expectations and actually enhance them by fostering effective problem solving.

There have been three main strands in memory rehabilitation in recent years, namely environmental adaptations, the implementation of new technology, and methods for improving learning. Memory rehabilitation includes the use of various memory aids and pharmacological treatments. Internal, cognitive-based memory aids such as mnemonics require a variety of other cognitive skills like motivation, concentration, attention, language, mental imagery, as well as the ability to develop new strategies, and are therefore not often suitable for patients with more advanced dementias. Despite these limitations, it has been observed that a significant number of patients with mild to moderate memory impairment due to AD were able to improve their performance on two everyday prospective memory tasks (Camp et al., 1996). The amount of memory improvement was not related to severity of dementia or demographic features, supporting the hypothesis that the type of memory involved appears to be related to implicit rather than declarative memory. Research using imaging technology shows that even in individuals who are more than 2 years post-brain-damage, relative increases in regional cerebral blood flow can be observed following individualised cognitive rehabilitation therapy (Laatsch et al., 1999). These changes can be related to improvements on neuropsychological tests that were maintained during the nontreatment period.

A large variety of external memory aids has been developed to alleviate the effects of amnesia

TABLE 11.1

Pharmacological approaches to treatment of memory dysfunctions

Neurotrasmitter systems	Disorders postulated to involve these systems	Drugs	References
Acetylcholine	Alzheimer's disease	Physostigmine	Cardenas et al., 1994; Minderhoud et al., 1996
		Lecithin	Levin et al., 1986; Weinberg et al., 1987
		Choline	Alvarez et al., 1997
		THA	Riekkinen & Riekkinen, 1999
		Rivastigmine	Rösler et al., 1999
		Galanthamine	MacGowan et al., 1998
		Nicotine	White & Levin, 1999
		Xanomeline	Bodick et al., 1997
Dopamine	Dementia with behavioural disturbance	Antipsychotics	Dobkin and Hanlon, 1993
Norepinephrine	Alzheimer's disease	Clonidine	Riekkinen & Riekkinen, 1999
	Behavioural disturbance	MAO inhibitors	
		Propranolol	
Serotonin	Alzheimer's disease	Antidepressants	
		Ondansetron	Arnsten et al., 1997
GABA	Behavioural disturbance Insomnia	Chlormethiazole	
Peptides	Alzheimer's disease	ACTH	Nicholson, 1990; McLean et al., 1991
		Vasopressin	
		CRF	
		TRH	
		Opioid antagonists	
Benzoquinones	Alzheimer's disease	Idebenone	Weyer et al., 1997
Xanthines	Alzheimer's disease	Propentofylline	Marcusson et al., 1997
Herbal medicines	Alzheimer's disease	Ginkgo biloba?	Oken et al., 1998

in everyday life, ranging from simple notepads and organisers, mechanical aids, electronic reminders, and dictation machines to sophisticated computer programs (Kapur, 1995). Given the apparently limited applicability of memory aids to patients with dementia, the treatment of amnesia in neurodegenerative disorders has mainly relied on pharmacological medications.

Concerning pharmacological treatment, research has led to a large number of drug trials involving a wide variety of drugs. In AD, most studies to date have involved attempts to enhance the effects of the damaged cholinergic nervous system.

PHARMACOLOGICAL TREATMENT

Pharmacological approaches encompass a wide range of drugs acting on many different neurotransmitter systems in the brain. Efforts have been focused on the following areas: acetylcholinesterase inhibitors, other cholinergic drugs, muscarinic receptor agonists, amyloid, anti-inflammatory drugs, excitatory amino acids, oestrogen, neurotropic drugs, antioxidants, and other drugs including monoamine oxidase-B (MAO-B) inhibitors. The major ones are listed in Table 11.1.

Cognitive enhancers

Patients with an MCI are also becoming of interest for treatment trials. Several pharmaceutical companies are embarking on multicentre trials of drugs intended to alter the progression of patients with MCI to AD (Grundman et al., 1996).

Cognitive enhancers is a term used loosely in the field of psychopharmacology to describe drugs that may enhance human memory in any of a number of conditions ranging from normal forgetfulness to AD. Until recently, discussions of cognitive enhancers focused primarily on the vasodilators, metabolic enhancers, and cholinergic drugs. Today, this class of drug includes numerous neurotransmitter-specific drugs, peptides, vitamins, channel blockers, second messenger drugs, and many others.

Treatment strategies developed for AD, specifically acetylcholinesterase inhibitors, have been among the first employed to treat MCI. It is hoped that by impeding the progression of MCI in this manner, fewer patients will convert to AD.

Old age

In human studies, the effects of oestrogen are frequently observed on measures of verbal memory (Sherwin, 1997). A double-blind, placebo-controlled study was designed to investigate the effects of oestrogen on brain activation patterns with fMRI in postmenopausal women (33–61 years, mean of 50.8 years) as they performed verbal (pronounceable nonsense words) and non-verbal working (complex geometric patterns such as Tamil letters) memory tasks (Sherwin, 1997). It was found that although oestrogen (conjugated equine estrogens, 1.25 mg/d) did not affect performance of the verbal and non-verbal memory tasks, it affected the brain organisation for memory. Treatment with oestrogen increased activation in the inferior parietal lobule during storage of verbal material and decreased activation in the inferior parietal lobule during storage of non-verbal material. Oestrogen also showed activation in the right superior frontal gyrus during retrieval tasks, accompanied by greater left-hemisphere activation during encoding. These alterations in brain activation in subjects taking oestrogen suggest functional plasticity of memory processes in mature women. It may also be possible that these changes

in brain organisation predict accompanying improvements in performance of memory tasks. However, this hypothesis needs confirmation in subsequent trials.

Results of a pharmacological study that assessed the efficacy of citicoline (cytidine-diphoscholine) in elderly subjects showed that it improves memory performance, and it was suggested that this molecule may be suitable for the treatment of memory deficits in old people (Alvarez et al., 1997). Citicoline improves memory performance in elderly subjects, mainly in free-recall tasks, at doses ranging from 300 to 1000 mg/day, probably by influencing brain neurotrophic mechanisms and processes of cerebrovascular regulation. Citicoline is a metabolic intermediate that completely dissociates to liberate choline, an acetylcholine precursor, and the ribonucleoside, cytidine; these compounds interact in cells to facilitate the repair and preservation of neuronal membranes by promoting phosphatidylcholine synthesis (Lopez-Coviella & Wartman, 1992). Citicoline may also enhance dopaminergic neurotransmission, an action that could improve the arousal and attention components of memory that depend on catecholaminergic systems (Fonlupt et al., 1985).

Some nutritional and botanical therapies such as phosphatidylserine, acetyl-L-carnitine, vinpocetine, *Ginkgo biloba* extract and *Bacopa monniera* are available which have some degrees of efficacy, although this needs to be demonstrated in large clinical trials based on statistical significance on all primary outcome variables (see Table 11.2).

Phosphatidylserine is a phospholipid enriched in the brain, validated through double-blind trials

---

TABLE 11.2

Five nutrients and botanicals that may enhance cognition

	Phosphatidylserine	Acetyl-L-carnitine	Vinpocetine	Ginkgo biloba extract	Bacopa monniera
Age-related cognitive decline	+	+	NT	NT	NT
Alzheimer dementia (non-vascular)	+	+	–	+	NT
Dementia (vascular)	NT	+	+	+	NT
Childhood	+	NT	NT	NT	+

"+" indicates some positive effects whereas "–" = no significant effects. NT = No trials available.

for improving memory, learning, concentration, word recall, and mood in middle-aged and elderly subjects with dementia or age-related cognitive decline (Amaducci, 1988; Cenacchi et al., 1993; Crook et al., 1992; Delwaide et al., 1986; Kidd, 1998). In animal studies, treatment with phosphatidylserine conserved the densities of receptors for NGF at higher levels characteristic of young rats (Angelucci et al., 1988; Nunzi et al., 1987). Simultaneously, phosphatidylserine improved the "intelligence" of these impaired rats towards levels resembling young, non-impaired rats. Effective intakes of phosphatidylserine range from 100 mg per day (for smaller children and for maintenance in healthy adults) through 300 mg/day for memory loss and up to 600 mg/day for mood enhancement (Kidd, 1998).

Acetyl-l-carnitine is an energiser and metabolic cofactor that also benefits various cognitive functions in the middle-aged and elderly but with a slightly less favourable benefit-to-risk profile (Sano et al., 1992; Spagnoli et al., 1991; Thal et al., 1996). As a general brain energiser, acetyl-l-carnitine partially protects against ischemic brain damage, and can be helpful for stroke victims (Patti, 1988). In one in vitro study, Acetyl-l-carnitine increased the production of NGF by cultured nerve cells and helped them respond better to NGF. Treatment of aged rats with acetyl-l-carnitine partially halted the loss of NGF receptors, while improving performance on maze tests (Rampello et al., 1992). In the trials with cognitively impaired subjects, intakes of acetyl-l-carnitine ranged from 1500 to 3000 mg per day, with most trials using two grams or more (Crayhon, 1998). However, at these intake levels, acetyl-l-carnitine can intensify dream activity and it may be contraindicated for subjects with epilepsy or bipolar conditions.

Vinpocetine, found in the lesser periwinkle *Vinca minor*, is an excellent vasodilator and cerebral metabolic enhancer with proven benefits for vascular-based cognitive dysfunction (Balestreri et al., 1987; Hindmarch et al., 1991; Nicholson, 1990). Vinpocetine is a highly potent vasodilator acting by direct relaxation of the vascular smooth muscle. It enhances cerebral blood flow in patients with cerebrovascular disorders (Tamaki et al., 1985). It partially blocks hypoxic damage to brain

tissue and is a good scavenger of hydroxy radicals. In animal models of anoxia, vinpocetine reduced cerebral oedema and prolonged survival (Nicholson, 1990). The clinically validated dose range for vinpocetine is 15–45 mg per day. Side effects may include skin eruptions, flushing, and sometimes gastrointestinal disturbances.

Ginkgo biloba is the most clinically used plant extract for the nutritional support of cognitive function. Two meta-analyses of *Ginkgo biloba* extract demonstrate that the best preparations offer limited benefits for vascular insufficiencies and even more limited benefits for AD, while "commodity" *Ginkgo biloba* products offer little benefit, if any at all (Kleijnen & Knipschild, 1992; Oken et al., 1998).

Bacopa monniera is an Ayurvedic botanical with apparent anti-anxiety, anti-fatigue, and memory-strengthening effects (Singh & Singh, 1980). In India, it is a revered Ayurvedic herbal popularly accepted for its effectiveness against mental illness and epilepsy (Badmaev, 1998). Bacopa can also be beneficial to children. A study showed that in children taking the drug, maze learning improved, as did immediate memory and perception as well as the children's reaction/performance times (Sharma et al., 1987). The dose given was 1.05 g per day for 3 months, of the dried plant extracted into a syrup. No side effects were seen.

Alzheimer's disease

Recent studies have suggested that various medications may favourably affect the course of AD (Rogers et al., 1998; Shadlen & Larson, 1999). The development of novel compounds designed to optimise synaptic acetylcholine levels remains an important approach for the amelioration of some of the symptoms of AD. The most widely studied drugs are the cholinesterase inhibitors (Rogers et al., 1998). The FDA has approved four such medications for the treatment of AD as follows: tacrine (tetrahydroaminoacridine; Cognex®), donepezil (Aricept®), rivastigmine (Exelon®), and galantamine (also called galanthamine; Reminyl®). The clinical trial of tacrine (10–40 mg *po qid*) was the first to demonstrate a small benefit in cognition, using an unusual enriched trial design complicated by a high dropout rate (Knapp et al., 1994). Tacrine, a mixed, reversible acetylcholinesterase inhibitor, received FDA approval in September 1993. It was subsequently approved in other nations including France, Sweden, Australia, Switzerland, Brazil, and Argentina for the treatment of mild to moderate AD. It is a centrally active, non-specific cholinesterase inhibitor and acts by increasing the amount of acetylcholine at the neuronal receptor by decreasing its degradation. In vitro studies have shown that tacrine also affects neuronal potassium and sodium channels and has effects on noradrenaline, dopamine, and serotonin neurotransmission. Clinical use of tacrine has been limited by the high rate of side effects. It causes serious side effects in up to 20% of patients, including liver toxicity and gastrointestinal disturbances such as nausea and diarrhoea. More recently, clinical trials of donepezil (5–10 mg po qd), rivastigmine (1.5–6 mg po bid), and galantamine (4–12 mg po bid) demonstrated benefits on cognitive and global measure (Raskind et al., 2000; Rogers et al., 1998a, b; Rogers & Friedhoff, 1996; Rösler et al., 1999; Wilcock et al., 2000).

Donepezil (previously referred to as E2020) has been approved in many countries including the United States, the United Kingdom, Canada, Germany, Italy, Spain, and France. Donepezil is a second-generation cholinesterase inhibitor, a piperidine-based compound that is chemically distinct from other drugs studied for the treatment of AD. This drug has greater specificity for the brain acetylcholinesterase enzyme than tacrine and a longer duration of action. This favourable profile of donepezil is complemented by its pharmacokinetic properties characterised by a long plasma half-life (70 h) and a bioavailability of 100% (Krall et al., 1999). The efficacy of donepezil in the treatment of patients with mild to moderate AD has been established in several double-blind, placebo-controlled studies (Greenberg et al., 2000; Homma et al., 2000; Rocca et al., 2002; Rogers et al., 1996, 1998). Some patients treated with donepezil have reported a reduction in loss of the activities of daily living and an improvement of neuropsychiatric and behavioural

symptoms (Cummings et al., 2000). Donepezil can lead to improved cognition and functional ability in a small minority of patients. It also attenuates the rate of decline in longitudinal cohort studies. It does not cure or reverse cognitive impairment and, thus, many patients and families may be disappointed by a lack of dramatic benefit. Galantamine was approved by the FDA for the treatment of AD in February 2001. Studies show significantly improved cognition compared with placebo at 6 months and little decline from baseline at 12 months (Raskind et al., 2000). Subjects also show improvements in activities of daily living, requiring less caretaker assistance.

Rivastigmine (formerly referred to as ENA-713) is a potent, pseudo-irreversible (slowly reversible) dual inhibitor of AChE and butyrylcholinesterase (BuChE) (Weinstock, 1999). It induces rapid, sustained, dose-dependent inhibition of AChE and BuChE levels in the cerebrospinal fluid of patients with AD (Giacobini et al., 2002). Rivastigmine has shown useful efficacy in patients with mild to moderate AD (Forette et al., 1999). Adverse events were generally gastrointestinal and mild to moderate following doses of up to 12 mg/day. A pooled analysis of the studies of the phase III programme ($n = 2126$) indicated a mean treatment difference of 3.2 points on the AD Assessment Scale–cognitive (ADAS–cog) in patients receiving rivastigmine at 6–12 mg/day (Schneider et al., 1998). These positive effects on cognitive abilities were supported by a pooled responder analysis in which the percentages of patients showing improvements of at least four points on the ADAS–cog were significantly greater with rivastigmine than with placebo.

The new acetylcholinesterase inhibitors (AChEIs) such as donepezil and rivastigmine show a long duration of inhibitory action and a greater specificity for brain tissues (Bryson & Benfield, 1997). Several studies have suggested beneficial effects on behavioural symptoms with improvement of the ADAS–cog score or other neuropsychological scales (Corey-Bloom et al., 1998; Cummings, 2000; Rogers et al., 1998a, b; Rosen et al., 1984). However, these AChEIs such as tacrine and donepezil have proven to be generally disappointing from a therapeutic standpoint. In addition to the peripheral side effects, they do not appear to reverse or retard the neurodegeneration nor do they significantly alter the eventual fatal outcome of the disease. However, AChEIs do provide modest improvements in cognitive function in some patients and thus offer some benefits. Use of AChEIs has been associated with a delay in nursing home placement and with improvement in a number of behavioural symptoms including depression, psychosis, and agitation even in the absence of significant cognitive improvement (Kauffer et al., 1996). Therefore, the development of new AChEIs, as well as other cholinergic compounds, seems warranted.

Oestrogen replacement may lower the risk of AD in women (Sano et al., 1997). The fact that oestrogen replacement can increase choline acetyltransferase mRNA and protein within specific regions of the basal forebrain projecting to the hippocampal formation and cortex suggests that oestrogen may have a significant impact on some learning and memory processes in women. In a retrospective study involving 253 women, the percentage of women diagnosed with AD was significantly greater among women who did not receive oestrogen therapy (18%) than for those that received estragon after menopause (7%) (Paganini-Hill et al., 1993). Thus, oestrogen may have some neuroprotective or maintenance effect, which in the long term can help reduce the incidence or rate of cognitive decline associated with ageing and disease. Whether any of the effects of oestrogen on cognitive function are related to oestrogen effects on NGF and/or basal forebrain cholinergic function is still unknown. Oestrogen has widespread effects in the brain, any or all of which may contribute in some way to effects on cognition (see Gibbs, 1994; Singh et al., 1995). There is, however, some evidence that interactions between oestrogen and NGF-related systems may play an important role in mediating some effects of oestrogen on brain function and behaviour (Yanase et al., 1988).

Non-steroidal anti-inflammatory drugs have been proposed as another candidate that could reduce the risk of AD. This is due to the observation that people on non-steroidal anti-inflammatory drugs for other reasons are less likely to develop AD.

This is probably due to the reduction of inflammation in the brain. Inflammation of the cerebral cortex is another cause of neuronal death. The anti-inflammatory medication ibuprofen reduced Aβ deposition in an amyloid precursor protein (APP) transgenic mouse model of AD (Lim et al., 2000). The odds ratio of developing AD with prednisone or non-steroidal anti-inflammatory drug (NSAID) use was 0.50–0.66 in a meta-analysis of case control studies (McGeer et al., 1997). NSAID use was associated with a 50% reduction in the relative risk of developing AD in the Baltimore Longitudinal Study of ageing (Stewart et al., 1996). A twin-sib study demonstrated an 11-year delay onset of AD in NSAID users (Anthony et al., 2000). However, larger clinical trials of prednisone and celecobix were unable to demonstrate a benefit in established AD (Sainati et al., 2000).

It is speculated that antioxidants may help prevent the progressive loss of brain neurons associated with AD. Antioxidants are vitamins, minerals, and enzymes that protect the body by neutralising free radicals, which are byproducts of our cells' normal metabolism. Free radicals are believed to be associated with age-related changes and certain diseases. The antioxidant that has shown the most promise in delaying the progression of AD is vitamin E (α-tocopherol). Vitamin E is a free-radical scavenger thought to have antioxidant properties. It has been suggested to delay important dementia milestones such as institutionalisation or progression to severe dementia by about 7 months (Sano et al., 1997). However, evidence to support the use of other antioxidants, anti-inflammatory agents, or herbal medications such as *Ginkgo biloba* is insufficient to recommend use as standard therapies (Doody et al., 2001).

Preliminary reports of the potential application of dietary cholinergic replacement regimens (lecithin, choline) for the treatment of memory dysfunctions associated with Alzheimer's and other dementias have appeared (Wurtman, 1980). Certainly this approach appears somewhat promising in view of animal studies showing increased brain acetylcholine content in animal treated with dietary lecithin or choline (Cohen & Wurtman, 1976; Hirsch & Wurtman, 1978). Dietary choline may also act to stimulate cholinergic receptors.

In several studies with oral choline therapy for memory dysfunction in presenile dementia, variable results have emerged. Some reduced confusional behaviour in approximately one-third of the patients receiving choline (9 g/day × 2 weeks) was observed, but no changes in memory tests were noted (Smith et al., 1978). Little cognitive benefit was observed from oral choline (5 g/day × 2 weeks + 10 g/day × 2 weeks) in elderly patients (Boyd et al., 1977). However, some improvement in younger patients with a shorter history of AD was noted after 3 weeks of choline (9 g/day) when memory tests were given (Signoret et al., 1978).

Other therapeutic agents are in development, undergoing clinical trials or being reviewed by the FDA for possible licensing and marketing. These new drug classes are drugs aimed to work with different mechanisms of action, such as acting on the apolipoprotein E, modulating the APP and amyloid β (Aβ) protein or the tau metabolism. Elimination of apolipoprotein E in APP transgenic mice reduces cerebral Aβ deposition (Bales et al., 1997). Apolipoprotein E levels can be modified pharmacologically by lipid-lowering drugs of the statin class (3-hydroxy-3-methylglutaryl-coenzyme A reductase inhibitors). In human and rodent studies, statins reduce plasma apo E levels by 29–43% (Cabezas et al., 1993; Bard et al., 1995). Statin use may reduce the risk of developing dementia in AD. Another primary target for AD-modifying therapies is the amyloid plaque, composed primarily of Aβ protein. A targeted approach to alter APP metabolism involves medications that affect γ-secretase (Felsenstein, 2000). Preliminary data demonstrate that γ-secretase inhibitors can reduce Aβ formation in vitro and in APP transgenic mice. γ-secretase inhibitors are currently in AD clinical trials. An Aβ clearance mechanism that has generated considerable enthusiasm over the past few years is antibody-mediated Aβ uptake. Compounds that can intercalate into amyloid deposits to prevent Aβ fibrillation and induce Aβ depolymerisation and subsequent clearance have also been conceived (Emilien et al., 2000).

Appropriate animal models were used to test the effects of anti-Aβ antibodies on both brain damage and the cognitive losses caused by AD (Chen et al., 2000; Janus et al., 2000; Morgan et al., 2000; Schenk et al., 1999). Indeed, immunisation with β-amyloid peptide improves learning and memory as well as diminishing brain damage in animal models. The results support a previously observed reduction in the formation of amyloid deposits. They also show that immunisation offered the mice some protection from the spatial learning deficits that normally accompany plaque formation. Therefore, these results suggest that such immunisation or vaccines could delay or prevent similar symptoms in people. Data from patients with AD who received a primary injection of preaggregated Aβ$_{42}$ followed by a booster injection in a placebo-controlled study showed that antibodies in immune sera recognised β-amyloid plaques, diffuse Aβ deposits, and vascular β-amyloid in brain vessels (Hock et al., 2002). Thus, vaccination of AD patients with Aβ$_{42}$ induces antibodies that have a high degree of selectivity for the pathogenic target structures. Long-term clinical assessment will be required to determine whether this approach will halt or improve cognition in the patients treated. The finding that vaccinated patients with AD generated antibodies against beta-amyloid encourages the further development of immunisation therapy, however, this study was suspended when clinical signs of post-vaccination meningoencephalitis were reported in several patients. Although it was pointed out that the meningoencephalitis suffered by some of the trial participants is unlikely to stem from an antibody-mediated response against cellular precursor protein, this study did not clarify the cause of the inflammation in the patients. Thus, additional research and efforts are clearly warranted. Other therapeutic Aβ vaccination strategies are being pursued, including immunoconjugates and monoclonal antibodies. The future of these and other Aβ immunisation approaches depend on a clear understanding of the mechanism of Aβ clearance and additional insight into the role of inflammation in the AD brain.

Some approaches to preventing neurofibrillary pathology include stabilisation, phosphorylation inhibitors, phosphatases, or tau anti-aggregants. Multiple kinases capable of phosphorylating tau in vitro—such as cyclin-dependent kinase 5, mitogen-activated protein kinase (MAPK), glycogen synthase kinase 3β and calcium/calmodulin-dependent protein kinase—may serve as therapeutic targets to prevent destabilisation of tau. Inhibitors of tau phosphorylation in vitro include cathepsin inhibitors, lithium, protein phosphatase 2A, and PD98059 (a MAPK kinase inhibitor) (Cutler & Sramek, 2001).

Psychotropic medications play a critical role in the management of behavioural disturbances of patients with AD. Recent double-blind, placebo-controlled trials have established the efficacy of the atypical antipsychotics risperidone and olanzapine for the treatment of psychosis and agitation in patients with AD (Katz et al., 1999; Street et al., 2000).

Strategies for traumatic brain injury

Primary neuronal injury occurs as a direct result of an initial insult (e.g., blunt trauma or embolus). Associated with this process is a dense area of focal ischaemia known as the core, which is surrounded by marginally perfused and perifocal tissue (the ischaemic penumbra), in which blood flow is adequate to maintain cellular integrity, but insufficient for maintaining normal cellular and neuronal functions (Astrup et al., 1981). Secondary neuronal injury (the consequence of delayed metabolic and biochemical changes that follow the primary insult), which begins within minutes and can persist for days after the initial injury, may exacerbate existing neurological deficits, thereby decreasing rehabilitation potential and increasing the likelihood of poor outcome. Drugs that interrupt the endogenous metabolic derangements are considered potential therapies for neuronal and memory protection (Fischer et al., 1994).

Preliminary clinical studies suggest that treatment with precursors of neurotransmitters (particularly physostigmine and L-dopa) can be useful in unconsciousness and amnesic syndromes (Cardenas et al., 1994; Minderhoud et al., 1996). Other proposed pharmacological treatment strategies for memory disorders consist of several classes of compounds including piracetam or co-dergocrine-type drugs, vasodilators, haemorrheological agents, cholinesterase inhibitors, ACTH,

vasopressin analogues, angiotensin II, and angiotensin-converting enzyme inhibitors (see McLean et al., 1991; Nicholson, 1990; Sze et al., 1998). Other potential new compounds include propentofylline, donepezil, and rivastigmine (Taverni et al., 1998). In the study with donepezil, two patients with TBI who were experiencing long-term static memory dysfunction refractory to conventional treatment showed an improvement in memory function within 3 weeks of starting donepezil (Taverni et al., 1998). These initial cases demonstrating the successful use of donepezil for treatment of memory dysfunction in TBI are quite encouraging. However, larger clinical trials to substantiate the safety and efficacy of donepezil for treatment of memory impairment in TBI are required.

A pharmacological study indicates that dopamine agonists may improve anterograde memory impairment (Dobkin & Hanlon, 1993). In a blinded, controlled, alternating repeated-measures protocol, bromocriptine significantly improved subject verbal learning, functional memory, and daily recall. A recent case report outlined the beneficial effect of citicoline, an investigational drug on the enhancement of cognition and recovery in severe TBI patients (Spiers & Hochanadel, 1999).

Increased understanding of TBI and memory impairment shows the importance of mechanisms such as increased intracellular calcium, excitotoxicity from excessive glutamate, and other excitatory amino acids (McIntosh, 1993). One of the most promising experimental strategies has been the use of antioxidants or free-radical scavengers. Free radicals are believed to contribute to subsequent tissue damage through a variety of proposed mechanisms, including peroxidation of lipid membranes, microvascular damage, oedema formation, and subarachnoid haemorrhage, including vasospasm (Hall & Braughler, 1996). Strong evidence from animal studies indicates that superoxide, hydroxyl, and nitric oxide radicals are produced in response to brain injuries and that treatment with antioxidants or free-radical scavengers such as superoxide dismutase or α-tocopherol limits secondary damage and promotes recovery (Chan, 1996; Faden, 1996; Hall & Braughler, 1996). However, a recent clinical trial of an oxygen radical scavenger, pegorgotein (polyethylene glycol-conjugated superoxide dismutase, formerly known as PEGSOD) shows no statistically significant difference in neurological outcome or mortality between patients treated with pegorgotein and those treated with placebo (Young et al., 1996). Nerve growth factor, acidic, and basic fibroblast growth factors may promote neuronal survival in both in vitro cell culture and in vivo animal models of neuronal injury (Barbin et al., 1987; Sendtner et al., 1990; Sievers et al., 1987). This discovery has provided new avenues of research in TBI and associated memory deficit.

A recent placebo-controlled phase II study in TBI patients suggests that dexanabinol, a cannabinoid, may be a potential pharmacological therapy (Bedell & Prough, 2002). Dexanabinol combines NMDA blockade, antioxidant effects, and anti-inflammatory actions. In a comparison of patients receiving placebo with those receiving dexanabinol, the dexanabinol group had a significantly lower mean time during which intracranial pressure exceeded 25 mm Hg and a significantly lower mean time during which systolic blood pressure was < 90 mm Hg. The importance of these results is underscored by the strong association of poor outcome after TBI with an intracranial pressure of > 25 mm Hg or systolic pressure of < 90 mm Hg (Chesnut et al., 1993). The potentially important reductions of intracranial hypertension and systemic hypotension could have an important impact on the clinical management of TBI patients if those secondary endpoints translate into an overall improvement in cognitive and neurological outcome. However, although these promising data on dexanabinol are exciting, further studies in larger TBI patient populations are required.

Despite the absence of a demonstrated effective treatment for human TBI and associated memory deficit in most studies performed, neuroprotection and even neurodegeneration may be achievable in the future. Pharmacological agents may not be the solitary solution for an injury process as heterogeneous as human TBI. However, improved understanding of the pathophysiological mechanisms involved creates the possibility of targeted strategies that could lead to an important contribution of neuroprotective compounds in

reducing morbidity and mortality. Patients with severe brain trauma reflect a heterogeneous population in terms of underlying mechanisms of secondary injury, and future research should pay specific attention to such factors. Another important variable may be the time at which pharmacological treatment is begun. Animal models suggest that an effective treatment requires immediate and early intervention. Through further understanding of the basic pathology of secondary neuronal damage and the pharmacology of various investigational drugs, possibilities of enhancement of neurological function and memory recovery may be achieved.

There have been reports in the neurological literature describing the use of physostigmine, an anticholinesterase with significant cardiovascular and autonomic side effects, to treat both confusional and memory deficits in TBI (Levin et al., 1986; Weinberg et al., 1987).

BEHAVIOURAL TREATMENT

The most common approach to intervention has been to attempt to remediate or retrain the cognitive skills lost through disease or injury. Clinical neuropsychology has emerged in response to a need to describe neurocognitive impairment associated with memory dysfunctions. Cognitive retraining may be described as a systematic attempt to improve resultant intellectual deficits that interfere with the processing of information at some level.

Interest in rehabilitation has increased and several programmes aimed at directly improving basic cognitive function have appeared. The term cognitive rehabilitation described a treatment approach designed to ameliorate deficits in problem-solving abilities in order to improve functional competence in everyday life conditions (Ben-Yishay & Prigatano, 1990). Thus, cognitive rehabilitation is broader in scope than cognitive retraining since the goal of rehabilitation is functional adaptation in daily life activities. Cognitive rehabilitation requires not only identifying specific operational problems but also determining how it is to be done, the methodology required, and strict adherence to training priorities (Luria et al., 1969). Cognitive neuropsychologists may treat impairments identified by scores on tests or disabilities that are the ways in which impairments manifest themselves, in the form of everyday problems encountered by the patient. The effectiveness of any particular rehabilitation programme may be measured in amounts of reduction in disability experienced by the patient (for example, by how much a particular patient who forgets to take medication has improved his or her ability to remember to take it). Focus on impairments may be measured by a reduction in a particular impairment, such as inability to name objects, as indicated by a particular naming test. However, this information may be of little importance to the patient or the patient's family. It may mean very little to staff treating the patient unless there has been a subsequent and measurable improvement in everyday language skills. Cognitive neuropsychological theoretical approaches are rehabilitation methods that use a cognitive model typically of language or reading to identify the specific deficit of an individual patient. The underlying rationale would appear to be that once a deficit can be identified, it can be treated (Coltheart, 1991; Seron et al., 1991).

Remediation programmes have focused on achieving a general or global improvement in memory. Examples of that type of training include the use of visual imagery mediation, semantic elaboration, rehearsal, study skills methods, or some combination of methods (Crovitz et al., 1979; Gianutsos & Gianutsos, 1979; Glasgow et al., 1977; Malec & Questad, 1983; Patten, 1972). Although global treatment strategies have been shown to produce gains in specific clinical trials, they have been criticised for failing to facilitate consistent, robust improvement in memory. More recently, some researchers have begun using the preserved abilities of amnesic patients to help them reduce the impact of memory deficits on their daily lives. Several methods of problem alleviation have shown promising results (Schacter & Graf, 1986). External memory devices such as memory books and calendars have been shown to be effective in helping patients to organise their daily activities,

and behaviour modification strategies have been used to shape situation-specific behaviours (Dolan & Norton, 1977; Harris, 1984; Schacter & Glisky, 1986; Wilson & Moffat, 1983).

One approach to improving cognitive function is to train the individual extensively to improve cognitive function, an approach that has been used and which has met with some success. Memory programmes designed for the elderly population operate on two basic assumptions. Older adults with impaired, or less than optimal, performance will benefit from intense exposure to memory aids. Participation in training will increase appropriate and spontaneous use of these memory aids. Memory-training programmes almost always include teaching mnemonic devices such as method of loci, pegword, and link systems. These devices are considered to be internal strategies for organising and/or encoding information with the sole purpose of making it more memorable (McDougall, 1995, 2002). An alternative approach is to alter the environment rather than the individual, and learn to present information and design environments to support diminished cognitive functions.

Significant improvement in memory-control beliefs following skills training plus appraisal modifying intervention in healthy older adults has been demonstrated (Lachman et al., 1992). West et al. (1992) compared memory skills training with practice to a memory skills training plus memory-control beliefs enhancement condition, and noted that both groups improved on measures of memory-control beliefs and on at least one memory performance task. Caprio-Prevette & Fry (1996) compared a cognitive restructuring intervention aimed at modifying participants' control beliefs concerning their memory to the traditional memory skills training in healthy older adults. By 9 weeks later the cognitive restructuring group outperformed the traditional memory skills group on several memory measures and perceived greater control over their memory. A brief, cognitive and behavioural group intervention targeting memory performance and memory appraisals can be effective at changing perceptions of memory ability in a high-risk population of older adults with cognitive impairment. Some older patients may need more skills training to achieve and maintain performance improvements.

Maintaining intentions in goal-directed behaviour depends on intact executive functions involving the frontal lobes (Duncan, 1986). To address the negative impact of goal-directed failures in TBI patients' day-to-day lives, Robertson (1996) developed goal management training (GMT), a five-stage, interactive rehabilitation protocol based on Duncan's theory of goal neglect (Duncan, 1986). During training, subjects are taught using paper-and-pencil versions of complex real-world activities to identify specific goals, and to organise those goals into sensible, more simplistic subgoals. They also need to keep the subgoals in mind while carrying out the respective tasks and to stay on task while avoiding distractions. In studies involving a randomised group trial of TBI patients and a case study of a postencephalic patient, GMT improved performance on both paper-and-pencil and real-life versions of everyday tasks (Levine et al., 2000). Animal and human research indicates that learning can occur and improve if attention is trained to focus on relevant task factors (Oakley, 1983). While it remains unclear as to whether loss of either short-term or long-term memory can be remediated, it is clear that the efficiency of the memory systems can be measurably enhanced in chronic brain-damaged populations.

For treatment of AD, a multifactorial therapeutic approach that includes both pharmacological and psychological interventions is being increasingly advocated in order to optimise cognition, affect, and global functioning of AD patients. This approach should comprehensively include most of their needs and those of their families (Winter & Hunkin, 1999). Three potential approaches with proven efficacy have been identified (De Vreese et al., 2001). The first approach bears on the facilitation of residual explicit memory with structured support both at encoding and at subsequent recall. The second method of memory facilitation exploits the relatively intact memory system (priming and procedural memory), and the last deals with finding methods of coping with the patient's limited explicit memory capacities through the use of external memory aids.

Mnemonics

Initial memory interventions focused on using internal strategies that primarily involved mental activity. Examples of internal strategies include imagery-based mnemonics such as the method of loci, face–name mnemonics, and pegwords. Such interventions have shown some success in elderly populations (Verhaeghen et al., 1992). Highly verbal techniques that do not involve imagery such as an organisation strategy have also been used with similar results. When internal strategies are spontaneously generated, older adults report using verbal strategies more frequently than imagery-based strategies (Camp et al., 1983).

There is some positive empirical evidence supporting the use of imagery mnemonics in rehabilitation programmes of mildly memory-impaired subjects. The large majority of these studies focused on learning new names and taught patients to apply imagery techniques to associate a name to a person's face. Generally, the subject is encouraged to look for a distinctive feature in the face and to think of an image in which that feature is associated with the person's name, or an appropriate transformation of that name. In everyday life, retrieving the names of familiar people is required much more frequently than learning a new name. Reliable strategies other than asking someone else for a name are rare. There is clear evidence that mental imagery can lead to consistent, reliable, and substantial improvements in memory performance in healthy individuals (Richardson, 1995). However, complex imagery techniques (e.g., loci) did not prove practicable with TBI adults (Richardson, 1995). A study designed to evaluate the efficacy of a simple visual imagery technique in a rehabilitation study over 7 months with a group of mildly memory-impaired patients showed that imagery training significantly improved delayed recall of everyday relevant verbal materials (Kaschel et al., 2002). Frequency of memory problems observed by relatives is reduced and each of these effects is stable at 3-month follow-up. Thus, a simple imagery technique can improve relevant aspects of everyday verbal memory performance.

Any benefits from imagery mnemonics training tend to vary with the severity of memory impairment. Therefore, the performance of the most profoundly impaired patients may simply remain at a floor level throughout their training. These patients may well benefit more from external aids and environmental restructuring (Wilson, 1987a, b). On the other hand, the performance of patients with minor TBI can be raised to the level of normal controls although in this population the memory impairment is quantitatively slight and typically resolves within the first few weeks following the injury (Richardson, 1990).

Although most intervention research has emphasised the use of internal aids, older adults seem to use external aids more frequently in their daily environments. The effects of using medication organisers in combination with organisational charts as a means of increasing medication compliance in young-old adults and old-old adults were studied (Park et al., 1992). It was found that two aids used in combination were more effective at improving medication regimen adherence in old-old adults than either aid alone or no aids. The cognitive effort necessary to adhere to a medication regimen in old-old subjects was reduced when two aids were used and thus fewer errors occurred.

Restructuring the environment

Older adults are very sensitive to cues in the environment. Some memory theorists have argued that older adults forget more easily because they do not remember the context or environment in which a memory occurs. It has been demonstrated repeatedly that young and old adults are equally sensitive to environmental cues that improve memory for information (Park et al., 1990a, b). This is an important finding because it suggests that changing aspects of the environment to improve cognition in older adults would be a fruitful endeavour.

The basic principle in the environmental adaptation model is to avoid or bypass problems caused by memory impairment. Restructuring the environment is a useful procedure for decreasing undesirable behaviour in people with developmental learning disabilities. If it becomes clear that

undesirable behaviour occurs in only one situation, it may be possible to modify the situation to prevent the behaviour occurring. This can be a very rapid and effective way of eradicating or reducing such behaviours, but it is not always possible to achieve it. Even when it is achievable it may not be ethical. For example, a memory-impaired person could be kept in a restrictive environment that is very structured and places no demands at all on memory, thus avoiding problems that would normally arise because of impairment. In some circumstances, however, this might be viewed as so restrictive as to be unethical. Perhaps, one of the most interesting developments in environmental control is the coming of "smart" houses that use technology to provide structure designed to disable the disabling environment. "Smart" houses, for example, employ computers and videos to monitor and control the living environments of people with dementia. The aim of people developing and using this technology is to increase independence and activity and to improve the quality of life for confused elderly people. If successful for this population, "smart" houses may be adopted for people with cognitive impairments.

Errorless learning

Some strategies from the field of study techniques and learning disability have been applied in neuropsychological rehabilitation, and work continues on ways to improve learning. One series of potentially important studies in recent years has involved errorless learning. As the name implies, errorless learning involves learning without errors or mistakes.

The errorless learning technique was first used by Terrace (1963). Through the errorless learning approach, pigeons were taught to peck at keys illuminated in red while ignoring presentations of keys illuminated in green. Initially steps were taken to minimise errors and reinforce the correct response to the red key by permitting the pigeons access to a bin of grain only while the key was lit in red. It was found that pigeons prevented from making errors during training responded more accurately and with reduced latency. Due to the success demonstrated by this study, researchers began applying the errorless learning technique to facilitate improved recall of information with a variety of conditions affecting memory.

Errorless learning has for many years been used to teach new skills to people with learning disabilities. Most people can learn or benefit from their errors because they remember their mistakes and, therefore, avoid making the same mistake repeatedly. Errorless learning techniques have been used in various memory-impaired conditions including anoxic brain damage, carbon monoxide poisoning, TBI, schizophrenia, and AD (Clare et al., 2000a; Hunkin et al., 1998; O'Carroll et al., 1999). Parkin et al. (1998) used the errorless training approach to facilitate recall of names of politicians and friends with a subject who had memory impairment secondary to the herpes simplex encephalitis. After six training sessions, the subject was able to recall six of the eight politicians' names that he was unable to recall at the beginning of the study. In addition, following the six training sessions the subject showed significant recall of friends' names that he could not recall initially. Follow-up data indicate that the subject was able to recall the names of politicians and friends 5 weeks after the completion of the study. This may suggest that information learned with the errorless training method remained stable over a period of time following the training sessions.

External aids

Explicit-external interventions involve the conscious use of external storage devices to retain and retrieve information. According to surveys, these are the mnemonics most often used by lay persons and memory researchers alike (Park et al., 1990a, b). External aids have been effective in interventions in memory-impaired populations (Bourgeois, 1990). Young adults and older adults seem to clearly prefer external to internal strategies as well as preferring verbal to imagery-based mnemonics (Park et al., 1990a, b). An example of such a mnemonic is an appointment book. A recent innovation is NeuroPage, an externally programmed paging system, which enables an individual to receive timed reminders or cues that appear on a portable pager carried by the subject. Evans et al. (1998) described a single-case investigation in which NeuroPage was effective in cueing behaviour. Wilson et al. (1997) found that all of 15 subjects benefited from the pager and showed significant improvements in task completion. Another study sought to evaluate a new electronic memory aid called the Voice Organiser and determine its utility in the rehabilitation of prospective memory impairment (Van den Broek et al., 2000). The Voice Organiser is a hand-held Dictaphone-type device which can be trained to recognise the patient's individual speech patterns and store messages dictated by the user. It can be programmed to replay messages at time periods specified orally by the patient. The results suggest that the Voice Organiser may be a useful aid in the neuropsychological rehabilitation of prospective memory impairment.

Despite general agreement that a compensatory approach is probably the most useful one to adopt, there is uncertainty about why some people use external aids efficiently and others do not. Simply providing aids and expecting them to be used appropriately is likely to lead to failure for many memory-impaired people, and patience and ingenuity may be required. Obviously age, severity of memory impairment, and additional cognitive deficits are important variables in predicting independence and use of compensations several years postrehabilitation.

The final approach to the management and rehabilitation of memory problems is to help people to use their residual, albeit damaged, skills more effectively. This can be done through the use of mnemonics, through rehearsal and study techniques, and perhaps through the use of games and exercises. Although memory games do not improve memory, they do enable people to realise they can do better if they use a strategy and have the opportunity of using these strategies in enjoyable situations.

Implicit self-stereotyping

Researchers have shown that most people have positive and negative stereotypes of old age, but the negative stereotypes are more prevalent (Levy & Langer, 1994). Older people tend to report feeling less of a sense of mastery over their memory abilities than do young people. Research on the nature of the relationship between these memory self-efficacy beliefs and memory performance in old age has been inconclusive. It has not been established whether these beliefs follow from inevitable biological decline of certain types of memory or whether these beliefs could contribute to the decline (Smith, 1996). In China, where the most positive views of ageing were expressed, no significant differences emerged on memory scores between the old and young Chinese participants, even though the types of memory selected were those for which researchers have documented a decline in old age (Schacter et al., 1991). A recent study examined whether cultural stereotypes can influence memory performance (Levy, 1996). It was demonstrated that subliminally activated stereotypes can alter judgements about oneself and can improve cognitive performance. It was shown that activated positive stereotypes of ageing without the participants' awareness tended to improve memory performance, memory self-efficacy, and views of ageing in old individuals. In contrast, an intervention that activated negative stereotypes of ageing worsened memory performance. This study highlights the potential for memory improvement in old individuals when the negative stereotypes of ageing that dominate are shifted to more positive stereotypes. This research suggests a direction in which treatment intervention for memory impairment in old age may be effective.

Comprehensive psychotherapy

Most studies agree on treatment strategies of dissociative amnesia. In the treatment of this disorder, it is important to avoid unnecessary therapeutic manipulation and maintain a consistent and comprehensive psychotherapy. A complete assessment of the patient should be performed. The premorbid personality, social adjustment, previous conflicts and traumatic events leading to amnesia, family environment, and suicidality should be assessed. Excessive haste to recover from amnesia may lead to a clinical destabilisation. Generally,

three approaches are described. Stabilisation with emphasis on safety and relief, exploration of traumatic memories with a focus on the reversal of the amnesia (e.g., using hypnotic techniques, stressing remembrance and mourning for the material that might come up), and reintegration with development of the self and reconnections (Siegel, 1995). Therapeutic psychotherapy strategies in dissociative amnesia therefore involve an effort to bridge the amnesia by providing emotional support and by helping the patients restructure their perspective on the information that was previously inaccessible, making it acceptable to integration into consciousness.

Memory rehabilitation for early Alzheimer's patients

A multifactorial therapeutic approach that includes both pharmacological and psychological interventions is being increasingly advocated in order to improve cognition and global functioning in AD patients. Concomitant psychological interventions may enable a reduction in the dosage, duration, or complexity of pharmacological treatment. It should be recognised that there was some initial scepticism about the use of cognition-orientated treatments that were not supported by much efficacy data (APA, 1997). However, recent evidence suggests that some AD patients can benefit substantially from various memory rehabilitation procedures (Bäckman et al., 1990; Bäckman & Small, 1998; De Vreese et al., 2001). This decrease in cognitive reserve capacity is due to both the overall severity of the episodic memory impairment in AD, and dementia-related deficits in the semantic network that guides encoding and retrieval of information. Nevertheless, AD patients are able to utilise cognitive support in episodic memory tasks, although they typically need more support than their healthy aged counterparts to show memory facilitation (Bäckman, 1998; Lipinska et al., 1994). Thus, the link between knowledge and remembering, though deficient, is existent. It is very important to provide cognitive support at both encoding and retrieval in order to induce performance gains in AD. Such cognitive and behavioural improvement appears to be maximised when the context prevailing during encoding is reinstated at retrieval. Successful use of retrieval support in AD is most likely to occur when the encoding needs force the AD patient to engage in elaborate cognitive activity (e.g., generation of task-relevant knowledge, categorical organisation).

The recommended first approach of treatment intervention represents the more traditional aspects of memory rehabilitation by improving explicit memory capacities with appropriate dual support both at encoding and at subsequent recall (De Vreese & Neri, 1999). This approach can demonstrably improve some residual explicit memory functions and by extension temporarily slow down the rate of overall cognitive decline and loss of functional abilities, at least when combined with pharmacological treatments.

Another approach of intervention techniques deals with strategies supposed to rely greatly on the implicit memory system. There have been numerous studies showing that amnesic subjects can learn some things normally or nearly normally, even though they may have no conscious recollection of learning anything at all (Baddeley, 1990). The intervention is restricted to relearning AD patients' domain-specific factual knowledge or to retaining specific skills that can be used directly to improve everyday life activities in particular areas. The aim of these approaches is not to restore memory ability *per se*, but rather to impart pragmatically useful information to better tackle everyday memory issues. Much evidence seems to suggest that teaching domain-specific old or new knowledge, exploiting predominantly the relatively preserved implicit memory system, is possible, at least in some AD patients (Clare et al., 1999, 2000a, b). Improvements are often of quite impressive magnitude even though the underlying memory ability remains unchanged and training effects are often well maintained for significant periods of time. Resulting gains are usually amenable to generalisation in ordinary life through the sustained and direct participation of a relative or carer as co-therapists. Techniques considered to exploit spared implicit memory abilities in AD to facilitate new learning for several kinds of information include the spaced-retrieval technique, the vanishing cues procedure, and the errorless learn-

ing method (Bjork, 1988; Camp et al., 2000; Clare et al., 2000; Van der Linden & Collette, 1995).

Reality orientation therapy

Reality orientation therapy (ROT) was developed to improve spatiotemporal disorientation and mental confusion in patients through mental stimulation, social interaction, and adjusting maladaptive behaviour of the patients (Powell-Procter & Miller, 1982). Rehabilitation staff are trained to present basic orientation information during the interactions with confused patients to involve them in what was happening around them and to reinforce their interest in their environment. In practice, patients are asked questions such as, "Who are you?", "Who is talking to you?", and "What is going on now?" and then their false responses are corrected by therapists. Information regarding time and place is also given to the patient. The therapists must present the information to the patient in a very clear and simple fashion. The patient is recommended to rehearse and talk to his or her own family and other patients. It is important that the therapist knows the details of the patient's family and their past history so that he or she can assess the patient's remarks and progress. Improvement in orientation is observed in well-structured formal reality orientation irrespective of whether it is conducted in groups or individually (Greene, 1984; Hanley, 1986). Combination of reality orientation with other memory training strategies may provide better results. For example, a combination of reality orientation with instruction using an alarm clock and a timetable was used successfully in training patients with early Alzheimer-type dementia (Kurlychek, 1983). Reality orientation combined with attention process training in rehabilitation for elderly dementia patients was also successfully applied (Honda & Kashima, 1992).

Reminiscence therapy

Reminiscence therapy was developed to facilitate recall of past experiences in order to improve daily functioning and well-being of AD patients (Thornton & Brotchie, 1987). This approach was originally developed for elderly people without dementia but it was also applied to demented individuals, with higher focus on socialisation functions than interpersonal functions (see Kasl-Godley & Gatz, 2000).

External memory aids

External memory aids may serve as external cueing devices to help patients with memory difficulties. This approach should provide the severe memory-disordered patient with a means of keeping track of time and for supporting the continuation of routinised performance. One important aspect to consider in the use of external aids with elderly people or AD patients is that people are more likely to use an aid with which they are familiar or with which they have experience prior to their memory problems. New learning is difficult for elderly people and even more difficult for those with AD. Therefore, therapists should try to build on earlier learning by applying familiar aids if possible.

According to Van der Linden and Juillerat, the most critical determinant in the learning procedure of these external memory devices consists of training the AD patient to react correctly to them (e.g., "Remember to look at your calendar; memory book, and so on") (Van der Linden & Juillerat, 1998).

The vanishing cues method

The vanishing cues method involves giving subjects a cue, in the form of a word stem. Across learning trials, cue information is gradually withdrawn until responses are eventually given in the absence of partial cues. A few studies have shown that this approach may also be efficient in the learning of new facts in AD patients (Fontaine, 1995; Moffat, 1989).

Errorless learning

The technique of errorless learning limits the opportunity to commit error by repeatedly exposing a patient to the correct response rather than

asking him or her to guess or explicitly retrieve it. Several recent studies have shown that it is possible to teach amnesic patients factual information by using this errorless learning method (Clare et al., 1999, 2000a). Arkin (1992) described an errorless learning approach to teach the use of external memory aids, specifically audio-tape training, with dementia patients. Errorless learning may be combined with other useful rehabilitation techniques (Wilson et al., 1994).

The spaced-retrieval technique

The spaced-retrieval technique prompted recall of information over increasingly longer retention intervals (Bjork, 1988). It was initially introduced to assist normal subjects with long-term retention of information (Landauer & Bjork, 1978). Following a recall failure, the intertrial interval is decreased to that of the previous trial. It has been noted that if the patients were able to successfully recall information over a critical interval (e.g., 8–10 minutes), the information seemed to be consolidated in LTM and could be retained across days. Bäckman (1992) suggested that this approach draws on automatised and strategy-free rehearsal operations. It is believed that spaced retrieval involves little cognitive effort and therefore is also beneficial when used with memory-impaired individuals. Thus, spaced retrieval is a therapy approach that facilitates new learning using implicit memory by having the learner practise recalling information over increasingly longer periods of time. When the patient is successful at retrieving the information, the preceding interval is doubled. If the patient fails to accurately recall the information, the patient is immediately told the right answer and asked to repeat it. The next interval then returns to the last interval that was successful for the patient (Camp et al., 1996). Therefore, the spaced-retrieval technique utilises implicit memory in conjunction with the errorless learning technique. The goal of spaced-retrieval therapy is to permit the patient to remember the information taught for extended periods of time.

Several studies in the literature have reported successful use of the spaced-retrieval technique with dementia patients. It has been used to train dementia patients to use a calendar as an external memory device to remember daily activities (Camp et al., 1996). This technique has also been found to be successful in training internal memory strategies with dementia patients (Schacter et al., 1985). McKitrick and Camp (1993) successfully used spaced retrieval to re-teach an AD patient names of objects encountered in her everyday life. This study involved training the patient's caregiver to implement the spaced-retrieval technique to maximise functionality. Brush and Camp (1998) trained nine patients, two with cerebral vascular accidents and seven with dementia, to learn the therapist's name and a compensatory technique that they could use to self-cue. The results showed that this form of therapy was effective for all patients even though they differed in terms of diagnoses, age, and gender. The spaced-retrieval technique has also been used to teach dementia patients to select and redeem a coupon for money (McKitrick et al., 1992). It has also been shown that the spaced-retrieval method is successful in teaching dementia patients associations between cues and specific tasks or behaviours (Bird et al., 1995; Bird & Kinsella, 1996).

The spaced-retrieval method has allowed AD patients to learn new face–name associations and to enhance prospective memory (Lekeu et al., 2000; Vanhalle et al., 1998). The technique appears to require little expenditure of cognitive effort (Camp & McKitrick, 1992). Taken together, these results suggest that spaced-retrieval technique is successful for dementia patients of varying severity levels (MMSE scores of 11–25) (Brush & Camp, 1998).

There are many advantages to using the spaced-retrieval technique. Professionals and caregivers can easily use the method because it requires minimal training prior to implementation. Intervals between trials can be filled with conversation, games, or whatever the participant enjoys, thus creating an excellent relaxed atmosphere for memory improvement. This technique does not require a great deal of cognitive effort on the part of the participant because it taps into unconscious learning (Camp et al., 1996).

NERVE STIMULATION TREATMENT

The vagus nerve carries most information about viscerosensory states to the brain. Electrical stimulation of the vagus nerve, delivered after an aversive learning experience, improves later retention performance in rats (Clark et al., 1995). A recent study extends that finding to human verbal learning (Clark et al., 1999). In a study that examined word-recognition memory in patients enrolled in a clinical study evaluating the capacity of vagus nerve stimulation to control epilepsy, it was observed that stimulation administered after learning significantly enhanced retention. These findings confirmed the hypothesis that vagus nerve activation modulates memory formation similarly to arousal. The capacity of vagal stimulation to enhance memory performance may be applied therapeutically to individuals experiencing cognitive impairments that result from TBI or disease.

DISCUSSION

Despite considerable investments in neuroscience research, only four medications, all cholinesterase inhibitors, have been approved for the symptomatic management of AD in the United States. Although basically safe and modestly effective, these drugs are not ideal, being neither universally efficacious nor disease-modifying. AD exacts a considerable toll in direct medical costs, reduced quality of life, and caregiver burden for persons and society.

Successful interventions for memory dysfunctions and amnesia are of substantial importance for a patient's quality of life and for reducing caregiving burden. One may adapt several useful strategies to improve memory (see Table 11.3). Although lost memory functioning cannot be restored, people can be helped to bypass problems and their difficulties compensated for. They can be helped to learn more efficiently, the effects of their problems in everyday life can be reduced, and society can be educated into what memory

TABLE 11.3	
Some memory strategies	
Intend to remember	Attitude has much to do with whether one remembers something or not. If one has to be in class, say to oneself, "I am going to remember everything I hear in class today." One may be amazed by how much one retains. Sit in front of the class and focus on the teacher. Get involved, participate, engage.
Selectivity	Determine what is most important and select those parts to study. This will condense the amount of material one has to study. Writing things down often facilitates recall.
Recitation	Saying ideas aloud is probably the most useful tool one has to transfer knowledge from STM to LTM. Working in a group is extremely helpful. Paraphrasing as one reads is important. If one can put the concepts in one's own words, it is more likely that one will understand the material better as one reads.
Basic background	Understanding of new material depends a great deal on how much one already knows about the subject. The more one increases one's basic knowledge, the easier it is to build new knowledge on this background. Reading about the same concept from a range of sources can expand one's understanding by allowing one to view it from various authors' perspectives.
Mnemonic devices	Mnemonic devices can be useful when one needs to remember a list of facts, or steps in a procedure.
Repetition	For some materials, repetition and drill is necessary. For example, if one has to remember how to identify all the muscles in the body, one needs to practise doing it. Memorisation is necessary.
Apply what has been learned	If the concepts are abstract, discussion is often the best way to fully understand the issues, ideas, or theories one needs to learn.

impairment means. Memory interventions that target the attitudes and beliefs of older adults have resulted in high satisfaction ratings by participants, even though objective gains in memory ability were only modest (Caprio-Prevette & Fry, 1996). For example, older adults' complaints include feelings that they are not in control of their memory ability. Therefore, educating them as to strategies they can use for a variety of memory situations appears to allay some of their fears and give them more confidence. In general, success with external memory aids appears to be enhanced when principles of applied behaviour analysis are incorporated (Phelps & Cheney, 1996). Clinicians should carefully observe behaviour, select techniques that fit the performance characteristics of a particular patient, address the training needs of the patient and his or her environment, and plan for generalisation (Wilson, 1999).

AD researchers are working on two parallel paths to understand and better treat the disease. The first involves identifying signs and symptoms of AD long before it develops. Identifying MCI was the first step towards that goal. The other path involves testing different drugs to determine if they can help delay the onset of AD in people with MCI. It is hoped this would allow people with MCI to live normal lives for longer. In the future, researchers hope to develop strategies to prevent AD. Currently, two such strategies, immunisation therapy and a drug to block an enzyme responsible for AD, have shown promise in the laboratory and human clinical trails have been started. Future studies should elucidate whether MRI-based evaluation of hippocampal atrophy can predict the efficacy of cholinergic replacement therapies to alleviate memory and cognitive dysfunctions during long-term pharmacological treatment.

The efficiency of rehabilitative techniques has been explored in several reviews (Miller & Morris, 1993; Spector et al., 2000). Even if these approaches proved relatively beneficial to patients with mild dementia, unfortunately they are based on the implicit principle that all demented patients suffer similar cognitive impairments and therefore will respond similarly to the same rehabilitative programmes (Van der Linden, 1989). However, recent progress in neuropsychological characterisation of AD patients has led to the conception of early neuropsychological interventions that consider the complexity of mental processes and heterogeneity of their disorganisation (Juillerat et al., 2000). Indeed, the purpose of rehabilitation is not to increase performance on cognitive tests but to improve the quality of life for the patient and family caregivers. Caregiver burden and quality of life in both the patient and the caregiver may constitute important treatment outcome measures. A therapeutic intervention that has proven successful for dementia associated with AD is spaced retrieval. This is a shaping paradigm applied to memory, and involves attempts to recall information over expanding time intervals (Camp & McKitrick, 1992). Spaced retrieval has been used successfully to train patients with AD to learn and remember names of individuals or objects, locations, and even a strategy for remembering to use a calendar for daily tasks (Stevens et al., 1993). Given its success in patients with AD, spaced retrieval was proposed for use in dementia associated with PD. This approach shows promise as an intervention for diverse memory impairments associated with PD. Obviously, the long-term maintenance and generalisation of the use of memory strategies is the most important and indispensable research topic in memory rehabilitation and further research in these areas is required.

Some AD patients can benefit substantially from various memory rehabilitation procedures that apply recent findings reported by experimental clinical research in the field of AD and neurorehabilitation intervention studies in learning-disabled individuals. However, some researchers remain sceptical about the value of rehabilitation treatments (Caramazza, 1989). Wilson and Patterson (1990) argued that the interest in treatment on the part of the neuropsychologists has been almost entirely for the benefit of the scientist rather than the patient. While many of the rehabilitation programmes proposed were encouraging, difficulties arose with respect to assessing their long-term benefits. Outcome studies were often hampered by one or more flaws such as lack of appropriate control groups, inadequate assessment measures, and inappropriate statistical analyses. Often there was failure to consider potentially confounding variables such as other treatments and psychosocial environment. Such methodological weaknesses need to be addressed in cognitive rehabilitation studies. An integrated rehabilitation programme should address not only cognitive functions but also social, emotional, functional, and affective difficulties. Cognition should not be separated from emotion, motivation, or other noncognitive functions. Cognitive neuropsychologists engaged in rehabilitation should encourage dialogue with other clinicians and disciplines. Critical determinants for future research and development relate to the domain of assessment as well as to the realisation of effective rehabilitation programmes. It is important to ensure proper evaluation of cognitive rehabilitation programmes at both focal and global levels.

Conclusion

12

DISCUSSION AND CONCLUSION

The exact neural structures and mechanisms underlying human memory remain uncertain. None of the current theories seems to encompass the full range or complexity of memory processes, which include memory for sights and sounds, for feelings, and for belief systems that integrate information on a larger number of concepts. However, current research has been very helpful in clarifying some of the aspects of the memory processes and functions. The classic dichotomy between STM and LTM emphasised the relative resistance of memories stored over long durations as compared with newly acquired memories that are held briefly and lost if not reinforced. Although this distinction is certainly valid on a functional basis, it may be less valid on a topographical basis, since the two types of memory share much of the same cerebral substrate (Fuster, 1995). What seems to have become obvious from the results of current research on neural basis of memory is that, although seminal in their time, the pioneering work of Brodmann and others will be substituted by the convergence of results of different disciplines (neuroanatomical as well as functional

neuroimaging, electrophysiology, and neuropsychology) resulting in new cortical maps. These new maps will overcome the inaccuracies we are committing at present when referring, for example, to activation in distinct Brodmann areas, which are based on a microscopic interpretation of only one brain. These new maps, finally, will appeal to the clinician as well as to the scientist due to their computer-enhanced representation in 3D as well as their connection to large databases.

Since the frontal region is also involved in non-verbal memory, regarding its relation to the medial temporal lobe it may be suggested that the critical cascade driving human memory formation occurs only when frontal activity provides information to medial temporal lobe structures. Therefore, both regions would be critical to the conception of a memory, and lack of participation of either brain region would disrupt memory formation. Activity within frontal cortex would fail to instil a memory if the medial temporal lobes are damaged. Consistent with this hypothesis, patients with amnesia due to medial temporal lobe damage can show normal frontal activity patterns associated with encoding, yet these patients fail to form new memories (Buckner & Koutstaal, 1998; Gabrieli et al., 1998). Correspondingly, normal subjects with intact medial temporal lobes fail to form memories when frontal activity is absent. Thus the interaction of frontal and medial temporal regions, rather than the isolated contribution of either region, seems to be crucial for the effective formation of memories that contribute to consciousness of past events.

Functional neuroimaging studies have contributed considerably to a better understanding of the central executive of working memory or executive functioning. Indeed, studies using these methodologies have clearly shown that the executive functioning requires both prefrontal and parietal regions. Moreover, these investigations have also shown that some cerebral areas are devoted to very general executive processes, while others would be involved in more specific executive processes. Both neuroimaging and lesion studies have already yielded evidence that the PFC plays an important role in episodic memory. In the case of PFC activity, most studies are consistent with the notion that neural activity is less asymmetric in older adults than in younger adults. Although the neural mechanisms and function of this hemispheric asymmetry reduction in old adults (HAROLD) are still unknown, the consistency of the pattern is noteworthy particularly when one takes into account the small number of studies performed.

Non-invasive in vivo neuroimaging techniques have been a significant advance for the study of human memory. They have allowed researchers to examine normal, healthy brain operation as never before. It is important to acknowledge that what is measured in human brain-imaging experiments is not neuronal activity. It is the local haemodynamic changes such as blood flow, in the case of PET, and blood oxygenation, in the case of fMRI that may seem to be an ideal technique to address assessment of memory systems in the individual patient. Localisation of primary sensorimotor cortices and lateralisation of language have been accomplished with fMRI. Localisation of episodic memory systems and delineation of the functional integrity of medial temporal lobe structures could have immediate applications in the clinical setting (e.g., the preoperative assessment of epilepsy surgery patients). Neuroimaging offers direct applications to clinical

practice by providing the clinician with non-invasive and in vivo benefits of fMRI to aid in the diagnosis of psychological and neurological disorders. By being able to view the actual functioning of a patient's brain, a clinician may be able to discern dysfunction or abnormality in certain regions or circuits. An obvious application for using neuroimaging to investigate pathological memory is the disorder of AD. This disorder's hallmark symptom is a profound episodic memory impairment. Some of the earliest brain changes in the disease occur in critical memory locations such as the hippocampus and neighbouring regions. One PET study compared patients with AD and normal controls on a word-stem cued recall task (Bäckman et al., 1999). In addition to the AD patients' marked performance deficit in the episodic memory task, only control participants exhibited activation in the left hippocampal formation. This finding seems to indicate a potential direct link between memory impairment and impaired functioning in a distinct anatomical region related to memory. Such kinds of studies may offer guidelines and suggestions as to how the relationship between memory impairment and cortical dysfunction can be realised and examined in AD.

In the understanding of the biology of memory, the degree of spatial and temporal resolution attained by the physiological and pharmacological approach is unmatched by any other techniques, including the now highly developed imaging techniques (Andreasen et al., 1995a, b; Buckner & Koutsaal, 1998; Gabrieli et al., 1998). The latter provide clues as to maps within given training or retrieval contexts, and bring into the field functional gross anatomy, which is a step forward from the lesion (Friston, 1998; Fredrikson et al., 1995). The discovery of dissociations between classes of memory function in amnesic patients led to the postulation that there are multiple memory systems which are functionally and neurologically independent. Gross anatomy, however, has great limitations; For example, many imaging studies suggest that the hippocampus is very little involved, if at all, in memory formation or retrieval, a conclusion that no other method would endorse. Evidence derived from studies of animals with hippocampal lesions demonstrates that the hippocampus is not necessary to form simple associations in memory, but becomes necessary when the associative information must be used in a novel, flexible way (Bunsey & Eichenbaum, 1996).

In the understanding of memory while we perform various tasks, it is critical not only to ask where changes in activity occur but also to understand the underlying mechanisms that produce the changes. New methods of analysis of brain-imaging data such as correlational, time series, and path analysis may provide powerful methodological approaches. However, the relation between these haemodynamic changes is still inadequately characterised. Although the picture of memory that is emerging from functional imaging studies is consistent with current physiological accounts, there are issues that will probably be solved only through a combination of human and animal studies. Even with these improvements on imaging technology, remarkable progress in brain-imaging techniques does not compete with psychological analysis of behaviour. Such approaches instead place a new premium upon the thoughtfulness and accuracy of such analysis.

Imaging and biochemical pharmacological techniques have indeed shown that many brain sites are involved in the making, storage, and retrieval of even very simple basic tasks such as one-trial inhibitory avoidance in rodents or classical conditioning in humans (Bevilaqua et al., 1997; Fredrikson et al., 1995). No single place in the brain is omniscient, and there really is nothing like "hippocampal tasks" as opposed to "amygdala-based tasks" or "purely neocortical tasks", as has too often been concluded from single-lesion studies. All tasks that have been studied to some depth have revealed a rather complex underlying circuitry, and also a necessary role of complex and sequential biochemical processes in one or more points of the circuits. Recent developments in imaging techniques have revolutionised human cognitive studies, since they have allowed the identification of the brain regions engaged during specific behavioural tasks.

Imaging studies revealed subregions within the medial temporal lobe involved in the encoding of novel as opposed to familiar visual data (Reber & Squire, 1994). An integration of lesion and imaging studies in humans appears to be desirable in order to provide bases for a more detailed molecular approach in hitherto unexplored forms of memory. A recent study designed to examine the alterations in brain activation associated with pharmacologically induced memory impairment used fMRI to study the effects of lorazepam and scopolamine on a face–name associative encoding paradigm (Sperling et al., 2002). With the administration of either lorazepam or scopolamine, significant decreases were observed in both the extent and magnitude of activation within the hippocampal, fusiform, and inferior prefrontal regions of interest but no significant alterations in activation in the striate cortex were observed. Both medications impaired performance on postscan memory measures, and significant correlations between memory performance and extent of activation were found in hippocampal and fusiform regions of interest. These findings suggest that pharmacological effects can be detected by fMRI in a reproducible experimental paradigm by using an associative encoding task and that activation is decreased in specific brain regions thought to subserve this cognitive function. Further work exploring optimal analysis techniques is required, but the reliability and importance of these data, using medications known to impair memory, suggest that fMRI eventually may prove a useful method for screening medications that are being developed to enhance memory and treat cognitive dysfunctions.

However, studies with amnesic patients have not been highly successful in pinpointing the exact source of the pathological forgetting that patients exhibit. Thus, for instance, investigations of anterograde amnesia have not yet resolved whether forgetting is attributable specifically to problems in encoding, storage, or retrieval of information, or some combination of these processes (Mayes & Downes, 1997). Neuropsychological assessment is of help for the early diagnosis of dementia to determine a profile that suggests its cause. A set of tests to assess dementia at an early stage is required. However, the results must be interpreted in the light of the patient's history, rate of progression, imaging, and the nature of any behavioural impairment. Follow-up of patients is necessary to improve diagnostic accuracy.

Current studies have revealed multiple relations between normal ageing, age-related diseases, and memory systems. Perceptual memory systems appear minimally, if at all, affected by either ageing or AD. Conceptual memory systems appear to be unaffected by ageing but impaired in AD. Strategic memory systems appear to show a continuous decline across the lifespan. Nonstrategic memory may be minimally unaffected for much of the adult lifespan. Thus, studies of intact and impaired memory in age-related diseases suggest that normal ageing has markedly different effects on different memory systems. Ageing may have little or no effect on neocortical memory systems that mediate perceptual and conceptual priming. Ageing has a continuous, lifelong effect on a frontal-lobe system that mediates critical aspects of working and strategic memory. Degeneration in this system may account for much of the age-related decline in declarative memory seen in healthy individuals in their 60s and 70s. Finally, the insidious, late onset of AD may account for the further declarative memory deficits in old age. The growing awareness of disorders leading to dementia, the increasing demands to retain learning capacity even in old age, and the necessity to live independently as long as possible all create personal concerns about possible changes in memory. Differentiation of mild dementia from the less severe changes has been difficult. Therefore, even persons without clear objective evidence of memory impairment may be looking for advice. The borderline between normal age-related changes and dementia has not been easy to draw. Patients with an MCI are also becoming of interest for treatment trials. Several pharmaceutical companies are initiating large trials on this group of patients.

FUTURE PERSPECTIVE

A better comprehension of cognition is key to our understanding of both normal function and the pathophysiology of cognitive disorders. With

regard to the advancement in understanding of the molecular basis of memory, the rush is on to understand the physiology of CREB in neurons. Clearly, neuronal activity induces phosphorylation of CREB in a calcium-dependent manner, but it is not known which of several candidate biochemical mechanisms regulates the CREB switch. In addition to cAMP signalling, calcium-dependent kinases, MAP kinases, and growth factors have been implicated in various model systems. More recent studies have also suggested that nuclear and cytoplasmic calcium signals produce distinct effects on CREB-dependent gene expression, and the coactivation of CREB's binding partner, CBP, may play a critical role (Chawla et al., 1998; Deisseroth et al., 1998). This approach presages the day when a specific memory will be visualised in cells and circuits, connecting gene function with neural networks and behaviour.

Although molecular–genetic analysis may some day clarify the nature of the mechanisms of memory storage and perhaps even the exact loci of storage, such reductionist analysis may not be able to tell us what the memories are. Only a detailed characterisation of the neural circuities that code, store, and retrieve the memories can do this.

Future research directions include the identification of critical phosphoproteins responsible for short- and long-term potentiation and depression of synaptic transmissions, and the identification of important genes whose activation contributes to synaptic plasticity and memory consolidation. The discovery of therapeutic interventions that can improve pathological conditions associated with brain injury and ageing is crucial.

Common sense suggests that LTM storage does not rely on the production of new proteins or other molecules, but must involve long-lasting functional alterations that make some synapses more efficient and, perhaps, others less efficient (Dunn, 1980). The need for the suppression of some behaviours in order to permit the acquisition and storage of new ones using the same brain systems is not given the attention it deserves, despite the fact that inhibitory avoidance, by description, involves precisely this.

Additional studies are needed to try to identify conditions under which normal individuals might draw on information available from priming to support recognition judgements, as well as conditions under which amnesic patients might improve their recognition performance by drawing on information available from the system that supports priming. It is our opinion that pharmacological studies, in combination with neuropsychological studies of brain-lesioned patients, will become increasingly useful in uncovering those brain systems that play a role in mediating and modulating different forms of memory.

An important development in the future is likely to be an increasing interest in the neuropsychiatric disorders of memory from a clinico-legal as well as a cognitive point of view. Reports of "recovered memories" of sexual abuse have provoked great interest and legal proceedings. Clinical neuropsychology will need to collaborate with experts from various scientific and medical disciplines to better understand the problems of memory function and false memory syndrome.

The need for more sophistication and specificity in memory assessment procedures and conceptualisations has been emphasised (Loring & Papanicolaou, 1987). Two continuing criticisms of memory assessment procedures are the need for more measures of nonverbal or visual memory and the need for the adaptation of tests designed for laboratory or research paradigms to clinical use. Concerning AD, obviously more research needs to be directed at the psychometric properties of standard neuropsychological tests. Neuro-imaging should focus on all areas in the brain. We also need longitudinal studies of neuro-imaging, neurotransmitting, and neuropathology. Finally, education, health, and social class should be studied in relation to cognitive decline. Equipped with this information, it would be possible to embark on a multifactor intervention trial in normal healthy individuals at risk of AD.

Substantial progress has been made in the identification and comprehension of cognitive and behavioural deficits of AD as well as the consequences of these deficits on daily life functioning and family caregivers' conditions. An important challenge in the near future would be to assess whether and how pharmacological interventions and neuropsychological rehabilitation approaches may combine to constitute a more efficient treatment strategy. To alleviate the daily living of AD patients, the creation of daycare centres in which a real-life environment can be reproduced, optimisation strategies put in place, and satisfying leisure activities proposed, would be favourable for treatment approaches to AD. Future research needs to explore the effectiveness of memory rehabilitation techniques with dementia patients. More specifically, longitudinal studies are needed to determine maintenance rates and retraining frequency, and large subject samples would also be beneficial.

References

Aarsland, D., Cummings, J. L., & Larsen, J. P. (2001). Neuropsychiatric differences between Parkinson's disease with dementia and Alzheimer's disease. *International Journal of Geriatric Psychiatry, 16*, 184–191.

Abe, K., Inokawa, M., Kashiwagi, A., & Yanagihara, T. (1998). Amnesia after a discrete basal forebrain lesion. *Journal of Neurology, Neurosurgery and Psychiatry, 65*(1), 126–130.

Abel, T., Martin, K. C., Bartsch, D., & Kandel, E. R. (1998). Memory suppressor genes: Inhibitory constraints on the storage of long-term memory. *Science, 279*, 338–341.

Abel, T., Nguyen, P. V., Barad, M., Deuel, T. A., Kandel, E. R., & Bourcouladze, R. (1997). Genetic demonstration of a role for PKA in the late phase of LTP and in hippocampus-based long-term memory. *Cell, 88*, 615–626.

Abrisqueta-Gomez, J., Bueno, O. F. A., Oliveira, M. G. M., & Bertolucci, P. H. F. (2002). Recognition memory for emotional pictures in Alzheimer's patients. *Acta Neurologica Scandinavica, 105*, 51–54.

Adamec, R. (1997). Transmitter systems involved in neural plasticity underlying increased anxiety and defence—implications for understanding anxiety following traumatic stress. *Neuroscience & Biobehavioural Reviews, 21*, 755–765.

Adams, J. W., & Hitch, G. J. (1997). Working memory and children's mental addition. *Journal of Experimental Child Psychology, 67*, 21–38.

Adolphs, R., Cahill, L., Schul, R., & Babinsky, R. (1997). Impaired declarative memory for emotional material following bilateral amygdala damage in humans. *Learning and Memory, 4*, 291–300.

Adolphs, R., Tranel, D., Damasio, H., & Damasio, A. (1994). Impaired recognition of emotion in facial expressions following bilateral damage to the human amygdala. *Nature, 372*, 669–672.

Adolphs, R., Tranel, D., Damasio, H., & Damasio, A. (1995). Fear and the human amygdala. *Journal of Neuroscience, 15*(9), 5879–5891.

Adolphs, R., Tranel, D., Hamann, S., Young, A. W., Calder, A. J., Phelps, E. A. et al. (1999). Recognition of facial emotion in nine individuals with bilateral amygdala damage. *Neuropsychologia, 37*(10), 1111–1117.

Aggleton, J. P., Blindt, H. S., & Rawlins, J. N. P. (1989). Effects of amygdaloid and amygdaloid-hippocampal lesions on object recognition and spatial working memory in rats. *Behavioral Neuroscience, 103*(5), 962–974.

Aggleton, J. P., & Brown, M. W. (1999). Episodic memory, amnesia and the hippocampal-anterior thalamic axis. *Behavioral Brain Sciences, 22*, 425–489.

Aggleton, J. P., Hunt, P. R., & Rawlins, J. N. P. (1986). The effects of hippocampal lesions upon spatial and non-spatial tests of working memory. *Behavioral Brain Research, 19*, 133–146.

Aggleton, J. P., & Sahgal, A. (1993). The contribution of the anterior thalamic nuclei to anterograde amnesia. *Neuropsychologia, 31*, 1001–1019.

Agid, Y., Ruberg, M., Dubois, B., & Pillon, B. (1987). Anatomoclinical and biochemical concepts of subcortical dementia. In S. M. Stahl, S. Iversen, & E. C. Goodman (Eds.), *Cognitive neurochemistry*, 248–271.

Ahtee, L., & Kaakkola, S. (1978). Effect of mecamylamine on the fate of dopamine in striatal and mesolimbic areas of rat brain: Interactions with morphine and haloperidol. *British Journal of Pharmacology, 62*, 213–218.

Aigner, T. G., Mitchell, S. J., Aggleton, J. P., DeLong, M. R., Struble, R. G., Price, D. L. et al. (1991). Transient impairment of recognition memory following ibotenic-acid lesions of the basal forebrain in macaques. *Experimental Brain Research, 86*(1), 18–26.

Aigner, T. G., Walker, D. L., & Mishkin, M. (1991). Comparison of the effects of scopolamine administered before and after acquisition in a test of visual recognition memory in monkeys. *Behavioral & Neural Biology, 55*(1), 61–67.

Aït Amara, D., Segu, L., Naili, S., & Buhot, M-C. (1995). Serotonin 1B receptor regulation after dorsal subiculum deafferentation. *Brain Research Bulletin, 38*, 17–23.

Albert, M. L. (1978). Subcortical dementia. In R. Katzman, R. D. Terry, & K. L. Bick (Eds.), *Alzheimer's disease: Senile dementia and related disorders* (pp. 173–180). New York: Raven Press.

Albert, M. L. (1997). The ageing brain: Normal and abnormal memory. *Philosophical Transactions of the Royal Society, London, B, 352*, 1703–1709.

Albert, M. L., Duffy, F., & Naeser, M. (1987). Non-linear changes in cognition with age and neurophysiological correlates. *Canadian Journal of Psychology, 41*, 141–157.

Albert, M. L., Goodglass, H., Helm, N. A., Rubens, A. B., & Alexander, M. P. (1981). *Clinical aspects of dysphasia*. New York: Springer-Verlag.

Albert, M. S., Butters, N., & Levin, J. (1979). Temporal gradients in the retrograde amnesia of patients with alcoholic Korsakoff's disease. *Archives of Neurology, 36*, 211–221.

Aleman, A., Hijman, R., de Haan, E. H. F., & Kahn, R. S. (1999). Memory impairment in schizophrenia: A meta-analysis. *American Journal of Psychiatry, 156*(9), 1358–1366.

Alexander, G. E., Delong, M. R., & Strick, P. L. (1986). Parallel organization of functionally segregated circuits linking basal ganglia and cortex. *Annual Review of Neuroscience, 9*, 357–381.

Alexander, G. E., Furey, M. L., Grady, C. L., Pietrini, P., Mentis, M. J., & Schapiro, M. B. (1997). Association of premorbid function with cerebral metabolism in Alzheimer's disease: Implications for the reserve hypothesis. *American Journal of Psychiatry, 154*, 165–172.

Alexander, M. P., & Freedman, M. (1984). Amnesia after anterior communicating artery aneurysm rupture. *Neurology, 34*, 752–757.

Allain, H., Lieury, A., Quemener, V., Thomas, V., Reymann, J-M., & Gandon, J-M. (1995a). Procedural memory and Parkinson's disease. *Dementia, 6*, 174–178.

Allain, H., Lieury, A., Thomas, V., Reymann, J. M., Gandon, J. M., & Belliard, S. (1995b). Explicit and procedural memory in Parkinson's disease. *Biomed and Pharmacology, 49*, 179–186.

Allain, P., Le Gall, D., Etcharry-Bouyx, F., Aubin, G., & Emile, J. (1999). Mental representation of knowledge following frontal-lobe lesion: Dissociation on tasks using scripts. *Journal of Clinical and Experimental Neuropsychology, 21*, 643–665.

Allen, H. A., Jolly, D., Comish, J., & Burns, A. (1997). Depression in dementia: A study of mood in a community sample and referrals to a community service. *International Journal of Geriatric Psychiatry, 12*, 513–518.

Allen, H. A., Liddle, P. F., & Frith, C. D. (1993). Negative features, retrieval processes and verbal fluency in schizophrenia. *British Journal of Psychiatry, 163*, 769–775.

Alloy, L. B., & Abramson, L. Y. (1988). Depressive realism: Four theoretical perspectives. In L. B. Alloy (Ed.), *Cognitive processes in depression* (pp. 223–265). New York: Guilford Press.

Almkvist, O., Bäckman, L., Basun, H., & Wahlund, L. O. (1993). Patterns of neuropsychological performance in Alzheimer's disease and vascular dementia. *Cortex, 29*, 661–673.

Alpert, M. (1986). Language processes and hallucination phenomenology. *Behavioral Brain Sciences, 9*, 518–519.

Altmann, E. M., & Gray, W. D. (2002). Forgetting to remember: The functional relationship of decay and interference. *Psychological Science, 13*(1), 27–33.

Alvarez, P., Zola-Morgan, S., & Squire, L. R. (1995). Damage limited to the hippocampal region produces long-lasting memory impairment in monkeys. *Journal of Neuroscience, 15*(5 II), 3796–3807.

Alvarez, X. A., Laredo, M., Corzo, D., Fernandez-Novoa, L., Mouzo, R., Perea, J. E. et al. (1997). Citicoline improves memory performance in elderly subjects. *Methods and Findings in Experimental and Clinical Pharmacology, 19*(3), 201–210.

Amaducci, L. (1988). Phosphatisylserine in the treatment of Alzheimer's disease: Results of a multicenter study. *Psychopharmacology Bulletin, 24*, 130–134.

American Psychiatric Association. (1994). *Diagnostic and statistical manual of mental disorders (4th Ed.)*. Washington, DC: American Psychiatric Association.

American Psychiatric Association (1997). Practice guidelines. Workgroup on Alzheimer's disease and related disorders. In P. Rabins (Ed.), *Practice guideline for the treatment of patients with Alzheimer's disease and other dementias. American Journal of Pychiatry, S 154*.

Amrhein, P. C., Bond, J. K., & Hamilton, D. A. (1999). Locus of control and the age difference in free recall from episodic memory. *Journal of General Psychology, 126*(2): 149–164.

Anagnostaras, S. G., Maren, S., & Fanselow, M. S. (1999). Temporally graded retrograde amnesia of contextual fear after hippocampal damage in rats: Within-subjects examination. *Journal of Neuroscience, 19*, 1106–1114.

Anderson, A. K., Spencer, D. D., Fulbright, R. K., & Phelps, E. A. (2000). Contribution of the anteromedial temporal lobes to the evaluation of facial emotion. *Neuropsychology, 14*, 526–536.

Anderson, M. C., & McCulloc, K. C. (1999). Integration as a general boundary condition on retrieval-induced forgetting. *Journal of Experimental Psychology: Learning, Memory and Cognition, 25*, 608–629.

Anderson, N. D., & Craik, F. I. M. (2000). Memory in the aging brain. In E. Tulving & F. I. M. Craik (Eds.), *The Oxford handbook of memory*. Oxford: Oxford University Press.

Anderson, N. D., Craik, F. I. M., & Naveh-Benjamin, M. (1998). The attentional demands of encoding and retrieval in younger and older adults: I. Evidence from divided attention costs. *Psychology and Aging, 13*, 405–423.

Anderson, S. W., Damasio, H., Jones, R. D., & Tranel, D. (1991). Wisconsin card sorting test performance as a measure of frontal lobe damage. *Journal of Clinical and Experimental Neurospychology, 13*, 909–992.

Andreasen, N. C. (1989). Neural mechanisms of negative symptoms. *British Journal of Psychiatry, 155*, 93–98.

Andreasen, N. C., O'Leary, D. S., Arndt, S., Cizadlo, T., Hurtig, R., Rezai, K. et al. (1996). Neural substrates of facial recognition. *Journal of Neurosychiatry, 8*, 139–146.

Andreasen, N. C., O'Leary, D. S., Arndt, S., Cizadlo, T., Rezai, K., Watkins, G. L. et al. (1995a). PET studies of memory—Novel and practiced free recall of complex narratives. *Neuroimage, 2*(4), 284–295.

Andreasen, N. C., O'Leary, D. S., Cizadlo, T., Arndt, S., Rezai, K., Watkins, G. L. et al. (1995b). Remembering the past: Two facets of episodic memory explored with positron emission tomography. *American Journal of Psychiatry, 152*, 1576–1585.

Andreasen, N. C., Rezai, K., Alliger, R., Swayze, V. W., Flaum, M., Kirchner, P. et al. (1992). Hypofrontality in neuroleptic-native patients and in patients with chronic schizophrenia:

Assessment with xenon 133 single-photon emission computed tomography and the Tower of London. *Archives of General Psychiatry, 49,* 943–958.

Andrés, P., & Van der Linden, M. (2000). Age-related differences in supervisory attentional system functions. *Journal of Gerontology: Psychological Sciences, 55*B, P373–P380.

Angelucci, L., Ramacci, M. T., Taglialatela, G., Hulsebosch, C., Morgan, B., Werrbach-Perez, K. et al. (1988). Nerve growth factor binding in aged rat central nervous system: Effect of acetyl-L-carnitine. *Journal of Neuroscience Research, 20*(4), 491–496.

Anlezark, G. M., Crow, T. J., & Greenway, A. P. (1973). Impaired learning and decreased cortical norepinephrine after bilateral locus coeruleus lesions. *Science, 181,* 662–684.

Anthony, E. W., & Nevins, M. E. (1993). Anxiolytic-like effects of *N*-methyl-D-aspartate-associated glycine receptor ligands in the rat potentiated startle test. *European Journal of Pharmacology, 250,* 317–324.

Anthony, J. C., Breitner, J. C., Zandi, P. P., Meyer, M. R., Jurasova, I., Norton, M. C. et al. (2000). Reduced prevalence of AD in users of NSAIDs and H2 receptor antagonists: The Cache County study. *Neurology, 54*(11), 2066–2071.

Antoniadis, E. A., & McDonald, R. J. (2001), Amygdala, hippocampus, and unconditioned fear. *Experimental Brain Research, 138*(2), 200–209.

Appolonio, I., Grafman, J., Clark, K., Nichelli, P., Zeffiro, T., & Hallett, M. (1994). Implicit and explicit memory in patients with Parkinson's disease with and without dementia. *Archives of Neurology, 51,* 359–367.

Ardenghi, P., Barros, D., Izquierdo, L. A., Bevilaqua, L., Schroder, N., Quevedo, J. et al. (1997). Late and prolonged post-training memory modulation in entorhinal and parietal cortex by drugs acting on the cAMP/protein kinase A signalling pathway. *Behavioural Pharmacology, 8*(8), 745–751.

Arenberg, D. (1978). Differences and changes with age in the Benton Visual Retention Test. *Journal of Gerontology, 33,* 534–540.

Arendt, T., Bigl, V., & Teanstedt, A. (1983). Loss of neurons in the nucleus basal of Meynert in Alzheimer's disease, paralysis agitans, and Korsakoff's disease. *Acta Neuropathologica, 61,* 101–108.

Arkin, S. (1992). Audio-assisted memory training with early Alzheimer's patients: Two single subject experiments. *Clinical Gerontologist, 12*(2), 77–96.

Arnaiz, E., Jelic, V., Almkvist, O., Wahlund, L-O., Winblad, B., Valind, S. et al. (2001). Impaired cerebral glucose metabolism and cognitive functioning predict deterioration in mild cognitive impairment. *NeuroReport, 12,* 851–855.

Arnsten, A. F., Cai, J. X., & Goldman-Rakic, P. S. (1988). The alpha-2 adrenergic agonist guanfacine improves memory in aged monkeys without sedative or hypotensive side effects: Evidence for alpha-2 receptor subtypes. *Journal of Neuroscience, 8,* 4287–4298.

Arnsten, A. F., Lin, C. H., Van Dyck, C. H., & Stanhope, K. J. (1997). The effects of 5-HT$_3$ receptor anatagonists on cognitive performance in aged monkeys. *Neurobiology of Aging, 18,* 21–28.

Astrup, J., Siesjö, B. K., & Symon, L. (1981). Thresholds in cerebral ischemia—the ischemic penumbra. *Stroke, 12,* 723–725.

Atkins, C. M., Selcher, J. C., Petraitis, J. J., Tzaskos, J. M., & Sweat, J. D. (1998). The MAPK cascade is required for mammalian associative learning. *Nature Neuroscience, 1,* 602–609.

Atkinson, R. C., & Juola, J. G. (1974). Search and decision processes in recognition memory. In R. C. Atkinson, R. D. Luce, D. H. Krantz, & Suppes (Eds.), *Contemporary developments in mathematical psychology. I. Learning, memory and thinking* (pp. 243–293). San Francisco: Freeman.

Atkinson, R. C., & Shiffrin, R. M. (1971). The control of short-term memory. *Scientific American, 225,* 82–90.

Austin, M. P., Mitchell, P., Wilhelm, K., Parker, G., Hickie, I., Brodaty, H. et al. (1999). Melancholic depression: A pattern of frontal cognitive impairment. *Psychological Medicine, 29,* 73–85.

Austin, M. P., Ross, M., Murray, C., O'Carrol, R. E., Ebmeier, K. P., & Goodwin, G. M. (1992). Cognitive function in major depression. *Journal of Affective Disorders, 25*, 21–30.

Awh, E., Jonides, J., Smith, E. E., & Koeppe, R. A. (1996). PET evidence for an amodal verbal working memory system. *Neuroimage, 3*(2), 79–88.

Babinsky, R., Calabresse, P., Durwen, H. F., Markowitsch, H. J., Brechtelsbauer, D., Heuser, L. et al. (1993). The possible contribution of the amygdala to memory. *Behavioral Neurology, 6*, 167–170.

Bäckman, L. (1992). Memory training and memory improvement in Alzheimer's disease: Rules and exceptions. *Acta Neurologica Scandinavica, 84*, 84–89.

Bäckman, L. (1998). The link between knowledge and remembering in Alzheimer's disease. *Scandinavian Journal of Psychology, 39*, 131–139.

Bäckman, L., Almkvist, O., Andersson, J., Nordberg, A., Winblad, B., Rineck, R. et al. (1997). Brain activation in young and older adults during implicit and explicit retrieval. *Journal of Cognitive Neuroscience, 9*(3), 378–391.

Bäckman, L., Almkvist, O., Nyberg, L., & Anderson, J. (2000a). Functional changes in brain activity during priming in Alzheimer's disease. *Journal of Cognitive Neuroscience, 12*(1), 134–141.

Bäckman, L., Andersson, J. L., Nyberg, L., Winblad, B., Nordberg, A., & Almkvist, O. (1999). Brain regions associated with episodic retrieval in normal aging and Alzheimer's disease. *Neurology, 52*, 1861–1870.

Bäckman, L., Ginovart, N., Dixon, R. A., Wahlin, T-B. R., Wahlin, A., Halldin, C. et al. (2000b). Age-related cognitive deficits mediated by changes in the striatal dopamine system. *American Journal of Psychiatry, 157*, 635–637.

Bäckman, L., & Lipinska, B. (1993). Monitoring of general knowledge: Evidence for preservation in early Alzheimer's disease. *Neuropsychologia, 31*, 335–345.

Bäckman, L., Mäntylä, T., & Herlitz, A. (1990). The optimization of episodic remembering in old age. In P. B. Baltes (Ed.), *Successful aging: Perspectives from the behavioral sciences* (pp. 118–163). Cambridge: Cambridge University Press.

Bäckman, L., & Nilsson, L-G. (1996). Semantic memory functioning across the adult life span. *European Psychologist, 1*, 27.

Bäckman, L., & Small, B. J. (1998). Influences of cognitive support on episodic remembering: Tracing the process of loss from normal aging to Alzheimer's disease. *Psychology and Aging, 13*, 267–276.

Bäckman, L., Small, B. J., & Fratiglioni, L. (2001). Stability of the preclinical episodic memory deficit in Alzheimer's disease. *Brain, 124*, 96–102.

Baddeley, A. D. (1982). Implications of neuropsychological evidence for theories of normal memory. In D. E. Broadbent & L. Weiskrantz (Eds.), *Philosophical Transactions of the Royal Society, London*, 59–72.

Baddeley, A. D. (1986). *Working memory*. Oxford: Clarendon Press.

Baddeley, A. D. (1988). Cognitive psychology and human memory. *Trends in Neurosciences, 11*(4), 176–181.

Baddeley, A. D. (1990). *Human memory: Theory and practice*. London: Lawrence Erlbaum Associates Ltd.

Baddeley, A. D. (1992). Working memory. *Science, 225*, 556–559.

Baddeley, A. D. (1995). The psychology of memory. In A. D. Baddeley, B. Wilson, & F. N. Watts (Eds.), *Handbook of memory disorders* (pp. 3–25). New York: Wiley.

Baddeley, A. D. (1996). The fractionation of working memory. *Proceedings of the National Academy of Sciences, USA, 93*, 13468–13472.

Baddeley, A. D., Della Salla, S., Logie, R., & Spinnler, H. (1991a). The decline of working memory in Alzheimer's disease. *Brain, 114*, 2521–2542.

Baddeley, A. D., Della Salla, S., & Spinnler, H. (1991b). The two-component hypothesis of memory deficit in Alzheimer's disease. *Journal of Clinical and Experimental Neuropsychology, 13*, 372–380.

Baddeley, A. D., Gathercole, S. E., & Papagno, C. (1998). The phonological loop as a language learning device. *Psychological Review, 105*, 158–173.

Baddeley, A. D., & Hitch, G. J. (1974). Working memory. In G. H. Bower (Ed.), *The psychology of learning and motivation: Advances in research and theory*. New York: Academic Press.

Baddeley, A. D., Lewis, V., Eldridge, M., & Thomson, N. (1984). Attention and retrieval from long-term memory. *Journal of Experimental Psychology: General, 113*, 518–540.

Baddeley, A. D., Logie, R., Bressi, S., Della Salla, S., & Spinnler, H. (1986). Dementia and working memory. *Quarterly Journal of Experimental Psychology, 38*, 603–618.

Baddeley, A. D., & Scott, D. (1971). Short term forgetting in the absence of proactive interference. *Quarterly Journal of Experimental Psychology, 23*, 275–283.

Baddeley, A. D., & Warrington, E. K. (1970). Amnesia and the distinction between long- and short-term memory. *Journal of Verbal Learning and Verbal Behavior, 9*, 176–189.

Baddeley, A. D., & Wilson, B. (1986). Amnesia, autobiographical memory and confabulation. In D. Rubin (Ed.), *Autobiographical memory*. Cambridge: Cambridge University Press.

Baddeley, A. D., & Wilson, B. A. (1994). When implicit learning fails: Amnesia and the problem of error elimination. *Neuropsychologia, 32*, 53–68.

Badmaev, V. (1998). *Bacopin* (Bacopa monniera): *A memory enhancer from Ayurveda*. Piscataway, NJ: Sabinsa Corporation.

Bailey, C. H., Bartsch, D., & Kandel, E. R. (1996). Toward a molecular definition of long-term memory storage. *Proceedings of the National Academy of Sciences USA*, 13445–13452.

Bailey, C. H., & Chen, M. (1989). Time course of structural changes at identified sensory neuron synapses during long-term sensitization in aplysia. *Journal of Neuroscience, 9*, 1774–1781.

Baker, S. C., Rogers, R. D., Owen, A. M., Frith, C. D., Dolan, R. J., Frackowiak, R. S. et al. (1996). Neural systems engaged by planning: A PET study of the Tower of London task. *Neuropsychologia, 34*(6), 515–526.

Bales, K. R., Verina, T., Dodel, R. C., Du, Y., Altstiel, L., Bender, M. et al. (1997). Lack of apolipoprotein E dramatically reduces amyloid beta-peptide deposition. *Nature Genetics, 17*(3), 263–264.

Balestreri, R., Fontana, L., & Astengo, F. (1987). A double-blind placebo controlled evaluation of the safety and efficacy of Vinpocetine in the treatment of patients with chronic vascular senile cerebral dysfunction. *Journal of the American Geriatrics Society, 35*, 425–430.

Baldo, J. V., & Shimamura, A. P. (1998). Letter and category fluency in patients with frontal lobe lesions. *Neuropsychology, 12*, 259–267.

Balota, D. A., Dolan, P. O., & Duchek, J. M. (2000). Memory changes in healthy older adults. In E. Tulving & F. I. M. Craik (Eds.), *Oxford handbook of memory*. Oxford: Oxford University Press.

Balota, D. A., Watson, J. M., Duchek, J. M., & Ferraro, F. R. (1999). Cross-modal priming with ambiguous and unambiguous words in young, healthy older adults, and in individuals with dementia of the Alzheimer's type: Explorations of semantic memory. *Journal of the International Neuropsychological Society, 5*, 626–640.

Baltes, P. B. (1991). The many faces of human ageing: Toward a psychological culture of old age. *Psychological Medicine, 21*, 837–854.

Baltes, P. B. (1993). The aging mind: Potential and limits. *Gerontologist, 33*, 580.

Bank, A. L., Yochim, B. P., MacNeill, S. E., & Lichtenberg, P. A. (2000). Expanded normative data for the Mattis Dementia Rating Scale for use with urban, elderly medical patients. *The Clinical Neuropsychologist, 14*(2), 149–156.

Banks, P. G., Dickson, A. L., & Plasay, M. T. (1987). The Verbal Selective Reminding Test: Preliminary data for healthy elderly. *Experimental Aging Research, 13*(4), 203–207.

Bannister, H., & Zangwill, O. L. (1941). Experimentally induced visual paramnesias. *British Journal of Psychology, 32*, 30–51.

Barber, R., McKeith, I., Ballard, C., & O'Brien, J. (2002). Volumetric MRI study of the caudate nucleus in patients with dementia with Lewy bodies, Alzheimer's disease, and vascular dementia. *Journal of Neurology, Neurosurgery & Psychiatry*, 72(3), 406–407.

Barbin, G., Manthorpe, M., & Varon, S. (1987). Purification of chicken ciliary neurotrophic factor. *Journal of Neurochemistry*, 43, 11468–11478.

Barch, D. M., & Berenbaum, H. (1997). The effect of language production manipulations on negative thought disorder and discourse coherence disturbances in schizophrenia. *Psychiatry Research*, 71, 115–127.

Barch, D. M., Csernansky, J. G., Conturo, T., & Snyder, A. Z. (2002). Working and long-term memory deficits in schizophrenia: Is there a common prefrontal mechanism? *Journal of Abnormal Psychology*, 111(3), 478–494.

Bard, J. M., Ose, L., Hagen, E., Duriez, P., Pfister, P., Fruchart, J. C. et al. (1995). Changes in plasma apolipoprotein B-containing lipoparticle levels following therapy with fluvastatin and cholestyramine. European Fluvastatin Study Group. *American Journal of Cardiology*, 76(2), 65A–70A.

Barker, A., Jones, R., & Jennison, C. (1995). A prevalence study of age-associated memory impairment. *British Journal of Psychiatry*, 167, 642–648.

Barkley, R., Murphy, K., & Kwasnik, D. (1996). Psychological adjustment and adaptive impairments in young adults with ADHD. *Journal of Attention Disorders*, 1, 41–54.

Barnes, J. M., Costall, B., Coughlan, J., Domeney, A. M., Gerrard, P. A., Kelly, M. E. et al. (1990). The effects of ondansetron, a 5-HT$_3$ receptor antagonist, on cognition in rodents and primates. *Pharmacology Biochemistry and Behavior*, 35, 955–962.

Barresi, B., & Lindfield, K. C. (2000). Short-term memory in a patient with conduction aphasia. *Brain and Language*, 74(3), 491–494.

Baron, J. C., D'Antona, R., Pantano, P., Serdaru, M., Samson, Y., & Bousser, M. G. (1986). Effects of thalamic stroke on energy metabolism of the cerebral cortex. A positron tomography study in man. *Brain*, 6, 1243–1259.

Baron-Cohen, S. (1995). *Mindblindness: An essay on autism and theory of mind*. Cambridge, MA: MIT Press.

Barsalou, L. W. (1988). The concept and organization of autobiographical memories. In U. Neisser & E. Winograd (Eds.), *Remembering reconsidered. Ecological and traditional approaches to memory* (pp. 193–243). Cambridge: Cambridge University Press.

Bartrés-Faz, D., Junque, C., Lopez, A., Valveny, N., Moral, P., Galvez, E. et al. (1999). Apo E influences declarative and procedural learning in age-associated memory impairment. *Neuroreport*, 10(14), 2923–2927.

Bartrés-Faz, D., Junqué, C., Lopez-Alomar, A., Valveny, N., Moral, P., Casamayor, R. et al. (2001). Neuropsychological and genetic differences between age-associated memory impairment and mild cognitive imapairment entities. *Journal of the American Geriatrics Society*, 49(7), 985–990.

Bartus, R. T., Dean, R. I., Beer, B., & Lippa, A. S. (1982). The cholinergic hypothesis of geriatric memory dysfunction. *Science*, 217, 408–414.

Bass, E. W. Jr., Means, L. W., & McMillen, B. A. (1992). Buspirone impairs performance of a three-choice working memory water escape task in rats. *Brain Research Bulletin*, 28(3), 455–461.

Bassett, S. S., & Folstein, M. F. (1991). Cognitive impairment and functional disability in the absence of psychiatric diagnosis. *Psychological Medicine*, 21, 77–84.

Baudry, M., & Davis, J. L. (Eds.) (1991). *Long-term potentiation: A debate of current issues*. Cambridge, MA: MIT Press.

Bauer, P. J. (1995). Recalling past events from infancy to early childhood. *Annals of Child Development*, 11, 25–71.

Bauer, R. J., & Wewerka, S. S. (1995). One-to two-year-olds recall of events. The more expressed, the more impressed. *Journal of Experimental Child Psychology*, 59, 475–496.

Bauer, R. M., Tobias, B., & Valenstein, E. (1993). Amnesic disorders. In: K. M. Heilman & E. Valenstein (Eds.), *Clinical neuropsychology*. New York: Oxford University Press.

Baum, K., Vanderploeg, R., & Curtis, G. (1996). Patterns of verbal memory deficits in traumatic brain injury using the CVLT (Abstract). *Clinical Neuropsychology*, 10, 340.

Baxter, M. G., Bucci, D. J., Wiley, R. G., Gorman, L. K., & Gallagher, M. (1995). Selective immunotoxic lesions of basal forebrain cholinergic cells: Effects on learning and memory in rats. *Behavioral Neuroscience, 109*, 714–722.

Baxter, M. G., & Gallagher, M. (1997). Cognitive effects of selective loss of basal forebrain cholinergic neurons: Implications for cholinergic therapies of Alzheimer's disease. In J. D. Brioni & M. W. Decker (Eds.), *Pharmacological treatment of Alzheimer's disease: Molecular and neurobiological foundations* (pp. 87–103). New York: Wiley.

Beatty, W. W. (1992). Memory dysfunction in the subcortical dementia. In L. Bäckman (Ed.), *Memory functioning in dementias* (pp. 153–173). Amsterdam: Elsevier.

Beatty, W. W., Hames, K. A., Blanco, C. R., Nixon, S. J., & Tivis, L. J. (1996a). Visuospatial perception, construction and memory in alcoholism. *Journal of Studies on Alcohol, 57*, 136–143.

Beatty, W. W., Jocic, Z., Monson, N., & Staton, R. D. (1993). Memory and frontal lobe dysfunction in schizophrenia and schizoaffective disorder. *Journal of Nervous and Mental Disease, 181*, 448–453.

Beatty, W. W., & Salmon, D. P. (1991). Remote memory for visuospatial information in patients with Alzheimer's disease. *Journal of Geriatric Psychiatry and Neurology, 4*, 14–17.

Beatty, W. W., Salmon, D. P., Butters, N., Heindel, W. C., & Granholm, E. L. (1988). Retrograde amnesia in patients with Alzheimer's disease or Huntington's disease. *Neurobiology of Aging, 9*, 181–186.

Beatty, W. W., Staton, R. D., Weir, W. S., Monson, N., & Whitaker, H. A. (1989). Cognitive disturbances in Parkinson's disease. *Journal of Geriatric Psychiatry and Neurology, 2*, 22–33.

Beatty, W. W., Wilbanks, S. L., Blanco, C. R., Hames, K. A., Tivis, R., & Paul, R. H. (1996b). Memory disturbance in multiple sclerosis: Reconsideration of patterns of performance on the Selective Reminding Test. *Journal of Clinical and Experimental Neuropsychology, 18*, 56–62.

Bechara, A., Tranel, D., Damasio, H., Adolphs, R., Rockland, C., & Damasio, A. R. (1995). Double dissociation of conditioning and declarative knowledge relative to the amygdala and hippocampus in humans. *Science, 269*, 1115–1118.

Beck, A. T. (1976). *Cognitive therapy and the emotional disorders*. New York: International Universities Press.

Beck, A. T., Brown, G., & Steer, R. A. (1989). Prediction of eventual suicide in psychiatric inpatients by clinical ratings of hopelessness. *Journal of Consulting and Clinical Psychology, 57*, 309–310.

Beck, A. T., Rush, A. J., Shaw, B. F., & Emery, G. (1979). *Cognitive therapy of depression*. New York: Guilford Press.

Becker, E. S., Roth, W. T., Andrich, M., & Margraf, J. (1999). Explicit memory in anxiety disorders. *Journal of Abnormal Psychology, 108*, 153–163.

Becker, J. T., Lopez, O. L. (1992). Episodic memory in Alzheimer's disease: Breakdown of multiple memory processes. In L. Bäckman (Ed.), *Memory functioning in dementia*. Amsterdam: Elsevier.

Becker, J. T., Walker, J. A., & Olton, D. S. (1980). Neuroanatomical bases of spatial memory. *Brain Research, 200*(2), 307–320.

Becker, M., Warr-Leeper, G. A., & Leeper, H. A. Jr. (1990). Fetal alcohol syndrome: A description of oral motor, articulatory, short-term memory, grammatical and semantic abilities. *Journal of Communication Disorders, 23*, 97–124.

Beckwith, B. E., Petros, T. V., Scaglione, C., & Nelson, J. (1986). Dose-dependent effects of hydrocortisone on memory in human males. *Physiology and Behaviour, 36*, 283–286.

Bedell, E. A., & Prough, D. S. (2002). Dexanabinol as a treatment for traumatic brain injury: Will another therapeutic promise be broken? *Critical Care Medicine, 30*(3), 710–711.

Beeson, P. M., Bayles, K. A., Rubens, A. B., & Kaszniak, A. W. (1993). Memory impairment and executive control in individuals with stroke-induced aphasia. *Brain and Language, 45*, 253–275.

Belger, A., Puce, A., Krystal, J. H., Gore, J. C., Goldman-Rakic, P., & McCarthy, G. (1998). Dissociation of mnemonic and perceptual processes during spatial and nonspatial working memory using fMRI. *Human Brain Mapping*, *6*, 14–32.

Bellack, L., & Black, R. B. (1992). Attention-deficit hyperactivity disorder in adults. *Clinical Therapeutics*, *14*(2), 138–147.

Belleville, S., Peretz, I., & Malefant, D. (1996). Examination of the working memory components in normal aging and in dementia of the Alzheimer type. *Neuropsychologia*, *3*, 195–207.

Bennett, D. A., Wilson, R. S., Schneider, J. A., Evans, D. A., Beckett, L. A., Aggarwal, N. T. et al. (2002). Natural history of mild cognitive impairment in older persons. *Neurology*, *59*, 198–205.

Benson, D. F., Kuhl, D. E., Hawkins, R. A., Phelps, M. E., Cummings, J. L., & Tsai, S. Y. (1983). The fluorodeoxyglucose 18F scan in Alzheimer's disease and multi-infarct dementia. *Archives of Neurology*, *40*, 711–714.

Bentin, S., Moscovitch, M., & Nirhod, O. (1998). Levels of processing, selective attention and memory: Encoding. *Acta Psychologica*, *98*, 311–341.

Benton, A. L. (1968). Differential behavioral effects in frontal lobe disease. *Neuropsychologia*, *5*, 53–60.

Benton, A. L. (1974). *Revised Visual Retention Test (4th Ed.)*. New York: Psychological Corporation.

Benton, A. L., & Hamsher, K. de S. (1976). *Multilingual aphasia examination*. Iowa City: University of Iowa.

Benton, A. L., & Van Allen, M. W. (1968). Impairment in facial recognition in patients with cerebral disease. *Cortex*, *4*, 344–358.

Benton, S. L., Kraft, R. G., Glover, J. A., & Plake, B. S. (1984). Cognitive capacity differences among writers. *Journal of Educational Psychology*, *76*, 820–834.

Ben-Yishay, Y., & Prigatano, G. P. (1990). Cognitive remediation. In M. Rosenthal, E. R. Griffith, M. R. Bond, & J. D. Miller (Eds.), *Rehabilitation of the adult and child with traumatic brain injury, Second edition* (pp. 393–409). Philadelphia: FA Davis.

Berent, E., Giordani, B., Lehtinen, S., Markel, D., Penny, J. B., Buchtel, H. D. et al. (1988). Positron emission tomographic scan investigations of Huntington's disease: Cerebral metabolic correlates of cognitive function. *Annals of Neurology*, *23*, 541–546.

Berg, E. (1948). A simple objective test for measuring flexibility in thinking. *Journal of General Psychology*, *39*, 15–22.

Berger, T. W., Alger, B. E., & Thompson, R. F. (1976). Neuronal substrate of classical conditioning in the hippocampus. *Science*, *192*, 483–485.

Berger, T. W., & Orr, W. B. (1983). Hippocampectomy selectively disrupts discrimination reversal conditioning of the rabbit nictitating membrane response. *Behavioral Brain Research*, *8*(1), 49–68.

Berger, T. W., Rinaldi, P. C., Weiss, D. J., & Thompson, R. F. (1983). Single-unit analysis of different hippocampal cell types during classical conditioning of rabbit nictitating membrane response. *Journal of Neuphysiology*, *50*, 1197–1219.

Berger, T. W., & Thompson, R. F. (1978). Identification of pyramidal cells as the critical elements in hippocampal neuronal plasticity during learning. *Proceedings of the National Academy of Science of the United States of America*, *75*, 1572–1576.

Berksun, O. E. (1999). Panic disorder and memory: Does panic disorder result from memory dysfunction? *European Psychiatry*, *14*, 54–56.

Berman, D. E., Hazvi, S., Rosenblum, K., Seger, R., & Dudai, Y. (1998). Specific and differential activation of mitogen-activated protein kinase cascades by unfamiliar taste in the insular cortex of the behaving rat. *Journal of Neuroscience*, *18*, 37–44.

Berman, I., Viegner, B., Merson, A., Allan, E., Pappas, D., & Green, A. I. (1997). Differential relationship between positive and negative symptoms and neuropsychological deficits in schizophrenia. *Schizophrenia Research*, *25*, 1–10.

Bernabeu, R., Cammarota, M., Izquierdo, I., & Medina, J. H. (1997). Involvement of hippocampal AMPA glutamate receptors changes and the cAMP/protein kinase A/CREB-P signalling pathway in memory consolidation of an avoidance task in rats. *Brazilian Journal of Medical and Biological Research, 30*, 961–965.

Berry, D. T. R., Allen, R. S., & Schmitt, F. A. (1991). Rey–Osterrieth Complex Figure: Psychometric characteristics in a geriatric sample. *The Clinical Neuropsychologist, 5*, 143–153.

Beversdorf, D. Q., Anderson, J. M., Manning, S. E., Anderson, S. L., Nordgren, R. E., Felopulos, G. J. et al. (1998). The effect of semantic and emotional context on written recall for verbal language in high functioning adults with autism spectrum disorder. *Journal of Neurology, Neurosurgery and Psychiatry, 65*(5), 685–692.

Bevilaqua, L., Ardenghi, P., Schroder, N., Bromberg, E., Schmitz, P. K., Schaeffer, E. et al. (1997). Drugs acting upon the cyclic adenosine monophosphate/protein kinase A signalling pathway modulate memory consolidation when given late after training into rat hippocampus but not amygdala. *Behavioural Pharmacology, 8*(4), 331–338.

Bickel, H., & Cooper, B. (1994). Incidence and relative risk of dementia in an urban elderly population: Findings of a prospective field study. *Psychological Medicine, 24*, 179–192.

Bigler, E. D., Rosa, L., Schultz, F., Hall, S., & Harris, J. (1989). Rey Auditory–Verbal Learning and Rey–Osterrieth Complex Figure Design performance in Alzheimer's disease and closed head injury. *Journal of Clinical Psychology, 24*, 277–280.

Binder, J. R., Frost, J. A., Hammeke, T. A., Cox, R. W., Rao, S. M., & Proeto, T. (1997). Human brain language areas identified by functional magnetic resonance imaging. *Journal of Neuroscience, 17*, 353–362.

Bird, M., Alexopoulos, P., & Adamowicz, J. (1995). Success and failure in five case studies; Use of cued recall to ameliorate behavior problems in senile dementia. *International Journal of Geriatric Psychology, 10*, 305–311.

Bird, M., & Kinsella, G. (1996). Long-term cued recall of tasks in senile dementia. *Psychology and Aging, 11*, 45–56.

Birren, J. E., Fisher, L. M. (1991). Aging and slowing of behavior: Consequences for cognition and survival. *Nebraska Symposium on Motivation, 39*, 1.

Bishop, J., Knights, R. M., & Stoddart, C. (1990). Rey Auditory–Verbal Learning Test: Performance of English and French children aged 5 to 16. *The Clinical Neuropsychologist, 4*(2), 133–140.

Bixler, E. O., Scharf, M. B., Soldatos, C. R., Mitsky, D. J., & Kales, A. (1979). Effects of hypnotic drugs on memory. *Life Sciences, 25*, 1379–1388.

Bjork, R. A. (1988). Retrieval practice and the maintenance of knowledge. In M. M. Gruneberg, P. E. Morris, & R. N. Sykes (Eds.), *Practical aspects of memory: Current research and issues* (pp. 396–401). New York: Academic Press.

Bjork, R. A. (1989). Retrieval inhibition as an adaptive mechanism in human memory. In H. L. Roediger & F. I. M. Craik (Eds.), *Varieties of memory and consciousness: Essays in honor of Endel Tulving* (pp. 283–288). London: Wiley.

Blachstein, H., Vakil, E., & Hoofien, D. (1993). Impaired learning in patients with closed-head injuries: An analysis of components in the acquisition process. *Journal of Clinical Psychology, 7*, 530–535.

Blanchard, J. J., & Neale, J. M. (1994). The neuropsychological signature of schizophrenia: Generalized or differential deficit? *American Journal of Psychiatry, 151*, 40–48.

Blanchard, R. J., Blanchard, D. C., & Fial, R. A. (1970). Innate and conditioned reactions to threats in rats with amygdaloid lesions. *Journal of Comparative and Physiological Psychology, 71*: 92–102.

Blackford, R. C., & La Rue, A. (1989). Criteria for diagnosing age associated memory impairment: Proposed improvements from the field. *Developmental Neuropsychology, 5*, 295–306.

Blaxton, T. A. (1985). *Investigating dissociations among memory measures: Support for a transfer-appropriate processing framework.* PhD thesis, Purdue University, IN, USA.

Blaxton, T. A. (1989). Investigating dissociations among memory measures: Support for a transfer-appropriate processing framework. *Journal of Experimental Psychology: Learning Memory & Cognition, 15*(4), 657–668.

Blaxton, T. A., Bookheimer, S. Y., Zeffiro, T. A., Figlozzi, C. M., William, D. D., & Theodore, W. H. (1996). Functional mapping of human memory using PET: Comparisons of conceptual and perceptual tasks. *Canadian Journal of Experimental Psychology, 50,* 42–56.

Bleecker, M. L., Bolla-Wilson, K., Agnew, J., & Meyers, D. A. (1988). Age-related sex differences in verbal memory. *Journal of Clinical Psychology, 44,* 403–411.

Bliss, T. V. P., & Collingridge, G. L. (1993). A synaptic model of memory: Long-term potentiation in the hippocampus. *Nature, 361,* 31–39.

Bliss, T. V. P., & Lomo, T. (1973). Long-lasting potentiation of synaptic transmission in the dentate area of the anaesthetized rabbit following stimulation of the perforant path. *Journal of Physiology, 232,* 331–356.

Blitzer, R. D., Connor, J. H., Brown, G. P., Wong, T., Shenolikar, S., Iyengar, R. et al. (1998). Gating of CaMKII by cAMP-regulated protein phosphatase activity during LTP. *Science, 280,* 1940–1942.

Blitzer, R. D., Wong, T., Nouranifar, R., Iyengar, R., & Landau, E. M. (1995). Postsynaptic cAMP pathway gates early LTP in hippocampal CA1 region. *Neuron, 15,* 1403–1414.

Block, R. I., & Berchou, R. (1984). Alprazolam and lorazepam effects on memory acquisition and retrieval processes. *Pharmacology Biochemistry and Behavior, 20,* 233–241.

Blokland, A. (1996). Acetylcholine: A neurotransmitter for learning and memory? *Brain Research Reviews, 21,* 285–300.

Blum, S., Morre, A. N., Adams, F., & Dash, P. A. (1999). Mitogen-activated protein kinase cascade in the CA1/CA2 subfield of the dorsal hippocampus is essential for long-term spatial memory. *Journal of Neuroscience, 19,* 3535–3544.

Bodamer, J. (1947). Die Prosopagnosie [Prosopagnosia]. *Archiv für Psychiatrie und Zeitschrift für Neurologie, 179,* 6–54.

Bodick, N. C., Offen, W. W., Levey, A. I., Cutler, N. R., Gauthier, S. G., Satlin, A. et al. (1997). Effects of xanomeline, a selective muscarinic receptor agonist, on cognitive function and behavioral symptoms in Alzheimer disease. *Archives of Neurology, 54,* 465–473.

Boeijinga, P. H., & Boddeke, H. W. G. M. (1996). Activation of 5-HT1B receptors suppresses low but not high frequency synaptic transmission in the rat subicular cortex in vitro. *Brain Research, 721,* 59–65.

Bohanon, J. N., & Simons, V. L. (1992). Flashbulb memories: Confidence, consistency and quantity. In E. Winograd & U. Neisser (Eds.), *Affect and accuracy* (pp. 65–91). Cambridge: Cambridge University Press.

Bohnstedt, M., Fox, P. J., & Kohatsu, N. D. (1994). Correlates of Mini-Mental Status Examination scores among elderly demented patients: The influence of race–ethnicity. *Journal of Clinical Epidemiology, 47,* 1381–1387.

Boller, F., El Massioui, F., Devouche, E., Traykov, L., Pomati, S., & Starkstein, S. E. (2002). Processing emotional information in Alzheimer's disease: Effects on memory performance and neurophysiological correlates. *Dementia & Geriatric Cognitive Disorders, 14*(2), 104–112.

Bondi, M. W., Monsch, A. U., Galasko, D., Butters, N., Salmon, D. P., & Delis, D. C. (1994a). Preclinical cognitive markers of dementia of the Alzheimer's type. *Neuropsychology, 8,* 374–384.

Bondi, M. W., Salmon, D. P., & Butters, N. (1994b). Neuropsychological features of memory disorders in Alzheimer's disease. In R. D. Terry, R. Katzman, & K. L. Bick (Eds.), *Alzheimer disease.* New York: Raven Press.

Bondi, M. W., & Tröster, A. I. (1997). Parkinson's disease: Neurobehavioral consequences of basal ganglia dysfunction. In P. D. Nussbaum (Ed.), *Handbook of neuropsychology and aging* (pp. 216–245). New York: Plenum Press.

Borkovec, T. D., Ray, W. J., & Stober, J. (1998). Worry: A cognitive phenomenon intimately linked to affective, physiological and interpersonal behavioral processes. *Cognitive Therapy and Research, 6,* 561–576.

Bortolotto, Z. A., Bashir, Z. I., Davies, C. H., Taira, T., Kaila, K., & Collingridge, G. L.

(1995). Studies on the role of metabotropic glutamate receptors in long-term potentiation: Some methodological considerations. *Journal of Neuroscience Methods, 59,* 19–24.

Boulton, T. G., Nye, S. H., Robbins, D. J., Ip, N. Y., Radziejewska, E., Morgenbesser, S. D. et al. (1991). ERKs: A family of protein-serine/threonine kinases that are activated and tyrosine phosphorylated in response to insulin and NGF. *Cell, 65*(4), 663–675.

Bourson, A., Boroni, E., Austin, R. H., Monsma, F. J. Jr., & Sleight, A. J. (1995). Determination of the role of the 5-HT6 receptor in rat brain: A study using antisense oligonucleotides. *Journal of Pharmacology and Experimental Therapeutics, 274,* 173–180.

Boyd, W., Graham-White, I., & Blackwood, G. (1977). Clinical effects of choline in Alzheimer senile dementia. *Lancet, 2,* 711.

Bogousslavsky, J., & Regli, F. (1988). Transient global amnesia and stroke. *European Neurology, 28*(2), 106–110.

Bolla, K. I., McCann, U. D., & Ricaurte, G. A. (1998). Memory impairment in abstinent MDMA ("Ecstasy") users. *Neurology, 51,* 1532–1537.

Boller, F., Marcie, P., Starkstein, S., & Traykov, L. (1998). Memory and depression in Parkinson's disease. *European Journal of Neurology, 5,* 291–295.

Boller, F., Mizutani, T., Roessmann, U., & Gambetti, P. (1980). Parkinson disease, dementia and Alzheimer disease. Clinicopathological correlations. *Annals of Neurology, 7,* 329–335.

Bonner, T. I., Buckley, N. J., Young, A. C., & Brann, M. R. (1987). Identification of a family of muscarinic acetylcholine receptor genes. *Science, 237*(4814), 527–532.

Boone, K. B., Ghaffarian, S., & Lesser, I. M. (1993). Wisconsin Card Sorting Test performance in healthy, older adults: Relationship to age, sex, education and IQ. *Journal of Clinical Psychology, 49,* 54–60.

Boschert, U., Aït Amara, D., Segu, L., & Hen, R. (1994). The mouse 5-hydroxytryptamine1B receptor is localized predominantly on axon terminals. *Neuroscience, 58,* 167–182.

Bourgeois, M. S. (1990). Enhancing conversation skills in patients with Alzheimer's disease using a prosthetic memory aid. *Journal of Applied Behavior Analysis, 23,* 29–42.

Bourtchuladze, R., Frenguelli, B., Blendy, J., Cioffi, D., Schutz, G., & Silva, A. (1994). Deficient long-term memory in mice with a targeted mutation of the cAMP-responsive element binding protein. *Cell, 79,* 59–68.

Bowers, J. S., & Schacter, D. L. (1990). Implict memory and test awareness. *Journal of Experimental Psychology: Learning, Memory & Cognition, 16,* 404–416.

Braak, H., & Braak, E. (1991). Neuropathological stageing of Alzheimer-related changes. *Acta Neuropathologica, 82*(4), 239–259.

Braak, H., & Braak, E. (1996). Evolution of the neuropathology of Alzheimer's disease. *Acta Neurologica Scandinavica, 165*(suppl.), 3–12.

Braak, H., Braak, E., Yilmazer, D., de Vos, R. A., Jansen, E. N., & Bohl, J. (1996). Pattern of brain destruction in Parkinson's and Alzheimer's diseases. *Journal of Neural Transmission, 103,* 455–490.

Bradford, J. W., & Smith, S. M. (1979). Amnesia and homicide: The Padola case and a study of thirty cases. *Bulletin of the American Academy of Psychiatry and Law, 7,* 219–231.

Brandimonte, M., Einstein, G. O., & McDaniel, M. A. (Eds.). (1996). *Prospective memory: Theory and applications.* Mahwah, NJ: Lawrence Erlbaum Associates Inc.

Brandt, J., & Bylsma, F. W. (1993). The dementia of Huntington's disease. In R. W. Parks, R. F. Zec, & R. S. Wilson (Eds.), *Neuropsychology of Alzheimer's disease and other dementias* (pp. 265–282). New York: Oxford University Press.

Brandt, J., Bylsma, F. W., Aylward, E. H., Rothlind, J., & Gow, C. A. (1995). Impaired source memory in Huntington's disease and its relation to basal ganglia atrophy. *Journal of Clinical and Experimental Neuropsychology, 17*(6), 868–877.

Bransford, J. D., & Franks, J. J. (1971). The abstraction of linguistic ideas. *Cognitive Psychology, 2,* 331–350.

Brébion, G., Amador, X., Smith, M. J., & Gorman, J. M. (1997). Mechanisms underlying memory impairment in schizophrenia. *Psychological Medicine*, *27*, 383–393.

Brédart, S., Brennen, T., & Valentine, T. (1997). Dissociations between the processing of proper and common names. *Cognitive Neuropsychology*, *14*, 209–217.

Bremner, J. D. (1999). Does stress damage the brain? *Biological Psychiatry*, *45*, 797–805.

Bremner, J. D., Krystal, J. H., Southwick, S. M., & Charney, D. S. (1995a). Functional neuro-anatomical correlates of the effects of stress on memory. *Journal of Trauma Stress*, *8*, 527–554.

Bremner, J. D., Randall, P., Scott, T. M., Bronen, R. A., Seitbyl, J. P., Southwick, S. M. et al. (1995b). MRI-based measurement of hippocampal volume in combat-related posttraumatic stress disorder. *American Journal of Psychiatry*, *152*, 973–981.

Bremner, J. D., Scott, T. M., Delaney, R. C., Southwick, S. M., Mason, J. W., Johnson, D. R. et al. (1993a). Deficits in short-term memory in posttraumatic stress disorder. *American Journal of Psychiatry*, *150*, 1015–1019.

Bremner, J. D., Steinberg, M., Southwick, S. M., Johnson, D. R., & Charney, D. S. (1993b). Use of the structured Clinical Interview for DSM–IV Dissociative Disorders for systematic assessment of dissociative symptoms in posttraumatic stress disorder. *American Journal of Psychiatry*, *150*, 1011–1014.

Brewer, J. B., Zhao, Z., Glover, G. H., & Gabrieli, J. D. E. (1998). Making memories: Brain activity that predicts how well visual experience will be remembered. *Science*, *281*, 1185–1187.

Brewer, W. (1996). What is recollective memory? In D. C. Rubin (Ed.), *Remembering our past: Studies of autobiographical memory* (pp. 19–26). New York: Cambridge University Press.

Brewer, W. F. (1992). The theoretical and empirical status of the flashbulb memory hypothesis. In E. Winograd & U. Neisser (Eds.), *Affect and accuracy in recall* (pp. 274–305). Cambridge: Cambridge University Press.

Brewin, C. R., & Andrews, B. (1998). Recovered memories of trauma: Phenomenology and cog-nitive mechanisms. *Clinical Psychology Review*, *18*(8), 949–970.

Briggs, S. D., Raz, N., & Marks, W. (1999). Age-related deficits in generation and manipulation of mental images: I. The role of sensorimotor speed and working memory. *Psychology and Aging*, *14*(3), 427–435.

Brinkman, S. D., Largen, J. W., Gerganoff, S., & Pomara, N. (1983). Russel's revised Wechsler memory scale in the evaluation of dementia. *Journal of Clinical Psychology*, *39*(6), 989–993.

Brittlebank, A. D., Scott, J., Williams, J. M. G., & Ferrier, I. N. (1993). Autobiographical memory in depression: State or trait marker? *British Journal of Psychiatry*, *162*, 118–121.

Broadbent, D. E., Cooper, P. F., FitzGerald, P., & Parkes, K. R. (1982). The Cognitive Failures Questionnaire (CFQ) and its correlates. *British Journal of Clinical Psychology*, *21*, 1–16.

Brodaty, H., Clarke, J., Ganguli, M., Grek, A., Jorm, A. F., Khachatyrian, Z. et al. (1998). Screening for cognitive impairment in general practice: Toward a consensus. *Alzheimer Disease Association Disorders*, *12*, 1–13.

Brody, L. R., & Hall, J. A. (1993). Gender and emotion. In M. Lewis & J. M. Haviland (Eds.), *Handbook of emotions* (pp. 447–462). New York: Guilford Press.

Brooks, D. N., & Baddeley, A. D. (1976). What can amnesic patients learn? *Neuropsychologia*, *14*, 111–122.

Brooks, N. (1984). Cognitive deficits after head injury. In N. Brooks (Ed.), *Closed head injury. Psychological, social and family consequences*. Oxford: Oxford University Press.

Brouwers, P., Cox, C., Martin, A., Chase, T., & Fedio, P. (1984). Differential perceptual-spatial impairments in Huntington's and Alzheimer's dementias. *Archives of Neurology*, *41*, 1073–1076.

Brown, A. S., & Nix, L. A. (1996). Age-related changes in the tip-of-the-tongue experience. *American Journal of Psychology*, *109*, 79–91.

Brown, H. D., Kosslyn, S. M., Breiter, H. C., Baer, L., & Jenike, M. A. (1994). Can patients with obsessive-compulsive disorder discriminate between percepts and mental images? A signal detection analysis. *Journal of Abnormal Psychology, 103*, 445–454.

Brown, J. (1958). Some tests of the decay theory of immediate memory. *Quarterly Journal of Experimental Psychology, 10*, 12–21.

Brown, J., & Brown, M. W. (1990). The effects of repeating a recognition test on lorazepam-induced amnesia: Evidence for impaired contextual memory as a cause of amnesia. *Quaterly Journal of Experimental Psychology, 42*A(2), 279–290.

Brown, J., Lewis, V., Brown, M. W., Horn, G., & Bowes, J. B. (1983). A comparison between transient amnesias induced by two drugs (diazepam and lorazepam) and amnesia of organic origin. *Neuropsychologia, 20*, 55–70.

Brown, M. W., & Aggleton, J. P. (2001). Recognition memory: What are the roles of the perirhinal cortex and the hippocampus? *Nature Reviews, Neuroscience, 2*, 51–61.

Brown, M. W., Brown, J., & Bowes, J. (1989). Absence of priming coupled with substantially preserved recognition in lorazepam induced amnesia. *Quarterly Journal of Experimental Psychology, 41*A, 599–617.

Brown, N., & Kulik, J. (1977). Flashbulb memories. *Cognition, 5*, 73–99.

Brown, R. G., & Marsden, C. D. (1988). Subcortical dementia: The neuropsychological evidence. *Neuroscience, 25*, 363–387.

Brown, T., & Zador, A. (1990). Hippocampus. In G. Shepherd (Ed.), *The synaptic organization of the brain*. New York: Oxford University Press.

Brozoski, T. J., Brown, R. M., Rosvold, H. E., & Goldman, P. S. (1979). Cognitive deficit caused by regional depletion of dopamine in prefrontal cortex of rhesus monkey. *Science*, 205, 929–932.

Bruce, V., & Young, A. (1986). Understanding face recognition. *British Journal of Psychology, 77*, 305–327.

Brush, J. A., & Camp, C. J. (1998). Using spaced retrieval as an intervention during speech-language therapy. *Clinical Gerontologist, 19*, 51–64.

Bruyn, G. W., Bots, G., & Dom, R. (1979). Huntington's chorea: Current neuropathological status. In F. Chase, N. Wexler, & A. Barbeau (Eds.), *Advances in neurology, Vol. 23:*

Huntington's disease. New York: Raven Press.

Bryan, J., & Luszcz, M. A. (1996). Speed of information processing as a mediator between age and free-recall performance. *Psychology and Aging, 11*(1), 3–9.

Bryson, H. M., & Benfield, P. (1997). Donepezil. *Drugs & Aging, 10*, 234–239.

Buchanan, T. W., & Lovallo, W. R. (2001). Enhanced memory for emotional material following stress-level cortisol treatment in humans. *Psychoneuroendocrinology, 26*, 307–317.

Büchel, C., & Dolan, R. J. (2000). Classical fear conditioning in functional neuroimaging. *Current Opinion in Neurobiology, 10*(2): 219–223.

Büchel, C., & Friston, K. J. (1997). Modulation of connectivity in visual pathways by attention: Cortical interaction evaluated with structural equation modelling and fMRI. *Cerebral Cortex, 7*, 768–778.

Buckner, R. L., & Koutsaal, W. (1998). Functional neuroimaging studies of encoding, priming, and explicit memory retrieval. *Proceedings of the National Academy of Science of the United States of America, 95*, 891–899.

Buckner, R. L., Petersen, S. E., Ojemann, J. G., Miezin, F. M., Squire, L. R., & Raichle, M. E. (1995). Functional anatomical studies of explicit and implicit memory retrieval tasks. *Journal of Neuroscience, 15*, 12–29.

Buckner, R. L., Raichle, M. E., Miezin, F. M., & Petersen, S. E. (1996). Medial parietal (precuneus) activation during episodic memory retrieval: One area that is involved and one that isn't. *NeuroImage, 3*, S533.

Budson, A. E., Daffner, K. R., Desikan, R., & Schacter, D. L. (2000). When false recognition is unopposed by true recognition: Gist-based memory distortion in Alzheimer's disease. *Neuropsychology, 14*, 277–287.

Bull, D. L. (1999). A verified case of recovered memories of sexual abuse. *American Journal of Psychotherapy, 53*(2), 221–224.

Bullock, M., & Lutkenhaus, P. (1990). Who am I? Self-understanding in toddlers. *Merrill-Palmer Quarterly, 36*, 217–239.

Bunsey, M., & Eichenbaum, H. (1996). Conservation of hippocampal memory function in rats and humans. *Nature, 379*, 255–257.

Burgess, P. W., & Shallice, T. (1996). Confabulation and the control of recollection. *Memory*, *4*, 359–411.

Burgess, P. W., Veitch, E., de Lacy Costello, A., & Shallice, T. (2000). The cognitive and neuroanatomical correlates of multitasking. *Neuropsychologia*, *38*(6), 848–863.

Burgio, F., & Basso, A. (1997). Memory and aphasia. *Neuropsychologia*, *35*(6), 759–766.

Burke, D. M., & Mackay, D. G. (1997). Memory, language and ageing. *Philosophical Transactions of the Royal Society: Biological Sciences*, *352*, 1845–1856.

Burke, D. M., Mackay, D. G., Worthley, J. S., & Wade, E. (1991). On the tip of the tongue: What causes word finding failures in young and older adults? *Journal of Memory and Language*, *30*, 542–579.

Burnham, W. H. (1889). Memory, historically and experimentally considered. III paramnesia. *American Journal of Psychology*, *2*, 431–494.

Burstein, A. (1985). Posttraumatic flashbacks, dream disturbances, and mental imagey. *Journal of Clinical Psychiatry*, *46*, 374–378.

Burt, D. B., Zembar, M. J., & Niederehe, G. (1995). Depression and memory impairment: A meta-analysis of the association, its pattern and specificity. *Psychological Bulletin*, *117*, 285–305.

Busatto, G. F., David, A. S., Costa, D. C., Ell, P. J., Pilowsky, L. S., Lucey, J. V. et al. (1995). Schizophrenic auditory hallucinations are associated with increased regional cerebral blood flow during verbal memory activation in a study using single photon emission computed tomography. *Psychiatry Research*, *61*, 255–264.

Busatto, G. F., Pilowski, L. S., Costa, D. C., Ell, P. J., David, A. S., & Kerwin, R. W. (1996). Reduced *in-vivo* benzodiazepine receptor binding correlates with severity of psychotic symptoms in schizophrenia. *American Journal of Psychiatry*, *154*, 56–63.

Buschke, H. (1973). Selective reminding for analysis of memory and learning. *Journal of Verbal Learning & Verbal Behavior*, *12*, 543–550.

Buschke, H. (1984). Cued recall in amnesia. *Journal of Clinical Neuropsychology*, *6*, 433–440.

Buschke, H., & Fuld, P. A. (1974). Evaluating storage, retention, and retrieval in disordered memory and learning. *Neurology*, *24*, 1019–1025.

Bussey, T. J., Muir, J. L., & Aggleton, J. P. (1999). Functionally dissociating aspects of event memory: The effects of combined perirhinal and postrhinal cortex lesions on object and place memory in the rat. *Journal of Neuroscience*, *19*, 495–502.

Butters, N. (1985). Alcoholic Korsakoff's syndrome: Some unresolved issues concerning etiology, neuropathology, and cognitive deficits. *Journal of Clinical and Experimental Neuropsychology*, *7*, 181–210.

Butters, N., Delis, D., & Lucas, J. A. (1995). Clinical assessment of memory disorders in amnesia and dementia. *Annual Review of Psychology*, *46*, 493–523.

Butters, N., & Granholm, E. (1987). The continuity hypothesis: Some conclusions and their implications for the etiology and neuropathology of alcoholic Korsakoff's syndrome. In O. A. Parsons, N. Butters, & P. E. Nathan (Eds.), *Neuropsychology of alcoholism: Implications for diagnosis and treatments*. New York: Guilford Press.

Butters, N., Salmon, D. P., Cullum, C. M., Cairns, P., Tröster, A. I., Jacobs, D. et al. (1988a). Differentiation of amnesic and demented patients with the Wechsler Memory Scale-Revised. *The Clinical Neuropsychologist*, *2*, 133–148.

Butters, N., Salmon, D. P., Heindel, W., & Granholm, E. (1988b). Episodic, semantic and procedural memory: Some comparisons of Alzheimer and Huntington disease patients. In R. D. Terry (Ed.), *Aging and the brain*. New York: Raven.

Butters, N., Sax, D. S., Montgomery, K., & Tarlow, S. (1978). Comparison of the neuropsychological deficits associated with early and advanced Hntington's disease. *Archives of Neurology*, *35*, 585–589.

Butters, N., Wolfe, J., Granholm, E., & Martone, M. (1986). An assessment of verbal recall, recognition and fluency abilities in patients with Huntington's disease. *Cortex*, *22*, 11–32.

Butters, N., Wolfe, J., Martone, M., Granholm, E., & Cermak, L. (1985). Memory disorders associated with Huntington's disease: Verbal recall, verbal recognition, and procedural memory. *Neuropsychologia, 23*, 729–743.

Buytenhuijs, E. L., Berger, H. J., Van Spaendonck, K. P., Horstink, W. I., Born, G. F., & Cools, A. R. (1994). Memory and learning strategies in patients with Parkinson's disease. *Neuropsychologia, 32*, 335–342.

Buzsaki, G. (1989). Two-stage model of memory trace formation: A role for "noisy" brain states. *Neuroscience, 31*, 551–570.

Bylsma, F. W., Brandt, J., & Strauss, M. E. (1990). Aspects of procedural memory are differentially impaired in Huntington's disease. *Archives of Clinical Neuropsychology, 5*, 287–297.

Byrne, D. G. (1977). Choice reaction times in depressive states. *British Journal of Social and Clinical Psychology, 15*, 149–156.

Cabeza, R. (2000). The neural bases of recognition memory. In E. Tulving (Ed.), *Memory, consciousness, and the brain: The Talinn Conference.* Philadelphia: Psychology Press.

Cabeza, R., Anderson, A. D., Mangels, J., Nyberg, L., & Houle, S. (2000). Age-related differences in neural activity during item and temporal-order memory retrieval: A positron emission tomography study. *Journal of Cognitive Neuroscience, 12*, 197–206.

Cabeza, R., Grady, C. L., Nyberg, L., McIntosh, A. R., Tulving, E., Kapur, S. et al. (1997). Age-related differences in neural activity during memory encoding and retrieval: A positron emission tomography study. *Journal of Neuroscience, 17*, 391–400.

Cabeza, R., & Nyberg, L. (2000). Imaging cognition II: An empirical review of 375 PET and fMRI studies. *Journal of Cognitive Neuroscience, 12*, 1–47.

Cabezas, M. C., De Bruin, T. W. A., Kock, L. A. W., Kortlandt, W., Trip, M. V. L. S., Jansen, H. et al. (1993). Simvastatin improves chylomicron remnant removal in familial combined hyperlipidemia without changing chylomicron conversion. *Metabolism: Clinical & Experimental, 42*(4), 497–503.

Cahill, L., Babinsky, R., Markowitsch, H. J., & McGaugh, J. L. (1995). The amygdala and emotional memory. *Nature, 377*, 295–296.

Cahill, L., Haier, R., Fallon, J., Alkire, M., Tang, C., Keator, D. et al. (1996). Amygdala activity at encoding correlated with long-term, free recall of emotional information. *Proceedings of the National Academy of Sciences, 93*, 8016–8021.

Cahill, L., Haier, R. J., White, N. S., Fallon, J., Kilpatrick, L., Lawrence, C. et al. (2001). Sex-related difference in amygdala activity during emotionally influenced memory storage. *Neurobiology of Learning & Memory, 75*(1), 1–9.

Cahill, L., & McGaugh, J. L. (1996). Modulation of memory storage. *Current Opinion in Neurobiology, 6*, 237–242.

Cahill, L., & McGaugh, J. L. (1998). Mechanisms of emotional arousal and lasting declarative memory. *Trends in Neurosciences, 21*, 294–299.

Cahill, L., Prins, B., Weber, M., & McGaugh, J. L. (1994). Beta-adrenergic activation and memory for emotional events. *Nature, 371*, 702–704.

Cahill, L., Weinberger, N. M., Roozendaal, B., & McGaugh, J. L. (1999). Is the amygdala a locus of "conditioned fear"? Some questions and caveats. *Neuron, 23*(2), 227–228.

Caine, E. D. (1993). Should aging-associated cognitive decline be included in DSM–IV. *Journal of Neuropsychiatry and Clinical Neuroscience, 5*, 1–5.

Caine, E. D., Ebert, M. H., & Weingartner, H. (1977). An outline for the analysis of dementia. *Neurology, 27*, 1087–1092.

Caine, E. D., Weingartner, H., Ludlow, C. L., Cudahy, E. A., & Wehry, S. (1981). Qualitative analysis of scopolamine-induced amnesia. *Psychopharmacology, 74*, 74–80.

Callahan, C. M., Hendrie, H. C., & Tierney, W. M. (1995). Documentation and evaluation of cognitive impairment in elderly primary care patients. *Annals of Internal Medicine, 122*(6), 422–429.

Callicott, J. H., Bertolino, A., Mattay, V. S., Langheim, F. J. P., Duyn, J., Coppola, R. et al. (2000). Physiological dysfunction of the dorsolateral prefrontal cortex in schizophrenia revisited. *Cerebral Cortex, 10*, 1078–1092.

Callicott, J. H., Mattay, V. S., Bertolino, A., Finn, K., Coppola, R., Frank, J. A. et al. (1999). Physiological characteristics of capacity constraints in working memory as revealed by functional MRI. *Cerebral Cortex, 9*(1), 20–26.

Calvo, M. G., Eysenck, M. W., Ramos, P. M., & Jimenez, A. (1994). Compensatory reading strategies in test anxiety. *Anxiety, Stress and Coping, 7*, 99–116.

Cammarota, M., Bernabeu, R., de Stein, M. L., Izquierdo, I., & Medina, J. H. (1998). Learning-specific, time-dependent increases in hippocampal Ca^{2+}/calmodulin-dependent protein kinase II activity and AMPA GluR1 subunit immunoreactivity. *European Journal of Neuroscience, 10*, 2669–2676.

Cammarota, M., Izquierdo, I., Wolfram, C., de Stein, M. L., Bernabeu, R., Jerusalinsky, D. et al. (1995). Inhibitory avoidance training induces rapid and selective changes in ^{3}H-AMPA binding in the rat hippocampal formation. *Neurobiology of Learning and Memory, 64*, 257–264.

Camp, C. J., Bird, M. J., & Cherry, K. E. (2000). Retrieval strategies as a rehabilitation aid for cognitive loss in pathological aging. In R. D. Hill, L. Bäckman, & A. Stigsdotter Neely (Eds.), *Cognitive rehabilitation in old age* (pp. 224–248). Oxford: Oxford University Press.

Camp, C. J., Foss, J. W., Stevens, A. B., & O'Hanlon, A. M. (1996). Improving prospective memory task performance in persons with Alzheimer's disease. In M. Brandimonte, G. O. Einstein, & M. A. McDaniel (Eds.), *Prospective memory: Theory and applications* (pp. 351–367). Mahwah, NJ: Lawrence Erlbaum Associates Inc.

Camp, C. J., Markley, R. P., & Kramer, J. J. (1983). Spontaneous use of mnemonics by elderly individuals. *Educational Gerontology, 9*, 57–71.

Camp, C. J., & McKitrick, L. A. (1992). Memory intervention in Alzheimer's type dementia populations: Methodological and theoretical issues. In R. L. West & J. D. Sinnott (Eds.), *Everyday memory and aging: Current research and methodology* (pp. 155–172). New York: Springer-Verlag.

Campodonico, J. R., Codori, A. M., & Brandt, J. (1996). Neuropsychological stability over two years in asymptomatic carriers of the Huntington's disease mutation. *Journal of Neurology, Neurosurgery and Psychiatry, 61*, 621–624.

Cansino, S., Ruiz, A., & Lopez-Alonso, V. (1999). What does the brain do while playing scrabble?: ERPs associated with a short-long term memory task. *International Journal of Psychophysiology, 31*, 261–274.

Cantani, M., Cherubini, A., Howard, R., Tarducci, R., Pelliccioli, G., Piccirrilli, M. et al. (2001). ^{1}H-MR spectoscopy differentiates mild cognitive impairment from normal brain aging. *NeuroReport, 12*(11), 2315–2317.

Caplan, D., & Waters, G. S. (1994). Syntactic processing in sentence comprehension by aphasic patients under dual-task conditions. *Brain and Language, 47*, 397–399.

Caplan, L., Chedru, F., Lhermitte, F., & Mayman, C. (1981). Transient global amnesia and migraine. *Neurology, 31*(9), 1167–1170.

Cappa, S. F., & Pasquali, P. (1998). Verbal short-term memory and repetition in aphasics. *Brain and Language, 65*, 230–233.

Caprio-Prevette, M. D., & Fry, P. S. (1996). Memory enhancement program for community-based older adults: Development and evaluation. *Experimental Aging Research, 22*, 281–303.

Caramazza, A. (1989). Cognitive neuropsychology and rehabilitation: An unfulfilled promise? In X. Seron & Deloche (Eds.), *Cognitive approaches in neuropsychological rehabilitation* (pp. 383–398). Hillsdale, NJ: Lawrence Erlbaum Associates Inc.

Cardenas, D. D., McLean, A. Jr., Farrel-Roberts, L., Baker, L., Brooke, M., & Haselkorn, J. (1994). Oral physostigmine and impaired memory in adults with brain injury. *Brain Injury, 8*(7), 579–587.

Carmelli, D., Swan, G. E., Reed, T., Miller, B., Wolf, P. A., Jarvik, G. P. et al. (1998). Midlife cardiovascular risk factors, ApoE, and cognitive decline in elderly male twins. *Neurology, 50*(6), 1580–1585.

Carrillo, M. C., Gabrieli, J. D. E., Hopkins, R. O., McGlinchey-Berroth, R., Fortier, C. B., Kesner,

R. P. et al. (2001). Spared discrimination and impaired reversal eyeblink conditioning in patients with temporal lobe amnesia. *Behavioral Neuroscience, 115*(6), 1171–1179.

Case, R., Kurland, M. D., & Goldberg, J. (1982). Operational efficiency and the growth of short-term memory span. *Journal of Experimental Child Psychology, 33*, 386–404.

Casey, B. J., Cohen, J. D., Jezzard, P., Turner, R., Noll, D. C., Trainor, R. J. et al. (1995). Activation of prefrontal cortex in children during a non-spatial working memory task with functional MRI. *Neuroimage, 2*, 221–229.

Caspari, I., Parkinson, S. R., LaPointe, L. L., & Katz, R. C. (1998). Working memory and aphasia. *Brain and Cognition, 37*, 205–223.

Cassel, J. C., & Jeltsch, H. (1995). Serotonergic modulation of cholinergic function in the central nervous system: Cognitive implications. *Neuroscience, 69*, 1–41.

Cassel, J-C., Jeltsch, H., Neufang, B., Lauth, D., Szabo, B., & Jackisch, R. (1995). Downregulation of muscarinic- and 5-HT$_{1B}$-mediated modulation of [^{3}H]acetylcholine release in hippocampal slices of rats with fimbria-fornix lesions and intrahippocampal grafts of septal origin. *Brain Research, 704*, 153–166.

Castellano, C. (1975). Effects of morphine and heroin on discrimination learning and consolidation in mice. *Psychopharmacology (Berl), 42*, 235–242.

Castellanos, F. X., Giedd, J. N., Eckburg, P., Marsh, W. L., Vaituzis, A. C., Kaysen, D. et al. (1994). Quantitative morphology of the caudate nucleus in attention deficit hyperactivity disorder. *American Journal of Psychiatry, 151*(12), 1791–1796.

Castellanos, F. X., Giedd, J. N., Marsh, W. L., Hamburger, S. D., Vaituzis, A. C., Dickstein, D. P. et al. (1996). Quantitative brain magnetic resonance imaging in attention-deficit hyperactivity disorder. *Archives of General Psychiatry, 53*(7), 607–616.

Cavanaugh, J. C., & Green, E. E. (1990). I believe, therefore I can: Self-efficacy beliefs in memory aging. In E. A. Lovelace (Ed.), *Aging and cognition: Mental processes, self-awareness and interventions* (pp. 189–230). Amsterdam: North Holland.

Cavanaugh, J. C., & Murphy, N. Z. (1986). Personality and metamemory performance in younger and older adults. *Educational Gerontology, 12*, 385–394.

Cave, C., & Squire, L. R. (1992). Intact verbal and non-verbal short-term memory following damage to the human hippocampus. *Hippocampus, 2*, 151–163.

Celcis, P., Agnies, A., Cardebat, D., Demonet, J. F., Ousset, P. J., & Puel, M. (1997). Age related cognitive decline: A clinical entity? A longitudinal study of cerebral blood flow and memory performance. *Journal of Neurology, Neurosurgery and Psychiatry, 62*(6), 601–608.

Cellucci, T., Evans, W. J., Cattaruzza, C., & Carter, S. (2001). Stability and correlates of the California verbal learning test for a sample of normal elderly persons. *Psychological Reports, 88*, 171–174.

Cenacchi, T., Bertoldin, T., Farina, C., Fiori, M. G., Crepaldi, G., Azzini, C. F. et al. (1993). Cognitive decline in the elderly: A double-blind, placebo-controlled multicenter study on efficacy of phosphatidylserine administration. *Aging-Clinical & Experimental Research, 5*(2), 123–133.

Cermak, L. S. (1984). The episodic-semantic distinction in amnesia. In L. R. Squire & N. Butters (Eds.), *Neuropsychology of memory*. New York: Guilford Press.

Cermak, L. S., Stiassny, D., & Uhly, B. (1984). Reconstructive retrieval deficits in Broca's aphasia. *Brain and Language, 21*, 95–104.

Chaikelson, J. S., & Schwartzman, A. E. (1983). Cognitive changes with aging in schizophrenia. *Journal of Consulting and Clinical Psychology, 39*, 25–30.

Chalfonte, B. L., & Johnson, M. K. (1996). Feature memory and binding in young and older adults. *Memory & Cognition, 24*, 403–416.

Chan, A. S., Butters, N., Paulsen, J. S., Salmon, D. P., Swenson, M. R., & Maloney, L. T. (1993). An assessment of the semantic network in patients with Alzheimer's disease. *Journal of Cognitive Neuroscience, 5*, 254–261.

Chan, A. S., Choi, A., Chiu, H., & Lam, L. (2003). Clinical validity of the Chinese version of Mattis Dementia Rating Scale in differentiating dementia of Alzheimer's type in Hong Kong. *Journal of the International Neuropsychological Society*, *9*(1), 45–55.

Chan, A. S., Ho, Y-C., & Cheung, M-C. (1998). Music training improves verbal memory. *Nature*, *396*(6707), 128.

Chan, P. H. (1996). Role of oxidants in ischemic brain damage. *Stroke*, *27*, 1124–1129.

Channon, S. (1997). Impairments in deductive reasoning and working memory in Parkinson's disease. *Behavioural Neurology*, *10*, 1–8.

Channon, S., Baker, J. E., & Robertson, M. M. (1982). Working memory in clinical depression: An experimental study. *Psychological Medicine*, *23*, 593–597.

Chan-Palay, V., & Asan, E. (1989). Quantitation of catecholamine neurons in the locus ceruleus in human brains of normal young and older adults in depression. *Journal of Comparative Neurology*, *287*, 357–372.

Chapin, K., McCown, J., Vann, L., Kenney, I., & Youssef, I. (1992). Activation and facilitation in the lexicon of schizophrenics. *Schizophrenia Research*, *6*, 251–255.

Chappell, J., McMahan, R., Chiba, A., & Gallagher, M. (1998). A re-examination of the role of basal forebrain cholinergic neurons in spatial working memory. *Neuropharmacology*, *37*, 481–487.

Charney, D. S., Deutch, A. Y., Krystal, J. H., Southwick, S. M., & Davis, M. (1993). Psychobiologic mechanisms of posttraumatic stress disorder. *Archives of General Psychiatry*, *50*, 294–299.

Chawla, S., Hardingham, G. E., Quinn, D. R., & Bading, H. (1998). CBP: A signal-regulated transcriptional coactivator controlled by nuclear calcium and CaM kinase IV. *Science*, *281*(5382), 1505–1509.

Chelune, G., & Baer, R. (1986). Developmental norms for the Wisconsin Card Sorting Test. *Journal of Clinical and Experimental Neuropsychology*, *8*, 219–228.

Chen, G., Chen, K. S., Knox, J., Inglis, J., Bernard, A., Martin, S. J. et al. (2000). A learning deficit related to age and beta-amyloid plaques in a mouse model of Alzheimer's disease. *Nature*, *408*(6815), 975–979.

Chen, L., Bao, S., Lockard, J. M., Kim, J. J., & Thompson, R. F. (1996). Impaired classical eyeblink conditioning in cerebellar-lesioned and Purkinje cell degeneration (pcd) mutant mice. *Journal of Neuroscience*, *16*(8), 2829–2838.

Chen, P., Ratcliff, G., Belle, S. H., Cauley, J. A., DeKosky, S. T., & Ganguli, M. (2001). Patterns of cognitive decline in presymptomatic Alzheimer disease. *Archives of General Psychiatry*, *58*, 853–858.

Cherrier, M. M., Mendez, M. F., Dave, M., & Perryman, K. M. (1999). Performance on the Rey–Osterrieth Complex Figure Test in Alzheimer disease and vascular dementia. *Neuropsychiatry, Neuropsychology and Behavioral Neurology*, *12*(2), 95–101.

Cherry, K. E., & Stadler, M. A. (1995). Implicit learning of a nonverbal sequence in younger and older adults. *Psychology and Aging*, *10*, 379–394.

Chertkow, H., & Bub, D. (1990). Semantic memory loss in dementia of the Alzheimer's type: What do various measures measure? *Brain*, *113*, 397–417.

Chesnut, R. M., Marshall, S. B., Piek, J., Blunt, B. A., Klauber, M. R., & Marshall, L. F. (1993). Early and late systemic hypotension as a frequent and fundamental source of cerebral ischemia following severe brain injury in the Traumatic Coma Data Bank. *Acta Neurochirurgica—Supplementum*, *59*, 121–125.

Chey, J., Lee, J., Kim, Y-S., Kwon, S-M., & Shin, Y-M. (2002). Spatial working memory span, delayed response and executive function in schizophrenia. *Psychiatry Research*, *110*, 259–271.

Cho, Y. H., Beracochea, D., & Jaffard, R. (1993). Extended temporal gradient for the retrograde and anterograde amnesia produced by ibotenate cortex lesions in mice. *Journal of Neuroscience*, *13*, 1759–1766.

Christensen, H., Hadzi-Pavlovic, D., & Jacob, P. (1991). The psychometric differentiation of dementia from normal aging: A meta-analysis. *Psychological Assessment*, *3*, 147–155.

Christensen, H., Kopelman, M. D., Stanhope, N., Lorentz, L., & Owen, P. (1998). Rates of forgetting in Alzheimer dementia. *Neuropsychologia, 36*, 547–557.

Christensen, H., Maltby, N., Jorm, A. F., Creasey, H., & Broe, G. A. (1992). Cholinergic "blockade" as a model of the cognitive deficits in Alzheimer's disease. *Brain, 115*(6), 1681–1699.

Christianson, S. A. (Ed.). (1991). *Handbook of emotion and memory.* Hillsdale, NJ: Lawrence Erlbaum Associates Inc.

Chu, L. W., Chiu, K. C., Hui, S. L., Yu, G. K. K., Tsui, W. J. C., & Lee, P. W. H. (2000). The reliability and validity of the Alzheimer's disease assessment scale cognitive subscale (ADAS–Cog) among the elderly Chinese in Hong Kong. *Annals Academy of Medicine Singapore, 29*, 474–485.

Chu, S., & Downes, J. J. (2000). Long live Proust. The odour-cued autobiographical memory bump. *Cognition, 75*, B41–B50.

Chu, Y., Cochran, E. J., Bennett, D. A., Mufson, E. J., & Kordower, J. H. (2001). Down-regulation of trKA mRNA within nucleus basalis neurons in individuals with mild cognitive impairment and Alzheimer's disease. *The Journal of Comparative Neurology, 437*, 296–307.

Cicerone, K. D. (2002). Remediation of "working attention" in mild traumatic brain injury. *Brain Injury, 16*(3), 185–195.

Ciompi, L., & Muller, C. (1976). *Lebensweg und Alter der Schizophrenen, Eine katamnestiche Langzeitstudie bis ins Senium.* Berlin: Springer.

Clare, L., McKenna, P. H., Mortimer, A. H., & Baddeley, A. D. (1993). Memory in schizophrenia: What is impaired and what is preserved. *Neuropsychologia, 31*, 1225–1241.

Clare, L., Wilson, B. A., Breen, K., & Hodges, J. R. (1999). Errorless learning of face–name associations in early Alzheimer's disease. *Neurocase, 5*, 37–46.

Clare, L., Wilson, B. A., Carter, G., Green, K., Gosses, A., & Hodges, J. R. (2000a). Intervening with everyday memory problems in dementia of Alzheimer type: An errorless learning approach. *Journal of Clinical and Experimental Neuropsychology, 22*, 132–146.

Clare, L., Wilson, B. A., Emslie, H., Tate, R., & Watson, P. (2000b). Adapting the Rivermead Behavioural Memory Test extended version (RBMT–E) for people with restricted mobility. *British Journal of Clinical Psychology, 39*, 363–369.

Clark, K. B., Krahl, S. E., Smith, D. C., & Jensen, R. A. (1995). Post-training unilateral vagal stimulation enhances retention performance in the rat. *Neurobiology of Learning and Memory, 63*, 213–216.

Clark, K. B., Naritoku, D. K., Smith, D. C., Browning, R. A., & Jensen, R. A. (1999). Enhanced recognition memory following vagus nerve stimulation in human subjects. *Nature Neuroscience, 2*, 94–98.

Cleland, P. G., Saunders, M., & Rosser, R. (1981). An unusual case of visual perseveration. *Journal of Neurology, Neurosurgery and Psychiatry, 44*, 226–263.

Cloitre, M., & Leibowitz, M. R. (1991). Memory bias in panic disorder: An investigation of the cognitive avoidance hypothesis. *Cognitive Therapy and Research, 15*, 371–386.

Clyman, R. B. (1991). The procedural organization of emotions: A contribution from cognitive science to the psychoanalytic theory of therapeutic action. *Journal of the American Psychoanalytic Associations, 39*(suppl.), 349–382.

Coblentz, J. M., Mattis, S., Zingesser, L. H., Kassofs, S. S., Wisniewski, H. M., & Katzman, R. (1973). Presenile dementia. *Archives of Neurology, 29*, 299–308.

Cockburn, J. (1995). Task interruption in prospective memory: A frontal lobe function? *Cortex, 31*, 87–97.

Cockburn, J., & Smith, P. T. (1989). *Rivermead Behavioural Memory Test (Suppl. 3): Elderly people.* Reading, UK: Thames Valley Test Company.

Cockburn, J., Wilson, B. A., & Baddeley, A. D. (1990). Assessing everyday memory in patients with dysphasia. *British Journal of Clinical Psychology, 29*, 353–360.

Cockburn, J., Wilson, B., Baddeley, A., & Hiorns, R. (1990). Assessing everyday memory in patients with dysphasia. *British Journal of Clinical Psychology, 29*(4), 353–360.

Coen, R. F., Kirby, M., Swanwick, G. R. J., Maguire, C. P., Walsh, J. B., Coakley, D. et al.

(1997). Distinguishing between patients with depression or very mild Alzheimer's disease using the delayed-word recall test. *Dementia and Geriatric Cognitive Disorders, 8,* 244–247.

Coen, R. F., Swanwick, G. R. J., Maguire, C., Kirby, M., Lawlor, B. A., Walsh, J. B. et al. (1996). Memory impairment in Alzheimer's disease: Replication and extension of the delayed word recall (DWR) test. *Irish Journal of Psychological Medicine, 13*(2), 55–58.

Coffey, C. E., Wilkinson, W. E., Parashos, I. A., Siady, S. A. R., Sullivan, R. J., Patterson, L. J. et al. (1992). Quantitative cerebral anatomy of the aging human brain. A cross-sectional study using magnetic resonance imaging. *Neurology, 42,* 527–536.

Cohen, E. L., & Wurtman, R. J. (1976). Brain acetylcholine: Control by dietary choline. *Science, 191,* 561–562.

Cohen, G., & Faulkner, D. (1988). Lifespan changes in autobiographical memory. In M. M. Gruneberg, P. E. Morris, & R. N. Sykes (Eds.), *Practical aspects of memory: Current research and issues: Vol. 1. Memory in everyday life* (pp. 277–282). Chichester, UK. Wiley.

Cohen, H., Bouchard, S., Scherzer, P., & Whitaker, H. (1994a). Language and verbal reasoning in Parkinson's disease. *Neuropsychiatry, Neuropsychology and Behavioral Neurology, 7,* 166–175.

Cohen, J. D., Forman, S. D., Braver, T. S. et al. (1994b). Activation of the prefrontal cortex in a nonspatial working memory task with functional MRI. *Human Brain Mapping, 1,* 293–304.

Cohen, J. D., Perlstein, W. M., Braver, T. S., Nystrom, L. E., Noll, D. C., Jonides, J. et al. (1997). Temporal dynamics of brain activation during a working memory task. *Nature, 386*(6625), 604–611.

Cohen, N. J., & Eichenbaum, H. (1993). *Memory, amnesia and the hippocampal system.* Cambridge, MA: MIT Press.

Cohen, N. J., Ryan, J., Hunt, C., Romine, L., Wszalek, T., & Nash, C. (1999). Hippocampal system and declarative (relational) memory: Summarizing the data from functional neuroimaging studies. *Hippocampus, 9*(1), 83–98.

Cohen, N. J., & Squire, L. R. (1980). Preserved learning and retention of pattern-analyzing skill in amnesia: Dissociation of knowing how and knowing that. *Science, 210,* 207–210.

Cohen, R. M., Weingartner, H., Smallberg, S. A., Pickard, D., & Murphy, D. L. (1982). Effort and cognition in depression. *Archives of General Psychiatry, 39,* 593–597.

Cole, S. O. (1986). Effects of benzodiazepines upon acquisition and performance: A critical assessment. *Neuroscience Biobehavioral Reviews, 10,* 265–272.

Collette, F., Salmon, E., Van der Linden, M., Chicherio, C., Belleville, S., Degueldre, C. et al. (1999a). Regional brain activity during tasks devoted to the central executive of working memory. *Cognitive Brain Research, 7,* 411–417.

Collette, F., Van der Linden, M., Bechet, S., & Salmon, E. (1999b). Phonological loop and central executive functioning in Alzheimer's disease. *Neuropsychologia, 37,* 905–918.

Collins, A., & Loftus, E. (1975). A spreading activation theory of semantic processing. *Psychological Review, 82,* 407–428.

Colombo, M., D'Amato, M. R., Rodman, H. R., & Gross, C. G. (1990). Auditory association cortex lesions impair auditory short-term memory in monkeys. *Science, 247,* 336–338.

Coltheart, M. (1991). Cognitive psychology applied to the treatment of acquired language disorders. In P. Martin (Ed.), *Handbook of behavior therapy and psychological science: An integrative approach* (pp. 216–226). New York: Pergamon Press.

Coman, E., Moses, J. A. Jr., Kraemer, H. C., Friedman, L., Benton, A. L., & Yesavage, J. (1999). Geriatric performance on the Benton Visual Retention Test: Demographic and diagnostic considerations. *The Clinical Neuropsychologist, 13*(1), 66–77.

Commissaris, R. L. (1993). Conflict behaviors as animal models for the study of anxiety. In F. van Haaren (Ed.), *Methods in behavioral pharmacology* (pp. 443–474). Amsterdam: Elsevier.

Connor, D. J., Salmon, D. P., Sandy, T. J., Galasko, D., Hansen, L. A., & Thal, L. J. (1998). Cognitive profiles of autopsy-confirmed Lewy body variant vs pure Alzheimer disease. *Archives of Neurology, 55*(7), 994–1000.

Connor, L. T., Dunlosky, J. & Hertzog, C. (1997). Age-related differences in absolute but not relative metamemory accuracy. *Psychology and Aging, 12*(1), 50–71.

Constans, J. I., Foa, E. B., Franklin, M. E., & Mathews, A. (1995). Memory for actual and imagined events in OC checkers. *Behaviour Research and Therapy, 33*, 665–671.

Conway, M. A. (1992). A structural model of autobiographical memory. In M. A. Conway, D. C. Rubin, H. Spinnler, & W. A. Wagenaar (Eds.), *Theoretical perspectives on autobiographical memory* (pp. 167–193). Dordrecht: Kluwer Academic Publishers.

Cooper, J. A., Saga, H. J., Jordan, N., Harvey, N. S., & Sullivan, E. V. (1991). Cognitive impairment in early untreated Parkinson's disease and its relationship to motor disability. *Brain, 114*, 2095–2122.

Corkin, S. (1968). Acquisition of motor skill after bilateral medial temporal-lobe excision. *Neuropsychologia, 6*, 255–265.

Corkin, S. (1998). Functional MRI for studying episodic memory in aging and Alzheimer's disease. *Geriatrics, 53*, S13–S15.

Corkin, S., Amaral, D. G., Gonzalez, R. G., Johnson, K. A., & Hyman, B. T. (1997). HM's medial temporal-lobe lesion: Findings from MRI. *Journal of Neuroscience, 17*, 3964–3979.

Cornblatt, B., & Keilp, J. (1994). Impaired attention, genetics, and the pathophysiology of schizophrenia. *Schizophrenia Bulletin, 20*, 31–46.

Conklin, H. M., Curtis, C. E., Katsanis, J., & Lacono, W. G. (2000). Verbal working memory impairment in schizophrenia patients and their first-degree relatives: Evidence from the digit span task. *American Journal of Psychiatry, 157*, 275–277.

Conway, M. A., Turk, D. A., Miller, S. L., Logan, J., Nebes, R. D., Meltzer, C. C. et al. (1999). A positron emission tomography (PET) study of autobiographical memory retrieval. *Memory, 7*, 679–702.

Corey-Bloom, J., Anand, R., & Veach, J., for the ENA 713 B352 Study Group. (1998). A randomized trial evaluating the efficacy and safety of ENA 713 (rivastigmine tartrate), a new acetylcholinesterase inhibitor, in patients with mild to moderate severe Alzheimer's disease. *International Journal of Geriatric Psychopharmacology, 1*, 55–65.

Cornell, D. G., Saurez, R., & Berent, S. (1984). Psychomotor retardation in melancholic and non-melancholic depression: Cognitive and motor components. *Journal of Abnormal Psychology, 932*, 150–157.

Costall, B., & Naylor, R. J. (1997). Neuropharmacology of 5-HT3 receptors ligands. In H. G. Baumgarten & M. Gother, (Eds.), *Serotonergic neurons and 5-HT receptors in the CNS* (pp. 409–438). Berlin: Springer.

Coull, J. T., Middleton, H. C., Robbins, T. W., & Sahakian, B. J. (1995). Contrasting effects of clonidine and diazepam on tests of working memory and planning. *Psychopharmacology, 120*(3), 311–321.

Courbon, P., & Fail, G. (1927). Syndrome d'illusion Frégoli et schizophrénie. *Bulletin Society Clinical Médicopsychologique Mentale, 90*, 1–12.

Courbon, P., & Tusques, J. (1932). Illusions d'intermétamorphose et de la charme. *Annals Médicopsychologique, 90*, 401–406.

Courtney, S. M., Petit, L., Maisog, J., Ungerleider, L., & Haxby, J. V. (1998). An area specialized for spatial working memory in human frontal cortex. *Science, 279*, 1347–1351.

Courtney, S. M., Ungerleider, L. G., Keil, K., & Haxby, J. V. (1997). Transient and sustained activity in a distributed neural system for human working memory. *Nature, 386*, 608–611.

Cowan, N. (1988). Evolving conceptions of memory storage, selective attention, and their mutual constraints within the human information processing system. *Psychological Bulletin, 104*, 163–191.

Cowan, N. (1995). *Attention and memory: An integrated framework*. Oxford: Oxford University Press.

Cowan, N. (1996). Short term memory, working memory and their importance in language processing. *Topics in Language Disorder, 17*, 1–18.

Coyle, J. T., Price, D. L., & DeLong, M. R. (1983). Alzheimer's disease: A disorder of cortical cholinergic innervation. *Science*, *219*, 1184–1190.

Craft, S., Asthana, S., Newcomer, J. W., Wilkinson, C. W., Matos, I. T., Baker, L. D. et al. (1999). Enhancement of memory in Alzheimer disease with insulin and somatostatin, but not glucose. *Archives of General Psychiatry*, *56*, 1135–1140.

Craig, A. M., Blackstone, C. D., Huganir, R. L., & Banker, G. (1993). The distribution of glutamate receptors in cultured rat hippocampal neurons: Postsynaptic clustering of AMPA-selective subunits. *Neuron*, *10*, 1055–1068.

Craik, F. I. M. (1977). Age differences in human memory. In J. E. Birren & K. W. Schaie (Eds.), *Handbook of the psychology of ageing*. Van Nostrand Reinhold.

Craik, F. I. M. (1983). On the transfer of information from temporary to permanent memory. *Philosophical transactions of the Royal Society of London, Series B*, *302*, 341–359.

Craik, F. I. M. (1986). A functional account of age differences in memory. In F. Klix & H. Hagendorf (Eds.), *Human memory and cognitive capabilities: Mechanisms and performance* (pp. 409–422). New York: Elsevier Science.

Craik, F. I. M. (2002). Levels of processing: Past, present . . . and future?. *Memory*, *10*(5–6), 305–318.

Craik, F. I. M., Byrd, M., & Swanson, J. M. (1987). Patterns of memory loss in three elderly samples. *Psychology and Aging*, *2*, 79.

Craik, F. I. M., & Dirkx, E. (1992). Age-related differences in three tests of visual imagery. *Psychology and Aging*, *7*, 661–665.

Craik, F. I. M., Govoni, R., Naveh-Benjamin, M., & Anderson, N. D. (1996). The effects of divided attention on encoding and retrieval processes in human memory. *Journal of Experimental Psychology: General*, *125*, 159–180.

Craik, F. I. M., & Jennings, J. M. (1992). Human memory. In F. I. M. Craik & T. A. Salthouse (Eds.), *The handbook of aging and cognition*. Hillsdale, NJ: Lawrence Erlbaum Associates Inc.

Craik, F. I. M., Morris, L. W., Morris, R. G., & Loewen, E. R. (1990). Relations between source amnesia and frontal lobe functioning. *Psychology and Aging*, *5*, 148–151.

Craik, F. I. M., Moscovitch, M., & McDowd, J. M. (1994). Contributions of surface and conceptual information to performance on implicit and explicit memory tasks. *Journal of Experimental Psychology: Learning, Memory and Cognition*, *20*, 864–875.

Cranberg, L. D., Filley, C. M., Hart, E. J., & Alexander, M. P. (1987). Acquired aphasia in childhood: Clinical and CT investigations. *Neurology*, *37*, 1165–1172.

Crayhon, R. (1998). *The carnitine miracle*. New York: M. Evans & Co.

Cronin-Golomb, A., Corkin, S., & Growdonm, J. H. (1994). Impaired problem-solving in Parkinson's disease: Impact of a set-shifting deficit. *Neuropsychologia*, *32*, 579–593.

Crook, T., Petrie, W., Wells, C., & Massari, D. C. (1992). Effects of phosphatidylserine in Alzheimer's disease. *Psychopharmacology Bulletin*, *28*, 61–66.

Crook, T. H., Bartus, R. T., Ferris, S. H., Whitehouse, P., Cohen, G. D., & Gershon, S. (1986). Age-associated memory impairment: Proposed diagnostic criteria and measures of clinical change—Report of a National Institute of Mental Health work group. *Developmental Neuropsychology*, *2*, 261–276.

Crook, T. H., & Larrabee, G. J. (1992). Normative data on a self-rating scale for evaluating memory in everyday life. *Archives of Clinical Neuropsychology*, *7*, 41–51.

Crook, T. H., Youngjohn, J. R., & Larrabee, G. J. (1992). Multiple, equivalent test forms in a computerized, everyday memory battery. *Archives of Clinical Neuropsychology*, *7*, 221–232.

Crook, T. H., III & Larrabee, G. J. (1990). A self-rating scale for evaluating memory in everyday life. *Psychology and Aging*, *5*, 48–57.

Crosson, B. (1992). *Subcortical functions in language and memory*. New York/London: Guilford Press.

Crosson, B., Novack, T. A., Trenerry, M. R., & Craig, P. L. (1988). California Verbal Learning Test (CVLT) performance in severely head-injured and neurologically normal adult males.

Journal of Clinical and Experimental Neuropsychology, 10, 754–768.

Crovitz, H. F., Harvey, M. T., & Horn, R. W. (1979). Problems in the acquisition of imagery mnemonics: Three brain-damaged cases. *Cortex, 15,* 225–234.

Crowder, R. G. (1989). Modularity and dissociations in memory systems. In H. L. Roediger III & F. I. M. Craik (Eds.), *Varieties of memory and consciousness: Essays in honor of Endel Tulving* (pp. 271–294). Hillsdale, NJ: Lawrence Erlbaum Associates Inc.

Crowell, G. F., Stump, D. A., Biller, J., McHenry, L. C., & Toole, J. F. (1984). The transient global amnesia–migraine connection. *Archives of Neurology, 41*(1), 75–79.

Crum, R., Anthony, J., Bassett, S. S., & Folstein, M. F. (1993). Population-based norms for the Mini-Mental State Examination by age and education level. *JAMA, 269,* 2386–2391.

Cruz-Morales, S. E., Quirarte, G. L., Diaz del Guante, M. A., & Prado-Alcala, R. A. (1993). Effects of GABA antagonists on inhibitory avoidance. *Life Sciences, 53,* 1325–1330.

Cuenod, C. A., Denys, A., Michot, J. L., Jehenson, P., Forette, F., Kaplan, D., Syrota, A., et al. (1993). Amygdala atrophy in Alzheimer's disease. An in vivo magnetic resonance imaging study. *Archives of Neurology, 50*(9), 941–945.

Cummings, J. L. (1988). Intellectual impairment in Parkinson's disease: Clinical, pathologic, and biochemical correlates. *Journal of Geriatric Psychiatry & Neurology, 1*(1), 24–36.

Cummings, J. L. (1990). Introduction. In J. L. Cummings (Eds.), *Subcortical dementia.* New York: Oxford University Press.

Cummings, J. L. (1993). Frontal-subcortical circuits and human behavior. *Archives of Neurology, 50,* 873–880.

Cummings, J. L. (2000). Cholinesterase inhibitors: A new class of psychotropic compounds. *American Journal of Psychiatry, 157,* 4–15.

Cummings, J. L., & Benson, D. F. (1984). Subcortical dementia: Review of an emerging concept. *Archives of Neurology, 41,* 874–879.

Cummings, J. L., Donohue, J. A., & Brooks, R. L. (2000). The relationship between donepezil and behavioural disturbances in patients with

Alzheimer's disease. *American Journal of Geriatric Psychiatry, 8*(Suppl 2), 134–140.

Cummings, J. L., & Duchen, L. W. (1981). Kluver-Bucy syndrome in Pick's disease: Clinical and pathological correlations. *Neurology, 31,* 1415–1422.

Curran, H. V. (1991). Benzodiazepines, memory and mood: A review. *Psychopharmacology, 105,* 1–8.

Curran, H. V., & Birch, B. (1991). Differentiating the sedative, psychomotor and amnesic effects of benzodiazepines: A study with midazeolam and the benzodiazepine antagonist, flumazenil. *Psychopharmacology, 1039,* 519–523.

Curran, H. V., Bond, A., O'Sullivan, G., Bruce, M., Marks, I., Lelliot, P. et al. (1994). Memory functions, alprazolam and exposure therapy: A controlled longitudinal study of patients with agoraphobia and panic disorder. *Psychological Medicine, 24,* 969–976.

Curran, H. V., & Gorenstein, C. (1993). Differential effects of lorazepam and oxazepam on priming. *International Clinical Psychopharmacology, 8,* 37–42.

Curran, H. V., Pooviboonsuk, P., Dalton, J., & Lader, M. H. (1998). Differentiating the effects of centrally acting drugs on arousal and memory: An event-related potentail study of scopolamine, lorazepam and diphenhydramine. *Psychopharmacology, 135,* 27–36.

Curran, H. V., Sakulsriprong, M., & Lader, M. (1988). Antidepressants and human memory: An investigation of four drugs with different sedative and anticholinergic profiles. *Psychopharmacology, 95,* 520–527.

Curran, H. V., Schifano, F., & Lader, M. (1991). Models of memory dysfunction? A comparison of the effects of scopolamine and lorazepam on memory, psychomotor performance and mood. *Psychopharmacology, 103,* 83–90.

Curran, H. V., Schiwy, W., & Lader, M. (1987). Differential amnesic effects of benzodiazepines: A dose-response comparison of two drugs with similar elimination half-lives. *Psychopharmacology, 92,* 358–364.

Curran, T., Schacter, D. L., Norman, K. A., & Gallucio, L. (1997). False recognition after a right frontal lobe infarction: Memory for general and specific information. *Neuropsychologia, 35,* 1035–1049.

Cutler, N. R., & Sramek, J. J. (2001). Review of the next generation of Alzheimer's disease therapeutics: Challenges for drug development. *Progress in Neuropsychopharmacology and Biological Psychiatry, 25,* 27–57.

Daigneault, S., & Braun, C. M. J. (1993). Working memory and the self-ordered pointing task: Further evidence of early prefrontal decline in normal aging. *Journal of Clinical and Experimental Neuropsychology, 15,* 881–895.

Dalla Barba, G., Frasson, E., Mantovan, M. C., Gallo, A., & Denes, G. (1996). Semantic and episodic memory in aphasia. *Neuropsychologia, 34*(5), 361–367.

Damasio, A. R. (1994). *Descarte's error: Emotion, reason and the human brain.* New York: Grosset, Putnam.

Damasio, A. R., Graff-Radford, N. R., Eslinger, P. J., Damasio, H., & Kassel, N. (1985). Amnesia following basal forebrain lesions. *Archives of Neurology, 42,* 263–271.

Damasio, A. R., Tranel, D., & Damasio, H. C. (1991). Somatic markers and the guidance of behavior: Theory and preliminary testing. In H. S. Levin, H. M. Eisenberg, & A. L. Benton (Eds.), *Frontal lobe function and dysfunction* (pp. 217–229). New York: Oxford University Press.

Damasio, H., & Damasio, A. R. (1980). The anatomical basis of conduction aphasia. *Brain, 103,* 337–350.

Damasio, H., Grabowski, T. J., Tranel, D., Hichwa, R. D., & Damasio, A. R. (1996). A neural basis for lexical retrieval. *Nature, 380,* 499–505.

d'Amato, T., Saoud, M., Triboulet, P., Bertaud, J. P., & Dalery, J. (1998). Vulnérabilité à la schizophrénie. I: Nature familiale des indicateurs neuropsychologiques. *L'Encéphale, XXIV,* 442–448.

Daneman, M., & Carpenter, P. A. (1980). Individual differences in working memory and reading. *Journal of Verbal Learning and Verbal Behavior, 19,* 450–466.

Daneman, M., & Carpenter, P. A. (1983). Individual differences in integrating information between and within sentences. *Journal of Experimental Psychology: Learning, Memory and Cognition, 9,* 561–584.

Daneman, M., & Merikle, P. M. (1996). Working memory and language comprehension: A meta-analysis. *Psychonomic Bulletin & Review, 3,* 422–433.

Danion, J. M., Kauffmann-Muller, F., Grange, D., Zimmermann, M. A., & Greth, P. (1995). Affective valence of words, explicit and implicit memory in clinical depression. *Journal of Affective Disorders, 34*(3), 227–234.

Danion, J. M., Rizzo, L., & Bruant, A. (1999). Functional mechanisms underlying impaired recognition memory and conscious awareness in patients with schizophrenia. *Archives of General Psychiatry, 56,* 639–644.

Danion, J. M., Zimmermann, M. A., Willard-Schroeder, D., Grange, D., & Singes, L. (1989). Diazepam induces a dissociation between explicit and implicit memory. *Psychopharmacology, 99,* 238–243.

Dannenbaum, S. E., Parkinson, S. R., & Inman, V. W. (1988). Short-term forgetting: Comparisons between patients with dementia of the Alzheimer type, depressed and normal elderly. *Cognitive Neuropsychology, 5,* 213–233.

Dantzer, R., & Bluthé, R. M. (1993). Vasopressin and behavior: From memory to olfaction. *Regulatory Peptides, 45,* 121–125.

Dash, P. K., Hochner, B., & Kandel, E. R. (1990). Injection of the cAMP-responsive element into the nucleus of *Aplysia* sensory neurons blocks long-term facilitation. *Nature, 345,* 718–721.

Daum, I., & Ackermann, H. (1994). Dissociation of declarative and nondeclarative memory after bilateral thalamic lesions: A case report. *International Journal of Neuroscience, 75,* 153–165.

Daum, I., Channon, S., & Gray, J. A. (1992). Classical conditioning after temporal lobe lesions in man: Sparing of simple discrimination and extinction. *Behavioural Brain Research, 52*(2), 159–165.

Daum, I., Channon, S., Polkey, C. E., & Gray, J. A. (1991). Classical conditioning after temporal lobe lesions in man: Impairment in conditional discrimination. *Behavioral Neuroscience, 105*(3), 396–408.

Daum, I., Schugens, M. M., Ackermann, H., Lutzenberger, W., Dichgans, J., & Birbaumer, N. (1993). Classical conditioning after cerebellar lesions in humans. *Behavioral Neuroscience, 107*, 748–756.

Davenport, L., Brown, F. F., Fein, G., & Van Dyke, C. (1988). A fifteen-item modification of the Fuld Object-Memory evaluation: Preliminary data from healthy middle-aged adults. *Archives of Clinical Neuropsychology, 3*, 345–349.

David, K. L., & Yamamura, H. I. (1978). Cholinergic under-activity in human memory disorders. *Life Sciences, 23*, 1729–1734.

Davies, K. G., Bell, B. D., Dohan, F. C., Schweitzer, J. B., & Hermann, B. P. (1999). Prediction of presence of hippocampal sclerosis from intracarotid amobarbital procedure memory asymmetry scores and epilepsy onset age. *Epilepsy Research, 33*(2–3), 117–123.

Davis, C. A., & Ball, H. E. (1996). Effects of age on comprehension of complex sentences in adulthood. *Journal of Speech and Hearing Research, 32*, 422–433.

Davis, H., Cohen, A., Gandy, M., Colombo, P., VanDusseldorp, G., Simolke, N. et al. (1990). Lexical priming deficits as a function of age. *Behavioral Neuroscience, 104*, 288–297.

Davis, H. P., & Squire, L. R. (1984). Protein synthesis and memory. *Psychological Bulletin, 96*, 518–559.

Davis, K. L., Davis, B. M., Greenwald, B. S., Mohs, R. C., Mathe, A. A., Johns, C. A. et al. (1986). Cortisol and Alzheimer's disease, I: Basal studies. *American Journal of Psychiatry, 143*(3), 300–305.

Davis, M. (1994). The role of the amygdala in emotional learning. *International Review in Neurobiology, 36*, 225–66.

Davis, M., Hitchcock, J. M., & Rosen, J. B. (1987). Anxiety and the amygdala: Pharmacological and anatomical analysis of the fear-potentiated startle response. In G. Bower (Ed.), *The psychology of learning and motivation*. Orlando FL: Academic Press.

Davis, P. J. (1999). Gender differences in autobiographical memory for childhood emotional experiences. *Journal of Personality and Social Psychology, 76*(3), 498–510.

Davis, S., Butcher, S. P., & Morris, R. G. M. (1992). The NMDA receptor antagonist D-2-amino-5-phosphonopentanoate (D-AP5) impairs spatial learning and LTP in vivo at intracerebral concentrations comparable to those that block LTP in vitro. *The Journal of Neuroscience, 12*(1), 21–34.

Davis, S., & Laroche, S. (1998). A molecular biological approach to synaptic plasticity and learning. *Comptes Rendes de l'Academie des Sciences Serie III—Sciences de la Vie-Life Sciences, 321*, 97–107.

Davis, S., Vanhoutte, P., Pagès, C., Caboce, J., & Laroche, S. (2000). The MAPK/ERK cascade targets both ERK-1 and cAMP response element-binding protein to control long-term potentiation-dependent gene expression in the dentate gyrus in vivo. *The Journal of Neuroscience, 20*(12), 4563–4572.

Dawe, B., Procter, A., & Phillipot, M. (1992). Concepts of mild memory impairment in the elderly and their relationship to dementia: A review. *International Journal of Geriatric Psychiatry, 7*, 473–479.

DeBettignies, B. H., Mahurin, R. K., & Pirozzolo, F. J. (1990). Insight for impairment in independent living skills in Alzheimer's disease and multi-infarct dementia. *Journal of Clinical and Experimental Neuropsychology, 12*, 355–363.

Deckersbach, T., Otto, M. W., Savage, C. R., Baer, L., & Jenike, M. A. (2000). The relationship between semantic organization and memory in obsessive-compulsive disorder. *Psychotherapy and Psychosomatics, 69*, 101–107.

Dehlin, O., Hedenrud, B., Jansson, P., & Norgard, J. (1985). A double-blind comparison of alaproclate and placebo in the treatment of patients with senile dementia. *Acta Psychiatrica Scandinavica, 71*, 190–196.

de Hoz, L., Knox, J., & Morris, R. G. (2003). Longitudinal axis of the hippocampus: Both septal and temporal poles of the hippocampus support water maze spatial learning depending on the training protocol. *Hippocampus, 13*(5), 587–603.

Deisseroth, K., Heist, E. K., & Tsien, R. W. (1998). Translocation of calmodulin to the nucleus supports CREB phosphorylation in hippocampal neurons. *Nature, 392*(6672), 198–202.

de Kloet, E. R. (1991). Brain corticosteroid receptor balance and homeostatic control. *Frontiers in Neuroendocrinology, 12*(2), 95–164.

de Kloet, E. R., Oitzl, M. S., & Joels, M. (1999). Stress and cognition: Are corticosteroids good or bad guys? *Trends in Neuroscience, 22,* 422–426.

De Kloet, E. R., & Veldhuis, H. D. (1984). Adrenocortical hormone action on the brain. In A. Lajtha (Ed.), *Handbook of neurochemistry, Vol. VIII* (pp. 47–91). New York: Pergamon Press.

DeKosky, S. T., Ikonomovic, M. D., Styren, S. D., Beckett, L., Wisniewski, S., Bennett, D. A. et al. (2002). Upregulation of choline acetyltransferase activity in hippocampus and frontal cortex of elderly subjects with mild cognitive impairment. *Annals of Neurology, 51,* 145–155.

Delacourte, A., David, J. P., Sergeant, N., Buee, L., Wattez, A., Vermersch, P. et al. (1999). The biochemical pathway of neurofibrillary degeneration in aging and Alzheimer's disease. *Neurology, 52*(6), 1158–1165.

de Leon, M. J., Golomb, J., George, A. E., Convit, A., Tarshish, C. Y., McRae, T. et al. (1993). The radiologic prediction of Alzheimer disease: The atrophic hippocampal formation. *American Journal of Neuroradiology, 14*(4), 897–906.

Delis, D. C., Kramer, J. H., Kaplan, E., & Ober, B. A. (1987). *California Verbal Learning Test.* New York: The Psychological Corporation.

Delis, D. C., Kramer, J. H., Kaplan, E., & Ober, B. A. (1994). *The California Verbal Learning Test–Children's Version.* New York: The Psychological Corporation.

Delis, D. C., & Lucas, J. A. (1996). Memory. In B. S. Fogel, R. B. Schiffer, & S. M. Rao (Eds.), *Neuropsychiatry* (pp. 365–399). Baltimore: Williams & Wilkins.

Delis, D. C., Masserman, P. J., Butters, N., Salmon, D. P., Kramer, J. H., & Cermak, L. (1991a). Profiles of demented and amnesic patients on the California Verbal Learning Test: Implications for the assessment of memory disorders. *Psychological Assessment, 3,* 19–26.

Delis, D. C., Masserman, P. J., Kaplan, E., McKee, R., Kramer, J. H., & Gettman, D. (1991b).

Alternate form of the California Verbal Learning Test: Development and reliability. *Clinical Neuropsychologist, 5,* 154–162.

Dellasega, C., & Morris, D. (1993). The MMSE to assess the cognitive state of elders. *Journal of Neuroscience Nursing, 25*(2), 147–152.

DeLuca, J., & Diamond, B. J. (1995). Aneurysm of the anterior communicating artery: A review of neuroanatomical and neuropsychological sequelae. *Journal of Clinical and Experimental Neuropsychology, 17,* 100–121.

DeLuca, J., Schultheis, M. T., Madigan, N. K., Christodoulou, C., & Averill, A. (2000). Acquisition versus retrieval deficits in traumatic brain injury: Implications for memory rehabilitation. *Archives of Physical Medicine and Rehabilitation, 81,* 1327–1333.

Delwaide, P. J., Gyselynck-Mambourg, A. M., Hurlet, A., & Ylieff, M. (1986). Double-blind randomized controlled study of phosphatidylserine in demented patients. *Acta Neurologica Scandinavica, 73,* 136–140.

Demb, J. B., Desmond, J. E., Wagner, A. D., Vaidya, C. J., Glover, G. H., & Gabrieli, J. D. (1995). Semantic encoding and retrieval in the left inferior prefrontal cortex: A functional MRI study of task difficulty and process specificity. *Journal of Neuroscience, 15,* 5870–5878.

Dempster, F. N. (1992). The rise and fall of the inhibitory mechanisms. Toward a unified theory of cognitive development and aging. *Developmental Review, 12,* 45–75.

Denman, S. B. (1984). *Neuropsychology memory.* Charleston, SC: S. B. Denman.

DePaulo, J. R., Folstein, M. F., & Gordon, B. (1980). Psychiatric screening on a neurological ward. *Psychological Medicine, 10,* 125–132.

Deptula, D., Singh, R., Goldsmith, S., Block, R., Bagne, C. A., & Pomara, N. (1990). Equivalence of five forms of the selective reminding test in young and elderly subjects. *Psychological Reports, 67,* 1287–1295.

De Renzi, E. (1986). Prosopagnosia in two patients with CT scan evidence of damage confined to the right hemisphere. *Neuropsychologia, 24,* 385–389.

De Renzi, E., Faglioni, P., & Previdi, P. (1977). Spatial memory and hemisphere locus of lesion. *Cortex, 13,* 424–433.

De Renzi, E., & Lucchelli, F. (1993). Dense retrograde amnesia, intact learning capability and abnormal forgetting rate: A consolidation deficit? *Cortex, 29,* 449–466.

De Renzi, E., Perani, D., Carlesimo, G. A., Silveri, M. C., & Fazio, F. (1994). Prosopagnosia can be associated with damage confined to the right hemisphere—An MRI and PET study and a review of the literature. *Neuropsychologia, 32,* 893–902.

Derrer, D. S., Howieson, D. B., Mueller, E. A., Camicioli, R. M., Sexton, G., & Kaye, J. A. (2001). Memory testing in dementia: How much is enough. *Journal of Geriatric Psychiatry Neurology, 14,* 1–6.

Derry, P. A., & Kuiper, N. A. (1981). Schematic processing and self-reference in clinical depression. *Journal of Abnormal Psychology, 90,* 286–297.

Desimone, R., Miller, E. K., Chelazzi, L. et al. (1995). Multiple memory systems in the visual cortex. In M. S. Gazzaniga (Ed.), *The cognitive neurosciences.* Cambridge, MA: MIT Press.

Desmond, J. E., Sum, J. M., Wagner, A. D., Demb, J. B., Shear, P. K., Glover, G. H. et al. (1995). Functional MRI measurement of language lateralization in Wada-tested patients. *Brain, 118*(Pt 6), 1411–1419.

D'Esposito, M. (2000). Functional neuroimaging of working memory. In R. Cabeza & A. Kingstone (Eds.), *Handbook of functional neuroimaging of cognition.* Cambridge, MA: MIT Press.

D'Esposito, M., Postle, B. R., Ballard, D., & Lease, J. (1999). Maintenance versus manipulation of information held in working memory: An event-related fMRI study. *Brain & Cognition, 41*(1), 66–86.

Des Rosiers, G., Hodges, J., & Berrios, G. (1995). The neuropsychological differentiation of patients with very mild Alzheimer's disease and/or major depression. *Journal of the American Geriatric Society, 43,* 1256–1263.

DeSteno, D., & Salovey, P. (1997). Structural dynamism in the concept of self: A flexible model for a malleable concept. *Review of General Psychology, 1,* 389–409.

Devinsky, O. (1995). Cognitive and behavioral effects of antiepileptic drugs. *Epilepsia, 36,* S46–S65.

De Vreese, L. P., & Neri, M. (1999). Ecological impact of combined cognitive training programs (CPT) and drug treatment (ChE-I) in Alzheimer's disease. *International Psychogeriatrics, 11*(Suppl.), S187.

De Vreese, L. P., Neri, M., Fioravanti, M., Belloi, L., & Zanetti, O. (2001). Memory rehabilitation in Alzheimer's disease: A review of progress. *International Journal of Geriatric Psychiatry, 16,* 794–809.

De Wied, D., Bohus. B., & van Wimersma Greidanus, T. J. B. (1975). Memory deficit in rats with hereditary diabetes insipidus. *Brain Research, 85,* 152–156.

De Wied, D., & Croiset, G. (1991). Stress modulation of learning and memory processes. *Methods and Achievements in Experimental Pathology, 15,* 167–199.

Diamond, D. M., Bennett, M. C., Fleshner, M., & Rose, G. M. (1992). Inverted-U relationship between the level of peripheral corticosterone and the magnitude of hippocampal primed burst potentiation. *Hippocampus, 2*(4), 421–430.

Dick, J. P., Guiloff, R. J., Stewart, A., Blackstock, J., Bielawska, C., Paul, E. A. et al. (1984). Mini-Mental State Examination in neurological patients. *Journal of Neurology, Neurosurgery and Psychiatry, 47,* 496–499.

Dickinson-Anson, H., Mesches, M. H., Coleman, K., & McGaugh, J. L. (1993). Bicuculline administered into the amygdala blocks benzodiazepine-induced amnesia. *Behavioral & Neural Biology, 60*(1), 1–4.

Dikmen, S. S., Machamer, J. E., Winn, H. R., & Tempkin, N. R. (1995). Neuropsychological outcome at 1-year post head injury. *Neuropsychology, 9,* 80–90.

Dirson, S., Bouvard, M., Cottraux, J., & Martin, R. (1996). Visual memory impairment in patients with obsessive-compulsive disorder. *Journal of Neuropsychiatry, 6,* 22–31.

Disterhoft, J. F., Coulter, D. A., & Alkon, D. L. (1986). Conditioning-specific membrane changes of rabbit hippocampal neurons measured in vitro. *Proceedings of the National Academy of Science of the United States of America, 83,* 2733–2737.

Dixit, N. K., Gerton, B. K., Khon, P., Meyer-Lindenberg, A., & Berman, K. F. (2000). Age-related changes in rCBF activation during an "N-Back" working memory paradigm occur prior to age 50. *Neuroimage, 5*(2): S94.

Dixon, R. A., Hultsch, D. F., & Hertzog, C. (1988). The metamemory in adulthood (MIA). *Psychopharmacology Bulletin, 24,* 671–688.

Dobkin, B. H., & Hanlon, R. (1993). Dopamine agonist of anterograde amnesia from a mediobasal forebrain injury. *Annals of Neurology, 33*(3), 313–316.

Dolan, R. J., & Fletcher, P. C. (1997). Dissociating prefrontal and hippocampal function in episodic memory encoding. *Nature, 388,* 582–585.

Dolan, R. J., & Fletcher, P. F. (1999). Encoding and retrieval in human medial temporal lobes: An empirical investigation using functional magnetic resonance imaging (fMRI). *Hippocampus, 9,* 25–34.

Dolan, M. P., & Norton, J. C. (1977). A programmed training technique that uses reinforcement to facilitate acquisition and retention in brain-damaged patients. *Journal of Clinical Psychology, 33,* 4967–5001.

Donaldson, W. (1999). The role of decision processes in remembering and knowing. *Memory and Cognition, 26,* 523–533.

Doody, R. S., Stevens, J. C., Beck, C., Dubinsky, R. M., Kaye, J. A., Gwythes, L., et al. (2001). Practice parameter: Management of dementia (an evidence-based review). *Neurology, 56,* 1154–1166.

Dorrego, M. F., Sabe, L., Cuerva, A. G., Kuzis, G., Tiberti, C., Boller, F., et al. (1999). Remote memory in Alzheimer's disease. *The Journal of Neuropsychiatry and Clinical Neurosciences, 11,* 490–497.

Double, K. L., Halliday, G. M., McRitchie, D. A., Reid, W. G., Hely, M. A., & Morris, J. G. (1996). Regional brain atrophy in idiopathic Parkinson's disease and diffuse Lewy body disease. *Dementia, 7*(6), 304–313.

Drachman, D. A. (1977). Memory and cognitive function in man: Does the cholinergic system have a specific role? *Neurology, 27,* 783–790.

Drachman, D. A., & Leavitt, J. (1974). Human memory and the cholinergic system. *Archives of Neurology, 30,* 113–121.

Drachman, D. A., & Sahakian, B. J. (1979). Effects of cholinergic agents on human learning and memory. In A. Barbeau, J. H. Growdon, & R. J. Wurtman (Eds.), *Nutrition and the brain. Vol. 5* (pp. 351–366). New York: Raven Press.

Drane, D. L., Loring, D. W., Lee, G. P., & Meador, K. J. (1998). Trial-length sensitivity of the Verbal Selective Reminding Test to lateralized temporal lobe impairment. *The Clinical Neuropsychologist, 12,* 68–73.

Driscoll, E. J., Smilack, Z. H., Lightbody, P. M., & Fiorucci, R. D. (1972). Sedation with intravenous diazepam. *Journal of Oral Surgery, 30,* 332–343.

Duka, T. (1991). Birectional activity of benzodiazepine-receptor ligands in cognitive functions in humans. In M. Briley & S. E. File (Eds.), *New concepts in anxiety* (pp. 440–457). Boston, MA: Macmillan.

Dunn, A. J. (1980). Neurochemistry of learning and memory: An evaluation of recent data. *Annual Review of Psychology, 31,* 434.

Dubois, B., Boller, F., Pillon, B., & Agid, Y. (1991). Cognitive deficits in Parkinson's disease. In F. Boller & J. Grafman (Eds.), *Handbook of neuropsychology, Vol. 5* (pp. 195–240). Amsterdam: Elsevier.

Dubois, B., Defontaines, B., Deweer, B., Malapani, C., & Pillon, B. (1995). Cognitive and behavioral changes in patients with focal lesions of the basal ganglia. In W. J. Weiner & A. E. Lang (Eds.), *Behavioral neurology of movement disorders, Advances in neurology, Vol. 65,* New York: Raven Press.

Dufouil, C., Clayton, D., Brayne, C., Chi, L. Y., Dening, T. R., Paykel, E. S. et al. (2000). Population norms for the MMSE in the very old. Estimates based on longitudinal data. *Neurology, 55,* 1609–1613.

Duncan, J. (1986). Disorganization of behavior after frontal lobe damage. *Cognitive Neuropsychology, 3,* 271–290.

Dupont, R. M., Jernigan, T. L., Butters, N., Delis, D. C., Hesselink, J. R., Heindel, W. et al. (1990). Subcortical abnormalities in bipolar affective disorder using magnetic resonance imaging. *Archives of General Psychiatry, 47,* 55–59.

Dywan, J., & Jacoby, L. L. (1990). Effects of aging on source monitoring: Differences in susceptibility to false fame. *Psychology and Aging, 5,* 379–387.

Dywan, J., Segalowitz, S., & Arsenault, A. (2002). Electrophysiological response during source memory decisions in older and younger adults. *Brain and Cognition, 49,* 322–340.

Dywan, J., Segalowitz, S. J., & Williamson, L. (1994). Source monitoring during name recognition in older adults. Psychometric and electrophysiological correlates. *Psychology and Aging, 9,* 568–577.

Eadie, K., & Shum, D. (1995). Assessment of visual memory: A comparison of Chinese characters and geometric figures as stimulus materials. *Journal of Clinical and Experimental Neuropsychology, 17,* 731–739.

East, S. J., & Garthwaite, J. (1991). NMDA receptor activation in rat hippocampus induces cyclic GMP formation through the L-arginine nitric oxide pathway. *Neuroscience Letters, 123,* 17–19.

Ebbinghaus, H. (1885/1909). Memory: A contribution to experimental psychology. (H. R. Ruger & C. Bussenius, Trans). New York: Teachers College. [Original work published 1885.]

Ebly, E., Hogan, D. B., & Parhad, I. M. (1995). Cognitive impairment in the nondememted elderly. *Archives of Neurology, 52,* 612–619.

Edelstyn, N. M. J., Riddoch, M. J., Oyebode, F., Humphreys, G. W., & Forde, E. (1996). Visual processing in patients with Frégoli syndrome. *Cognitive Neuropsychiatry, 1,* 103–124.

Eglen, R. M., Wong, E. H. F., Dumuis, A., & Bockaert, J. (1995). Central 5-HT$_4$ receptors. *Trends in Pharmacological Sciences, 16,* 391–398.

Eichenbaum, H. (1997). Declarative memory: Insights from cognitive psychology. *Annunciation Review Psychology, 48,* 547–572.

Eichenbaum, H. (2000). A cortical-hippocampal system for declarative memory. *Nature Reviews Neuroscience, 1*(1), 41–50.

Eichenbaum, H., Dudchenko, P., Wood, E., Shapiro, M., & Tanila, H. (1999). The hippocampus, memory and place cells: Is it spatial memory or a memory space? *Neuron, 23,* 209–226.

Eichenbaum, H., Fagan, A., & Cohen, N. J. (1986). Normal olfactory discrimination learning set and facilitation of reversal learning after medial-temporal damage in rats: Implications for an account of preserved learning abilities in amnesia. *Journal of Neuroscience, 6*(7), 1876–1884.

Eichenbaum, H., & Harris, K. (2000). Toying with memory in the hippocampus. *Nature Neuroscience, 3*(3), 205–206.

Einstein, G. O., & McDaniel, M. A. (1990). Normal aging and prospective memory. *Journal of Experimental Psychology: Learning, Memory and Cognition, 16,* 717–726.

Einstein, G. O., McDaniel, M. A., Richardson, S. L., Guynn, M. J., & Cunfer, A. R. (1995). Aging and prospective memory: Examining the influences of self-limited retrieval processes. *Journal of Experimental Psychology: Learning, Memory & Cognition, 21,* 996–1007.

Eisen, M. L., & Goodman, G. S. (1998). Trauma, memory and suggestibility in children. *Development and Psychopathology, 10,* 717–738.

Elbert, T., Pantev, C., Wienbruch, C., Rockstroh, B., & Taub, E. (1995). Increased cortical representation of the fingers of the left hand in string players. *Science, 270*(5234), 305–307.

Elias, M. F., Wolf, P. A., D'Agostino, R. B., Cobb, J., & White, L. R. (1993). Untreated blood pressure level is inversely related to cognitive functioning: The Framingham Study. *American Journal of Epidemiology, 138*(6), 353–364.

Elliot, R., Sahakian, B. J., McKay, A. P. et al. (1996). Neuropsychological impairments in unipolar depression: The influence of perceived failure on subsequent performance. *Psychological Medicine, 26,* 975–989.

Ellis, R. J., & Oscar-Berman, M. (1989). Alcoholism, aging and functional cerebral asymmetries. *Psychological Bulletin, 106,* 128–147.

Ellis, R. W. (1911). Neurologic aspects of hyperventilation syndrome. *Seminars in Neurology*, *15*, 115–125.

Elwood, R. W. (1991). The Wechsler Memory Scale—Revised. Psychometric characteristics and clinical application. *Neuropsychology Review*, *2*, 179–201.

Elwood, R. W. (1995). The California Verbal Learning Test: Psychometric characteristics and clinical application. *Neuropsychology Review*, *5*, 173–201.

Emilien, G., Beyreuther, K., Masters, C. L., & Maloteaux, J. M. (2000). Prospects for pharmacological intervention in Alzheimer disease. *Archives of Neurology*, *57*, 454–459.

Engen, T., & Ross, B. M. (1973). Long-term memory for odors with and without verbal descriptors. *Journal of Experimental Psychology*, *100*, 221–227.

Engle, R. W., Kane, M. J., & Tuholski, S. W. (1999a). Individual differences in working memory capacity and what they tell us about controlled attention, general fluid intelligence, and functions of the prefrontal cortex. In A. Miyake & P. Shah (Eds.), *Models of working memory: Mechanisms of active maintenance and executive control*. New York: Cambridge University Press.

Engle, R. W., Tuholski, S. W., Laughlin, J. E., & Conway, A. R. A. (1999b). Working memory, short-term memory, and general fluid intelligence: A latent variable approach. *Journal of Experimental Psychology: General*, *128*, 309–331.

Epstein, J. N., Conners, C. K., Erhardt, D., March, J. S., & Swanson, J. M. (1997). Asymmetrical hemispheric control of visual-spatial attention in adults with attention deficit hyperactivity disorder. *Neuropsychology*, *11*(4), 467–473.

Ergis, A. M., Van der Linden, M., Boller, F., & Deweer, B. (1995). Memoire visuo-spatiale à court terme et à long terme dans la maladie d'Alzheimer débutante. *Neuropsychologica Latina*, *1*, 18–25.

Ergis, A. M., Van der Linden, M., & Deweer, B. (1998). Priming for new associations in normal aging and in mild dementia of the Alzheimer type. *Cortex*, *34*, 357–373.

Erkinjuntti, T., Laaksonen, R., Sulkava, R., Syrjalainen, R., & Palo, J. (1986). Neuropsychological differentiation between normal aging, Alzheimer's disease and vascular dementia. *Acta Neurologica Scandinavica*, *74*, 393–403.

Ernst, M., Zametkin, A. J., Matochik, J. A., Liebenauer, L., Fitzgerald, G. A., & Cohen, R. M. (1994). Effects of intravenous dextroamphetamine on brain metabolism in adults with attention-deficit hyperactivity disorder (ADHD). Preliminary findings. *Psychopharmacology Bulletin*, *30*(2), 219–225.

Eslinger, P. J., & Damasio, A. R. (1986). Preserved motor learning in Alzheimer's disease: Implications for anatomy and behavior. *Journal of Neuroscience*, *6*, 3006–3009.

Espino, D. V., Lichtenstein, M. J., Palmer, R. F., & Hazuda, H. P. (2001). Ethnic differences in Mini-Mental State Examination (MMSE) scores: Where you live makes a difference. *JAGS*, *49*, 538–548.

European Pentoxifylline Multi-Infarct Dementia Study. (1996). *European Neurology*, *36*(5), 315–321.

Eustache, F., Desgranges, B., Giffard, B., de la Sayette, V., & Baron, J-C. (2000). Entorhinal cortex disruption causes memory deficit in early Alzheimer's disease as shown by PET. *NeuroReport*, *12*(4), 683–685.

Eustache, F., Desgranges, B., Laville, P., Guillery, B., Lalevée, C., Schaeffer S. et al. (1999). Episodic memory in transient global amnesia: Encoding, storage or retrieval deficit? *Journal of Neurology, Neurosurgery and Psychiatry*, *66*, 148–154.

Eustache, F., Desgranges, B., Petit-Taboué, M. C., de la Sayette, V., Piot, V., Sablé, C. et al. (1997). Transient global amnesia: Implicit/explicit memory dissociation, and PET assessment of brain perfusion and oxygen metabolism in the acute stage. *Journal of Neurology, Neurosurgery and Psychiatry*, *63*, 357–367.

Evans, D. A., Beckett, L. A., Albert, M. S., Hebert, L. E., Scherr, P. A., Funkenstein, H. H. et al. (1993). Level of education and change in cognitive function in a community population of older persons. *Annals of Epidemiology*, *3*(1), 71–77.

Evans, J. J., Emslie, H., & Wilson, B. A. (1998). External cueing systems in the rehabilitation of executive impairments of action. *Journal of the International Neuropsychological Society*, 4, 399–408.

Evans, J. J., Heggs, A. J., Antoun, N., & Hodges, J. R. (1995). Progressive prosopagnosia with selective right temporal lobe atrophy: A new syndrome? *Brain*, 118, 1–13.

Everett, J., Lavoie, K., Gagnon, J-F., & Gosselin, N. (2001). Performance of patients with schizophrenia on the Wisconsin Card Sorting Test (WCST). *Journal of Psychiatry and Neuroscience*, 26(2), 123–130.

Eysenck, M. W. (1982). *Attention and arousal*. Berlin: Springer-Verlag.

Eysenck, M. W., & Calvo, M. G. (1992). Anxiety and performance: The processing efficiency theory. *Cognition and Emotion*, 6, 409–434.

Fadda, F., & Rossetti, Z. L. (1998). Chronic ethanol consumption: From neuroadaptation to neurodegeneration. *Progress in Neurobiology*, 56(4), 385–431.

Faden, A. I. (1996). Pharmacological treatment of central nervous trauma. *Pharmacological Toxicology*, 78, 12–17.

Fama, R., Sullivan, E. V., Shear, P. K., Stein, M., Yesavage, J. A., Tinklenberg, J. R. et al. (2000). Extent, pattern, and correlates of remote memory impairment in Alzheimer's disease and Parkinson's disease. *Neuropsychology*, 14(2), 265–276.

Fang, J. C., Hinrichs, J. V., & Ghoneim, M. M. (1987). Diazepam and memory: Evidence for spared memory function. *Pharmacology Biochemistry and Behavior*, 28, 347–352.

Fanselow, M. S., & Kim, J. J. (1994). Acquisition of contextual Pavlovian fear conditioning is blocked by application of an NMDA receptor antagonist D, L-2-amino-5-phosphonovaleric acid to the basolateral amygdala. *Behavioral Neuroscience*, 108, 210–212.

Fanselow, M. S., & LeDoux, J. E. (1999). Why we think plasticity underlying Pavlovian fear conditioning occurs in the basolateral amygdala. *Neuron*, 23(2), 229–232.

Fastenau, P. S. (1996). Development and preliminary standardization of the "Extended Complex Figure Test" (ECFT). *Journal of Clinical and Experimental Neuropsychology*, 18, 63–76.

Fastenau, P. S., Bennett, J. M., & Denburg, N. L. (1996). Application of psychometric standards to scoring system evaluation: Is "new" necessarily "improved"? *Journal of Clinical and Experimental Neuropsychology*, 18, 462–472.

Fastenau, P. S., Denburg, N. L., & Hufford, B. J. (1999). Adult norms for the Rey-Osterrieth complex Figure Test and for supplemental recognition and matching trials from the extended complex figure test. *The Clinical Neuropsychologist*, 13(1), 30–47.

Fastenau, P. S., & Fisk, J. L. (1997). Use of memory scores to predict side of resection in epilepsy surgery (Abstract). *Journal of Neuropsychiatry and Clinical Neurosciences*, 9, 168–169.

Felsenstein, K. M. (2000). Abeta modulation: The next generation of AD therapeutics. *Annals of the New York Academy of Sciences*, 920, 269–273.

Fendt, M., & Fanselow, M. S. (1999). The neuroanatomical and neurochemical basis of conditioned fear. *Neuroscience and Biobehavioral Reviews*, 23, 743–760.

Fernandes, M. A., & Moscovitch, M. (2000). Divided attention and memory: Evidence of substantial interference effects at retrieval and encoding. *Journal of Experimental Psychology: General*, 129(2), 155–176.

Ferraro, F. R., Balota, D. A., & Connor, T. (1993). Implicit memory and the formation of new associations in nondemented Parkinson's disease individuals and individuals with senile dementia of the Alzheimer type: A serial reaction time (SRT) investigation. *Brain and Cognition*, 21, 163–180.

Fery, P., Vincent, E., & Brédart, S. (1995). Personal name anomia: A single case study. *Cortex*, 31, 191–198.

Fibiger, H. C. (1991). Cholinergic mechanisms in learning, memory and dementia: A review of recent evidence. *Trends in Neurosciences*, 14, 220–223.

Fiez, J. A., Raichle, M. E., Balota, D. A., Tallal, P., & Petersen, S. E. (1996). PET activation of posterior temporal regions during auditory word presentation and verb generation. *Cerebral Cortex, 6*(1), 1–10.

File, S. E., Sharma, R., & Shaffer, J. (1992). Is lorazepam-induced amnesia specific to the type of memory or to the task used to assess it? *Journal of Psychopharmacology, 6,* 76–82.

Filley, C. M. (1997). Alzheimer's disease in women. *American Journal of Obstetrics and Gynecology, 176,* 1–7.

Filley, C. M., Heaton, R. K., Nelson, L. M., Burks, J. S., & Franklin, G. M. (1989). A comparison of dementia in Alzheimer's disease and multiple sclerosis. *Archives of Neurology, 46,* 157–161.

Fink, G. R., Markowitsch, H. J., Reinkemeier, M., Bruckbauer, T., Kessler, J., & Heiss, W-D. (1996). Cerebral representation of one's own past: Neural networks involved in autobiographical memory. *The Journal of Neuroscience, 16*(13), 4275–4282.

Finkenauer, C., Luminet, O., Gisle, L., El-Ahmadi, A., Van der Linden, M., & Philippot, P. (1998). Flashbulb memories and the underlying mechanisms of their formation: Toward an emotional-integrative model. *Memory & Cognition, 26*(3), 516–531.

Fiore, R. S., Bayer, V. E., Pelech, S. L., Posada, J., Cooper, J. A., & Baraban, J. M. (1993). P42 mitogen-activated protein kinase in brain: Prominent localization in neuronal cell bodies and dendrites. *Neuroscience, 55,* 463–472.

Fischer, W. A., Björklund, A., Chen, K., & Gage, F. H. (1991). NGF improves spatial memory in aged rodents as a funcion of age. *Journal of Neuroscience, 11,* 1889–1906.

Fisher, C. M., & Adams, R. D. (1964). Transient global amnesia. *Acta Neurologica Scandinavica, 40*(Suppl. 9), 1–83.

Fischer, M., Jones, S., & Sacco, R. L. (1994). Prophylactic neuroprotection for cerebral ischemia. *Stroke, 25,* 1075–1080.

Fisher, C. M. (1982). Transient global amnesia: Precipitating activities and other observations. *Archives Neurology, 39*(10), 605–608.

Fisher, N. J., Rourke, B. P., Bieliauskas, L. A., Giordani, B., Berent, S., & Foster, N. L. (1997). Unmasking the heterogeneity of Alzheimer's disease: Case studies of individuals from distinct neuropsychological subgroups. *Journal of Clinical and Experimental Neuropsychology, 19,* 713–754.

Fisk, A. D. (1986). Frequency encoding is not inevitable and is not automatic: A reply to Hasher and Zacks. *American Psychologist, 41,* 215–216.

Fivush, R. (1998). Children's recollections of traumatic events. *Development and Psychopathology, 10,* 699–716.

Fivush, R., Gray, J. T., & Fromhoff, F. A. (1987). Two-year-olds talk about the past. *Cognitive Development, 2,* 393–409.

Fivush, R., & Reese, E. (1992). The social construction of autobiographical memory. In M. A. Conway, D. C. Rubin, H. Spinner, & W. A. Wagenaar (Eds.), *Theoretical perspectives on autobiographical memory* (pp. 115–132). Dordrecht, the Netherlands: Kluwer Academic.

Flemming, K., Goldberg, T. E., Gold, J. M., & Weinberger, D. R. (1995). Verbal working memory dysfunction in schizophrenia—use of Brown-Peterson paradigm. *Psychiatry Research, 56,* 155–161.

Fletcher, P. C., Frith, C. D., Baker, S. C., Shallice, T., Frackowiak, R. S. J., & Dolan, R. J. (1995a). The mind's eye—precuneus activation in memory-related imagey. *Neuroimage, 2,* 195–200.

Fletcher, P. C., Frith, C. D., Grasby, P. M., Shallice, T., Frackowiak, R. S. J., & Dolan, R. J. (1995b). Brain systems for encoding and retrieval of auditory-verbal memory. *Brain, 118,* 401–416.

Fletcher, P. C., Frith, C. D., & Rugg, M. D. (1997). The functional neuroanatomy of episodic memory. *Trends in Neurosciences, 20*(5), 213–218.

Fletcher, P. C., McKenna, P. J., Frith, C. D., Grasby, P. M., Friston, K. J., & Dolan, R. J. (1998). Brain activations in schizophrenia during a graded memory task studied with functional neuroimaging. *Archives of General Psychiatry, 55,* 1001–1008.

Flicker, C., Ferris, S. H., & Reisberg, B. (1991). Mild cognitive impairment in the elderly: Predictors of dementia. *Neurology, 41,* 1006–1009.

Flood, J. F., Farr, U. K., & Morley, J. E. (1998). Age-related changes in septal serotonergic,

GABAergic and glutamatergic facilitation of retention in SAMP8 mice. *Mechanisms of Ageing and Development, 105*, 173–188.

Flood, J. F., Smith, G. E., & Roberts, E. (1988). Dehydroepiandrosterone and its sulfate enhance memory retention in mice. *Brain Research, 447*, 269–278.

Folstein, M. F., Anthony, C., Perhed, I., Duffy, B., & Gruenberg, E. M. (1985). The meaning of cognitive impairment in the elderly. *Journal of the American Geriatrics Society, 33*, 228–235.

Folstein, M. F., & Blysma, F. W. (1994). Non-cognitive symptoms of Alzheimer's disease. In R. D. Terry & R. Katzman (Eds.), *Alzheimer's disease* (pp. 27–40). New York: Raven Press.

Folstein, M. F., Folstein, S. E., & McHugh, P. R. (1975). Mini-Mental State: A practical method for grading the cognitive state of patients for the clinician. *Journal of Psychiatric Research, 12*, 189–198.

Fonlupt, P., Martinet, M., & Pacheco, H. (1985). Effect of CDP-choline on dopamine metabolism in central nervous system. In V. Zappia, E. P. Kennedy, B. I. Nilsson, & P. Galetti (Eds.), *Novel biochemical, pharmacological, and clinical aspects of CDP-choline* (pp. 169–177). New York, Elsevier Science.

Fontaine, F. (1995). *Apprentissage de nouvelles connaissances chez les patients Alzheimer.* Thèse de Doctorat, Département de Psychologie, Université de Montréal.

Fontana, D. J., Daniels, S. E., Henderson, C., Eglen, R. M., & Wong, E. H. F. (1995). Ondansetron improves cognitive performance in the Morris water maze spatial navigation task. *Psychopharmacology, 120*, 409–417.

Foos, P. W., & Sarno, A. J. (1998). Adult age differences in semantic and episodic memory. *Journal of Genetic Psychology, 159*(3), 297–312.

Forette, F., Anand, R., & Gharabawi, G. (1999). A phase II study in patients with Alzheimer's disease to assess the preliminary efficacy and maximum tolerated dose of rivastigmine (Exelon®). *European Journal of Neurology, 6*, 423–429.

Forette, F., Bert, P., Breuil, V. et al. (1992). Therapeutic drug trials and heterogeneity of Alzheimer's disease. In F. Boller, F. Forette, Z. Khatchaturian, et al. (Eds.), *Heterogeneity of Alzheimer's disease: Research and perspectives in Alzheimer's disease* (pp. 67–73). Berlin: Springer-Verlag.

Förstl, H., Hentschel, F., Sattel, H., Geiger-Kabisch, C., Besthorn, C., Czech, C. et al. (1995). Age-associated memory impairment and early Alzheimer's disease. Only time will tell the difference. *Arzneimittel-Forschung, 45*(3A), 394–397.

Foundas, A. L., Eure, K. F., & Seltzer, B. (1996). Conventional MRI volumetric measures of parietal and insular cortex in Alzheimer's disease. *Progress in Neuropsychopharmacology and Biological Psychiatry, 20*, 1131–1144.

Fox, N. C., Warrington, E. K., Seiffer, A. L., Agnew, S. K., & Rossor, M. N. (1998). Presymptomatic cognitive deficits in individuals at risk of familial Alzheimer's disease. A longitudinal prospective study. *Brain, 121*, 1631–1639.

Fowler, K. S., Saling, M. M., Conway, E. L., Semple, J. M., & Louis, W. J. (1995). Computerized delayed matching to sample and paired associate performance in the early detection of dementia. *Applied Neuropsychology, 2*, 72–78.

Fowler, K. S., Saling, M. M., Conway, E. L., Semple, J. M., & Louis, W. J. (1997). Computerized neuropsychological tests in the early detection of dementia: Prospective findings. *Journal of the International Neuropsychological Society, 3*, 139–146.

Franceschi, M., & Canal, N. (1996). AAMI [Letter]. *Neurology, 46*(5), 1490–1491.

Francis, P. T., Palmer, A. M., Snape, M., & Wilcock, G. K. (1999). The cholinergic hypothesis of Alzheimer's disease: A review of progress. *Journal of Neurology, Neurosurgery and Psychiatry, 66*, 137–147.

Frank, D. A., & Greenberg, M. E. (1994). CREB: A mediator of long-term memory from mollusks to mammals. *Cell, 79*, 5–8.

Franke, P., Maier, W., Hain, C., & Klinger, T. (1992). Wisconsin Card Sorting Test: An indicator of vulnerability to schizophrenia. *Schizophrenia Research, 6*, 243–249.

Frankel, F. (1994). The concept of flashbacks in historical perspective. *International Journal of*

Clinical and Experimental Hypnosis, 42, 321–336.

Fredrikson, M., Wik, G., Fischer, H., & Andersson, J. (1995). Affective and attentive neural networks in humans: A PET study of Pavlovian conditioning. *NeuroReport, 7*(1), 97–101.

Freud, S. (1922). *Introductory lectures on psychoanalysis* (1st Ed.) London: Allen & Unwin.

Freud, S. (1905/1953). Three essays on the theory of sexuality. In J. Strachey (Ed.), *The standard edition of the complete psychological works of Sigmund Freud* (Vol. 7, pp. 135–243). London: Hogarth Press [original work published 1905].

Frey, U., Frey, S., Schollmeier, F., & Krug, M. (1996). Influence of actinomycin D, an RNA synthesis inhibitor on rat hippocampal neurons in vivo and in vitro. *Journal of Physiology (London), 490*, 703–711.

Friedland, R. P. (1993). Epidemiology, education, and the ecology of Alzheimer's disease. *Neurology, 43*(2), 246–249.

Friedman, B. H., Thayer, J. F., & Borkovec, T. D. (2000). Explicit memory bias for threat words in generalized anxiety disorder. *Behavior Therapy, 31*, 745–756.

Friedman, H. R., Janas, J. D., & Goldman-Rakic, P. S. (1990). Enhancement of metabolic activity in the diencephalon of monkeys performing working memory tasks: A 2-deoxyglucose study in behaving rhesus monkeys. *Journal of Cognitive Neuroscience, 2*, 18–31.

Friedman, R. (1993). Alzheimer's disease: Clinical features and differential diagnosis. *Neurology, 43*, 45–51.

Friston, K. J. (1998). Imaging neuroscience—principles or MAPS. *Proceedings of the National Academy of Sciences of the United States of America, 95*(3), 796–802.

Frith, C. D., Dowdy, J., Ferrier, I. N., & Crow, T. J. (1985). Selective impairment of associate learning after administration of a centrally acting adrenergic agonist (clonidine). *Psychopharmacology, 87*, 490–493.

Frith, C. D., Richardson, J. T. E., Samuel, M., Crow, T. J., & McKenna, P. J. (1984). The effects of intravenous diazepam and hyoscine upon human memory. *Quarterly Journal of Experimental Psychology, 36*A, 133–144.

Frith, U., & Happe, F. (1994). Autism: Beyond "theory of mind". *Cognition, 50*(1–3), 115–132.

Fromm, D., & Schopflocher, D. (1984). Neuropsychological test performance in depressed patients before and after drug therapy. *Biological Psychiatry, 19*, 55–71.

Fuld, P. A. (1981). *The Fuld Object-Memory Evaluation*. Chicago: Stoeling Instrument.

Fuld, P. A. (1983). Word intrusions as a diagnostic sign in Alzheimer's disease. *Geriatric Medicine Today, 2*, 33–41.

Fuld, P. A., Katzman, R., Davies, P., & Terry, R. D. (1982). Intrusions as a sign of Alzheimer dementia: Chemical and pathological verification. *Annals of Neurology, 11*, 155–159.

Fuld, P. A., Masur, D. M., Blau, A. D., Crystal, H., & Aronson, M. K. (1990). Object-memory evaluation for prospective detection of dementia in normal functioning elderly: Predictive and normative data. *Journal of Clinical and Experimental Neuropsychology, 12*, 520–528.

Fuld, P. A., Muramato, O., Blau, A., Westbrook, L., & Katzman, R. (1988). Cross-cultural and multi-ethnic evaluation by mental status and memory testing. *Cortex, 24*, 511–519.

Furey, M. L., Pietrini, P., Alexander, G. E., Schapiro, M. B., & Horwitz, B. (2000). Cholinergic enhancement improves performance on working memory by modulating the functional activity in distinct brain regions: A positron emission tomography regional cerebral blood flow study in healthy humans. *Brain Research Bulletin, 51*(3), 213–218.

Furey, M. L., Pietrini, P., Haxby, J. V., Alexander, G. E., Lee, H. C., VanMeter, J. et al. (1997). Cholinergic stimulation alters performance and task-specific regional cerebral blood flow during working memory. *Proceedings of the National Academy of Sciences of the United States of America, 94*(12), 6512–6516.

Fuster, J. M. (1995). *Memory in the cerebral cortex*. Cambridge, MA: MIT Press.

Gabrieli, J. D. E., Brewer, J. B., Desmond, J. E., & Glover, G. H. (1997). Separate neural bases of two fundamental memory processes in the human medial temporal lobe. *Science, 276*, 264–266.

Gabrieli, J. D. E., Cohen, N. J., & Corkin, S. (1988). The impaired learning of semantic knowledge following bilateral medial temporal-lobe resection. *Brain and Cognition*, 7, 525–539.

Gabrieli, J. D. E., Desmond, J. E., Demb, J. B., Wagner, A. D., Stone, M. W., Vaidya, C. J. et al. (1996a). Functional magnetic resonance imaging of semantic memory processes in the frontal lobes. *Psychological Science*, 7, 278–283.

Gabrieli, J. D. E., Milberg, W., Keane, M. W., & Corkin, S. (1990). Intact priming of patterns despite impaired memory. *Neuropsychologia*, 28, 417–428.

Gabrieli, J. D. E., Poldrack, R. A., & Desmond, J. E. (1998). The role of left prefrontal cortex in language and memory. *Proceedings of the National Academy of Science of the United States of America*, 95, 906–913.

Gabrieli, J. D. E., Singh, J., Stebbins, G. T., & Goetz, C. G. (1996b). Reduced working memory span in Parkinson's disease: Evidence for the role of frontostriatal system in working and strategic memory. *Neuropsychology*, 10, 321–332.

Gaffan, D. (1993). Additive effects of forgetting and fornix transection in the temporal gradient of retrograde amnesia. *Neuropsychologia*, 31, 1055–1066.

Gaffan, D., & Harrison, S. (1989). Place memory and scene memory: effects of fornix transection in the monkey. *Experimental Brain Research*, 74, 202–212.

Gaffan, E. A., Gaffan, D., & Harrison, S. (1988). Disconnection of the amygdala from visual association cortex impairs visual reward-association learning in monkeys. *Journal of Neuroscience*, 8, 3144–3150.

Gainotti, G., Marra, C., & Villa, G. (2001). A double dissociation between accuracy and time of execution on attentional tasks in Alzheimer's disease and multi-infarct dementia. *Brain*, 124, 731–738.

Gainotti, G., Parlato, V., Monteleone, D., & Carlomagno, S. (1989). Verbal memory disorders in Alzheimer's disease and multi-infarct dementia. *Journal of Neurolinguistics*, 4, 327–345.

Gainotti, G., Parlato, V., Monteleone, D., & Carlomagno, S. (1992). Neuropsychological markers of dementia on visual-spatial tasks: A comparison between Alzheimer's type and vascular forms of dementia. *Journal of Clinical and Experimental Neuropsychology*, 14, 239–252.

Gais, S., Sommer, M., Fischer, S., Perras, B., & Born, J. (2002). Post-trial administration of vasopressin in humans does not enhance memory formation (vasopressin and memory consolidation). *Peptides*, 23, 581–583.

Galasko, D., Corey-Bloom, J., & Thal, L. J., (1991). Monitoring progression in Alzheimer's disease. *Journal of the American Geriatrics Society*, 39, 932–941.

Gallo, J. J., Fulmer, T., Paveza, G., & Reichel, W. (2000). *Handbook of geriatric assessment* (3rd Edition). Gaithersburg, MD: Aspen Publishers.

Gardiner, J. M. (1988). Functional aspects of recollective experience, *Memory and Cognition*, 16, 309–313.

Gardiner, J. M., & Parkin, A. J. (1990). Attention and recollective experience in recognition memory. *Memory and Cognition*, 18, 579–583.

Gardiner, J. M., Ramponin, C., & Richardson-Klavehn, A. (1999). Response deadline and subjective awareness in recognition memory. *Consciousness and Cognition*, 8, 484–496.

Gardiner, J. M., & Richardson-Klavehn, A. (2000). Remembering and knowing. In E. Tulving & F. I. M. Craik (Eds.), *Handbook of memory*. New York: Oxford University Press.

Gash, D., Herman, J., & Thomas, G. (1987). Vasopressin and animal behavior. In D. M. Gash & G. J. Boer (Eds.), *Vasopressin: Principles and properties*. New York: Plenum Press.

Gasquoine, P. G., & Gibbons, T. A. (1994). Lack of awareness of impairment in institutionalised, severely and chronically disabled survivors of traumatic brain injury: A preliminary investigation. *Journal of Head Trauma Rehabil*, 9, 16–24.

Gass, C. S. (1995). A procedure for assessing storage and retrieval on the Wechsler Memory Scale–Revised. *Archives of Clinical Neuropsychology*, 10, 475–487.

Gass, C. S., & Russell, E. W. (1986). Differential impact of brain damage and depression on memory test performance. *Journal of Consulting.*

Gathercole, S. E., & Baddeley, A. D. (1989). Evaluation of the role of phonological STM in the development of vocabulary in children: A longitudinal study. *Journal of Memory and Language, 28,* 200–213.

Gathercole, S. E., & Baddeley, A. D. (1994). *Working memory and language.* Hove, UK: Lawrence Erlbaum Associates Ltd.

Gazzaley, A., Siegel, S., Kordower, J., Mufson, E., & Morrison, J. (1996). Circuit-specific alterations of N-methyl-D-aspartate receptor subunit 1 in the dentate gyrus of aged monkeys. *Proceedings of the National Academy of Science of the United States of America, 93,* 3121–3125.

George, L., Landerman, R., Blazer, D., & Anthony, J. (1991). Cognitive impairment. In L. Robins & D. Regier (Eds.), *Psychiatric disorders in America.* New York: The Free Press.

Gershberg, F. B., & Shimamura, A. P. (1995). Impaired use of organizational strategies in free recall following frontal lobe damage. *Neuropsychologia, 33,* 1305–1333.

Ghaem, O., Mellet, E., Crivello, F., Tzourio, N., Mazoyer, B., Bethoz, A. et al. (1997). Mental navigation along memorized routes activates the hippocampus, precuneus, and insula. *NeuroReport, 8,* 739–744.

Ghoneim, N. M., & Mewaldt, S. P. (1977). Studies on human memory. The interactions of diazepam, scopolamine, and physostigmine. *Psychopharmacology, 52,* 1–6.

Ghoneim, N. M., & Mewaldt, S. P. (1990). Benzodiazepines and human memory: A review. *Anesthesiology, 72,* 926–938.

Giacobini, E., Spiegel, R., Enz, A., Veroff, A. E., & Cutler, N. R. (2002). Inhibition of acetyl- and butyryl-cholinesterase in the cerebrospinal fluid of patients with Alzheimer's disease by rivastigmine: Correlation with cognitive benefit. *Journal of Neural Transmission, 109*(7–8), 1053–1065.

Giambra, L. M., Arenberg, D., Zonderman, A. B., Kawas, C., & Costa, P. T. (1995). Adult lifespan changes in immediate visual memory and verbal intelligence. *Psychology and Aging, 10,* 123–139.

Gianutsos, R., & Gianutsos, J. (1979). Rehabilitating the verbal recall of brain-injured patients by mnemonic training: An experimental demonstration using single-case methodology. *Journal of Clinical Neuropsychology, 1,* 117–135.

Gibbs, R. B. (1994). Estrogen and nerve growth factor-related systems in brain. Effects on basal forebrain cholinergic neurons and implications for learning and memory processes and aging. *Annals of the New York Academy of Sciences, 743,* 165–196; discussion 197–199.

Gilewski, M. J., Zelinski, E. M., & Schaie, K. W. (1990). The Memory Functioning Questionnaire for assessment of memory complaints in adulthood and old age. *Psychology and Aging, 5,* 482–490.

Gilman, S., & Newman, S. (1992). The hypothalamus and limbic system. In J. Manter & A. Gatz (Eds.), *Essentials of clinical neuroanatomy and neurophysiology.* Philadelphia: Davis.

Gilmore, R. O., & Johnson, M. H. (1995). Working memory in infancy: Six-month-olds' performance on two versions of the oculomotor delayed response task. *Journal of Experimental Child Psychology, 59,* 397–418.

Glaser, R. (1987). Thoughts on expertise. In C., Schooler & K. Schaie (Eds.), *Cognitive functioning and social structure over the life course.* New York: Ablex Publishing Co.

Glasgow, R. E., Zeiss, R. A., Barrera, M. Jr., & Lewinsohn, P. M. (1977). Case studies on remediating memory deficits in brain-damaged individuals. *Journal of Clinical Psychology, 33*(4), 1049–1054.

Glenn, M. J., & Mumby, D. G. (1998). Place memory is intact in rats with perirhinal cortex lesions. *Behavioral Neuroscience, 112*(6), 1353–1365.

Glenn, M. J., & Mumby, D. G. (1999). Place memory is intact in rats with perirhinal cortex in two versions of the radial arm maze task. *Behavioral Neuroscience, 113,* 512–524.

Glisky, E. L. (1996). Prospective memory and the frontal lobes. In M. Brandimonte, G. O.

Einstein & M. A. McDaniel (Eds.), *Prospective memory: Theories and applications*.

Glisky, E. L., Rubin, S. R., & Davidson, P. S. R. (2001). Source memory in older adults: An encoding or retrieval problem? *Journal of Experimental Psychology: Learning, Memory, and Cognition, 27*(5), 1131–1146.

Glisky, E. L., Schacter, D. L., & Tulving, E. (1986). Learning and retention of computer-related vocabulary in memory-impaired patients: Method of vanishing cues. *Journal of Clinical and Experimental Neuropsychology, 8*, 292–312.

Glosser, G. (2001). Neurobehavioral aspects of movement disorders. *Neurologic Clinics, 19*, 535–551.

Gloor, P., Olivier, A., Quesney, L. F., Anderman, F., & Horowitz, S. (1982). The role of the limbic system in experiential phenomena of temporal lobe epilepsy. *Annals of Neurology, 12*, 129–144.

Glozman, Zh. M., Artem'ev, D. V., Damulin, I. V., & Kovyazina, M. S. (1994). *Vest, MGU Series 14 (Psychology), 3*, 25–36.

Gobbo, C., Mega, C., & Pipe, M-E. (2002). Does the nature of the experience influence suggestibility? A study of Children's Event Memory. *Journal of Experimental Child Psychology, 81*, 502–530.

Goddard, L., Dritschel, B., & Burton, A. (1996). Role of autobiographical memory in social problem solving and depression. *Journal of Abnormal Psychology, 105*, 609–616.

Gold, J. M., Randolph, C., Carpenter, C. J., Goldberg, T. E., & Weinberger, D. R. (1992). Forms of memory failure in schizophrenia. *Journal of Abnormal Psychology, 101*, 487–494.

Gold, P. E., & Van Buskirk, R. (1975). Facilitation of time-dependent memory processes with posttrial epinephrine injection. *Behavioral Biology, 13*, 145–153.

Goldberg, E., Antin, S. P., Bilder, R. M. Jr., Gerstman, L. J., Hughes, J. E., & Mattis, S. (1981). Retrograde amnesia: possible role of mesencephalic reticular activation in long-term memory. *Science, 213*(4514), 1392–1394.

Goldberg, T. E., Aloia, M. S., Gourovitch, M. L., Missar, D., Pickar, D., & Weinberger, D. R. (1998). Cognitive substrates of thought disorder, I: The semantic system. *American Journal of Psychiatry, 155*, 1671–1676.

Goldberg, T. E., & Gold, J. M. (1995). Neurocognitive deficits in schizophrenia. In S. R. Hirsch & D. R. Weinberger (Eds.), *Schizophrenia*. London: Blackwell Science Ltd.

Goldberg, T. E., Gold, J. M., & Braff, D. L. (1991). Neuropsychological functioning and time-linked information processing in schizophrenia. In A. Tasman & S. M. Goldfinger (Eds.), *Review of Psychiatry, Vol. 10*. Washington (DC): American Psychiatric Press.

Goldberg, T. E., Karson, C. N., Leleszi, J. P., & Weinberger, D. R. (1988). Intellectual impairment in adolescent psychosis. A controlled psychometric study. *Schizophrenia Research, 1*(4), 261–266.

Goldberg, T. E., Torrey, E. S., Gold, J. M., Ragland, J. E., Bigelow, L. C., & Weinberger, D. R. (1993). Learning and memory in monozygotic discordant for schizophrenia. *Psychological Medicine, 23*, 71–85.

Goldberg, T. E., Weinberger, D. R., Berman, K. F., Pliskin, N. H., & Podd, M. H. (1987). Further evidence for dementia of the prefrontal type in schizophrenia? A controlled study of teaching the Wisconsin Card Sorting Test. *Archives of General Psychiatry, 44*, 1008–1014.

Goldberg, T. E., Weinberger, D. R., & Pliskin, N. H. (1989). Recall memory deficit in schizophrenia: A possible manifestation of prefrontal dysfunction. *Schizophrenia Research, 2*, 251–257.

Goldenberg, G., Dettmers, H., Grothe, C., & Spart, J. (1994). Influence of linguistic and and nonlinguistic capacities on spontaneous recovery of aphasia and on success of language therapy. *Aphasiology, 8*, 443–456.

Goldman-Rakic, P. S. (1987). Circuitry of primate prefrontal cortex and regulation of behavior by representational memory. In V. B. Mountcastle & F. Plum (Eds.), *Handbook of physiology, Sect. 1, Vol. 5, pt 1* (pp. 373–417). Bethesda, MD: American Physiological Society.

Goldman-Rakic, P. S. (1984). Modular organization of prefrontal cortex. *Trends in Neuroscience, 7*, 419–424.

Goldman-Rakic, P. S. (1988). Topography of cognition: parallel distributed networks in primate association cortex. *Annual Review of Neuroscience, 11*, 137–156.

Goldman-Rakic, P. S. (1990). Cellular and circuit basis of working memory in prefrontal cortex of nonhuman primates. In H. B. M. Uylings, C. G. Van Eden, J. P. C. De Bruin, M. A. Corner, & M. G. P. Feenstra (Eds.), *Progress in brain research, Vol. 85* (pp. 325–336). Amsterdam: Elsevier Science Publishers, BV.

Goldman-Rakic, P. S. (1995a). Architecture of the prefrontal cortex and the central executive. *Annals of the New York Academy of Sciences, 769*, 71–83.

Goldman-Rakic, P. S. (1995b). Cellular basis of working memory. *Neuron, 14*, 477–485.

Goldman-Rakic, P. S. (1998). The prefrontal landscape: Implications of functional architecture for understanding human mentation and the central executive. In A. C. Roberts, T. W. Robbins, & L. Weiskrantz (Eds.), *The prefrontal cortex: Executive and cognitive functions* (pp. 87–102). Oxford: Oxford University Press.

Goldman-Rakic, P. S., & Porrino, L. J. (1985). The primate mediodorsal (MD) nucleus and its projections to the frontal lobe. *Journal of Comparative Neurology, 242*, 535–560.

Goldman-Rakic, P. S., Selemon, L. D., & Schwartz, M. L. (1984). Dual pathways connecting the dorsolateral prefrontal cortex with the hippocampal formation and parahippocampal cortex in the rhesus monkey. *Neuroscience, 12*, 719–743.

Goldstein, F. C., Levin, H. S., & Boake, C. (1989). Conceptual encoding following severe closed head injury. *Cortex, 25*, 541–554.

Golebiowski, M., Barcikowska, M., & Pfeffer, A. (1999). Magnetic resonance imaging-based hippocampal volumetry in patients with dementia of the Alzheimer type. *Dementia and Geriatric Cognitive Disorders, 10*, 284–288.

Golombok, S., Moodley, P., & Lader, M. (1988). Cognitive impairment in long-term benzodiazepine users. *Psychological Medicine, 18*, 365–374.

Gomez-Isla, T., Price, J. L., McKeel, D. W., Morris, J. C., Growdon, J. H., & Hyman, B. T. (1996). Profound loss of layer II entorhinal cortex neurons distinguishes very mild Alzheimer's disease from nondemented aging. *Journal of Neuroscience, 16*, 4491–4500.

Goodglass, H. (1993). *Understanding aphasia.* San Diego, CA: Academic Press.

Goodglass, H., & Kaplan, E. (1972). *Assessment of aphasia and related disorders.* Philadelphia: Lea & Febiger.

Goodin, D. S. (1990). Clinical utility of long latency "cognitive" event-related potentials (P300): the pros. *Electroencephalography and Clinical Neurophysiology, 76*, 2–5.

Goodlett, C. R., Hamre, K. M., & West, J. R. (1992). Dissociation of spatial navigation and visual guidance performance in Purkinje cell degeneration (pcd) mutant mice. *Behavioural Brain Research, 47*(2), 129–141.

Goodman, A. M., Delis, C. D., & Mattson, S. N. (1999). Normative data for 4-year-old children on the California Verbal Learning Test–Children's Version. *The Clinical Neuropsychologist, 13*(3), 274–282.

Goodman, G. S., & Reed, R. S. (1986). Age differences in eyewitness testimony. *Law and Human Behavior, 10*, 317–332.

Goodwin, G. M. (1997). Neuropsychological and neuroimaging evidence for the involvement of the frontal lobes in depression. *Journal of Psychopharmacology, 11*, 115–122.

Gordon, W. P. (1983). Memory disorders in aphasia: I. Auditory immediate recall. *Neuropsychologia, 21*, 325–339.

Gosche, K. M., Mortimer, J. A., Smith, C. D., Markesbery, W. R., & Snowdon, D. A. (2002). Hippocampal volume as an index of Alzheimer neuropathology. Findings from the Nun Study. *Neurology, 58*, 1476–1482.

Gotham, A. M., Brown, R. G., & Marsden, C. D. (1988). "Frontal" cognitive functions in patients with Parkinson's disease "on" and "off" levodopa. *Brain, 111*, 299–321.

Gottfries, C. G. (1988). Dementia: Classification and aspects of treatment. *Psychopharmacology Series, 5*, 187–195.

Gottfries, C. G., Brane, G., Gullberg, B., & Steen, G. (1982). A new rating scale for dementia syndromes. *Archives of Gerontology Geriatrics, 1,* 311–330.

Grady, C. L., Bernstein, L. J., Beig, S., & Siegenthaler, A. L. (2002). The effects of encoding strategy on age-related changes in the functional neuroanatomy of the memory. *Psychology and Aging,* 7–23.

Grady, C. L., McIntosh, A. R., Horwitz, B., Maisog, J. M., Ungerleider, L. G. G., Mentis, M. J. et al. (1995). Age-related reductions in human recognition memory due to impaired encoding. *Science, 269,* 218–221.

Grady, C. L., McIntosh, A. R., Rajah, M. N., & Craik, F. I. M. (1998). Neural correlates of the episodic encoding of pictures and words. *Proceedings of the National Academy of Sciences of the United States of America, 95,* 2703–2708.

Graf, P. (1990). Life-span changes in implicit and explicit memory. *Bulletin of Psychonomic Society, 28,* 353–358.

Graf, P., & Mandler, G. (1984). Activation makes words more accessible but not necessarily more retrievable. *Journal of Verbal Learning & Verbal Behavior, 23,* 553–568.

Graf, P., Mandler, G., & Haden, M. (1982). Simulating amnesic symptoms in normal subjects. *Science, 218,* 1243–1244.

Graf, P., & Ryan, L. (1990). Transfer-appropriate processing for implicit and explicit memory. *Journal of Experimental Psychology: Learning, Memory & Cognition, 16*(6), 978–992.

Graf, P., & Schacter, D. L. (1985). Implicit and explicit memory for new associations in normal and amnesic subjects. *Journal of Experimental Psychology: Learning, Memory & Cognition, 11,* 501–518.

Graf, P., Squire, L. R., & Mandler, G. (1984). The information that amnesic patients do not forget. *Journal of Experimental Psychology: Learning, Memory, and Cognition, 10,* 164–178.

Graf, P., & Uttl, B. (1995). Component processes of memory: Changes across the adult lifespan. *Swiss Journal of Psychology, 54,* 113.

Graf, P., & Uttl, B. (2001). Prospective memory: A new focus for research. *Consciousness and Cognition, 10,* 437–450.

Graff-Radford, N. R., Damasio, A. R., Hyman, B. T., Hart, M. N., Tranel, D., Damasio, H. et al. (1990). Progressive aphasia in a patient with Pick's disease: A neuropsychological, radiologic, and anatomic study. *Neurology, 40*(4), 620–626.

Grafman, J. (1994). Alternative frameworks for the conceptualization of prefrontal lobe functions. In F. Boller & J. Grafman (Eds.), *Handbook of neuropsychology, Vol. 9* (pp. 187–201). Amsterdam: Elsevier.

Grafton, S. T., Mazziotta, J. C., Presty, S., Friston, K. J., Frackowiak, R. S. J., & Phelps, M. E. (1992). Functional anatomy of human procedural learning determined with regional cerebral blood flow and PET. *Journal of Neuroscience, 12*(7), 2542–2548.

Graham, K. S., & Hodges, J. R. (1997). Differentiating the roles of the hippocampal complex and the neocortex in long-term memory storage: Evidence from the study of semantic dementia and Alzheimer's disease. *Neuropsychology, 11,* 77–89.

Graham, K. S., Simons, J. S., Pratt, K. H., Patterson, K., & Hodges, J. R. (2000). Insights from semantic dementia on the relationship between episodic and semantic memory. *Neuropsychologia, 38,* 313–324.

Granholm, E., & Butters, N. (1988). Associative encoding and retrieval in Alzheimer's and Huntington's disease. *Brain and Cognition, 7,* 335–347.

Grasby, P. M., Frith, C. D., Paulesu, E., Friston, K. J., Frackowiak, R. S., & Dolan, R. J. (1995). The effect of the muscarinic antagonist scopolamine on regional cerebral blood flow during the performance of a memory task. *Experimental Brain Research, 104*(2), 337–348.

Graybiel, A. M. (1995). Building action repertoires: Memory and learning functions of the basal ganglia. *Current Opinion Neurobiology, 5,* 733–741.

Green, E., & Howes, D. H. (1978). The nature of conduction aphasia: A study of anatomic and clinical features and of underlying mechanisms. In H. Whitaker & H. A. Whitaker (Eds.), *Studies in neurolinguistics. Vol. 3* (pp. 123–156). New York: Academic Press.

Green, R. C. (1995). Alzheimer's disease and other dementing disorders in adults. *Clinical Neurology, 3,* 1–83.

Greenberg, S. M., Tennis, M. K., Brown, L. B., Gomez-Isla, T., Hayden, D. L., Schoenfeld, D. A. et al. (2000). Donepezil therapy in clinical practice. *Archives of Neurology, 57,* 94–99.

Greene, J. D. W., Baddeley, A. D., & Hodges, J. R. (1996). Analysis of the episodic memory deficit in early Alzheimer's disease: Evidence from the doors and people test. *Neuropsychologia, 34,* 537–551.

Greene, J. D. W., & Hodges, J. R. (1996). The fractionation of remote memory: Evidence from a longitudinal study of dementia Alzheimer type. *Brain, 119,* 129–142.

Greene, J. D. W., Hodges, J. R., & Baddeley, A. D. (1995). Autobiographical memory and executive function in early dementia of Alzheimer type. *Neuropsychologia, 33,* 1647–1670.

Greene, J. G. (1984). The evaluation of reality orientation. In I. Hanley & J. Hodge (Eds.), *Psychological approaches to the care of the elderly* (pp. 192–212). London: Croom, Helm.

Greenstein, R. J., Ybanez, M. M., Zhang, R. L., & Bauman, W. A. (1991). Is ageing preprogrammed? Observations from the brain/gut axis. *Mechanisms of Ageing and Development, 61,* 113–121.

Greenstock, J., & Pipe, M. E. (1996). Interviewing children about past events: The influence of peer support and misleading questions. *Child Abuse and Neglect, 20,* 69–80.

Gregg, J. M., Ryan, D. E., & Levin, K. H. (1974). The amnesic actions of diazepam. *Oral Surgery, 32,* 651–664.

Greve, K. W. (2001). The WCST-64: A standardized short-form of the Wisconsin Card Sorting Test. *The Clinical Neuropsychologist, 15*(2), 228–234.

Grillon, C., Ameli, R., Woods, S. W., Merikangas, K., & Davis, M. (1991). Fear-potentiated startle in humans: Effects of anticipatory anxiety on the acoustic blink reflex. *Psychophysiology, 28*(5), 588–595.

Grober, E., Lipton, R. B., Hall, C., & Crystal, H. (2000). Memory impairment on free and cued selective reminding predicts dementia. *Neurology, 54,* 827–832.

Grober, E., Lipton, R. B., Katz, M., & Sliwinski, M. (1998). Demographic influences on free and cued selective reminding performance in older persons. *Journal of Clinical and Experimental Neuropsychology, 20,* 221–226.

Grober, E., Merling, A., Heimlich, T., & Lipton, R. B. (1997). Free and cued selective reminding and selective reminding in the elderly. *Journal of Clinical & Experimental Neuropsychology, 19*(5), 643–654.

Grön, G., Bittner, D., Schmitz, B., Wunderlich, A. P., & Riepe, M. W. (2002). Subjective memory complaints: Objective neural markers in patients with Alzheimer's disease and major depressive disorder. *Annals of Neurology, 51,* 491–498.

Grön, G., Wunderlich, A. P., Spitzer, M., Tomczak, R., & Riepe, M. W. (2000). Brain activation during human navigation: Gender-different neural networks. *Nature Neuroscience, 3,* 404–408.

Grossman, M., Carvell, S., Peltzer, L., Stern, M. B., Gollomp, S., & Hurtig, H. I. (1993). Visual constructional impairments in Parkinson's disease. *Neuropsychology, 7,* 536–547.

Grossman, M., Cooke, A., DeVita, C., Alsop, D., Detre, J., Chen, W. et al. (2002). Age-related changes in working memory during sentence comprehension: An fMRI study. *NeuroImage, 15,* 302–317.

Grossman, M., Robinson, K., Bernharddt, N., & Koenig, P. (2001). A rule-based categorization deficit in Alzheimer's disease. *Brain and Cognition, 45,* 265–276.

Grundman, M., Petersen, R., Morris, J. et al. (1996). Rate of dementia of the Alzheimer type (DAT) in subjects with mild cognitive impairment (abstract). *Neurology, 46,* A 403.

Grut, M., Jorm, A. F., Fratiglioni, L., Forsell, Y., Viitanen, M., & Winblad, B. (1993). Memory complaints of elderly people in a population survey: Variation according to dementia stage and depression. *Journal of American Geriatric Society, 41,* 1295–1300.

Guillemin, R. (1978). Peptides in the brain: The new endocrinology of the neuron. *Science, 202,* 390–402.

Gulya, M., Rossi-George, A., Hartshorn, K., Vieira, A., Rovee-Collier, C., Johnson, M. K. et al. (2002). The development of explicit memory for basic perceptual features. *Journal of Experimental Child Psychology, 81*, 276–297.

Gustafsson, B., & Wigström, H. (1988). Physiological mechanisms underlying long-term potentiation. *Trends in Neuroscience, 11*, 156–162.

Guzowski, J. F., & McGaugh, J. L. (1997). Antisense oligodeoxynucleotide-mediated disruption of hippocampal cAMP response element binding protein levels impairs consolidation of memory for water maze training. *Proceedings of the National Academy of Sciences of the United States of America, 94*(6), 2693–2698.

Haaland, K. Y., Vranes, L. F., Goodwin, J. S., & Garry, P. J. (1987). Wisconsin Card Sort Test performance in a healthy elderly population. *Journal of Gerontology, 42*, 345–346.

Haas, H. S., & Schauenstein, K. (1997). Neuroimmunomodulation via limbic structures—The neuroanatomy of psychoimmunology. *Progress in Neurobiology, 51*, 195–222.

Haddad, L. B., & Nussbaum, P. (1990). Predictive utility of the Rey Auditory-Verbal Learning Test with Alzheimers patients. *Clinical Gerontologist, 9*(2), 53–59.

Hadjiivanova, C., Kehayov, R., Petkov, V. V., Amblard, M., & Martinez, J. (1995). Behavioural effects of the cyclic cholecystokinin peptide analogue JMV-320. *Peptides, 5*, 815–819.

Hahn-Barma, V., Deweer, B., Durr, A., Dode, C., Feingold, J., Pillon, B. et al. (1998). Are cognitive changes the first symptoms of Huntington's disease? A study of gene carriers. *Journal of Neurology, Neurosurgery & Psychiatry, 64*(2), 172–177.

Haikala, H., & Ahtee, L. (1988). Antagonism of the nicotine-induced changes of the striatal dopamine metabolism in mice by mecamylamine and pempidine. *Naunyn Schmiedbergs Archiv fur Pharmakologie, 338*, 169–173.

Haist, F., Bowden Gore, J., & Mao, H. (2001). Consolidation of human memory over decades revealed by functional magnetic resonance imaging. *Nature Neuroscience, 4*(11), 1139–1145.

Hale, S., Bronik, M. D., & Fry, A. F. (1997). Verbal and spatial working memory in school-age children: Developmental differences in susceptibility to interference. *Developmental Psychology, 33*, 364–371.

Haley, J. E., Malen, P. L., & Chapman, P. F. (1993). Nitric oxide synthase inhibitors block long-term potentiation induced by weak but not strong tetanic stimulation at physiological brain temperatures in rat hippocampal slices. *Neuroscience Letters, 160*, 85–88.

Haley, J. E., Wilcox, G. L., & Chapman, P. F. (1992). The role of nitric oxide in hippocampal long-term potentiation. *Neuron, 8*, 211–216.

Halgren, E., Babb, T. L., & Crandall, P. H. (1978). Activity of human hippocampal formation and amygdala neurons during memory testing. *Electroencephalography and Clinical Neurophysiology, 45*, 585–601.

Hall, E. D., & Braughler, J. M. (1996). Free radicals and lipid peroxidation. In R. K. Narayan, J. E. Wilberger & J. T. Povlishock, (Eds.), *Neurotrauma* (pp. 1405–1419). New York: McGraw Hill.

Hall, J., Thomas, K. L., & Everitt, B. J. (2000). Rapid and selective induction of BDNF expression in the hippocampus during contextual learning. *Nature Neuroscience, 3*, 533–535.

Hall, J. L., Gonder-Frederick, L. A., Chewning, W. W., Silveira, J., & Gold, P. E. (1989). Glucose enhancement of performance on memory tests in young and aged humans. *Neuropsychologia, 27*, 1129–1138.

Hamann, S. B., Cahill, L., McGaugh, J. L., & Squire, L. R. (1997). Intact enhancement of declarative memory for emotional material in amnesia. *Learning & Memory, 4*(3), 301–309.

Hamann, S. B., Cahill, L., & Squire, L. R. (1997). Emotional perception and memory in amnesia. *Neuropsychology, 11*(1), 104–113.

Hamann, S. B., Ely, T. D., Grafton, S. T., & Kilts, C. D. (1999). Amygdala activity related to enhanced memory for pleasant and aversive stimuli. *Nature Neuroscience, 2*(3), 289–293.

Hamann, S. B., & Squire, L. R. (1997). Intact perceptual memory in the absence of conscious memory. *Behavioral Neuroscience, 111*(4), 850–854.

Hamann, S. B., Squire, L. R., & Schacter, D. L. (1995). Perceptual thresholds and priming in amnesia. *Neuropsychologia*, *9*, 3–15.

Hambrick, D. Z., & Engle, R. W. (2002). Effects of domain knowledge, working memory capacity and age on cognitive performance: An invesigation of the knowledge-is-power hypothesis. *Cognitive Psychology*, *44*, 339–387.

Hampel, H., Teipel, S., Bayer, W., Alexander, G. E., Schwarz, R., Schapiro, M. B. et al. (2002). Age transformation of combined hippocampus and amygdalar volume improves diagnostic accuracy in Alzheimer's disease. *Journal of the Neurological Sciences*, *194*, 15–19.

Han, J., Lee, J. D., Bibbs, L., & Ulevitch, R. J. (1994). A MAP kinase targeted by endotoxin and hyperosmolarity in mammalian cells. *Science*, *265*, 808–811.

Han, L., Cole, M., Bellavance, F., McCusker, J., & Primeau, F. (2000). Tracking cognitive decline in Alzheimer's disease usingg the Mini-Mental State Examination: A meta-analysis. *International Psychogeriatrics*, *12*(2), 231–247.

Hanley, I. (1986). Reality orientation in the care of the elderly patient with dementia—three case studies. In I. Hanley & M. Gilhoorly (Eds.), *Psychological therapies for the elderly* (pp. 65–79). London: Croom Helm.

Hannay, H. J., & Levin, H. S. (1985). Selective reminding test: An examination of the equivalence of four forms. *Journal of Clinical and Experimental Neuropsychology*, *7*, 251–263.

Hänninen, T., Hallikainen, M., Koivisto, K., Helkala, E. L., Reinikainen, K. J., Soininen, H. et al. (1995). A follow-up study of age-associated memory impairment: Neuropsychological predictors of dementia. *Journal of the American Geriatrics Society*, *43*(9), 1007–1015.

Hansen, J., & Bowey, J. A. (1994). Phonological analysis skills, verbal working memory, and reading ability in second-grade children. *Children Development*, *65*, 938–950.

Harasty, J. A., Halliday, G. M., Code, C., & Brooks, W. S. (1996). Quantification of cortical atrophy in a case of progressive fluent aphasia. *Brain*, *119*, 181–190.

Harding, C. M., Brooks, G. W., Ashikaga, T., Strauss, J. S., & Breier, A. (1987). The Vermont Longitudinal Study of Persons with Severe Mental Illness, I: Methodology, study sample, and overall status 32 years later. *American Journal of Psychiatry*, *144*, 718–726.

Harley, C. W., & Martin, G. M. (1999). Open field motor patterns and object marking, but not object sniffing, are altered by ibotenate lesions of the hippocampus. *Neurobiology of Learning & Memory*, *72*(3), 202–214.

Harley, K., & Reese, E. (1999). Origins of autobiographical memory. *Developmental Psychology*, *35*(5), 1338–1348.

Harrell, L. E., Marson, D., Chatterjee, A., & Parrish, J. A. (2000). The severe Mini-Mental State Examination: A new neuropsychologic instrument for the bedside assessment of severely impaired patients with Alzheimer's disease. *Alzheimer Disease and Associated Disorders*, *14*(3), 168–175.

Harrington, D. L., Haaland, K. Y., Yeo, R. A., & Marder, E. (1990). Procedural memory in Parkinson's disease: Impaired motor but not visuoperceptual learning. *Journal of Clinical and Experimental Neuropsychology*, *12*, 323–339.

Harris, J. (1984). Methods of improving memory. In B. A. Wilson & N. Moffat (Eds.), *Clinical management of memory problems* (pp. 46–62). Rockville, MD: Aspen.

Harro, J., & Oreland, L. (1993). Cholecystokinin receptors and memory: A radial maze study. *Pharmacology Biochemistry and Behavior*, *44*, 509–517.

Hart, J., & Gordon, B. (1990). Delineation of single-word semantic comprehension deficits in aphasia, with anatomical correlation. *Annals of Neurology*, *27*, 226–231.

Harvey, J. A. (1993). Serotonergic regulation of associative learning. *Behavioral Brain Research*, *73*, 47–50.

Harvey, J. A. (1996). Serotonergic regulation of associative learning. *Behavioral Brain Research*, *73*, 47–50.

Harvey, P. D., White, L., Parrella, M., Putnam, K. M., Kincaid, M. M., Powchik, P. et al. (1995). The longitudinal stability of cognitive impairment in schizophrenia. Mini-Mental scores at one-and two-year follow-ups in geriatric in-patients. *British Journal of Psychiatry, 166*, 630–633.

Hasher, L., & Zacks, R. T. (1979). Automatic and effortful processes in memory. *Journal of Experimental Psychology: General, 108*(3), 356–388.

Hasher, L., & Zacks, R. T. (1988). Working memory, comprehension and aging: A review and a new view. In G. H. Bower (Ed.), *The psychology of learning and motivation* (Vol. 22). San Diego, CA: Academic Press.

Hashtroudi, S., Johnson, M. K., & Chrosniak, L. D. (1989). Aging and source monitoring. *Psychology and Aging, 4*, 106–112.

Hasselmo, M. E., & Bower, J. M. (1993). Acetylcholine and memory. *Trends in Neuroscience, 16*, 218–222.

Haug, H., Barmwater, U., Eggers, R., Fischer, D., Kuhl, S., & Sass, N. L. (1983). Anatomical changes in aging brain. Morphometric analysis of the human prosencephalon. In J. Cervos-Navarro & H. I. Sarkander (Eds.), *Neuropharmacology (Aging Vol. 21)* (pp. 1–12). New York: Raven Press.

Haug, H., & Eggers, R. (1991). Morphometry of the human cortex cerebri and corpus striatum during aging. *Neurobiology of Aging, 12*, 336–338.

Hawkins, K. A. (1999). Memory deficits in patients with schizophrenia: Preliminary data from the Wechsler Memory scale—Third Edition support earlier findings. *Journal of Psychiatry and Neuroscience, 24*(4), 341–347.

Haxby, J. V., Grady, C. L., Koss, E., Horwitz, B., Heston, L., Schapiro, M. et al. (1990). Longitudinal study of cerebral metabolic asymmetries and associated neuropsychological patterns in early dementia of the Alzheimer type. *Archives of Neurology, 47*(7), 753–760.

Haxby, J. V., Ungerleider, L. G., Horwitz, B., Maisog, J. M., Rapoport, S. I., & Grady, C. L. (1996). Face encoding and recognition in the human brain. *Proceedings of the National Academy of Sciences of the United States of America, 93*(2), 922–927.

Hayman, C. A., MacDonald, C. A., & Tulving, E. (1993). The role of repetition and associative interference in new semantic learning in

amnesia: A case experiment. *Journal of Cognitive Neuroscience, 5*, 375–389.

Haynes, C., & Naidoo, S. (1991). *Children with specific speech and language impairments.* Oxford: Blackwell.

Heaton, R. K. (1981). *Wisconsin Card Sorting Test: Manual.* Odessa, FL: Psychological Assessment Resources, Inc.

Heaton, R. K., Baade, L. E., & Johnson, K. L. (1978). Neuropsychological test results associated with psychiatric disorders in adults. *Psychological Bulletin, 85*, 141–162.

Heaton, R. K., Chelune, G. J., Talley, J. L., Kay, G. G., & Curtis, G. (1993). *Wisconsin Card Sorting Test manual: Revised and expanded.* Odessa, FL: Psychological Assessment Resources Inc.

Heaton, R. K., & Drexler, M. (1987). Clinical and neuropsychological findings in schizophrenia and aging. In N. E. Miller & C. D. Cohen (Eds.), *Schizophrenia and aging: Schizophrenia, paranoia, and schizophreniform disorders in later life.* New York: Guilford Press.

Hebb, D. O. (1949). *The organization of behavior.* Chichester, UK: John Wiley and Sons, Inc.

Heilman, K. M., Scholes, R., & Watson, R. T. (1976). Defects of immediate memory in Broca's and conduction aphasia. *Brain and Language, 3*, 201–208.

Heindel, W. C., Butters, N., & Salmon, D. P. (1988). Impaired learning of a motor skill in patients with Huntington's disease. *Behavioral Neuroscience, 102*, 141–147.

Heindel, W. C., Salmon, D. P., & Butters, N. (1993). Cognitive approaches to the memory disorders of demented patients. In P. B. Sutker & H. E. Adams (Eds.), *Comprehensive handbook of psychopathology* (2nd Edn). New York: Plenum Press.

Heindel, W. C., Salmon, D. P., Shults, C. W., Walicke, P. A., & Butters, N. (1989). Neuropsychological evidence for multiple implicit memory systems: A comparison of Alzheimer's, Huntington's, and Parkinson's disease patients. *The Journal of Neuroscience, 9*, 582–587.

Heine, M. K., Ober, B. A., & Shenaut, G. K. (1999). Naturally occurring and experimentally induced tip-of-the-tongue experiences in three adult age groups. *Psychology and Aging, 14,* 445–457.

Heinrichs, R. W. (1990). Variables associated with Wisconsin Card Sorting Test performance in neuropsychiatric patients referred for assessment. *Neuropsychiatry Neuropsychology and Behavioral Neurology, 3,* 107–112.

Helkala, E-L., Koivisto, K., Hänninen, T., Vanhanen, M., Kervinen, K., Kuusisto, J. et al. (1996). Memory functions in human subjects with different apolipoprotein E phenotypes during a 3-year population-based follow-up study. *Neuroscience Letters, 204,* 177–180.

Helmstaedter, C., Grunwald, T., Lehnertz, K., Gleissner, U., & Elger, C. E. (1997). Differential involvement of left temporolateral and temporomesial structures in verbal declarative learning and memory: Evidence from temporal lobe epilepsy. *Brain & Cognition, 35*(1), 110–131.

Henderson, D. (1996). *Emotion and memory in women with and without a history of childhood sexual abuse.* D Clin Psy thesis, University of Wales, Bangor.

Henson, R. N., Rugg, M. D., Shallice, T., Josephs, O., & Dolan, R. J. (1999). Recollection and familiarity in recognition memory: An event-related functional magnetic resonance imaging study. *The Journal of Neuroscience, 19*(10), 3962–3972.

Herremans, A. H. J., Hijzen, T. H., Olivier, B., & Slangen, J. L. (1995). Serotonergic drug effects on a delayed conditional discrimination task in the rat: Involvement of the $5HT_{1A}$ receptor in working memory. *Journal of Psychopharmacology, 9,* 242–250.

Herman, J. P., & Cullinan, W. E. (1997). Neurocircuitry of stress: Central control of the hypothalamus-pituitary-adrenocortical axis. *Trends in Neurobiology, 51,* 195–222.

Hermann, B. P., Wyler, A. R., Steenman, H., & Richey, E. T. (1988). The interrelationship between language function and verbal learning/memory performance in patients with complex partial seizures. *Cortex, 24,* 245–253.

Hermelin, B., & O'Connor, N. (1970). *Psychological experiments with autistic children.* Oxford: Oxford University Press.

Hertel, P. T., & Hardin, T. S. (1990). Remembering with and without awareness in a depressed mood: Evidence of deficits in initiative. *Journal of Experimental Psychology, 119,* 45–59.

Hertzog, C., & Dixon, R. A. (1994). Metacognitive development in adulthood and old age. In J. Metcalfe & A. P. Shimamura (Eds.), *Metacognition: Knowing about knowing.* Cambridge, MA: MIT Press.

Hertzog, C., & Rypma, B. (1991). Age differences in components of mental-rotation task performance. *Bulletin of the Psychonomic Society, 29,* 209–212.

Herz, R. S., & Cupchik, G. C. (1992). An experimental characterization of odor-evoked memories in humans. *Chemical Senses, 17,* 519–528.

Hetem, L. A. B., Danion, J. M., Diemunsch, P., & Brandt, C. (2000). Effect of a subanesthetic dose of ketamine on memory and conscious awareness in healthy volunteers. *Psychopharmacoloy, 152,* 283–288.

Hettinger, T. P., & Frank, M. E. (1992). Information processing in mammalian gustatory systems. *Current Opinions in Neurobiology, 2,* 469–478.

Heuer, F., & Reisberg, D. (1992). Remembering the details of emotional events. In E. Winograd & U. Neisser (Eds.), *Affect and accuracy in recall: Studies of "flashbulb" memories* (pp. 162–190). Cambridge, UK: Cambridge University Press.

Hildebrandt, H., Brand, A., & Wilfried, S. (1998). Profiles of patients with left prefrontal and left temporal lobe lesions after cerebrovascular infarctions on California Verbal Learning Test-Like indices. *Journal of Clinical and Experimental Neuropsychology, 20*(5), 673–683.

Hilsabeck, R. C., Schrager, D. A., & Gouvier, W. D. (1999). Cross-validation of the Two- and Three-subtest short forms of the Wechsler Memory Scale–Revised. *Applied Neuropsychology, 6*(4), 247–254.

Hindmarch, I. (1980). Psychomotor function and psychoactive drugs. *British Journal of Clinical Pharmacology, 10,* 189–209.

Hindmarch, I., Fuchs, H., & Erzigkeit, H. (1991) Efficacy and tolerance of Vinpocetine in ambulant patients suffering from mild to moderate organic psychosyndromes. *International Clinical Psychopharmacology*, 6, 31–43.

Hinshaw, S. P. (1994). *Attention deficits and hyperactivity in children.* London: Sage Publications.

Hirano, H., Day, J., & Fibiger, H. C. (1995). Serotonergic regulation of acetylcholine release in rat frontal cortex. *Journal of Neurochemisty*, 65, 1139–1145.

Hirsch, M. J., & Wurtman, R. J. (1978). Lecithin consumption elevates acetylcholine concentrations in rat brain and adrenal gland. *Science*, 202, 223–225.

Hirsh, R. (1974). The hippocampus and contextual retrieval of information from memory: A theory. *Behavioral Biology*, 12, 421–444.

Hirshman, E., & Master, S. (1997). Modeling the conscious correlates of recognition memory: Reflections on the remember–know paradigm. *Memory and Cognition*, 25, 345–351.

Hitch, G. J., & Ferguson, J. (1991). Prospective memory for future intentions: Some comparisons with memory for past events. *European Journal of Cognitive Psychology*, 3, 285–295.

Hobson, J. (1992). The brain as a dream machine: An activation-synthesis hypothesis of dreaming. In M. Lansky (Ed.), *Essential papers on dreams* (pp. 452–473). New York: New York University Press.

Hock, C., Konietzko, U., Papassotiropoulos, A., Wollmer, A., Streffer, J., Von Rotz, R. C. et al. (2002). Generation of antibodies specific for β-amyloid by vaccination of patients with Alzheimer disease. *Nature Medicine, Advance online publication, October 15.*

Hodes, R. L., Cook, E. W., & Liang, P. J. (1985). Individual differences in autonomic response: Conditioned association or conditioned fear? *Psychophysiology*, 22, 545–560.

Hodges, J. R., Garrard, P., & Patterson, K. (1998). Semantic dementia. In A. Kertesz & D. G., Munoz (Eds.), *Pick's disease and Pick complex* (pp. 83–104). New York: Wiley-Liss.

Hodges, J. R., & McCarthy, R. A. (1993). Autobiographical amnesia resulting from bilateral paramedian thalamic infarction. A study in cognitive neurobiology. *Brain*, 116, 921–940.

Hodges, J. R., Patterson, K., Oxbury, S., & Funnell, E. (1992). Semantic dementia: Progessive fluent aphasia with temporal lobe atrophy. *Brain*, 115, 1783–1806.

Hodges, J. R., Patterson, K., & Tyler, L. (1994). Loss of semantic memory: Implications for the modularity of mind. *Cognitive Neuropsychology*, 11, 505–542.

Hodges, J. R., Salmon, D. P., & Butters, N. (1990). Differential impairment of semantic and episodic memory in Alzheimer's and Huntington's diseases: A controlled prospective study. *Journal of Neurology, Neurosurgery and Psychiatry*, 53, 1089–1095.

Hodges, J. R., Salmon, D. P., & Butters, N. (1991). The nature of the naming deficit in Alzheimer's and Huntington's disease. *Brain*, 114, 1547–1558.

Hohl, U., Grundman, M., Salmon, D. P., Thomas, R. G., & Thal, L. J. (1999). Mini-Mental State Examination and Mattis Dementia Rating Scale performance differs in Hispanic and non-Hispanic Alzheimer's disease patients. *Journal of the International Neuropsychological Society*, 5, 301–307.

Hökfelt, T., Zhang, X., & Wiesenfeld-Halin, Z. (1994). Messenger plasticity in primary sensory neurons following axotomy and its functional implications. *Trends in Neuroscience*, 17, 22–30.

Hollman, M., & Heinemann, S. (1994). Cloned glutamate receptors. *Annual Review of Neuroscience*, 17, 31–108.

Holmes, P. V., & Drugan, R. C. (1991). Differential effects of anxiogenic central and peripheral benzodiazepine receptor ligands in tests of learning and memory. *Psychopharmacology*, 104, 249–254.

Holmgren, B., & Condi, C. (1964). Conditioned avoidance reflex under pentobarbital. *Boletin de Estudios Medicos y Biologicos*, 22, 21–38.

Holscher, C. (1997). Nitric oxide, the enigmatic neuronal messenger: Its role in synaptic plasticity. *Trends in Neuroscience*, 20, 298–303.

Holzman, P. S., Solomon, C. M., Levin, S., & Waternaux, C. S. (1984). Pursuit eye movement dysfunctions in schizophrenia. Family evidence for specificity. *Archives of General Psychiatry, 41,* 136–139.

Homma, A. (1992). Assessment and treatment of patients with dementia of the Alzheimer type. *Nippon Ronen Igakkai Zasshi, 29,* 264–270.

Homma, A., Takeda, M., Imai, Y., Udaka, F., Hasegawa, K., Kameyama, M. et al. (2000). E2020 Study Group. Clinical efficacy and safety of donepezil on cognitive and global function in patients with Alzheimer's disease. *Dementia and Geriatric Cognitive Disorders, 11,* 299–313.

Honda, T., & Kashima, H. (1992). Cognitive rehabilitation program for demented patients. *Ronen Seishin Igaku Zasshi (Japanese Journal of Geriatric Psychiatry), 3,* 301–306.

Horn, J. L. (1982). The theory of fluid and crystallized intelligence in relation to concepts of cognitive psychology and aging in adulthood. In F. I. M. Craik & S. Therub (Eds.), *Aging and cognitive processes* (pp. 237–278). New York: Plenum Press.

Horowitz, M. (1969). Flashbacks: Recurrent intrusive images after the use of LSD. *American Journal of Psychiatry, 126,* 565–559.

Houk, J. C., & Wise, S. P. (1995). Distributed modular architectures linking basal ganglia, cerebellum and cerebral cortex: Their role in planning and controlling action. *Cerebral Cortex, 5,* 95–110.

Howard, D. V., & Howard, J. H. (1992). Adult age differences in the rate of learning serial patterns: Evidence from direct and indirect tests. *Psychology and Aging, 7,* 232–241.

Howe, M. L. (2000). *The fate of early memories: Developmental science and the retention of childhood experiences.* Washington, DC: American Psychological Association.

Howe, M. L., & Courage, M. L. (1993). On resolving the enigma of infantile amnesia. *Psychological Bulletin, 113*(7), 305–326.

Howe, M. L. & Courage, M. L. (1997). The emergence and early development of autobiographical memory. *Psychological Review, 104,* 499–523.

Howe, M. L., & O'Sullivan, J. T. (1990). The development of strategic memory: Coordinating knowledge, metamemory, and resources. In

D. F. Bjorklund (Ed.), *Children's strategies: Contemporary views of cognitive development* (pp. 129–155). Hillsdale, NJ: Lawrence Erlbaum Associates Inc.

Howe, M. L., & O'Sullivan, J. T. (1997). What children's memories tell us about recalling our childhoods: A review of storage and retrieval processes in the development of long-term retention. *Developmental Review, 17,* 148–204.

Howard, D. V. (1988). Implicit and explicit assessment of cognitive aging. In M. L. Howe & C. J. Brainerd (Eds.), *Cognitive development in adulthood* (pp. 3–37). New York: Springer–Verlag.

Hoyer, W. J. (1987). Acquisition of knowledge and the decentralisation of "g" in adult intellectual development. In C. Schooler & K. Schaie (Eds.), *Cognitive functioning and social structure over the life course.* New York: Ablex Publishing Co.

Huang, Y. Y., Nguyen, P. V., Abel, T., & Kandel, E. R. (1996). Long lasting forms of synaptic potentiation in the mammalian hippocampus. *Learning and Memory, 3,* 74–85.

Huff, F. J., Corkin, S., & Growdon, J. H. (1986). Semantic impairment and anomia in Alzheimer's disease. *Brain and Language, 28,* 235–249.

Hultsch, D. F., Hertzog, C., & Dixon, R. A. (1987). Age differences in metamemory: Resolving the inconsistencies. *Canadian Journal of Psychology, 41*(2), 193–208.

Hultsch, D. F., Masson, M. E., & Small, B. J. (1991). Adult age differences in direct and indirect tests of memory. *Journal of Gerontology, 46,* 22–30.

Humphreys, G., & Bruce, V. (1989). *Visual cognition: Computational, experimental and neuropsychological perspectives.* Hove, UK: Lawrence Erlbaum Associates Ltd.

Hunkin, N. M., Parkin, A. J., Bradley, V. A., Burrows, E. H., Aldrich, F. K., Jansari, A. et al. (1995). Focal retrograde amnesia following closed head injury: A case study and theoretical account. *Neuropsychologia, 33*(4), 509–523.

Hunkin, N. M., Squires, E. J., Parkin, A. J., & Tidy, J. A. (1998). Are the benefits of errorless learning dependent on implicit memory? *Neuropsychologia, 36*(1), 25–36.

Huppert, F. A., & Piercy, M. (1978). Dissociation between learning and remembering in organic amnesia. *Nature, 275*(5678), 317–318.

Huppert, F. A., & Piercy, M. (1979). Normal and abnormal forgetting in organic amnesia: Effect of locus of lesion, *Cortex, 15*(3), 385–390.

Huppert, F. A., & Beardsall, L. (1993). Prospective memory impairment as an early indicator of dementia. *Journal of Clinical and Experimental Neuropsychology, 15*, 805–821.

Huppert, F. A., & Whittington, J. E. (1995). Symptoms of psychological distress predict 7-year mortality. *Psychological Medicine, 25*, 1037–1086.

Huron, C., Danion, J. M., Giacomoni, F., Grangé, D., Robert, P., & Rizzo, L. (1995). Impairment of recognition memory with, but not without, conscious recollection in schizophrenia. *American Journal of Psychiatry, 152*, 1737–1742.

Hutton, U. M. Z., & Towse, J. N. (2001). Short-term memory and working memory as indices of children's cognitive skills. *Memory, 9*, 383–394.

Hyde, T., Nawroz, S., Goldberg, T. E., Bigelow, L. B., Strong, D., Ostrem, J. L. et al. (1994). Is there cognitive decline in schizophrenia? *British Journal of Psychiatry, 164*, 494–500.

Hyman, B. T., Van Hoesen, G. W., Damasio, A. R., & Barnes, C. L. (1984). Alzheimer's disease: Cell-specific pathology isolates the hippocampal formation. *Science, 225*, 1168–1170.

Ikeda, M., Mori, E., Hirono, N., Imamura, T., Shimomura, T., Ikejiri, Y., & Yamashita, H. (1998). Amnestic people with Alzheimer's disease who remembered the Kobe earthquake. *British Journal of Psychiatry, 172*, 425–428.

Ikegami, S., & Inokuchi, K. (2000). Antisense DNA against calcineurin facilitates memory in contextual fear conditioning by lowering the threshold for hippocampal long-term potentiation induction. *Neuroscience, 98*, 637–646.

Ilsley, J. E., Moffoot, A. P. R., & O'Carrol, R. E. (1995). An analysis of memory dysfunction in major depression. *Journal of Affective Disorders, 35*, 1–9.

Ilyutchenok, R. Y., & Dubrovina, N. I. (1995). Memory retrieval enhancement by kappa opioid agonist and mu, delta antagonists. *Pharmacology, Biochemistry & Behavior, 52*(4), 683–687.

Incisa Della Rochetta, A., & Milner, B. (1993). Strategic search and retrieval inhibition: The role of the frontal lobes. *Neuropsychologia, 31*, 503–524.

Introini-Collison, I. B., Dalmaz, C., & McGaugh, J. L. (1996). Amygdala beta-noradrenergic influences on memory storage involve cholinergic activation. *Neurobiology of Learning & Memory, 65*(1), 57–64.

Introini-Collison, I. B., Miyazaki, B., & McGaugh, J. L. (1991). Involvement of the amygdala in the memory-enhancing effects of clenbuterol. *Psychopharmacology, 104*(4), 541–544.

Introini-Collison, I. B., Nagahara, A. H., & McGaugh, J. L. (1989). Memory-enhancement with intra-amygdala posttraining naloxone is blocked by concurrent administration of propranolol. *Brain Research, 476*, 94–101.

Introini-Collison, I., Saghafi, D., Novack, G. D., & McGaugh, J. L. (1992). Memory-enhancing effects of post-training dipivefrin and epinephrine: Involvement of peripheral and central adrenergic receptors. *Brain Research, 572*(1–2), 81–86.

Isaacs, E. B. & Vargha-Khadem, F. (1989). Differential course of development of spatial and verbal memory span: A normative study. *British Journal of Developmental Psychology*, 377–380.

Isaacson, R. (1987). Hippocampus. In G. Adelman (Ed.), *Encyclopedia of neuroscience, Vol 1*. Cambridge: Birkhäuse Boston.

Isingrini, M., Fontaine, R., Taconnat, L., & Duportal, A. (1995). Aging and encoding in memory: False alarms and decision criteria in a word-pair recognition task. *International Journal of Aging and Human Development, 41*, 79–88.

Ito, M. (1984). *The cerebellum and the neural control*. New York: Appleton Century-Crofts.

Ito, M. (1989). Long-term depression. *Annual Review of Neuroscience, 12*, 85–102.

Ito, M. (1994). In M. Baudry, J. L. Davis, & R. F. Thompson (Eds.), *Synaptic plasticity: Molecular and functional aspects* (pp. 117–128). Cambridge, MA: MIT Press.

Ito, M., Sakurai, M., & Tongroach, P. (1982). Climbing fibre induced depression of both mossy fibre responsiveness and glutamate sensitivity of cerebellar Purkinje cells. *Journal of Physiology, 324,* 113–134.

Itoh, S., & Katsuura, G. (1987). Cholecystokinin octapeptide prevents extinction of active avoidance behaviour in the rat. *Drug Development Research, 10,* 171–175.

Itoh, S., Takashima, A., Igano, K., & Inouye, K. (1989). Memory effects of caerulein and its analogs in active and passive avoidance responses in the rat. *Peptides, 10,* 843–848.

Itoh, S., Takashima, A., & Maeda, Y. (1992). Memory impairments induced by peripherally administered cholecystokinin A-type receptor anatagonists in rats. *Drug Development Research, 26,* 89–99.

Itoh, J., Ukai, M., & Kameyama, T. (1994). Dynorphin A-(1–13) potently improves the impairment of spontaneous alternation performance induced by the mu-selective opioid receptor agonist DAMGO in mice. *Journal of Pharmacology & Experimental Therapeutics, 269*(1), 15–21.

Ivnik, R. J., Smith, G. E., Lucas, J. A., Tangalos, E. G., Kokmen, E., & Petersen, R. C. (1997). Free and Cued Selective Reminding Test: MOANS norms. *Journal of Clinical and Experimental Neuropsychology, 18*(5), 676–691.

Izquierdo, I., Barros, D. M., Mello e Souza, T., de Souza, M. M., Izquierdo, L. A., & Medina, J. H. (1998). Mechanisms for memory types differ. *Nature, 393*(6686), 635–636.

Izquierdo, I., Bianchin, M., Silva, M. B. E., Zanatta, M. S., Walz, R., Ruschel, A. C. et al. (1993). CNQX infused into rat hippocampus or amygdala disrupts the expression of memory of two different tasks. *Behavioral & Neural Biology, 59*(1), 1–4.

Izquierdo, I., Da Cunha, C., Huang, C. H., Walz, R., Wolfman, C., & Medina, J. H. (1990). Post-training down-regulation of memory consolidation by a GABA-A mechanism in the amygdala modulated by endogenous benzodiazepines. *Behavioral & Neural Biology, 54*(2), 105–109.

Izquierdo, I., & Medina, J. H. (1991). GABA$_A$ receptor modulation of memory: The role of endogenous benzodiazepines. *Trends in Pharmacological Science, 121,* 260–265.

Izquierdo, I., & Medina, J. H. (1997). Memory formation: The sequence of biochemical events in the hippocampus and its connection to activity in other brain structures. *Neurobiology of Learning and Memory, 68,* 285–316.

Izquierdo, I., Medina, J. H., Izquierdo, L. A., Barros, D. M., de Souza, M. M., & Mello e Souza, T. (1998). Short- and long-term memory are differentially regulated by monoaminergic systems in the rat brain. *Neurobiology of Learning & Memory, 69*(3), 219–224.

Izquierdo, I., Quillfeldt, J. A., Zanatta, M. S., Quevedo, J., Schaeffer, E., Schmitz, P. K. et al. (1997). Sequential role of hippocampus and amygdala, entorhinal cortex and parietal cortex in formation and retrieval of memory for inhibitory avoidance in rats. *European Journal of Neuroscience, 9*(4), 786–793.

Izumi, S-I., Yasueda, M., Hihara, N., Yamamoto, E., Sawatari, M., & Ishida, A. (1998). An individual patient comparison of response to a memory training program—psychogenic v organic amnesia. *American Journal of Physical Medicine & Rehabilitation, 77,* 458–462.

Jack, C. R. Jr., Petersen, R. C., Xu, Y. C., O'Brien, P. C., Smith, G. E., Ivnik, R. J. et al. (1999). Prediction of AD with MRI-based hippocampal volume in mild cognitive impairment. *Neurology, 52*(7), 1397–1403.

Jacobs, D., Salmon, D. P., Tröster, A. I., & Butters, N. (1990). Intrusion error in the figural memory of patients with Alzheimer's and Huntington's disease. *Archives of Clinical Neuropsychology, 5,* 49–57.

Jacobs, J. (1887). Experiments on "prehension". *Mind, 12,* 75–79.

Jacobson, L. L., & Sapolsky, R. M. (1991). The role of the hippocampus in feedback regulation of the hypothalamic-pituitary-adrenal axis. *Endocrine Reviews, 12,* 118–134.

Jacoby, L. L. (1983). Perceptual enhancement: Persistent effects of an experience. *Journal of Experimental Psychology: Learning, Memory and Cognition, 9,* 21–38.

Jacoby, L. L. (1983). Remembering the data: Analyzing interactive processes in reading. *Journal of Verbal Learning & Verbal Behavior, 22*, 485–508.

Jacoby, L. L. (1991). A process-dissociation framework: Separating automatic from intentional uses of memory: *Journal of Memory and Language, 30*, 513–541.

Jacoby, L. L. (1998). Invariance in automatic influences in memory: Toward a user's guide for the process-dissociation procedure. *Journal of Experimental Psychology: Learning, Memory and Cognition, 24*, 3–26.

Jacoby, L. L. (1999). Ironic effects of repetition: Measuring age-related differences in memory. *Journal of Experimental Psychology: Learning, Memory and Cognition, 25*, 3–22.

Jacoby, L. L., & Dallas, M. (1981). On the relationship between autobiographical memory and perceptual learning. *Journal of Experimental Psychology: General, 3*, 306–340.

Jacoby, L. L., & Kelley, C. M. (1992). A process dissociation framework for investigating unconscious influences: Freudian slips, projective tests, subliminal perception, and signal detection theory. *Current Disorder Psychology Sciences, 1*, 174–178.

Jacoby, L. L., Toth, J. P., & Yonelinas, A. P. (1993). Separating conscious and unconscious influences of memory: Measuring recollection. *Journal of Experimental Psychology: General, 122*, 139–154.

Jacoby, L. L., Yonelinas, A. P., & Jennings, J. M. (1997). The relation between conscious and unconscious (automatic) influences: A declaration of independence. In J. D. Cohen & J. W. Schooler (Eds.), *Scientific approaches to the question of consciousness*. Hillsdale, NJ: Lawrence Erlbaum Associates Inc.

James, W. (1890). *Principles of psychology*. New York: Holt.

James, W. (1892). *Psychology. Briefer course*. New York: Holt.

Janowsky, J. S., Shimamura, A. P., Kritchevsky, M., & Squire, L. R. (1989). Cognitive impairment following frontal lobe damage and its relevance to human amnesia. *Behavioral Neuroscience, 103*, 548–560.

Janowsky, J. S., Shimamura, A. P., & Squire, L. R. (1989). Source memory impairment in patients with frontal lobe lesions. *Neuropsychologia, 27*, 1043–1056.

Jansari, A., & Parkin, A. J. (1996). Things that go bump in your life. Explaining the reminiscence bump in autobiographical memory. *Psychology and Aging, 11*, 85–91.

Janus, C., Pearson, J., McLaurin, J., Mathews, P. M., Jiang, Y., Schmidt, S. D. et al. (2000). A beta peptide immunization reduces behavioural impairment and plaques in a model of Alzheimer's disease. *Nature, 408*(6815), 979–982.

Jason, G. W., Suchowersky, O., Pajurkova, E. M., Graham, L., Klimek, M. L., Garber, A. T. et al. (1997). Cognitive manifestations of Huntington disease in relation to genetic structure and clinical onset. *Archives of Neurology, 54*(9), 1081–1088.

Jelicic, M., Craik, F. I. M., & Moscovitch, M. (1996). Effects of ageing on different explicit and implicit memory tasks. *European Journal of Cognitive Psychology, 8*, 225.

Jenkins, L., Myerson, J., Hale, S., & Fry, A. F. (1999). Individual and developmental differences in working memory across the life span. *Psychonomic Bulletin & Review, 6*(1), 28–40.

Jernigan, T. L., & Ostergaard, A. L. (1993). Word priming and recognition memory are both affected by medial temporal lobe damage. *Neuropsychology, 1*, 14–26.

Jernigan, T. L., Ostergaard, A. L., & Fennema-Notestine, C. (2001). Mesial temporal, diencephalic, and striatal contributions to deficits in single word reading, word priming and recognition memory. *Journal of the International Neuropsychological Society, 7*, 63–78.

Jeste, D. V., Wragg, R. E., Salmon, D. P., Harris, M. J., & Thal, L. J. (1992). Cognitive deficits of Alzheimer disease patients with and without delusions. *American Journal of Psychiatry, 149*, 184–189.

Jetter, W., Poser, U., Freeman, R. B., & Markowitsch, H. J. (1986). A verbal long-term memory deficit in frontal lobe damaged patients. *Cortex, 22*, 229–242.

Joanette, Y., Goulet, P., & Hannequin, D. (1990). *Right hemisphere and verbal communication.* New York: Springer-Verlag.

Jobst, K. A., Smith, A. D., Szatmari, M., Molyneux, A., Esiri, M. E., King, E. et al. (1992). Detection in life of confirmed Alzheimer's disease using a simple measurement of medial temporal lobe atrophy by computed tomography. *Lancet, 340*(8829), 1179–1183.

Johansson, B., Zarit, S. H., & Berg, S. (1992). Changes in cognitive functioning of the oldest old. *Journal of Gerontology, 47*, 75–80.

Johnson, L. C., & Chernik, D. A. (1982). Sedative hypnotics and human performance. *Psychopharmacology, 76*, 101–113.

Johnson, M. K., Hashtroudi, S., & Lindsay, D. S. (1993). Source monitoring. *Psychological Review, 114*, 3–28.

Johnson, M. K., Kounios, J., & Nolde, S. F. (1996). Electrophysiological brain activity and memory source monitoring. *NeuroReport, 7*, 2929–2932.

Johnson, M. K., & Raye, C. L. (1981). Reality monitoring. *Psychological Review, 88*, 67–85.

Johnston, D., Williams, S., Jaffe, D., & Gray, R. (1992). NMDA-receptor-independent long-term potentiation. *Annual Review of Physiology, 54*, 489–505.

Johnston, M. V. (1992). Cognitive disorders. In M. V. Johnston, R. L. McDonald, & A. B. Young (Eds.), *Principles of drug therapy in neurology* (pp. 226–267). Philadelphia, PA: FA Davis.

Jones, D., Jones, M., Lewis, M., & Spriggs, T. (1979). Drugs and human memory: Effects of low doses of nitrazepam and hyoscine on retention. *British Journal of Clinical Pharmacology, 7*, 479–483.

Jones, M. W., Erington, M. L., French, P. J., Fine, A., Bliss, T. V. P., Garel, S. et al. (2001). A requirement for the immediate early gene Zif268 in the expression of late LTP and long-term memories. *Nature Neuroscience, 4*, 289–296.

Jones-Gotman, M. (1986). Memory for designs: The hippocampal contribution. *Neuropsychologia, 24*, 193–202.

Jonides, J. (1995). In E. E. Smith & D. Osherson (Eds.), *An invitation to cognitive science: Thinking.* Cambridge, MA: MIT Press.

Jonides, J., Reuter-Lorenz, P., Smith, E. E., Awh, E., Barnes, L., Drain, M. et al. (1996). In D. Medin (Ed.), *The psychology of learning and motivation.* New York: Academic Press.

Jonides, J., Smith, E. E., Koeppe, R. A., Awh, E., Minoshima, S., & Mintun, M. A. (1993). Spatial working memory in humans as revealed by PET. *Nature, 363*, 623–625.

Jorm, A. F. (1986). Controlled and automatic information processing in senile dementia: A review. *Psychology Medicine, 16*, 77–88.

Josselyn, S. A., Shi, C., Carlezon, W. A. J., Neve, R. L., Nestler, E. J., & Davis, M. (2001). Long-term memory is facilitated by cAMP response element-binding protein overexpression in the amygdala. *Journal of Neuroscience, 21*, 2404–2412.

Juillerat, A. C., Van der Linden, M., Seron, X., & Adam, S. (2000). La prise en charge des patients Alzheimer au stade debutant. In X. Seron & M. Van der Linden (Eds.), *Traité de Neuropsychologie Clinique, Tome 2.* Marseille: Solal.

Juottonen, K., Laakso, M. P., Partanen, K., & Soininen, H. (1999). Comparative MR analysis of the entorhinal cortex and hippocampus in diagnosing Alzheimer disease. *American Journal of Neuroradiology, 20*, 139–144.

Kabani, N. J., Sled, J. G., & Chertkow, H. (2002). Magnetization transfer ratio in mild cognitive impairment and dementia of Alzheimer's type. *Neuroimage, 15*, 604–610.

Kahn, R. I., & Rowe, J. W. (1998). *Successful aging.* New York: Pantheon.

Kail, P., & Hall, L. (2001). Distinguishing short-term memory from working memory. *Memory & Cognition, 29*(1), 1–9.

Kalska, H., Punamäki, R-L., Mäkinen-Pelli, T., & Saarinen, M. (1999). Memory and meta-memory functioning among depressed patients. *Applied Neuropsychology, 6*(2), 96–107.

Kandel, E. R. (1989). Genes, nerve cells and the remembrance of things past. *Journal of Neuropsychiatry and Clinical Neuroscience, 1*, 103–125.

Kane, M. J., Bleckley, M. K., Conway, A. R. A., & Engle, R. W. (2001). A controlled-attention view of working-memory capacity. *Journal of*

Experimental Psychology: General, 130, 169–183.

Kane, M. J., & Engle, R. W. (2002). The role of prefrontal cortex in working-memory capacity, executive attention, and general fluid intelligence: an individual-differences perspective. *Psychonomic Bulletin & Review, 9*(4), 637–671.

Kantarci, K., Reynolds, G., Petersen, R. C., Boeve, B. F., Knopman, D. J., Edland, S. et al. (2003). Proton MR spectroscopy in mild cognitive impairment an Alzheimer disease: A comparison of 1.5 and 3T. *American Journal of Neuroradiology, 24*(5), 843–849.

Kaplan, E., Goodglass, H., & Weintraub, S. (1983). *The Boston Naming Test.* Philadelphia: Lea & Febiger.

Kapp, B. S., Frysinger, R. C., Gallagher, M., & Haselton, J. R. (1979). Amygdala central nucleus lesions: Effects on heart rate conditioning in the rabbit. *Physiology and Behaviour, 23,* 1109–1117.

Kapur, N. (1992). Focal retrograde amnesia in neurological disease: A critical review. *Cortex, 29,* 217–234.

Kapur, N. (1995). Memory aids in the rehabilitation of memory disordered patients. In A. D., Baddeley, B. A., Wilson, & F. N. Watts (Eds.), *Handbook of memory disorders.* New York: Wiley.

Kapur, N., Ellison, D., Parkin, A. J., Hunkin, N. M., & Burrowe, E. (1994a). Bilateral temporal lobe pathology with sparing of medial temporal lobe structures: Lesion profile and pattern of memory disorder. *Neuropsychologia, 32,* 23–38.

Kapur, N., Millar, J., Abbott, P., & Carter, M. (1998). Recovery of function processes in human amnesia: Evidence from transient global amnesia. *Neuropsychologia, 36*(1), 99–107.

Kapur, N., Young, A., Bateman, D., & Kennedy, P. (1989). Focal retrograde amnesia: A long term clinical and neuropsychological follow-up. *Cortex, 25,* 387–402.

Kapur, S., Craik, F. I., Jones, C., Brown, G. M., Houle, S., & Tulving, E. (1995). Functional role of the prefrontal cortex in retrieval of memories: A PET study. *Neuroreport, 6*(14), 1880–1884.

Kapur, S., Craik, F. I. M., Tulving, E., Wilson, A. A., Houle, S., & Brown, G. M. (1994b). Neuroanatomical correlates of encoding in episodic memory: Levels of processing effect. *Proceedings of the National Academy of Science of the United States of America, 91,* 2008–2011.

Kapur, S., Rose, R., Liddle, P. F., Zipursky, R. B., Brown, G. M., Stuss, D. et al. (1994c). The role of the left prefrontal cortex in verbal processing: Semantic processing or willed action? *NeuroReport, 5*(16), 2193–2196.

Karaken, D. A., Moberg, P. J., & Gur, R. C. (1996). Proactive inhibition and semantic organization: Relationship with verbal memory in patients with schizophrenia. *Journal of the International Neuropsychological Society, 2,* 486–493.

Karamat, E., Ilmberger, J., Poewe, W., & Gerstenbrand, F. (1991). Memory dysfunction in Parkinson patients: An analysis of verbal learning processes. *Journal of Neural Transmission, 33*(suppl.), 93–97.

Karlsson, I., Brane, G., Melin, E., Nyth, A. L., & Rybo, E. (1988). Effects of environmental stimulation on biochemical and psychological varibales in dementia. *Acta Psychiatrica Scandinavica, 77,* 207–213.

Kartsounis, L. R., Rudge, P., & Stevens, J. M. (1995). Bilateral lesion of CA1-CA2 fields of the hippocampus are sufficient to cause a severe amnesic syndrome in humans. *Journal of Neurology, Neurosurgery and Psychiatry, 59,* 95–98.

Kaschel, R., Della Sala, S., Cantagallo, A., Fahlböck, A., Laaksonen, R., & Kazen, M. (2002). Imagery mnemonics for the rehabilitation of memory: A randomised group controlled trial. *Neuropsychological Rehabilitation, 12*(2), 127–153.

Kasl-Godley, J., & Gatz, M. (2000). Psychosocial interventions for individuals with dementia: An integration of theory, therapy and a clinical understanding of dementia. *Clinical Psychological Review, 20,* 755–782.

Katsuura, G., & Itoh, S. (1986). Prevention of experimental amnesia by peripherally administered cholecystokinin octapeptide in the rat. *Drug Development Research, 7,* 269–276.

Katz, I. R., Jeste, D. V., Mintzer, J. E. et al. (1999). Comparison of risperidone and placebo for psychosis and behavioural disturbances associated with dementia. *Journal of Clinical Psychiatry*, *60*, 107–115.

Katzman, R., & Kawas, C. (1994). The epidemiology of dementia and Alzheimer's disease. In R. D. Terry, R. Katzman, & K. L. Bick (Eds.), *Alzheimer's disease* (pp. 104–122). New York: Raven Press.

Kauffer, D. I., Cummings, J. L., & Christine, D. (1996). Effect of tacrine on behavioral symptoms in Alzheimer's disease: An open label study. *Journal of Geriatric Psychiatry Neurology*, *9*, 1–6.

Kausler, D. H. (1990). Automaticity of encoding and episodic memory processes. In E. A. Lovelace (Ed.), *Aging and cognition. Mental processes, self-awareness and interventions* (pp. 29–67). New York: Elsevier Science.

Kausler, D. H., & Lichty, W. (1988). Memory for activities: Rehearsal-independence and aging. In M. L. Howe & C. J. Brainerd (Eds.), *Cognitive development in adulthood* (pp. 93–131). New York, Springer-Verlag.

Kazui, H., Mori, E., Hashimoto, M., Hirono, N., Imamura, T., Tanimukai, S. et al. (2000). Impact of emotion on memory. Controlled study of the influence of emotionally charged material on declarative memory in Alzheimer's disease. *British Journal of Psychiatry*, *177*, 343–347.

Keane, M., Gabrieli, J. D. E., Fennema, A. C., Growden, J. H., & Corkin, S. (1991). Evidence for a dissociation between perceptual and conceptual priming in Alzheimer's disease. *Behvioral Neuroscience*, *105*(2), 326–342.

Keane, M. M., Gabrieli, J. D., Mapstone, H. C., Johnson, K. A., & Corkin, S. (1995). Double dissociation of memory capacities after bilateral occipital-lobe or medial temporal-lobe lesions. *Brain*, *118*(Pt 5), 1129–1148.

Keane, M. M., Gabrieli, J. D. E., Monti, L. A., Fleischman, D. A., Cantor, J. M., & Noland, J. S. (1997). Intact and impaired conceptual memory processes in amnesia. *Neuropsychology*, *11*, 59–69.

Kear-Caldwell, J. J., & Heller, M. (1980). The Wechsler Memory Scale and closed head injury. *Journal of Clinical Psychology*, *36*, 782–787.

Keele, S. W., & Ivry, R. B. (1990). In A. Diamond (Ed.), *The development and neural bases of higher cognitive functions* (pp. 179–211). New York: New York Academy of Science Press.

Keiburtz, K., McDermott, M., & Growdon, J. (1994). In *IX International Workshop on Parkinson's Disease*, Rome.

Kelley, W. M., Miezin, F. M., McDermott, K. B., Buckner, R. L., Raichle, M. E., Cohen, N. J. et al. (1998). Hemispheric specialization in human dorsal frontal cortex and medial temporal lobe for verbal and nonverbal memory encoding. *Neuron*, *20*, 927–936.

Kendler, K. S., & Diehl, S. R. (1993). The genetics of schizophrenia: A current genetic-epidemiological perspective. *Schizophrenia Bulletin*, *19*, 261–285.

Kennedy, M. B. (1993). The postsynaptic density. *Current Opinion in Neurobiology*, *3*, 732–737.

Kenny, J. T., & Meltzer, H. Y. (1991). Attention and higher cortical functions in schizophrenia. *Journal of Neuropsychiatry and Clinical Neuroscience*, *3*, 269–275.

Keppel, G., & Underwood, B. J. (1962). Proactive inhibition in short-term retention of single items. *Journal of Verbal Learning and Verbal Behavior*, *1*, 153–161.

Kertesz, A., & Clydesdale, S. (1994). Neuropsychological deficits in vascular dementia vs Alzheimer's disease. *Archives of Neurology*, *51*, 1226–1231.

Kesner, R. P., Walser, R. D., & Winzenried, G. (1989). Central but not basolateral amygdala mediates memory for positive affective experiences. *Behavioral Brain Research*, *33*, 189–195.

Kia, H. K., Brisorgueil, M. J., Daval, G., Langlois, X., Hamon, M., & Vergé, D. (1996). Serotonin 1A receptors are expressed by a subpopulation of cholinergic neurons in the rat medial septum and diagnoal band of broca—a double immunocytochemical study. *Neuroscience*, *74*, 143–154.

Kidd, P. M. (1998). *Phosphatidylserine, number one brain booster*. New Canaan, CT: Keats Publishing.

Kihlstrom, J. F. (1994). Hypnosis, delayed recall, and the principles of memory. *International Journal of Clinical and Experimental Hypnosis, 42*, 337–345.

Kihlstrom, J. F. (1997). Hypnosis, memory and amnesia. *Philosophical Transactions of the Royal Society, London, 352*, 1727–1732.

Kihlstrom, J. F., Glisky, M. L., & Angiulo, M. J. (1994). Dissociative tendencies and dissociative disorders. *Journal of Abnormal Psychiatry, 103*, 117–124.

Kilander, L., Nyman, H., Boberg, M., Hansson, L., & Lithell, H. (1998). Hypertension is related to cognitive impairment: A 20-year follow-up of 999 men. *Hypertension, 31*(3), 780–786.

Kim, J. J., Andreasen, N. C., O'Leary, D. S., Wiser, A. K., Ponto, L. L., Watkins, G. L. et al. (1999). Direct comparison of the neural substrates of recognition memory for words and faces. *Brain, 122*, 1069–1083.

Kim, J. J., Clark, R. E., & Thompson, R. F. (1995). Hippocampectomy impairs the memory of recently, but not remotely, acquired trace eyeblink conditioned responses. *Behavioral Neuroscience, 109*(2), 195–203.

Kim, J. J., & Fanselow, M. S. (1992). Modality-specific retrograde amnesia of fear. *Science, 256*, 675–677.

Kim, M., Campeau, S., Falls, W. A., & Davis, M. (1993). Infusion of the non-NMDA receptor antagonist CNQX into the amygdala blocks the expression of fear-potentiated startle. *Behavioral & Neural Biology, 59*(1), 5–8.

Kimberg, D. Y., Aguirre, G. K., Lease, J., & D'Esposito, M. (2001). Cortical effects of bromocriptine, a D2 dopamine receptor agonist in human subject, revealed by fMRI. *Human Brain Mapping, 12*, 246–257.

Kinsella, G., Murtagh, D., Landry, A., Homfray, K., Hammond, M., Obeirne, L. et al. (1996). Everyday memory following traumatic brain injury. *Brain Injury, 10*(7), 499–507.

Kirkwood, S. C., Siemers, E., Stout, J. C., Hodes, M. E., Conneally, P. M., Christian, J. C. et al. (1999). Longitudinal cognitive and motor changes among presymptomatic Huntington disease gene carriers. *Archives of Neurology. 56*(5), 563–568.

Kitchener, E. G., Hodges, J. R., & McCarthy, R. (1998). Acquisition of post-morbid vocabulary and semantic facts in the absence of episodic memory. *Brain, 121*, 1313–1327.

Kivipelto, M., Helkala, E-L., Hänninen, T., Laakso, M. P., Hallikainen, M., Alhainen, K. et al. (2001). Midlife vascular risk factors and late-life mild cognitive impairment. A population-based study. *Neurology, 56*, 1683–1689.

Kivipelto, M., Helkala, E-L., Hallikainen, M. et al. (2000). Elevated systolic blood pressure and high cholesterol levels at midlife are risk factors for late-life dementia. *Neurobiology of Aging, 21*(suppl. 1), S174, Abstract.

Kixmiller, J. S., Verfaellie, M., Mather, M. M., & Cermak, L. S. (2000). Role of perceptual and organizational factors in amnesics' recall of the Rey-Osterrieth Complex Figure: A comparison of three amnesic groups. *Journal of Clinical and Experimental Neuropsychology, 22*(2), 198–207.

Kiyak, H. A., Teri, L., & Borson, S. (1994). Physical and functional health assessment in normal aging and in Alzheimer's disease: Self-reports vs family reports. *Gerontologist, 34*, 324–330.

Kleijnen, J., & Knipschild, P. (1992). Ginkgo biloba for cerebral insufficiency. *British Journal of Clinical Pharmacology, 34*, 352–358.

Klisz, D. K., & Parsons, O. A. (1977). Hypothesis testing in younger and older alcoholics. *Journal of Studies on Alcohol, 38*, 1718–1729.

Knapp, M., Knopman, D., Solomon, P., Pendlebury, W., Davis, C., & Gracon, S. (1994). A 30-week randomized controlled trial of high-dose tacrine in patients with Alzheimer's disease. *Journal of the American Medical Association, 271*, 985–991.

Knight, R. G. (1992). *The neuropsychology of degenerative brain diseases*. Hillsdale, NJ: Lawrence Erlbaum Associates Inc.

Knopman, D. J. (1991). Unaware learning versus preserved learning in pharmacological amnesia: similarities and differences. *Journal of Experimental Psychology: Learning, Memory & Cognition, 17*, 1017–1029.

Knopman, D. S., & Nissen, M. J. (1987). Implicit learning in patients with probable Alzheimer's disease. *Neurology, 37,* 784–788.

Knopman, D. S., & Ryberg, S. (1989). A verbal memory test with high predictive accuracy for dementia of the Alzheimer type. *Archives of Neurology, 46,* 141–145.

Knowlton, B. J., & Squire, L. R. (1993). The learning of categories: Parallel brain systems for time memory and category level knowledge. *Science, 262,* 1747–1749.

Knowlton, B. J., & Squire, L. R. (1995). Remembering and knowing: Two different expressions of declarative memory. *Journal of Experimental Psychology, 21,* 699–710.

Knowlton, B. J., & Squire, L. R. (1996). Artificial grammar learning depends on implicit acquisition of both abstract and exemplar-specific information. *Journal of Experimental Psychology: Learning, Memory and Cognition, 22,* 169–181.

Kogan, J. H., Frankland, P. W., Blendy, J. A., Coblentz, J., Marowitz, Z., Schutz, G. et al. (1997). Spaced training induces normal long-term memory in CREB mutant mice. *Current Biology, 7*(1), 1–11.

Koh, S. D. (1978). Remembering of verbal materials by schizophrenic young adults. In S. Schwartz (Ed.), *Language and cognition in schizophrenia* (pp. 59–69). Hillsdale, NJ: Lawrence Erlbaum Associates Inc.

Kohn, S. E. (1992). Conclusions: Toward a working definition of conduction aphasia. In S. E. Kohn (Ed.), *Conduction aphasia.* Hillsdale, NJ: Lawrence Erlbaum Associates Inc.

Koivisto, K., Reinikainen, K. J., Hanninen. T., Vanhanen, M., Helkala, E. L., Mykkanen, L. et al. (1995). Prevalence of age-associated memory impairment in a randomly selected population from eastern Finland. *Neurology,* 45(4), 741–747.

Kolb, B. & Wishaw, I. (1991). *Fundamentals of human neuropsychology* (3rd Ed.). New York: Freeman.

Kopelman, M. D. (1985). Rates of forgetting in Alzheimer type dementia and Korsakoff's syndrome. *Neuropsychology, 23,* 623–638.

Kopelman, M. D. (1986). The cholinergic neurotransmitter system in human memory and dementia: A review. *Quarterly Journal of Experimental Psychology Section A–Human Experimental Psychology, 38*(4), 535–573.

Kopelman, M. D. (1987a). Amnesia: Organic and psychogenic. *British Journal of Psychiatry, 150,* 428–442.

Kopelman, M. D. (1987b). Two types of confabulation. *Journal of Neurology, Neurosurgery and Psychiatry, 50,* 1482–1487.

Kopelman, M. D. (1994). The great escape: A neuropsychological study of psychogenic amnesia. *Neuropsychologia, 32,* 675–691.

Kopelman, M. D. (1995). The assessment of psychogenic amnesia. In A. D. Baddeley, B. A. Wilson, & F. N. Watts (Eds.), *Handbook of memory disorders* (pp. 427–448). Chichester: John Wiley & Sons.

Kopelman, M. D., & Corn, T. H. (1988). Cholinergic "blockade" as a model for cholinergic depletion. A comparison of the memory deficits with those of Alzheimer-type dementia and the alcoholic Korsakoff syndrome. *Brain, 111*(Pt 5), 1079–1110.

Kopelman, M. D., Stevens, T. G., Foli, S., & Grasby, P. (1998). PET activation of the medial temporal lobe in learning. *Brain, 121,* 875–887.

Koponen, H., Stenbäck, U., Mattila, E., Soininen, H., Reinikainen, K., & Riekkinen, P. J. (1989). Delirium among elderly persons admitted to a psychiatric hospital: Clinical course during the acute stage and one-year follow-up. *Acta Psychiatrica Scandinavica, 79,* 579–585.

Kordower, J. H., Chu, Y., Stebbins, G. T., DeKosky, S. T., Cochran, E. J., Bennett, D. et al. (2001). Loss and atrophy of layer II entorhinal cortex neurons in elderly people with mild cognitive impairment. *Annals of Neurology, 49*(2), 202–213.

Korsakova, N. K., & Moskvichyute, L. I. (1985). *Subcortical structures of the brain and mental processes.* Moscow: Moscow State University.

Kosslyn, S. M. (1980). *Image and mind.* Cambridge, MA: Harvard University Press.

Kosslyn, S. M. (1994). *Image and brain.* Cambridge, MA: MIT Press.

Kotler-Cope, S., Camp, C. J. (1995). Anosognosia in Alzheimer disease. *Alzheimer's Disease, 9,* 52–56.

Koukolik, F. (1992). Relation of dementia, Alzheimer's disease and aging. *Ceskoslovenska Patologie, 28*(1), 14–20.

Koutstaal, W., & Schacter, D. L. (1997). Inaccuracy and inaccessibility in memory retrieval: Contributions from cognitive psychology and cognitive neuropsychology. In P. S. Appelbaum, L. Uyehara, & M. Elin (Eds.), *Trauma and memory: Clinical and legal controversies* (pp. 93–137). New York: Oxford University Press.

Kraepelin, E. (1887). Uber Erinnerungsfälschungen. *Archiv für Psychiatrie und Nervenkrankheiten, 17,* 830–843.

Kral, V. A. (1958). Neuropsychiatric observations in an old people home. Studies of memory dysfunction in senescence. *Journal of Gerontology, 13,* 169–176.

Kral, V. A. (1962). Senescent forgetfulness. Benign and malignant. *Canadian Medical Association Journal, 86,* 257–260.

Krall, W. J., Sramek, J. J., & Cutler, N. R. (1999). Cholinesterase inhibitors: A therapeutic strategy for Alzheimer's disease. *Annals of Pharmacotherapy, 33,* 441–450.

Kramer, A. F., Humphrey, D. G., Larish, J. F., Logan, G. D., & Strayer, D. L. (1994). Aging and inhibition. Beyond a unitary view of inhibitory processing in attention. *Psychology and Aging, 9,* 491–512.

Kramer, J. H., Blusewicz, M. J., & Preston, K. A. (1989a). The premature aging hypothesis: Old before its time? *Journal of Consulting and Clinical Psychology, 57,* 257–262.

Kramer, J. H., Delis, D. C., Blusewicz, M. J., Brandt, J., Ober, B. A., & Strauss, M. (1988). Verbal memory errors in Alzheimer's and Huntington's dementias. *Developmental Neuropsychology, 4,* 1–15.

Kramer, J. H., Levin, B. E., Brandt, J., & Delis, D. C. (1989b). Differentiation of Alzheimer's, Huntington's and Parkinson's disease patients on the basis of verbal learning characteristics. *Neuropsychology, 3,* 111–120.

Kroll, N., Markowitsch, H. J., Knight, R. K., & von Cramon, C. Y. (1997). Retrieval of old memories—The temporo-frontal hypothesis. *Brain, 120,* 1377–1399.

Kruskal, J. B., & Wish, M. (1978). *Multidimensional scaling.* Beverly Hills, CA: Sage Publications.

Krystal, J. H., Southwick, S. M., & Charney, D. S. (1995). Post traumatic stress disorder: Psychobiological mechanisms of traumatic remembrance. In D. L. Schachter (Ed.), *Memory distortion: How minds, brains, and societies reconstruct the past* (pp. 150–172). Cambridge, MA: Harvard University Press.

Kuhl, D. E., Small, G. W., Riege, W. H. et al. (1987). Cerebral metabolic patterns before the diagnosis of probable Alzheimer's disease. *Journal of Cerebral Blood Flow and Metabolism 7,* (suppl. 1), S406.

Kukull, W. A., Larsow, E. B., Teri, L., Bowen, J., McCormick, W., & Pfanschmidt, M. L. (1994). The mini-mental state examination score and the clinical diagnosis of dementia. *Journal of Clinical Epidemiology, 47,* 1061–1067.

Kurlychek, R. T. (1983). Use of a digital alarm chronograph as a memory aid in early dementia. *Clinical Gerontologist, 1,* 93–94.

Kuyken, W., & Brewin, C. R. (1995). Autobiographical memory functioning in depression and reports of early abuse. *Journal of Abnormal Psychology, 104,* 585–591.

Kuyken, W., & Dalgliesh, T. (1995). Autobiographical memory and depression. *British Journal of Clinical Psychology, 34,* 89–92.

Kyllonen, P. C., & Christal, R. E. (1990). Reasoning ability (is little more than) working memory capacity? *Intelligence, 14,* 389–433.

Kyriakis, J. M., Banerjee, P., Nikolakaki, E., Dai, T., Rubie, E. A., Ahmad, M. F. et al. (1994). The stress-activated protein kinase subfamily of c-Jun kinases. *Nature, 369*(6476), 156–160.

Laatsch, L., Pavel, D., Jobe, T., Lin, Q., & Quintana, J-C. (1999). Incorporation of SPECT imaging in a longitudinal cognitive rehabilitation therapy programme. *Brain Injury, 13*(8), 555–570.

LaBar, K. S., LeDoux, J. E., Spencer, D. D., & Phelps, E. A. (1995). Impaired fear conditioning following unilateral temporal lobectomy in humans. *Journal of Neuroscience, 15*(10), 6846–6855.

Lachman, M. E. (2000). Promoting a sense of control over memory aging. In R. D. Hill, L. Backman, & A. S. Neely (Eds.), *Cognitive rehabilitation in old age* (pp. 106–122). New York: Oxford University Press.

Lachman, M. E., Weaver, S. L., Bandura, M., Elliot, E., & Lewkowicz, C. J. (1992). Improving memory and control beliefs through cognitive restructuring and self-generated strategies. *Journal of Gerontology Psychological Sciences, 47*, 293–299.

Ladurelle, N., Keller, G., Blommaert, A., Roques, B. P., & Daugé, V. (1997). The CCK-B agonist, BC264, increases dopamine in the nucleus accumbens and facilitates motivation and attention after intraperitoneal injection in rats. *European Journal of Neuroscience, 9*, 1804–1814.

Lalonde, R., & Botez, M. I. (1990). The cerebellum and learning processes in animals. *Brain Research—Brain Research Reviews, 15*(3), 325–332.

Lambon Ralph, M. A., Graham, K. S., Hodges, J. R., & Patterson, K. (1998). Naming in semantic dementia: What matters? *Neuropsychologia, 36*, 775–784.

Lamprecht, R., Hazvi, S., & Dudai, Y. (1997). cAMP response element-binding protein in the amygdala is required for long- but not short-term conditioned taste aversion memory. *Journal of Neuroscience, 17*(21), 8443–8450.

Lancaster, J. S., & Barsalou, L. W. (1997). Multiple organisations of events in memory. *Memory, 5*(5), 569–599.

Landauer, T. K., & Bjork, R. A. (1978). Optimal rehearsal patterns and name learning. In M. Gruneberg, P. Morris, & R. Sykes (Eds.), *Practical aspects of memory*. London: Academic Press.

Landis, S. C., & Mullen, R. J. (1978). The development and degeneration of Purkinje cells in pcd mutant mice. *Journal of Comparative Neurology, 177*(1), 125–143.

Landis, T., Cummings, J. G., Christen, L., Bogen, J. E., & Imhof, H. G. (1986). Are unilateral right posterior cerebral lesions sufficient to cause prosopagnosia? Clinical and radiological findings in six additional patients. *Cortex, 22*, 243–252.

Lang, P. J., Ohman, A., & Vaitl, D. (1988). *The International Affective Picture System* [photographic slides]. Gainesville: University of Florida, Center for Research in Psychophysiology.

Lange, K. W., Sahakian, B. J., Quinn, N. P., Marsden, C. D., & Robbins, T. W. (1995). Comparison of executive and visuospatial memory function in Huntington's disease and dementia of Alzheimer type matched for degree of dementia. *Journal of Neurology, Neurosurgery and Psychiatry, 58*, 598–606.

Larrabee, G. J., & Crook, T. H. (1994). Estimated prevalence of age-associated memory impairment derived from standardized tests of memory function. *International Psychogeriatrics, 6*, 95–104.

Larrabee, G. J., Kane, R. L., Schuck, J. R., & Francis, D. L. (1985). Construct validity of various memory testing procedures. *Journal of Clinical and Experimental Neuropsychology, 7*, 239–250.

Larrabee, G. L., Trahan, D. E., & Levin, H. S. (2000). Normative data for a six-trial administration of the Verbal Selective Reminding Test. *The Clinical Neuropsychologist, 14*(1), 110–118.

La Rue, A. (1989). Patterns of performance on the Fuld Object Memory Evaluation in elderly inpatients with depression or dementia. *Journal of Clinical and Experimental Neuropsychology, 11*(4), 409–422.

La Rue, A., D'Elia, L. F., Clark, E. O., Spar, J. E., & Jarvik, L. F. (1986). Clinical tests of memory in dementia, depression and healthy aging. *Psychology and Aging, 1*, 69–77.

Launer, L. J., Masaki, K., Petrovitch, H., Foley, D., & Havlik, R. J. (1995a). The association between midlife blood pressure levels and late-life cognitive function. The Honolulu–Asia Aging Study. *JAMA, 274*(23), 1846–1851.

Launer, L. J., Ross, G. W., Petrovitch, H., Masaki, K., Foley, D., White, L. R. et al. (2000). Midlife blood pressure and dementia: The Honolulu–Asia aging study. *Neurobiology of Aging, 21*(1), 49–55.

Launer, L. J., Scheltens, P., Lindeboom, J., Barkhof, F., Weinstein, H. C., & Jonker, C. (1995b). Medial temporal lobe atrophy in an open population of very old persons. Cognitive, brain atrophy and sociomedical correlates. *Neurology, 45*, 747–752.

La Voie, D., & Light, L. L. (1994). Adult age differences in repetition priming. A meta-analysis. *Psychology and Aging, 9*, 539–553.

Laws, K., McKenna, P., & Kondel, T. (1998). On the distinction between access and store disorders in schizophrenia: A question of deficit severity? *Neuropsychologia, 36*, 313–321.

Layton, B., & Krikorian, R. (2002). Memory mechanisms in posttraumatic stress disorder. *Journal Neuropsychiatry and Clinical Neuroscience, 14*, 254–261.

Leather, C. V., & Henry, L. A. (1994). Working memory span and phonological awareness tasks as predictors of early reading ability. *Journal of Experimental Child Psychology, 58*(1), 88–111.

LeBoeuf, A., Lodge, J., & Eames, P. (1978). Vasopressin and memory in Korsakoff syndrome. *Lancet, 2*, 1370.

Leconte, P., & Hennevin, E. (1981). Post-learning paradoxical sleep, reticular activation and noradrenergic activity. *Physiology and Behaviour, 26*, 587–594.

LeDoux, J. E. (1984). Fear and the brain: Where have we been, and where are we going? *Biology and Psychiatry, 44*, 1229–1238.

LeDoux, J. E. (1995). Emotion: Clues from the brain. *Annual Review of Psychology, 46*, 209–235.

LeDoux, J. E. (1998). Fear and the brain: Where have we been, and where are we going? *Biological Psychiatry, 44*, 1229–1238.

LeDoux, J. E. (2000). Emotional circuits in the brain. *Annual Review of Neuroscience, 23*, 155–184.

LeDoux, J. E., Iwata, J., Cicchetti, P., & Reis, D. J. (1988). Different projections of the central amygdaloid nucleus mediate autonomic and behavioral correlates of conditioned fear. *Journal of Neuroscience, 8*, 2517–2529.

Lee, G. P., Loring, D. W., & Thompson, J. L. (1989). Construct validity of material specific memory measures following unilateral temporal lobe ablations. *Psychological Assessment, 1*, 192–197.

Lee, H. K., Barbarosie, M., Kameyama, K., Bear, M. F., & Huganir, R. L. (2000). Regulation of distinct AMPA receptor phosphorylation sites during bi-directional synaptic plasticity. *Nature, 405*, 955–959.

Legros, J. J., Gilot, P., Seron, X., Claessens, J., Adam, A., Moeglen, J. M. et al. (1978). Influence of vasopressin on learning and memory. *Lancet, 1*, 41–42.

Lehnung, M., Leplow, B., Herzog, A., Benz, B., Ritz, A., Stolze, H. et al. (2001). Children's spatial behavior is differentially affected after traumatic brain injury. *Child Neuropsychology, 7*(2), 59–71.

Lehrner, J. P., Walla, P., Laska, M., & Deecke, L. (1999). Different forms of human odor memory: A developmental study. *Neuroscience Letters, 272*, 17–20.

Leininger, B. E., Gramling, S. E., Farrell, A. D., Kreutzer, J. S., & Peck E. A. III (1990). Neuropsychological deficits in symptomatic minor head injury patients after concussion and mild concussion. *Journal of Neurology, Neurosurgery and Psychiatry, 53*, 293–296.

Lekeu, F., Chicherio Ch, Van der Linden, M. & Salmon, E. (2000). Prise en charge des difficultés de mémoire prospective dans la maladie d'Alzheimer. *Alzheimer, 3*, 17–20.

Lemaire, M., Böhme, G. A., Piot, O., Roques, B. P., & Blanchard, J. C. (1994). CCK-A and CCKB selective receptor agonists and antagonists modulate olfactory recognition in male rats. *Psychopharmacology, 115*, 435–440.

Lemaire, M., Piot, O., Roques, B. P., Böhme, G. A., & Blanchard, J. C. (1992). Evidence for endogenous cholecystokinergic balance in social memory. *NeuroReport, 3*, 925–932.

Leonard, B. W., Amaral, D. G., Squire, L. R., & Zola-Morgan, S. (1995). Transient memory impairment in monkeys with bilateral lesions of the entorhinal cortex. *Journal of Neuroscience, 15*, 5637–5659.

Lepage, M., Ghaffar, O., Nyberg, L., & Tulving, E. (2000). Prefrontal cortex and episodic memory retrieval mode. *Proceedings of the National*

Academy of Sciences of the United States of America, 97, 506–511.

Lepage, M., Habib, R., & Tulving, E. (1998). Hippocampal PET activation of memory encoding and retrieval: The HIPER Model. *Hippocampus*, 8, 313–322.

Le Roi, S., Kirby, K. C., Montgomery, I. M., & Daniels, B. A. (1999). Differential effects of lorazepam and diazepam on explicit and implicit memory. *The Australian Journal of Psychopharmacology*, 9, 48–54.

Letenneur, L., Commenges, D., Dartigues, J. F., & Barberger-Gateau, P. (1994). Incidence of dementia and Alzheimer's disease in elderly community residents of south-western France. *International Journal of Epidemiology*, 23, 1256–1261.

Levelt, W. J. (1989). *Speaking: From intention to articulation*. Cambridge, MA: MIT Press.

Levin, E. D. (1992). Nicotinic systems and cognitive function. *Psychopharmacology*, 108, 417–431.

Levin, H. S., Grossman, R. G., Rose, J. E., & Teasdale, G. (1979). Long-term neuropsychological outcome of closed head injury. *Journal of Neurosurgery*, 50, 412–422.

Levin, H. S., Peters, B. H., Kalisky, Z., High, W. M. Jr., von Laufen, A. Eisenberg, H. M. et al. (1986). Effects of oral physostigmine and lecithin on memory and attention in closed head-injured patients. *Central Nervous System Trauma*, 3(4), 333–342.

Levine, B., Robertson, I. H., Clare, L., Carter, G., Hong, J., Wilson, B. A. et al. (2000). Rehabilitation of executive functioning: An experimental-clinical validation of goal management training. *Journal of the International Neuropsychological Society*, 6(3), 299–312.

Levy, B. (1996). Improving memory in old age through implicit self-stereotyping. *Journal of Personality and Social Psycology*, 17(6), 1092–1107.

Levy, B., & Langer, E. (1994). Aging free from negative stereotypes: Successful memory in China and among American Deaf. *Journal of Personality and Social Psychology*, 66, 989–998.

Levy, D. L., Holzman, P. S., Matthysse, S., & Mendell, N. R. (1993). Eye tracking dysfunc-

tion and schizophrenia: A critical perspective. *Schizophrenia Bulletin*, 19, 462–536.

Levy, D. L., Holzman, P. S., Matthysse, S., & Mendell, N. R. (1994). Eye tracking and schizophrenia: A selective review. *Schizophrenia Bulletin*, 20, 47–62.

Levy, R. (1994). Aging-associated cognitive decline. *International Psychogeriatrics*, 6, 63–68.

Lewis, P., & Shute, L. (1967). The cholinergic limbic system: Projections to hippocampal formation, medial cortex, nuclei of the ascending cholinergic, reticular system and the subfornical organ and supraoptic crest. *Brain*, 90, 521–539.

Lewis-Jack, O. O., Campbell, A. L., Ridley, S., & Ocampo, C. (1997). Unilateral brain lesions and performance on Russel's version of the Wechsler Memory Scale in an African American population. *International Journal of Neuroscience*, 9, 229–240.

Lezak, M. D. (1982). The problem of assessing executive functions. *International Journal of Psychology*, 17, 281–297.

Lezak, M. D. (1983). *Neuropsychological assessment* (2nd ed). New York: Oxford University Press.

Lezak, M. D. (1995). *Neuropsychological assessment* (3rd ed). New York: Oxford University Press.

Liang, K. C., Chen, L. L., & Huang, T. E. (1995). The role of amygdala norepinephrine in memory formation: Involvement in the memory enhancing effect of peripheral epinephrine. *Chinese Journal of Physiology*, 38(2), 81–91.

Liang, K. C., Juler, R. G., & McGaugh, J. L. (1986). Modulating effects of posttraining epinephrine on memory: Involvement of the amygdala noradrenergic system. *Brain Research*, 368, 125–133.

Liang, K. C., McGaugh, J. L., & Yao, H. Y. (1990) Involvement of amygdala pathways in the influence of post-training intra-amygdala norepinephrine and peripheral epinephrine on memory storage. *Brain Research*, 508, 225–233.

Light, L. L. (1991). Memory and aging: Four hypotheses in search of data. *Annual Review of Psychology*, 42, 333–376.

Light, L. L., & Singh, V. (1987). Implicit and explicit memory in young and older adults. *Journal of Experimental Psychology: Learning, Memory & Cognition, 13*, 531–541.

Liljequist, R., & Mattila, M. J. (1979). Effect of physostigmine and scopolamine on the memory functions of chess players. *Medical Biology, 57*, 402–405.

Lim, G. P., Yang, F., Chu, T., Chen, P., Beech, W., Teter, B. et al. (2000). Ibuprofen suppresses plaque pathology and inflammation in a mouse model for Alzheimer's disease. *Journal of Neuroscience, 20*(15), 5709–5714.

Lindenmayer, J. P., Negron, A. E., Shah, S., Lowinger, R., Kennedy, G., Bark, N. et al. (1997). Cognitive deficits and psychopathology in elderly schizophrenic patients. *The American Journal of Geriatric Psychiatry, 5*(1), 31–42.

Lindsay, D. S., Johnson, M. K., & Kwon, P. (1991a). Developmental changes in source memory. *Journal of Experimental Child Psychology, 52*, 297–318.

Lindsay, R. M., Alderson, R. F., Friedman, B., & Ip, C. H. (1991b). The neurotrophin family of NGF-related neurotrophic factors. *Resorative Neurology & Neuroscience, 2*, 211–220.

Linn, R. T., Wolf, P. A., Bachman, D. L., Knoefel, J. E., Cobb, J. L., Belanger, A. J. et al. (1995). The "preclinical phase" of probable Alzheimer's disease. A 13-year prospective study of the Framingham cohort. *Archives of Neurology, 52*(5), 485–490.

Lipinska, B., & Bäckman, L. (1996). Feeling of knowing in fact retrieval: Further evidence for preservation in early Alzheimer's disease. *Journal of the International Neuropsychological Society, 2*, 350–358.

Lipinska, B., Bäckman, L., Mäntylä, T., & Viitanen, M. (1994). Effectiveness of self-generated cues in early Alzheimer's disease. *Journal of Clinical and Experimental Neuropsychology, 16*, 809–819.

Lister, R. G. (1985). The amnesic action of benzodiazepines in man. *Neuroscience Biobehavioral Reviews, 9*, 87–93.

Lister, R. G. (1990). Ethologically-based animal models of anxiety disorders. *Pharmacology Therapeutics, 46*, 321–340.

Lister, R. G., & File, S. E. (1984). The nature of lorazepam-induced amnesia. *Psychopharmacology, 83*, 183–187.

Little, R. E., & Streissguth, A. P. (1981). Effects of alcohol on the fetus: Impact and prevention. *Canadian Medical Association Journal, 125*, 149–164.

Liu, P., & Bilkey, D. K. (1998). Perirhinal cortex contributions to performance in the Morris water maze. *Behavioral Neuroscience, 112*, 304–315.

Liu, P., & Bilkey, D. K. (1999). The effects of excitotoxic lesions centred on perirhinal cortex in two versions of the radial arm task. *Behavioral Neuroscience, 113*, 512–524.

Llonen, T., Taiminen, T., Lauerma, H., Karlsson, H., Helenius, H. Y. M., Tuimala, P. et al. (2000). Impaired Wisconsin Card Sorting Test performance in first-episode schizophrenia: Resource or motivation deficit? *Comprehensive Psychiatry, 41*(5), 385–391.

Locascio, J. J., Growdon, J. H., & Corkin, S. (1995). Cognitive test performance in detecting, staging, and tracking Alzheimer's disease. *Archives of Neurology, 52*, 1087–1099.

Loewenstein, D. A., Duara, R., Argüelles, T., & Argüelles, S. (1995). Use of the Fuld Object-Memory evaluation in the detection of mild dementia among Spanish- and English-speaking groups. *American Journal of Geriatric Psychiatry, 3*, 300–307.

Loftus, E. F., Joslyn, S., & Polage, D. (1998). Repression: A mistaken impression? *Development and Psychopathology, 10*, 781–792.

Loftus, E. F., & Loftus, G. R. (1980). On the permanence of stored information in the human brain. *American Psychologist, 35*, 409–420.

Loftus, E. F., Loftus, G. R., & Messo, J. (1987). Some facts about "weapon focus". *Law and Human Behavior, 11*, 55–62.

Loftus, E. F., Polonsky, S., & Fullilove, M. T. (1994). Memories of childhood sexual abuse: Remembering and repressing. *Psychology of Women Quarterly, 18*, 67–84.

Logan, C. G., & Grafton, S. T. (1995). Functional anatomy of human eyeblink conditioning determined with regional cerebral glucose metabolism and positron-emission tomography. *Proceedings of the National Academy of Science of the United States of America, 92*, 7500–7504.

Logan, W., & Sherman, D. G. (1983). Transient global amnesia. *Stroke, 14*(6), 1005–1007.

Loge, D. V., Staton, R. D., & Beatty, W. W. (1990). Performance of children with ADHD on tests sensitive to frontal lobe dysfunction. *Journal of the American Academy of Child and Adolescent Psychiatry, 29*, 540–545.

Logie, R. H. (1995). *Visual working memory*. Hilldsale, NJ: Lawrence Erlbaum Associates Inc.

Logie, R. H. (1996). The seven ages of working memory. In M. Richards, R. W. Engle, L. Hasher, R. H. Logie, E. R. Stoltzfus, & R. T. Zacks (Eds.), *Working memory and human cognition* (pp. 31–65). Oxford: Oxford University Press.

Logie, R. H., Baddeley, A., Mane, A., Donchin, E., & Sheptak, R. (1989). Working memory in the acquisition of complex cognitive skills. *Acta Psychologica, 71*, 53–87.

Logie, R. H., Gilhooly, K. J., & Wynn, V. (1994). Counting on working memory in mental arithmetic. *Memory and Cognition, 22*, 395–410.

Logue, P., & Wyrick, L. (1979). Initial validation of Russel's revised Wechsler Memory Scale: A comparison of normal aging versus dementia. *Journal of Consulting and Clinical Psychology, 47*, 176–178.

Looi, J. C., & Sachdev, P. S. (1999). Differentiation of vascular dementia from AD on neuropsychological test (Review). *Neurology, 53*, 670–678.

Lopez-Coviella, I., & Wurtman, R. J. (1992). Enhancement by cytidine of membrane phospholipid synthesis. *Journal of Neurochemistry, 59*, 338–343.

Lord, C., Rutter, M., & Le Couteur, A. (1994). Autism Diagnostic Interview–Revised: A revised version of a diagnostic interview for caregivers of individuals with possible pervasive developmental disorders. *Journal of Autism & Developmental Disorders, 24*(5), 659–685.

Loring, D. (1989). The Wechsler Memory Scale–Revised or the Wechsler Memory Scale–

revisited. *The Clinical Neyropsychologist, 3*, 59–69.

Loring, D. W., & Papanicolaou, A. C. (1987). Memory assessment in neuropsychology: Theoretical considerations and practical utility. *Journal of Clinical and Experimental Neuropsychology, 9*, 340–358.

Louis, E. D., Marder, K., Cote, L., Tang, M., & Mayeux, R. (1997). Mortality from Parkinson's disease. *Archives of Neurology, 54*, 260–264.

Lovelace, E. A. (1990). Aging and metacognition concerning memory function. In E. A. Lovelace (Ed.), *Aging and cognition: Mental processes, self-awareness and interventions* (pp. 157–187). Amsterdam: North-Holland.

Lovelace, E. A., & Twohig, P. T. (1990). Healthy older adults' perceptions of their memory functioning and use of mnemonics. *Bulletin of the Psychonomic Society, 28*, 115–118.

Loveland, K. A. (1987). Behavior of young children with Down syndrome before the mirror: Finding things reflected. *Child Development, 58*, 928–936.

Lucas, J. A., Ivnik, R. J., Smith, G. E., Bohac, D. L., Tangalos, E. G., Kokmen, E. et al. (1998). Normative data for the Mattis Dementia Scale. *Journal of Clinical and Experimental Neuropsychology, 20*, 536–547.

Luciana, M., Collins, P. F., & Depue, R. A. (1998). Opposing roles for dopamine and serotonin in the modulation of human spatial working memory functions. *Cerebral Cortex, 8*, 218–226.

Luciana, M., Depue, R. A., Arbisi, P., & Leon, A. (1992). Facilitation of working memory in humans by a D2 dopamine receptor agonist. *Journal of Cognitive Neuroscience, 4*, 58–68.

Luciana, M., & Nelson, C. A. (1998). The functional emergence of prefrontally-guided memory systems in four- to-eight-year-old children. *Neuropsychologia, 36*, 272–293.

Luine, V., Villegas, M., Martinez, C., & McEwen, B. S. (1994). Stress-dependent impairments of spatial memory. Role of 5-HT. *Annals of the New York Academy of Sciences, 746*, 403–404.

Lupien, S. J., de Leon, M., de Santi, S., Convit, A., Tarshish, C., Nair, N. P. V. et al. (1998). Cortisol levels during human aging predict hippocampal atrophy and memory deficits. *Nature Neuroscience, 1*, 69–73.

Lupien, S. J., Gillin, C., Frakes, D., Soefje, S., & Hauger, R. L. (1995). Delayed but not immediate effects of a 100 minutes hydrocortisone infusion on declarative memory performance in young normal adults. *International Society Psychoneuroendocrinol Abstract, 25.*

Lupien, S. J., Gillin, C. J., & Hauger, R. L. (1999). Working memory is more sensitive than declarative memory to the acute effects of corticosteroids: A dose-response study in humans. *Behavioural Neuroscience, 113*, 420–430.

Lupien, S. J., Lecours, A. R., Schwartz, G., Sharma, S., Hauger, R. L., Meaney, M. J. et al. (1995). Longitudinal study of basal cortisol levels in healthy elderly subjects: Evidence for subgroups. *Neurobiology of Aging, 17*, 95–105.

Lupien, S. J., & McEwen, B. S. (1997). The acute effects of corticosteroids on cognition: Integration of animal and human model studies. *Brain Research Reviews, 24*, 1–27.

Luria, A. R., Naydin, V. L., Tsvetkova, L. S., & Vinarskaya, E. N. (1969). Restoration of higher cortical function following local brain damage. In P. J. Vinken & G. W. Bruyn (Eds.), *Handbook of clinical neurology* (pp. 368–433). Amsterdam, the Netherlands: North-Holland Publishing Co.

Lynch, G. S. (1986). *Synapses, circuits and the beginnings of memory*. Cambridge, MA: MIT Press.

Lynch, G. S., & Baudry, M. (1984). The biochemistry of memory: A new and specific hypothesis. *Science, 224*, 1057–1063.

Lynch, G. S., Larson, J., Kelso, S., Barrionuevo, G., & Schottler, F. (1983). Intracellular injections of EGTA block induction of hippocampal long-term potentiation. *Nature, 305*, 719–721.

Lyon, G. R., & Krasnegor, N. A. (Eds.) (1996). *Attention, memory and executive function*. Baltimore, MD: Paul, H. Brookes.

Lysaker, P. H., Bryson, G. J., Lancaster, R. S., Evans, J. D., & Bell, M. D. (2003a). Insight in schizophrenia: Associations with executive function and coping style. *Schizophrenia Research, 59*(1):41–47.

Lysaker, P. H., Wilt, M. A., Plascak-Hallberg, C. D., Brenner, C. A., & Clements, C. A. (2003b). Personality dimensions in schizophrenia: Associations with symptoms and coping. *Journal of Nervous & Mental Disease, 191*(2), 80–86.

Lyubomirsky, S., Caldwell, N. D., & Nolen-Hoeksema, S. (1998). Effects of ruminative and distracting responses to depressed mood on retrieval of autobiographical memories. *Journal of Personality and Social Psychology, 75*, 166–177.

MacDonald, J. M. A., Just, M. A., & Carpenter, P. A. (1992). Working memory constraints on the processing of syntactic ambiguity. *Cognitive Psychology, 24*, 56–98.

MacGowan, S. H., Wilcoci, G. K., & Scott, M. (1998). Effect of gender and apolipoprotein E genotype on response to anticholinesterase therapy in Alzheimer's disease. *International Journal of Geriatric Psychiatry, 13*, 625–630.

MacKay, D. G. (1987). *The organization of perception and action: A theory for language and other cognitive skills*. New York: Springer-Verlag.

MacLeod, C., & McLaughlin, K. (1995). Implicit and explicit bias in anxiety: A conceptual replication. *Behaviour Research and Therapy, 33*, 1–14.

Madakasira, S., & O'Brian, K. (1987). Acute post-traumatic stress disorder in victims of a natural disaster. *Journal of Nervous and Mental Disease, 175*, 286–290.

Madden, D. J., Turkington, T. G., Provenzale, J. M., Denny, L. L., Hawk, T. C., Gottlob, L. R. et al. (1999). Adult age differences in the functional neuroanatomy of verbal recognition memory. *Human Brain Mapping, 7*(2), 115–135.

Maddock, R. J., Garrett, A. S., & Buonocore, M. H. (2001). Remembering familiar people: The posterior cingulate cortex and autobiographical memory retrieval: *Neuroscience, 104*(3), 667–676.

Maguire, E. A. (1997). Hippocampal involvement in human topographical memory: Evidence from functional imaging. *Philosophical Transactions of the Royal Society, London, 352*, 1475–1480.

Maguire, E. A., Frackowiak, R., & Frith, C. (1996). Learning to find your way: A role for the human hippocampal formation. *Proceedings of the Royal Society of London B Biological Science*, *263*, 1745–1750.

Maguire, E. A., & Mummery, C. J. (1999). Differential modulation of a common memory retrieval network revealed by positron emission tomography. *Hippocampus*, *9*, 54–61.

Magnusson, K. R., & Cotman, C. W. (1993). Age-related changes in excitatory amino acid receptors in two mouse strains. *Neurobiology of Aging*, *14*, 197–206.

Mahler, M. E., & Cummings, J. L. (1990). Alzheimer's disease and the dementia of Parkinson's disease: Comparative investigations. *Alzheimer's Disease and Associated Disorders*, *4*, 133–149.

Mai, F. M. (1995). "Hysteria" in clinical neurology. *Canadian Journal of Neurological Sciences*, *22*, 101–110.

Maillot, F., Belin, C., Perrier, D., & Larmande, P. (1993). Visual perseveration and palinopsia: A visual memory disorder? *Revue Neurologique (Paris)*, *149*, 794–796.

Makatura, T. J., Lam, C. S., Leahy, B. J., Castillo, M. T., & Kalpakjian, C. Z. (1999). Standardized memory tests and the appraisal of everyday memory. *Brain Injury*, *13*(5), 355–367.

Malapani, C., Pillon, B., Dubois, B., & Agid, Y. (1994). Impaired simultaneous cognitive task performance in Parkinson's disease: A dopamine-related dysfunction. *Neurology*, *44*(2), 319–326.

Malec, J., & Questad, K. (1983). Rehabilitation of memory after craniocerebral trauma: Case report. *Archives of Physical Medicine and Rehabilitation*, *64*, 436–438.

Malenka, R. C. (1994). Synaptic plasticity in the hippocampus: LTP and LTD. *Cell*, *78*, 535–538.

Malenka, R. C., & Nicoll, R. A. (1993). NMDA-receptor-dependent synaptic plasticity: Multiple forms and mechanisms. *Trends in Neurosciences*, *16*, 521–527.

Malone, G. L., & Leiman, H. I. (1983). Differential diagnosis of palinacusis in a psychiatric patient. *American Journal of Psychiatry*, *140*, 1067–1068.

Mandler, G. (1980). Recognizing: The judgment of previous occurrence. *Psychological Review*, *87*, 252–271.

Mandler, J. M. (1983). Representation. In P. Mussen (Series Ed.) and J. Flavell & E. Markman (Vol. Eds.), *Handbook of child psychology, Vol. 3, Cognitive development* (pp. 420–494). New York: Wiley.

Manning, C. A., Ragozzino, M. E., & Gold, P. E. (1993). Glucose enhancement of memory in patients with probable senile dementia of the Alzheimer's type. *Neurobiology of Aging*, *14*, 523–528.

Manzano, J. M., Llorca, G., Ledesma, A., & Lopez-Ibor, J. J. (1994). Spanish adaptation of the Alzheimer's disease assessment scale (ADAS). *Actas Luso Espanolas de Neurologia Psiquiatria Ciencias Afines*, *22*, 64–70.

Mao, Z-M., Arnsten, A. F. T., & Li, B-M. (1999). Local infusion of an α-1 adrenergic agonist into the prefrontal cortex impairs spatial working memory performance in monkeys. *Biological Psychiatry*, *46*, 1259–1265.

Maquet, P., Laureys, S., Peigneux, P., Fuchs, S., Petiau, C., Phillips, C. et al. (2000). Experience-dependent changes in cerebral activation during human REM sleep. *Nature Neuroscience*, *3*(8), 831–836.

Marcopulos, B. A., McLain, C. A., & Giuliano, A. J. (1997). Cognitive impairment or inadequate norms? A study of health, rural, older adults with limited education. *The Clinical Neuropsychologist*, *11*, 111–131.

Marcusson, J., Rother, M., Kittner, B., Rossner, M., Smith, R. J., Babic, T. et al. (1997). A 12-month, randomized, placebo-controlled trial of propentofylline (HWA 285) in patients with dementia according to DSM III–R. *Dementia and Geriatric Cognitive Disorders*, *8*, 320–328.

Maren, S. (1999). Neurotoxic basolateral amygdala lesions impair learning and memory but not performance of conditional fear in rats. *Journal of Neuroscience*, *19*, 8696–9703.

Maren, S. (2000). Reply to Vazdarjanova. *Trends in Neuroscience*, *23*(8), 345–346.

Maren, S. (2001). Neurobiology of Pavlovian fear conditioning. *Annual Review in Neuroscience, 24,* 897–931.

Maren, S., & Fanselow, M. S. (1995). Synaptic plasticity in the basolateral amygdala induced by hippocampal formation stimulation in vivo. *Journal of Neuroscience, 15*(11), 7548–7564.

Maren, S., Tocco, G., Standley, S., Baudry, M., & Thompson, R. F. (1993). Postsynaptic factors in the expression of long-term potentiation (LTP): Increased glutamate receptor binding following LTP induction in vivo. *Proceedings of the National Academy of Science of the United States of America, 90,* 9654–9658.

Markowitsch, H. J. (Ed.) (1990). *Transient global amnesia and related disorders.* Toronto: Hogrefe & Huber Publishers.

Markowitsch, H. J. (1995). Anatomical basis of memory disorders. In M. S. Gazzaniga (Ed.), *The cognitive neurosciences* (pp. 665–679). Cambridge, MA: MIT Press.

Markowitsch, H. J., Calabresse, P., Haupts, M., Durwen, H. F., Liess, J., & Gehlen, W. (1993a). Searching for the anatomical basis of retrograde amnesia. *Journal of Clinical and Experimental Neuropsychology, 15*(6), 947–967.

Markowitsch, H. J., Calabresse, P., Wurker, M., Durwen, H. F., Kessler, J., Babinsky, R. et al. (1994). The amygdala's contribution to memory—a study on two patients with Urbach-Wiethe disease. *NeuroReport, 5,* 1349–1352.

Markowitsch, H. J., Kessler, J., Russ, M. O., Frölich, L., Schneider, B., & Maurer, K. (1999). Mnestic block syndrome. *Cortex, 35,* 219–230.

Markowitsch, H. J., Kessler, J., Van Der Ven, C., Weber-Luxenburger, B., & Heiss, W. D. (1998). Psychic trauma causing grossly reduced brain metabolism and cognitive deterioration. *Neuropsychologia, 36,* 77–82.

Markowitsch, H. J., von Cramon, D. Y., & Schuri, U. (1993b). Mnestic performance profile of a bilateral diencephalic infarct patient with preserved intelligence and severe amnesic disturbances. *Journal of Clinical & Experimental Neuropsychology, 15*(5), 627–652.

Marks, G. A., Shaffery, J. P., Oksenberg, A., Speciale, S. G., & Roffwarg, H. P. (1995). A functional role for REM sleep in brain maturation. *Behavioral Brain Research, 69,* 1–11.

Marsh, R. L., & Landau, J. D. (1995). Item availability in cryptomnesia: Assessing its role in two paradigms of unconscious plagiarism. *Journal of Experimental Psychology: Learning, Memory and Cognition, 21,* 1568–1582.

Martin, A. (2000). Functional neuroimaging of semantic memory. In R. Cabeza & A. Kingstone (Ed.), *Handbook of functional neuroimaging of cognition.* Cambridge, MA: MIT Press.

Martin, A., Brouwers, P., Lalonde, F., Cox, C., Teleska, P., Fedio, P. et al. (1986). Towards a behavioral typology of Alzheimer's patients. *Journal of Clinical & Experimental Neuropsychology, 8*(5), 594–610.

Martin, A., & Fedio, P. (1983). Word production and comprehension in Alzheimer's disease: The breakdown of semantic knowledge. *Brain and Language, 19,* 124–141.

Martin, A., Haxby, J. V., Lalonde, F. M., Wiggs, C. L., & Ungerleider, L. G. (1995). Discrete cortical regions associated with knowledge of color and knowledge of action. *Science, 270*(5233), 102–105.

Martin, A., Wiggs, C. L., Ungerleider, L. G., & Haxby, J. V. (1996). Neural correlates of category-specific knowledge. *Nature, 379,* 649–652.

Martin, G. R., Eglen, R. M., Hamblin, M. W., Hoyer, D., & Yocca, F. (1998). The structure and signaling properties of 5-HT receptors: And endless diversity? *Trends in Pharmacological Sciences, 19,* 2–4.

Martin, M. (1986). Ageing and patterns of change in everyday memory and cognition. *Human Learning, 5,* 63–74.

Martin, M., Williams, R. M., & Clark, D. M. (1991). Does anxiety lead to selective processing of threat-related information? *Behaviour Research and Therapy, 29,* 147–160.

Martin, N., & Saffran, E. M. (1997). Language and auditory-verbal short-term memory impairments: Evidence for common underlying processes. *Cognitive Neuropsychology, 14,* 641–682.

Martin, R. C. (1987). Articulatory and phonological deficits in short-term memory and their relation to syntactic processing. *Brain and Language, 32*, 159–191.

Martin, R. C., & Feher, E. (1990). The consequences of reduced memory span for the comprehension of semantic versus syntactic information. *Brain and Language, 38*, 1–20.

Martone, M., Butters, N., Payne, M., Becker, J. T., & Sax, D. S. (1984). Dissociations between skill learning and verbal recognition in amnesia and dementia. *Archives of Neurology, 41*, 965–970.

Masserman, P. J., Delis, D. C., Butters, N., Levin, B. E., & Salmon, D. P. (1990). Are all subcortical dementias alike? Verbal learning and memory in Parkinson's and Huntington's disease patients. *Journal of Clinical and Experimental Neuropsychology, 12*, 729–744.

Massoud, F., Chertkow, H., Whitehead, V., Overbury, O., & Bergman, H. (2002). Word-reading thresholds in Alzheimer disease and mild memory loss: A pilot study. *Alzheimer Disease and Associated Disorders, 16*(1), 31–39.

Masuo, O., Maeshima, S., Kubo, K., Terada, T., Nakai, K., Itakura, T. et al. (1999). A case of amnestic syndrome caused by a subcortical haematoma in the right occipital lobe. *Brain Injury, 13*, 213–216.

Masur, D. M., Fuld, P. A., Blau, A. D., Crystal, H., & Aronson, M. K. (1990). Predicting development of dementia in the elderly with the Selective Reminding Test. *Journal of Clinical and Experimental Neuropsychology, 12*, 529–538.

Masur, D. M., Fuld, P. A., Blau, A. D., Thal, L. J., Levin, H. S., & Aronson, M. K. (1989). Distinguishing normal and demented elderly with the Selective Reminding Test. *Journal of Clinical and Experimental Neuropsychology, 11*, 615–630.

Mateer, C. A., Sohlberg, M. M., & Crinean, J. (1987). Perceptions of memory functioning in individuals with closed head injury. *Journal of Head Trauma Rehabilitation, 2*, 74–84.

Mateer, C., Sohlberg, M. M., & Youngman, P. K. (1990). The management of acquired attention and memory deficits. In R. L. Wood & I. Fussey (Ed.), *Cognitive rehabilitation in perspective* (pp. 68–95). New York: Taylor & Francis.

Mathews, A., Mogg, K., May, J., & Eysenck, M. (1989). Implicit and explicit memory bias in anxiety. *Journal of Abnormal Psychology, 98*, 236–240.

Mattis, S. (1976). Mental status examination for organic mental syndrome in the elderly patients. In L. Bellak & T. B. Karasu (Eds.), *Geriatric psychiatry: A handbook for psychiatrists and primary care physicians* (pp. 77–121). New York: Grune & Stratton.

Mattson, S. N., Riley, E. P., Delis, D. C., Stern, C., & Jones, K. L. (1996). Verbal learning and memory in children with fetal alcohol syndrome. *Alcoholism: Clinical and Experimental Research, 20*, 810–816.

Matzel, L. D., Muzzio, I. A., & Talk, A. C. (1996). Variations in learning reflect individual differences in sensory function and synaptic integration. *Behavioral Neuroscience, 110*(5), 1084–1095.

Mayberg, H. S., Brannan, S. K., Mahurin, R. K., Jerabek, P. A., Brickman, J. S., Tekell, J. L., et al. (1997). Cingulate function in depression: A potential predictor of treatment response. *NeuroReport, 8*(4), 1057–1061.

Mayberg, H. S., Liotti, M., Brannan, S. K., McGinnis, S., Mahwin, R. K., Jerabek, P. A. et al. (1999). Reciprocal limbic-cortical function and negative mood: Converging PET findings in depression and normal sadness. *American Journal of Psychiatry, 156*, 675–682.

Mayer, M. L., & Westbrook, G. L. (1987). The physiology of excitatory amino acids in the vertebrate central nervous system. *Progress in Neurobiology, 28*, 197–276.

Mayer, R. E. (1977). Problem solving performance with task overload: Effects of self-pacing and trait anxiety. *Bulletin of the Psychonomic Society, 9*, 283–286.

Mayes, A. R., Daum, I., Markowitsch, H. J., & Sauter, B. (1997). Retrograde memory performance in a group of anterogradely amnesic patients. *Cortex, 33*, 197–217.

Mayes, A. R., & Downes, J. J. (1997). What do theories of the functional deficit(s) underlying amnesia have to explain? *Memory, 5*, 3–36.

Mayes, A. R., Gooding, P. A., & van Eijk, R. (1997). A new theoretical framework for explicit and implicit memory. *Psyche*, *3*(2), 1–43.

Mayes, A. R., & Warburg, R. (1992). Memory assessment in clinical practice and research. In J. R. Crawford, D. M. Parker, & W. W. McKinlay (Eds.), *A handbook of neuropsychological assessment*. Hove, UK: Lawrence Erlbaum Associates Ltd.

Maylor, E. A. (1990). Recognizing and naming faces: Aging, memory retrieval and the tip of the tongue state. *Journal of Gerontology: Psychological Sciences*, *46*, 207–217.

Mazurek, M. F., & Beal, F. (1991). Cholecystokinin and somatostatin in Alzheimer's disease postmortem cerebral cortex. *Neurology*, *41*, 716–719.

Mazziotta, J. C., Frackowiak, R. S. J., & Phelps, M. E. (1992). The use of positron emission tomography in the clinical assessment of dementia. *Seminars in Nuclear Medicine*, *22*, 233–246.

McAdams, D. P., Hoffman, B. J., Mansfield, E. D., & Day, R. (1996). Themes of agency and communion in significant autobiographical scenes. *Journal of Personality*, *64*, 339–377.

McCann, U. D., Ridenour, A., Shaham, Y., & Ricaurte, G. A. (1994). Serotonin neurotoxicity after (±) 3, 4-methylenedioxymethamphetamine (MDMA; "Ecstasy"): A controlled study in humans. *Neuropsychopharmacology*, *10*(2), 129–138.

McCarthy, G., Blamire, A. M., Rothman, D. L., Gruetter, R., & Shulman, R. G. (1993). Echoplanar magnetic resonance imaging studies of frontal cortex activation during word generation in humans. *Proceedings of the National Academy of Sciences of the United States of America*, *90*(11), 4952–4956.

McCarthy, G., Puce, A., Constable, R. T., Krystal, J. H., Gore, J. C., & Goldman-Rakic, P. (1996). Activation of human prefrontal cortex during spatial and nonspatial working memory tasks measured by functional MRI. *Cerebral Cortex*, *6*, 600–611.

McClelland, J. L., McNaughton, B. L., & O'Reilly, R. C. (1995). Why are there complementary learning systems in the hippocampus and neocortex: Insights from the successes and failures of connectionist models of learning and memory. *Psychological Review*, *102*, 419–457.

McCormick, D. A., & Thompson, R. F. (1987). Neuronal responses of the rabbit cerebellum during acquisition and performance of a classically conditioned NM-eyelid response. *Journal of Neuroscience*, *4*, 2811–2822.

McDaniel, M. A., Glisky, E. L., Rubin, S. R., Guynn, M. J., & Routhieaux, B. C. (1999). Prospective memory: A neuropsychological study. *Neuropsychology*, *13*(1), 103–110.

McDonald, J. W., & Johnston, M. V. (1990). Physiological and pathophysiological roles of excitatory amino acids during central nervous system development. *Brain Research Reviews*, *15*, 41–70.

McDougall, G. J. (1995). Memory self-efficacy and strategy use in sucessful elders. *Educational Gerontology*, *21*, 357–373.

McDougall, G. J. (2002). Memory improvement in octogenarians. *Applied Nursing Research*, *15*(1), 2–10.

McDowell, J. E., & Clementz, B. A. (1996). Ocular-motor delayed response task performance among schizophrenia patients. *Neuropsychobiology*, *34*, 67–71.

McDowell, S., Whyte, J., & D'Esposito, M. (1997). Working memory impairments in traumatic brain injury: Evidence from a dual-task paradigm. *Neuropsychologia*, *35*, 1341–1353.

McEntee, W. J., & Crook, T. H. (1990). Age-associated memory impairment. A role for catecholamines. *Neurology*, *40*, 526–530.

McEvoy, J. P., & Freter, S. (1989). The dose–response relationship for memory impairment by cholinergic drugs. *Comprehensive Psychiatry*, *30*(2), 135–138.

McEwen, B. S., De Kloet, E. R., & Rostene, W. (1986). Adrenal steroid receptors and actions in the nervous system. *Physiological Reviews*, *66*(4), 1121–1188.

McGaugh, J. L. (1973). Drug facilitation of learning and memory. *Annual Review of Pharmacology*, *13*, 229–241.

McGaugh, J. L. (1983). Hormonal influences on memory. *Annual Review of Psychology*, *34*, 297–323.

McGaugh, J. L. (1989). Dissociating learning and performance: Drug and hormone enhancement of memory storage. *Brain Research Bulletin, 23*(4–5), 339–345.

McGaugh, J. L. (2000). Memory—a century of consolidation. *Science, 287*, 248–251.

McGaugh, J. L., & Cahill, L. (1997). Interaction of neuromodulatory systems in modulating memory storage. *Behavioural Brain Research, 83*(1–2), 31–38.

McGaugh, J. L., Cahill, L., Parent, M. B., Mesches, M. H., Coleman-Mesches, K., & Salinas, J. A. (1995). In J. L. McGaugh, F. Bermudez-Rattoni, & R. A. Prado-Alcala (Eds.), *Plasticity in the central nervous system: Learning and memory.* Mahwah, NJ: Lawrence Erlbaum Associates Inc.

McGaugh, J. L., Cahill, L., & Roozendaal, B. (1996). Involvement of the amygdala in memory storage: Interaction with other brain systems. *Proceedings of the National Academy of Science of the United States of America, 26,* 93(24), 13508–13514.

McGaugh, J. L., & Gold, P. E. (1989). In R. B. Brush & S. Levine (Eds.), *Psychoendocrinology* (pp. 305–339). New York: Academic Press.

McGaugh, J. L., & Herz, M. J. (1972). *Memory consolidation.* San Francisco: Albion.

McGaugh, J. L., Introini-Collison, I. B., Cahill, L. F., Castellano, C., Dalmaz, C., Parent, M. B. et al. (1993). Neuromodulatory systems and memory storage: Role of the amygdala. *Behavioral Brain Research, 58,* 81–90.

McGaugh, J. L., Introini-Collison, I. B., & Nagahara, A. H. (1988). Memory-enhancing effects of posttraining naloxone: Involvement of beta-noradrenergic influences in the amygdaloid complex. *Brain Research, 446*(1), 37–49.

McGeer, P., McGeer, E., & Suzuki, J. (1977). Ageing and extra-pyramidal function. *Archives of Neurology, 34,* 33–35.

McGeer, P., Schulzer, M., & McGeer, E. (1997). Arthritis and anti-inflammatory agents as possible protective factors for Alzheimer's disease. A review of 17 epidemiologic studies. *Neurology, 47,* 425–432.

McGinnis, D., & Roberts, P. (1996). Qualitative characteristics of vivid memories attributed to real and imagined experiences. *American Journal of Psychology, 109*(1), 59–77.

McGlynn, S. M., & Schachter, D. L. (1989). Unawareness of deficits in neuropsychological syndromes. *Journal of Clinical and Experimental Neuropsychology, 11,* 143–205.

McHugh, P. R., & Folstein, M. F. (1975). Psychiatric syndromes of Huntington's chorea: A clinical and phenomenologic study. In D. F. Benson & D. Blumer (Eds.), *Psychiatric aspects of neurologic disease* (pp. 267–285). New York: Grune & Stratton.

McIntosh, T. K. (1993). Novel pharmacological therapies in the treatment of experimental traumatic brain injury: A review. *Journal of Neurotrauma, 10,* 215–261.

McIntyre, J. S., & Craik, F. I. M. (1987). Age differences in memory for item and source information. *Canadian Journal of Psychology, 41,* 175–192.

McKay, A. C., & Dundee, J. W. (1980). Effect of oral benzodiazepines on memory. *British Journal of Anaesthesia, 52,* 1247–1257.

McKenna, P., Clare, L., & Baddeley, A. D. (1995). Schizophrenia. In A. D., Baddeley, B. A. Wilson, & F. N. Watts (Eds.), *Handbook of memory disorders.* New York: John Wiley & Sons.

McKenna, P. J., Tamlyn, D., Lund, C. E., Mortimer, A. M., Hammond, S., & Baddeley, A. D. (1990). Amnesic syndrome in schizophrenia. *Psychological Medicine, 20,* 967–972.

McKernan, M. G., & Shinnick-Gallagher, P. (1997). Fear conditioning induces a lasting potentiation of synaptic currents in vitro. *Nature, 390,* 607–611.

McKhann, G., Drachman, D., Folstein, M., Katzman, R., Price, D., & Stadlan, E. M. (1984). Clinical diagnosis of Alzheimer's disease: Report of the NINCDS-ADRDA Work Group under the auspices of Department of Health and Human Services Task Force on Alzheimer's Disease. *Neurology, 34,* 939–944.

McKinlay, W., & Watkiss, A. J. (1999). Cognitive, and behavioural effect of brain injury. In M. Rosenthal, E. R. Griffith, J. S. Kreutzer, & B. Pentland (Eds.), *Rehabilitation of the adult and child with traumatic brain injury, 3rd Edn* (pp. 74–86). Philadelphia: F. A. Davis.

McKitrick, L. A., & Camp, C. J. (1993). Relearning the names of things: The spaced-retrieval intervention implemented by a caregiver. *Clinical Gerontologist, 14*, 60–62.

McKitrick, L. A., Camp, C. J., & Black, F. W. (1992). Prospective memory intervention in Alzheimer's disease. *Journal of Gerontology, 47*, 337–343.

McLean, A. Jr., Cardenas, D. D., Burgess, D., & Gamzu, E. (1991). Placebo-controlled study of pramiracetam in young males with memory and cognitive problems resulting from head injury and anoxia. *Brain Injury, 5*(4), 375–380.

McNally, R. J., Foa, E. B., & Donnel, C. D. (1989). Memory bias for anxiety information in patients with panic disorder. *Cognition and Emotion, 3*, 27–44.

McNally, R. J., Lasko, N. B., Macklin, M. L., & Pitman, R. K. (1995). Autobiographical memory disturbance in combat-related posttraumatic stress disorder. *Behaviour Research and Therapy, 33*, 619–630.

McNally, R. J., Litz, B. T., Prassas, A., Shin, L. M., & Weathers, F. W. (1994). Emotional priming of autobiographical memory in posttraumatic stress disorder. *Cognition and Emotion, 8*, 351–367.

McNamara, R. K., & Skelton, R. W. (1992). Like diazepam, CL 218, 872 a selective ligand for the benzodiazepine ω_1 receptor subtype impairs place learning in the Morris water maze. *Psychopharmacology, 107*, 347–351.

McNaughton, B. L. (1983). Activity dependent modulation of hippocampal synaptic efficacy. Some implications for memory processes. In W. Seifert (Ed.), *The neurobiology of the hippocampus* (pp. 233–253). London: Academic Press.

Meacham, J. A., & Leiman, B. (1982). Remembering to perform future actions. In U. Neisser (Ed.), *Memory observed: Remembering in natural contexts* (pp. 327–336). San Francisco: WH Freeman.

Media, K. R., Ryabinin, A. E., Corodimas, K. P., Wilson, M. C., & LeDoux, J. E. (1996). Alcohol, C-fos, context, fear conditioning and memory. Hippocampal-dependent learning and experience-dependent activation of the hippocampus are preferentially disrupted by ethanol. *Neuroscience, 74*, 313–322.

Mehta, M. A., Sahakian, B. J., McKenna, P. J., & Robbins, T. W. (1999). Systematic sulpiride in young adult volunteers simulates the profile of cognitive deficits in Parkinson's disease. *Psychopharmacology, 146*, 162–174.

Meier, E., Cohen, R., & Koemeda-Lutz, M. (1990). Short-term memory of aphasics in comparing token stimuli. *Brain and Cognition, 12*, 161–181.

Meiri, N., & Rosenblum, K. (1998). Lateral ventricle injection of the protein synthesis inhibitor anisomycin impairs long-term memory in a spatial memory task. *Brain Research, 789*, 48–55.

Mellet, E., Bricogne, S., Tzourio-Mazoyer, N., Ghaem, O., Petit, L., Zago, L. et al. (2000). Neural correlates of topographic mental exploration: The impact of route versus survey perspective learning. *NeuroImage, 12*, 588–600.

Mellon, S. H. (1994). Neurosteroids: Biochemistry, modes of action, and clinical relevance. *Journal of Clinical Endocrinology and Metabolism, 78*, 1003–1008.

Mendiondo, M. S., Ashford, J. W., Kryscio, R. J., & Schmitt, F. A. (2000). Modelling Mini Mental State Examination changes in Alzheimer's disease. *Statistics in Medicine, 19*, 1607–1616.

Meneses, A. (1998). Physiological, pathophysiological and therapeutic roles of 5-HT systems in learning and memory. *Reviews in the Neurosciences, 9*(4), 275–289.

Meneses, A. (1999a). Review of 5-HT system and cognition. *Neuroscience Biobehavioral Reviews, 23*, 1111–1125.

Meneses, A. (1999b). Are 5-HT1B/1D and 5-HT2A/2B/2C receptors involved in learning and memory processes? *IDrugs, 2*(8), 796–801.

Meneses, A., & Hong, E. (1997). Effects of 5-HT4 receptor agonists and antagonists in learning. *Pharmacology Biochemistry and Behavior, 56*, 347–351.

Meneses, A., Terron, J. A., & Hong, E., (1997). Effects of 5-HT receptor antagonists GR127935T (5-HT1B/1D) and MDL 100, 907 (5-HT2A) in the consolidation of learning. *Behavioral Brain Research, 89*, 217–223.

Mesulam, M. M. (1998). From sensation to cognition. *Brain*, *121*, 1013–1052.

Meudell, P. R., Mayes, A. R., Ostergaard, A., & Pickering, A. (1985). Recency and frequency judgments in alcoholic amnesics and normal people with poor memory. *Cortex*, *21*, 487–511.

Meulemans, T., & Van der Linden, M. (1997). Does the artificial grammar learning paradigm involve the acquisition of complex information? *Psychologica Belgica*, *37*, 69–88.

Meunier, M., Bachevalier, J., & Mishkin, M. (1997). Effects of orbital frontal and anterior cingulate lesions on object and spatial memory in rhesus monkeys. *Neuropsychologia*, *35*(7), 999–1015.

Meunier, M., Bachevalier, J., Murray, E. A., Malkova, L. & Mishkin, M. (1999). Effects of aspiration versus neurotoxic lesions of the amygdala on emotional responses in monkeys. *European Journal of Neuroscience*, *11*(12), 4403–4418.

Mewaldt, S., & Ghoneim, M. (1979). The effects and interactions of scopolamine, physostigmine and methamphetamine on human memory. *Pharmacology, Biochemistry and Behavior*, *10*, 205–210.

Meyers, J. E., & Meyers, K. R. (1995). *Rey Complex Figure Test and Recognition Trial: Professional manual*. Odessa, FL: Psychological Assessment Resources.

Micco, D. J., & McEwen, B. S. (1980). Glucocorticoids, the hippocampus, and behavior: Interactive relation between task activation and steroid hormone binding specificity. *Journal of Comparative and Physiological Psychology*, *94*, 624–633.

Miceli, G., Capasso, R., Daniele, A., Esposito, T., Magarelli, M., & Tomaiulo, F. (2000). Selective deficit for people's names following left temporal damage: An impairment of domain-specific conceptual knowledge. *Cognitive Neuropsychology*, *17*, 489–516.

Michel, E. M., & Troost, T. (1980). Pallinopsia cerebral localization with computed tomography. *Neurology*, *30*, 887–889.

Migliorelli, R., Teson, A., Sabe, L., Petraachi, M., Leiguarda, R., & Starkstein, S. (1995). Prevalence and correlates of dysthymia and major depression among patients with Alzheimer's disease. *American Journal of Psychiatry*, *152*, 37–44.

Miles, C., Morgan, M. J., Milne, A. B., & Morris, E. D. M. (1996). Developmental and individual differences in visual memory span. *Current Psychology: Developmental, Learning, Personality, Social*, *15*, 53–67.

Miller, E., & Morris, R. G. (1993). *The psychology of dementia*. Chichester: John Wiley & Sons.

Miller, L. A., Munoz, D. G., & Finmore, M. (1993). Hippocampal sclerosis and human memory. *Archives of Neurology*, *50*, 391–394.

Milner, B. (1962). Les troubles de la mémoire accompagnant des lésions hippocampiques bilatérales. In P. Passouant (Ed.), *Physiologie de l'hippocampe*. Paris: Centre National de la Recherche Scientifique.

Milner, B. (1963). Effects of different brain lesions on card sorting. *Archives of Neurology*, *9*, 90–100.

Milner, B. (1972). Disorders of learning and memory after temporal lobe lesion in man. *Clinical Neurosurgery*, *19*, 421–446.

Milner, B. (1985). Memory and the human brain. In M. Shaffo (Ed.), *How we know*. San Francisco: Harper & Row.

Milner, B., Petrides, M., & Smith, M. L. (1985). Frontal lobes and the temporal organization of memory. *Human Neurobiology*, *4*, 137–142.

Milner, B., Squire, L. R., & Kandel, E. R. (1998). Cognitive neuroscience and the study of memory. *Neuron*, *20*, 445–468.

Mimura, M., Kato, M., Watanabe, R., Tanabe, A., Isbii, K., & Kashima, H. (1997). Autobiographical memory loss following herpes encephalitis. *Brain & Nerve*, *49*(8), 759–764.

Minderhoud, J. M., Van Zomeren, A. H., & Van der Naalt, J. (1996). The fronto-temporal component in mild and moderately severe head injury. *Acta Neurologica Belgica*, *96*(1), 31–34.

Mineka, S., & Nugent, K. (1995). Mood-congruent memory biases in anxiety and depression. In D. L., Schacter (Ed.), *Memory distortion: How minds, brains and societies reconstruct the past*. Cambridge, MA: Harvard University Press.

Minoshima, S., Giordani, B., Berent, S., Frey, K., Foster, N., & Kuhl, D. (1997). Metabolic reduction in the posterior cingulate cortex in very early Alzheimer's disease. *Annals of Neurology, 42*, 85–94.

Minshew, N. J., & Goldstein, G. (1993). Is autism an amnesic disorder? Evidence from the California Verbal Learning Test. *Neuropsychology, 7*, 209–216.

Mischel, W. (1979). In the interface of cognition and personality. Beyond the person–situation debate. *American Psychologist, 34*, 740–754.

Mishkin, M. (1982). A memory system in the monkey. *Philosophical Transactions of the Royal Society, London, B, 298*, 85.

Mishkin, M., Ungerleider, L. G., & Macko, M. A. (1983). Object vision and spatial vision: Two cortical pathways. *Journal of Verbal Learning Behavior, 6*, 414, 417.

Mitchell, T. W., Mufson, E. J., Schneider, J. A., Cochran, E. J., Nissanov, J., Han, L. Y., Bienias, J. L., et al. (2002). Parahippocampal tau pathology in healthy aging, mild cognitive impairment, and early Alzheimer's disease. *Annals of Neurology, 51*(2), 182–189.

Mitrushina, M., Satz, P., Chervinsky, A., & D'elia, L. (1991). Performance of four age groups of normal elderly on the Rey Auditory-Verbal Learning Test. *Journal of Clinical Psychology, 47*(3), 351–357.

Miyashita, Y., Kameyama, M., Hasegawa, I., & Fukushima, T. (1998). Consolidation of visual associative long-term memory in the temporal cortex of primates. *Neurobiology of Learning Memory, 70*, 197–211.

Moayeri, S. E., Cahill, L., Jin, Y., & Potkin, S. G. (2000). Relative sparing of emotionally influenced memory in Alzheimer's disease. *Neuroreport, 11*, 653–655.

Moffat, N. J. (1989). Home-based cognitive rehabilitation with the elderly. In L. W. Poon, D. C. Rubin, & B. A. Wilson (Eds.), *Everyday cognition in adulthood and late life* (pp. 659–680). New York: Cambridge University Press.

Moffoot, A. P. R., O'Carroll, R. E., Bennie, J., Carroll, S., Dick, H., Ebmeier, K. P. et al. (1994). Diurnal variation of mood and neuropsychological function in major depression with melancholia. *Journal of Affective Disorders, 32*(4), 257–269.

Mogg, K., & Mathews, A. (1990). Is there a self-referent mood congruent recall bias in anxiety? *Behaviour Research and Therapy, 28*, 91–92.

Mohr, E., Feldman, H., & Gauthier, S. (1995a). Canadian guidelines for the development of antidementia therapies: A conceptual summary. *Canadian Journal of Neurological Sciences, 22*(1), 62–71.

Mohr, E., Mendis, T., & Grimes, J. D. (1995b). Late cognitive changes in Parkinson's disease with an emphasis on dementia. In W. J. Weiner & A. E. Lang (Eds.), *Behavioral neurology of movement disorders, advances in neurology, 65*, New York: Raven Press.

Mohs, R. C., & Cohen, L. (1988). Alzheimer's disease assessment scale (ADAS). *Psychopharmacology Bulletin, 24*, 627–628.

Molloy, D., Alemayehu, E., & Roberts, R. (1991). Reliability of a standardized Mini-Mental State Examination compared with the Traditional Mini-Mental State Examination. *American Journal of Psychiatry, 148*(1), 102–105.

Molloy, R., Brownell, H. H., & Gardner, H. (1990). Discourse comprehension by right-hemisphere stroke patients: Deficits of prediction and revision. In Y. Joanette & H. H. Brownell (Eds.), *Discourse ability and brain damage: Theoretical and empirical perspectives* (pp. 113–130). New York: Springer-Verlag.

Monti, L. A., Gabrieli, J. D. E., Reminger, S. L., Rinaldi, J. A., Wilson, R. S., & Fleischman, D. A. (1996). Differential effects of aging and Alzheimer's disease on conceptual implicit and explicit memory. *Neuropsychology, 10*(1), 101–112.

Montminy, M. R., Gonzalez, G. A., & Yamamoto, K. K. (1990). Regulation of cAMP-inducible genes by CREB. *Trends in Neuroscience, 13*, 184–188.

Monyer, H., Sprengel, R., Schoepfer, R., Herb, A., Higuchi, M., Lomeli, H. et al. (1992). Heteromeric NMDA receptors: Molecular and functional distinction of subtypes. *Science, 256*(5060), 1217–1221.

Moradi, A. R., Doost, H. T. N., Taghavi, M. R., Yule, W., & Dagleish, T. (1999). Everyday memory deficits in children and adolescents with PTSD: Performance on the Rivermead Behavioural Memory Test. *Journal of Child Psychiatry, 40*(3), 357–361.

Morales, M., Battenberg, E., de Lecea, L., Sanna, P. P., & Bloom, F. E. (1996). Cellular and subcellular immunolocalization of the type 3 serotonin receptor in the rat central nervous system. *Molecular Brain Research, 36,* 251–260.

Morgan, D., Diamond, D. M., Gottschall, P. E., Ugen, K. E., Dickey, C., Hardy, J. et al. (2000). A beta peptide vaccination prevents memory loss in an animal model of Alzheimer's disease. [erratum appears in *Nature*, 2001, Aug 9; *412*(6847), 660]. *Nature, 408*(6815), 982–985.

Morgan, M. J. (2000). Ecstasy (MDMA): A review of its possible persistent psychological effects. *Psychopharmacology, 152,* 230–248.

Mori, E., Ikeda, M., Hirono, N., Kitagaki, H., Imamura, T., & Shimomura, T. (1999). Amygdalar volume and emotional memory in Alzheimer's disease. *American Journal of Psychiatry, 156,* 216–222.

Mori, E., Lee, K., Yasuda, M., Hashimoto, M., Kazui, H., Hirono, N. et al. (2002). Accelerated hippocampal atrophy in Alzheimer's disease with apolipoprotein E ε4 allele. *Annals of Neurology, 51,* 209–214.

Morice, R. (1990). Cognitive inflexibility and pre-frontal dysfunction in schizophrenia and mania. *British Journal Psychiatry, 157,* 50–54.

Morice, R., & Delahunty, A. (1996). Frontal/executive impairments in schizophrenia. *Schizophrenia Bulletin, 22,* 125–137.

Morris, C. D., Bransford, J. D., & Franks, J. J. (1977). Levels of processing versus transfer appropriate processing. *Journal of Verbal Learning & Verbal Behavior, 16,* 519–533.

Morris, J. C. (1993). The clinical dementia rating (CDR): Current version and scoring rules. *Neurology, 43*(11), 2412–2414.

Morris, J. C., Heyman, A., Mohs, R. C., Hughes, J. P., van Belle, G., Fillenbaum, G. et al. (1989). The consortium to establish a registry for Alzheimer's disease (CERAD). Part I. Clinical and neuropsychological assessment of Alzheimer's disease. *Neurology, 39,* 1159–1165.

Morris, J. C., & Price, J. L. (2001). Pathologic correlates of nondemented aging, mild cognitive impairment, and early stage Alzheimer's disease. *Journal of Molecular Neuroscience, 17,* 101–118.

Morris, J. C., Storandt, M., McKeel, D. W. Rubin, E. H., Price, J. L., Grant, E. A. et al. (1996a). Cerebral amyloid deposition and diffuse plaques in "normal" aging: Evidence for presymptomatic and very mild Alzheimer's disease. *Neurology, 46,* 707–719.

Morris, J. S., Frith, C. D., Perrett, D. I., Rowland, D., Young, A. W., Calder, A. J. et al. (1996b). A differential neural response in the human amygdala to fearful and happy facial expressions. *Nature, 383*(6603), 812–815.

Morris, R. G. (1994). Working memory in Alzheimer-type dementia. *Neuropsychology, 8,* 544–554.

Morris, R. G. M. (1986). Short-term forgetting in senile dementia of the Alzheimer's type. *Cognitive Neuropsychology, 3,* 77–97.

Morris, R. G. M. (1989). Synaptic plasticity and learning: Selective impairment of learning in rats and blockade of long-term potentiation in vivo by the N-methyl-D-aspartate receptor antagonists AP5. *Journal of Neuroscience, 9,* 3040–3057.

Morris, R. G. M., Anderson, E., Lynch, G. S., & Baudry, M. (1986). Selective impairment of learning and blockade of long-term potentiation by an N-methyl-D-aspartate receptor antagonist AP5. *Nature, 319,* 774–776.

Morse, C. K. (1993). Does variability increase with age? An archival study of cognitive measures. *Psychology and Aging, 8,* 156–164.

Morton, J. (1969). Interaction of information in word recognition. *Psychological Review, 76,* 165–178.

Moscovitch, M. (1989). Confabulations and the frontal system: Strategic vs. associative retrieval in neuropsychological theories of memory. In H. L. Roediger III & F. I. M. Craik (Eds.), *Varieties of memory and consciousness: Essays in honour of Endel Tulving* (pp. 133–160). Hillsdale, NJ: Lawrence Erlbaum Associates Inc.

Moscovitch, M. (1992). Memory and working-with-memory: A component process model based on modules and central systems. *Journal of Cognitive Neuroscience, 4*, 257–267.

Moscovitch, M. (1994). Cognitive resources and DA interference effects at retrieval in normal people: The role of the frontal lobes and medial temporal cortex. *Neuropsychology, 8*, 524–534.

Moscovitch, M., Kapur, S., Kohler, S., & Houle, S. (1995). Distinct neural correlates of visual long-term memory for spatial location and object identity: A positron emission tomography study in humans. *Proceedings of the National Academy of Sciences of the United States of America, 92*(9), 3721–3725.

Moscovitch, M., & Melo, B. (1997). Strategic retrieval and the frontal lobes: Evidence from confabulation and amnesia. *Neuropsychologia, 35*, 1017–1034.

Moscovitch, M., & Umilta, C. (1990). Modularity and neuropsychology: Implications for the organization of attention and memory in normal and brain-damaged people. In M. F. Schwartz (Ed.), *Modular processes in dementia* (pp. 1–59). Cambridge, MA: MIT/Bradford.

Moscovitch, M., & Umilta, C. (1991). Conscious and nonconscious aspects of memory: A neuropsychological framework of modules and central systems. In R. Lister & H. Weingartner (Eds.), *Perspectives in cognitive neuroscience* (pp. 229–266). London: Oxford University Press.

Moscovitch, M., & Winocur, G. (1992). The neuropsychology of memory and aging. In T. A. Salthouse & F. I. M. Craik (Eds.), *The handbook of aging and cognition*. Hillsdale, NJ: Lawrence Erlbaum Associates Inc.

Moscovitch, M., Winocur, G., & Behrmann, M. (1997). What is special about face recognition? Nineteen experiments on a person with visual object agnosia and dyslexia but normal face recognition. *Journal of Cognitive Neurosciences, 9*, 555–604.

Moseley, M. E., & Glover, G. H. (1995). Functional MR imaging: Capabilities and limitations. *Neuroimaging Clinics of North America*, 161–191.

Moss, M. B., Albert, M. S., Butters, N., & Payne, M. (1986). Differential patterns of memory loss among patients with Alzheimer's disease, Huntington's disease and alcoholic Korsakoff's syndrome. *Archives of Neurology, 43*, 239–246.

Moulin, C. J. A., Perfect, T. J., & Jones, R. W. (2000). Evidence for intact memory monitoring in Alzheimer's disease: Metamemory sensitivity at encoding. *Neuropsychologia, 38*, 1242–1250.

Mowry, D. J., & Burvill, P. W. (1988). A study of mild dementia in the community using a wide range of diagnostic criteria. *British Journal of Psychiatry, 153*, 328–334.

Moyer, J. R. Jr., Deyo, R. A., & Disterhoft, J. F. (1990). Hippocampectomy disrupts trace eyeblink conditioning in rabbits. *Behavioral Neuroscience, 104*(2), 243–252.

Mu, Q., Xie, J., Wen, Z., Weng, Y., & Shuyun, Z. (1999). A quantitative MR study of the hippocampal formation, the amygdala horn of the lateral ventricle in healthy subjects 40 to 90 years of age. *American Journal of Neuroradiology, 20*, 207–211.

Mufson, E. J., Ma, S. Y., Cochran, E. J., Bennett, D. A., Beckett, L. A., Jaffar, S. et al. (2000). Loss of nucleus basalis neurons containing trkA immunoreactivity in individuals with mild cognitive impairment and early Alzheimer's disease. *Journal of Comparative Neurology, 427*, 19–30.

Muller, U., Yves von Cramon, D., & Pollman, S. (1998). D1 versus D2 receptor modulation of visuospatial working memory in humans. *Journal of Neuroscience, 18*, 2720–2737.

Mungas, D. (1983). Differential clinical sensitivity of specific parameters of the Rey Auditory-Verbal Learning Test. *Journal of Consulting and Clinical Psychology, 51*(6), 848–855.

Murden, R. A., McRae, T. D., Kaner, S., & Bucknam, M. E. (1991). Mini-Mental State exam scores vary with education in blacks and whites. *Journal of the American Geriatrics Society, 39*, 149–155.

Murray, E. A., & Mishkin, M. (1998). Object recognition and location memory in monkeys with excitotoxic lesions of the amygdala and hippocampus. *Journal of Neuroscience, 18,* 6568–6582.

Murray, J. B. (1984). Effects of valium and librium on human psychomotor and cognitive functions. *Genetic Psychology Monographs, 109,* 167–197.

Murray, L. L., Ramage, A. E., & Hopper, T. (2001). Memory impairments in adults with neurogenic communication disorders. *Seminars in Speech and Language, 22,* 127–136.

Musleh, W. Y., Shahi, K., & Baudry, M. (1993). Further studies concerning the role of nitric oxide in LTP induction and maintenance. *Synapse, 13,* 370–375.

Myers, P. S. (1999). *Right hemisphere damage: Disorders of communication and cognition.* San Diego, CA: Singular.

Nachson, I. (1995). On the modularity of face recognition: The riddle of domain specificity. *Journal of Clinical and Experimental Neuropsychology, 17,* 256–275.

Nadel, L., & Moscovitch, M. (1997). Memory consolidation, retrograde amnesia and the hippocampal complex. *Current Opinion in Neurobiology, 7,* 217–227.

Nadin, G., & Coulthard, P. (1997). Memory and midazolam conscious sedation. *British Dental Journal, 183*(11/12), 399–407.

Nagaraja, D., & Jayashree, S. (2001). Randomized study of the dopamine receptor agonist piribedil in the treatment of mild cognitive impairment. *American Journal of Psychiatry, 158,* 1517–1519.

Nakanishi, S. (1992). Molecular diversity of glutamate receptors and implications for brain function. *Science, 258,* 597–603.

National Head Injury Foundation Task Force on Special Education. (1989). *An educator's manual: What educators need to know about students with traumatic brain injury.* Southborough, MA: NHIF.

Nausieda, P. A., & Sherman, I. C. (1979). Long-term prognosis in transient global amnesia. *Journal of the American Medical Association, 24*(4), 392–393.

Neary, D., Snowden, J. S., Gustafson, L., Passant, U., Stuss, D., Black, S., Freedman, M., et al. (1998). Frontotemporal lobar degeneration: A consensus on clinical diagnostic criteria. *Neurology, 51*(6), 1546–1554.

Nebes, R. D. (1989). Semantic memory in Alzheimer's disease. *Psychological Bulletin, 106,* 377–394.

Nebes, R. D., Boller, F., & Holland, A. (1986). Use of semantic context by patients with Alzheimer's disease. *Psychology and Aging, 1,* 261–269.

Nebes, R. D., Brady, C. B., & Huff, F. J. (1989). Automatic and attentional mechanisms of semantic priming in Alzheimer's disease. *Journal of Clinical and Experimental Neuropsychology, 11,* 219–230.

Nebes, R. D., & Brady, C. B. (1989). Focused and divided attention in Alzheimer's disease. *Cortex, 25,* 305–315.

Nehlig, A. (2000). Caffeine effects on the brain and behavior: A metabolic approach. In T. H. Parliament, C. Ho. & P. Scheiberle (Eds.), *Caffeinated beverages: Health benefits, physiological effects and chemistry* (pp. 46–53). Washington, DC: American Chemical Society.

Nehlig, A., Daval, J. L., & Debry, G. (1992). Caffeine and the central nervous system: Mechanisms of action, biochemical, metabolic and psychostimulant effects. *Brain Research Review, 17,* 139–170.

Neisser, U., & Libby, L. K. (2000). Remembering life experiences. In E. Tulving & F. I. M. Craik (Eds.), *The Oxford handbook of memory* (pp. 315–332). Oxford: Oxford University Press.

Nelson, C. A., Monk, C. S., Lin, J., Carver, L. J., Thomas, K. M., & Truwit, C. L. (2000). Functional neuroanatomy of spatial working memory in children. *Developmental Psychology, 36,* 109–116.

Nelson, H. E. (1976). A modified card sorting test sensitive to frontal lobe defects. *Cortex, 12*(4), 313–324.

Nelson, K. (1993). The psychological and social origins of autobiographical memory. *Psychological Science, 4,* 7–14.

Nelson, O. T. (1996). Consciousness and metacognition. *American Psychologist, 51,* 102–116.

Neppe, V. M. (1983). *The psychology of déjà vu have I been here before?* Johannesburg: Witwatersrand University Press.

Neshige, R., Barrett, G., & Shibasaki, H. (1988). Auditory long latency event-related potentials in Alzheimer's disease and multiinfarct dementia. *Journal of Neurology, Neurosurgery and Psychiatry, 51*, 1120–1125.

Netherton, S. D., Elias, J. W., Albrecht, N. N., Acosta, C., Hutton, T., & Albrecht, W. (1989). Changes in the performance of Parkinsonian patients and normal aged on the Benton Visual Retention Test. *Experimental Aging Research, 15*(1), 13–18.

Neuschatz, J. S., Payne, D. G., Lampinen, J. M., & Toglia, M. P. (2001). Assessing the effectiveness of warnings and the phenomenological characteristics of false memories. *Memory, 9*(1), 53–71.

Nevo, I., & Hamon, M. (1995). Neurotransmitter and neuromodulatory mechanisms involved in alcohol abuse and alcoholism. *Neurochemistry International, 26*, 305–336.

Newcombe, F. (1969). *Missile wounds of the brain.* London: Oxford University Press.

Newcomer, J. W., Farber, N. B., Jevtovic-Todorovic, V., Selke, G., Melson, A. K., Hershey, T. et al. (1999). Ketamine-induced NMDA receptor hypofunction as a model of memory impairment and psychosis. *Neuropsychopharmacology, 20*, 106–118.

Nichol, C. G. (1995). Mild memory impairment. *Current Opinion in Psychiatry, 8*, 258–263.

Nicholson, C. D. (1990). Pharmacology of nootropics and metabolically active compounds in relation to their use in dementia. *Psychopharmacology, 101*, 147–159.

Nicoll, R. A., & Malenka, R. C. (1995). Contrasting properties of two forms of long-term potentiation in the hippocampus. *Nature, 377*, 115–117.

Niederehe, G., & Yoder, C. (1989). Metamemory perceptions in depressions of young and older adults. *Journal of Nervous and Mental Disease, 177*, 4–14.

Nielsen, H., Lolk, A., & Kragh-Sorensen, P. (1998). Age-associated memory impairment—Pathological memory decline or normal aging? *Scandinavian Journal of Psychology, 39*, 33–37.

Nilsson, L-G., Backman, L., Erngrund, K., Nyberg, L., Adolfsson, R., Bucht, G. et al. (1997). The betula prospective cohort study: Memory, health, and aging. *Aging Neuropsychology & Cognition, 4*(1), 1–32.

Nilsson, O. G., & Gage, F. H. (1993). Anticholinergic sensitivity in the aging rat septohippocampal system as assesed in a spatial memory task. *Neurobiology of Aging, 14*, 487–497.

Nilsson, O. G., Leanza, G., Rosenblad, C., Lapri, D. A., Wiley, R. G., & Björklund, A. (1992). Spatial learning impairments in rats with selective immunolesion of the forebrain cholinergic system. *NeuroReport, 3*, 1005–1008.

Nishiyama, K., Sugishita, M., Kurisaki, H., & Sakuta, M. (1998). Reversible memory disturbance and intelligence impairment induced by long-term anticholinergic therapy. *Internal Medicine, 37*(6), S14–S18.

Nissen, M. J., Knopman, D. S., & Schacter, D. L. (1987). Neurochemical dissociation of memory systems. *Neurology, 37*, 789–794.

Nolan, K. A., Lino, M. M., Seligmann, A. W., & Blass, J. P. (1998). Absence of vascular dementia in an autopsy series from a dementia clinic. *Journal of the American Geriatrics Society, 46*, 597–604.

Nolde, S. F., Johnson, M. K., & Raye, C. L. (1998). The role of prefrontal cortex during tests of episodic memory. *Trends in Cognitive Sciences, 2*(10), 399–406.

Noonberg, A., Goldstein, G., & Page, H. A. (1985). Premature aging in male alcoholics: "Accelerated aging" or "increased vulnerability"? *Alcoholism: Clinical and Experimental Research, 9*, 334–338.

Norman, D. A., & Shallice, T. (1986). Attention to action, willed and automatic control of behavior (Center for Human Information Processing Technical Report No. 99, rev. ed.). In R. J. Davidson, G. E. Schartz, & D. Shapiro (Eds.), *Consciousness and self-regulation: Advances in research* (pp. 1–18). New York: Plenum Press.

Norman, K. A., & Shachter, D. L. (1996). In L. M. Reder (Ed.), *Implicit memory and metacognition.* Hillsdale, NJ: Lawrence Erlbaum Associates Inc.

Norman, K. A., & Shacter, D. L. (1997). False recognition in younger and older adults: Exploring the characteristics of illusory memories. *Memory & Cognition, 25*, 838–848.

Norman, M. A., Evans, J. D., Miller, S. W., & Heaton, R. K. (2000). Demographically corrected norms for the California Verbal Learning Test. *Journal of Clinical and Experimental Neuropsychology, 22*(1), 80–94.

Numan, B., Sweet, J. J., & Ranganath, C. (2000). Use of the California Verbal Learning Test to detect proactive interference in the traumatically brain injured. *Journal of Clinical Psychology, 56*(4), 553–562.

Nunzi, M. G., Milan, F., Guidolin, D., & Toffano, G. (1987). Dendritic spine loss in hippocampus of aged rats. Effect of brain phosphatidylserine administration. *Neurobiology of Aging, 8*, 501–510.

Nyberg, L., Cabeza, R., & Tulving, E. (1996). Pet studies of encoding and retrieval: The HERA model. *Psychonomic Bulletin and Review, 3*, 135–148.

Nyberg, L., Cabeza, R., & Tulving, E. (1998). Assymetric frontal activation during episodic memory: What kind of specificity? *Trends in Cognitive Science, 2*, 419–420.

Nyberg, L., Tulving, E., Habib, R., Nilsson, L. G., Kapur, S., Houle, S. et al. (1995). Functional brain maps of retrieval mode and recovery of episodic information. *NeuroReport, 7*(1), 249–252.

Oakley, D. A. (1983). The varieties of memory: A phylogenetic approach. In A. Mayes (Ed.), *Memory in animals and humans.* New York: Van Nostrand Reinhold Co.

Ober, B. A., & Shenaut, G. K. (1988). Lexical decision and priming in Alzheimer's disease. *Neuropsychologia, 26*, 273–286.

Obler, L., Fein, D., Nicholas, M., & Albert, M. L. (1991). Auditory comprehension and aging: Decline in syntactic processing. *Applied Psycholinguistics, 12*, 433–452.

Obler, L. K., Fein, D., Nicholas, M., & Albert, M. L. (1991). Auditory comprehension and aging: Decline in syntactic processing. *Applied Psycholinguistics, 12*, 433–452.

O'Brien, J. T. (1994). Age-associated memory impairment. A real disease entity? *CNS Drugs, 1*, 89–94.

O'Brien, J. T., & Levy, R. (1992). Age-associated memory impairment. Too broad an entity to justify drug treatment yet. *Lancet, 304*, 5–6.

O'Brien, M., & Nutt, D. (1998). Loss of consciousness and post-traumatic stress disorder. A clue to aetiology and treatment. *British Journal of Psychiatry, 173*, 102–104.

O'Carroll, R. E., Conway, S., Ryman, A., & Prentice, N. (1997). Performance on the delayed word recall test (DWR) fails to differentiate clearly between depression and Alzheimer's disease in the elderly. *Psychological Medicine, 27*, 967–971.

O'Carroll, R. E., Russell, H. H., Lawrie, S. M., & Johnstone, E. C. (1999). Errorless learning and the cognitive rehabilitation of memory-impaired schizophrenic patients. *Psychological Medicine, 29*, 105–112.

O'Connor, D. W., Pollitt, P. A., Roth, M., Brook, P. B., & Reiss, B. B. (1990). Memory complaints and impairment in normal, depressed, and demented elderly persons identified in a community survey. *Archives of General Psychiatry, 47*, 224–227.

O'Connor, M., Butters, N., Miliotis, P., Eslinger, P., & Cermak, L. S. (1992). The dissociation of anterograde and retrograde amnesia in a patient with herpes encephalitis. *Journal of Clinical and Experimental Neuropsychology, 14*, 159–178.

O'Connor, N., & Hermelin, B. (1967). Auditory and visual memory in autistic and normal children. *Journal of Mental Deficiency Research, 11*(2), 126–131.

O'Craven, K. M., & Kanwisher, N. (2000). Mental imagery of faces and places activates corresponding stimulus-specific brain regions. *Journal of Cognitive Neuroscience, 12*, 1013–1023.

Oddy, M., Coughlan, T., Tyerman, A., & Jenkins, D. (1985). Social adjustment after closed head injury: A further follow-up seven years after injury. *Journal of Neurology, Neurosurgery and Psychiatry, 48*, 564–568.

O'Donovan, K. J., Tourtellotte, W. G., Milbrandt, J., & Baraban, J. M. (1999). The EGR family of transcription-regulatory factors: Progress at the interface of molecular and systems neuroscience. *Trends in Neuroscience, 22,* 167–173.

Ogle, S. E. (1986). Memory and ageing: A review and application of current theories. *Lifelong Learning, 9*(6), 8–10.

Ohkura, T., Isse, K., Akazawa, K., Hamamoto, M., Yaoi, Y., & Hagino, N. (1995). Long-term estrogen replacement therapy in female patients with dementia of the Alzheimer type: 7 cases. *Dementia, 6*(2), 99–107.

Öhman, A. (1992). Fear and anxiety as emotional phenomena: Clinical phenomenology, evolutionary perspectives, and information-processing mechanisms. In M. Lewis & J. M. Haviland (Eds.), *Handbook of emotions* (pp. 511–536). New York: Guilford Press.

Ohno, M., Yoshimatsu, A., Kobayashi, M., & Watanabe, S. (1996). β-adrenergic dysfunction exacerbates impairment of working memory induced by hippocampal NMDA receptor blockade in rats. *European Journal of Pharmacology, 307,* 21–26.

Oitzl, M. S., de Kloet, E. R., Joels, M., Schmid, W., & Cole, T. J. (1997). Spatial learning deficits in mice with a targeted glucocorticoid receptor gene disruption. *European Journal of Neuroscience, 9*(11), 2284–2296.

Oitzl, M. S., Fluttert, M., & de Kloet, E. R. (1994). The effect of corticosterone on reactivity to spatial novelty is mediated by central mineralocorticosteroid receptors. *European Journal of Neuroscience, 6*(7), 1072–1079.

Oitzl, M. S., Reichardt, H. M., Joëls, M., & de Kloet, R. (2001). Point mutation in the mouse glucocorticoid receptor preventing DNA binding impairs spatial memory. *Proceedings of the National Academy of Sciences of the United States of America, 98*(22), 12790–12795.

Okazaki, H. (1989). *Fundamentals of neuropathology.* New York: Agaku-Shoin.

O'Keefe, J., & Dostrovsky, J. (1971). The hippocampus as a spatial map: Preliminary evidence from unit activity in the freely-moving rat. *Brain Research, 34,* 171–175.

O'Keefe, J., & Nadel, L. (1978). *The hippocampus as a cognitive map.* Oxford: Clarendon Press.

Oken, B. S., Storzbach, D. M., & Kaye, J. A. (1998). The efficacy of Ginkgo biloba on cognitive function in Alzheimer's disease. *Archives of Neurology, 55,* 1409–1415.

Olds, J. L., Anderson, M. L., McPhee, D. L., Staten, L. D., & Alken, D. L. (1989). Imaging of memory-specific changes in the distribution of protein kinase C in the hippocampus. *Science, 245,* 866–869.

Oliveros, J. C., Jandali, M. K., Timsit, J. R., Berthier, M., Remy, R., Behghezal, A. et al. (1978). Vasopressin in amnesia. *Lancet, 1,* 42.

Olton, D. S., Meck, W. H., & Church, R. M. (1987). Separation of hippocampal and amygdaloid involvement in temporal memory dysfunctions. *Brain Research, 404*(1–2), 180–188.

Olton, D. S., Wenk, G. L., Church, R. M., & Meck, W. H. (1988). Attention and the frontal cortex as examined by simulataneous temporal processing. *Neuropsychologia, 26,* 307–318.

Ornstein, P. A., Baker-Ward, L., Gordon, B. N., & Merritt, K. A. (1997). Children's memory for medical experiences. *Applied Cognitive Psychology, 11,* S87–S104.

Ostergaard, A. L. (1994). Dissociations between word priming effects in normal subjects and patients with memory disorders: Multiple memory systems or retrieval? *Quarterly Journal of Experimental Psychology: Human Experimental Psychology, 47A,* 331–364.

Ostergaard, A. L. (1999). Priming deficits in amnesia: Now you see them, now you don't. *Journal of the International Neuropsychological Society, 5,* 175–190.

Ostergaard, A. L., & Jernigan, T. L. (1993). Are word priming and explicit memory mediated by different brain structures? In P. Graf & M. E. J. Masson (Eds.), *Implicit memory* (pp. 327–349). Hillsdale NJ: Lawrence Erlbaum Associates Inc.

Ott, A., Breteler, M. M., van Harskamp, F., Stijnen, T., & Hofman, A. (1998). Incidence and risk of dementia. The Rotterdam Study. *American Journal of Epidemiology, 147,* 574–580.

Ouvrier, R. A., Goldsmith, R. F., Ouvrier, S., & Williams, I. C. (1993). The value of the Mini-Mental State Examination in childhood: A preliminary study. *Journal of Child Neurology, 8,* 145–148.

Owen, A. (1997). The functional orgnanization of working memory processes within lateral frontal cortex: The contribution of functional neuroimaging. *European Journal of Neuroscience, 9*, 1329–1339.

Owen, A. M., Evans, A. C., & Petrides, M. (1996). Evidence for a two-stage model of spatial working memory processing within the lateral frontal cortex: A positron emission tomography study. *Cerebral Cortex, 6*, 31–38.

Owen, A. M., Iddon, J. L., Hodges, J. R., Summers, B. A., & Robbins, T. W. (1997). Spatial and non-spatial working memory at different stages of Parkinson's disease. *Neuropsychologia, 35*, 519–532.

Owen, A. M., Stern, C. E., Look, R. B., Tracey, I., Rosen, B. R., & Petrides, M. (1998). Functional organisation of spatial and nonspatial working memory processing within the human lateral frontal cortex. *Proceedings of the National Academy of Science of the United States of America, 95*, 7721–7726.

Packard, M. G., Cahill, L., & McGaugh, J. L. (1994). Amygdala modulation of hippocampal-dependent and caudate nucleus-dependent memory processes. *Proceedings of the National Academy of Science of the United States of America, 91*(18), 8477–8481.

Packard, M. G., & Knowlton, B. J. (2002). Learning and memory functions of the basal ganglia. *Annunciation Review Neuroscience, 25*, 563–593.

Packard, M. G., & Teather, L. A. (1998). Amygdala modulation of multiple memory systems: Hippocampus and caudate putamen. *Neurobiology of Learning and Memory, 69*, 163–203.

Paganini-Hill, A., Buckwalter, J. G., Logan, C. G., & Hendersen, V. W. (1993). Estrogen replacement and Alzheimer's disease in women. *Social Neuroscience, Abstract, 19*, 425.12.

Palfrey, J. S., Levine, M. D., Walker, D. K., & Sullivan, M. (1985). The emergence of attention deficits in early childhood: A prospective study. *Journal of Developmental and Behavioral Pediatrics, 6*, 339–348.

Palmer, A. M., & Gerson, S. (1990). Is the neuronal basis of Alzheimer's disease cholinergic or glutamatergic? *The FASEB Journal, 4*, 2745–2752.

Palumbo, C. L., Alexander, M. P., & Naeser, M. A. (1992). CT scan lesion sites associated with conduction aphasia. In S. E. Kohn (Ed.), *Conduction aphasia*. Hillsdale, NJ: Lawrence Erlbaum Associates Inc.

Pang, K., Williams, M. J., Egeth, H., & Olton, D. S. (1993). Nucleus basalis magnocellularis and attention: Effects of muscimol infusions. *Behavioral Neuroscience, 107*, 1031–1038.

Pappas, B. A., Sunderland, T., Weingartner, H. M., Vitiello, B., Martinson, H., & Putnam, K. (1992). Alzheimer's disease and feeling of knowing for knowledge and episodic memory. *Journal of Gerontology: Psychological Sciences, 47*, 159–164.

Parasuraman, R., & Haxby, J. V. (1993). Attention and brain function in Alzheimer's disease: A review. *Neuropsychology, 7*, 242–272.

Paratcha, G., Furman, M., Bevilaqua, L., Cammarota, M., Vianna, M., De Stein, M. L. et al. (2000). Involvment of hippocampal PKCβI isoform in the early phase of memory formation of an inhibitory avoidance learning. *Brain Research, 855*, 199–205.

Park, D. C., Cherry, K. E., Smith, A. D., & Lafronza, V. N. (1990a). Effects of distinctive context on memory for objects and their locations in young and older adults. *Psychology and Aging, 5*, 250–255.

Park, D. C., Hertzog, C., Kidder, D. P., Morrell, R. W., & Mayhorn, C. B. (1997). Effect of age on event-based and time-based prospective memory. *Psychology and Aging, 12*, 314–327.

Park, D. C., & Kidder, D. P. (1996). Prospective memory and medication adherence. In M. Brandimonte, G. O. Einstein, & M. A. McDaniel (Eds.), *Prospective memory: Theory and applications* (pp. 369–390). Mahwah, NJ: Lawrence Erlbaum Associates Inc.

Park, D. C., Morrell, R. W., Frieske, D., & Kincaid, D. (1992). Medication adherence behaviors in older adults: Effects of external cognitive supports. *Psychology and Aging, 7*, 252–256.

Park, D. C., Smith, A. D., & Cavanaugh, J. C. (1990b). Metamemories of memory researchers. *Memory & Cognition, 18*, 321–327.

Park, D. C., Smith, A. D., Dudley, W. N., & Lafronza, V. N. (1989). Effects of age and a divided attention task presented during encoding and retrieval on memory. *Journal of Experimental Psychology: Learning, Memory and Cognition, 15,* 1185–1191.

Park, R. J., Goodyer, I. M., & Teasdale, J. D. (2002). Categoric overgeneral autobiographical memory in adolescents with major depressive disorder. *Psychological Medicine, 32,* 267–276.

Park, S., & Holzman, P. S. (1992). Schizophrenics show spatial working memory deficits. *Archives of General Psychiatry, 49,* 975–982.

Park, S., & Holzman, P. S. (1993). Association of working memory deficit and eye tracking dysfunction in schizphrenia. *Schizophrenia Research, 11,* 55–61.

Park, S., Holzman, P. S., & Goldman-Rakic, P. S. (1995). Spatial working memory deficits in the relatives of schizophrenic patients. *Archives of General Psychiatry, 52,* 821–828.

Parker, L. N., Levin, E. R., & Lifrak, E. T. (1985). Evidence for adrenocortical adaptation to severe illness. *Journal of Clinical Endocrinology and Metabolism, 60,* 947–952.

Parkin, A. J., Dunn, J. C., Lee, C., O'Hara, P. F., & Nussbaum, L. (1993). Neuropsychological sequelae of Wernicke's encephalopathy in a 20-year-old woman: Selective impairment of a frontal memory system. *Brain and Cognition, 21,* 1–19.

Parkin, A. J. (1987). *Memory and amnesia.* New York: Blackwell.

Parkin, A. J. (1991). Recent advances in the neuropsychology of memory. In J. Weinman & J. Hunter (Eds.), *Memory: Neurochemical and abnormal perspectives.* London: Harwood Academic Publishers.

Parkin, A. J. (1996). Focal retrograde amnesia: A multi-faceted disorder? *Acta Neuropathologica Belgica, 96,* 43–50.

Parkin, A. J., Hunkin, N. M., & Squires, E. J. (1998). Unlearning John Mayor: The use of errorless learning in the reacquisition of proper names following herpes simplex encephalitis. *Cognitive Neuropsychology, 15*(4), 361–375.

Parkin, A. J., Rees, J., Hunkin, N. M., & Rose, P. E. (1994). Impairment of memory following discrete thalamic infarction. *Neuropsychologia, 32,* 39–51.

Parkin, A. J., & Russo, R. (1990). Implicit and explicit memory and the automatic/effortful distinction. *European Journal of Cognitive Psychology, 2,* 71–80.

Parkinson, J. K., Murray, E. A., & Mishkin, M. (1988). A selective mnemonic role for the hippocampus in monkeys: Memory for the location of objects. *Journal of Neuroscience, 8,* 4159–4167.

Parnetti, L., Lowenthal, D. T., Presciutti, O., Pelliccioli, G., Gobbi, G., Chiarini, P. et al. (1996). 1H-MRS, MRI-based hippocampal volumetry, and 99mTc-HMPAO-SPECT in normal aging, age-associated memory impairment and probable Alzheimer's disease. *Journal of the American Geriatrics Society, 44,* 133–138.

Parsons, O. A., & Nixon, S. J. (1993). Neurobehavioral sequelae of alcoholism. *Neurologic Clinics, 11,* 205–218.

Pasquier, F. (1996). Neuropsychological features and cognitive assessment in frontotemporal dementia. In F. Pasquier, F. Lebert, & P. Scheltens (Eds.), *Frontotemporal dementia.* Dordrecht: ICG.

Pasquier, F., Grymonprez, L., Lebert, F., & Van der Linden, M. (2001). Memory impairment differs in frontotemporal dementia and Alzheimer's disease. *Neurocase, 7,* 161–171.

Passafiume, D., Boller, F., & Keefe, N. C. (1986). Neuropsychological impairment in patients with Parkinson's disease. In I. Grant & K. M. Adams (Eds.), *Neuropsychological assessment of neuropsychiatric disorders.* New York: Oxford University Press.

Patten, B. M. (1972). The ancient art of memory-usefulness in treatment. *Archives of Neurology, 26,* 25–31.

Patti, F. (1988). Effects of L-acetylcarnitine on functional receovery of hemiplegic patients. *Clinical Trials Journal, 25,* 87–101.

Paulesu, E., Frith, C. D., & Frackowiak, R. S. J. (1993). The neural correlates of the verbal component of working memory. *Nature, 362,* 342–345.

Paulsen, J. S., Salmon, D. P., Monsch, A. U., Butters, N., Swenson, M. R., & Bondi, M. W.

(1995). Discrimination of cortical from sub-cortical dementias on the basis of memory and problem-solving tests. *Journal of Clinical Psychology, 51,* 48–58.

Pavlides, C., Watanabe, Y., & McEwen, B. S. (1993). Effects of glucocorticoids on hippo-campal long-term potentiation. *Hippocampus, 3,* 183–192.

Peigneux, P., Maquet, P., Meulemans, T., Destrebecqz, A., Laureys, S., Degueldre, C. et al. (2000). Striatum forever, despite sequence learning variability: A random effect analysis of PET data. *Human Brain Mapping, 10,* 179–194.

Pellegrino, L. J., & Altman, J. (1979). Effects of differential interference with postnatal cerebel-lar neurogenesis on motor performance, activity level, and maze learning of rats: A develop-mental study. *Journal of Comparative & Physi-ological Psychology, 93*(1), 1–33.

Pelosi, L., & Blumhardt, L. D. (1999). Effects of age on working memory: An event-related potential study. *Brain Research, Cognitive Brain Research, 7*(3), 321–34.

Pena-Casanova, J. (1997). Alzheimer's Disease Assessment Scale—Cognitive in clinical practice. *International Psychogeriatrics, 9*(S1), 105–114.

Pennington, B. F., Bennetto, L., McAleer, O. K., & Roberts, R. J. Jr. (1996). Executive func-tions and working memory: Theoretical and measurement issues. In G. R. Lyon & N. A. Krasnegor (Eds.), *Attention, memory and exec-utive function* (pp. 327–348). Baltimore, MD: Paul H Brookes Publishing Company.

Pérez, M., & Godoy, J. (1998). Comparison between a "traditional" memory test and a "behavioral" memory battery in Spanish pati-ents. *Journal of Clinical and Experimental Neuropsychology, 20*(4), 496–502.

Perlick, D., Stastny, P., Mattis, S., & Teresi, J. (1992). Contribution of family, cognitive and clinical dimensions to long-term outcome in schizophrenia. *Schizophrenia Research, 6,* 257–265.

Perlmutter, M. (1978). What is memory aging the aging of? *Developmental Psychology, 14,* 330.

Perlmutter, M., & Hall, E. (1985). Learning and memory across adulthood. In M. Perlmutter & E. Hall (Eds.), *Adult development and ageing.* Chichester, UK: Wiley.

Perlstein, W. M., Carter, C. S., Noll, D. C., & Cohen, J. D. (2001). Relation of prefrontal cor-tex dysfunction to working memory and symp-toms in schizophrenia. *American Journal of Psychiatry, 158*(7), 1105–1113.

Perner, J., & Ruffman, T. (1995). Episodic memory and autonoetic consciousness: Developmental evidence and a theory of childbood amnesia. *Journal of Experimental Child Psychology, 59,* 516–548.

Perry, R. J., & Hodges, J. R. (1996). Spectrum of memory dysfunction in degenerative disease. *Current Opinion in Neurology, 9,* 281–285.

Perry, W., Potterat, E. G., & Braff, D. (2001). Self-monitoring enhances Wisconsin Card Sorting Test performance in patients with schizophrenia: Performance is improved by simply asking patients to verbalize their sort-ing stragtey. *Journal of the International Neuro-psychological Society, 7,* 344–352.

Peters, B. H., & Levin, H. A. (1977). Memory enhancement after physostigmine treatment in the amnestic syndrome. *Archives of Neurology, 34,* 215–219.

Peters, B. H., & Levin, H. A. (1979). Effects of physostigmine and lecithin on memory in Alzheimer disease. *Annals of Neurology, 6,* 219–221.

Petersen, L. R., & Petersen, M. J. (1959). Short term retention of individual items. *Journal of Experimental Psychology, 91,* 341–343.

Petersen, R., Smith, G., Kokmen, E., Ivnik, R., & Tangalos, E. (1992). Memory function in normal ageing. *Neurology, 42,* 396–401.

Petersen, R. C. (1995). Normal aging, mild cog-nitive impairment, and early Alzheimer's dis-ease. *Neurologist, 1,* 326–344.

Petersen, R. C., & Ghoneim, M. M. (1980). Diazepam and human memory: Influence on acquisition, retrieval and state dependent learn-ing. *Progress in Neuropsychopharmacology, 4,* 81–89.

Petersen, R. C., Smith, G. E., Ivnik, R. J., Kokmen, E., & Tangalos, E. G. (1994). Memory function in very early Alzheimer's disease. *Neurology*, *44*, 867–872.

Petersen, R. C., Smith, G. E., Ivnik, R. J., Tangalos, E. G., Schaid, D. J., Thibodeau, S. N. et al. (1995). Apolipoprotein E status as a predictor of the development of Alzheimer's disease in memory-impaired individuals. *Journal of the American Medical Association*, *273*, 1274–1278.

Petersen, R. C., Smith, G. E., Waring, S. C., Ivnik, R. J., Kokmen, E., & Tangelos, E. G. (1997). Aging, memory, and mild cognitive impairment. *International Psychogeriatrics*, *9*(Suppl 1), 65–69.

Petersen, R. C., Smith, G. E., Waring, S. C., Ivnik, R. J., Tangalos, E. G., & Kokmen, E. (1999). Mild cognitive impairment. Clinical characterization and outcome. *Archives of Neurology*, *56*, 303–308.

Petersen, R. C., Waring, S. C., Smith, G. E., Tangalos, E. G., & Thibodeau, S. N. (1996). Predictive value of APOE genotyping in incipient Alzheimer's disease. *Annals of the New York Academy of Sciences*, *802*, 58–69.

Petersen, S. E., Fox, P. T., Posner, M. I., Mintun, M., & Raichle, M. E. (1988). Positron emission tomographic studies of the cortical anatomy of single-word processing. *Nature*, *331*, 585–589.

Petersen, S. E., Fox, P. T., Posner, M. I., Mintun, M., & Raichle, M. E. (1989). Positron emission tomographic studies of the processing of single words. *Journal of Cognitive Neuroscience*, *1*, 153–170.

Peterson, L. R., & Peterson, M. J. (1959). Short-term retention of individual verbal items. *Journal of Experimental Psychology*, *58*, 193–198.

Petrides, M. (1994). Frontal lobes and working memory: Evidence from investigations of the effects of cortical excisions in nonhuman primates. In F. Boller & J. Grafman (Eds.), *Handbook of neuropsychology, Vol. 9*. Amsterdam: Elsevier.

Petrides, M. (1995a). Impairment on non-spatial self-ordered and externally ordered working memory tasks after lesions of the mid-dorsal part of the lateral frontal cortex in the monkey. *Journal of Neuroscience*, *15*, 359–375.

Petrides, M. (1995b). Functional organization of the human frontal cortex for mnemonic processing: Evidence from neuroimaging studies. *Annals of the New York Academy of Sciences*, *769*, 85–96.

Petrides, M., Alivisatos, B., Meyer, E., & Evans, A. C. (1993). Functional activation of the human frontal cortex during performance of verbal working memory tasks. *Proceedings of the National Academy of Sciences of the United States of America*, *90*, 878–882.

Petrie, K., Chamberlain, K., & Clarke, D. (1988). Psychological predictors of future suicidal behavior in hospitalised suicide attempters. *British Journal of Clinical Psychology*, *27*, 247–258.

Pfefferbaum, A., Ford, J., & Kraemer, H. C. (1990). Clinical utility of long latency "cognitive" event-related potentials (P300): The cons. *Electroencephalography and Clinical Neurophysiology*, *76*, 6–12.

Phelps, B. J., & Cheney, C. D. (1996). Memory rehabilitation techniques with brain-injured individuals. In J. R. Cautela & W. Ishaq (Eds.), *Contemporary issues in behavior therapy: Improving the human condition*. New York: Plenum.

Phelps, E., & Gazzaniga, M. S. (1992). Hemispheric differences in mnemonic processing: The effects of left hemisphere interpretation. *Neuropsychologia*, *30*, 293–297.

Phillips, C. D., Chu, C. W., Morris, J. N., & Hawes, C. (1993). Effects of cognitive impairment on the reliability of geriatric assessments in hursing homes. *Journal of the American Geriatrics Society*, *41*(2), 136–142.

Phillips, R. G., & LeDoux, J. E. (1992). Differential contributions of amygdala and hippocampus to cued and contextual fear conditioning. *Behavioral Neuroscience*, *106*, 274–285.

Piaget, J. (1954). *The construction of reality in the child*. New York: Basic Books.

Pick, A. (1903). Clinical studies. III. On reduplicative paramnesia. *Brain*, *26*, 260–267.

Pickens, R. W., & Johanson, C-E. (1992). Craving: Consensus of status and agenda for future research. *Drug Alcohol Dependence*, *30*, 127–131.

Piggott, M. A., Perry, E. K., Perry, R. H., & Court, J. A. (1992). [3H]MK-801 binding to the NMDA receptor complex, and its modulation in human frontal cortex during development and aging. *Brain Research, 588,* 277–286.

Pillemer, D. B. (1998). *Momentous events, vivid memories.* Cambridge, MA: Harvard University Press.

Pillon, B., Deweer, B., Agid, Y., & Dubois, B. (1993). Explicit memory in Alzheimer's, Huntington's and Parkinson's disease. *Archives of Neurology, 50,* 374–379.

Pillon, B., Deweer, B., Vidailhet, M., Bonnet, A-M., Hahn-Barma, V., & Dubois, B. (1998). Is impaired memory for spatial location in Parkinson's disease domain specific or dependent on "strategic" processes? *Neuropsychologia, 36*(1), 1–9.

Pillon, B., Dubois, B., Lhermitte, F., & Agid, Y. (1986). Heterogeneity of cognitive impairments in progressive supranuclear palsy, Parkinson's disease, and Alzheimer's disease. *Neurology, 36,* 1179–1185.

Pillon, B., Ertle, S., Deweer, B., Bonnet, A. M., Vidailhet, M., & Dubois, B. (1997). Memory for spatial location in "*de novo*" parkinsonian patients. *Neuropsychologia, 35,* 221–228.

Pillon, B., Ertle, S., Deweer, B., Sarazin, M., Agid, Y., & Dubois, B. (1996). Memory for spatial location is affected in Parkinson's disease. *Neuropsychologia, 34,* 77–85.

Pipe, M. E., Dean, J., Canning, J., & Murachver, T. (1996). *Narrating events and telling stories.* Paper presented at the second International Conference on Memory, Albano, Italy.

Pitman, R. K., Orr, S. P., & Lasko, N. B. (1993). Effects of intranasal vasopressin and oxytocin on physiologic responding during personal combat imagery in Vietnam veterans with post-traumatic stress disorder. *Psychiatry Research, 48,* 107–117.

Podoll, K., Caspary, P., Lange, H. W., & Noth, J. (1988). Störungen der Objectbenennung bei Chorea Huntington. *Zeitschrift für Experimentelle und Angewandte Psychologie, 35,* 242–258.

Poldrack, R. A., Wagner, A. D., Prull, M. W., Desmond, J. E., Glover, G. H., & Gabrieli, J. D. (1999). Functional specialization for semantic and phonological processing in the left inferior prefrontal cortex. *Neuroimage, 10,* 15–35.

Polich, J. (1996). Meta-analysis of P300 normative aging studies. *Psychophysiology, 33,* 334–353.

Polich, J., Ladish, C., & Bloom, F. E. (1990). P300 assessment of early Alzheimer disease. *Electroencephalography and Clinical Neurophysiology, 77,* 179–189.

Polster, M. R. (1993). Drug-induced amnesia: Implications for cognitive neuropsychological investigations of memory. *Psychological Bulletin, 114,* 477–493.

Pomara, N., Deptula, D., Medel, M., Block, R. I., & Greenblatt, D. J. (1989). Effects of diazepam on recall memory: Relationship to aging, dose and duration of treatment. *Psychopharmacology Bulletin, 25,* 144–148.

Poole, D. A., Lindsay, O. S., Memon, A., & Bull, R. (1995). Psychotherapy and the recovery of memories of childhood sexual abuse: US and British practitioners' opinions, practices and experiences. *Journal of Consulting and Clinical Psychology, 63*(3), 426–437.

Poon, L. W. (1985). Differences in human memory with aging: Nature, causes, and clinical implications. In J. E. Birren & K. W. Schaie (Eds.), *Handbook of the psychology of aging, Ed 2.* New York: Van Nostrand Reinhold.

Pope, H. G. Jr., & Hudson, J. I. (1996). "Recovered memory" therapy for eating disorders: Implications of the Ramona verdict. *International Journal of Eating Disorders, 19*(2), 139–145.

Porter, S., Birt, A. R., Yuille, J. C., & Lehman, D. (2000). The negotiation of false memories: Interviewer and rememberer characteristics relate to memory distortion. *Psychological Science, 11,* 513–516.

Posner, M. I., & Keele, S. W. (1968). On the genesis of abstract ideas. *Journal of Experimental Psychology, 77,* 353–363.

Postle, B. R., & D'Esposito, M. (1999). "What" then "Where" in visual working memory: An event-related fMRI study. *Journal of Cognitive Neuroscience, 11,* 585–597.

Postman, L., & Underwood, B. J. (1973). Critical issues in interference theory. *Memory & Cognition, 1,* 19–40.

Powell, J. B., Cripe, L. I., & Dodrill, C. B. (1991). Assessment of brain impairment with the Rey Auditory Verbal Learning Test: A comparison with other neuropsychological measures. *Archives of Clinical Neuropsychology, 6*, 241–249.

Powell-Proctor, L., & Miller, E. (1982). Reality orientation: A critical appraisal. *British Journal of Clinical Psychology, 26*, 83–91.

Prabhakaran, V., Smith, J. A. L., Desmond, J. E., Glover, G. H., & Gabrieli, J. D. E. (1997). Neural substrates of fluid reasoning: An fMRI study of neocortical activation during performance of the Raven's Progressive Matrices Test. *Cognitive Psychology, 33*, 46–63.

Prather, P. L., Forster, M. J., & Lal, H. (1992). Learning and memory-enhancing effects of Ro 15-4513: A comparison with flumazeil. *Neuropharmacology, 31*, 299–306.

Pratico, D. (1999). F2-isopropanes: Sensitive and specific non-invasive indices of lipid peroxidation in vivo. *Atherosclerosis, 147*, 1–10.

Pratico, D., Clark, C. M., Lee, VM-Y., Trojanowski, J. Q., Rokach, J., & FitzGerald, G. A. (2000). Increased 8, 12-iso-iPF2α-VI in Alzheimer's disease: Correlation of a noninvasive index of lipid peroxidation with disease severity. *Annals of Neurology, 48*, 809–812.

Pratico, D., Clark, C. M., Liun, F., Lee, VM-Y., & Trojanowski, J. Q. (2002). Increases of brain oxidative stress in mild cognitive impairment. *Archives of Neurology, 59*, 972–976.

Press, A., Amaral, D. G., & Squire, L. R. (1989). Hippocampal abnormalities in amnesic patients revealed by high-resolution magnetic resonance imaging. *Nature, 341*, 54–57.

Preston, G. C., Broks, P., Traub, M., Ward, C., Poppleton P., & Stahl, S. M. (1988). Effects of lorazepam on memory, attention and sedation in man. *Psychopharmacology, 95*(2), 208–215.

Preston, G. C., Ward, C. E., Broks, P., Traub, M., & Stahl, S. M. (1989). Effects of lorazepam on memory, attention and sedation in man: Antagonism by Ro 15-1788. *Psychopharmacology, 97*(2), 222–227.

Price, J. L., Ko, A. I., Wade, M. J., Tsou, S. K., McKeel, D. W., & Morris, J. C. (2001). Neuron number in the entorhinal cortex and CA1 in preclinical Alzheimer disease. *Archives of Neurology, 58*, 1395–1402.

Prigatano, G. P. (1996). Behavioral limitations that TBI patients tend to underestimate: A replication and extension to patients with lateralized cerebral dysfunction. *Clinical Neuropsychologist, 10*, 191–201.

Prigatano, G. P., Fordyce, D. J., Zeiner, H. K., Roueche, J. R., Pepping, M., & Wood, B. C. (1984). Neuropsychological rehabilitation after closed head injury in young adults. *Journal of Neurology, Neurosurgery and Psychiatry, 47*, 505–513.

Prior, M., & Hoffmann, W. (1990). Neuropsychological testing of autistic children through an exploration with frontal lobe tests. *Journal of Autism and Developmental Disorders, 20*, 581–590.

Puglisi, J. T., & Morrell, R. W. (1986). Age-related slowing in mental rotation of three-dimensional objects. *Experimental Aging Research, 12*, 217–220.

Quarton, G. C., & Talland, G. A. (1962). The effects of methamphetamine and pentobarbital on two measures of attention. *Psychopharmacologia, 3*, 66–71.

Query, W. T., & Megran, J. (1983). Age-relaetd norms for AVLT in a male patient population. *Journal of Clinical Psychology, 39*, 136–138.

Quirarte, G. L., Roozendaal, B., & McGaugh, J. L. (1997). Glucocorticoid enhancement of memory storage involves noradrenergic activation in the basolateral amygdala. *Proceedings of the National Academy of Science of the United States of America, 94*, 14048–14053.

Quirk, G. J., Armony, J. L., & LeDoux, J. E. (1997). Fear conditioning enhances different temporal components of tone-evoked spike trains in auditory cortex and lateral amygdala. *Neuron, 19*(3), 613–624.

Quirk, G. J., Repa, C., & LeDoux, J. E. (1995). Fear conditioning enhances short-latency auditory responses of lateral amygdala neurons: Parallel recordings in the freely behaving rat. *Neuron, 15*(5), 1029–1039.

Rabinowitz, J. C. (1986). Priming in episodic memory. *Journal of Gerontology, 41*, 204–213.

Rabinowiz, J. C. (1989). Judgments of origin and generation effects: Comparisons between young and elderly adults. *Psychology and Aging, 4,* 259–268.

Rack, J. P., Snowling, M. J., & Olson, R. K. (1992). The nonword reading deficit in developmental dyslexia: A review. *Reading Research Quarterly, 27,* 28–53.

Ragneskog, H., Brane, G., Karlsson, I., & Kihlgren, M. (1996). Influence of dinner music on food intake and symptoms common in dementia. *Scandinavian Journal of Caring Sciences, 10*(1), 11–17.

Raichle, M. E. (1994). Images of the mind: Studies with modern imaging techniques. *Annals Reviews Psychology, 45,* 333–356.

Raichle, M. E., Fiez, J. A., Videen, T. O., MacLeod, A. M., Pardo, J. V., Fox, P. T. et al. (1994). Practice-related changes in human brain functional anatomy during nonmotor learning. *Cerebral Cortex, 4*(1), 8–26.

Räihä, I., Isoaho, R., Ojanlatva, A., Viramo, P., Sulkava, R., & Kivelä, S-L. (2001). Poor performance in the Mini-Mental State examination due to causes other than dementia. *Scandinavian Journal of Primary Health Care, 19,* 34–38.

Rajaram, S. (1993). Remembering and knowing: Two means of access to the personal past. *Memory & Cognition, 21*(1), 89–102.

Rajaram, S., & Roediger, H. L. (1993). Direct comparison of four implicit memory tests. *Journal of Experimental Psychology: Learning, Memory, and Cognition, 19,* 765–776.

Ramirez, M. J., Cenarruzabeitia, E., Lasheras, B., & Del Rio, J. (1996). Involvement of GABA systems in acetylcholine release induced by 5-HT3 receptor blockade in slices from rat entorhinal cortex. *Brain Research, 712,* 274–280.

Rammsayer, T. H., Rodewald, S., & Groh, D. (2000). Dopamine-antagonistic, anticholinergic, and GABAergic effects on declarative and procedural memory functions. *Cognitive Brain Research, 9,* 61–71.

Rampello, L., Giammona, G., Aleppo, G., Favit, A., & Fiore, L. (1992). Trophic action of acetyl-L-carnitine in neuronal cultures. *Acta Neurologica, 14*(1), 15–21.

Randolph, C. (1991). Implicit, explicit and semantic memory functions in Alzheimer's disease and Huntington's disease. *Journal of Clinical and Experimental Neuropsychology, 13*(4), 479–494.

Randolph, C., Braun, A. R., Goldberg, T. E., & Chase, T. N. (1993). Semantic fluency in Alzheimer's, Parkinson's and Huntington's disease: Dissociation of storage and retrieval failures. *Neuropsychology, 7,* 82–88.

Raoul, P., Lieury, A., Decombe, R., Chauvel, P., & Allain, H. (1992). Déficit mnésique au cours de la maladie de Parkinson. Vieillissement accéléré des processus de rappel. *Presse Médicale, 21,* 69–73.

Rapcsak, S. Z., Reminger, S. L., Glisky, E. L., Kaszniak, A. W., & Comer, J. F. (1999). Neuropsychological mechanisms of false recognition following frontal lobe damage. *Cognitive Neuropsychology, 16,* 267–292.

Rapee, R. M. (1994). Failure to replicate a memory bias in panic disorder. *Journal of Anxiety Disorder, 8,* 291–300.

Rapee, R. M., McCallum, S. L., Melville, L. F., Ravenscroft, H., & Rodney, J. M. (1994). Memory bias in social phobia. *Behaviour Research and Therapy, 32,* 89–99.

Rapp, P. R., & Amaral, D. G. (1992). Individual differences in the cognitive and neurobiological consequences of normal aging. *Trends in Neuroscience, 15,* 340–345.

Raskin, S. A., & Sohlberg, M. M. (1996). The efficacy of prospective memory training in two adults with brain injury. *Journal of Head Trauma Rehabilitation, 11,* 32–51.

Raskind, M. A., Peskind, E. R., Wessel, T., & Yuan, W. (2000). Galantamine in AD: A 6-month randomized, placebo-controlled trial with a 6-month extension. The Galantamine USA-1 Study Group. *Neurology, 54,* 2261–2268.

Rausch, R. (1985). Differences in cognitive function with left and right temporal lobe dysfunction. In D. F. Benson & E. Zaidel (Eds.), *The dual brain: Hemispheric specialization in humans.* New York: Guilford Press.

Rausch, R., Serafetinides, E. A., & Crandall, P. H. (1977). Olfactory memory in patients with anterior temporal lobectomy. *Cortex, 13,* 445–453.

Raven, J. C. (1962). *Coloured progressive matrices sets A, AB, B*. London: Lewis.

Rawlins, J. N. P. (1985). Associations across time. The hippocampus as a temporary memory store. *Behavioral Brain Sciences, 8,* 479–496.

Rawlins, J. N. P., & Olton, D. S. (1982). The septohippocampal system and cognitive mapping. *Behavioral Brain Research, 5,* 331–358.

Rawlins, J. N. P., & Tsaltas, E. (1983). The hippocampus, time and working memory. *Behavioural Brain Research, 10,* 233–262.

Raz, N., Gunning, F. M., Head, D., Dupuis, J. H., McQuain, J., Briggs, S. D. et al. (1997). Selective aging of the human cerebral cortex observed in vivo: Differential vulnerability of the prefrontal gray matter. *Cerebral Cortex, 7*(3), 268–282.

Reber, P. J., & Squire, L. R. (1994). Parallel brain systems for learning with and without awareness. *Learning & Memory, 1*(4), 217–229.

Reed, E. S. (1994). Perception is to self as memory is to selves. In U. Neisser & R. Fivush (Eds.), *The remembering self: Construction and accuracy in the life narrative* (pp. 278–292). New York: Cambridge University Press.

Reed, G. (1979). Everyday anomalies of recall and recognition. In J. F. Kihlstrom & F. J. Evans (Eds.), *Functional disorders of memory*. Hillsdale, NJ: Lawrence Erlbaum Associates Inc.

Reed, J. M., & Squire, L. R. (1998). Retrograde amnesia for facts and events: Findings from four new cases. *Journal Neuroscience, 18,* 3493–3954.

Regier, D. A., Boyd, J. H., Burke, J. D. Jr., Rae, D. S., Myers, J. K., Kramer, M. et al. (1988). One month prevalence of mental disorders in the US: Based on five epidemiologic catchment area (ECA) sites. *Archives of General Psychiatry, 45,* 977–986.

Reid, W. G., Broe, G. A., Hely, M. A., Morris, J. G., Williamson, P. M., O'Sullivan, D. J. et al. (1989). The neuropsychology of de novo patients with idiopathic Parkinson's disease: The effects of age of onset. *International Journal of Neuroscience, 48*(3–4), 205–217.

Reisberg, B., Ferris, S. H., de Leon, M. J., & Crook, T. (1982). The global deterioration scale for assessment of primary degenerative dementia. *American Journal of Psychiatry, 139,* 1136–1139.

Reisberg, B., Ferris, S. H., de Leon, M. J., & Crook, T. (1988a). The global deterioration scale (GDS). *Psychopharmacology Bulletin, 24,* 661–663.

Reisberg, B., Ferris, S. H., de Leon, M. J., Sinaiko, E., Franssen, E., Kluger, A. et al. (1988b). Stage-specific behavioral, cognitive, and in vivo changes in community residing subjects with age-associated memory impairment and primary degenerative dementia of the Alzheimer type. *Drug Development Research, 15,* 101–114.

Rempel-Clower, N. L., Zola, S. M., Squire, L. R., & Amaral, D. G. (1996). Three cases of enduring memory impairment after bilateral damge limited to the hippocampal formation. *Journal of Neuroscience, 16,* 5233–5255.

Reneman, L., Booij, J., de Bruin, K., Reitsma, J. B., de Wolff, F. A., Gunning, W. B. et al. (2001). Effects of dose, sex and long-term abstention from use on toxic effects of MDMA (ecstasy) on brain serotonin neurons. *The Lancet, 358,* 1864–1869.

Resnick, S. M., Trotman, K. M., Kawas, C., & Zonderman, A. B. (1995). Age-associated changes in specific errors on the Benton Visual Retention Test. *Journal of Gerontology: Psychological Sciences, 50*B(3), P171–P178.

Reuter-Lorenz, P., Jonides, J., Smith, E. S. et al. (2000). Age differences in the frontal lateralization of verbal and spatial working memory revealed by PET. *Journal of Cognitive Neuroscience, 12,* 174–187.

Rey, A. (1941). L'examen psychologique dans les cas d'encéphalopathie traumatique. *Archives de Psychologie, 28,* 286–340.

Rey, A. (1964). *L'Examen clinique en psychologie*. Paris: Presses Universitaires de France.

Ricardo, J. A., & Koh, E. T. (1978). Anatomical evidence of direct projections from the nucleus of the solitary tract to the hypothalamus, amygdala, and other forebrain structures in the rat. *Brain Research, 153*(1), 1–26.

Rich, J. B., & Brown, G. G. (1992). Selective dissociations of sedation and amnesia following ingestion of diazepam. *Psychopharmacology, 106,* 346–350.

Richardson, J. T. E. (1990). *Clinical and neuropsychological aspects of closed head injury.* London: Taylor & Francis.

Richardson, J. T. E. (1995). The efficacy of imagery mnemonics in memory remediation. *Neuropsychologia, 33*, 1345–1357.

Richardson, J. T. E. (2000). *Clinical and neuropsychological aspects of closed head injury.* Philadelphia: Taylor & Francis.

Richardson-Klavehn, A., & Bjork, R. A. (1988). Measures of memories. *Annual Review of Psychology, 39*, 475–543.

Riklan, M., Reynolds, C. M., & Stellar, S. (1989). Correlates of memory in Parkinson's disease. *Journal of Nervous & Mental Disease, 177*(4), 237–240.

Riedel, G., & Micheau, J. (2001). Function of the hippocampus in memory formation: Desperately seeking resolution. *Progress in Neuropsychopharmacology and Biological Psychiatry, 25*, 835–853.

Riedel-Heller, S. G., Matschinger, H., Schork, A., & Angermeyer, M. C. (1999). Do memory complaints indicate the presence of cognitive impairment? Results of a field study. *European Archives of Psychiatry, 249*, 197–204.

Riege, W. H., Metter, E. J., & Hanson, W. R. (1980). Verbal and nonverbal recognition memory in aphasic and nonaphasic stroke patients. *Brain and Language, 10*, 60–70.

Riekkinen, M., Jäkälä, P., Kejonen, K., & Riekkinen, J. R. P. (1999). The α_2 agonist, clonidine, improves spatial working memory performance in Parkinson's disease. *Neuroscience, 92*, 983–989.

Riekkinen, M., Soininen, H., Riekkinen, P. Sr., Kuikka, J., Laakso, M., Helkala, E-L. et al. (1998a). Tetrahydroaminoacridine improves the recency effect in Alzheimer's disease. *Neuroscience, 83*(2), 471–479.

Riekkinen, P. Jr., Kejonen, K., Laakso, M. P., Soininen, H., Partanen, K., & Riekkinen, M. (1998b). Hippocampal atrophy is related to impaired memory, but not frontal functions in non-demented Parkinson's disease patients. *NeuroReport, 9*, 1507–1511.

Riekkinen, P. Jr., & Riekkinen, M. (1999). THA improves word priming and clonidine enhances fluency and working memory in Alzheimer's disease. *Neuropsychopharmacology, 20*, 357–364.

Risse, G. L., Rubens, A. B., & Jordan, L. S. (1984). Disturbances of long-term memory in aphasic patients. A comparison of anterior and posterior lesions. *Brain, 107*, 605–617.

Ritchie, K., Artero, S., & Touchon, J. (2001). Classification criteria for mild cognitive impairment. A population-based validation study. *Neurology, 56*, 37–42.

Ritchie, K., & Touchon, J. (2000). Mild cognitive impairment: Conceptual basis and current nosological status. *Lancet, 335*, 225–228.

Rizzolatti, G., Umilta, C., & Berlucchi, G. (1971). Opposite superiorities of the right and left cerebral hemispheres in discriminative reaction time to physiognomical and alphabetic material. *Brain, 94*, 431–442.

Robbins, T. W., Everitt, B. J. Fray, P. J., Gaskin, M., Carli, M., & de la Riva, C. (1982). The roles of the central catecholamines in attention and learning. In M. V. Spiegelstein & A. Levy (Eds.), *Behavioral models and the analysis of drug action.* Amsterdam: Elsevier.

Robbins, T. W., Semple, J., Kumar, R., Truman, M. I., Shorter, J., Ferraro, A. et al. (1997). Effects of scopolamine on delayed matching to sample and paired associates tests of visual memory and learning in human subjects: Comparison with diazepam and implications for dementia. *Psychopharmacology, 134*, 95–106.

Roberson, E. D., English, J. D., Adams, J. P., Selchher, J. C., Kondratick, C., & Sweat, J. D. (1999). The mitogen-activated protein kinase cascade couples PKA and PKC to cAMP response element binding protein phosphorylation in area CA1 of the hippocampus. *Journal Neuroscience, 19*, 4337–4348.

Roberts, E. (1986). Guides through the labyrinth of AD: Dehydroepiandrosterone, potassium channels and the C4 component of complement. In T. Crook, R. T. Bartus, S. Ferris, & S. Gershon (Eds.), *Treatment development strategies for Alzheimer's disease* (pp. 173–219). Madison, CT: Mark Powley & Associates.

Robertson, I. H. (1996). *Goal management training: A clinical manual.* Cambridge: PsyConsult.

Robertson-Tchabo, E. A., & Arenberg, D. (1989). Assessment of memory in older adults. In T. Hunt & C. J. Lindley (Eds.), *Testing older adults* (pp. 200–231). Kansas City, MO: Test Corporation of America.

Rocca, P., Cocuzza, E., Marchiaro, L., & Bogetto, F. (2002). Donepezil in the treatment of Alzheimer's disease. Long-term efficacy and safety. *Progress in Neuropsychopharmacology and Biological Psychiatry, 26,* 369–373.

Roediger, H. L. III, & Blaxton, T. A. (1987). Retrieval modes produce dissociations in memory for surface information. In D. S. Gorfein & R. R. Hoffman (Eds.), *Memory and cognitive processes: The Ebinghaus Centennial Conference.* Hillsdale, NJ: Lawrence Erlbaum Associates Inc.

Roediger, H. L., & McDermott, K. B. (1993a). Implicit memory in normal human subjects. In F. Boller & J. Grafman (Eds.), *Handbook of neuropsychology, Vol. 8.* New York: Elsevier.

Roediger, H. L., & McDermott, K. B. (1993b). The problem of differing false alarm rates for the process dissociation procedure: Comment on Verfaellie and Treadwell (1993). *Neuropsychology, 8,* 284–288.

Roediger, H. L., McDermott, K. B. (1995). Creating false memories: Remembering words not presented in lists. *Journal of Experimental Psychology: Learning, Memory & Cognition, 21,* 803–814.

Roediger, H. L., & Srinivas, K. (1993). Specificity of operations in perceptual priming. In P. Graf & M. E. Masson (Eds.), *Implicit memory: New directions in cognition, development and neuropsychology.* Hillsdale, NJ: Lawrence Erlbaum Associates Inc.

Roediger, H. L., Weldon, M. S., & Challis, B. H. (1989). Explaining dissociations between implicit and explicit measures of retention: A processing account. In H. L. Roediger & F. I. M. Craik (Eds.), *Varieties of memory and consciousness: Essays in honor of Endel Tulving.* Hillsdale, NJ: Lawrence Erlbaum Associates Inc.

Rogan, M. T., Stäubli, U. V., & LeDoux, J. E. (1997). Fear conditioning induces associative long-term potentiation in the amygdala. *Nature, 390,* 604–607.

Rogers, S. L., Doody, R. S., Mohs, R. C., & Friedhoff, L. T. (1998a). Donepezil improves cognition and global function in Alzheimer disease: A 15-week, double-blind, placebo-controlled study. Donepezil Study Group. *Archives of Internal Medicine, 158*(9), 1021–1031.

Rogers, S. L., Farlow, M., Doody, R., Mohs, R., & Friedhoff, L. (1998b). A 24-week, double-blind, placebo-controlled trial of donepezil in patients with Alzheimer's disease. Donepezil Study Group. *Neurology, 50,* 136–145.

Rogers, S. L., Friedhoff, L., & The Donepezil Study Group. (1996). The efficacy and safety of donepezil in patients with Alzheimer's disease. *Dementia, 7,* 293–303.

Rohrer, D., Paulsen, J. S., Salmon, D., & Wixted, J. T. (1999). The disparate effects of Alzheimer's disease and Huntington's disease on semantic memory. *Neuropsychology, 13*(3), 381–388.

Roman, G. C., Tatemichi, T. K., Erkinjuntti, T., Cummings, J. L., Masdeu, J. C., Garcia, J. H. et al. (1993). Vascular dementia: Diagnostic criteria for research studies. Report of the NINDS-AIREN International Workshop. *Neurology, 43*(2), 250–260.

Roozendaal, B. (2000). Glucocorticoids and the regulation of memory consolidation. *Psychoneuroendocrinology, 25,* 213–238.

Roozendaal, B., Cahill, L., & McGaugh, J. L. (1996). In K. Ishikawa, J. L. McGaugh, & H. Sakata (Eds.), *Brain processes and memory* (pp. 39–54). Amsterdam: Elsevier.

Roozendaal, B., Carmi, O., & McGaugh, J. L. (1996). Adrenocortical suppression blocks the memory-enhancing effects of amphetamine and epinephrine. *Proceedings of the National Academy of Science of the United States of America, 93,* 1429–1433.

Roozendaal, B., Koolhaas, J. M., & Bohus, B. (1991). Central amygdala lesions affect behavioral and autonomic balance during stress in rats. *Physiology & Behavior, 50*(4), 777–781.

Roozendaal, B., & McGaugh, J. L. (1996). Amygdaloid nuclei lesions differentially affect glucocorticoid-induced memory enhancement in an inhibitory avoidance task. *Neurobiology of Learning & Memory, 65*(1), 1–8.

Roozendaal, B., & McGaugh, J. L. (1997). Glucocorticoid receptor agonist and antagonist administration into the basolateral but not central amygdala modulates memory storage. *Neurobiology of Learning & Memory, 67*(2), 176–179.

Rosen, W. G., Mohs, R. C., & Davis, K. L. (1984). A new rating scale for Alzheimer's disease. *American Journal of Psychiatry, 141*, 1356–1364.

Rosenblum, K., Meiri, N., & Dudai, Y. (1993). Taste memory: The role of protein synthesis in gustatory cortex. *Behavioural Neural Biology, 59*, 49–56.

Rosene, D. (1993). Comparing age-related changes in the basal forebrain and hippocampus of the rhesus monkey. *Neurobiology of Aging, 14*, 669–670.

Rosenfeld, J. P., Ellwanger, J., & Sweet, J. J. (1995). Detecting simulated amnesia with event-related brain potentials. *International Journal of Psychophysiology, 19*, 1–11.

Rösler, M., Anand, R., Cicin-Sain, A., Gauthier, S., Agid, Y., Dal-Bianco, P. et al. (1999). Efficacy and safety of rivastigmine in patients with Alzheimer's disease: International randomized controlled trial. *British Medical Journal, 318*, 633–638.

Ross, D. F., Ceci, S. J., Dunning, D., & Toglia, M. P. (1994). Unconscious transference and mistaken identity: When a witness misidentifies a familiar but innocent person. *Journal of Applied Psychology, 79*, 918–930.

Ross, R. T., Orr, W. B., Holland, P. C., & Berger, T. W. (1984). Hippocampectomy disrupts acquisition and retention of learned conditional responding. *Behavioral Neuroscience, 98*(2), 211–225.

Rosselli, M., & Ardila, A. (1993). Developmental norms for the Wisconsin Card Sorting Test in 5- to 12-year-old children. *The Clinical Neuropsychologist, 7*, 145–154.

Roth, D., & Rehm, L. P. (1980). Relationship among self-monitoring processes, memory and depression. *Cognitive Therapy and Research, 4*, 149–157.

Rothi, L. J., & Hutchinson, E. C. (1981). Retention of verbal information by rehearsal in rela-tion to the fluency of verbal output in aphasia. *Brain and Language, 12*, 347–359.

Rothlind, J. C., Brandt, J., Zee, D., Codori, A. M., & Folstein, S. (1993). Unimpaired verbal memory and oculomotor control in asymptomatic adults with the genetic marker for Huntington's disease. *Archives of Neurology, 50*, 799–802.

Rovee-Collier, C., Hayne, H. H., & Colombo, M. (2001). *The development of implicit and explicit memory.* Amsterdam: John Benjamins.

Rovee-Collier, C., & Shyi, G. (1992). A functional and cognitive analysis of infant long-term reten-tion. In M. L. Howe, C. J. Brainerd, & V. F. Reyna (Eds.), *Development of long-term reten-tion* (pp. 3–55). New York: Springer-Verlag.

Rowe, J. W., & Kahn, R. L. (1987). Human aging. Usual and successful. *Science, 237*, 143–149.

Rowley, V. N., & Baer, P. E. (1961). Visual Reten-tion Test performance in emotionally disturbed and brain-damged children. *American Journal of Orthopsychiatry, 31*, 579–583.

Rubin, D. C. (1995). *Memory in oral traditions: The cognitive psychology of epic, ballads and counting-out rhymes.* New York: Oxford University Press.

Rubin, D. C., & Greenberg, D. L. (1998). Visual memory-deficit amnesia: A distinct amnesic presentation and etiology. *Proceedings of the National Academy of Sciences of the United States of America, 95*, 5413–5416.

Rubin, D. C., & Kozin, M. (1984). Vivid memor-ies. *Cognition, 16*, 81–95.

Rubin, S. R., Van Petten, C., Glisky, E. L., & Newberg, W. M. (1999). Memory conjunction errors in younger and older adults. Event-related potentials and neuropsychological data. *Cognitive Neuropsychology, 16*, 459–488.

Rubin, D. C., Wetzler, S. E., & Nebes, R. D. (1986). Autobiographical memory across the lifespan. In D. C. Rubin (Ed.), *Autobiographi-cal memory* (pp. 202–221). Cambridge: Cambridge University Press.

Ruchkin, D. S., Johnson, R. Jr., Grafman, J., Canoune, H., & Ritter, W. (1997). Multiple visuospatial working memory buffers: Evid-ence from spatiotemporal patterns of brain activity. [erratum appears in *Neuropsychologia,*

35(4), 572]. *Neuropsychologia*, 35(2), 195–209.

Rugg, M. D., Fletcher, P. C., Frith, C. D., Frackowiak, R. S. J., & Dolan, R. J. (1996). Differential activation of the prefrontal cortex in successful and unsuccessful memory retrieval. *Brain*, 119, 2073–2083.

Rund, B. R. (1989). Distractibility and recall capability in schizophrenics: A 4 year longitudinal study of stability in cognitive performance. *Schizophrenia Research*, 2, 265–275.

Rush, A. J., Weissenburger, J., Vinson, D. B., & Giles, D. E. (1983). Neuropsychological dysfunctions in unipolar nonpsychotic major depressions. *Journal of Affective Disorders*, 5(4), 281–287.

Russel, P. N., & Beekhuis, M. E. (1976). Organization in memory: A comparison of psychotics and normals. *Journal of Abnormal Psychology*, 85, 527–534.

Russell, E. W. (1975). A multiple scoring method for the assessment of complex memory functions. *Journal of Consulting and Clinical Psychology*, 43, 800–809.

Russell, W. R. (1971). *The traumatic amnesias*. Oxford: Oxford University Press.

Russo, R., & Spinnler, H. (1994). Implicit verbal memory in Alzheimer's disease. *Cortex*, 30, 359–375.

Rusted, J., Graupner, L., & Warburton, D. (1995). Effects of post-trial administration of nicotine on human memory: Evaluating the conditions for improving memory. *Psychopharmacology*, 119, 405–413.

Rusted, J., & Sheppard, L. (2002). Action-based memory in Alzheimer's disease: A longitudinal look at tea making. *Neurocase*, 8, 111–126.

Rusted, J. M., Eaton-Williams, P., & Warburton, D. M. (1991). A comparison of scopolamine and diazepam on working memory. *Psychopharmacology*, 105, 442–445.

Rusted, J. M., & Warburton, D. M. (1988). The effects of scopolamine on working memory in healthy young volunteers. *Psychopharmacology*, 96, 145–152.

Rusted, J. M., & Warburton, D. M. (1989). Effects of scopolamine on verbal memory: A retrieval or acquisition deficit? *Neuropsychobiology*, 21, 76–83.

Ryan, C. M., & Williams, T. M. (1993). Effects of insulin-dependent diabetes on learning and memory efficiency in adults. *Journal of Clinical & Experimental Neuropsychology*, 15, 685–700.

Ryan, T. V., Sautter, S. W., Capps, C. F., Menees, W., & Barth, J. T. (1992). Utilizing neuropsychological measures to predict vocational outcome in a head trauma population. *Brain Inj*, 6, 175–182.

Ryback, R. S. (1970). Alcohol amnesia. *Journal of American Medical Association*, 212, 1524.

Rypma, B., & D'Esposito, M. (1999). The role of prefrontal brain regions in components of working memory: Effects of memory load and individual differences. *Proceedings of the National Academy of Science of the United States of America*, 96, 6558–6563.

Rypma, B., Prabhakaran, V., Desmond, J. E., Glover, G. H., & Gabrieli, J. D. (1999). Load-dependent roles of frontal brain regions in the maintenance of working memory. *Neuroimage*, 9(2), 216–226.

Sagar, H. J., Cohen, N. J., Sullivan, E. V., Corkin, S., & Growdon, J. H. (1988). Remote memory function in Alzheimer's disease and Parkinson's disease. *Brain*, 111, 201–222.

Sahakian, B. J., Downes, J. J., Eagger, S., Evenden, J. L., Levy, R., Philpot, M. P. et al. (1990). Sparing of attentional relative to mnemonic function in a subgroup of patients with dementia of the Alzheimer type. *Neuropsychologia*, 28, 1197–1213.

Sahakian, B. J., Morris, R. G., Evenden, J. L., Heald, A., Levy, R., Philpot, M. et al. (1988). A comparative study of visuospatial memory and learning in Alzheimer-type dementia and Parkinson's disease. *Brain*, 111, 695–718.

Sainati, S. M., Ingram, D. M. M., Talwalker, S. et al. (2000). *Results of a double-blind, randomized, placebo-controlled study of celecoxib in the treatment of progression of Alzheimer therapy*. Proceedings of the sixth international Stockholm/Springfield Symposium on advances in Alzheimer's therapy, Sweden.

Saint-Cyr, J. A., Taylor, A. E., & Lang, A. E. (1988). Procedural learning and neostriatal function in man. *Brain, 111*, 941–959.

Saletu, B., Moller, H-J., Grunberger, J., Deutsch, H., & Rossner, M. (1990). Propentofylline in adult-onset cognitive disorders: Double-blind, placebo-controlled, clinical, psychometric and brain mapping studies. *Neuropsychobiology, 24*, 173–184.

Salomon, A. R., Marcinowski, K. J., & Zagorski, M. (1996). Nicotine inhibits amyloid formation by the beta-peptide. *Biochemistry, 35*, 13568–13578.

Salmon, D. P., & Butters, N. (1995). Neurobiology of skill and habit learning. *Current Opinion in Neurobiology, 5*, 184–190.

Salmon, D. P., Shimamura, A. P., Butters, N., & Smith, S. (1988). Lexical and semantic priming deficits in patients with Alzheimer's disease. *Journal of Clinical and Experimental Neuropsychology, 10*, 477–494.

Salter, D., & Platt, S. (1990). Suicidal intent, hopelessness and depression in parasuicide population: The influence of social desirability and elapsed time. *British Journal of Clinical Psychology, 29*, 361–371.

Salthouse, T. A. (1985). *A theory of cognitive ageing*. Amsterdam: North Holland.

Salthouse, T. A. (1990). Working memory as a processing resource in cognitive aging. *Developmental Review, 10*, 101–124.

Salthouse, T. A. (1992). Shifting levels of analysis in the investigation of cognitive aging. *Human Development, 35*, 321–342.

Salthouse, T. A. (1994). The aging of working memory. *Neuropsychology, 8*, 535–543.

Salthouse, T. A. (1996). The processing-speed theory of adult age differences in cognition. *Psychological Review, 103*, 403–428.

Samuels, S. C., & Davis, K. L. (1998). Experimental approaches to cognitive disturbance in Alzheimer's disease. *Harvard Review of Psychiatry, 6*, 11–22.

Sandi, C., Loscertales, M., & Guaza, C. (1997). Experience-dependent facilitating effect of corticosterone on spatial memory formation in the water maze. *European Journal of Neuroscience, 9*(4), 637–642.

Sandi, C., & Rose, S. P. (1994). Corticosterone enhances long-term retention in one-day-old chicks trained in a weak passive avoidance learning paradigm. *Brain Research, 647*(1), 106–112.

Sandor, T., Jolesz, F., Tieman, J., Kikinis, R., Jones, K., & Albert, M. (1992). Comparative analysis of computed tomographic and magnetic resonance imaging scans in Alzheimer patients and controls. *Archives of Neurology, 49*, 381–384.

Sanfey, A. G., Hastie, R., Colvin, M. K., & Grafman, J. (2003). Phineas gauged: Decision-making and the human prefrontal cortex. *Neuropsychologia, 41*(9), 1218–1229.

Sano, M., Bell, K., Cote, L., Dooneief, G., Lawton, A., Legler, L. et al. (1992). Double-blind parallel design pilot study of acetyl levocarnitine in patients with Alzheimer's disease. *Archives of Neurology, 49*(11), 1137–1141.

Sano, M., Ernesto, C., Thomas, R. G., Klauber, M. R., Schafer, K., Grundman, M. et al. (1997). A controlled trial of selegiline, alpha-tocopherol, or both as treatment for Alzheimer's disease. The Alzheimer's Disease Cooperative Study. *New England Journal of Medicine, 336*(17), 1216–1222.

Sapolsky, R. M. (1992). *Stress, the aging brain, and the mechanisms of neuron death*. Cambridge, MA: MIT Press.

Sapolsky, R. M. (1996). Why stress is bad for your brain. *Science, 273*, 749–750.

Sapolsky, R. M., Armanini, M. P., Packan, D. R., Sutton, S. W., & Plotsky, P. M. (1990). Glucocorticoid feedback inhibition of adrenocorticotropic hormone secretagogue release. Relationship to corticosteroid receptor occupancy in various limbic sites. *Neuroendocrinology, 51*(3), 328–336.

Sapolsky, R. M., & McEwen, B. S. (1986). Stress, glucocorticoids and their role in degenerative changes in the aging hippocampus. In T. Crook, R. T. Bartus, S. Ferris, & S. Gershon (Eds.), *Treatment development strategies for Alzheimer's disease* (pp. 151–171). Madison: Mark Powley Associates.

Saransaari, P., & Oja, S. S. (1995). Dizocilpine binding to cerebral cortical membranes from developing and ageing mice. *Mechanisms of Ageing and Development*, *85*, 171–181.

Sass, K. J., Buchanan, C. P., Kraemer, S., Westerveld, M., Kim, J. H., & Spencer, D. D. (1995). Verbal memory impairment resulting from hippocampal neuron loss among epileptic patients with structural lesions. *Neurology*, *45*, 2154–2158.

Savage, C. R. (1998). Neuropsychology of OCD: Research findings and treatment implications. In M. A. Jenike, L. Baer, & W. E. Minichello (Eds.), *Obsessive-compulsive disorders* (pp. 254–275). St Louis: Mosby.

Savage, C. R., Baer, L., Keuthen, N. J., Brown, H. D., Rauch, S. L., & Jenike, M. A. (1999). Organizational strategies mediate nonverbal memory impairment in obsessive-compulsive disorder. *Biological Psychiatry*, *45*(7), 905–916.

Savage, C. R., Keuthen, N. J., Jenike, M. A., Brown, H., Baer, L., Kendrick, A. D. et al. (1996). Recall and recognition in obsessive-compulsive disorder. *Journal of Neuropsychiatry*, *8*, 99–103.

Savage, J. M., Sweet, A. J., Castillo, R., & Langlais, P. J. (1997). The effects of lesions to thalamic lateral internal medullary lamina and posterior nuclei on learning, memory and habituation in the rat. *Behavioral Brain Research*, *82*, 133–147.

Saykin, A., Ruben, C., Raquel, E., et al. (1992). Neuropsychological function in schizophrenia: Selective impairment in memory and learning. *Archives of General Psychiatry*, *48*, 618–624.

Saykin, A. J., Johnson, S. C., Flashman, L. A., McAllister, T. W., Sparling, M., Darcey, T. M. et al. (1999). Functional differentiation of medial temporal and frontal regions involved in processing novel and familiar words: An fMRI study. *Brain*, *122*(Pt 10), 1963–1971.

Saykin, A. J., Shtasel, D. L., Gur, R. E., Kestel, D. P., Mozley, L. H., Stafiniak, P. et al. (1994). Neuropsychological deficits in neuroleptic naïve patients with first-episode schizophrenia. *Archives of General Psychiatry*, *51*, 124–131.

Schacter, D. L. (1977). The cognitive neuroscience of memory: Perspectives from neuroimaging research. *Philosophical Transactions of the Royal Society, London*, *352*, 1689–1695.

Schacter, D. L. (1987). Memory, amnesia and frontal lobe dysfunction. *Psychobiology*, *15*, 21–36.

Schacter, D. L. (1990). Perceptual representation systems and implicit memory: Toward a resolution of the multiple memory systems debate. In A. Diamond (Ed.), *The development and neural bases of higher cognitive functions* (pp. 543–571). New York: New York Academy of Sciences.

Schacter, D. L. (1992). Understanding implicit memory. *American Psychologist*, *47*, 559–569.

Schacter, D. L. (1994). Priming and multiple memory systems: Perceptual mechanisms of implicit memory. In D. L. Schacter & E. Tulving (Eds.), *Memory systems, Vol. 407* (pp. 233–268). Cambridge, MA: MIT Press.

Schacter, D. L. (1996). *Searching for memory: The brain, the mind and the past*. New York: Basic Books.

Schacter, D. L. (1997). The cognitive neuroscience of memory: perspectives from neuroimaging research. *Philosophical Transactions of the Royal Society of London—Series B: Biological Sciences*, *352*(1362), 1689–1695.

Schacter, D. L. (1999). The seven sins of memory. Insights from Psychology and Cognitive Neuroscience. *American Psychologist*, *54*(3), 182–203.

Schacter, D. L., Alpert, N. M., Savage, C. R., Rauch, S. L., & Albert, M. S. (1996a). Conscious recollection and the human hippocampal formation: Evidence from positron emission tomography. *Proceedings of the National Academy of Science of the United States of America*, *93*, 321–325.

Schacter, D. L., Bowers, J., & Booker, J. (1989). Intention, awareness and implicit memory: The retrieval intentionality criterion. In S. Lewandowsky, J. C. Dunn, & K. Kirsner (Eds.), *Implicit memory: Theoretical issues* (pp. 47–65). Hillsdale, NJ: Lawrence Erlbaum Associates Inc.

Schacter, D. L., Buckner, R. L., Koutstaal, W., Dale, A. M., & Rosen, B. R. (1997a). Late onset of anterior prefrontal activity during retrieval of veridical and illusory memories: An event-related fMRI study. *NeuroImage*, *6*, 259–269.

Schacter, D. L., Curran, T., Galluccio, L., Milberg, W. P., & Bates, J. F. (1996b). False recognition and the right frontal lobe: A case study. *Neuropsychologia, 34,* 793–808.

Schacter, D. L., Chiu, P., & Ochsner, K. N. (1993). Implicit memory: A selective review. *Annual Review of Neuroscience, 16,* 159–182.

Schacter, D. L., Church, B. A., & Treadwell, J. (1994). Implicit memory in amnesic patients: Evidence for spared auditory priming. *Psychological Science, 5,* 20–25.

Schacter, D. L., & Glisky, B. L. (1986). Memory remediation: Restoration, alleviation, and the acquisition of domain-specific knowledge. In B. P. Uzzell & Y. Gross (Eds.), *Clinical neuropsychology of intervention* (pp. 257–280). Boston: Martinus Nijhoff.

Schacter, D. L., & Graf, P. (1986). Preserved learning in amnesic patients: Perspectives from research on direct priming. *Journal of Clinical and Experimental Neuropsychology, 8,* 727–743.

Schacter, D. L., Harbluk, J. L., & McLachlan, D. R. (1984). Retrieval without recollection: An experimental analysis of source amnesia. *Journal of Verbal Learning and Verbal Behavior, 23,* 593–611.

Schacter, D. L., Kaszniak, A., & Kilstrom, J. (1991a). Models of memory and the understanding of memory disorders. In T. Yanagiara & R. Petersen (Eds.), *Memory disorders: Research and clinical practice* (pp. 111–133). New York: Marcel Dekker.

Schacter, D. L., Kaszniak, A. W., Kihlstrom, J. F., & Valdiserri, M. (1991b). The relation between source memory and aging. *Psychology and Aging, 6,* 559–568.

Schacter, D. L., & Kihlstrom, J. F. (1989). Functional amnesia. In F. Boller & J. Grafman (Eds.), *Handbook of neuropsychology (Vol. 3)* (pp. 209–231). Amsterdam: Elsevier.

Schacter, D. L., Koutstaal, W., Johnson, M. K., Gross, M. S., & Angell, K. A. (1997b). False recollection induced by photographs: A comparison of older and younger adults. *Psychology and Aging, 12,* 203–215.

Schacter, D. L., Koutstaal, W., & Norman, K. A. (1996c). Can cognitive neuroscience illuminate the nature of traumatic childhood memories? *Current Opinion in Neurobiology, 6*(2), 207–214.

Schacter, D. L., Osowiecki, D., Kazniak, A. W., Kihlstrom, J. F., & Valdiserri, M. (1994). Source memory: Extending the boundaries of age-related deficits. *Psychology and Aging, 9,* 81–89.

Schacter, D. L., Reiman, E., Curran, T., Yun, L. S., Bandy, D., McDermott, K. B. et al. (1996d). Neuroanatomical correlates of veridical and illusory recognition memory: Evidence from positron emission tomography. *Neuron, 17,* 267–274.

Schacter, D. L., Reiman, E., Uecker, A., Polster, M. R., Yun, L. S., & Cooper, L. A. (1995). Brain regions associated with retrieval of structurally coherent visual information. *Nature, 376,* 587–590.

Schacter, D. L., Rich, S. A., & Stampp, M. S. (1985). Remediation of memory disorders: Experimental evaluation of the spaced-retrieval technique. *Journal of Clinical and Experimental Neuropsychology, 7,* 79–96.

Schacter, D. L., & Tulving, E. (Eds.) (1994). *Memory systems.* Cambridge, MA: MIT Press.

Schacter, D. L., Verfaelli, M., & Anes, M. D. (1997). Illusory memories in amnesic patients: Conceptual and perceptual false recognition. *Neuropsychology, 11,* 331–342.

Schacter, D. L., & Wagner, A. D. (1999). Medial temporal lobe activations in fMRI and PET studies of episodic encoding and retrieval. *Hippocampus, 9,* 7–24.

Schafe, G. E., Atkins, C. M., Swank, M. W., Bauer, E. P., Sweat, J. D., & LeDoux, J. E. (2000). Activation of ERK/MAP kinase in the amygdala is required for memory consolidation of Pavlovian fear conditioning. *Journal of Neuroscience, 20,* 8177–8187.

Schafe, G. E., Nadel, N. V., Sullivan, G. M., Harris, A., & Ledoux, J. E. (1999). Memory consolidation for contextual and auditory fear conditioning is dependent on protein synthesis, PKA and MAP kinase. *Learning & Memory, 6,* 97–110.

Schafe, P., Fan, J., Choih, J., Fetter, R., & Serafini, T. (2000). Neuroligin expressed in nonneuronal cells triggers presynaptic development in contacting axons. *Cell, 101,* 657–669.

Schaie, K. W. (1983). The Seattle longitudinal study: A 21-year exploration of psychometric intelligence in adulthood. In K. W. Schaie (Ed.), *Longitudinal studies of adult psychological development.* New York: Guilford Press.

Schank, R. (1982). *Dynamic memory: A theory of reminding and learning in computers and people.* Cambridge: Cambridge University Press.

Scheltens, P., Hazenberg, G. J., Lindeboom, J., Valk, J., & Wolters, E. C. (1990). A case of progressive aphasia without dementia: "Temporal" Pick's disease? *Journal of Neurology, Neurosurgery and Psychiatry, 53,* 79–80.

Schenk, D., Barbour, R., Dunn, W., Gordon, G., Grajeda, H., Guido, T. et al. (1999). Immunization with amyloid-beta attenuates Alzheimer-disease-like pathology in the PDAPP mouse. *Nature, 400*(6740), 173–177.

Schlaug, G., Jancke, L., Huang, Y., & Steinmetz, H. (1995). In vivo evidence of structural brain asymmetry in musicians. *Science, 267*(5198), 699–701.

Schmahmann, J. (Ed.) (1997). *The cerebellum and cognition.* New York: Academic Press.

Schmidt, R., Freidl, W., Fazekas, F., Reinhart, B., Grieshofer, P., Koch, M. et al. (1994). The Mattis Dementia Rating Scale: Normative data from 1,001 healthy volunteers. *Neurology, 44*(5), 964–966.

Schneider, L. S., Anand, R., & Farlow, M. R. (1998). Systematic review of the efficacy of rivastigmine for patients with Alzheimer's disease. *International Journal of Geriatric Psychopharmacology, 1*(Suppl. 1), S26–S34.

Schneider, W., & Bjorklund, D. F. (1998). Memory. In W. Damon (Ed.), *Handbook of child psychology, Vol. 2. Cognition, perception and language* (5th Ed.) (pp. 467–521). New York: Wiley.

Schneider, L. S., Olin, J. T., Doody, R. S., Clark, C. M., Morris, J. C., Reisberg, B. et al. (1997). Validity and reliability of the Alzheimer's Disease Cooperative Study—Clinical global impression of change. The Alzheimer's Disease Cooperative Study. *Alzheimer Disease and Associated Disorders, 11*(Suppl. 2), S22–32.

Schneider, W., & Pressley, M. C. (1989). *Memory development between 2 and 20.* New York: Springer-Verlag.

Schneider, W., & Shiffrin, R. M. (1977). Controlled and automatic human information processing. I. Detection search and attention. *Psychological Review, 84,* 1–66.

Schnider, A., & Ptak, R. (1999). Spontaneous confabulators fail to suppress currently irrelevant memory traces. *Nature Neuroscience, 2*(7), 677–681.

Schnider, A., Ptak, R., Von Däniken, C., & Remonda, L. (2000). Recovery from spontaneous confabulations parallels receevery of temporal confusion in memory. *Neurology, 55,* 74–83.

Schnider, A., Regard, M., & Landis, T. (1994). Anterograde and retrograde amnesia following bitemporal infarction. *Behavioral Neurology, 7,* 87–92.

Schnider, A., von Däniken, C., & Gutbrod, K. (1996). The mechanisms of spontaneous and provoked confabulations. *Brain, 119,* 1365–1375.

Schofield, P. W., Marder, K., Dooneief, G., Jacobs, D. M., Sano, M., & Stern, Y. (1997). Association of subjective memory complaints with subsequent cognitive decline in community-dwelling elderly individuals with baseline cognitive impairment. *American Journal of Psychiatry, 154*(5), 609–615.

Scholey, A. B., Harper, S., & Kennedy, D. O. (2001). Cognitive demand and blood glucose. *Physiology & Behavior, 73,* 585–592.

Schooler, J. W., & Hermann, D. J. (1992). There is more to episodic memory than just episodes. In M. A. Conway, D. C. Rubin, H. Spinnler, & W. A. Wagenaar (Eds.), *Theoretical perspectives on autobiographical memory* (pp. 241–261). Dordrecht: Kluwer Academic Publishers.

Schooler, C., & Schaie, K. W. (1987). *Cognitive functioning and social structure over the life course.* New York: Ablex Publishing Co.

Schore, A. N. (1994) *Affect regulation and the origin of the self: The neurobiology of emotional development.* Hillsdale, NJ: Lawrence Erlbaum Associates Inc.

Schotte, D. E., Cools, J., & Payvar, S. (1990). Problem-solving skills in suicidal patients:

Trait vulnerability or state dependent phenomenon? *Journal of Consulting and Clinical Psychology*, *58*, 562–564.

Schreiber, H., Stolz-Born, G., Pietrowsky, R., Kornhuber, H. H., Fehm, H. L., & Born, J. (1995). Improved event-related potential signs of selective attention after the administration of the cholecystokinin analog ceruletide in healthy persons. *Biological Psychiatry*, *37*, 702–712.

Schugens, M. M., Daum, I., Spindler, M., & Birbaumer, N. (1997). Differential effects of aging on explicit and implicit memory. *Aging Neuropsychology & Cognition*, *4*(1), 33–44.

Schwartz, B. L., Deutsch, L. H., & Cohen, C. (1991). Memory for temporal order in schizophrenia. *Biological Psychiatry*, *29*, 329–339.

Schwartz, A. F., & McMillan, T. M. (1989). Assessment of everyday memory after severe head injury. *Cortex*, *25*, 665–671.

Schwartz, M. F., Montgomery, M. W., Buxbaum, L. J., Lee, S. S., Carew, T. G., Coslett, H. B. et al. (1998). Naturalistic action impairment in closed head injury. *Neuropsychology*, *12*, 13–28.

Schwartzman, A. E., Gold, D., Andres, D., Arbuckle, T. Y., & Chaikelson, J. (1987). Stability of intelligence. A 40-year follow-up. *Canadian Journal of Psychology*, *41*, 244–256.

Schweinberger, S. R. (2002). Personal names and the human right hemisphere: An illusory link? *Brain and Language*, *80*, 111–120.

Schweitzer, J. B., Faber, T. L., Grafton, S. T., Tune, L. E., Hoffman, J. M., & Kilts, C. D. (2000). Alterations in the functional anatomy of working memory in adult attention deficit hyperactivity disorder. *American Journal of Psychiatry*, *157*, 278–280.

Scott, S. K., Young, A. W., Calder, A. J., Hellawell, D. J., Aggleton, J. P., & Johnson, M. (1997) Impaired auditory recognition of fear and anger following bilateral amygdala lesions. *Nature*, *385*, 254–257.

Scoville, W., & Milner, B. (1957). Loss of recent memory after bilateral hippocampal lesions. *Journal of Neurology, Neurosurgery and Psychiatry*, *20*, 11–21.

Seamon, J. G., Luo, C. R., & Gallo, D. A. (1998). Creating false memories of words with or without recognition of list items: Evidence for nonconscious processes. *Psychological Science*, *9*, 20–26.

Sebastian, M. V., Menor, J., & Elosua, R. (2001). Patterns of errors in short-term forgetting in AD and ageing. *Memory*, *9*, 223–231.

Selcher, J. C., Atkins, C. M., Trzaskos, J. M., Paylor, R., & Sweat, J. D. (1999). A necessity for MAP kinase activation in mammalian spatial learning. *Learning & Memory*, *6*, 478–490.

Selden, N. R. W., Everitt, B. J., Jarrard, L. E., & Robbins, T. W. (1991). Complementary roles for the amygdala and hippocampus in aversive conditioning to explicit and contextual cues. *Neuroscience*, *42*, 2335–2350.

Sellal, F., Danion, J. M., Kauffmann-Muller, F., Grangé, D., Imbs, J. L., Van Der Linden, M. et al. (1992). Differential effects of diazepam and lorazepam on repetition priming in healthy volunteers. *Psychopharmacology*, *108*, 371–379.

Semenza, C., Mondini, S., & Zettin, M. (1995). The anatomical basis of proper name processing: A critical review. *Neurocase*, *1*, 183–188.

Sendtner, M., Kreutzberg, G. W., & Thoenen, H. (1990). Ciliary neurotrophic factor prevents the degeneration of motor neurons after axotomy. *Nature*, *345*, 440–441.

Seron, X., Van der Linden, M., & de Partz, M-P. (1991). In defence of cognitive approaches in neuropsychological therapy. *Neuropsychological Rehabilitation*, *1*, 303–318.

Severson, J., Marcusson, J., Winblad, B., & Finch, C. (1982). Age-correlated loss of dopaminergic binding sites in human basal ganglia. *Journal of Neurochemistry*, *39*, 1623–1631.

Shadlen, M. F., & Larson, E. B. (1999). What's new in Alzheimer's disease treatment? *Postgraduate Medicine*, *105*, 109–118.

Shah, P. J., O'Carroll, R. E., & Rogers, A. (1999). Abnormal response to negative feedback in depression. *Psychological Medicine*, *29*, 63–72.

Shah, P. J., & Miyake, A. (1996). The separability of working memory resources for spatial thinking and language processing: An individual differences approach. *Journal of Experimental Psychology: General*, *125*, 4–27.

Shallice, T. (1982). Specific impairments of planning. *Philosophical Transactions of the Royal Society, London Ser B, 298*, 199–209.

Shallice, T., & Butterworth, B. (1977). Short-term memory impairment and spontaneous speech. *Neuropsychologia, 15*, 729–735.

Shallice, T., Fletcher, P. C., Frith, C. D., Grasby, P., Frackowiak, R. S. J., & Dolan, R. J. (1994). Brain regions associated with acquisition and retrieval of verbal episodic memory. *Nature, 368*, 633–635.

Shallice, T., & Warrington, E. K. (1977). Auditory-verbal short-term memory impairment and conduction aphasia. *Brain and Language, 4*, 479–491.

Shapiro, M., & Caramanos, Z. (1990). NMDA antagonist MK-801 impairs acquisition but not performance of spatial working and reference memory. *Psychobiology, 18*, 231–243.

Shapiro, L. P., McNamara, P., Zurif, E., Lanzoni, S., & Cermak, L. (1992). Processing complexity and sentence memory: Evidence from amnesia. *Brain and Language, 42*, 431–453.

Sharma, R., Chaturvedi, C., & Tewari, P. V. (1987). Efficacy of Bacopa monniera in revitalizing intellectual functions in children. *Journal of Research Education Individual Medicine*, 1–12.

Shay, K. A., Kuke, L. W., Conboy, T., Harrell, L. E., Callaway, R., & Folks, D. G. (1991). The clinical validity of the Mattis Dementia Rating Scale in Alzheimer's dementia. *Journal of Geriatric Psychiatry and Neurology, 4*, 18–25.

Shean, G., Burnett, T., & Eckman, F. S. (2002). Symptoms of schizophrenia and neurocognitive test performance. *Journal of Clinical Psychology, 58*(7), 723–731.

Shepard, R. N., Romney, A. K., & Nerlove, S. B. (1972). *Multidimensional scaling: Theory and application in the behavioral sciences, Vol. I*. New York: Seminar Press.

Sherwin, B. (1997). Estrogen effects on cognition in menopausal women. *Neurology, 48*(Suppl. 7), S21–S26.

Shiffrin, R. M., & Schneider, W. (1977). Controlled and automatic human information processing. II. Perceptual learning automatic attending and a general theory. *Psychological Review, 84*, 127–190.

Shimamura, A. P. (1994). Memory and frontal lobe function. In M. S. Gazzaniga (Ed.), *The cognitive neurosciences* (pp. 803–813.) Cambridge, MA: MIT Press.

Shimamura, A. P., Janowsky, J. S., & Squire, L. R. (1990). Memory for the temporal order of events in patients with frontal lobe lesions and amnesic patients. *Neuropsychologia, 28*, 803–814.

Shimamura, A. P., Janowsky, J. S., & Squire, L. R. (1991). What is the role of frontal lobe damage in memory disorders? In H. S. Levin, H. M. Eisenberg, & A. L. Benton (Eds.), *Frontal lobe function and dysfunction*. New York: Oxford University Press.

Shimamura, A. P., Jernigan, T., & Squire, L. R. (1988). Memory for temporal order in patients with frontal lobe lesions and patients with amnesia. *Society for Neuroscience Abstracts, 14*, 1043.

Shimamura, A. P., & Squire, L. R. (1984). Paired-associate learning and priming effects in amnesia: A neuropsychological study. *Journal of Experimental Psychology: General, 113*, 556–570.

Shimamura, A. P., & Squire, L. R. (1987). A neuropsychological study of fact memory and source amnesia. *Journal of Experimental Psychology: Learning Memory & Cognition, 13*, 464–473.

Shimizu, E., Tang, Y. P., Rampon, C., & Tsien, J. Z. (2000). NMDA receptor-dependent synaptic reinforcement as a crucial process for memory consolidation. *Science, 290*, 1170–1174.

Shindler, A. G., Caplan, L. R., & Heir, D. B. (1984). Intrusions and perseverations. *Brain and Language, 23*, 148–158.

Shoqeirat, M. A., & Mayes, A. R. (1991). Disproportionate incidental spatial-memory and recall deficits in amnesia. *Neuropsychologia, 29*, 749–769.

Shors, T. J. (2001). Acute stress rapidly and persistently enhances memory formation in the male rat. *Neurobiology of Learning & Memory, 75*(1), 10–29.

Shors, T. J., Servatius, R. J., Thompson, R. F., Rogers, G., & Lynch, G. (1995). Enhanced glutamatergic neurotransmission facilitates classical conditioning in the freely moving rat. *Neuroscience Letters*, *186*, 153–156.

Shu, B-C., Tien, A. Y., Lung, F-W., & Chang, Y-Y. (2000). Norms for the Wisconsin Card Sorting Test in 6- to 11-year old children in Taiwan. *The Clinical Neuropsychologist*, *14*(3), 275–286.

Shue, K. L., & Douglas, V. I. (1992). Attention deficit hyperactivity disorder and the frontal lobe syndrome. *Brain & Cognition*, *20*(1), 104–124.

Shum, D. H. K., Harris, D., & O'Gorman, J. G. (2000). Effects of severe traumatic brain injury on visual memory. *Journal of Clinical and Experimental Neuropsychology*, *22*, 25–39.

Shute, C. C. (1975). Chemical transmitter system in the brain. *Modern Trends in Neurology*, *6*, 183–203.

Sieber, F. E., & Traystman, R. J. (1992). Special issues: Glucose and the brain. *Critical Care Medicine*, *20*, 104–114.

Siegel, D. J. (1995). Memory, trauma and psychotherapy: A cognitive science view. *Journal of Psychotherapy Practice and Research*, *4*, 93–122.

Sievers, J., Hasumann, B., Unsicker, K., & Berry, M. (1987). Fibroblast growth factors promote the survival of adult retinal ganglion neurons after transection of the optic nerve. *Neuroscience Letters*, *76*, 157–162.

Signoret, J., Whiteley, A., & Lhermitte, F. (1978). Influence of choline on amnesia in early Alzheimer's disease. *Lancet*, *2*, 837.

Silva, A. J., Kogan, J. H., Frankland, P. W., & Kida, S. (1998). CREB and memory. *Annual Review of Neuroscience*, *21*, 127–148.

Silva, A. J., Paylor, R., Wehner, J. M., & Tonnegawa, S. (1992). Impaired spatial learning in alpha-calcium-calmodulin kinase II mutant mice. *Science*, *257*, 206–211.

Silverstein, S. M., Osborn, L. M., & Palumbo, D. R. (1998). Rey-Osterrieth complex figure test performance in acute, chronic and remitted schizophrenia patients. *Journal of Clinical Psychology*, *54*(7), 985–994.

Simmons, M. L., & Chavkin, C. (1996). Endogenous opioid regulation of hippocampal function. *International Review of Neurobiology*, *39*, 145–196.

Simon, E., Leach, L., Winocur, G., & Moscovitch, M. (1994). Intact primary memory in mild to moderate Alzheimer's disease: Indices from the California Verbal Learning Test. *Journal of Clinical and Experimental Neruopsychology*, *16*, 414–422.

Simons, J. S., & Graham, K. S. (2000). New learning in semantic dementia: Implications for cognitive and neuroanatomical models of long-term memory. *Revue de Neuropsychologie*, *10*, 199–215.

Simons, J. S., Graham, K. S., Galton, C. J., Patterson, K., & Hodges, J. R. (2001). Semantic knowledge and episodic memory for faces in semantic dementia. *Neuropsychology*, *15*(1), 101–114.

Singh, M., Meyer, E. M., & Simpkins, J. W. (1995). The effect of ovariectomy and estradiol replacement on brain-derived neurotrophic factor messenger ribonucleic acid expression in cortical and hippocampal brain regions of female Sprague-Dawley rats. *Endocrinology*, *136*, 2320–2324.

Singh, R. H., & Singh, L. L. (1980). Studies on the anti-anxiety effect of the mehyda rasayana drug, Brahmi (*Bacopa monniera* Wettst.) part I. *Journal Research Ayur Siddhama*, *1*, 133–148.

Sitaram, W., Weingartner, H., & Gillin, J. C. (1978). Human serial learning: Enhancement with arecoline and choline and impairment with scopolamine. *Science*, *201*, 274–275.

Sivan, A. B. (1992). *Benton Visual Retention Test, 5th Ed.* San Antonio, CA: The Psychological Corporation.

Skingle, M., Beattie, D. T., Scopes, D. I. C., Starkey, S. J., Connor, H. E., Feniuk, W. et al. (1996). GR127935: A potent and selective 5-HT1D receptor antagonist. *Behavioral Brain Research*, *73*, 249–252.

Skoog, I., Lernfelt, B., Landahl, S., Palmertz, B., Andreasson, L. A., Nilsson, L. et al. (1996). 15-year longitudinal study of blood pressure and dementia. *Lancet*, *347*(9009), 1141–1145.

Slife, B. D., & Weaver, C. A. III. (1992). Depression, cognitive skill, and metacognitive skill in problem solving. *Cognition & Emotion*, *6*, 1–22.

Slooter, A. J., Cruts, M., Kalmijn, S., Hofman, A., Breteler, M. M., Van Broeckhoven, C. et al. (1998). Risk estimates of dementia by apolipoprotein E genotypes from a population-based incidence study: The Rotterdam Study. *Archives of Neurology*, *55*(7), 964–968.

Small, B. J., Viitanen, M., & Bäckman, L. (1997). Mini-Mental State Examination item scores as predictors of Alzheimer's disease: Incidence data from the Kungsholmen Project, *Stockholm. Journals of Gerontology Series A—Biological Sciences and Medical Sciences*, *52*, M299–304.

Smirne, S., Ferini-Strambi, L., Pirola, R., Tancredi, O., Franceschi, M., Pinto, P. et al. (1989). Effects of flunitrazepam on cognitive functions. *Psychopharmacology*, *98*, 251–256.

Smith, A. (1996). Memory. In J. E. Birren & K. W. Scaie (Eds.), *Handbook of psychology of aging* (pp. 236–250). New York: Academic Press.

Smith, C. D., Malcein, M., Meurer, K., Schmitt, F. A., Markesbery, W. R., & Pettigrew, L. C. (1999). MRI temporal lobe volume measures and neuropsychologic function in Alzheimer's disease. *Journal of Neuroimaging*, *9*, 2–9.

Smith, C. M., Swash, M., Exton-Smith, A. N., Phillips, M. J., Overstall, P. W., Piper, M. E. et al. (1978). Choline in Alzheimer's disease. *Lancet*, *2*, 318.

Smith, E. E., & Jonides, J. (1995a). Working memory in humans: Neuropsychological evidence. In M. S. Gazzaniga (Ed.), *The cognitive neurosciences*. Cambridge, MA: MIT Press.

Smith, E. E., & Jonides, J. (1995b). Spatial versus object working memory: PET investigations. *Journal of Cognitive Neuroscience*, *7*, 337–356.

Smith, E. E., Jonides, J., & Koeppe, R. A. (1996a). Dissociating verbal and spatial working memory using PET. *Cerebral Cortex*, *6*, 11–20.

Smith, E. E., Jonides, J., Marshuetz, C., & Koeppe, R. (1998). Components of verbal working memory: Evidence from neuroimaging. *Proceedings of the National Academy of Science of the United States of America*, *95*, 876–882.

Smith, G. E., Ivnik, R. J., Malec, J. F., Kokmen, E., Tangalos, E., & Petersen, R. C. (1994). Psychometric properties of the Mattis Dementia Rating Scale. *Assessment*, *1*(2), 123–131.

Smith, G. E., Ivnik, R. J., Petersen, R. C., Malec, J. F., Kokmen, E., & Tangalos, E. (1991). Age-associated memory impairment diagnoses: Problems of reliability and concerns for terminology. *Psychology & Aging*, *6*(4), 551–558.

Smith, G. E., Petersen, R. C., Parisi, J. E., Ivnik, R. J., Kokmen, E., Tangalos, E. G. et al. (1996b). Definition, course, and outcome of mild cognitive impairment. *Aging Neuropsychology & Cognition*, *3*(2), 141–147.

Smith, M. L., & Milner, B. (1988). Estimation of frequency of occurrence of abstract designs after frontal or temporal lobectomy. *Neuropsychologia*, *26*, 297–306.

Smith, M. L., & Milner, B. (1989). Right hippocampal impairment in the recall of spatial location: Encoding deficit or rapid forgetting? *Neuropsychologia*, *27*, 71–81.

Smith, R. L., Goode, K. T., La Marche, J. A., & Boll, T. J. (1995). Selective Reminding Test short form administration: A comparison of two through twelve trials. *Psychological Assessment*, *7*, 177–182.

Snow, J. H. (1998). Clinical use of the Benton Visual Retention Test for Children and adolescents with learning disabilities. *Archives of Clinical Neuropsychology*, *13*(7), 629–636.

Snowden, J. S., Goulding, P. J., & Neary, D. (1989). Semantic dementia. A form of circumscribed cerebral atrophy. *Behavioural Neurology*, *2*, 167–182.

Snowden, J. S., Neary, D., & Mann, D. M. A. (1996). *Fronto-temporal lobar degeneration: Fronto-temporal dementia, progressive aphasia, semantic dementia*. New York: Churchill Livingstone.

Snowdon, D. A., Greiner, L. H., Mortimer, J. A., Riley, K. P., Greiner, P. A., & Markesbery, W. R. (1997). Brain infarction and the clinical expression of Alzheimer disease. *Journal of the American Medical Association*, *277*, 813–817.

Snyder, S. H., & Bredt, D. S. (1991). Nitric oxide as a neuronal messenger. *Trends in Pharmacological Sciences*, *12*, 125–128.

Soderling, T. R., & Derkach, V. A. (2000). Postsynaptic protein phosphorylation and LTP. *Trends in Neuroscience*, *23*, 75–80.

Sofroniew, M. V., Pearson, R. C., & Powell, T. P. (1987). The cholinergic nuclei of the basal forebrain of the rat: normal structure, development and experimentally induced degeneration. *Brain Research*, *411*(2), 310–331.

Soininen, H., Partanen, K., Pitkanen, A., Hallikainen, M., Hanninen, T., Helisalmi, S. et al. (1995). Decreased hippocampal volume asymmetry on MRIs in nondemented elderly subjects carrying the apolipoprotein E4 allele. *Neurology*, *45*, 391–392.

Soininen, H. S., Partanen, K., Pitkanen, A., Vainio, P., Hanninen, T., Hallikainen, M. et al. (1994). Volumetric MRI analysis of the amygdala and the hippocampus in subjects with age-associated memory impairment: Correlation to visual and verbal memory. *Neurology*, *44*(9), 1660–1668.

Soliveri, P., Brown, R. G., Jahanshani, M., & Marsden, C. D. (1992). Procedural memory and neurological disease. *European Journal of Cognitive Psychology*, *4*, 161–193.

Solomon, P. R., Vander Schaaf, E. R., Thompson, R. F., & Weisz, D. J. (1986). Hippocampus and trace conditioning of the rabbits classically conditioned nictitating membrane response. *Behavioral Neuroscience*, *100*, 729–744.

Son, H., Hawkins, R. D., Martin, K., Kiebler, M., Huang, P. L., Fishman, M. C. et al. (1996). Long-term potentiation is reduced in mice that are doubly mutant in endothelial and neuronal nitric oxide synthase. *Cell*, *87*, 1015–1023.

Spagnoli, A., Lucca, U., Menasce, G., Bandera, L., Cizza, G., Forloni, G. et al. (1991). Long-term acetyl-L-carnitine treatment in Alzheimer's disease. *Neurology*, *41*(11), 1726–1732.

Spector, A., Davies, S., Woods, B., & Orrell, M. (2000). Reality orientation for dementia: A systematic review of the evidence of effectiveness from randomised controlled trials. *The Gerontologist*, *40*, 206–212.

Spenceley, A., & Jerrom, W. (1997). Intrusive traumatic childhood memories in depression: A comparison between depressed, recovered and never depressed women. *Behavioural and Cognitive Psychotherapy*, *25*, 309–318.

Spencer, W. D., & Raz, N. (1995). Differential effects of aging on memory for content and context. A meta-analysis. *Psychology & Aging*, *10*, 527–539.

Sperling, R., Greve, D., Dale, A., Killiany, R., Holmes, J., Rosas, H. D. et al. (2002). Functional MRI detection of pharmacologically induced memory impairment. *PNAS*, *99*(1), 455–460.

Spiegel, D., Frischholz, E. J., & Spira, J. (1993). Functional disorders of memory. In J. M. Oldham, M. B. Riba, & A. Tasman (Eds.), Review of psychiatry, Vol. 12. Washington, DC: American Psychiatric Press.

Spiers, P. A., & Hochanadel, G. (1999). Citicoline for traumatic brain injury: Report of two cases, including my own. *Journal of the International Neurospsychology Society*, *5*, 260–264.

Spreen, O., & Strauss, E. (1991). *A compendium of neuropsychological tests*. New York: Oxford University Press.

Squire, L. R. (1981). Two forms of human amnesia: An analysis of forgetting. *Journal of Neuroscience*, *1*(6), 635–640.

Squire, L. R. (1987). *Memory and brain*. New York: Oxford University Press.

Squire, L. R. (1992). Memory and the hippocampus: A synthesis from findings with rats, monkeys and humans. *Psychological Review*, *99*, 195–231.

Squire, L. R., & Alvarez, P. (1995). Retrograde amnesia and memory consolidation: A neurobiological perspective. *Current Opinion in Neurobiology*, *5*, 169–177.

Squire, L. R., Amaral, D. G., & Press, G. (1990). Magnetic resonance imaging of the hippocampal formation and mamillary nuclei distinguish medial temporal lobe and diencephalic amnesia. *Journal of Neuroscience*, *10*, 3106–3117.

Squire, L. R., Cohen, N. J., & Nadel, L. (1984). The medial temporal region and memory consolidation: A new hypothesis. In H. Weingartner & E. Parker (Eds.), *Memory consolidation*. Hillsdale, NJ; Lawrence Erlbaum Associates Inc.

Squire, L. R., Haist, F., & Shimamura, A. P. (1989). The neurology of memory: Quantitative assessment of retrograde amnesia in two groups of amnesic patients. *Journal of Neuroscience*, *9*(3), 828–839.

Squire, L. R., Hamann, S. B., & Schacter, D. L. (1996). Intact baseline performance and priming in amnesia: Reply to Ostergaard and Jernigan. *Neuropsychology, 10*(1), 131–135.

Squire, L. R., & Knowlton, B. J. (1994). Memory, hippocampus and brain systems. In M. Gazzaniga (Ed.), *The cognitive neurosciences.* Cambridge, MA: MIT Press.

Squire, L. R., Ojemann, J. G., Miezin, F. M., Petersen, S. E., Videen, T. O., & Raichle, M. E. (1992). Activation of the hippocampus in normal humans: A functional anatomical study of memory. *Proceedings of the National Academy of Science of the United States of America, 89,* 1837–1841.

Squire, L. R., & Slater, P. C. (1978). Bilateral and unilateral ECT: Effects on verbal and nonverbal memory. *American Journal of Psychiatry, 135,* 1316–1320.

Squire, L. R., Slater, P. C., & Chace, P. M. (1975). Retrograde amnesia: Temporal gradient in very long term memory following electroconvulsive therapy. *Science, 187,* 77–79.

Squire, L. R., & Zola, S. M. (1996a). Ischemic brain damage and memory impairment: A commentary. *Hippocampus, 6*(5), 546–552.

Squire, L. R., & Zola, S. (1996b). Structure and function of declarative and nondeclarative memory systems. *Proceedings of the National Academy of Science of the United States of America, 93,* 13515–13522.

Squire, L. R., & Zola, S. M. (1998). Episodic memory, semantic memory and amnesia. *Hippocampus, 8,* 205–211.

Squire, L. R., & Zola-Morgan, S. (1991). The medial temporal lobe memory system. *Science, 253,* 1380–1386.

Stadtlander, L. M., Murdoch, L. D., & Heiser, S. M. (1998). Visual and haptic influences on memory: Age differences in recall. *Experimental Aging Research, 24*(3), 257–272.

Starkman, M. N., Gebarski, S. S., Berent, S., & Schteingart, D. E. (1992). Hippocampal formation volume, memory dysfunction, and cortisol levels in patients with Cushing's syndrome. *Biological Psychiatry, 32*(9), 756–765.

Starkman, M. N., & Schteingart, D. E. (1981). Neuropsychiatric manifestations of patients with Cushing's syndrome: Relationship to cortisol and adrenocorticotropic hormone levels. *Archives of Internal Medicine, 141,* 215–219.

Starkstein, S., & Mayberg, H. (1993). Depression in Parkinson's disease. In S. Starkstein & R. Robinson, (Eds.), *Depression in neurologic disease.* Baltimore: Johns Hopkins University.

Starkstein, S. E., Brandt, J., Bylsma, F., Peyser, C., Folstein, M., & Folstein, S. E. (1992). Neuropsychological correlates of brain atrophy in Huntington's disease: A magnetic resonance imaging study. *Neuroradiology, 34,* 487–489.

Starkstein, S. E., Preziosi, T. J., Berthier, M. L., Bolduc, P. L., Mayberg, H. S., & Robinson, R. G. (1989) Depression and cognitive impairment in Parkinson's disease. *Brain, 112,* 1141–1153.

Staubli, U., Perez, Y., Xu, F., Rogers, G., Inguar, M., Stone-Elander, S. et al. (1995). Centrally active modulators of glutamate (AMPA) receptors facilitate the induction of LTP in vivo. *Proceedings of the National Academy of Science of the United States of America, 91*(23), 11158–11182.

Staubli, U., Rogers, G., & Lynch, G. (1994). Facilitation of glutamate receptors enhances memory. *Proceedings of the National Academy of Science of the United States of America, 91,* 777–781.

Stebbins, G. T., Gabrieli, J. D. E., Masciari, F., Monti, L., & Goetz, C. G. (1999). Delayed recognition memory in Parkinson's disease: A role for working memory? *Neuropsychologia, 37,* 503–510.

Steele, R. J., & Morris, R. G. M. (1999). Delay-dependent impairment of a matching-to-place task with chronic and intrahippocampal infusion of the NMDA-antagonist D-AP5. *Hippocampus, 9*(2), 118–136.

Steele, T., McCann, U. D., & Ricaurte, G. A. (1994). 3,4-Methylenedioxy-methamphetamine (MDMA, "Ecstasy"): Pharmacology and toxicology in animals. *Addiction, 89,* 539–551.

Stefanis, L., Desmond, D. W., & Tatemichi, T. K. (1997). Crossed conduction aphasia associated with impairment of visuospatial memory. *Neurocase, 3,* 201–207.

Steinberg, R., Brun, P., Fournier, M., Souilhac, J., Rodier, D., Mons, J. et al. (1994). SR 48692, a non-peptide neurotensin receptor antagonist differentially affects neurotensin-induced behavior and changes in dopaminergic transmission. *Neuroscience, 59,* 921–929.

Steinmetz, J. E., Logue, S. F., & Miller, D. P. (1993). Using signaled barpressing tasks to study the neural substrates of appetitive and aversive learning in rats: Behavioral manipulations and cerebellar lesions. *Behavioral Neuroscience, 107*(6), 941–954.

Ste-Marie, D. M., Jennings, J. M., & Finalyson, A. J. (1996). Process dissociation procedure: Memory testing in populations with brain damage. *Clinical Neuropsychologist, 10,* 25–36.

Stern, Y., Albert, S., Tang, M-X., & Tsai, W-Y. (1999). Rate of memory decline in AD is related to education and occupation. Cognitive reserve? *Neurology, 53,* 1942–1947.

Stern, C. E., Corkin, S., Gonzalez, R. G., Guimaraes, A. R., Baker, J. R., Jennings, P. J. et al. (1996). The hippocampal formation participates in novel picture encoding: Evidence from functional magnetic resonance imaging. *Proceedings of the National Academy of Sciences of the United States of America, 93*(16), 8660–8665.

Stern, Y., Andrews, H., Pittman, J., Sano, M., Tatemichi, T., Lantigua, R. et al. (1992a). Diagnosis of dementia in a heterogenous population. Development of a neuropsychological paradigm-based diagnosis of dementia and quantified correction for the effects of education. *Archives of Neurology, 49,* 453–460.

Stern, Y., Alexander, G. E., Prohovnik, I., & Mayeux, R. (1992b). Inverse relationship between education and parietotemporal perfusion deficit in Alzheimer's disease. *Annals of Neurology, 32,* 371–375.

Stern, Y., Alexander, G. E., Prohovnik, I., Stricks, L., Link, B., Lennon, M. C. et al. (1995). Relationship between lifetime occupation and parietal flow: Implications for a reserve against Alzheimer's disease pathology. *Neurology, 45*(1), 55–60.

Stern, Y., Gurland, B., Tatemichi, T. K., Tang, M. X., Wilder, D., & Mayeux, R. (1994). Influence of education and occupation on the incidence of Alzheimer's disease. *Journal of the American Medical Association, 271,* 1004–1010.

Stern, Y., Sano, M., & Mayeux, R. (1987). Clinical efficacy of oral physostigmine in Alzheimer's disease. *Annals of Neurology, 22,* 306–310.

Sternberg, S. (1969). Memory-scanning: Mental processes revealed by reaction-time expriments. *American Scientist, 57*(4), 421–457.

Stevens, A. B., O'Hanlon, A. M., & Camp, C. J. (1993). The spaced-retrieval method: A case study. *Clinical Gerontologist, 13,* 106–109.

Stevens, C. F. (1994). CREB and memory consolidation. *Neuron, 13,* 769–770.

Stewart, S. H., Rioux, G. F., & Connolly, J. F. (1996). Effects of oxazepam and lorazepam on implicit and explicit memory: Evidence for possible influences of time course. *Psychopharmacology, 128,* 139–149.

Stewart, W. F., Kawas, C., Corrada, M., & Metter, E. J. (1996). Risk of Alzheimer's disease and duration of NSAID use. *Neurology, 48,* 626–632.

Stip, E., Lussier, I., Babai, M., & Debruille, B. (1995). Cognitive decline in young drug-naïve schizophrenia. *Schizophrenia Research, 15,* 135.

Stokes, L. C., & Pankowski, M. L. (1988). Incidental learning of ageing adults via television. *Adult Education Quaterly, 38*(2), 88–89.

Storandt, M., & Hill, R. (1989). Very mild senile dementia of the Alzheimer type. II. Psychometric test performance. *Archives of Neurology, 46,* 383–386.

Stork, O., Stork, S., Pape, H-C., & Obata, K. (2001). Identification of genes expressed in the amygdala during the formation of fear memory. *Learning & Memory, 8,* 209–219.

Strange, B. A., Fletcher, P. C., Henson, R. N., Friston, K. J., & Dolan, R. J. (1999). Segregating the functions of human hippocampus. *Proceedings of the National Academy of Sciences of the United States of America, 96*(7), 4034–4039.

Stratta, P., Daneluzzo, E., Mattei, P., Bustini, M., Casacchia, M., & Rossi, A. (1997). No deficit in Wisconsin Card Sorting Test performance of schizophrenic patients' first-degree relatives. *Schizophrenia Research, 26,* 147–151.

Strauss, G. D. (1995). Diagnosis and psychiatry: Examination of the psychiatric patient. In H. I. Kaplan & B. J. Sadock (Eds.), *Comprehensive textbook of psychiatry, 6th Edn. Vol. I.* Baltimore, Williams & Wilkins.

Street, J., Clark, W. S., Gannon, K. S., Cummings, J. L., Bymaster, F. P., Tamura, R. N. et al. (2000). Olanzapine treatment of psychotic and behavioural symptoms in patients with Alzheimer's disease in nursing care facilities. *Archives of General Psychiatry, 57,* 968–976.

Stringer, A. Y., & Goldman, M. S. (1988). Experience-dependent recovery of block design performance in male alcoholics. Strategy training versus unstructured practice. *Journal of Studies on Alcohol, 49,* 406–411.

Stuss, D. T., & Benson, D. F. (1986). *The frontal lobes.* New York: Raven Press.

Suchy, Y., & Sweet, J. J. (2000). Information/Orientation Subtest of the Wechsler Memory Scale–Revised as an indicator of suspicion of insufficient effort. *The Clinical Neuropsychologist, 14*(1), 56–66.

Sullivan, E. V., Mathalon, D. H., Ha, C. N., Zipursky, R. B., & Pfefferbaum, A. (1992). The contribution of constructional accuracy and oranization strategy to nonverbal recall in schizophrenia and chronic alcoholism. *Biological Psychiatry, 32,* 312–333.

Summerfelt, A. T., Alphs, L. D., Funderburk, F. R., Strauss, M. E., & Wagman, A. M. I. (1991). Impaired Wisconsin card sort performance in schizophrenia may reflect motivational deficits. *Archives of General Psychiatry, 48,* 282–283.

Summers, J. D., Lichtenberg, P. A., & Vangel, S. J. (1995). Fuld object-memory evaluation in an urban geriatric population. *Clinical Gerontologist, 15*(4), 21–34.

Supple, W. F. Jr., & Leaton, R. N. (1990). Lesions of the cerebellar vermis and cerebellar hemispheres: Effects on heart rate conditioning in rats. *Behavioral Neuroscience, 104*(6), 934–947.

Sutherland, R. J., & McDonald, R. J. (1990). Hippocampus, amygdala, and memory deficits. *Behavioural Brain Research, 34,* 57–79.

Sutherland, R. J., McDonald, R. J., & Hill, C. R. (1989). Damage to the hippocampal formation in rats selectively impairs the ability to learn cue relationships. *Behavioral & Neural Biology, 52*(3), 331–356.

Sutherland, R. J., & Rudy, J. W. (1989). Configural association theory: The role of the hippocampal formation in learning, memory, and amnesia. *Psychobiology, 17,* 129–144.

Suzuki, W. A. (1996). The anatomy, physiology and functions of the perirhinal cortex. *Current Opinion in Neurobiology, 6*(2), 179–186.

Suzuki, W. A., & Amaral, D. G. (1994). Perirhinal and para-hippocampal cortices of the macaque monkey: Cortical afferents. *Journal of Comparative Neurology, 350,* 497–533.

Suzuki, W. A., Zola-Morgan, S., Squire, L. R., & Amaral, D. G. (1993). Lesions of the perirhinal and parahippocampal cortices in the monkey produce long-lasting memory impairment in the visual and tactual modalities. *Journal of Neuroscience, 13,* 2430–2451.

Swainson, R., Hodges, J. R., Galton, C. J., Semple, J., Michael, A., Dunn, B. D. et al. (2001). Early detection and differential diagnosis of Alzheimer's disease and depression with neuropsychological tasks. *Dementia and Geriatric Cognitive Disorders, 12,* 265–280.

Swan, G. E., Morrison, E., & Eslinger, P. J. (1990). Interrater agreement on the Benton Visual Retention Test. *The Clinical Neuropsychologist, 4,* 37–44.

Swanson, H. L. (1999). Reading comprehension and working memory in learning-disabled readers: Is the phonological loop more important than the executive system? *Journal of Experimental Child Psychology, 72,* 1–31.

Swanson, H. L., & Alexander, J. (1997). Cognitive processes that predict reading in learning disabled readers. Revisiting the specificity hypothesis. *Journal of Educational Psychology, 89,* 128–158.

Swick, D., & Knight, R. T. (1995). Contributions of right inferior temporal-occipital cortex to visual word and non-word priming. *Neuroreport, 7,* 11–16.

Swick, D., & Knight, R. T. (1996). Is prefrontal cortex involved in cued recall? A neuropsychological test of PET findings. *Neuropsychologia, 34,* 1019–1028.

Szatmari, P., Offord, D. R., & Boyle, M. (1989). Correlates associated impairments and patterns of service utilization of children with attention deficit disorders: Findings from the Ontario Child Health Study. *Journal of Child Psychology and Psychiatry, 30,* 205–217.

Sze, K. H., Sim, T. C., Wong, E., Cheng, S., & Woo, J. (1998). Effect of nimodipine on memory after cerebral infarction. *Acta Neurologica Scandinavica, 97,* 386–392.

Tabert, M. H., Albert, S. M., Borukhova-Milov, L., Camacho, Y., Pelton, G., Liu, X. et al. (2002). Functional deficits in patients with mild cognitive impairment. Prediction of AD. *Neurology, 58,* 758–764.

Takashima, A., Yokota, T., Maeda, Y., & Itoh, S. (1991). Pretreatment with caerulein protects against memory impairment induced by protein kinase C inhibitors in the rat. *Peptides, 12,* 699–703.

Talland, G. A., & Quarton, G. C. (1965). The effects of methamphetamine and pentobarbital on the running memory span. *Psychopharmacologia, 7,* 379–382.

Tallis, F. (1997). The neuropsychology of obsessive-compulsive disorder: A review and consideration of clinical implications. *British Journal of Clinical Psychology, 36,* 3–20.

Tamaki, N., Kusunoki, T., & Matsumoto, S. (1985). The effect of Vinpocetine on cerebral blood flow in patients with cerebraovascular disorders. *Therapia Hungaria, 33,* 13–21.

Tamkin, A. S., & Kunce, J. T. (1985). A comparison of three neuropsychological tests: The Weigl, Hooper, and Benton. *Journal of Clinical Psychology, 41,* 660–664.

Tamlyn, D., McKenna, C. J., Morgentheimer, A. N., Lund, C. E., Hammond, S., & Baddeley, A. D. (1992). Memory impairment in schizophrenia: Its extent, affiliations, and neuropsychological character. *Psychological Medicine, 22,* 101–115.

Tang, Y-P., Shimizu, E., Dube, G. R., Rampon, C., Kerchner, G. A., Zhuo, M. et al. (1999). Genetic enhancement of learning and memory in mice. *Nature, 401*(6748), 63–69.

Tangalos, E. G., Smith, G. E., Ivnik, R. J., Petersen, R. C., Kokmen, E., Kurland, E. et al. (1996). The Mini-Mental State Examination in general practice: Clinical utility and acceptance. *Mayo Clinic Proceedings, 71,* 829–837.

Tata, P. R., Rollings, J., Collins, M., Pickering, A., & Jacobson, R. R. (1994). Lack of cognitive recovery following withdrawal from long-term benzodiazepine use. *Psychological Medicine, 24,* 203–213.

Taubenfeld, S. M., Wiig, K. A., Bear, M. F., & Alberini, C. M. (1999). A molecular correlate of memory and amnesia in the hippocampus. *Nature Neuroscience, 2*(4), 309–310.

Taverni, J. P., Seliger, G., & Lichtman, S. W. (1998). Donepezil mediated memory improvements in traumatic brain injury during post acute rehabilitation. *Brain Injury, 12*(1), 77–80.

Taylor, A. E., Saint-Cyr, J. A., & Lang, A. E. (1986). Frontal lobe dysfunction in Parkinson's disease. *Brain, 109,* 845–883.

Taylor, A. E., Saint-Cyr, J. A., & Lang, A. E. (1987). Parkinson's disease. Cognitive changes in relation to treatment response. *Brain, 110*(Pt 1), 35–51.

Taylor, A. E., Saint-Cyr, J. A., & Lang, A. E. (1990). Memory and learning in early Parkinson's disease: Evidence for a "frontal lobe sybdrome". *Brain and Cognition, 13,* 211–232.

Taylor, J., Hunt, E., & Cogan, P. (1967). Effects of diazepam on the speed of mental rotation. *Psychopharmacology, 91,* 369–371.

Taylor, J. E. (Ed.) (1958). *Selected writings of John Hughlings Jackson, Vol. 2,* London: Staples.

Teasdale, J. D., Howard, R. J., Cox, S. G., Ha, Y., Brammer, M. J., Williams, S. C. et al. (1999). Functional MRI study of the cognitive generation of affect. *American Journal of Psychiatry, 156*(2), 209–215.

Teccott, L. H., Logue, S. F., Wehner, J. M., & Kauer, J. A. (1998). Perturbed dentate gyrus function in serotonin 5-HT2C receptor mutant mice. *Proceedings of the National Academy of Sciences of the United States of America, 95,* 15026–15031.

Terrace, H. S. (1963). Discrimination learning with and without "errors". *Journal of the Experimental Analysis of Behavior, 6,* 1–27.

Terry, A. V. J., Buccafusco, J. J., Jackson, W. J., Prendergast, M. A., Fontana, D. J., Wong, E. H. P. et al. (1998). Enhanced delayed matching performance in younger and older macaques administered the 5-HT$_4$ receptor agonist, RS 17017. *Psychopharmacology*, *135*, 407–415.

Terry, A. V. J., Jackson, W. J., & Buccafusco, J. J. (1993). Effects of concomitant cholinergic and adrenergic stimulation on learning and memory performance by young and aged monkeys. *Cerebral Cortex*, *3*, 304–312.

Tessler, M., & Nelson, K. (1994). Making memories: The influence of joint encoding on later recall by young children. *Consciousness and Cognition*, *3*, 307–326.

Teyler, T. J., & DiScenna, P. (1986). The hippocampal memory indexing theory. *Behavioral of Neuroscience*, *100*, 147–154.

Teyler, T. J., & DiScenna, P. (1987). Long-term potentiation. *Annual Review of Neuroscience*, *10*, 131–161.

Thach, W. T., Goodkin, H. P., & Keating, J. G. (1992). The cerebellum and the adaptive coordination of movement. *Annual Review of Neuroscience*, *15*, 403–442.

Thal, L. J., Carta, A. Clarke, W. R., Ferris, S. H., Friedland, R. P., Petersen, R. C. et al. (1996). A 1-year multicenter placebo-controlled study of acetyl-L-carnitine in patients with Alzheimer's disease. *Neurology*, *47*(3), 705–711.

Thal, L. J., & Fuld, P. A. (1983). Memory enhancement with oral physostigmine in Alzheimer's disease. *New England Journal of Medicine*, *308*, 720–721.

Thal, L. J., Fuld, P. A., Masur, D. M., & Sharpless, N. S. (1983). Oral physostigmine and lecithin improve memory in Alzheimer's disease. *Annals of Neurology*, *13*, 491–496.

The Psychological Corporation. (1997). *WAIS-III/WMS-III technical manual*. San Antonio, TX: Psychological Corporation.

Thomas-Antérion, C., Jacquin, K., & Laurent, B. (2000). Differential mechanisms of impairment of remote memory in Alzheimer's and frontotemporal dementia. *Dementia and Geriatric Cognitive Disorders*, *11*, 100–106.

Thomas, V., Reymann, J-M., Lieury, A., & Allain, H. (1996). Assessment of procedural memory in Parkinson's disease. *Progress in Neuropsychopharmacology and Biological Psychiatry*, *20*, 641–650.

Thompson, L. T., Deyo, R. A., & Disterhoft, J. F. (1990). Nimodipine enhances spontaneous activity of hippocampal pyramidal neurons in aging rabbits at a dose that facilitates associative learning. *Brain Research*, *535*(1), 119–130.

Thompson-Schill, S. L., Swick, D., Farah, M. J., D'Esposito, M., Kan, I. P., & Knight, R. T. (1998). Verb generation in patients with focal frontal lesions: A neuropsychological test of neuroimaging findings. *Proceedings of the National Academy of Sciences of the United States of America*, *95*, 15855–15860.

Thornton, S., & Brotchie, J. (1987). Reminiscence: A critical review of the empirical literature. *British Journal of Clinical Psychology*, *26*, 93–111.

Tierney, M. C., Snow, W. G., Reid, D. W., Zorzitto, M. L., & Fisher, R. H. (1987). Psychometric differentiation of dementia: Replication and extension of the findings of Storandt and coworkers. *Archives of Neurology*, *44*, 720–722.

Tierney, M. C., Szalai, J. P., Snow, W. G., Fisher, R. H., Nores, A., Nadon, G. et al. (1996a). Prediction of probable Alzheimer's disease in memory-impaired patients: A prospective longitudinal study. *Neurology*, *46*, 661–665.

Tierney, M. C., Szalai, J. P., Snow, W. G., Fisher, R. H., Tsuda, T., Chi, H. et al. (1996b). A prospective study of the clinical utility of ApoE genotype in the prediction of outcome in patients with memory impairment. *Neurology*, *46*, 149–154.

Tillfors, M., Furmark, T., Marteinsdottir, I., Fischer, H., Pissiota, A., Langstrom, B. et al. (2001). Cerebral blood flow in subjects with social phobia during stressful speaking tasks: A PET study. *American Journal of Psychiatry*, *158*(8), 1220–1226.

Tiplady, B., Faineteau, H., Loganathan, A., Spiegelberg, M., Taylor, Z., & Wright, P. (1998). Effects of ethanol and temazepam on performance in memory and psychomotor tasks: A dose–response comparison. *Human Psychopharmacology*, *13*, 285–291.

Tocco, G., Devgan, K. K., Hauge, S. A., Weiss, C., Baudry, M., & Thopson, R. F. (1991). Classical conditioning selectively increases AMPA receptor-binding in rabbit hippocampus. *Brain Research, 559*(2), 331–336.

Tocco, G., Maren, S., Shors, T. J., Baudry, M., & Thompson, R. F. (1992). Long-term potentiation is associated with increased [3H]AMPA binding in rat hippocampus. *Brain Research, 573*(2), 228–234.

Todd, C. M., & Perlmutter, M. (1980). Reality recalled by preschool children. In M. Perlmutter (Ed.), *Children's memory: New directions for child development* (pp. 69–85). San Francisco, Jossey-Bass.

Todd, J., Dewhurst, K., & Wallis, G. (1981). The syndrome of Capgras. *British Journal of Psychiatry, 139*, 319–327.

Tolman, E. C. (1917). Retroactive inhibition as affected by conditions of learning. *Psychological Monographs, 18*, 107.

Tomaz, C., Dickinson-Anson, H., & McGaugh, J. L. (1992). Bilateral amygdala lesions block diazepam-induced anterograde amnesia in an inhibitory avoidance task. *Proceedings of the National Academy of Science of the United States of America, 89*, 3615–3619.

Tombaugh, T. N., & McIntyre, N. J. (1992). The Mini-Mental State Examination: A comprehensive review. *Journal of the American Geriatrics Society, 40*, 922–935.

Tompkins, C. A. (1995). *Right hemisphere communication disorders: Theory and management*. San Diego, CA: Singular Publishing Group.

Tonkiss J., Morris, R. G. M., & Rawlins, J. N. P. (1988). Intra-ventricular infusion of the NMDA antagonist AP5 impairs performance on a non-spatial operant DRL task in the rat. *Experimental Brain Research, 73*, 181–188.

Tonkiss, J., & Rawlins, J. N. P. (1991). The competitive NMDA antagonist AP5, but not the non-competitive antagonist MK-801 induces a delay-related impairment in spatial working memory in rats. *Experimental Brain Research, 85*, 349–358.

Tounsi, H., Deweer, B., Ergis, A-M., Van der Linden, M., Pillon, B., Michon, A. et al. (1999). Sensitivity to semantic cuing: An index of episodic memory dysfunction in early Alzheimer disease. *Alzheimer Disease and Associated Disorders, 13*(1), 38–46.

Traupmann, K. L., Berzofsky, M., & Kesselman, M. (1976). Encoding of taxonomic word categories by schizophrenics. *Journal of Abnormal Psychology, 85*, 350–355.

Treisman, R. (1996). Regulation of transcription by MAP kinase cascade. *Current Opinion in Cell Biology, 8*, 205–215.

Tronche, F., Kellendonk, C., Kretz, O., Gass, P., Anlag, K., Orban, P. C. et al. (1999). Disruption of the glucocorticoid receptor gene in the nervous system results in reduced anxiety. *Nature Genetics, 23*(1), 99–103.

Tröster, A. I., & Fields, J. A. (1995). Frontal cognitive function and memory in Parkinson's disease: Toward a distinction between prospective and declarative memory impairments. *Behavioral Neurology, 8*, 59–74.

Tröster, A. I., Stalp, L. D., Paolo, A. M., Fields, J. A., & Koller, W. C. (1995). Neuropsychological impairments in Parkinson's disease with and without depression. *Archives of Neurology, 52*, 1164–1169.

Trott, C. T., Friedman, D., Ritter, W., & Fabiani, M. (1997). Item and source memory: Differential age effects revealed by event-related potentials. *NeuroReport, 8*, 3373–3378.

Trott, C. T., Friedman, D., Ritter, W., Fabiani, M., & Snodgrass, J. G. (1999). Episodic priming and memory for temporal source: Event-related potentials reveal age-related differences in prefrontal functioning. *Psychology and Aging, 14*, 390–413.

Troyer, A. K., & Rich, J. B. (2002). Psychometric properties of a new metamemory questionnaire for older adults. *Journal of Gerontology. Psychological Sciences, 57*B(1), P19–P27.

Tsai, C-H., Lu, C-S., Hua, M-S., Lo, W-L., & Lo, S-K. (1994). Cognitive dysfunction in early onset Parkinsonism. *Acta Neurologica Scandinavica, 89*, 9–14.

Tsolaki, M., Fountaoulakis, K., Nakopoulou, E., Kazis, A., & Mohs, R. C. (1997). Alzheimer's Disease Assessment Scale: The validation of the scale in Greece in elderly demented patients and normal subjects. *Dementia and Geriatric Cognitive Disorders, 8*, 273–280.

Tucker, D. M., Luu, P., & Pribram, K. H. (1995). Social and emotional self-regulation. *Annals of the New York Academy of Sciences, 769,* 213–239.

Tuholski, S. W., Engle, R. W., & Baylis, G. C. (2001). Individual differences in working memory capacity and enumeration. *Memory & Cognition, 29,* 484–492.

Tulving, E. (1972). Episodic and semantic memory. In E. Tulving & W. Donaldson (Eds.), *Organization of memory.* New York: Academic Press.

Tulving, E. (1983). *Elements of episodic memory.* New York: Oxford University Press.

Tulving, E. (1984). Precis of elements of episodic memory. *Behavioral Brain Sciences, 7,* 223–268.

Tulving, E. (1985). Memory and consciousness. *Canadian Psychology, 26,* 1–12.

Tulving, E. (1987). Introduction: Multiple memory systems and consciousness. *Human Neurobiology, 6,* 67–80.

Tulving, E. (1989). Remembering and knowing the past. *American Scientist, 77,* 361–367.

Tulving, E. (1995). Organization of memory: Quo vadis? In M. S. Gazzaniga (Ed.), *The cognitive neurosciences* (pp. 839–847). Cambridge, MA: MIT Press.

Tulving, E., Kapur, S., Craik, F. I. M., Moscovitch, M., & Houle, S. (1994a). Hemispheric encoding/retrieval asymmetry in episodic memory: Positron emission tomography findings. *Proceedings of the National Academy of Sciences of the United States of America, 91,* 2016–2020.

Tulving, E., Kapur, S., Markowitsch, H. J., Craik, F. I., Habib, R., & Houle, S. (1994b). Neuroanatomical correlates of retrieval in episodic memory: Auditory sentence recognition. *Proceedings of the National Academy of Sciences of the United States of America, 91,* 2012–2015.

Tulving, E., & Markowitsch, H. J. (1998). Episodic and declarative memory: Role of the hippocampus. *Hippocampus, 8*(3), 198–204.

Tulving, E., Markowitsch, H. J., Craik, F. I. M., Habib, R., & Houle, S. (1996). Novelty and familiarity activations in pet studies of memory encoding and retrieval. *Cerebral Cortex, 6,* 71–79.

Tulving, E., Markowitsch, H. J., Kapur, S., Habib, R., & Houle, S. (1994c). Novelty encoding networks in the human brain: Positron emission tomography data. *NeuroReport, 5*(18), 2525–2528.

Tulving, E., & Schacter, D. L. (1990). Priming and human memory systems. *Science, 247,* 301–306.

Tulving, E., & Thomson, D. M. (1973). Encoding specificity and retrieval processes in episodic memory. *Psychological Review, 80,* 352–373.

Tun, P. A., Wingfield, A., Rosen, M. J., & Blanchard, L. (1998). Response latencies for false memories: Gist-based processes in normal aging. *Psychology and Aging, 13,* 230–241.

Tuokko, H., Vernon-Wilkinson, R., Weir, J., & Beattie, B. L. (1991). Cued recall and early identification of dementia. *Journal of Clinical and Experimental Neuropsychology, 13,* 871–879.

Turner, M. L., & Engle, R. W. (1989). Is working memory capacity task dependent? *Journal of Memory and Language, 28,* 127–154.

Ukai, M., Itoh, J., Kobayashi, T., Shinkai, N., & Kameyama, T. (1997). Effects of the kappa-opioid dynorphin A(1-13) on learning and memory in mice. *Behavioural Brain Research, 83*(1–2), 169–172.

Ullsperger, M., Mecklinger, A., & Müller, U. (2000). An electrophysiological test of directed forgetting: The role of retrieval inhibition. *Journal of Cognitive Neuroscience, 12*(6), 924–940.

Unger, J. W., Lapham, L. W., McNeill, T. H., Eskin, T. A., & Hamill, R. W. (1991). The amygdala in Alzheimer's disease: Neuropathology and Alz 50 immunoreactivity. *Neurobiology of Aging, 12*(5), 389–399.

Ungerleider, L. G. (1995). Functional brain imaging studies of cortical mechanisms for memory. *Science, 270,* 760–775.

Ungerleider, L. G., & Mishkin, M. (1982). Two cortical visual systems. In D. J. Ingle, M. A. Goodale, & R. J. W. Mansfield (Eds.), *Analysis of visual behavior.* Cambridge MA: MIT Press.

Uno, H., Tarara, R., Else, J. G., Suleman, M. A., & Sapolsky, R. M. (1989). Hippocampal damage asociated with prolonged and fatal stress in primates. *Journal of Neuroscience, 9*, 1705–1711.

Urakami, K., Shimomura, T., Ohshima, T., Okada, A., Adachi, Y., Takahashi, K. et al. (1993). Clinical effect of WEB 1881 (nebracetam fumarate) on patients with dementia of the Alzheimer type and study of its clinical pharmacology. *Clinical Neuropharmacology, 16*, 347–358.

Ursin, H. (1965). The effect of amygdaloid lesions on flight and defense behavior in cats. *Experimental Neurology, 11*, 298–317.

Ursin, H., Jellestead, F., & Cabrera, I. G. (1981). The amygdala, exploration and fear. In Y. BenAri (Ed.), *The amygdaloid complex* (pp. 672–681). Elsevier: Amsterdam.

Uttl, B., Graf, P., Miller, J., & Tuokko, H. (2001). Pro- and retrospective memory in late adulthood. *Consciousness and Cognition, 10*, 451–472.

Vallar, G., & Baddeley, A. D. (1984). Phonological short-term store, phonological processing and sentence comprehension: A neuropsychological case study. *Cognitive Neuropsychology, 1*, 121–141.

Vallar, G., & Papagno, C. (1995). Neuropsychological impairments of short-term memory. In A. D. Baddeley, B. A. Wilson, & F. N. Watts (Eds.), *Handbook of memory disorders*. Chichester, UK: Wiley.

Van Balen, H. G. G., Westzaan, P. S. H., & Mulder, T. (1996). Stratified norms for Rivermead Behavioural Memory Test. *Neuropsychological Rehabilitation, 6*(3), 203–217.

Vandenberghe, R., Price, C., Wise, R., Josephs, O., & Frackowiak, R. S. (1996). Functional anatomy of a common semantic system for words and pictures. *Nature, 383*, 254–256.

Van den Broek, M. D., Downes, J., Johnson, Z., Dayus, B., & Hilton, N. (2000). Evaluation of an electronic memory aid in the neuropsychological rehabilitation of prospective memory deficits. *Brain Injury, 14*(5), 455–462.

Van den Broek, A., Golden, C. J., Loonstra, A., Ghinglia, K., & Goldstein, D. (1998). Short forms of the Wechsler Memory Scale—Revised: Cross-validation and derivation of a two-subtest form. *Psychological Assessment, 10*, 38–40.

Van der Kolk, B. A., & Kadish, W. (1987). Amnesia, dissociation and the return of the repressed. In B. A. Van der Kolk (Ed.), *Psychological trauma* (pp. 173–190). Washington DC: American Psychiatric Press.

Van der Linden, M. (1989). *Les troubles de la mémoire*. Bruxelles: Mardaga.

Van der Linden, M. (1994). Neuropsychologie des syndromes démentiels. In M. Jeannerod & X. Seron (Eds.), *Neuropsychologie de la mémore humaine*. Brussels: Mardaga.

Van der Linden, M. (1998). The relationship between working memory and long-term memory. *Comptes Rendes de l'Academie des Sciences de la Vie/Life Sciences, 321*, 175–177.

Van der Linden, M., Brédart, S., & Beerten, A. (1994). Age-related differences in updating working memory. *British Journal of Psychology, 85*, 145–152.

Van der Linden, M., & Collette, F. (1999). The neural correlates of updating information in verbal working memory. *Memory, 7*(5/6), 549–560.

Van der Linden, M., & Coyette, F. (1995). Acquisition of word processing knowledge in an amnesic patient: Implications for theory and rehabilitation. In R. Campbell & M. Conway (Eds.), *Broken memories. Neuropsychological case studies* (pp. 54–80). Oxford: Blackwell.

Van der Linden, M., & Juillerat, A. C. (1998). Prise en charge des déficits cognitifs chez les patients atteints de maladie d'Alzheimer (Management of cognitive deficits in patients with Alzheimer's disease). *Revue Neurologique, 154*(2S), 137–143.

Vanderploeg, R. D., & Eichler, S. R. (1990). *Performance of the severely traumatic brain injured on the CVLT*. Paper presented at the annual meeting of the American Psychological Association, Boston, MA.

Van der Zee, E. A., Luiten, P. G., & Disterhoft, J. F. (1997). Learning-induced alterations in hippocampal PKC-immunureactivity: A review and hypothesis of its functional significance. *Progress in Neuropsychopharmacology and Biological Psychiatry, 21*, 531–572.

Van Duijm, C. M., Hofman, A., & Kay, D. W. (1991). Risk factors for Alzheimer's disease: A collaborative re-analysis of case-control studies. *International Journal of Epidemiology*, *20*, 4–12.

Van Ge, J., & Barnes, N. M. (1996). 5-HT$_4$ receptor-mediated modulation of 5-HT release in the rat hippocampus in vivo. *British Journal of Pharmacology*, *117*, 1475–1480.

Van Gorp, W. G., & Mahler, M. (1990). Subcortical features of normal aging. In J. L. Cummings (Ed.), *Subcortical dementia*. New York: Oxford University Press.

Van Gorp, W. G., Marcotte, T. D., Sultzer, D., Hinkin, C., Mahler, M., & Cummings, J. L. (1999). Screening for dementia: Comparison of three commonly used instruments. *Journal of Clinical & Experimental Neuropsychology*, *21*(1), 29–38.

Vanhalle, C., Van der Linden, M., Belleville, S., & Gilbert, B. (1998). Putting names on faces: Use of spaced retrieval strategy in patient with dementia of Alzheimer type. *ASHA, American Speech & Hearing Association, Special Interest Division 2, Neurophysiology and Neurogenic Speech and Language Disorders*, *8*, 17–21.

Van Herwaarden, G., Berger, H. J. C., & Horstink, W. I. M. (1993). Short-term memory in Parkinson's disease after withdrawal of long-term anticholinergic therapy. *Clinical Neuropharmacology*, *16*(5), 438–443.

Van Hoesen, G. W., Hyman, B. T., & Damasio, A. R. (1991). Entorhinal cortex pathology in Alzheimer's disease. *Hippocampus*, *1*, 1–8.

VanLancker, D. (1991). Personal relevance and the human right hemisphere. *Brain and Cognition*, *17*, 64–92.

VanLancker, D., Klein, K., Hanson, W., Lanto, A., & Metter, E. J. (1991). Preferential representation of personal names in the right hemisphere. *Clinical Aphasiology*, *20*, 181–190.

Van Zomeren, A. H., & Brouwer, W. H. (1994). *Clinical neuropsychology of attention*. New York: Oxford University Press.

Vaphiades, M. S., Celesia, G. G., & Brigell, M. G. (1996). Positive spontaneous visual phenomena limited to the hemianopic field in lesions of central visual pathways. *Neurology*, *47*, 408–417.

Varney, N. R., Alexander, B., & Macindoe, J. H. (1981). Reversible steroid dementia in patients without steroid psychosis. *Americal Journal of Psychiatry*, *141*, 215–219.

Vazdarjanova, A., & McGaugh, J. L. (1998). Basolateral amygdala is not critical for cognitive memory of contextual fear conditioning. *Proceedings of the National Academy of Science of the United States of America*, *95*, 15003–15007.

Venault, P., Chapouthier, G., de Carvalho, L., & Rosier, J. (1986). Benzodiazepine impairs and beta-carboline enhances performance in learning and memory tasks. *Nature*, *321*, 864–866.

Verfaellie, M., Gabrieli, J. D. E., Vaidya, C., & Croce, P. (1996). Implicit memory for pictures in amnesia: Role of etiology and priming task. *Neuropsychology*, *10*, 517–537.

Verfaellie, M., & Treadwell, J. R. (1993). Status of recognition memory in amnesia. *Neuropsychology*, *7*, 5–13.

Verhaeghen, P., Marcoen, A., & Goossens, L. (1992). Improving memory performance in the aged through mnemonic training. A meta-analytic study. *Psychology and Aging*, *7*, 242–251.

Veroff, A. E. (1980). The neuropsychology of aging. Qualitative analysis of visual reproductions. *Psychology Research*, *41*, 259–268.

Victor, M., Adams, R. D., & Collins, G. H. (1989). *The Wernicke-Korsakoff syndrome. 2nd Ed.* Philadelphia: FA Davis.

Vidailhet, P., Danion, J. M., Kauffmann-Muller, F., Grange, D., Giersch, A., Van Der Linden, M. et al. (1994). Lorazepam and diazepam effects on memory acquisition in priming tests. *Psychopharmacology*, *115*, 397–406.

Vigliocco, G., Antonini, T., & Garrett, M. F. (1997). Grammatical gender is on the tip of Italian tongues. *Psychological Science*, *8*, 314–317.

Villardita, C. (1993). Alzheimer's disease compared with cerebrovascular dementia: neuropsychological similarities and differences (Review). *Acta Neurologica Scandinavica*, *87*, 299–308.

Visser, P. J., Scheltens, P., Verhey, F. R., Schmand, B., Launer, L. J., Jolles, J. et al. (1999). Medial temporal lobe atrophy and memory dysfunction as predictors for dementia in subjects with mild cognitive impairment. *Journal of Neurology*, *246*(6), 477–485.

Vogt, B. A., Absher, J. R., & Bush, G. (2000). Human retrosplenial cortex: Where is it and is it involved in emotion? *Trends in Neurosciences*, *23*, 195–196.

Vogt, B. A., Finch, D. M., & Olson, C. R. (1992). Functional heterogeneity in cingulate cortex: The anterior executive and posterior evaluative regions. *Cerebral Cortex*, *2*, 435–443.

Voits, M., Fink, H., Gerhardt, P., & Huston, J. P. (1995). Application of "nose-poke habituation" validation with post-trial diazepam and cholecystokinin-induced hypo- and hypermnesia. *Journal of Neuroscience Methods*, *57*, 101–105.

Volkow, N. D., Gur, R. C., Wang, G. J., Fowler, J. S., Moberg, P. J., Ding, Y. S. et al. (1998). Association between decline in brain dopamine activity with age and cogntive and motor impairment in healthy individuals. *American Journal of Psychiatry*, *155*, 344–349.

Volkow, N. D., Logan, J., Fowler, J. S., Wang, G. J., Gur, R. C., Wong, C. et al. (2000). Association between age-related decline in brain dopamine activity and impairment in frontal and cingulate metabolism. *American Journal of Psychiatry*, *157*, 75–80.

Volpe, B. T., & Hirst, W. (1983). Amnesia following the rupture and repair of an anterior communicating artery aneurysm. *Journal of Neurology, Neurosurgery and Psychiatry*, *46*, 704–709.

Von Dras, D. D., & Blumenthal, H. T. (1992). Dementia of the aged. Disease or atypical accelerated aging? Biopathological and psychological perspectives. *Journal of the American Geriatrics Society*, *40*, 285–294.

Vonsattel, J. P., Meyers, R. H., Stevens, T. J., Ferrante, R. J., Bird, E, D., & Richardson, E. P. (1985). Neuropathological classification of Huntington's disease. *Journal of Neuropathology and Experimental Neurology*, *44*, 59–577.

Voytko, M. L., Olton, D. S., Richardson, R. T., Gorman, L. K., Tobin, J. T., & Price, D. L.

(1994). Basal forebrain lesions in monkeys disrupt attention but not learning and memory. *Journal of Neuroscience*, *14*, 167–186.

Waber, D. P., & Holmes, J. M. (1986). Assessing children's memory productions of the Rey-Osterrieth Complex Figure. *Journal of Clinical and Experimental Neuropsychology*, *8*, 563–580.

Wall, J. R., Deshpande, S. A., MacNeilll, S. E., & Lichtenberg, P. A. (1998). The Fuld Object Memory Evaluation, a useful tool in the assessment of urban geriatric patients. *Clinical Gerontologist*, *19*(1), 39–48.

Wallace, W. P. (1965). Review of historical, empirical and theoretical status of the von Restorff phenomenon. *Psychological Bulletin*, *63*, 410–424.

Warburton, D. M. (1987). Drugs and the processing of information. In S. M. Stahl, S. D. Iversen, & E. C. Goodman (Eds.), *Cognitive neurochemistry*. Oxford: Oxford University Press.

Warburton, D. M. (1992). Nicotine issues. *Psychopharmacology*, *108*, 393–396.

Wagner, A. D. (1999). Working memory contributions to human learning and remembering. *Neuron*, *22*, 19–22.

Wagner, A. D., Gabrieli, J. D. E., & Verfaellie, M. (1997). Dissociations between familiarity processes in explicit-recognition and implicit-perceptual memory. *Journal of Experimental Psychology: Learning, Memory & Cognition*, *23*, 305–323.

Wagner, A. D., Koutstaal, W., Maril, A., Schacter, D. L., & Buckner, R. L. (2000). Task specific repetition priming in left inferior prefrontal cortex. *Cerebral Cortex*, *10*, 1176–1184.

Wagner, A. D., Poldrack, R. A., Eldridge, L. L., Desmond, J. E., Glover, G. H., & Gabrieli, J. D. (1998). Material-specific lateralization of prefrontal activation during episodic encoding and retrieval. *Neuroreport*, *9*, 3711–3717.

Wagner, A. D., Schacter, D. L., Rotte, M., Koutstaal, W., Maril, A., Dale, A. M. et al. (1998). Building memories: Remembering and forgetting of verbal experiences as predicted by brain activity. *Science*, *281*(5380), 1188–1191.

Wahlin, A., Backman, L., & Winblad, B. (1995). Free recall and recognition of slowly and rapidly presented words in very old age: A community-based study. *Experimental Aging Research, 21,* 251.

Wallace, K. J., & Rosen, J. B. (2001). Neurotoxic lesions of the lateral nucleus of the amygdala decrease conditioned fear but not unconditioned fear of a predator odor: Comparison with electrolytic lesions. *The Journal of Neuroscience, 21*(10), 3619–3627.

Wang, Q-S., & Zhou, J-N. (2002). Retrieval and encoding of episodic memory in normal aging and patients with mild cognitive impairment. *Brain Research, 924,* 113–115.

Warrington, E. K. (1975). The selective impairment of semantic memory. *Quarterly Journal of Experimental Psychology, 27,* 635–657.

Warrington, E. K. (1984). *Recognition memory test.* Windsor, UK: NEFR-Nelson.

Warrington, E. K., & Shallice, T. (1984). Category specific semantic impairments. *Brain, 107,* 829–854.

Warrington, E. K., & Weiskrantz, L. (1974). The effects of prior learning on subsequent retention in amnesic patients. *Neuropsychologia, 12,* 419–428.

Watanabe, Y., Gould, E., Cameron, H. A., Daniels, D. C., & McEwen, B. S. (1992). Phenytoin prevents stress- and corticosterone-induced atrophy of CA3 pyramidal neurons. *Hippocampus, 2*(4), 431–435.

Waters, G. S., & Caplan, D. (1996). The measurement of verbal working memory capacity and its relation to reading comprehension. *The Quarterly Journal of Experimental Psychology, 49*A, 51–79.

Watson, J. M., Balota, D. A., & Sergent-Marshall, S. D. (2001). Semantic, phonological, and hybrid veridical and false memories in healthy older adults and in individuals with dementia of the Alzheimer type. *Neuropsychology, 15*(2), 254–267.

Watts, F. N., & Coyle, K. (1993). Phobics show poor recall of anxiety words. *British Journal of Medicine Psychology, 66,* 373–382.

Wechsler, D. (1945). A standardized memory scale for clinical use. *Journal of Psychology, 19,* 87–95.

Wechsler, D. (1981). *Wechsler Adult Intelligence Scale—Revised: Test manual.* New York: The Psychological Corporation.

Wechsler, D. (1987). *Wechsler Memory Scale—Revised. Manual.* New York: The Psychological Corporation.

Wechsler, D. (1997). *The Wechsler Memory Scale—Third Edition.* San Antonio, CA: The Psychological Corporation.

Ween, J. E., Verfaellie, M., & Alexander, M. P. (1996). Verbal memory function in mild aphasia. *Neurology, 47,* 795–801.

Wegner, D. M., & Erber, R. (1992). The hyperaccessibility of suppressed thoughts. *Journal of Personality and Social Psychology, 63,* 903–912.

Weinberg, R. M., Auerbach, S. H., & Moore, S. (1987). Pharmacologic treatment of cognitive deficits: A case study. *Brain Injury, 1,* 57–59.

Weinberger, D. R., Berman, K. F., & Zec, R. F. (1986). Physiological dysfunction of dorsolateral prefrontal cortex in schizophrenia: I. Regional cerebral blood flow evidence. *Archives of General Psychiatry, 43,* 114–125.

Weingartner, H. (1985). Models of memory dysfunctions. *Annals of the New York Academy of Sciences, 444,* 359–369.

Weingartner, H., & Wolkowitz, O. M. (1998). Pharmacological strategies for exploring psychobiologically distinct cognitive systems. *Psychopharmacology, S125.*

Weingartner, H. J., Hommer, D., Lister, R. G., Thompson, K., & Wolkowitz, O. (1992). Selective effects of triazolam on memory. *Psychopharmacology, 106*(3), 341–345.

Weinstock, M. (1999). Selectivity of cholinesterase inhibition. *CNS Drugs, 12,* 307–323.

Weiskrantz, L., & Warrington, E. K. (1979). Conditioning in amnesic patients. *Neuropsychologia, 17,* 187–194.

Weisskopf, M. G., Zalutsky, R. A., & Nicoll, R. A. (1993). The opioid peptide dynorphin mediates heterosynaptic depression of hippocampal mossy fibre synapses and modulates long-term potentiation. *Nature, 362*(6419), 423–427.

Weldon, M. S., & Roediger, H. L. (1987). Altering retrieval demands reverses the picture superiority effect. *Memory and Cognition, 15,* 269–280.

Welsh, K. A., Butters, N., Hughes, J. P., Mohs, R., & Heyman, A. (1991). Detection of abnormal memory decline in mild cases of Alzheimer's disease using CERAD neuropsychological measures. *Archives of Neurology, 48*, 278–281.

Wenk, G. L. (1989). An hypothesis on the role of glucose in the mechanism of action of cognitive enhancers. *Psychopharmacology, 99*, 431–438.

Wessel, I., Meeren, M., Peeters, F., Arntz, A., & Merckelbach, H. (2001). Correlates of auto-biographical memory specificity: The role of depression, anxiety and childhood trauma. *Behaviour Research and Therapy, 39*, 409–421.

West, M. J., Coleman, P. D., Flood, D. G., & Troncoso, J. C. (1994). Differences in the pattern of hippocampal neuronal loss in normal aging and Alzheimer's disease. *Lancet, 344*, 769–772.

West, R. L., Bramlett, J. P., Welch, D. C., & Bellott, B. (1992). *Memory training for the elderly: An intervention designed to improve memory skills and memory self-evaluation.* Paper presented at the Cognitive Aging Conference, Atlanta.

West, R. L., Welch, D. C., & Yassuda, M. S. (2000). Innovative approaches to memory training for older adults. In R. D. Hill, L. Backman, & A. S. Neely (Eds.), *Cognitive rehabilitation in old age* (pp. 81–105). New York: Oxford University Press.

Wetzel, C. D., & Squire, L. R. (1980). Encoding in anterograde amnesia. *Neuropsycholgia, 18*(2), 177–184.

Wexler, B. E., Anderson, M., Fulbright, R. K., & Gore, J. C. (2000). Preliminary evidence of improved verbal working memory performance and normalization of task-related frontal lobe activation in schizophrenia following cognitive exercises. *American Journal of Psychiatry, 157*, 1694–1697.

Wexler, B. E., Stevens, A. A., Bowers, A. A., Sernyak, M. J., & Goldman-Rakic, P. S. (1998). Word and tone memory deficits in schizophrenia. *Archives of General Psychiatry, 55*, 1093–1096.

Weyer, G., Erzigkeit, H., Kanowski, S., Ihl, R., & Hadler, D. (1997). Alzheimer's disease assessment scale: Reliability and validity in a multicenter clinical trial. *International Psychogeriatrics, 9*(2), 123–138.

Wheeler, M. A., Stuss, D. T., & Tulving, E. (1995). Frontal lobe damage produces episodic memory impairment. *Journal of the International Neuropsychological Society, 1*, 525–536.

Wheeler, M. A., Stuss, D. T., & Tulving, E. (1997). Toward a theory of episodic memory: Frontal lobes and autonoetic consciousness. *Psychological Bulletin, 121*, 331–354.

White, H. K., & Levin, E. D. (1999). Four-week nicotine skin patch treatment effects on cognitive performance in Alzheimer's disease. *Psychopharmacology, 143*, 158–165.

White, N. M. (1991). Peripheral and central memory enhancing actions of glucose. In R. C. A. Frederickson, I. L. McGaugh, & D. L. Felten (Eds.), *Peripheral signaling of the brain: Role in neural-immune interactions and learning and memory.* Toronto: Hogrefe & Huber.

White, T. L. (1998). Olfactory memory. The long and the short of it. *Chemical Senses, 23*, 433–441.

Whitehouse, P. J. (1986). The concept of subcortical and cortical dementia: Another look. *Annals of Neurology, 19*, 1–6.

Whitfield, K. (1996). Studying cognition in older African Americans: Some conceptual considerations. *Journal of Aging and Ethnicity, 1*, 41–52.

Widlocher, D., & Hardy-Bayle, M. C. (1989). Cognition and control of action in psychopathology. *Cahiers de psychologie cognitive (European Bulletin of Cognitive Psychology), 9*, 583–615.

Wiegner, S., & Donders, J. (1999). Performance on the California Verbal Learning Test after traumatic brain injury. *Journal of Clinical and Experimental Neuropsychology, 21*(2), 159–170.

Wierazko, & Ball, G. F. (1993). Long-term potentiation in the avian hippocampus does not require activation of the N-methyl-D-aspartate (NMDA) receptor. *Synapse, 13*, 173–178.

Wiggins, E., & Brandt, J. (1988). The detection of simulated amnesia. *Law and Human Behavior, 12*, 57–78.

Wilcock, G. K., Lilienfeld, S., & Gaens, E. (2000). Efficacy and safety of galantamine in patients with Alzheimer's disease: Multicentre randomised controlled trial. Galantamine International-1 Study Group. *British Journal of Medicine, 321*, 1445–1449.

Wilde, M. C., Boake, C., & Sherer, M. (1995). Do recognition-free discrepancies detect retrieval deficits in closed head injury? An exploratory analysis with the California Verbal Learning Test. *Journal of Clinical and Experimental Neuropsychology, 17,* 849–855.

Wilding, E. L., & Rugg, M. D. (1996). An event-related potential study of recognition memory with and without retrieval of source. *Brain, 119,* 889–905.

Wilhelm, S., McNally, R. J., Baer, L., & Florin, I. (1997). Autobiographical memory in obsessive-compulsive disorder. *British Journal of Clinical Psychology, 36,* 21–31.

Williams, C. L., & McGaugh, J. L. (1993). Reversible lesions of the nucleus of the solitary tract attenuate the memory-modulating effects of posttraining epinephrine. *Behavioral Neuroscience, 107*(6), 955–962.

Williams, J. M. (1991). *MAS: Memory Assessment Scales professional manual.* Odessa, FL: Psychological Assessment Resources.

Williams, J. M. G. (1996). Depression and the specificity of autobiographical memory. In D. Rubin (Eds.), *Remembering our past: Studies in autobiographical memory,* Cambridge: Cambridge University Press.

Williams, J. M. G., & Broadbent, K. (1986). Autobiographical memory in attempted suicide patients. *Journal of Abnormal Psychology, 95,* 144–149.

Williams, J. M. G., Ellis, N. C., Tyers, C., & Healy, H. (1996). The specificity of autobiographical memory and imageability of the future. *Memory and Cognition, 24*(1), 116–125.

Williams, J. M. G., Healy, H. G., & Ellis, N. C. (1999). The effect of amageability and predictability of cues in autobiographical memory. *The Quarterly Journal of Experimental Psychology, 52*A(3), 555–579.

Williams, J. M. G., Teasdale, J. D., Segal, Z. V., & Soulsby, J. (2000). Mindfulness-based cognitive therapy reduces overgeneral autobiographical memory in formerly depressed patients. *Journal of Abnormal Psychology, 109*(1), 150–155.

Williams, J. M. G., Watts, F. N., MacLeod, C., & Mathews, A. (1997). *Cognitive psychology and emotional disorders* 2nd Ed. Chichester: John Wiley.

Williams, L. M. (1995). Recovered memories of abuse in women with documented child sexual victimization histories. *Journal of Traumatic Stress, 8,* 649–676.

Williams, L. R., Rylett, R. J., Moises, H. C., & Tang, A. H. (1991). Exogenous NGF affects cholinergic transmitter function and Y-maze behavior in aged Fischer 344 male rats. *Canadian Journal of Neurological Sciences, 18,* 403–407.

Williams, M. (1997). *Cry of pain.* London: Penguin.

Wilkins, R. H., & Brody, I. A. (1969). Alzheimer's disease. *Archives of Neurology, 21,* 109–110.

Wilkinson, C. B. (1983). Aftermath of a disaster: The collapse of the Hyatt Regency Hotel skywalks. *American Journal of Psychiatry, 140,* 1134–1139.

Willner, P., Sanger, D., & Oglesby, M. (1997). The behavioural pharmacology of anxiety and depression. *Behavioural Pharmacology, 8*(6–7), 475–476.

Wills, P., Clare, L., Shiel, A., & Wilson, B. A. (2000). Assessing subtle memory impairments in the everyday memory performance of brain injured people: Exploring the potential of the Extended Rivermead Behavioural Memory Test. *Brain Injury, 14*(8), 693–704.

Wilson, B. A. (1987a). Memory therapy in practice. In B. Wilson & N. Moffat (Eds.), *Clinical management of memory problems.* London: Croom Helm.

Wilson, B. A. (1987b). *Rehabilitation of memory.* New York: Guilford Press.

Wilson, B. A. (1991). Long term prognosis of patients with severe memory disorders. *Neuropsychological Rehabilitation, 1,* 117–134.

Wilson, B. A. (1999). Memory rehabilitation in brain-injured people. In D. Stuss, G. Winocur, & I. H. Robertson (Eds.), *Cognitive Neurorehabilitation.* Cambridge: Cambridge University Press.

Wilson, B. A., Baddeley, A., & Evans. J. (1994). Errorless learning in the rehabilitation of memory impaired people. *Neuropsychological Rehabilitation, 4*(3), 307–326.

Wilson, B. A., Clare, L., Baddeley, A. D., Cockburn, J., Watson, P., & Tate, R. (1999). *The Rivermead Behavioural Memory Test—Extended Version. (RBMT—E)*. Bury St Edmunds, UK: Thames Valley Test Company.

Wilson, B. A., Cockburn, J., & Baddeley, A. (1985). *The Rivermead Behavioral Memory Test*. Titchfield, UK: Thames Valley Test Company.

Wilson, B. A., Cockburn, J., & Baddeley, A. D. (1991). *The Rivermead Behavioural Memory Test, 2nd Ed*. Titchfield, UK: Thames Valley Test Company.

Wilson, B. A., Cockburn, J., Baddeley, A., & Hiorns, R. (1989). The development and validation of a test battery for detecting and monitoring everyday memory problems. *Journal of Clinical and Experimental Neuropsychology, 11*, 855–870.

Wilson, B. A., Evans, J. J., Emslie, H., & Malinek, V. (1997). Evaluation of NeuroPage: A new memory aid. *Journal of Neurology, Neurosurgery and Psychiatry, 63*, 113–115.

Wilson, B. A., Ivani-Chalian, R., & Aldrich, F. (1991). *The Rivermead Behavioural Memory Test for children aged 5 to 10 years*. Bury St Edmunds, UK: Thames Valley Test Company.

Wilson, B. A., Ivani-Chalian, R., Besag, F. M., & Bryant, T. (1993). Adapting the Rivermead Behavioural Memory Test for use with children aged 5 to 10 years. *Journal of Clinical & Experimental Neuropsychology, 15*(4), 474–486.

Wilson, B. A., & Moffat, N. (1983). Rehabilitation of memory for everyday life. In J. E. Harris & P. Morris (Eds.), *Everyday memory: Actions and absentmindedness*. London: Academic Press.

Wilson, B. A., & Patterson, K. E. (1990). Rehabilitation and cognitive neuropsychology: Does cognitive psychology apply? *Journal of Applied Cognitive Psychology, 4*, 247–260.

Wilson, R., Bacon, L., Fox, J., & Kazniak, A. (1983). Primary and secondary memory in dementia of the Alzheimer type. *Journal of Clinical Neuropsychology, 5*, 337–344.

Wilson, R. S., Schneider, J. A., Bienias, J. L., Evans, D. A., & Bennett, D. A. (2003). Parkinsonianlike signs and risk of incident Alzheimer disease in older persons. *Archives of Neurology, 60*(4), 539–544.

Wilson, S. P., & Kipp, K. (1998). The development of efficient inhibition: Evidence from directed-forgetting tasks. *Developmental Review, 18*, 86–123.

Winbolt, B. (1996). False memory syndrome—an issue clouded by emotion. *Medicine, Science and the Law, 36*(2), 100–109.

Winner, E., Brownell, H., Happé, F., Blum, A., & Pincus, D. (1998). Distinguishing lies from jokes: Theory of mind deficits and discourse interpretation in right hemisphere brain-damaged patients. *Brain and Language, 62*, 89–106.

Winocur, G. (1995). The hippocampus and thalamus: Their roles in short- and long-term memory and the effects of interference. *Behavioral Brain Research, 16*, 135–152.

Winocur, G. (1990). Anterograde and retrograde amnesia in rats with dorsal hippocampal or dorsomedial thalamic lesions. *Behavioral Brain Research, 38*, 145.

Winocur, G. (1995). Glucose-enhanced performance by aged rats on a test of conditional discrimination-learning. *Psychobiology, 23*, 270–276.

Winocur, G., Pfohl, B., & Tsuang, M. (1987). A 40-year follow-up of hebephrenic-catatonic schizophrenia. In N. E. Miller & C. D. Cohen (Eds.), *Schizophrenia and aging: Schizophrenia, paranoia, and schizophreniform disorders in later life*. New York: Guilford Press.

Winson, J. (1993). The biology and function of rapid eye movement sleep. *Current Opinion in Neurobiology, 3*, 243–248.

Winter, J., & Hunkin, N. M. (1999). Re-learning in Alzheimer's disease. *International Journal of Geriatric Psychiatry, 14*, 988–990.

Wittenberg, G. M., & Tsien, J. Z. (2002). An emerging molecular and cellular framework for memory processing by the hippocampus. *Trends in Neurosciences, 25*(10), 501–505.

Woike, B. A. (1994). Vivid recollection as a technique to arouse implicit motive-related affect. *Motivation and Emotion, 18*, 335–349.

Wolff, S. D., & Balaban, R. S. (1989). Magnetization transfer contrast (MTC) and tissue water proton relaxation in vivo. *Magnetic Resonance in Medicine, 10,* 135–144.

Wolkowitz, O. M., Reus, VI., Canick, J., Levin, B., & Lupien, S. J. (1997). Glucocorticoid medication, memory and steroid psychosis in medical illness. *Annals of the New York Academy of Sciences, 823,* 81–96.

Wong, EHF., Reynolds, G. P., Bonhaus, D. W., Hsu, S., & Eglen, R. M. (1996). Characterization of [3H]GR 113808 binding to 5-HT$_4$ receptors in brain tissues from patients with neurodegenerative disorders. *Behavioral Brain Research, 73,* 249–252.

Wonnacott, S. (1997). Presynaptic nicotinic ACh receptors. *Trends in Neuroscience, 20,* 92–98.

Wonnacott, S., Irons, J., Rapier, C., Thorne, B., & Lunt, G. G. (1989). Presynaptic modulation of transmitter release by nicotinic receptors. In A. Nordberg, K. Fuxe, B. Holmstedt, & A. Sundwall (Eds.), *Progress in Brain Research.* Amsterdam: Elsevier Science Publishers.

Woodard, J. L., & Axelrod, B. N. (1995). Parsimonious prediction of Wechsler Memory Scale —Revised memory indices. *Psychological Assessment, 7,* 445–449.

Woodard, J. L., Salthouse, T. A., Godsall, R. E., & Green, R. C. (1996). Confirmatory factor analysis of the Mattis Dementia Rating Scale in patients with Alzheimer's disease. *Psychological Assessment, 8*(1), 85–91.

Woodruff-Pak, D. S., Finkbiner, R. G., & Sasse, D. K. (1990). Eyeblink conditioning discriminates Alzheimer's patients from nondemented aged. *Clinical Neuroscience Neuropathology, 1,* 45–49.

Woodruff-Pak, D. S., & Papka, M. (1996). Huntington's disease and eyeblink classical conditioning: Normal learning but abnormal timing. *Journal of the International Neuropsychological Society, 2,* 323–334.

Woodruff-Pak, D. S., & Thompson, R. F. (1988). Classical conditioning of the eyeblink response delay paradigm in adults aged 18–83 years. *Psychology & Aging, 3,* 219–229.

Woods, B. T., & Carey, S. (1979). Language deficits after apparent clinical recovery from childhood aphasia. *Annals of Neurology, 6,* 405–409.

Wurtman, R. (1980). Memory disorders. *Trends in Neurosciences,* 8–10.

Yanase, M. A., Honmura, T., Akaishi, T., & Sakuma, Y. (1988). Nerve growth factor-mediated sexual differentiation of the rat hypothalamus. *Neuroscience Research, 6,* 181–185.

Yang, C-H., Hwang, J-P., Tsai, S-J., & Liu, C-M. (2000). The clinical application of Mini-Mental State Examination in geropsychiatric inpatients. *International Journal of Psychiatry in Medicine, 30*(3), 277–285.

Yeates, K. O., Blumenstein, E., Patterson, C. M., & Delis, D. C. (1995). Verbal learning and memory following pediatric closed-head injury. *Journal of the International Neuropsychological Society, 1,* 78–87.

Yesavage, J. A., & Brooks, J. O. (1991). On the importance of longitudinal research in Alzheimer's disease. *Journal of the American Geriatrics Society, 39,* 942–944.

Yoneda, Y., Yamadori, A., Mori, E., & Yamashita, H. (1992). Isolated prolonged retrogade amnesia. *European Neurology, 32,* 340–342.

Yonelinas, A. P. (1994). Receiver-operating characteristics in recognition memory: Evidence for a dual-process model. *Journal of Experimental Psychology: Learning, Memory & Cognition, 20,* 1341–1354.

Yonelinas, A. P., Kroll, N. E., Dobbins, I., Lazzara, M., & Knight, R. T. (1998). Recollection and familiarity deficits in amnesia: Convergence of remember-know, process dissociation, and receiver operating characteristic data. *Neuropsychology, 12,* 323–339.

Young, A. W., Aggleton, J. P., Hellawell, D. J., Johnson, M., Broks, P., & Hanley, J. R. (1995). Face-processing impairments after amygdalotomy. *Brain, 118*(Pt 1), 15–24.

Young, A. W., Flude, B. M., Hay, D. C., & Ellis, A. W. (1993). Impaired discrimination of familiar from unfamiliar faces. *Cortex, 29,* 65–75.

Young, B., Runge, J. W., Waxman, K. S., Harrington, T., Wilberger, J., Muizelaar, J. P. et al. (1996). Effects of pegorgotein on neurologic outcome of patients with severe head injury. A multicenter, randomised controlled trial. *Journal of the American Medical Association, 276*(7), 538–543.

Youngjohn, J. R., Larrabee, G. J., & Crook, T. H. (1992a). Discriminating age-associated memory impairment from Alzheimer's disease. *Psychological Assessment, 4,* 54–59.

Youngjohn, J. R., Larrabee, G. J., & Crook, T. H. (1992b). Test–retest reliability of computerized, everyday memory measures and traditional memory tests. *The Clinical Neuropsychologist, 6,* 276–286.

Youngjohn, J. R., Larrabee, G. J., & Crook, T. H. (1993). New adult age- and education-correction norms for the Benton Visual Retention Test. *The Clinical Neuropsychologist, 7,* 155–160.

Zaborszky, L., Pang, K., Somogyi, J., Nadasdy, Z., & Kallo, I. (1999). The basal forebrain corticopetal system revisited. *Annals of the New York Academy of Sciences, 877,* 339–367.

Zacks, R. T., Hasher, L., & Li, K. Z. H. (2000). Human memory. In F. I. M. Craik & T. A. Salthouse (Eds.), *The handbook of aging and cognition.* Hillsdale, NJ: Lawrence Erlbaum Associates Inc.

Zacks, R. T., Radvansky, G., & Hasher, L. (1996). Studies of directed forgetting in older adults. *Journal of Experimental Psychology: Learning, Memory and Cognition, 22,* 143–156.

Zakzanis, K. K. (1998). Quantitative evidence for neuroanatomic and neuropsychological markers in dementia of the Alzheimer's type. *Journal of Clinical and Experimental Neuropsychology, 20,* 259–269.

Zametkin, A. J., & Rapoport, J. L. (1986). The pathophysiology of attention deficit disorders. In B. B. Lahey & A. E. Kadzin (Eds.), *Advances in clinical child psychology.* New York: Plenum.

Zaudig, M. (1992). A new systematic method of measurement and diagnosis of "mild cognitive impairment" and dementia according to ICD–10 and DSM–III–R criteria. *International Psychogeriatrics, 4,* Suppl. 2, 203–219.

Zec, R. F., Landreth, E. S., Vicari, S. K., Feldman, E., Belman, J., Andrise, A. et al. (1992). Alzheimer's Disease Assessment Scale: Useful for both early detection and staging of dementia of the Alzheimer's type. *Alzheimer Disease and Associated Disorders, 6,* 89–102.

Zelinski, E. M., Gilewski, M. J., & Anthony-Bergstone, C. R. (1990). The Memory Functioning Questionnaire: Concurrent validity with memory performance and self-reported memory failures. *Psychology and Aging, 5,* 388–399.

Zhou, G., Bao, Z. Q., & Dixon, J. E. (1995). Components of a new human protein kinase signal transduction pathway. *Journal of Biological Chemistry, 270*(12), 665–669.

Zola-Morgan, S., & Squire, L. R. (1990). The primate hippocampal formation: Evidence for a time-limited role in memory storage. *Science, 250,* 288–290.

Zola-Morgan, S., & Squire, L. R. (1993). Neuroanatomy of memory. *Annual Review of Neurosciences, 16,* 547–563.

Zola-Morgan, S., Squire, L. R., Clower, R. P., & Rempel, N. L. (1993). Damage to the perirhinal cortex but not the amygdala exacerbates memory impairment following lesions to the hippocampal formation. *Journal of Neurosciences, 12,* 2582–2596.

Zucker, R. S. (1989). Short-term synaptic plasticity. *Annunciation Review of Neurosciences, 12,* 13–31.

Zurif, E., Swinney, D., Prather, P., Wingfield, A., & Pownell, H. (1995). The allocation of memory resources during sentence comprehension: Evidence from the elderly. *Journal of Psycholinguistic Research, 24,* 165–182.

Zurif, E. B., Caramazza, A., Foldi, N. S., & Gardner, H. (1979). Lexical semantics and memory for words. *Journal of Speech and Hearing Research, 22,* 456–467.

Author Index

Hertzog, C. 27, 68, 70, 167
Herz, M. J. 3
Herz, R. S. 31
Herzog, A. 209
Hesselink, J. R. 62
Heston, L. 106
Hetem, L. A. B. 118
Hettinger, T. P. 128
Heuer, F. 162
Heuser, L. 112
Heyman, A. 55, 173
Hichwa, R. D. 78, 98
Hickie, I. 224, 226
High, W. M., Jr. 232, 239
Higuchi, M. 117
Hihara, N. 163
Hijman, R. 217
Hildebrandt, H. 62
Hill, C. R. 80
Hill, R. 180
Hilsabeck, R. C. 51
Hilton, N. 243
Hindmarch, I. 135, 234
Hinkin, C. 56
Hinrichs, J. V. 138
Hinshaw, S. P. 227
Hiorns, R. 52
Hirano, H. 113
Hirono, N. 85, 169, 179, 183, 190
Hirsch, M. J. 236
Hirsh, R. 5
Hirshman, E. 28
Hirst, W. 87
Hitch, G. J. 19, 20, 26, 44, 203
Hitchcock, J. M. 86
Ho, Y.-C. 101
Hobson, J. 37
Hochanadel, G. 136, 238
Hochner, B. 128
Hock, C. 237
Hodes, M. E. 197
Hodes, R. L. 37
Hodges, J. R. 26, 71, 76, 105, 155, 178, 180, 182, 184, 185, 187, 188, 190, 191, 192, 195, 199, 243, 245, 246
Hoffman, B. J. 31
Hoffman, J. M. 227
Hoffmann, W. 59
Hofman, A. 177, 179
Hogan, D. B. 170
Hohl, U. 69
Hökfelt, T. 122
Holland, A. 188

Holland, P. C. 80
Hollman, M. 117
Holmes, J. 253
Holmes, J. M. 59
Holmes, P. V. 135
Holmgren, B. 138
Holscher, C. 119
Holzman, P. S. 216, 219
Homfray, K. 53
Homma, A. 67, 235
Hommer, D. 138
Honda, T. 245
Hong, E. 113
Hong, J. 241
Honmura, T. 236
Hoofien, D. 210
Hopkins, R. O. 35
Hopper, T. 154
Horn, G. 137
Horn, J. L. 42
Horn, R. W. 240
Horowitz, M. 162
Horowitz, S. 75
Horstink, W. I. M. 139, 194, 195
Horwitz, B. 43, 84, 91, 92, 106, 116
Houk, J. C. 101
Houle, S. 11, 78, 83, 84, 91, 92, 96, 97, 99, 100, 103, 105, 154
Howard, D. V. 46, 70
Howard, J. H. 46
Howard, R. J. 171, 226
Howe, M. L. 1, 30, 40, 70
Howes, D. H. 205
Howieson, D. B. 71
Hoyer, D. 113
Hoyer, WJ. 71
Hsu, S. 114
Hua, M.-S. 194
Huang, C. H. 122, 134
Huang, P. L. 119
Huang, T. E. 111
Huang, Y. 101, 120
Hudson, J. I. 161
Huff, F. J. 187, 188
Huganir, R. L. 118, 131
Hughes, J. E. 77
Hughes, J. P. 55, 173
Hui, S. L. 67
Hulsebosch, C. 234
Hultsch, D. F. 68, 70, 174
Humphrey, D. G. 43
Humphreys, G. W. 32, 153
Hunkin, N. M. 77, 91, 154, 155, 241, 243

Hunt, C. 105
Hunt, E. 135
Hunt, P. R. 120
Huppert, F. A. 28, 52, 53, 88
Hurlet, A. 234
Huron, C. 29, 216
Huston, J. P. 126
Hutchinson, E. C. 204
Hutton, T. 193
Hutton, U. M. Z. 24
Hwang, J.-P. 54
Hyde, T. 220
Hyman, B. T. 76, 78, 175, 192

Iddon, J. L. 195
Ihl, R. 67, 232
Ikeda, M. 85, 183, 190
Ikegami, S. 131
Ikejiri, Y. 183
Ikonomovic, M. D. 116, 171
Ilmberger, J. 195
Ilsley, J. E. 225
Ilyutchenok, R. Y. 123
Imai, Y. 235
Imamura, T. 85, 183, 190
Imbs, J. L. 134, 138
Imhof, H. G. 209
Incisa Della Rochetta, A. 90
Inglis, J. 237
Ingram, D. M. M. 236
Inguar, M. 130
Inman, V. W. 186
Inokawa, M. 148
Inokuchi, K. 131
Introini-Collison, I. B. 110, 111, 112, 123
Ip, C. H. 123
Ip, N. Y. 127
Irons, J. 117
Isaacs, E. B. 23
Isaacson, R. 80
Isbii, K. 148
Ishida, A. 163
Isingrini, M. 150
Isoaho, R. 55
Isse, K. 57
Itakura, T. 75
Ito, M. 100
Itoh, J. 123
Itoh, S. 126
Ivani-Chalian, R. 52
Ivnik, R. J. 41, 54, 56, 57, 166, 169, 171, 172
Ivry, R. B. 101

Subject Index

Note: page numbers in **bold** refer to information contained in figures and tables.